Guide to
Linux Installation and Administration
Second Edition

Nicholas Wells

THOMSON

COURSE TECHNOLOGY

Australia • Canada • Mexico • Singapore • Spain • United Kingdom • United States

THOMSON

COURSE TECHNOLOGY

Guide to Linux Installation and Administration, Second Edition is published by Course Technology

Senior Editor:
William Pitkin III

Senior Editor:
Lisa Egan

Product Manager:
Amy M. Lyon

Developmental Editor:
Deb Kaufmann

Production Editor:
Lesley Rock, Viewtistic

Technical Editor:
Edward Sawicki, Accelerated
Learning Center

Manufacturing Coordinator:
Trevor Kallop

MQA Technical Leader:
Nicole Ashton

Product Marketing Manager:
Jason Sakos

Associate Product Manager:
Tim Gleeson

Editorial Assistant:
Nick Lombardi

Cover Design:
Abby Scholz

Text Designer:
GEX Publishing Services

Compositor:
GEX Publishing Services

Disclaimer
Course Technology reserves the right to revise this publication and make changes from time to time in its content without notice.

ISBN 0-619-13095-4

BRIEF Contents

TABLE OF

Contents

CHAPTER FIVE
Using Linux Graphical Environments   **169**

CHAPTER SIX
Using the Shell and Text Files   **211**

CHAPTER THIRTEEN
Backing Up System Data

APPENDIX A
Linux Certification Objectives

Preface

The growth of Linux as a widely used operating system is the most important event to occur in the computer industry since the rise of the Internet. Linux continues to expand its technical prowess and marketing reach as companies deploy it in mission-critical situations around the globe. Most hardware vendors are working to ensure compatibility with Linux, and most software vendors who produce server-oriented products are seriously considering Linux versions if they have not already released them. At the same time, some computer professionals may have the mistaken impression that knowledge of systems beyond the world of Microsoft Windows is not really necessary. Most networks, however, include multiple operating systems, and system administrators planning for the long term are well-advised to include Linux as a core competency to offer to potential employers, many of whom have already installed Linux and are looking for staff to maintain it.

This book guides you through the basics of Linux technology and trains you as a system administrator to maintain a Linux server that other users rely on for e-mail, Web, database, networking, or other system services. The book begins by introducing basic Linux concepts that may be unfamiliar to you, and then explains the installation and use of a Linux-based computer from the viewpoint of a system administrator.

This book is the first in a two-volume set, the second being *Guide to Linux Networking and Security* (Course Technology, 2003, ISBN 0-619-00094-5). This volume assumes no background in Linux, but for a more complete picture of the world of Linux system administration (and as preparation for Linux certification exams), you should consider studying the second volume as well as this book.

One aim of the material presented here is to prepare you to pass a Linux certification exam, to demonstrate to potential employers that you have mastered important theoretical and practical knowledge about Linux-based computers. Several certification programs for Linux are currently available. This book and its companion volume provide more than enough material for you to pass both the Linux Professional Institute (LPI) Level 1 certification and the SAIR/GNU Linux Certified Administrator (LCA) certification program. Two other Linux certifications are not covered explicitly. The Linux+ certification from CompTIA (see *www.comptia.com*) is a less technically demanding program that this book and its companion should also prepare you for. The Red Hat Certified Engineer certification is a more demanding program that may require additional study of Red Hat Linux before taking the hands-on certification exam.

The Linux Professional Institute (LPI) is sponsored by several major vendors, including SCO, Hewlett-Packard, and IBM. It is a nonprofit organization that operates with a board of directors who gather input from members of the Linux community to develop over-all certification goals, testing objectives, and future plans. LPI has planned a three-level certification program. The first level, addressed by this book, consists of two tests aimed at basic Linux proficiency.

The Sair/GNU certification effort was started by Tobin Maginnis, a professor at the University of Mississippi. With cooperation from leading free software enthusiasts, his organization created the LCA testing objectives and testing program. To obtain LCA cer-tification, you must pass a series of four tests. The material in the first two tests is cov-ered in this book. The material in the second two tests is covered in *Guide to Linux Networking and Security*.

Appendix A provides the most current information about the LPI and LCA certifica-tion objectives available at this writing, with references tying each objective in both pro-grams to sections of this book or its companion volume.

The Intended Audience

This book is intended for students and professionals who need to install Linux and understand basic system administration tasks on UNIX or Linux-based servers. Though it begins with the conceptual foundations of operating systems and some historical notes on Linux, the focus is on practical, hands-on descriptions of system administra-tion tasks and the utilities—both command-line and graphical when available—that an administrator would use to complete daily work managing a Linux-based server. This book is ideal as the text for introductory courses on operating systems and system administration; it assumes the reader has no experience with Linux and only minimal experience with Windows-based computers. The text and pedagogical features are designed to provide an interactive learning experience, so that further self-study of Linux documentation, Internet documents, and computer industry resources will pre-pare readers for more advanced education or work assignments in system and network administration. Each chapter includes Hands-on Projects that lead readers through var-ious tasks in a step-by-step fashion. Each chapter also contains Case Projects that place readers in the role of problem solver, requiring them to apply concepts presented in the chapter in a situation that might occur in a real-life work environment.

Chapter Descriptions

The chapters in this book discuss the following topics:

Chapter 1, "Introducing Linux" introduces the free software model and provides a basic history on UNIX and Linux, with some comparisons to other operating systems and descriptions of the features of Linux.

Chapter 2, "Planning Your System" describes how to gather hardware information that may be helpful during the installation of Linux. It also explains installation concepts such as hard disk partitioning that the reader should be familiar with to understand the questions presented during installation of Linux.

Chapter 3, "Installing Linux" describes the installation process step-by-step, including how to select among the options presented, and how to start up and use the system after the installation is completed.

Chapter 4, "Running a Linux System" introduces additional operating system concepts related to working in the Linux file system, managing Linux software packages, and understanding how the Linux system is initialized. This material forms a basis for more advanced descriptions of related material in later chapters.

Chapter 5, "Using Linux Graphical Environments" presents the Linux graphical environment in detail, including configuration details, a conceptual overview of the X Window System, and a description of some of the major graphical desktop interfaces available for Linux.

Chapter 6, "Using the Shell and Text Files" includes more information about using the shell, or command-line environment, to complete work in Linux such as editing text files, processing text files using filter commands, and customizing the shell environment to suit a user's individual preferences.

Chapter 7, "The Role of the System Administrator" introduces Linux system administration as a role distinct from simply using a Linux system. It describes the daily work of a system administrator, the skills and personal attributes that a system administrator will find useful to make a successful career, and a few additional administration tasks, building on those presented in chapters 4 and 6.

Chapter 8, "Basic Administration Tasks" focuses on three key areas of Linux system administration: user accounts—creating, deleting, modifying, and maintaining them; file systems—creating new file systems, watching them for errors, modifying them, keeping them running efficiently; and processes started within a single shell—tracking them, modifying their status and ending them when necessary.

Chapter 9, "Preparing for Emergencies" describes how to safeguard information on a Linux-based computer against hardware failure using a UPS, rescue floppy, and other tools. It explains concepts such as redundancy and introduces Linux tools that you can use to protect data. It also describes how to use software tools to check the integrity of your file systems if problems occur.

Chapter 10, "Managing System Resources" covers the management of two important system resources: processes (CPU time used by programs), and memory (both RAM and virtual memory). In addition, system logging is described in some detail.

Chapter 11, "Using Advanced Administration Techniques" explains how to write shell scripts in Linux using loops, decision statements, and variables. You learn how to then use those scripts to schedule tasks for execution at any time using the Linux scheduling system. Kernel recompilation is also described in this chapter.

Chapter 12, "Printing in Linux" focuses on printing within Linux. Both traditional LPRng and the newer CUPS printing systems are described, in addition to printing from command line and graphical programs and managing print jobs using command-line, graphical, and browser-based tools.

Chapter 13, "Backing up System Data" explains why backing up system data is a critical feature of good system administration. It then describes how to perform backups using either standard Linux command line utilities or popular commercial tools. Details are provided on a number of hardware backup devices.

Appendix A, "Linux Certification Objectives" lists all certification objectives for the Linux Professional Institute LPI Level 1 certification and the SAIR/GNU Linux Certified Administrator (LCA) certification, each with corresponding references to chapter and heading within this book and its companion volume, *Guide to Linux Networking and Security*. Check *www.lpi.org* and *www.linuxcertification.com* to see if updated certification objectives have been announced.

Appendix B, "Linux Command Summary" contains an alphabetical list of all command-line utilities referenced in this book and in *Guide to Linux Networking and Security*.

Appendix C, "Graphical Administration Utilities" contains a brief description of popular Gnome and KDE graphical utilities used for system administration.

Features

To aid you in fully understanding networking concepts, this book includes many features designed to enhance your learning experience.

- **Chapter Objectives.** Each chapter begins with a detailed list of the concepts to be mastered within that chapter. This list provides you with both a quick reference to the chapter's contents and a useful study aid.

- **Illustrations and Tables.** Numerous illustrations of Linux utilities as well as conceptual diagrams help you to visualize and better understand Linux tools and technical concepts. In addition, the many tables included provide concise references on essential topics such as command options and online information resources.

- **Chapter Summaries.** Each chapter's text is followed by a summary of the concepts introduced in that chapter. These summaries provide a helpful way to recap and revisit the ideas covered in each chapter.

- **Key Terms.** All of the terms within the chapter that were introduced with boldfaced text are gathered together in the Key Terms list at the end of the chapter. This provides you with a method of checking your understanding of all the terms introduced.

- **Review Questions.** A list of review questions is included to reinforce the ideas introduced in each chapter. Answering these questions will ensure that you have mastered the important concepts.

- **Hands-on Projects.** Although it is important to understand the theory behind the Linux operating system, nothing can improve upon real-world experience. To this end, along with thorough explanations, each chapter provides numerous Hands-on Projects aimed at providing you with practical implementation experience and real-world solutions.

Case Projects. Located at the end of each chapter are several case projects. To complete these exercises, you must draw on real-world common sense as well as your knowledge of the technical topics covered to that point in the book. Your goal for each project is to come up with answers to problems similar to those you will face as a working network administrator.

Text and Graphic Conventions

Wherever appropriate, additional information and exercises have been added to this book to help you better understand the topic at hand. Icons throughout the text alert you to additional materials. The icons used in this textbook are described below.

 The Note icon draws your attention to additional helpful material related to the subject being described.

 Each hands-on activity in this book is preceded by the Hands-On icon and a description of the exercise that follows.

 Tips based on the author's experience provide extra information about how to attack a problem or what to do in real-world situations.

 The Caution icon warns you about potential mistakes or problems and explains how to avoid them.

 The Case Project icon marks case projects, which are more involved, scenario-based assignments. In these case examples, you are asked to implement independently what you have learned.

Instructor's Resources

The following supplemental materials are available when this book is used in a classroom setting. All of the supplements available with this book are provided to the instructor on a single CD-ROM.

Electronic Instructor's Manual. The Instructor's Manual that accompanies this textbook includes additional instructional material to assist in class preparation, including suggestions for classroom activities, discussion topics, and additional projects.

Solutions to all end-of-chapter material, including the Review Questions, and where applicable, Hands-on Projects.

ExamView® This textbook is accompanied by ExamView, a powerful testing software package that allows instructors to create and administer printed, computer (LAN-based), and Internet exams. ExamView includes hundreds of questions that correspond to the topics covered in this text, enabling students to generate detailed study guides that include page references for further review. The computer-based and Internet testing components allow students to take exams at their computers, and also save the instructor time by grading each exam automatically.

PowerPoint Presentations. This book comes with Microsoft PowerPoint slides for each chapter. These are included as a teaching aid for classroom presentation, to make available to students on the network for chapter review, or to be printed for classroom distribution. Instructors, please feel at liberty to add your own slides for additional topics you introduce to the class.

Figure Files: All of the figures in the book are reproduced on the Instructor's Resources CD, in bit-mapped format. Similar to the PowerPoint presentations, these are included as a teaching aid for classroom presentation, to make available to students for review, or to be printed for classroom distribution.

Read This Before You Begin

The Hands-on Projects in this book help you to apply what you have learned about Linux. The following section lists the minimum hardware requirements that allow you to complete all the Hands-on Projects in this book. In addition to those requirements, students must have administrator (root) privileges on their workstations in order to complete many of the projects.

Although this book includes a copy of Red Hat Linux 7.3 Publisher's Edition, the Linux certification programs that the book tracks are not focused on Red Hat Linux, and the information in the book applies in most cases to all current versions of Linux, such as United Linux, Caldera/SCO, SuSE, Debian, TurboLinux, Mandrake, and many others. The exceptions occur in some of the utilities used as examples and in the location of certain files in the directory structure. Red Hat is referenced particularly in many cases—users of other versions of Linux should check the location of the corresponding files on their systems or check their system documentation. In particular, the projects generally assume that the reader has installed Red Hat Linux 7.3. By making this assumption, the projects could be more complex than would be possible if they were aimed at the lowest common denominator among all versions of Linux.

Minimum Lab Requirements

Hardware

- Each student workstation and each server computer requires at least 64 MB of RAM, an Intel Pentium or compatible processor running at 200 MHz or higher, and a minimum of 1.5 GB of free space on the hard disk. More hard disk space is useful, but 1.5 GB will allow Linux to be installed as directed in the chapter text.

- It may be useful to have workstations in a lab networked together, though detailed instructions and troubleshooting on network configuration are not provided in this book. No particular cabling system or speed requirements apply. Internet access or the ability to communicate with another workstation is assumed for several of the book's hands-on projects (this is noted in the introduction to any such project). If Linux is installed in a lab with newer computers and networking hardware installed, networking is generally very easy to set up using the basic descriptions in Chapters 2 and 3.

- Care should be taken that security is not compromised in allowing workstations to access the Internet through a larger organizational LAN. Linux includes many utilities that, if used carelessly, are likely to make administrators on the LAN quite unhappy. (None of these utilities are the focus on this book, but they are available on the default system nevertheless.)

Software

■ RED HAT LINUX 7.3 PUBLISHER'S EDITION

This book includes a copy of the Publisher's Edition of Red Hat® Linux® from Red Hat, Inc., which you may use in accordance with the license agreement. Official Red Hat® Linux®, which you may purchase from Red Hat, includes the complete Red Hat® Linux® distribution, Red Hat's documentation, and may include technical support for Red Hat® Linux®. You also may purchase technical support from Red Hat. You may purchase Red Hat® Linux® and technical support from Red Hat through the company's web site (www.redhat.com) or its toll-free number 1.888.REDHAT1. There is a sticker on the top of the envelope containing the Red Hat® Linux® CD-ROMs (this sticker may also be on the inside back cover of the text). By ripping this seal, you agree to the terms listed above.

DEDICATION

This book is dedicated to my favorite teacher, Quentin T. Wells. Thanks, Dad.

ACKNOWLEDGMENTS

A second edition is a great thing. It means both that the subject matter continues to develop in interesting ways and that the first edition was well received. To that end, I wish to thank those instructors and readers who gave such a positive reception to the first edition of this book. I hope this second edition will meet expectations in effectively teaching the latest that Linux has to offer.

This is my second book with Senior Editor Will Pitkin and Production Manager Amy Lyon. Both are always a pleasure to work with and excel at handling all the details so that I can concentrate on the content of the book without worrying about the myriad other steps that go into making the finished product come together so well. Amy has juggled my changing academic and travel schedule in addition to managing all the reviewers and editorial steps during the entire past year. And always with good cheer. Likewise, my development editor, Deb Kaufmann, was always full of forbearance and encouragement during revision after revision as I used her suggestions to improve on the first edition and try to make the text enjoyable to read as well as technically useful. I feel much better sending this book into the world knowing that her skillful editing is part of every page.

I also had the pleasure of working again with Ed Sawicki, my technical editor. I wish I could have included all of his historical commentary and well-informed (and humorous) opinions in the text instead of just enjoying them myself. His expertise and teaching experience added a great deal to the finished product. Other members of the team put together by Amy included Production Editor Lesley Rock and two Quality Assurance Testers: team lead Nicole Ashton and tester Chris Scriver. These three went through the final product with a fine-tooth comb checking the text to save readers from the trouble I frequently caused them. Their efforts often went beyond what I considered their "job" as they worked to save my time and improve the book.

Amy and her staff also recruited several instructors to review the material as writing progressed. I considered their input invaluable in tailoring the material presented here to the needs of students based on their many years of experience in the classroom. My thanks to each of them:

Dick Breault	Mid-Plains Community College
Denny Brown	Ozarks Technical Community College
Jan Curtis	College of Eastern Utah
Randy Weaver	Everest College

Back in the trenches of producing each draft and responding to editorial comments on schedule, my wife deserves more thanks than she typically gets for watching the kids and for smiling day after day while I studied as a full-time law student and wrote a textbook in my "free time."

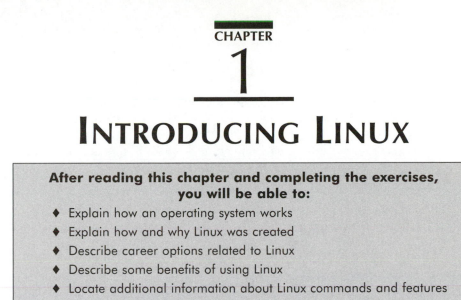

CHAPTER 1

INTRODUCING LINUX

After reading this chapter and completing the exercises, you will be able to:

♦ Explain how an operating system works

♦ Explain how and why Linux was created

♦ Describe career options related to Linux

♦ Describe some benefits of using Linux

♦ Locate additional information about Linux commands and features

In this chapter you learn what an operating system is and how the Linux operating system compares to others that you may have already used. You learn about the unusual background of Linux and why many people feel so strongly about the way it continues to be developed. Finally, you learn about where you can find additional information regarding Linux.

UNDERSTANDING OPERATING SYSTEMS

If you are like most computer users, your experience is limited to working on one of the popular graphical computers such as an Apple Macintosh or a computer running Microsoft Windows (NT, XP, ME, 2000, etc.). These platforms are popular and easy to use, but no product can be all things to all people. Linux was developed as an alternative for people whose computing needs require something other than the platforms most people are familiar with.

To appreciate the features and benefits that Linux offers, you should first understand what an operating system is, and how an operating system interacts with the applications that you run on your computer (such as your word processor or Web browser).

Defining an Operating System

When computers were first created 50 or so years ago, everything the computer needed to do was **hard wired**, meaning that the instructions were arranged in the wires and other components that made up the computer. Because of this, a computer was able to complete only a single task—the one that it was hard wired to perform. For example, a computer might be designed to accept two numbers as inputs and add those numbers together. A computer that was hard wired for this task could not subtract one number from the other without being rebuilt by rearranging the wires in the computer. As more powerful computer hardware became available, computer scientists demanded more flexibility. Once computers included the capability both to store information and to alter it electronically, computer designers could create software. **Software** is a collection of instructions that control the tasks that a computer performs. Unlike a hard-wired system, software can be changed without disassembling the computer and applying a soldering iron to the wiring. Obviously, this was real progress compared to hard-wired systems.

Early software programs contained every instruction that a computer needed to complete a given task. Before long, however, programmers decided it would be more efficient to create reusable software that provided core functionality such as reading keystrokes from the keyboard or writing characters to a screen. Specialized programs could then be written more quickly by taking advantage of these core functions.

A set of core functionality that many programs can use to control a computer is called an operating system. Although operating systems have advanced a great deal in the last 50 years, the basic purpose remains the same: an **operating system** is software that helps other programs control the computer hardware and interact with users.

With an operating system to take care of common tasks, programmers can more easily write applications. An **application** is a software program that provides a service to the person using the computer, rather than simply controlling the computer's hardware. For example, word processors and accounting software are applications. So are Web browsers and e-mail readers. In the case of a Web browser, the operating system manages networking, the keyboard, the screen display, and dozens of other issues. The programmer who created the Web browser is free to focus on problems specific to the browser, such as how to process Web pages or how to store Web page bookmarks.

A good operating system makes it easier to create application software, but you still must learn how to interact with the services provided by the operating system. This is quite a complex task in itself.

The operating system controls applications running on the computer. An application cannot act without "permission" from the operating system. But as long as the applications avoid unreasonable requests (such as "delete everything in memory"), the operating system spends most of its time acting on requests of the applications. Figure 1-1 shows the relationship of the user, the application software, the operating system, and the computer hardware.

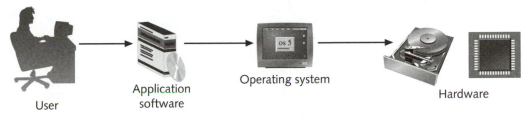

User   Application software   Operating system   Hardware

Figure 1-1   Relationship between the user, applications, operating system, and hardware

Operating System Functions

Today you can choose from many operating systems. Although they vary in appearance and functionality, they do have many similarities. For instance, as described previously, an operating system provides basic services to every application running on the computer. These services are likely to include the following:

- Initialize (or prepare) the computer hardware so that the operating system and other programs can function correctly.

- Allocate system resources, such as memory and processing time, to the programs that are using the operating system.

- Keep track of multiple programs running at the same time.

- Provide an organized method for all programs to use system devices (such as the hard disk, printer, and keyboard).

The effectiveness with which an operating system handles these basic tasks determines how powerful and useful it is.

An operating system consists of multiple parts or components. The most essential part is the kernel. Additional components assist the kernel in managing the computer's resources and in controlling application software. The major components of an operating system include:

- **Kernel**: The core of the operating system, which allocates computer resources such as memory and CPU time between multiple applications.

- **Device drivers**: Software that permits the kernel access to hardware devices such as a keyboard, mouse, hard disk, scanner, or network card.

- **Shell**: Software that accepts input from a user via a command line and processes that input to manage system resources.

- **Utility programs**: Software programs that manage the hardware and operating system features. A utility is similar to an application such as a Web browser, but the purpose of a utility is to manage the computer system rather than perform a task that is independently useful (such as display a Web page or calculate a mortgage payment).

- **Graphical User Interface** (**GUI**; sometimes just called a graphical interface): Software that provides a mouse-driven interface in which graphical applications can operate using menu bars, buttons, and so forth.

The precise line between an operating system component and an application is vague. For example, many utility programs are included when you install an operating system, but they may also fulfill specific needs you have such as counting the lines in a file or searching for a word. But this vagueness won't cause any problems if you understand the purpose of an operating system as outlined above.

Commonly Used Operating Systems

Some of the better known operating systems are described in this section. Many other operating systems are also used around the world, sometimes within specific industries or on specific types of computers. This section only summarizes a few key developments in the last 40 or so years as they relate to the emergence of Linux.

The **UNIX** operating system was created at AT&T Bell Labs (now part of Lucent Technologies) in the early 1970s by Ken Thompson and Dennis Ritchie. It was designed to control networked computers that were shared by many users. UNIX development has continued since it was first introduced, and versions of UNIX are currently sold by dozens of large companies, such as IBM, Hewlett-Packard, and Sun Microsystems. The Internet was developed on UNIX and is still based around the UNIX operating system.

One reason that many versions of UNIX exist is because of government restrictions on what AT&T—being a monopoly at the time—could do with technology that it developed. Today you will sometimes see reference to *nix or *unices*, meaning all of the versions of UNIX collectively. If something is compatible with most unices (most versions of UNIX), it is also likely compatible with Linux, as described later in this section.

The first version of the Disk Operating System (**DOS**) for IBM personal computers was created in about 1980 by Microsoft. Despite very limited functionality, it gained widespread acceptance when IBM introduced the first personal computer, the IBM PC, in August 1981. DOS was designed to make efficient use of very limited hardware resources for a single user on one computer.

Neither UNIX nor DOS included a graphical interface. The operating system provided only character-based screens, which required the user to type commands at the keyboard. Eventually, graphical interfaces were developed for each operating system. These graphical interfaces provided core graphical functionality that other programs could draw upon. The leading graphical interface for UNIX was called the **X Window System**. This system is still in use today and is also used for graphical displays on the Linux operating system. The leading graphical interface for DOS became **Microsoft Windows**.

In 1984 Apple Computer introduced the **Macintosh**, which integrated the operating system and the graphical interface so that users were essentially unaware of the operating system. Rather than having to type text commands that had to be memorized, users navigated a graphical user interface that prompted them to point and click with a mouse to indicate commands they wanted to perform. The Macintosh was designed to make new computer users comfortable with technology. Although the popularity of the Macintosh never equaled that of Microsoft Windows (perhaps because Macintosh computers were more expensive than IBM-compatible PCs), the idea of hiding the complexity of the operating system from users took root. In August 1995 Microsoft introduced the Windows 95 operating system, which integrated a copy of DOS and a copy of Windows (both updated many times since earlier versions). In Windows 95, Microsoft attempted to "hide" the command-line interface to the operating system. All but the most expert users were expected to perform all tasks through the graphical interface.

While all this was happening in the world of personal computers, businesses continued to use computers running the UNIX operating system (and other, specialized operating systems). These operating systems were much more powerful than DOS, Windows, or Macintosh systems, but they were also very expensive and many of them ran only on costly computer hardware.

Microsoft continued development of its operating systems by creating a business-oriented product called **Windows NT**. Unlike the earlier version of Windows, Windows NT did not include DOS as an underlying operating system. Instead, Windows NT was conceptually modeled on the VMS operating system, a business-oriented operating system that had been used for years on expensive minicomputers. (A minicomputer, which is a multiuser computer midway between a personal computer and a mainframe, cost between about $20,000 and $100,000 in the early 1990s.) Windows NT developers sought to include UNIX features to capture the market of business users who wanted more power than a Macintosh or Windows 95/98 system provided. Windows NT technology was also used in later versions of Windows such as Windows XP and Windows 2000.

Linux Arrives

Linux is a relative newcomer in the operating systems market, and it is one with an unusual background. In 1991 **Linus Torvalds** was a college student in Helsinki, Finland. He wanted to use a UNIX operating system (UNIX has always been popular on many college and university campuses), but he couldn't afford his own UNIX system. Torvalds decided to create a UNIX-like operating system kernel for his IBM-compatible PC as a school project. This in itself would not be different from the efforts of many other students working to create something useful and save a few dollars.

But instead of trying to complete the project on his own, Torvalds solicited help via the Internet. Soon hundreds of programmers around the world were working together to create a new UNIX operating system kernel. (For a photograph of Torvalds, see Figure 1-2.) Their work was dubbed Linux, in honor of Linus, the founder of this cooperative software development project.

Figure 1-2   Linus Torvalds, originator of the Linux kernel

THE WORLD OF LINUX

Several factors were working in favor of Linus Torvalds as he sought to create an operating system kernel for his PC:

- Even back in 1991, Finland had excellent Internet service, especially on its college campuses. This gave Torvalds access to a worldwide network of people who could help him develop Linux.

- As a computer science student, Torvalds (and those who helped him) could draw on nearly 30 years of shared experience with the UNIX operating system on which they modeled their work. All of the design and experimentation

1

that had gone into creating UNIX could be implemented in the kernel that Torvalds created from scratch.

- Torvalds was working as an individual, with other individuals. Decisions about how to do things were based on technical merit rather than on immediate market needs, a factor that often drives the actions of commercial software companies, sometimes to the detriment of those using the software.

- Many users of other operating systems (such as Microsoft Windows) were becoming frustrated with some of their features and with lack of stability. Users were also frustrated by delays in Microsoft's promised upgrades to Windows.

- Torvalds decided to base the software license for the Linux kernel on a model created by Richard Stallman and the Free Software Foundation.

The last item in this list may surprise you. In fact, the software license selected by Torvalds is an important part of the history of Linux and bears further explanation.

The Linux Software License

A **software license** is a legal definition of who can use a piece of software and how it can be used. The creator of a piece of software—either an individual programmer or a company—decides how the software will be licensed. Licenses for commercial software usually state that you can use one copy of the software (the one you paid for), that you may not copy the software, that the author of the software is not responsible for how you use it, and so forth. The license for Linux is quite different, as you will learn in the following sections.

The Free Software Foundation and the GNU Project

In 1983 **Richard Stallman** at the Massachusetts Institute of Technology founded an organization called the **Free Software Foundation (FSF)**. Stallman's motivating idea was that software should be freely available, without restrictions on copying. He proposed that companies and individuals could make money by charging for services and customization, but that the software itself should not be restricted in its distribution by a standard commercial license agreement. To back up his opinions, Stallman and those working with the FSF created hundreds of utilities that run on most versions of the UNIX operating system and distributed them freely around the world. This effort was called the **GNU project**. With the GNU project, Stallman intended to create a completely free version of UNIX, written from scratch. When most of the project was finished and the FSF was working on a UNIX kernel, Linus Torvalds and his co-developers appeared with a complete kernel already developed.

Stallman had started with the utilities; Torvalds with the kernel. Stallman had a complete philosophical agenda; Torvalds didn't want to pay for UNIX. Between them, they created the pieces necessary for rapid development of Linux.

One of the best known products of the GNU project is the C language compiler called **gcc**. This is a software program for converting C language programming instructions into code that a computer can execute. The gcc compiler is the most widely used, highly regarded compiler in the world.

For more information about the philosophy of free software and the relationship between GNU and Linux, visit *www.fsf.org*.

The GNU General Public License (GPL)

The license that Richard Stallman designed for the programs created as part of the GNU project is called the **GNU General Public License**, often abbreviated as the **GPL**. The GPL is very different from a standard commercial software license. It includes the following points:

- When software is licensed under the GPL, the author gives away the source code to the software. The **source code** is the set of human-readable programming instructions used to create the program. Normally, only the machine-readable **binary code** used to execute a program is distributed. By including the source code, the software author makes it possible for anyone to modify the original program.

- Anyone who obtains a copy of the software can redistribute it in any form they choose (on CD-ROM, via the Internet, in retail stores, etc.). They can also charge any amount of money for it. But they must also include the original source code, and they cannot restrict the redistribution rights of anyone who obtains the software from them. (This keeps the prices low.)

- Anyone can modify the software, since the source code is included. But any modifications (including modified source code) must be made freely available as well; the modifications are automatically subject to the GPL.

The last point here is sometimes referred to as the "viral" nature of the GPL—any changes to the code are also "infected" with the GPL. Once you start with software licensed under the GPL, you can't get away from it. On the other hand, some have mistakenly assumed that any program that is used with GPL software is also infected. That is not the case. For example, if you wrote a business software program for Linux and used a standard commercial license, running on Linux doesn't mean that your software is part of the same collection of source code as Linux itself.

Software called *system libraries* may be shared by both free programs and commercial programs operating in memory at the same time. The use of these libraries is covered by a separate version of the GPL called the Library GPL (or the **LGPL**).

Because of its community-oriented nature, Torvalds decided to released the Linux kernel under the GPL. The GPL allowed Linux to develop rapidly because everyone who worked on the project knew that they would benefit from everyone else's efforts: because they were all working on the same program, the GPL guaranteed that everyone's work would be shared. The result was rapid progress in a friendly, professional atmosphere.

Almost from the beginning, the term *copyleft* was associated with the GPL. The legal process called *copyright* has always protected creative work by authors, artists, musicians, and others. A copyright lets the creator of a work control how that work is used, so that others cannot rob a creative person of his or her livelihood by using creative works without permission. Conversely, the GPL does not let an author (that is, a programmer) *control* a creative work; instead it lets the author maintain *credit* for a work, while letting everyone benefit without charge for what the author has done. The term **copyleft** is used ironically to describe this radical departure from the customary copyright arrangement. Legally, the author of a GPL program still maintains the program's copyright. By choosing to release software under the GPL, the author does not choose to give up the copyright; instead, he or she is simply stating who can use the software and how. The author's name always remains associated with the software that he or she created.

Some software is placed in the public domain by its author. **Public domain** means that no one has copyright to the software. Most things produced by the U.S. government are in the public domain because they were produced using tax dollars. If software is in the public domain, anyone can modify it, keep the modifications secret, and copyright the modifications under a standard commercial software license. Because the GPL is a type of license that is maintained by the software author, GPL is very different from software in the public domain, though some journalists confuse the two concepts.

The GPL was not the first license to allow free redistribution of software. Nor will it be the last. Other similar licenses are used for the Berkeley version of UNIX (called FreeBSD), the Apache Web server, the PERL programming language, the X Window System, and many other programs.

 The name **OpenSource** is often used to refer to software licensed under the GPL. The OpenSource initiative is a consortium of people who support free software principles, but they have approved many different licenses as being valid expressions of those principles. The Free Software Foundation, which maintains the GPL, makes a distinction between the GPL and the term OpenSource, though in practice they are used synonymously in the Linux industry. For more information visit, *www.opensource.org*.

How Linux Is Developed

Linux kernel development follows the model of most free software projects. To begin a project, a person identifies a need and begins writing a program. At some point, the software developer announces the project on the Internet. Developers who share an interest in that project respond, and soon they begin to work together on different parts of the project. One programmer or team of programmers might develop the user interface, another the networking capabilities. Another group might work on documentation for the software. All of the individual developers and writers share code, documentation, and their views on how the project should move forward through e-mail. One person acts as the project lead.

After the software being developed reaches a certain level of stability, the project lead releases the software (including source code) on the Internet. This part of the process has become both easier and more formalized in recent years. Most projects have their own Web site and can use free software sites to announce progress and software updates. Some of these sites include:

- *slashdot.org*

- *freshmeat.net*

- *sourceforge.net*

 Since the inception of Linux, the source code has been distributed via the Internet site *ftp://ftp.funet.fi*, based in Finland, and many other sites around the world.

After a software project (or an update to it) has been announced, people download the source code and try out the program. Some of those people send back information about problems they have encountered (software bugs). The team of developers fixes the bugs, occasionally working with other developers who have submitted bug fixes or specific enhancements to the software. These fixes and enhancements are the basis for the next version of the software, which may be announced and released anywhere from a few days to many months later.

Linus Torvalds continues to work on the Linux kernel, along with a small group of developers who control what is included in Linux. Some commercial users of Linux have posed the unpleasant question of what will happen to Linux if something happens to Linus Torvalds. The answer is simple: another of the core developers of the Linux kernel would take over management of the project. Each member of that team is a recognized expert in Linux. Torvalds leads them now, but he could conceivably retire from that position, leaving another qualified individual to continue the work.

Sometimes a participant in a project decides that he or she doesn't like the direction the project is going. If the larger project membership doesn't share his or her views, that person can start a new project based on the existing source code. This is sometimes called **forking** the source code. Forking is how many new projects begin. For example, suppose a group of developers is working on a driver for a network card. A new card from the same company is announced. One of the developers decides he would like to work on a driver for that project. He starts a new team, using the original team's source code as a beginning point. Because no one is being paid, everyone chooses to work on whatever is most interesting to them.

Linux Distributions

The Linux kernel originally created by Linus Torvalds did not provide the functionality of a full-blown commercial operating system. To be really useful, the Linux kernel also requires:

- Hardware drivers

- Installation tools

- Networking utilities

- System administration utilities

- Documentation

- Technical support information

- A graphical environment (like the X Window System mentioned previously)

- Graphical tools

- Personal productivity applications such as word processors or spreadsheets

Given the method used to develop Linux (with developers all over the world creating and documenting its various parts), you might wonder how the many pieces of Linux could be combined into a complete operating system. Such a "productized" version of Linux, which includes many software components, installation tools, documentation, and so forth, is called a **Linux distribution**.

A Linux distribution has the Linux kernel at its core, plus hundreds or thousands of additional programs that run on Linux. Most of these are related to managing the Linux system—in other words, they are **system utilities**. Many of these system utilities are taken from the GNU project. For this reason, some people refer to a Linux distribution as the GNU/Linux operating system. When taken as a whole, a Linux distribution makes it possible for nonprogrammers to install and use Linux. Figure 1-3 shows how different components are collected into a Linux distribution.

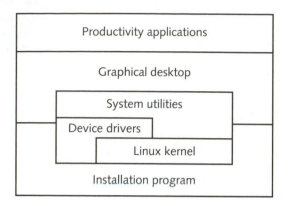

Figure 1-3   Many components together create a Linux distribution

Distributions in the Marketplace

Many companies have created Linux distributions. In accordance with the GPL, these companies include in their distributions the source code for the Linux kernel, as well as many other utilities. They can charge as much as they choose for their Linux distributions; because the software is freely available from other sources, one view of Linux companies is that they act essentially as packaging services that save users the trouble of downloading a large number of files from the Internet. This is an oversimplified view of their role, however, given the large variety of programs that Linux companies add to a typical distribution, including installation tools, professional documentation, technical support, and specialized software that Linux itself doesn't include.

Nevertheless, the fact that Linux itself is freely available has kept prices for Linux quite low—generally between $2 and $100. Because the Linux kernel and utilities offered by the many Linux vendors are practically identical, vendors use commercial components (such as specialized Web utilities) or services (such as installation technical support) to make their products more attractive to consumers.

Table 1-1 lists several popular Linux distributions, along with a Web site for each where you can learn more. Each company tends to focus on a specific part of the Linux market. For example, The SCO Group provides a business-oriented Linux product in association with their brand-name UNIX software and professional services. TurboLinux is aimed at those requiring specialized high-end Linux servers. SuSE is a distribution with an international background that includes thousands of software packages. You can see a more complete list of Linux products by visiting *www.distrowatch.com*.

Table 1-1   Popular Linux Distributions

Name	Comments	Web site
Red Hat Linux	The most widely used distribution in the world, from Red Hat Software.	*www.redhat.com*
OpenLinux	Produced by The SCO Group (formerly Caldera International). Aimed at business users.	*www.sco.com*
UnitedLinux	A Linux distribution created by multiple Linux vendors as a common base product on which numerous Linux applications can be designed to run.	*www.unitedlinux.com*
TurboLinux	Focused on providing high-end, specialized server software to businesses.	*www.turbolinux.com*
Mandrake	Built on Red Hat Linux with many additional packages. Popular at retail outlets.	*www.mandrakelinux.com*
Stampede	A distribution optimized for speed.	*www.stampede.org*
Debian	A noncommercial Linux distribution targeted specifically to free software enthusiasts. Debian does not have a company behind it. It is created and maintained by developers of free software.	*www.debian.org*
SuSE	The leading German distribution. Increasingly popular in the United States.	*www.SuSE.com*
Yellow Dog Linux	A version of Linux for Macintosh computers—written for the PowerPC processor.	*www.yellowdoglinux.com*
Linux Router Project	A minimal version of Linux designed to create a dedicated router appliance.	*www.linuxrouter.org*

The Future of Linux Development

Some Linux developers claim that commercial Linux distributions exploit the work of unpaid Linux developers solely for commercial profit. Most Linux developers, however, are glad to see their work widely distributed and enjoy the prestige that comes from having millions of people using their software. These developers also recognize that large organizations cannot afford to take the risk involved in using software that has been freely downloaded from the Internet—even if that software is reputedly of very high quality. Furthermore, Linux companies like Red Hat Software make Linux a viable commercial option for large organizations; Red Hat and others also contribute money and personnel toward developing and refining the free software on which their business is built. They provide services that commercial buyers require. Examples include the Volution management software (from The SCO Group—formerly Caldera International) or the Red Hat Network service for automated system upgrades.

Competition in the marketplace pushes Linux vendors to create more integrated, easier-to-use products. This competition benefits all Linux users. And because the core Linux and GNU technologies are licensed as free software (under the GPL or similar licenses), Linux vendors can't raise prices in the same way that vendors of proprietary software can. Thus, Linux users can be sure they are paying a fair price for a particular distribution. If the price of a particular distribution were to rise too high, many users would choose to download Linux for free or switch to a lower cost distribution. New companies could also create other Linux distributions. (In the language of business schools, the barrier to entry as a new Linux vendor is fairly low—anyone can create a Linux distribution by assembling a collection of free software from the Internet with an installation program.)

Linux is still too complex for many users—your grandmother probably wouldn't want to prepare her taxes with Linux. But Linux does have increasingly broad support in the business world. Companies like IBM and Hewlett-Packard have invested millions of dollars in Linux initiatives and have publicly proclaimed their support of free software and of the Linux operating system in particular as a viable business model. Some versions of Linux are even being sold at Walmart! (Specifically, the Lindows version of Linux is sold on a low-end PC. See *www.lindows.com* for details.)

Standardized Versions of Linux

Although the different Linux distributions are very similar, the complexities of the distribution system mean that an application designed to run on one distribution is unlikely to run flawlessly on another distribution. Some large companies that are committed to the Linux market created different versions of their applications optimized for each of the most popular distributions. But that requirement divides potential Linux purchasers into segments that are too small for most software vendors to consider as viable markets. Linux vendors are always working to distinguish themselves from each other by making what they consider to be the best technical decisions about how to create a Linux distribution. But in this case, a slight technical advantage still left the market fragmented.

The solution to this dilemma is to have a single foundation on which multiple Linux distributions are built. Multiple companies can use this foundation and add value to it to make their own products. But applications can be tied to the foundation distribution and be assured of a large market supported by multiple Linux vendors.

The first major effort in this direction was called Linux Standard Base (LSB). Although it had many supporters, a number of detractors (most notably Red Hat Software, the market leader) refused both active participation in its development and a commitment to using LSB as the foundation of their future products.

A more recent effort along the same lines as LSB is **UnitedLinux**. This project was started by four Linux companies that have very strong products but suffer in the market because third parties must currently support applications for each of their versions of Linux. UnitedLinux has created a single Linux distribution that will form the basis of each company's future products. At this writing, the UnitedLinux distribution is in beta testing. You can learn more about this project by visiting *www.unitedlinux.com*. The participants are:

- The SCO Group (formerly Caldera International)
- SuSE Linux
- TurboLinux
- Conectiva

Version Numbering

The version numbers associated with Linux products can be confusing. Each release of the Linux kernel is assigned a version number. Each component of a Linux distribution is also assigned a version number by the team that develops that component. The Linux distributions themselves also have version numbers, which are chosen for marketing reasons, based on how often the distribution is updated.

Most users will select the latest available version of the distribution that they choose to use. For example, Red Hat 7.3 is the latest version of Red Hat Linux available as of this writing. But the version number of the Linux kernel is also important because it defines some of the key capabilities of the operating system, such as what hardware is supported and what security model is used. The kernel version includes three parts:

- A major version number, which changes very rarely. The major version of Linux has been 2 for the last five or six years.
- A minor version number, which changes infrequently, perhaps every 10–18 months. Even-numbered minor versions are stable operating systems that are used for creating commercial Linux distributions. Odd-numbered minor versions are development versions of Linux that should not be used except by experienced Linux users because they may crash at any time. Development versions of Linux are interim releases—they allow advanced users to experiment with new features before they are stable.
- A patch level number, which changes very frequently for development versions of Linux, perhaps once per day or once per week. For stable versions of Linux, this number changes only a few times (about six to ten times in a year) as problems are located and fixed to make the stable Linux kernel even more solid.

A version number for the Linux kernel might look like this: 2.4.18. This is a stable release of the kernel (as indicated by the 4). It is also patch level 18, indicating that the 2.4 kernel has had several minor updates for stability or improvements in hardware support. Another Linux kernel version might look like this: 2.5.67. In this case the second number is odd, indicating that it is a development release of the kernel, which should not be used in a business environment. The 67 indicates that 67 versions of this release have occurred, each with fixes or enhancements added by the kernel developers. After a certain number of enhancements have been added and made stable, the kernel developers will decide to release a kernel version 2.6.0. The process then begins again as they work on adding new features with the 2.7 series of kernels.

 Don't run the development kernels on your servers unless you want to experiment with new features that might crash your system. Commercial Linux distributions always use stable Linux kernel releases.

Linux distributions created by companies such as Red Hat Software and The SCO Group are composed of hundreds of programs. The version of the Linux kernel included with a product is important, but a separate version number for each component could also be mentioned, for example, the version number of the Apache Web server or the version of the gcc compiler. To avoid the need to specify which version of each component is included in a distribution, vendors of commercial Linux distributions assign a version number to the distribution as a whole. For example, Red Hat Linux 7.3 contains a 2.4.18 Linux kernel. The 7.3 designation for the Red Hat product is a creation of Red Hat Software; it has no direct relation to the version of the kernel or any other package. It does provide a shorthand for users, however, since anyone who has Red Hat 7.3 can easily determine which version of other programs they are using by consulting the Red Hat Software Web site.

Don't worry about the version number of a distribution when comparing products. Instead, look at the versions for the individual components that matter most to you, including the Linux kernel, the graphical system, and specific services you need to use. You can get information about all these specific version numbers from the vendor's Web site.

Motivating Free Software Developers

As Linux is discussed in business and computer publications, those unfamiliar with the software development model used by Linux and other free software ask a reasonable question: "Why would so many people devote so much effort to something without expecting any reward? It just doesn't make sense."

Of course, the business world that asks these questions is driven mainly by money, and when considering money alone, free software development does not make much sense. Linux developers, however, have other motivations. After reading the first half of this chapter, you can probably compile a list of these motivations yourself. They include things such as the following:

- Creating a piece of software often fills a developer's specific technical need. Since they may have used the work of other free software developers at some point, releasing their own work as free software is a way to thank everyone who has made their life easier.

- Developers who create the highest quality, most useful programs are regarded very highly by their peers in the free software community. The respect of like-minded professionals whom you respect in turn is a powerful motivating factor.

- The Linux community and other similar online communities devoted to products like the Apache Web server are very popular in the news. Participating in free software development gives a sense of contribution and community to developer's. What begins as a small project to fulfill a developer's own technical requirements may be discussed in the *Wall Street Journal* a year later.

- As products like Linux receive increased support from mainstream software vendors (such as IBM and Hewlett-Packard), experience with Linux is a valuable boost to any developer's resume. Having your name associated with the development of a widely known free software project indicates both proven technical ability and strength at working in a team and organizing the work of others.

CAREERS IN LINUX

After reviewing the list of factors that motivate free software developers, you might be thinking, "That's fine for some people, but I still need to earn a living." In that case, you'll be happy to learn that Linux can set you on the path to a fulfilling and profitable career. Examples of the work you can do with a strong understanding of Linux and its related technologies include:

- *System administrator*: Each of the thousands of companies that use Linux needs at least one qualified system administrator to keep that Linux server running smoothly, day after day. This book will prepare you to become a Linux system administrator.

- *Network administrator*: Network administrators focus on the networking needs of multiple Linux servers, or on providing network services (such as Web access) to computers running many different operating systems. To learn more about Linux networking, consult the companion volume to this book, *Guide to Linux Networking and Security* (Course Technology, ISBN 0-619-00094-5).

- *Software engineer*: Many companies are using Linux as a development platform or Internet server and need qualified programmers to create software to run on Linux. The information in this book provides a good first step towards becoming a Linux developer.

- *Trainer*: As more companies begin using Linux, they require training for both technical and nontechnical specialists who will be using Linux to complete their work. Trainers work in all types of companies, teaching people how to use Linux.

- *Writer*: If you enjoy writing, you can share your knowledge about Linux with others. You might consider a career as a technical writer for a company, as a writer for a business-oriented computer publication, or some combination of these two. In addition, writers are often employed for magazine articles and books about Linux.

- *Business consultant*: By combining Linux knowledge with business experience you can consult for organizations that need to know how to add Linux to their information technology infrastructure. Consultants may create plans for how to use new systems and may also implement those plans.

- *Industry analyst*: A small number of business-savvy Linux specialists analyze the Linux industry, reporting their views to investment publications, the public at large, or individual organizations that have an ongoing interest in how Linux technology and markets are developing.

Even if you are not seeking a job in a field directly related to Linux, many companies now recognize Linux expertise as a sign of generally strong computer knowledge. Such companies list knowledge of Linux as a qualifying skill for many types of jobs, including training, marketing, sales, and technical management.

You can visit any of the following Web sites to research jobs related to Linux. Just search on the keyword *Linux*, or refine your search criteria further based on your specific interests.

- *www.dice.com*

- *www.careerjournal.com*

- *www.careerbuilder.com*

- *www.careermosaic.com*

Linux Certification

One of the best ways to show potential employers that you have Linux skills is by obtaining a Linux certification. As outlined in the Preface, several Linux certification programs are available, including programs from:

- SAIR/GNU (the LCA program); see *www.linuxcertification.com*

- Linux Professional Institute (the LPI program); see *www.lpi.org*

- CompTIA (the Linux+ program); see *www.comptia.com*

- Red Hat Software (the Red Hat Certified Engineer program); see *www.redhat.com*

Each program has similar objectives designed to show employers that you have mastered important work skills related to using Linux. Some programs are directed more toward end-users, others have tracks for software developers. This book focuses on the SAIR/GNU and LPI programs, which are aimed at providing a solid foundation for training Linux system administrators.

THE STRENGTHS OF LINUX

In previous sections you learned about the history of Linux and the license under which it is distributed. These are certainly contributing factors to the ongoing popularity of Linux. But people do not choose to use Linux simply because it is free. They choose Linux because it is a high-quality operating system. As noted previously, no operating system is perfect for every user; some may still find Linux difficult to use or lacking in the applications they want to run. But the following sections describe features of Linux that appeal to a growing number of computer professionals.

Stability

Linux has a strong reputation for stability. Many businesses have run a Linux server continuously for several years without rebooting (restarting) the system. This stability is due to both the quality and the design of Linux. Because the GNU General Public License requires that source code be distributed with Linux, thousands of developers review each new version of Linux. Programming errors that might cause the system to crash are discovered during the development stage and are fixed before the stable system is released. With no market-driven deadlines or fixed release schedules, a new version of the Linux kernel appears only when the developers are confident that it is ready for widespread use.

Security

The same development process that yields a highly stable operating system also yields a very secure operating system. Some journalists have erroneously concluded that an operating system with freely available source code could not possibly be secure. On the contrary, the fact that the source code is available, released in a controlled manner by well-known, respected professionals, means that all interested developers can help identify and fix security problems.

Proponents of other operating systems may point to the fact that many security holes have been identified on Linux systems. In truth, these security problems almost always relate to programs running on Linux, such as the `sendmail` e-mail server program. And in any case, when users do discover security problems, Linux developers will create a software update to fix the problem within about 24 hours. These updates are posted on the Internet so that all Linux users can download them. In contrast, developers of commercial operating systems seek to create secure systems by hiding the security problems that have been identified.

 After you install a copy of Linux, you can subscribe to receive free e-mail alerts of relevant security warnings through a Linux vendor such as Red Hat Software (see *www.redhat.com*). Other important computer security sites include *www.sans.org* and *www.cert.org*. To learn more about Linux security, consult the companion volume to this text, *Guide to Linux Networking and Security*.

Speed

Linux was designed to use limited hardware resources efficiently. As a result, Linux makes better use of hardware resources than almost any other operating system. Although few users will need to experiment with a computer having only 16 MB of memory, Linux can operate in such small systems. The efficiency of Linux when operating with such limited resources translates into speed when more extensive resources are available. Given a certain piece of computer hardware (such as a CPU running at 2 GHz with 512 MB of RAM), you will see better performance from Linux than from any other general-purpose operating system. Linux developers feel pressure from comparisons with Windows systems; they continually work to refine and improve system performance.

Cost

Price is usually not the deciding factor for an organization that selects Linux. A system administrator who manages a large budget and dozens or hundreds of servers must make decisions based on overall value to the organization, and some low-cost options are not a good value. But because Linux offers features like stability, speed, and security that are similar to other operating systems costing thousands of dollars, price can be an important factor weighting in favor of Linux.

A Multitasking, Multiuser, Multiprocessing System

Linux is a true multitasking operating system. This means that it can run many programs simultaneously. (A typical Linux system will have from 25 to 150 programs running at the same time.)

Linux manages multiple programs through a technology called **preemptive multitasking**, in which the Linux kernel controls which program is being executed at a given moment. Once a program has had a small time to work, the kernel intervenes and gives control to another program for a time. The Linux kernel maintains overall control of each program and of the system resources used by each program. The result is that even if a single program crashes because of poor design, networking problems, or other issues, the Linux operating system itself virtually never crashes. (In future chapters you learn how to handle a single crashed application.) Because of this design, other programs are not affected when one program has a problem and must be shut down.

 Compare this description to your experience with other multitasking operating systems that permit many programs to run simultaneously but that also permit a single application to crash the entire operating system.

Instead of preemptive multitasking, some operating systems use **cooperative multitasking**, in which the kernel is forced to wait for a program to yield control. Cooperative multitasking can be very efficient because it removes some of the overhead requirements of preemptive multitasking. But it is also problematic because a poorly written program can prevent the kernel from regaining control of the system, disabling all other programs running on the system.

In addition to being a multitasking system, Linux was designed from the beginning as a **multiuser system**, meaning that multiple users can log in to the same Linux system over a network connection and run programs, use the Internet, or complete other work. Programs run by one user do not affect the work of other users. A superuser, or administrative account, can configure and control all user accounts.

 As a security feature, users must log in to a Linux system using a valid username and password before doing any work. You cannot simply cancel the password entry or use a Guest account as in many versions of Windows.

Linux also supports multiple CPUs on the same computer using a technology called **symmetrical multiprocessing**. Systems with multiple processors perform faster than single-CPU systems because the processors can combine forces to work on one task at the same time. To use symmetrical multiprocessing, a software developer divides the components of a task into **threads**, or subtasks. Linux can then assign each thread of an application to a separate processor via a technique called **multithreading**; the various threads of one program are then run simultaneously on multiple processors. On commercial operating systems, using multiple processors adds significantly to the cost of the operating system. In contrast, all versions of Linux provide multiprocessing capability. Figure 1–4 illustrates the concept of a multiuser, multitasking, multiprocessing operating system.

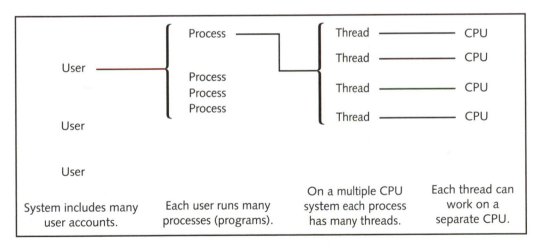

Figure 1-4   A multiuser, multitasking, multiprocessing operating system

Flexibility

Linux distributions are extremely flexible because they always include the source code to the operating system, allowing technically oriented system administrators and software developers to modify a system any way they choose. More in-depth modifications may require outside help, but Linux developers are easily consulted via the Internet, and they are generally more than willing to help. (Sometimes as a favor, sometimes for a fee.)

By comparison, operating systems that do not include source code offer little in the way of flexibility. Administrators are limited to asking the operating system vendor for an update that meets a specific need. The answer to such a request is usually, "Sorry, we can't do that," or "That feature is scheduled for our 2007 release."

 Although you are free to modify a Linux system as much as you want, you certainly don't have to make changes to keep your system running smoothly. If a Linux server is meeting your needs, you shouldn't feel any pressure to upgrade to a newer version.

Some organizations might opt for a more restrictive, commercial operating system because they are intimidated by the flexibility of Linux and all the options it provides. But in fact, commercial Linux vendors such as SuSE and Red Hat Software provide the technical support commonly associated with commercial operating systems. Management teams can be confident that a Linux expert is only a phone call away. (Technically oriented individuals might prefer the Internet resources described later in this chapter.)

Applications

Years ago, Linux was used almost exclusively for developing UNIX software or for specialized Internet servers. Back then, critics of Linux might have argued, "What good is an operating system that doesn't run the applications I need?"

Today that concern is unfounded, because Linux supports thousands of applications and because the focus of many Linux servers is on providing core Internet applications that are part of the global economy. As examples, consider some of the applications available on Linux:

- StarOffice, a complete graphical office suite similar to Microsoft Office, from Sun Microsystems

- Adobe Acrobat document reader

- Popular games from top entertainment companies like Loki

- Database products from Oracle, Sybase, IBM, and many others

- Java technology, both within browsers and stand-alone

- Web server software and supporting development tools

- E-mail servers with graphical configuration interfaces
- Security tools such as routers and firewalls

To see information about commercial and free applications available for Linux, visit one of these sites:

- *www.linuxapps.com*
- *linux.tucows.com*
- *www.linuxworld.com* (under the ProductFinder link)
- *linux.zdnet.com*

LEARNING MORE ABOUT LINUX

This book introduces you to the most important topics you need to know about to work as a Linux system administrator. You can learn more details than we have room for in this book, and also explore additional Linux topics, using the resources described in this section.

Reading Linux Documentation

Because the developers of Linux and other free software projects were working entirely via the Internet, they shared descriptions of their software via electronic or online documentation. This documentation was typically incorporated into the project when it was distributed for everyone's use. Most Linux distributions include all of this documentation—thousands of pages of material that you can quickly access using a few simple commands.

When you read Linux documentation, remember that much of it was written by software developers. Because of that, much of the documentation for Linux software is written as if you already have read all of the *other* documentation on the system. You can find a wealth of useful detail, but as a newcomer to Linux, you should expect to read many things that you don't initially understand. Returning to material later will make everything much clearer.

The Linux Documentation Project

The **Linux Documentation Project (LDP)** was begun by Matt Welsh in the early 1990s, when Linux was just becoming well-known in technical circles. The LDP was one of the first efforts to document how Linux works and continues to provide Linux documentation today in a variety of formats. The LDP currently contains over 6000 pages of documentation, all of which is available online, free of charge, under a version of the GPL modified for use with documentation. The LDP consists of several types of documents. Some of these, such as the *Network Administrator's Guide* and the *Kernel Hacker's Guide*, are complete online reference manuals. (Figure 1-5 shows a sample documentation Web site.)

Initially you will probably find the HOWTO documents to be the most useful part of the LDP. The **HOWTOs** cover specific topics, such as sharing a system between Windows XP and Linux, or maintaining network security. Each document is written by one person, or a small group, with expertise in that topic. Documents called mini-HOWTOs focus on narrower subjects than do regular HOWTOs. HOWTO documents are usually written by software developers, but they are intended for readers who are not familiar with the topic being discussed.

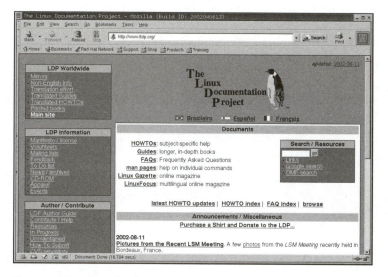

Figure 1-5   Sample documentation site

The LDP and all of the HOWTO documents are included with many Linux distributions, though they are generally not installed by default because of their size. You can also read them on many Web sites. A good place to begin researching the documentation available as part of the LDP is *www.linuxhq.com/info.html*. The LDP is also available at *www.tldp.org*.

Linux Command Information

As you learn in future chapters, Linux includes many different commands, each with numerous options. It makes little sense to memorize all of the commands and options, because you will only use a small percentage of them regularly. When you do need to use a new command or option, you can learn about it through the Linux command information that is available online. This information is provided in two formats. You can access online manual pages (called **man pages**) for most Linux commands by using the `man` command. For some Linux commands, the definitive source of information is in the second format: an info page. You can view info pages using the `info` command. These commands will be described in later chapters.

Documentation Included with Software Packages

Most of the software packages included with a Linux distribution provide at least some documentation. This documentation is installed on your system along with the software itself. You can normally view the documentation either in a text editor or a Web browser. In most distributions of Linux, the documentation is stored in the `/usr/doc` or `/usr/share/doc` subdirectory of the file system.

Linux on the Internet

Linux was created on the Internet, and the Internet is still a great place to find out more about Linux. Every day on the Internet, developers release new software, companies make announcements about Linux products, and software documenters provide new or revised information. Table 1-2 lists some Web sites that you will find useful as you explore the world of Linux.

Table 1-2   Linux-Related Web Sites

Web site	Description
www.linuxjournal.com	A high-quality companion Web site to the monthly printed magazine; contains additional Linux links and information (mostly technically oriented).
www.linuxworld.com	A business-oriented online magazine with interviews, links, technical reports, and other up-to-date information.
www.slashdot.org	An eclectic collection of news items related to free software and other topics (such as Star Wars, new music technologies, cryptography legislation, etc.) of interest to free software developers.
www.linuxhq.com	A collection of information about work on the Linux kernel, with useful links to many other sites and Linux resources.
www.lwn.net	Linux Weekly News, a collection of news items related to Linux and other free software.

The Web sites for each of the Linux distributions (listed in Table 1-1) are also great resources for learning about Linux. You learn about additional Web sites in later chapters.

CHAPTER SUMMARY

❑ An operating system provides an interface between the computer hardware and the applications run by the user.

❑ In its most basic form, an operating system manages the use of memory, CPU time, and other system resources. A complete operating system includes many other features to provide additional hardware support, a graphical environment, and utility programs.

❑ The Linux kernel was created by many talented individuals from around the world working under the leadership of Linus Torvalds, who continues to maintain the Linux kernel.

❑ The Free Software Foundation, led by Richard Stallman, created hundreds of software programs as part of its GNU project. These are included with the Linux kernel in each copy of a complete Linux operating system.

❑ The General Public License (GPL) is responsible in large part for the phenomenal growth of Linux in the last few years. It requires that source code be distributed with each copy of the Linux kernel (and many other free software projects). The so-called viral nature of the GPL means that anyone who changes part of the Linux kernel must also give away their work under the GPL.

❑ Various companies have created commercial products, called distributions, that are built around the Linux kernel and GNU software.

❑ Efforts to standardize Linux distributions could make it easier for software developers to write applications for the larger Linux market. The UnitedLinux project is one effort aimed at creating a foundation Linux distribution for multiple Linux vendors.

❑ Linux offers key features such as stability, speed, security, flexibility, and low cost.

❑ Careers in Linux include system administrators, software developers, technical writers, industry analysts, and others.

❑ Several Linux certification programs are currently available. Obtaining a Linux certification demonstrates to potential employers that you have mastered basic Linux skills.

❑ Information about Linux is available online as part of the Linux Documentation Project, which includes many HOWTO documents on specific topics. Online documentation for Linux commands is included with every copy of Linux. Many publications and Web sites maintain daily news updates about what is happening in the world of Linux and free software.

1

KEY TERMS

application — A program (such as a word processor or spreadsheet) that provides a service to a person using the computer, rather than simply managing the computer's resources.

binary code — Machine-readable instructions used to execute a program.

cooperative multitasking — A technique in which an operating system kernel must wait for a program to yield control to other programs.

copyleft — An ironic term that refers to the GNU General Public License (the GPL), signifying a radical departure from standard copyright.

device drivers — Software that provides access to additional hardware, beyond core device support provided by the kernel.

DOS — An operating system developed for personal computers in about 1980 by Microsoft. It gained widespread acceptance when IBM introduced the first IBM PC.

forking — Starting a new free software project based on an existing project.

Free Software Foundation (FSF) — An organization founded by Richard Stallman to promote his ideals of freely available software and to create and distribute that software.

gcc — A C language compiler. Probably the best-known product of the GNU project.

GNU General Public License (GPL) — The free software license that Richard Stallman of the Free Software Foundation developed for the programs created by the GNU project.

GNU project — An effort by the Free Software Foundation to create a free UNIX-like operating system. Many of the programs in every Linux distribution come from the GNU project.

Graphical User Interface (GUI) — Software that provides mouse-driven applications with menu bars, buttons, and so forth.

hard wired — Computer functionality that is arranged in the wires and other components that make up a computer. Hard-wired functionality cannot be easily altered.

HOWTOs — Documents within the Linux Documentation Project that cover specific topics.

kernel — The core of the operating system. The kernel interacts directly with the computer hardware and manages computer memory, the time allocated to each program running on a system, and other system resources.

LGPL — A special version of the GNU General Public License intended to govern both free and commercial software use of software libraries.

Linux distribution — A Linux operating system product that includes the Linux kernel plus many software components, installation tools, documentation, and so forth.

Linux Documentation Project (LDP) — One of the first efforts to document how Linux is used. Started by Matt Welsh.

Macintosh — A computer developed by Apple Computer that integrated the operating system and the graphical interface.

man pages — Online manual pages for Linux commands. The man pages are accessed using the `man` command.

Microsoft Windows — The leading graphical interface for DOS.

multithreading — A technique used within multiprocessing operating systems to divide a larger task between multiple processors.

multiuser system — An operating system on which numerous users can log in to the same computer (usually over a network connection).

OpenSource — A trademarked name often used to refer to software licensed under the GPL.

operating system — Software that provides a set of core functionality for other programs to use in working with the computer hardware and interfacing with the user running the computer.

preemptive multitasking — A technique used by the Linux kernel to control which program is running from moment to moment.

public domain — Creative work (such as a software program) to which no one has a copyright ownership interest.

shell — Software that accepts input from a user via a command line and processes that input to manage system resources.

software — Instructions that control the physical computer components, but can be changed because they reside on a changeable media such as a hard disk.

software license — A legal definition of who can use a piece of software and how it can be used.

source code — A set of human-readable programming instructions used to create a piece of software.

Stallman, Richard — Founder of the Free Software Foundation and the GNU project.

symmetrical multiprocessing — A technique that allows an operating system to support multiple CPUs on the same computer.

system utilities — Programs that are used to manage a Linux system. See also utility programs.

threads — Parts of a task. Used in the context of multiprocessing operating systems.

Torvalds, Linus — Originator of the Linux kernel; formerly a student in Helsinki, Finland.

UnitedLinux — A Linux distribution created by multiple Linux vendors as a common base product on which numerous Linux applications can be designed to run.

UNIX — An operating system created at AT&T Bell Labs (now part of Lucent Technologies) about 30 years ago by Ken Thompson and Dennis Ritchie. UNIX is still widely used, and it provided the technical basis for Linux.

utility programs — Software that provides assistance in managing the hardware and operating system features (as opposed to doing other types of work such as word processing). *See also* system utilities.

Windows NT — A business-oriented operating system product developed by Microsoft. Windows NT, 2000, and XP do not use DOS as an underlying operating system, as previous versions of Windows did (such as Windows 95 and 98).

X Window System — A graphical software environment used by almost all UNIX and Linux operating systems.

REVIEW QUESTIONS

1. Explain the difference between a computer that is solely hard wired and one that uses an operating system.

2. An operating system does *not* do which of the following:

   a. Allocate system resources such as memory and CPU time

   b. Initialize computer hardware so it can be used by software running on the computer

   c. Keep track of multiple programs running at the same time

   d. Provide word processing features for users

3. Name four career paths where a strong knowledge of Linux is useful.

4. Which of the following operating systems included a graphical interface when first released?

   a. UNIX

   b. Macintosh

   c. Linux

   d. DOS

5. Linus Torvalds began to create Linux because:

   a. He was hired as an operating system consultant by a major corporation.

   b. He wanted a powerful operating system but could not afford one.

   c. His professor required that each student create a basic operating system.

   d. He felt it would be a good career move.

6. The Free Software Foundation is dedicated to the idea that:

   a. No company should be able to charge money for any software.

   b. The real value of software is in customization, not in selling mass-produced copies.

   c. Richard Stallman's C compiler is the best in the world.

   d. Linux is an important development in operating systems.

7. The GNU project is important to Linux because:

   a. It provides the majority of the system utilities used by Linux.

   b. GNU software is the only software compatible with Linux.

   c. The media attention generated by the GNU project has made Linux popular.

   d. Richard Stallman is a strong supporter of the Linux movement.

8. The GPL includes all of the following facets *except*:

   a. GPL software must include source code.

   b. Modifications to GPL-licensed software must also be licensed under the GPL.

   c. Software that runs on a GPL operating system must be given away.

   d. A company cannot charge money for GPL-licensed software.

9. Explain why the term "copyleft" came to be used as an ironic comparison to "copyright."

10. In general usage, the name OpenSource software refers to:

    a. Only programs that are licensed explicitly under the GPL.

    b. Programs that don't have source code included.

    c. Software that has source code included and follows a set of general principles espoused by the OpenSource consortium.

    d. Only programs released as part of the GNU Project.

11. Two efforts to standardize Linux distributions are:

    a. LSB and UnitedLinux

    b. Conective and SuSE Linux

    c. The Apache server license and the Perl artistic license

    d. Those of IBM and Hewlett-Packard to influence Linux development

12. Why might Linux provide better security than operating systems that do not provide source code to users?

13. Name five things that a Linux distribution vendor might add to the Linux kernel when creating a product to sell.

14. Market dynamics (competition) keep the price of Linux low because it can be freely downloaded. True or False?

15. In the Linux kernel version 2.6.10, the second digit, 6, indicates:

    a. A major kernel release number

    b. A minor kernel release number for a stable kernel

    c. A minor kernel release number for a development kernel

    d. A patch release number

16. Version numbers for Linux distributions don't track Linux kernel version numbers because:

    a. Distributions include many components, so the vendor assigns a version number to the collection of software as a whole.

    b. Developers of the Linux kernel want to avoid having too close a tie with any single Linux vendor by using the same numbering scheme.

    c. Linux kernel versions change too quickly for standard retail cycles to keep up.

    d. Not all kernels are stable and no commercial distribution wants to create an image of poor stability.

17. Which of the following is not a likely motivating factor for those who develop free software?

    a. Greed

    b. Altruism or thanks

    c. Peer acceptance

    d. Desire for interesting work

18. Name five Linux distributions and comment on any specific purposes or background for each one.

19. Which of the following statements is *not* true?

    a. More businesses are using Linux and related products to run their businesses.

    b. Writing free software teaches marketable programming skills.

    c. Thousands of servers running Linux require competent system administrators.

    d. Linux is not based on any other operating system.

20. Linux systems have been known to run for months or years without crashing. True or False?

21. Compare preemptive multitasking to cooperative multitasking.

22. What is multithreading used for?

23. Linux certification programs include:

    a. SAIR/GNU and LPI

    b. GNU and LDP

    c. SuSE and TurboLinux

    d. dice.com and wsj.com

24. The _____ and _____ commands provide information about Linux commands.

    a. `HOWTO` and `mini-HOWTO`

    b. `man` and `info`

    c. `http` and `ftp`

    d. `GPL` and `LGPL`

25. HOWTO documents discuss a variety of specific subjects. They are written for:

    a. Software developers

    b. Journalists

    c. Anyone new to the subject being discussed

    d. Computer novices

HANDS-ON PROJECTS

Project 1-1

In this project, you review several sources of documentation for Linux. You may want to save the results of this project for future use. To complete this project, you should have a computer with access to the Internet and a functioning Web browser.

1. Open your Web browser and connect to the Internet.

2. Go to the homepage of the Linux Documentation Project, at *www.tldp.org.*

3. Click on the **Mirrors** link under LDP Worldwide on the left column of the screen.

    You see a list of sites that contain a copy of the LDP. Find the site that is physically closest to you. (If you have a reason to believe that you would have faster access to a different site, choose it instead.)

4. Note how frequently the mirror site is updated, and then click on your chosen mirror site link.

5. Save the information on your mirror site for future access. For example, choose the **Bookmark** option in your Web browser to record the Web address of the mirror site.

6. Review the home page of the LDP mirror site until you find the HOWTOs link.

7. Explore the HOWTO documents. What different formats are available?

Project 1-2

In this project, you look at some of the different Linux HOWTOs. To complete this project, you should have a computer with access to the Internet and a functional Web browser.

1. Open your Web browser and connect to the Internet.

2. Go to the mirror site for the Linux Documentation Project that you selected in Project 1-1.

3. Click the **HOWTOs** link, then click the **alphabetical index** link to browse the titles of the HOWTO documents in HTML format.

4. Open up a HOWTO document that interests you. Review the table of contents. Note the author and the date of the last update to the HOWTO.

5. Read one section of the HOWTO. Return to the Contents page and select another section to review. Summarize the main points of the document.

6. Use the Back button on your browser to return to the index of HOWTO documents. Select a second HOWTO document to review. Note the date of the last update. Is a link provided so that you could contact the author to obtain more recent information if needed?

Project 1-3

In this project, you review the Web sites for several Linux distributions. To complete this project, you should have a computer with access to the Internet and a functional Web browser.

1. Open your Web browser and connect to the Internet.

2. Visit the following Web sites: *www.debian.org*, *www.sco.com*, *www.suse.com*, *www.redhat.com*.

   Information on the Linux distribution for each company will be listed under a Product link or something similar. For some vendors you can select from among several different versions of Linux for the next step.

3. For each Web site, answer the following questions:

   a. Can you determine the focus of the Linux distribution provided by that vendor? To whom is the company trying to sell products?

   b. What key features of its distribution does each vendor highlight?

   c. What supporting documents (such as magazine articles) can you find on the Web site?

   d. Which Web site and distribution appeal most to you and why?

4. Locate information about signing up for an e-mail list on each Web site. What is the purpose of these mailing lists?

Project 1-4

In this project, you review the Web sites for Linux certification programs. To complete this project, you should have a computer with access to the Internet and a functional Web browser.

1. Open your Web browser and connect to the Internet.

2. Go to *www.comptia.com*.

3. Choose the **certification** link, then click on **Linux+** among the list of certifications.

4. Click on the **Linux+Objectives** link to review the objectives for the **Linux+** certification program.

5. Now visit the Web site *www.lpi.org*. Click on the **The LPI Program** link and then click on the link in the main part of the page to review the objectives for the LPI Level 1 certification.

6. Finally, visit *www.redhat.com/training/rhce/courses*.

7. Review the objectives for the Red Hat Certified Engineer program.

8. What differences do you see between these programs? Does one seem more difficult? Easier? Do the goals of one program seem more in line with your own goals than another? Is one or more program vendor-neutral or dedicated to a single version of Linux?

CASE PROJECTS

Based on your enthusiasm and strong analytical skills, you have just been hired as a consultant by a major international consulting firm, McKinney and Co. Because you are interested in technology, your boss explains that you will be assigned to work on several information technology projects in the coming months. Although you are a junior consultant at the moment, your responsibilities weigh heavily on you. You realize that companies will spend millions of dollars based on your recommendations, and thousands of people will either lead highly productive lives or will soon be laid off based on how you enable their company to succeed.

Your first project assignment is with a small technology startup called PixelDust that sells digital photo services online. In talking with the president of the company, you determine that the company doesn't have a large budget for technology purchases, but that the company's entire reputation depends on having a successful online presence.

1. As the main Web server, your client is considering several platforms, including an IBM AIX system (a version of UNIX) running on an RS/6000 minicomputer, Windows XP running on a large Pentium system, and Linux, also running on a large Pentium system. You lean towards Linux, but the president hesitates because of concerns about the way Linux is developed. (She's just been reading about it in

Business Week.) She asks you to explain why Linux is more stable and secure than other systems, and how the company can run the new Web server on free software. Write a brief report summarizing your thoughts on the matter. What useful information might you find on the vendor Web sites in Project 1-3? What concerns might remain unresolved at this point?

2. The president of PixelDust has started to use Linux as the new Web server, and things are going well. Your manager at McKinney informs you that PixelDust has entered a new consulting agreement in which your team will create a new piece of software to add certain database features to their Web server. As you plan the project, you realize that much of what you need to do has already been done using free software. You are considering using this software to speed development of your project. What considerations will affect your decision? If you decide to use the free software and must make your own project available freely because of the GPL, what justification would you give PixelDust (who is paying you to write the software) and McKinney management? What concerns might both of these parties have? Under what circumstances do you feel that a piece of software should *not* use the GPL?

3. You have used Linux on a number of McKinney projects in the last few months. Do you anticipate problems in the future as Linux becomes more commercial and popular, with mainstream applications, advertising, etc.? How might this affect the attitude of free software developers? How would you feel about the increasing popularity of Linux if you were participating in Linux development? What could commercial Linux vendors do to help alleviate potential problems? What can you do as a consultant who relies on Linux?

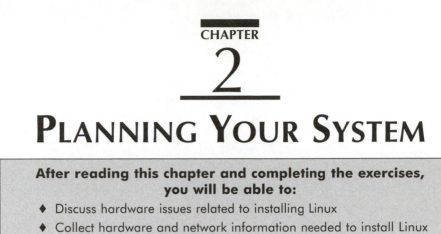

CHAPTER 2

PLANNING YOUR SYSTEM

After reading this chapter and completing the exercises, you will be able to:

♦ Discuss hardware issues related to installing Linux

♦ Collect hardware and network information needed to install Linux

♦ Organize a hard disk efficiently for a Linux installation

In the previous chapter you learned about the development of Linux and the unusual license terms under which Linux (and other free software) is distributed. You also learned about the technical advantages of the Linux operating system and some of the benefits that knowledge of Linux provides in your career plans.

In this chapter you learn more about how Linux uses the hardware resources in your computer system, such as memory and hard disk space. By learning about how Linux uses hardware resources, you can effectively plan how you want to install Linux on a single system or on multiple computers.

PREPARING TO INSTALL LINUX

Most of the computer systems that you have used or purchased yourself probably had an operating system pre-installed. You didn't have to think about how the operating system ended up on the computer's hard disk or how it was configured to use components such as the mouse, the video display capabilities, and the keyboard.

Although you can purchase computers with Linux pre-installed, you will learn a great deal about your computer system and about how Linux operates by installing the operating system yourself.

 Companies that sell systems with Linux pre-installed include VA Software (*www.vasoftware.com*), Penguin Computing (*www.penguincomputing.com*), and Sun Microsystems (their Cobalt network appliances; see *www.sun.com/ hardware/serverappliances*).

Before you install Linux (see Chapter 3), you must plan your installation. This means you must gather information about your computer hardware so that you can answer questions that arise during the installation process. It also means you must determine the best way to organize Linux on your computer—you will learn later in this chapter about completing both of these tasks.

Although the information in this chapter is useful for installing Linux on a single computer, it is even more important to understand installation planning issues when you install Linux on multiple computers, or on a large server with multiple hard disks and advanced hardware components.

You will soon discover that Linux is quite easy to install, especially on newer computers, on which Linux can automatically determine much of the needed information about your system. But the more you know about how the installation process functions, the better you can deal with problems that arise, and the more flexibility you will have when complex installation scenarios present themselves.

Understanding Computer Hardware

Linux treats your computer hardware as a collection of devices. Information is stored on a hard disk device, output is written to a video card device, input is read from a keyboard device, and so forth. Linux must be configured to use all of the devices on your computer system in order to function correctly. Sometimes the task of configuring your hardware is a challenge, although normally you don't need to do much at all.

 Linux can be used on many types of computers, including those that use different types of microprocessors (CPUs), such as Alpha, SPARC, and PowerPC. The discussion in this chapter is devoted solely to computers using Intel and Intel-compatible microprocessors—in other words, standard PCs.

2

Different types of hardware devices communicate with the operating system in different ways. This means that you must gather an array of information about your computer system before you can install Linux. The section "Creating a System Inventory," later in this chapter, explains how to locate the information you need.

It will be helpful to know a few common terms that describe your computer hardware. Space or capacity on a computer system is measured in bytes. A **byte** is enough space to store one character. Each byte is typically composed of eight bits. A **bit** is binary digit; it can hold a value of either one or zero. Eight bits together—a byte—can represent one of 256 different codes, or characters.

Because computers store many characters, space is commonly measured in **megabytes**, abbreviated **MB**. One megabyte is 1,048,576 bytes, or enough space to store roughly 1 million characters. Another common term is **gigabyte**, abbreviated **GB**. One gigabyte is 1024 MB, or roughly enough space to store 1 billion characters. For comparison, this chapter has about 75,000 characters in it. A 400-page novel would contain about 600,000 characters, or less than 1 MB.

Storing Information

One type of electronic computer memory is called **random access memory**, or **RAM**. Information in RAM is only available when the computer is turned on. When you turn the computer off, everything stored in RAM is lost. RAM is normally measured in MB, with most computers having from 32 MB to 512 MB of RAM.

Another type of electronic memory is called **read-only memory**, or **ROM**. ROM stores instructions controlling how the computer starts up and how the computer's devices are configured. Like RAM, ROM is stored on a computer chip, but information in ROM is not lost when the computer is turned off; it is permanent, or nonvolatile. One of the key things stored in ROM is the **Basic Input/Output System**, or **BIOS**, which provides instructions to the operating system for using the devices on the computer. The BIOS itself cannot be changed—it is permanent. But the computer also contains a special type of RAM that stores parameters to control parts of the computer configuration. You may hear this special storage referred to by its technical name, **CMOS RAM**. CMOS RAM depends on a tiny battery to maintain configuration data when the computer is turned off. You can change settings in the CMOS RAM using a utility that is part of the BIOS. Information stored in CMOS RAM by the BIOS utility might include the setting for the computer's clock, information about the structure of each disk drive, a start-up password, and many other details.

 CMOS RAM is an acronym for Complementary Metal Oxide Silicon Random Access Memory. It is usually pronounced "sea-moss-ram." This term describes the technique used to manufacture these memory chips.

You can usually access a menu to view and reconfigure settings related to the BIOS by pressing a key or key sequence while the computer is starting. To find out which key, watch the screen when you turn your computer on. You should see a message like "Press Del for Setup." You then have a few seconds during the system start-up to press the specified key, at which point the computer will display the BIOS configuration menus rather than starting the operating system. You will only need to change your BIOS settings in rare cases before installing Linux.

The hard disk is a magnetic storage space for data such as the operating system and data files that you create. You can think of magnetic storage as being like the stripe on the back of a credit card, except that a hard disk in a typical new computer holds from 20 billion or more characters (20 GB or more of data). Hard disk storage is not permanent—you can make changes to information on the hard disk. But it is also non-volatile—storage on the hard disk remains intact when the computer is turned off. When you turn on your computer, the instructions stored in ROM (the BIOS) load information from the hard disk into RAM for regular operations. When the computer is switched off, the information in RAM is discarded, but the data on the hard disk remains, ready to be reloaded the next time the computer is turned on. Table 2-1 highlights the differences between RAM, ROM (where the BIOS is stored), and the hard disk.

Table 2-1   Computer Storage Components

Component	Permanent (cannot be changed by a computer user)	Volatile (disappears when the power is turned off)
RAM	No	Yes
ROM	Yes	No
Hard disk space	No	No

A computer can have multiple hard disks. Each one is configured as a separate device. In an operating system like Windows, two disk drives would be called C: and D:. The naming scheme is different in Linux, as you will see in Chapter 3.

When you see a reference to Windows in this chapter, the reference applies to all versions of Windows (95, 98, ME, 2000, NT, XP) unless otherwise noted.

Communicating with Devices

Many computer devices communicate with the microprocessor and software programs via interrupt requests. An **interrupt request**, or **IRQ**, is a numbered signal that a device sends to the operating system to request service. A PC has only 16 IRQs, numbered from 0 to 15. Newer devices automatically communicate the correct IRQ number to

Linux; to configure some devices, especially older devices, you may have to determine which IRQ the device uses and specify it for Linux. Later in this chapter you will learn how to determine the IRQ used by a device.

Once a device sends an IRQ signal to the processor, the device and the CPU can communicate data and status information between them. This is done using two methods: direct memory access and port-mapped input/output.

A **direct memory access (DMA) channel** allows a device to read and write directly to the computer's RAM, rather than asking the microprocessor to perform that action for the device. DMA allows a device such as a sound card to read and write information to memory much more quickly than if the microprocessor were involved in each data transaction.

Only a few devices, such as sound cards, use DMA. Most devices use **port-mapped input/output (port-mapped I/O)**—a technique that uses a separate range of memory addresses devoted to device access as a place for a device to send and receive data. Essentially, each device-specific address works like a post office box. The device places data in a specific location called an **I/O port**; software programs retrieve the data from that location using special CPU commands and also place new data there. The device can then retrieve the data placed by the software. For a device to use port-mapped I/O, it must have a port number assigned to it. Most devices can use several different ports, so you can configure your computer to avoid a conflict between two devices that try to use the same ports. A few devices, including sound cards, use both a DMA channel and an I/O port, but this is unusual.

To refer to the I/O port for a device, you use a special numbering system because of the way bytes store information. You may have heard of binary numbers, in which everything is represented by zeros and ones (recall that each bit stores a single binary digit: a zero or a one). Another numbering system used with computer hardware is called hexadecimal. **Hexadecimal** numbering is a base-16 counting system. It uses the letters A through F (usually capitalized) to count the numbers 10 through 15. Using hexadecimal (often called **hex**) numbers is strange at first. For now, remember that when you encounter strange numbers that contain letters, they are simply hexadecimal numbers. Be certain to write them down carefully and enter them in Linux using the format that you see them in, including all the letters.

Hexadecimal numbers are often written with a prefix of 0x to identify them as base-16 numbers. For example, you might see the number 0x220 used as an I/O port address. The 0x indicates that this is a hexadecimal number. You don't need to convert it to a normal (decimal, or base-10) number. Just use it in Linux as it's written.

The range of IRQ numbers from 0 to 15 can be represented by single hexadecimal digits. The possible IRQ numbers in hex are 0, 1, 2, 3, 4, 5, 6, 7, 8, 9, A, B, C, D, E, F.

Hard Disk Devices

The hard disk in a computer must communicate with the microprocessor using an electronic interface that controls how data is sent and received. Two interfaces are used for hard disks in PCs: IDE (integrated drive electronics) and SCSI (small computer systems interface).

IDE is a low-cost, easy-to-manage interface used on virtually all new computers to connect hard disks and CD-ROMs to the CPU. Standard new PCs always include one IDE hard disk. An **IDE controller** is a device that handles communication between the hard disk and the microprocessor. The IDE controller is normally integrated into the system board rather than being a separate expansion card. To use an IDE controller card to connect to the CPU, the hard disk must be compatible with the IDE interface. You will hear such hard disks referred to as IDE hard disks. Each IDE controller can be connected to two IDE devices, such as hard disks and CD-ROM drives. Many computers come with two IDE controllers. Figure 2-1 shows how two IDE controllers, each with a separate cable, can be connected to hard disk and CD-ROM devices.

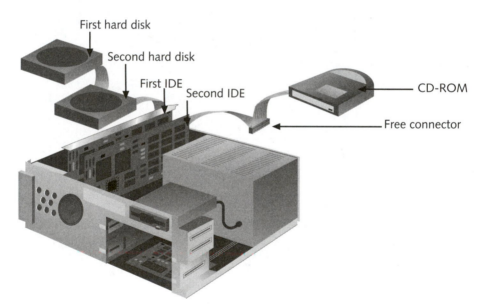

Figure 2-1   Hard disk and CD-ROM devices on multiple IDE interfaces

 In reviewing hardware on newer computers, you will see references to IDE-U, UltraIDE, and ATA-100. These terms all refer to IDE-compatible devices. The latest versions of IDE (such as UltraIDE) improve the speed and configuration flexibility of the IDE interface. All of these should be supported by Linux.

SCSI is a high–performance interface used to connect many types of devices to a computer. SCSI is designed for higher performance than IDE. A single SCSI controller can support many more devices, and performance doesn't degrade as new devices are added as on an IDE controller. But SCSI devices are much more expensive than IDE devices. SCSI devices include hard disks, scanners, plotters, tape backup drives, and other devices. As with IDE, a SCSI controller card provides the connection between SCSI-compatible devices and the CPU of the computer. A single SCSI controller card can connect up to 15 devices, each linked by a cable, as illustrated in Figure 2-2.

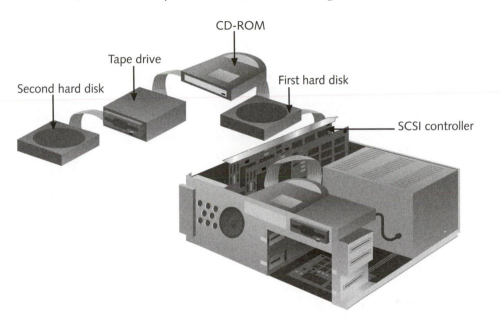

Figure 2-2   Multiple SCSI devices linked together by cables

Supported Linux Hardware

Linux works with thousands of different hardware devices, from very old proprietary CD-ROM drives to the latest high-speed networking cards. But not all devices work with Linux. Although Linux is growing in popularity, relatively few companies that manufacture hardware devices provide software to support their products on Linux. Instead, they rely on the free software community to create that software, often based on technical information provided by the manufacturer. As a result, if no free software developer has taken an interest in supporting a hardware product that you need, that product might not be supported in Linux.

The software used to support a hardware device in Linux is usually called a driver, or **device driver**. You must have the appropriate driver in order to use any hardware device, including something as simple as a keyboard. Many device drivers are standardized and included by default in Linux; only a few devices require special efforts to locate driver software.

This overstates the problem, however, since nearly all hardware devices you would be interested in are supported by Linux. In fact, with the most recent kernel version, Linux has strong support for USB devices, Firewire (IEEE-1394 video), and a variety of other fairly recent and popular types of hardware.

The exceptions to Linux hardware support are found in areas such as these:

- Windows-proprietary devices, such as WinModems and WinPrinters. These devices rely on part of the Windows operating system to provide the "brains" of the device. Some of these are supported in Linux, but it has been hard for developers to duplicate the software to operate these devices without technical specifications from the manufacturers and from Microsoft (neither of which has been forthcoming).

- Very old hardware that was not supported in early Linux kernels and is not used widely enough to have warranted later effort to add support.

- Very new hardware for which software is still under development but has not been released. Examples include new video cards and some digital cameras.

- Unusual or specialized hardware that relatively few users are interested in. There are few areas, however, where Linux developers haven't created the software to suit their interests. For example, Linux *does* support things like specialized data acquisition cards, scanners, high-end music hardware, computer telephony hardware, amateur radio networking hardware, and many other devices you might not have even heard of.

The list of hardware that Linux supports is too long to include in this book. But before starting a Linux installation, it's a good idea to check on the Web site of a Linux vendor to see if the hardware that you want to include on your Linux system is supported.

One of the most comprehensive sites for exploring Linux hardware compatibility is located at *http://hardware.redhat.com*. Although this site is run by Red Hat Software, the information that you find here applies to all Linux distributions. This is true because hardware support is provided through the Linux kernel, and all versions of Linux rely on essentially the same kernel. A sample Web page showing information on this hardware compatibility site is shown in Figure 2-3.

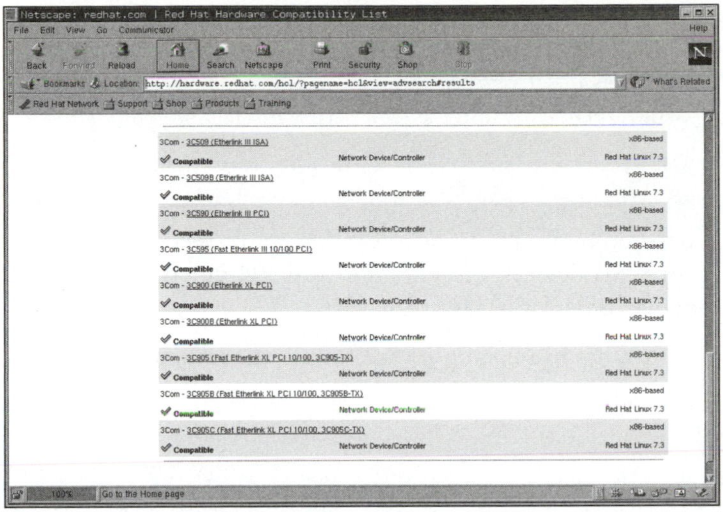

Figure 2-3 Linux hardware compatibility information on the Red Hat Software Web site

Understanding Networking

Many Linux systems are connected to networks so that they can communicate and share resources with other users connected to the network. Linux is often used to provide access to a printer or an Internet connection for many networked computers. Linux also works well as a **file server**, a computer on which many users store their data files for access across a network.

Sometimes a networked computer relies on another computer on the network to provide configuration details. In this situation, the computer that has no networking configuration is set up to "configure itself" when it is turned on by searching the network for the configuration data it needs. This is called **dynamic network configuration**. It is provided through a protocol called the **Dynamic Host Configuration Protocol (DHCP)**. The computer that provides networking configuration data for other computers is called the **DHCP server**.

If your system administrator has set up a DHCP server on your network, configuring networking when you install Linux is easy; you can just specify an option such as "Use DHCP" or "Use Dynamic Configuration."

Setting up a DHCP server is described in Chapter 3 of *Guide to Linux Networking and Security*.

If you do not have a DHCP server on your network and you plan on using Linux on a network, you need to define basic networking parameters when you install Linux. Even if you are using DHCP for your first installation, a basic knowledge of networking concepts is critical for your work as a Linux system administrator.

To communicate with each other effectively, computer systems use networking protocols. A **protocol** is an organized pattern of signals or words. Linux networking involves many different protocols. One protocol provides basic communication between network adapters (hardware in the computer that provides an interface between the computer and the network). Another lets Web browsers communicate with Web servers. Altogether, Linux supports dozens of networking protocols, each one designed for a different purpose. Some of the most important protocols are discussed in the following sections.

IP Networking

The most important protocol for Linux networking is called the Internet Protocol, or IP. **IP** is a networking protocol used to send packets of information across a network connection. IP is the basis on which most Linux networking (as well as the Internet) is built. In order to use IP networking, each computer on the network must be assigned an identifying number, called an **IP address**. Each packet of data sent across the network includes two IP addresses: the address of the computer that sent the packet and the address of the computer that should receive the packet.

An IP address consists of four numbers, each separated by a period. For example, 207.29.12.1 is an IP address; so is 192.168.100.15. Each of the four numbers can be a value from 0 to 255, though many addresses and address ranges are reserved for special purposes.

A new version of IP networking is under development. This version is called IPv6 (for version 6), or IPng (for Next Generation). IPv6 addresses are four times as large as regular IP addresses (which are sometimes called IPv4, for version 4). Having larger addresses means that IPv6 can support many more networked devices. IPv6 also has many other advanced features to improve the Internet. IPv6 is an advanced topic that is not discussed in this book, but Linux fully supports IPv6 networking. You can learn more about it by visiting *www.6bone.net*.

IP addresses are used all over the world, but if any two users have identical IP addresses, their networks can malfunction. To avoid these problems, you must only use an IP address that has been assigned to the computer on which you install Linux. Typically, your instructor or your Internet Service Provider (ISP) will assign you an IP address from a range of addresses that they have been assigned.

2

All of the IP addresses on a single network are related; for example, their first three numbers may be the same. Several special IP addresses are associated with setting up Linux networking so that packets can be passed around the network. These special IP addresses are listed here:

- A **network mask** tells the networking system in Linux how to identify IP numbers that are part of the local network, as opposed to IP numbers that are assigned to computers outside the local network.

- A **network address** identifies the local network that the computer is a part of. This address is used to determine how data is routed to its intended destination.

- A **broadcast address** identifies a special IP address that will send a packet of data to all computers on the local network.

- A **gateway address** identifies the computer that can send packets of data outside the local network, to the Internet, or to other networks in an organization.

Most Linux installation programs will calculate default values of the above addresses after you enter your assigned IP address. Check the values on-screen as you install Linux and be certain they match the information provided by your system administrator or instructor. If you received only an IP address, accept the default values that the installation program provides.

Domain Names and Hostnames

Transmitting data across a network would be difficult if you had to remember the IP address for every computer you wanted to access. To simplify matters, we use a system of human-readable names for computers and networks. Each name is mapped to (is associated with) a specific IP address. As described in the next section, a special network server does the work of translating computer and network names into IP addresses, and vice versa.

A name assigned to a collection of computers is called a **domain name**. Some examples of domain names are *ibm.com*, *linux.org*, and *nasa.gov*. Domain names within a large organization may be longer than this. For example, within IBM, you may find domains called *marketing.ibm.com*, *sales.ibm.com*, and *research.ibm.com*. The last word of a domain name will always be one of the standard top-level (most generalized) domain names. Table 2-2 shows a few of the top-level domains you are likely to see. Not all of the top-level domain names are listed, because each nation has a separate top-level domain name. Also, other top-level domain names are occasionally added, such as .info and .biz. You can learn more about current domain names by visiting the Domain Name Services link at *www.iana.net*.

Table 2-2   Top-Level Domains

Name	Description
.com	Commercial/business entities
.org	Noncommercial organizations
.net	Organizations whose work relates to the Internet
.edu	Educational institutions, usually colleges and universities in the United States
.gov	U.S. government organizations
.mil	U.S. military organizations
.us	Top-level domain for networks in the United States; used mostly for local governments and schools
.de	Top-level domain of Germany (Deutschland)
.uk	Top-level domain of the United Kingdom

Each computer in a domain is assigned a name. Computers involved in networking are often called **hosts**; so the name of a computer on the network is referred to as the computer's hostname. The **hostname** is a single word used to name a computer. Your instructor or system administrator may let you choose a hostname, or may assign one, such as lab13, or training01.

The hostname is combined with the domain name to create a **fully qualified domain name (FQDN)**. An example of an FQDN would be *lab13.myschool.edu*. Using the longer domain names given previously as examples, a sample FQDN might be *taco.research.ibm.com*. Web page addresses take the form of FQDNs. For example, the Web address *www.ibm.com* consists of a hostname (*www*) and a domain name (*ibm.com*). How can you tell that this is not simply a long domain name? By using a Web browser to successfully access a system using that FQDN. (You can't tell by looking at the name.) In theory, IBM could have a sub-domain named *www.ibm.com*. A host in that sub-domain with a hostname such as *florida* would yield a FQDN of *florida.www.ibm.com*.

Domain Name Service (DNS)

For the computers on your local network, you may decide to maintain a file that lists each hostname and the corresponding IP address of that computer. This is convenient for small networks, but quickly becomes unmanageable as the network grows in size. Even on a small network, making a change in one hostname means you must update the configuration file on every computer on the network.

A better approach for large networks and the Internet as a whole is the **Domain Name Service (DNS)**, a network service devoted to the task of mapping human-readable domain names and hostnames to the IP addresses of specific networks and computers. A **DNS server** is the computer that actually performs this conversion. The process works like this: When you enter the address *www.ibm.com* in a Web browser, the browser sends a network packet to a DNS server asking for the IP address of *www.ibm.com*. Once that address is returned by the DNS server, the Web browser can establish a connection to the IBM Web server using the IP address.

Generally, you must provide the IP address of a DNS server as you configure Linux networking. This allows your Linux system to use DNS to convert hostnames and domain names into IP addresses.

Creating a Shared System

You can install Linux on a system that already uses another operating system, such as Windows XP. This allows you to experiment with Linux and take advantage of its features while still using another operating system to support other needs, such as running applications that are not available for Linux. Such a shared system is also called a **dual-boot system**. It allows you to choose which operating system to start each time you boot (turn on) your computer. You can actually have numerous operating systems installed on one computer, not just two. The name dual-boot is commonly used to refer to any system with more than one operating system installed.

A program called a **boot manager** lets you select an operating system each time you boot the computer. Two popular boot managers used by Linux distributions are **GRUB** and **LILO (Linux Loader)**. You can also use commercial boot manager programs such as System Commander (see *www.v-com.com*) or BootMagic (see *www.powerquest.com*). Installing a Linux boot manager is part of every Linux installation, as you will learn in Chapter 3.

To create a dual-boot system, you must decide where on the computer's hard disk(s) each operating system will reside. Two basic options are available:

- Store multiple operating systems on a single hard disk.
- Store each operating system on a separate hard disk.

To use multiple operating systems on a single hard disk, you must first decide how much space you need for each operating system. The first operating system installed on the computer (often a version of Windows) probably takes up a lot of space already. You can determine the amount of hard disk space used on a Windows XP system as follows:

1. Click **start**, **All Programs**, **Accessories**, **Windows Explorer** to open a file system explorer window.

2. Click the plus sign "+" next to **My Computer**, then right-click on the **Local Disk** item.

3. Click **Properties**. The Properties dialog box opens.

4. View the information on the General tab of the Properties dialog box, which is shown in Figure 2-4. This window shows the amount of used space and free space, as well as other information that will be covered later in this chapter.

5. Click **Cancel** to close the Properties dialog box.

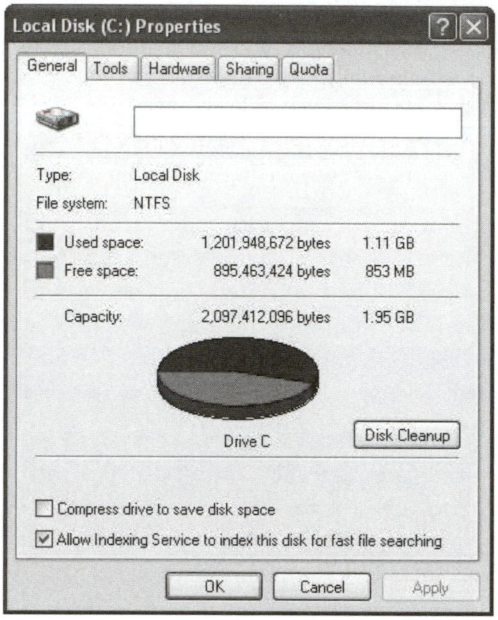

Figure 2-4   Hard disk information in the Windows Properties dialog box

Once you know how much space is available on the hard disk where Windows is stored, you can consider how much of the available free space you could use for your Linux operating system.

As with other operating systems, the exact components you need to install depend on what you intend to do with Linux. The more components you add, the more space you need on the hard disk. Each Linux distribution offers different standard installation options. Usually you can select a standard installation (such as Desktop or Server), or you can select more precisely which software packages you want to install. If you are familiar with Linux software, you may want to specify one or more packages to install; otherwise, you should simply indicate a general type of installation, such as Desktop or Server system.

The sizes of a few standard options that you might see as you install different Linux distributions are shown in Table 2-3. Most distributions inform you of the amount of disk space needed as you select different options.

Table 2-3 Typical Linux Installation Options

Type of installation	Typical hard disk space required	Comments
Server installation without graphics support	200–300 MB	A server system doesn't require graphical support, which saves hard disk space. The amount of space required depends on which network services are provided (for example, e-mail server, Web server, file server, etc.). For many servers, you should also calculate the amount of hard disk space needed for data storage (such as Web pages or e-mail messages).
Standard installation with graphics and common utilities	500–800 MB	You will probably start with a typical installation that includes a graphical desktop, some networking capabilities, common utilities, and documentation.
Developer's workstation	700 MB–1.3 GB	A developer typically uses a standard graphical workstation but adds many packages to aid in software development.
Complete installation	1.3 GB–4+ GB	A "complete installation" combines all packages for a graphical workstation, a developer, a network server and more. It typically does not actually install *all* packages in the distribution, however, because some are experimental, or highly specialized, or conflict with each other (that is, you can choose one or the other but not both). If you have plenty of hard disk space, a complete installation is a nice way to have everything to explore Linux.

A basic guideline for new Linux users is to have around 1.5 GB of free hard disk space to install a standard distribution comfortably with enough disk space left to experiment with your system.

Graphical Systems

For years, the most challenging part of installing Linux was configuring the video hardware to provide a graphical interface. Fortunately, Linux vendors such as Caldera (now The SCO Group), SuSE, and Red Hat Software have created installation programs that automatically detect video settings and let you quickly choose the display type that you prefer.

The one exception to easy graphical configuration is when you install Linux on a laptop. In that case, you may want to consult the Web site *www.linux-laptop.net* to see how Linux experts who own the same model of laptop as you have managed to get Linux running properly.

Despite the easy steps for installation, it's a good idea to understand some video card concepts for those times when the installation doesn't go as smoothly as planned. Video cards are inherently a challenging topic because very few standards exist—every vendor tries to create something newer and better using proprietary technology that requires special software for each new product. And although some video card vendors are dedicated to supporting Linux, most leave the Linux market on its own, providing at best occasional technical assistance.

The graphical environment in Linux is provided by the X Window System. Software from the **XFree86 Project** adds the X Window System to Linux. (For more information on this free software project, visit *www.xfree86.org*.)

You can read about the two major commercial X Window System products for Linux by visiting Xi Graphics at *www.xig.com* and MetroLink at *www.metrolink.com*.

The Web page for the XFree86 Project contains a complete list of video cards supported by their software. New video cards are added regularly as new versions of XFree86 are released. Video card manufacturers are slowly beginning to recognize the fact that having support in XFree86 software helps to sell more video cards, and so they are becoming more open about providing technical information to the free software community.

Monitors and the Graphical System

Because the X Window System is flexible enough to use all the features of a video card, it may be able to produce better graphics than your monitor can display. This can cause a newer, powerful video card to send signals that damage older monitors. For example, if you have a video card that supports a high-resolution display of 1240 × 1024 pixels, but your monitor is not capable of displaying that resolution, the signal from the video card might damage the monitor.

The solution to this potential problem is to configure Linux with the correct information about your monitor's capabilities. Thus, Linux will calculate what the monitor can support and block any signals that the monitor cannot handle. In the example just given, a suitable lower resolution mode would be selected to display graphics.

Most new monitors are **multisync monitors**, which means that the monitor can accept data in a range of frequencies. Three specifications identify a monitor's capabilities:

- The number of screen redraws per second (called the refresh rate). This number is expressed in hertz, or Hz. An example range for refresh rates is 50 to 90.

- The number of lines per second that can be redrawn. This number is expressed in kilohertz, or KHz.

- The clock speed of the monitor's electronics, which determines the rate at which data can be transferred between a video card and the monitor. (Indirectly, this also determines how many colors the monitor can support, since displaying more colors requires more information per screen.) This number is expressed in megahertz, or MHz.

If you have problems with the automated graphical configuration, having the above numbers can help you set up the system manually.

CREATING A SYSTEM INVENTORY

The Linux installation program may automatically detect all of your hardware and proceed without a hitch. While working as a system administrator, however, you're sure to encounter a few system components that Linux doesn't recognize. The information in this section helps you learn about your computer system in anticipation of those times. The more you understand about your hardware, the better you can help the installation proceed smoothly by answering questions and locating any additional software that Linux needs to support your hardware.

Table 2-4 lists hardware information that can be helpful during an installation that isn't proceeding smoothly. Example values for each item appear in the middle column; the far right column is blank, so you can enter data from your own system. The following sections explain how to locate the information.

The information in Table 2-4 can also be valuable *after* you have installed Linux, when you need to update configurations for the boot manager, the graphical system, or other parts of the Linux operating system.

Table 2-4   Useful Hardware Information for Installing Linux

Hardware information	Sample value	Your system
Amount of RAM	128 MB	
Hard disk interface type	IDE	
Hard disk size	20 GB	
Serial port used by modem	COM1 (first serial port)	
IRQ used by modem	4	
Printer port	LPT1 (first parallel port)	
CD-ROM interface type	IDE	
Type of mouse	Microsoft serial	
Port used by mouse	COM2 (second serial port)	
Monitor make and model	NEC Multisync C400	
Monitor scan rate range	50–90	
Video card make and model	Starfighter AGP	
Video card chipset	Intel i740	
Amount of video RAM	8 MB	
SCSI card make and model (if you have one in your system)	Adaptec AIC-7850	
Network adapter make and model	3Com Fast Etherlink XL 10/100	
IRQ used by the network adapter	11	
Sound card make and model	SoundBlaster	
IRQ, DMA channel, and memory addresses used by the sound card	10, 3, 220	

In addition to information about your hardware, you should ask your system administrator or instructor to provide any networking information needed for installation. If your network uses DHCP, you may not need any further information. For manual network configuration, you might need any or all of the items listed in Table 2-5.

Table 2-5   Information Needed to Set Up Linux Networking

Network information	Sample value	Your system
Domain name	xmission.com	
Hostname	brighton	
DHCP server address	207.49.12.1	
Static IP address	192.168.100.13	
Network mask	255.255.255.0	
Broadcast address	192.168.100.255	
Gateway address	192.168.100.1	
DNS server address	192.168.100.1	
Secondary DNS server address	207.29.12.2	

Some computer labs may be set up to provide all of the Linux installation data on a central server. Installations that use a network connection to access installation data may also require that you provide the information in Table 2-6.

Table 2-6   Information Needed for a Networked Installation

Network installation information	Sample value	Your system
NFS or SMB server IP address	192.168.100.4	
Path to the installation files on the remote server	/mnt/cdrom	

You can get the information described in these tables from a variety of sources. It's probably easiest to ask a technician or system administrator who is familiar with the hardware you are working on. However, if you use the methods described in the following sections, you will learn more about how your system functions and be better prepared to become a system administrator yourself.

Finding the Manuals

Most computer systems include some type of printed manual that describes how to set up and use the system. Unfortunately, this documentation is usually filed in some forgotten corner. Although manuals seem to be getting smaller every year, yours probably contains at least a few key specifications for your system. If you can locate your computer's manual, do the following:

- Look in the index under the name of the hardware component from Table 2-4 that you want to learn more about.

- Check the Table of Contents for a section named Specifications or Troubleshooting.

- Review the first few pages of the section on setting up the system. It may contain other details about the hardware.

Most computers come with separate manuals for each component; each of these manuals is provided by a different manufacturer. (Sometimes these manuals are tucked inside a sleeve with a CD-ROM full of software for the device.) Look for separate manuals on the following items:

- Main system (the CPU)

- Monitor

- Mouse

- Video card

- Modem

- CD-ROM drive

- Sound card

If you can't locate the printed manuals, try going online. Visit the Web site for the manufacturer of the component. Search under Products, Technical Support, or a related topic. Locating technical information on a huge Web site can be time-consuming, but this information is generally free. A sample Web page showing the specifications for a Toshiba laptop is shown in Figure 2-5.

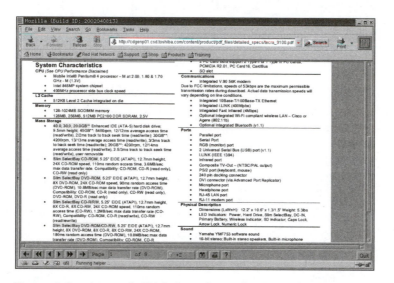

Figure 2-5   A sample Web-based specifications sheet

Reviewing BIOS Settings

Sometimes you can find information that is not evident in the printed or online documentation by reviewing the BIOS of the computer itself. Different systems use various methods of accessing the BIOS configuration menus, where you can learn about system status and devices. An on-screen message normally explains how to enter the Setup or BIOS information screen when you first boot the computer. Depending on your system, you might be asked to press F2, Del, Esc, or some other key or combination of keys to enter the BIOS menus. Review the system documentation if you don't see a message explaining how to enter the BIOS menus.

The exact steps for exploring the BIOS menus are not given here because each manufacturer uses a different interface for configuring the BIOS. A sample screen for BIOS configuration is shown in Figure 2-6.

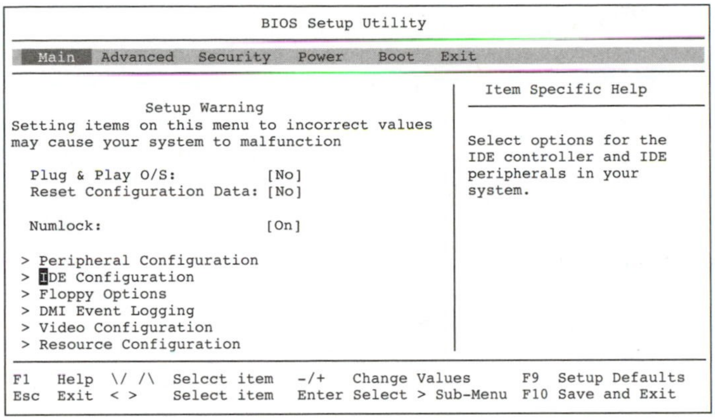

```
                          BIOS Setup Utility

  Main   Advanced   Security   Power   Boot   Exit

                                        │  Item Specific Help
                  Setup Warning          │
Setting items on this menu to incorrect values │
may cause your system to malfunction    │  Select options for the
                                        │  IDE controller and IDE
  Plug & Play O/S:           [No]        │  peripherals in your
  Reset Configuration Data: [No]         │  system.
                                        │
  Numlock:                  [On]         │
                                        │
> Peripheral Configuration              │
> IDE Configuration                     │
> Floppy Options                        │
> DMI Event Logging                     │
> Video Configuration                   │
> Resource Configuration                │

F1   Help  \/ /\  Selcct item   -/+   Change Values     F9  Setup Defaults
Esc  Exit  < >    Select item   Enter Select > Sub-Menu F10 Save and Exit
```

Figure 2-6   BIOS configuration menus

Keep the following points in mind as you examine the BIOS menus for hardware information:

- Most BIOS configurations include a number of options that are not relevant to installing Linux. These include things like the time to wait before entering low-power mode and whether to include a power-on password. You can ignore these options and focus on locating the information in Table 2-4.

- Different levels of information may be provided in different menus. The details in Table 2-4 are often in the Advanced portion of the BIOS configuration, because most users don't need to know this information to use a system that is already up and running.

- You can make changes to the settings in the BIOS and save them as you exit the BIOS setup utility. Don't do this unless you have studied the system documentation and are familiar with the features you are altering. Watch carefully as you exit the BIOS menus to make sure you do not accidentally choose a Save and Exit option unless you intend to. If you make changes, write down the settings that you alter so that you can change them back to their original values if the computer doesn't function as expected.

You should find the following information as you review your BIOS settings:

- Amount of RAM on the system.

- Hard disk interface type and size of each hard disk.

- Serial ports available on the system and the IRQ used by each one.

- IRQ numbers used by other devices that might conflict with devices such as a sound card or network adapter. (You usually can't see the IRQ used by these devices in the BIOS menus.)

- SCSI card make and model.

Without accessing the BIOS, you can use a related method for locating system information: simply watch the screen carefully as the system starts. Many devices, especially SCSI cards and video cards, print identification messages to the screen as they are initialized at system boot time. You may have to power the system off and on several times to read the messages, but you can often gain much useful information from these small "advertisements" that are printed on screen.

Studying Microsoft Windows

If your computer is already running a Windows operating system, you have an advantage in preparing for installation: the Windows operating system has already collected all of the hardware configuration information for you. Before installing Linux, you can start your computer in Windows and write down all the configuration information you'll need to use when installing Linux.

Device information in Windows is available from the Windows Control Panel, which you can view by clicking Start, then Settings, then Control Panel. You can also double-click the My Computer icon on the Desktop, and then double-click the Control Panel icon. The Windows Control Panel (Classic view in Windows XP) is shown in Figure 2-7. The icons on each Windows system vary slightly based on the hardware and software that you have installed; so your screen will likely vary from the figure.

Figure 2-7   The Windows Control Panel

2

Different versions of Windows (such as 98, NT, XP, ME, and 2000) arrange information differently in the Control Panel. You can explore several of the Control Panel sections by double-clicking on icons that appear to have useful information. For example, you might try double-clicking on one or more of the following Control Panel icons (not every icon is available on every version of Windows):

- Devices
- Display, via the Settings tab (choose the Display Type or Advanced Settings button)
- Multimedia, via the Devices tab
- Network, via the Adapters tab
- Ports
- Printers
- SCSI Adapters
- System

In the various lists of devices, you may be able to see the manufacturer and model name in some cases. Within some Windows dialog boxes, you can further research your system's hardware by selecting a hardware device and choosing the Properties button at the bottom of the dialog box or selecting Properties from a right-click pop-up menu.

You can also use Windows to find details about your networking configuration. Because a computer cannot run both Windows and Linux at the same time, you can normally use the same networking information for Linux that you use for Windows.

Within the Windows Control Panel, the Network Connections item opens a window in which you can select a network connection to review. If you have a Local Area Connection listed in this Network Connections window, double-click that item. A Local Area Connection Status dialog box appears.

Within the Local Area Connection Status dialog box, select the Support tab to view basic TCP/IP networking information. You can also change back to the General tab in that dialog box and click Properties to open a Local Area Connection Properties dialog box. This dialog box is shown in Figure 2-8.

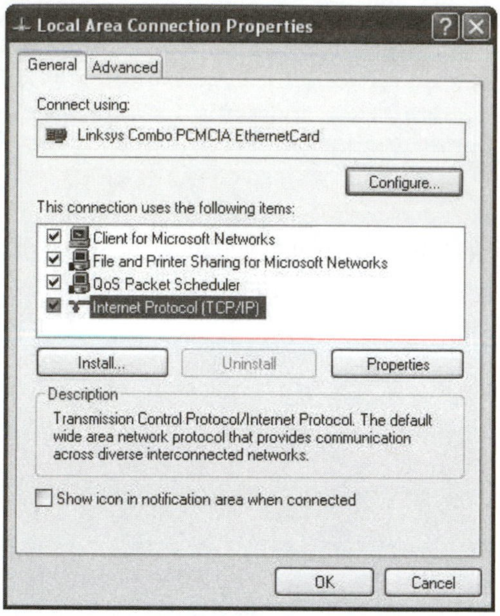

Figure 2-8   Local Area Connection Properties dialog box in Window XP

With the Internet Protocol (TCP/IP) item selected in the General tab, click the Properties button to open an Internet Protocol Properties dialog box. In this dialog box you may see that your computer is obtaining network information automatically. If your computer has manually configured network settings, you can collect them here. They include the following:

- The IP address of the computer.

- The subnet mask for the network on which the computer sits.

- The default gateway that the computer uses to access computers outside your local network.

- A DNS server to resolve between IP addresses and domain names.

- An alternate DNS server to contact when the main DNS server cannot be reached.

On some versions of Windows, you can find the IP address information used by Windows by choosing the Network icon in the Control Panel and then choosing the Protocols tab. Within that tab, double-click the TCP/IP Protocol item and view the IP Address and DNS tabs.

 Exit all of the Windows dialog boxes described here by choosing the Cancel button. This way you won't accidentally alter your Windows settings and cause problems with your hardware or networking configurations.

Asking Networking Questions

The only way to obtain some network settings is to ask the person (or organization) that assigns that setting. For instance, you cannot simply choose a network address, nor is the network address of your gateway or other servers something that you can guess. To get most of the networking information listed in Table 2-5 and Table 2-6, you will need to ask the authority who originally set up your network connection—that is, you need to consult either your instructor, system administrator, or ISP.

In some cases, you will be allowed to select a hostname for your Linux installation. You can choose any brief name that you want for the hostname. System administrators often use a pattern of names for setting up multiple computers, such as the names of animals, cities, foods, colors, or something similar. The names are arbitrary, but you must provide the name to the person who manages the DNS name server on your network so that e-mail and other services can be directed to your computer.

PREPARING YOUR HARD DISK

You must install Linux in a dedicated partition on the hard disk. A **partition** is a distinct area of a hard disk that has been prepared to store a particular type of data. For example, a computer that only contains Windows normally has only one partition on its hard disk. That partition is marked as containing Windows data. To install Linux you must prepare another partition that is marked as containing Linux data. You must create a Linux partition whether you plan to establish a dual-boot system or install only Linux on your computer.

You can think of a partition as an empty space on the disk with a label attached to it. Before a partition can hold information, it must be formatted with a particular file system type. The term **file system** refers to the arrangement of information on a device such as a hard disk. The organization usually takes the form of files and directories. In theory, you could create a partition that was marked as holding a certain file system type, then format that partition with a different file system type than the partition specified. In practice, however, the operating system prevents this sort of mistake.

Figure 2-9 shows how three partitions might be arranged on a hard disk, with marks indicating the file system type and a file system format inside each partition. Linux uses one of two default file system types: `ext2` or `ext3` (extended file system version 2 or version 3). The default file system type for older versions of DOS and Windows is called **FAT** (File Allocation Table). Windows NT and newer versions of Windows use **NTFS** (NT file system) or FAT32 (32-bit File Allocation Table).

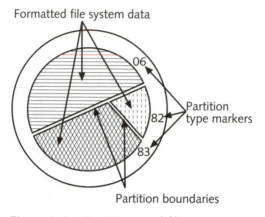

Formatted file system data

Partition type markers

Partition boundaries

Figure 2-9   Partitions and file systems on a hard disk

Because of limitations in how hard disks were designed years ago, each hard disk can have only four partitions. These are called **primary partitions** and are numbered 1 through 4. To avoid the limitation of four primary partitions, you can set up multiple **logical partitions** within a single primary partition. Logical partitions are numbered beginning with 5. A logical partition is the same as a primary partition as far as your operating system is concerned, but the software used to configure your hard disk must set up logical partitions differently than primary partitions.

Some Linux distributions such as Red Hat Linux use logical partitions by default so that a complex Linux installation on a large hard disk doesn't use all the available partitions.

Among all of the partitions on a hard disk, one can be marked as the **active partition**, or the bootable partition. If you haven't modified the default settings, the BIOS passes control to the operating system in this partition.

In Chapter 3 you will learn in detail about the tools you can use to create Linux partitions. To use these tools, you must have free space available on your hard disk. For computers that will be dual-boot systems, you must prepare the free space for Linux before you start the Linux installation. For computer systems that will have only Linux installed, the partitions can be created during the installation. The information in the following sections will help you understand how to use the partitioning tools discussed in Chapter 3 and how to create free space on a hard disk that is initially dedicated to Windows.

2

Booting the System

When you turn on a computer, the BIOS initializes the devices on the system, then passes control to whatever program is located on a small area of the first hard disk called the **Master Boot Record**, or **MBR**. The MBR contains a small program that decides how to start an operating system. Normally, the MBR does this by passing control to the program located on the boot record of the active partition. The **boot record** is a small area on each partition that contains a boot manager program to launch the operating system on that partition. For partitions containing Linux, the boot record contains a copy of GRUB, LILO, or a commercial boot manager.

The Linux boot manager can be stored on either the Master Boot Record or on the boot record of the active partition. The boot manager on a Linux partition can include instructions that pass control to another partition, such as a partition containing a Windows operating system. This creates a dual-boot system in which you choose the operating system to start each time you turn on the computer.

Figure 2-10 shows how a hard disk is arranged to include an MBR and a boot record on multiple partitions, with one partition being marked as active. Sometimes the boot record is called the boot sector, or the root sector, of the partition.

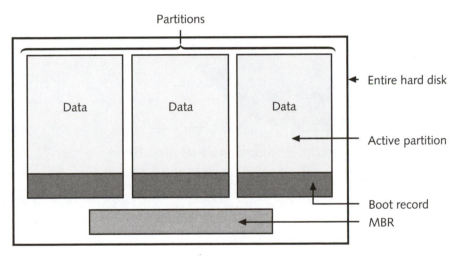

Figure 2-10　A hard disk with an MBR and boot records on each partition

Hard Disk Geometry

The operating system stored on a hard disk arranges information according to the file system used on that partition. Each operating system has a default file system. But the hard disk itself is designed to store information according to the physical characteristics of the hard disk. Sometimes you need to know about the disk drive layout to configure the system properly.

A hard disk is composed of multiple flat platters that hold magnetic data. These platters are stacked together, with small devices moving between the platters to read the data on each platter. Each concentric circle on a platter is called a **track**. When you format a hard disk, each track is divided into multiple sectors. A **sector** is a unit of data storage on a hard disk. Normally a sector contains 512 bytes. Sectors are often grouped together into larger units called clusters or blocks. A default hard disk **block** in Linux is a unit of hard disk space that contains 1024 bytes, or two sectors. Figure 2-11 shows a single platter of a hard disk with the tracks, sectors, and blocks illustrated.

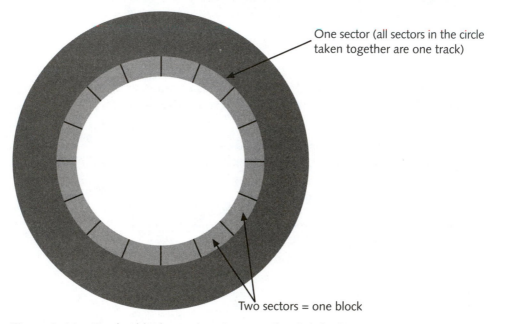

One sector (all sectors in the circle taken together are one track)

Two sectors = one block

Figure 2-11   Tracks, blocks, and sectors on a hard disk platter

Taken together, all of the tracks at the same position on each platter are called a **cylinder**. If you imagine a hollow cylinder being inserted from the top of a stack of platters, all of the tracks that the cylinder intersects as it passes through the platters are collectively called a cylinder. Figure 2-12 illustrates this concept.

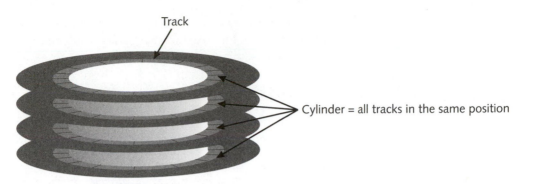

Figure 2-12   A cylinder on a hard disk

Figures 2-11 and 2-12 illustrate the concepts behind hard disk layout, but they are some-what deceptive. A hard disk often has over 1000 cylinders, or concentric tracks, on each platter. This is an important point. Hard disks with many cylinders can cause special installation problems for Linux because of limitations in the BIOS of many computers. The next section explains this problem.

Swap Partitions

The Linux operating system and the files that you create in Linux are stored in a parti-tion of type `ext2` or `ext3`. In addition to this partition, you create a separate partition used as a swap partition for the Linux kernel's virtual memory. **Virtual memory** is a special area of the hard disk that the operating system treats as if it were RAM, storing programs there temporarily when they are not being used. The **swap partition** (also called **swap space**) is the designated area used as virtual memory by the Linux kernel. For example, you might start several programs in Linux, but if one of the programs is sitting idle and the RAM memory that the program uses is needed by another program, the Linux kernel will copy part of the program or its data to the swap partition. When the program is activated again, the program and data are moved back to RAM so they can continue operating.

Using a separate partition controlled by the Linux kernel allows the virtual memory fea-ture to work very quickly, without interfering with other hard disk operations that read from or write to the Linux partition where regular data files are stored. A swap partition is normally from 32 MB to 256 MB in size, though it can be smaller or larger depend-ing on how much hard disk space you have and how busy the Linux system is.

If you have multiple hard disks in your system, configure your swap partition to be on a different hard disk than the bulk of your data files. This allows more efficient access to both virtual memory and data files because the two disks can work in tandem.

You create a swap partition just as you create a regular Linux partition, using the tools provided with the installation program. The partition is marked with the code 0x82 to indicate that it is to be used for Linux virtual memory.

Preparing a Shared Hard Disk

To create a dual-boot system running Linux and Windows (or another operating system), you must have a separate hard disk on which Linux will be installed, or else you must use some of the hard disk space currently occupied by Windows to install Linux. If you choose the latter approach, you can use the **FIPS** program to split a single Windows partition into two Windows partitions, the second being empty. Then you can reconfigure that empty partition for use by Linux.

 Before using the FIPS program, you should back up any important data on your Windows system by copying it to disks, tape, or to a network server. FIPS is considered stable and safe, but altering hard disk partition information always puts your data at risk.

The FIPS program is a DOS program that is included with every Linux distribution, usually in a separate directory called `utils`, `dostools`, or something similar. On CD 1 of Red Hat Linux 7.3, you can use the `fips.exe` program in the `dosutils` subdirectory.

Before using FIPS, you should arrange all the data on your Windows partition so that it is grouped together. This leaves a contiguous area of free space at one end of the hard disk. To accomplish this, you must defragment the Windows system. **Defragmenting** is a procedure that arranges each file on your hard disk so that all parts of the file are next to each other (as opposed to the parts of a file being fragmented, or spread across the entire hard disk). When you defragment a Windows system, all of the files are placed at the beginning of the hard disk. Figure 2-13 shows conceptually how a Windows partition is arranged before and after the defragmenting operation.

 On some Windows systems, defragmenting the hard disk will leave a few blocks of data spread throughout the disk, even though *most* files are defragmented. Depending on the position of these blocks, you may not be able to use FIPS to create a large enough empty partition to install Linux. In this case, you'll need to rely on more advanced software than FIPS to create a dual-boot system. Consider using the PartitionMagic product mentioned at the end of this section.

2

Before defragmenting After defragmenting

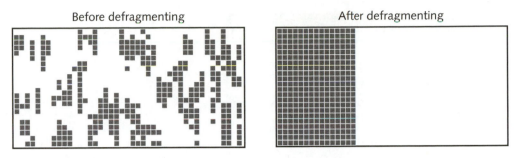

Figure 2-13 A Windows partition before and after defragmentation

 Defragmenting is also called optimizing a hard disk, because some operating systems (such as Windows) work much more efficiently (optimally) if you defragment your hard disk on a regular basis. Linux hard disks are not subject to fragmentation because Linux arranges data differently than Windows.

Many versions of Windows include a utility for defragmenting your Windows partitions. The steps to defragment a Windows partition vary based on the version of Windows you are using. The following procedure is for Windows XP:

1. Click **start**, **All Programs**, **Accessories**, **Windows Explorer** to open a file system explorer window.

2. Click the plus sign "+" next to **My Computer**.

3. Right-click on the **Local Disk** item.

4. Click **Properties**. The Properties dialog box for the selected hard drive opens.

5. Click the **Tools** tab to display the options shown in Figure 2-14. The last item on the Tools tab describes the Defragment utility.

6. Click the **Defragment Now** button. The Defragmentation program runs on the selected hard disk. You see a progress indicator as the program works.

 If you do not have a defragmentation utility installed on your copy of Windows, the Defragment Now button will not be available.

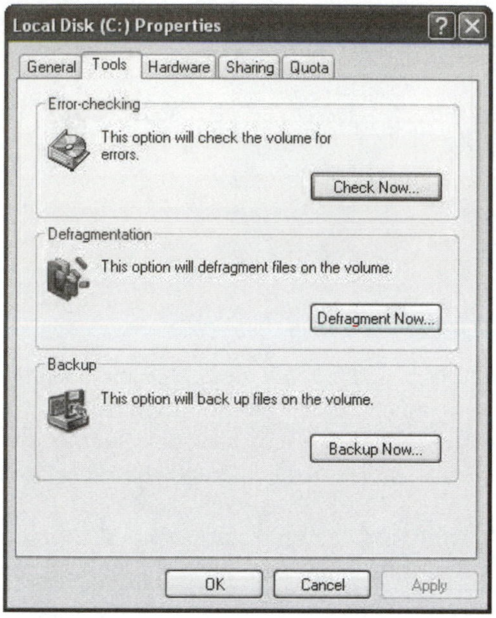

Figure 2-14   The Tools tab for a Windows XP hard disk

7. Click the **Analyze** button in the Disk Defragmenter window as shown in Figure 2-15.

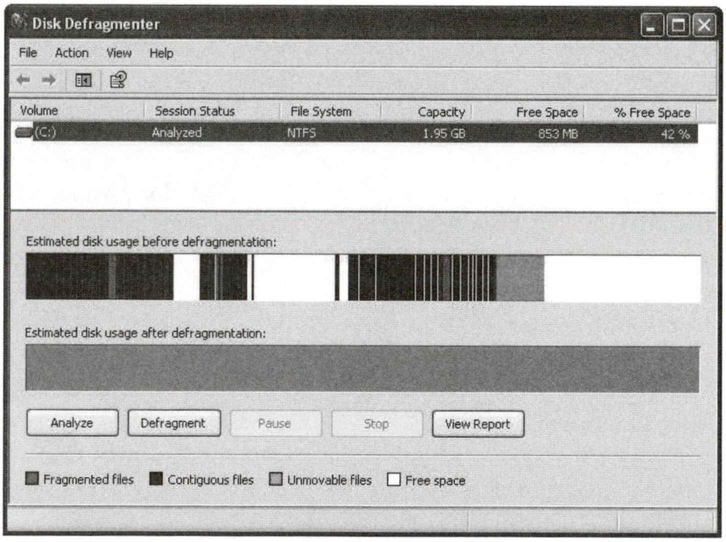

Figure 2-15   Disk Defragmenter window

8. Click the **Defragment** button and follow on-screen prompts to complete the defragmentation process.

If you are using an older version of Windows (Windows 98 or before), you can use the FIPS program as described below to create free space for a Linux partition. For systems running newer versions of Windows, such as XP or 2000, you will need to use a commercial tool such as PartitionMagic (*www.powerquest.com*) or System Commander (*www.v-com.com*) to partition your drive. (Defragmentation is needed for all Windows systems, though some commercial partitioning programs may be able to defragment as part of the partitioning process.)

To run FIPS to split an older Windows partition that has been defragmented, follow these steps:

1. Obtain two floppy disks.

2. Boot Windows and copy the FIPS program from Red Hat Linux CD 1 to a floppy disk. The program is located at DOSUTILS\FIPS.EXE.

    If you are using another version of Linux, the location on your Linux CD will vary, but the program name is typically still FIPS.EXE.

3. Click the **Start** button in Windows, click **Shut Down**, then click **Restart in MS-DOS mode**. After a moment, the C:\ prompt appears.

4. Start the FIPS program using the command **FIPS** preceded by the drive letter for your floppy drive (for example, A:\FIPS).

    FIPS must be run in MS-DOS mode to avoid conflicting with other programs. Because the CD-ROM drive is normally not available in MS-DOS mode, you must copy the FIPS program to a floppy disk.

5. Read the messages on-screen, and then press a key to continue.

6. Using the second floppy disk mentioned in Step 1, back up your disk information by following the instructions on-screen. (Keep this disk until you have finished installing Linux and made certain that you can start both Windows and Linux.)

7. If you have multiple hard disks, select the one you want FIPS to alter.

8. The partition table for the hard disk is displayed. You can review this information, but you don't need to do anything about it. Press a key to continue.

9. FIPS presents you with two numbers showing the size of the current Windows partition (on the left) and the size of the new Windows partition (on the right). Use the Up and Down arrow keys to adjust the space on each partition. Because you are changing the point at which the partition is to be split in two, one number goes up as the other goes down. The number on the right (shown in MB) should be large enough for your Linux partition *and* swap partition.

FIPS does not allow you to reduce the original Windows partition to a smaller size than is needed for the data residing on that Windows partition. If the number on the left for the size of the original Windows partition does not go low enough to allow space for Linux when the second Windows partition is deleted, you have not effectively moved all the data to the front of the Windows partition. Or the Windows partition may simply be too full to store Linux on the same computer.

10. Press **Enter** to accept your settings.

11. The partition table is displayed again as it will appear when updated by FIPS. If you are comfortable with the sizes shown, press **C** to confirm that you want to write this information to the hard disk. You can press **Ctrl+C** to exit FIPS without making any changes to your hard disk.

12. Reboot your computer immediately so that the updated hard disk information is reread into your system.

After using FIPS, you should have a smaller Windows partition containing the Windows operating system and your Windows data; you should also have a second Windows partition that contains no data. During the Linux installation you will use a tool such as `fdisk` or Disk Druid (discussed in Chapter 3) to delete this second, empty Windows partition and configure the resulting free space on the hard disk into the Linux partition and Linux swap partition.

As mentioned previously, commercial programs are available to help you prepare partitions for Linux. The most popular is PartitionMagic, from PowerQuest (*www.powerquest.com*). PartitionMagic provides a graphical interface to create new partitions, and helps you back up data before altering the hard disk. However, PartitionMagic is commercial software that costs money. (The OpenLinux distribution includes a reduced version of PartitionMagic to help prepare a Windows system for a Linux installation.)

CHAPTER SUMMARY

❐ Many Linux installation programs detect a computer's hardware for you, but understanding computer hardware helps you when Linux install doesn't proceed smoothly.

❐ Components of a computer are called devices in Linux. Each is controlled by software called a driver.

❐ Memory and hard disk space are measured in bytes, typically in megabytes or gigabytes.

❐ Devices communicate with the CPU of a computer using interrupts, direct memory access, or port-mapped input/output. Sometimes information about these techniques must be provided to the Linux kernel to use a device correctly.

❑ Linux supports thousands of hardware components (devices). It's a good idea to research the specific devices you want to use to see if they are supported.

❑ To use Linux networking, you must assign an IP address to your computer or else have a DHCP server available to provide dynamic network configuration.

❑ Other networking information may be required, such as a network mask and the IP address of a gateway system. A system administrator, instructor, or ISP can provide this information.

❑ Protocols define how devices and parts of an operating system communicate with each other. Linux uses many different protocols.

❑ The domain name service (DNS) converts between IP addresses and the hostnames and domain names that people generally use to refer to systems on a network.

❑ You can compile a system inventory by referring to the computer documentation or a vendor's Web site, or by checking computer settings in Windows (if it is already installed on the computer where Linux will be installed).

❑ Hard disks are composed of platters, each divided into tracks and sectors. Tracks on multiple platters that are vertically aligned are called a cylinder. Cylinders are used to define partitions.

❑ You can use Linux on the same computer as another operating system by setting up a dual-boot system. Each time you boot such a system, you select which operating system to launch.

❑ If you intend to create a dual-boot system, you must prepare the hard disk before you start to install Linux. You create partitions for the Linux file system and swap partition using a utility such as FIPS or PartitionMagic.

❑ The BIOS controls the boot process by passing control to the MBR, which in turn may contain a Linux boot manager such as GRUB or LILO, or may pass control on to the boot record of the active partition.

KEY TERMS

active partition — The bootable partition; the partition that the MBR passes control to if the MBR does not itself contain a boot manager.

BIOS (Basic Input/Output System) — Information stored in ROM that provides instructions to the operating system for using the devices on a computer.

bit — A binary digit; a bit can hold a value of either one or zero.

block — A unit of hard disk space; typically one that contains 1024 bytes, or two sectors.

boot manager — A program that lets you launch one or more operating systems each time you boot a computer. (Examples include GRUB and LILO.)

boot record — A small area on each partition that contains a program to launch the operating system on that partition.

broadcast address — An IP address that sends a packet of data to all computers on a network.

byte — Storage space sufficient to store one character; eight bits.

CMOS RAM — A special memory chip in which computer configuration details are stored. The data is maintained by a tiny battery and is modified as needed using a BIOS utility.

cylinder — A set of tracks at the same location on all the platters of a hard disk.

defragment — A procedure that arranges each file so that the parts of the file are next to each other on the hard disk; places all sectors comprising a file into contiguous disk locations.

DHCP server — A computer that provides networking configuration data for other computers via the DHCP protocol.

direct memory access (DMA) channel — A communication method within a computer that allows a device to read and write directly to the computer's RAM, without going through the microprocessor first.

DNS server — A computer that uses the DNS protocol to convert from domain names and hostnames to IP addresses.

domain name — A name assigned to a collection of computers on a network.

Domain Name Service (DNS) — A protocol that maps human-readable domain names and hostnames to IP addresses that correspond to individual computers.

device driver — Software used to communicate with or control a hardware component.

dual-boot system — A computer that allows a user to choose which operating system to start each time the computer is booted (turned on).

Dynamic Host Configuration Protocol (DHCP) — A protocol that allows a computer to obtain networking information (such as an IP address) dynamically from a network server at the time the computer is turned on.

dynamic network configuration — Configuring the networking services of a computer by automatically obtaining networking parameters when the system is turned on; typically done using DHCP.

ext2 — A file system type used by Linux.

ext3 — A newer file system type used by Linux.

FAT — The file system type used by older versions of Windows (such as Windows 3.1).

FAT32 — The file system type used by some newer versions of Windows (such as Windows 98 and XP).

file server — A computer on which many users store their data files for access across a network.

file system — An organized arrangement of information on a device such as a hard disk.

FIPS — A program that creates two separate partitions from an existing Windows partition. Used to create an empty partition that can be deleted and the resulting free space used for installing Linux.

fully qualified domain name (FQDN) — The hostname of a computer and the domain name of the network to which the computer is attached.

gateway address — The IP address of the computer on a local network that can send packets of data outside that network.

gigabyte (GB) — A measure of space on computers equal to 1024 megabytes, or roughly enough space to store 1 billion characters.

GRUB — A Linux boot manager; used by default on Red Hat Linux 7.3.

hexadecimal (hex) — A numbering system using base-16. Hex uses 0 to 9, plus the letters *A* through *F* (usually capitalized) to count the numbers 10 through 15.

host — A computer attached to a network.

hostname — A single word used to name a computer.

IDE — A low-cost, easy-to-manage interface used by most computers to connect hard disks and CD-ROM drives to the CPU.

IDE controller — A hardware component used to communicate between an IDE-compatible hard disk or other IDE device and the microprocessor.

interrupt request (IRQ) — A numbered signal that a device sends to the operating system to request service.

I/O ports — Special addresses (resembling memory addresses) used by a device for port-mapped I/O.

IP — (Internet Protocol) A networking protocol used to send packets of information across a network connection.

IP address — An identifying number assigned to a computer or device that uses IP to communicate across a network.

logical partition — A hard disk partition that exists within one of the four partitions that a hard disk can traditionally manage. Logical partitions are numbered beginning with 5. See also *primary partition*.

LILO (Linux Loader) — A Linux boot manager.

Master Boot Record (MBR) — A small area on the first hard disk partition that contains a program to decide how to start an operating system. Control passes from the BIOS to the program in the MBR when a computer is first booted.

megabyte (MB) — A measure of space on computers equal to 1,048,576 bytes, or enough space to store roughly 1 million characters.

multisync monitor — A monitor that can accept data using a range of frequencies (resulting in varying resolutions and color depths).

network address — An address that identifies the local network that a computer is a part of. This address is used to determine how data is routed to its intended destination.

network mask — A set of numbers that tells the networking system in Linux how to identify IP addresses that are part of the local network.

NTFS — The default file system type for Windows NT, Windows 2000, and Windows XP.

partition — A distinct area of a hard disk that has been prepared to store a particular type of data.

port-mapped input/output (port-mapped I/O) — A device communication technique that uses a separate range of memory addresses called I/O ports as a place for a device to send and receive data. Essentially, each device-specific port address works like a post office box.

primary partition — One of the four partitions that traditional hard disk electronics can effectively manage. See also *logical partition*.

protocol — An organized pattern of signals or words used to communicate efficiently.

random access memory (RAM) — Volatile electronic storage within a computer.

read-only memory (ROM) — Nonvolatile electronic storage within a computer. Used to store information about how the computer starts and how the devices in the computer are configured.

SCSI — A high-performance interface used by many types of devices to connect to a computer.

sector — A unit of data storage on a hard disk. Normally a sector contains 512 bytes.

swap partition (swap space) — A designated area on a hard disk used as virtual memory by the Linux kernel.

track — One of many concentric circles of data storage area on each platter of a hard disk.

virtual memory — A feature of the Linux kernel that allows Linux to treat a partition of the hard disk as if it were RAM, storing programs there temporarily when they are not being used.

XFree86 Project — A free software project that creates software to provide X Window System functionality to Linux.

REVIEW QUESTIONS

1. Name three vendors that sell computer systems with Linux preinstalled.

2. Why is Linux sometimes considered more difficult to install than other operating systems?

3. A byte is enough space to store:

    a. One character

    b. One hexadecimal digit

    c. One sector

    d. One megabyte

2

4. When you see a value in gigabytes, it probably refers to:

   a. An IRQ number

   b. A monitor refresh rate

   c. Hard disk size

   d. RAM size

5. Which of the following cannot be changed by a user?

   a. Magnetic data on a hard disk

   b. Electronic storage in RAM

   c. The configuration settings in the BIOS

   d. The BIOS stored in ROM

6. What is the difference between IDE and Ultra IDE?

7. Which of the following is *not* part of the communications scheme between a device and the CPU?

   a. IRQ

   b. FIPS

   c. I/O ports

   d. DMA channel

8. The _____ numbering system is often used to refer to information about computer hardware.

   a. hexadecimal

   b. MBR

   c. binary

   d. SCSI

9. Which of the following is *not* a valid hexadecimal digit?

   a. E

   b. D

   c. A

   d. H

10. The _____ interface is a high-cost, high-performance method of connecting hard disks to a computer.

    a. LILO

    b. SCSI

    c. IDE

    d. MBR

11. Which is *not* a valid IP address?

    a. 0.0.0.0

    b. 12.456.27.198

    c. 207.198.27.1

    d. 10.10.255.255

12. Name four items of information about the network that may be required to complete a Linux installation.

13. By using DHCP, a Linux system can:

    a. Convert a domain name to an IP address

    b. Pass packets outside the local network to the Internet

    c. Send broadcast messages to all computers on the network

    d. Obtain an IP address from a server on the network

14. An FQDN includes:

    a. A hostname and an IP address

    b. A hostname and a domain name

    c. A domain name and an IP address

    d. The IP address provided by DHCP

15. A DNS server provides the following service to computers on the network:

    a. It converts domain names to IP addresses

    b. It provides IP addresses when a computer is turned on

    c. It sends data packets to the Internet

    d. It configures independent file systems on the hard disk

16. Specifications of a monitor are expressed in:

    a. Hz, KHz, and MHz

    b. RAM and ROM

    c. TCP, UDP, and IP

    d. BIOS, LILO, and GRUB

17. Name four methods of obtaining system hardware specifications prior to installing Linux.

18. The Windows _____ can provide many hardware details about a computer.

    a. Search dialog box

    b. FIPS program

    c. Start menu

    d. Control Panel

19. Assuming a Windows system is using TCP/IP networking, which networking information is not included in any Windows dialog boxes accessible through the Control Panel?

    a. The IP address of the system

    b. The IP address of one or more DNS servers

    c. The IP address of the NFS server to use for installation

    d. The IP address of one or more gateway servers

20. Explain why you must receive an IP address assignment rather than simply choosing one you like (as you may be able to do with a hostname).

21. A file system resides within a:

    a. Partition

    b. Track

    c. Block

    d. Sector

22. DMA is one method of device communication, but most devices communicate with the CPU using special addresses called:

    a. Channels

    b. Ports

    c. Active partitions

    d. Blocks

23. Briefly define the purpose of a swap partition in Linux.

24. The FIPS program is used to:

    a. Split a single Windows partition into two Windows partitions

    b. Create a partition marked for the `ext2` file system

    c. Combine two Windows partitions into a single Windows partition

    d. Resize `ext2`, `ext3`, or Linux swap partitions once Windows data has been successfully defragmented

25. When a file system is defragmented, the files are arranged so that:

    a. They are alphabetical in the directory structure

    b. All parts of a file are next to each other on the hard disk

    c. Compatible files are next to each other on the hard disk

    d. Linux can easily use the files from Windows

HANDS-ON PROJECTS

Project 2-1

In this project you use the Windows Control Panel to learn information about your computer system. To complete this activity you need a computer with Windows installed. You can complete this activity as an exercise even if you are not going to install Linux on the same computer later on. The steps here should apply to the most recent versions of Windows. If you are using an older version (such as Windows 95), you may need to experiment and explore the options provided in your Control Panel.

1. Click **Start**, **All programs**, **Control Panel**.

2. Click **Switch to Classic View**.

3. Double-click the **System** icon in the Control Panel window. The System Properties dialog box opens.

4. You see the General tab. On that tab, locate the amount of system memory in your computer. Convert this number to MB if it is displayed in another form (such as KB).

5. Close the **System Properties** dialog box.

6. Double-click the **System** icon in the Control Panel, click the **Hardware** tab, and then click the **Device Manager** button in the **System Properties** dialog box.

7. Double-click the **Ports (COM+LPT)** button.

8. Double-click the **Communications Port (COM1)** button.

9. Click the **Resources** tab to see the Input/Output Range and the Interrupt Request.

10. Use the **Cancel** button(s) to close all open dialog boxes so that you see only the Control Panel again.

11. Double-click the **Display** icon in the Control Panel.

12. Select the **Settings** tab.

13. Notice the number of colors and the resolution of your current Windows display. Linux can operate at the same level, or perhaps better (higher resolution or more colors), depending on what hardware you have on your computer.

14. Click the **Advanced** button, then click the **Adapter** tab. Review the information in the dialog box that appears to see what information about your video card is provided. You might see the video card model, the video chipset used on the card, the amount of video memory on the card, the manufacturer, or other details.

15. Use the **Cancel** button(s) to close all open dialog boxes so that you see only the Control Panel again.

Project 2-2

In this activity you review the information provided on your Linux installation CD about the FIPS program. The documentation for FIPS includes information about how hard disks are organized and explains how to use FIPS. To complete this activity you need a CD containing a Linux distribution and a computer with a CD-ROM drive. This exercise assumes that you are using the Red Hat Linux 7.3 CD and a computer with Windows installed and a CD-ROM drive. Other types of Linux CDs can be used, but the location of the FIPS program on the CD will differ.

1. Insert your Linux CD into the CD-ROM drive.
2. Double-click the **My Computer** icon on the Windows Desktop.
3. Double-click the icon for the drive in which the Linux CD is located.
4. Double-click the **dosutils** icon.
5. Double-click the **fipsdocs** icon.
6. Double-click the **fips** document icon. (This icon may be labeled fips.doc, depending on your Windows configuration). The FIPS documentation appears in a word processing program.
7. Press **Alt+Tab** to switch back to the window showing the files in the fipsdocs directory.
8. Double-click on another document icon such as the techinfo (or techinfo.txt) icon.
9. Review the document files that you have opened to learn more about how FIPS operates. Open other files in the fipsdocs directory to learn additional information.

Project 2-3

In this activity you use the Windows Control Panel to gather information about how networking is set up on your computer. To complete this activity your computer must have Windows installed, and it must be connected to a network running TCP/IP, either via a network adapter such as an Ethernet card, or via a modem. You can complete this activity as an exercise on a Windows computer even if you are not going install Linux on the same computer later on. The steps here apply to the latest versions of Windows, such as Windows 2000. If you have an older version, the steps will differ because the arrangement of the Network dialog box has changed.

1. Right-click **My Network Places**, then choose **Properties** from the shortcut menu.
2. Right-click the network connection, then choose **Properties** from the shortcut menu.
3. In the Properties window, highlight **Internet Protocol (TCP/IP)**, then click **Properties**.
4. On the **General** tab, you should see your IP address and DNS server information.
5. Use the **Cancel** button(s) to close all open dialog boxes without making any changes.

Project 2-4

In this activity you explore hardware compatibility on the Red Hat Software Web site. To complete this activity, you need a working browser and an Internet connection. Assume for this project that you have an existing computer system that you want to convert for use as a Linux server. You need to ascertain whether the network card and video card are both supported by Red Hat Linux 7.3.

1. Log in to your system and open a Web browser.

2. Go to *hardware.redhat.com*.

3. Click the **Hardware Compatibility List** link.

4. Click the **Complete Listing** link. If you were selecting which hardware to buy for a new Linux system, you might choose the Certified Hardware link to be certain that the hardware you selected worked well with Linux. Since you already have the hardware in question, you will look at the Complete Listing to see if it is supported at all, even if Red Hat Software has not "certified" it.

5. Scroll to the bottom of the Web page and from the **By Manufacturer** drop-down list, choose **3Com**.

6. After a moment, a list of categories for which 3Com devices exist in the list appears. Click the **Network Device/Controller** link.

7. The device you want to verify is a 3C590 card with a PCI interface. The label also calls it an Etherlink III card. Find this device in the list and click on its link.

8. What is the name of the kernel module that supports this card?

9. Use the **back** button on your browser to return one page. Scroll up until you see the **Complete List** link again. Click that link.

10. Choose **Intel** as the manufacturer.

11. Choose **Video Device/Controller** as the hardware type.

12. Look for the **i740** video card in the list and click on its link.

13. Use the **back** button, then scroll up again until you see the **Certified Hardware** link.

14. Click on that link, then choose **Intel** as the manufacturer.

15. Are any Intel video cards certified?

16. What types of storage devices has Intel taken the trouble to have certified by Red Hat Software?

17. Choose one of the storage devices that looks interesting and click on its link to learn more about it.

CASE PROJECTS

2

Your work as a consultant for McKinney & Co. has been well received. The folks at PixelDust are excited about the success they have had with their digital photo services and are ready to upgrade their Linux Web servers.

1. The Web servers need much more hard disk space to work efficiently in the coming 12–18 months. Go online and research available hard disks. Determine whether IDE or SCSI drives are a better choice for this project. What effect do these factors have on your decision: cost, ability to upgrade later (scalability), Linux support, reliability?

2. Having decided on a type of hard drive, you now must determine how much hard disk space to add to the servers. You learn that each of the photos that PixelDust processes averages 0.8 MB. They have 560 current customers and process an average of 3 new photos a week for each one. They also anticipate obtaining 50 new customers per week during the coming year, each of which will process the same number of photos. If PixelDust wants to add hard disk space that will be sufficient for the next 12 months, with a 15% safety margin (that much extra space), how much hard disk space will you need to provide? How might your answer alter your decision in question 1 above?

3. PixelDust is wondering about the possibility of using some older computers they have found on sale as part of their collection of Web servers. What concerns would you have about using them? How would you determine if you could, in fact, use them?

3

INSTALLING LINUX

> **After reading this chapter and completing the exercises, you will be able to:**
>
> ♦ Install a popular distribution of Linux
> ♦ Start using a new Linux system
> ♦ Troubleshoot problems with a Linux installation

In the previous chapter you learned how to gather information about hardware components and networking protocols to prepare for installing Linux. You also learned about creating free hard disk space on a computer running Microsoft Windows in order to use that computer as a dual-boot system with Linux.

In this chapter you learn how to prepare for and install a new Linux operating system. Among other things, you learn how to configure Linux partitions, set up a user account, select which software packages to install, and answer other questions posed during the installation process. You also learn what to do when the installation process doesn't work correctly. Finally, you learn about starting Linux for the first time, after completing the installation.

UNDERSTANDING INSTALLATION ISSUES

The bulk of this chapter addresses general issues related to installing Linux and explains how to answer questions that are posed during the installation process. This information is applicable to virtually all versions of Linux, though each distribution arranges its installation programs a bit differently, and some installations may ask technical questions during the installation that are not covered here. (Generally, the more flexible an installation, the more knowledge you must have to complete it.) Project 3-3 at the end of the chapter walks you through a complete installation of Red Hat Linux 7.3 from the CDs included with this book.

Linux Distributions

People like having favorites: one person insists that Ford trucks are better; another buys only Chevrolet. One person always drinks Coke; another chooses Pepsi every time. The differences between products may be slight, but the loyalty they inspire is not. Linux users often have similar feelings about the version or distribution they have chosen. One person insists that Debian Linux is the only reasonable choice; another uses Red Hat exclusively.

 If you are curious about the different Linux distributions that are available, visit *www.distrowatch.com*.

Although having a favorite is fine, remember that Linux distributions are very similar to each other technically. Each one takes the Linux kernel from the same location on the Internet, and each uses the same set of supporting utilities. The organization or individual creating a distribution often has a specific goal that determines which parts of the distribution are highlighted, or what additional items are added to the basic Linux software. For example, some distributions focus on ease of use, others on security, others on completeness; still others focus on a particular technical purpose, such as creating the perfect e-mail server.

Table 1-1 (in Chapter 1) names several of the better known distributions. The list below highlights the major differences among Linux distributions. As this list indicates, you can choose a distribution with characteristics that fit your preferences.

- The installation program for each distribution is different. Commercial Linux vendors such as Red Hat Software, SuSE, and TurboLinux put a lot of time and money into designing an installation program. These programs focus on ease of use for new Linux users. Other distributions such as Debian and Slackware have an installation program that focuses on flexibility for users who are very familiar with Linux features.

3

■ The arrangement of the files that make up a standard Linux system is fairly standard, but some variations are possible. Different vendors place configuration files in different locations. These differences can be traced to the preferences of the software developers who assemble a particular distribution—each group of software developers has its own idea of the best way to arrange the files. For example, Caldera OpenLinux places configuration files for the Samba network service in the directory `/etc/samba.d`; Red Hat Linux places these files in the directory `/etc/samba`. Because you will become accustomed to finding configuration files in a certain location, you may not want to begin using another Linux distribution once you are familiar with one. But these differences are small compared to the total number of files installed on a typical Linux system.

■ The default configuration values and the default services started on a new Linux system vary by distribution. One vendor might choose to start up a Web server, firewall, e-mail server, and graphical desktop; another might start only a basic command line interface as the default environment. On many distributions, you have some flexibility during the installation in selecting which services you want to install or activate by default. You can also change these options after installing Linux.

■ Some configuration utilities were developed by the creator of a particular distribution and won't be available on other distributions. This is true even though the underlying configuration files that the utilities manage are the same in all distributions. As one example of the differences in utilities, consider that only Red Hat Linux includes the `neat` network administration utility; and only SuSE Linux includes the YAST utility. You will learn more about configuration utilities beginning in Chapter 7.

■ In general, each Linux distribution targets a certain type of user. The intended customer might be very technical or very new to Linux; the customer might be business-oriented or a home user; the customer might be in the United States or in another country. Of course, some distributions still try to be all things to all people. You must decide if you prefer a popular distribution that is generally appealing, or a more specialized product that caters to your preferences.

■ Some Linux vendors focus on creating products with the most recent versions of all software from the Internet, but they must sacrifice the time-consuming testing and documentation that other vendors choose to invest in. Having the very latest Linux features as soon as possible is a big concern for some Linux users; others prefer software that has been more thoroughly prepared for stable long-term use.

Red Hat Linux

Red Hat Linux 7.3 Publisher's Edition is included with this book. Red Hat Linux is the most widely used distribution in the world and has been around since about 1993. Although many other excellent distributions are available, Red Hat Linux has proven itself to be a stable, long-term participant in the Linux market.

If you are interested in using another version of Linux, you can obtain a copy in any of the following ways:

- Use the CD provided with another book on Linux.

- Receive a free copy of Linux on CD at a trade show, user group meeting, or other event sponsored by a Linux vendor.

- Purchase an inexpensive Linux product from a company such as Linux Mall (at *www.linuxmall.com*).

- Purchase a retail copy of Linux at a software store or bookstore, either online or in person. (Retail versions often include a printed user manual.) Visit *www.elinux.com*, *www.compusa.com*, and others.

- Download Linux from the FTP site of a Linux vendor, such as *ftp.redhat.com*. (This option is free but takes a long time to download unless you have a very fast Internet connection.)

An Overview of Linux Installation

Installing an operating system on a computer is different from installing an application like a word processor. When you install an application, the existing operating system provides a foundation for the installation process. When you install a new operating system, only the hardware is available—no other software can assist the installation program. The new operating system must somehow initialize itself sufficiently to install itself on the computer.

When you launch a Linux installation program to install Linux onto the hard disk of a computer, the general procedure runs like this:

1. You start the installation program by booting the computer from a Linux CD or floppy disk.

2. The installation program runs a copy of Linux within the computer's RAM.

3. The installation program determines where the files for the installation are located, either by asking you or automatically probing the system.

4. The installation program determines where the Linux operating system should be installed, again, by either asking you or by automatically probing the system for available space. A **target hard disk partition** (the target partition) is the location on the system's hard disk where Linux will be installed.

5. You answer questions posed by the installation program about which software packages should be installed and how core system services should be configured. (For example, you create an administrator password and enter the network addresses to use.)

6. The installation program copies the Linux software packages from the **installation source** (the set of files from which Linux is installed) to the target partition.

7. You answer a few remaining questions about initial system configuration.

8. The installation program configures the system based on your input and installs a boot manager so Linux can be launched.

9. You launch the newly installed Linux operating system, either by pressing a key or restarting the computer.

Installation Source Options

The procedures in this book assume that you will be installing Linux from a CD-ROM. But Linux supports other installation methods. If your installation source files are stored on another medium or in another location, you can specify this as you begin the installation program. The most common installation sources are:

- CD-ROM: Use files from the CD-ROM drive attached to the system on which you are installing Linux.

- Hard disk: Use files stored on a hard disk within the system on which you are installing Linux. This must be a hard disk partition or hard disk that is distinct from the location where Linux will be installed. A system administrator copies files from a Linux CD-ROM or downloads files from an Internet site, storing them on a hard disk for convenience or to overcome technical problems that make other installation methods impractical.

- Floppy disks: Use files stored on a series of floppy disks. This method is rarely used for standard Linux distributions because it would require hundreds of disks. It may still be useful when installing Linux on an older computer without a CD-ROM drive, or on one where a Linux CD-ROM driver cannot be found.

 A few specialized versions of Linux occupy only a single floppy disk. One of the most popular is the Linux Router Project (see *www.linuxrouter.org*); another is Tom's Boot Disk (see *www.toms.net/rb*).

- Network installation: Use files that are located on a server connected to the same network as the computer on which you are installing Linux. Depending on the version of Linux you are installing, you may be able to connect to the server on which the files are located using any of the following network protocols: FTP (a standard Internet format); SMB (used by Microsoft Windows servers); or NFS (the Network File System protocol, commonly available on all Linux and UNIX systems). Performing a network installation requires additional configuration on the server that will provide the installation source, but this method allows a system administrator to install multiple Linux systems from a single networked copy of the installation source.

 Some Linux products include applications that use standard commercial copyrights. Be careful not to violate these copyrights by installing Linux from a network onto multiple systems.

To perform a network installation, you must prepare another computer so it can provide the installation data. Because this involves setting up networking services that are beyond the scope of this book, you should contact the system administrator of the networked server you want to use. Here are a few hints:

- To use a Microsoft Windows server as the Linux installation source, ask the system administrator of the Windows system to prepare a share containing the CD-ROM drive (or a hard disk onto which the Linux installation CD data has been copied).

- To use the NFS protocol on a Linux or UNIX server, ask the system administrator to export the CD or hard disk directory containing the Linux installation source.

- Some Linux vendors provide FTP servers so you can install Linux directly from their Internet sites. If the version of Linux you are installing supports FTP-based installation, you will see an option for selecting FTP during the installation program.

Red Hat Linux supports installation from CD-ROM or hard disk, plus network installations using NFS, SMB, or FTP servers.

Options for Starting the Installation

When you turn on a computer, the BIOS checks the status of the system and then passes control to one of the disk drives, depending on how it is configured. Normally, it first checks whether a floppy disk is inserted; on newer computers, the CD-ROM may also be checked. If neither contains a bootable disk, control passes to the program contained in the Master Boot Record (MBR) of the first hard disk.

To launch the Linux installation program, you must pass control directly to the Linux installation program located on either a floppy disk or a CD-ROM, so that the BIOS never passes control to the MBR and launches an operating system that is already installed. You can do this by creating a boot disk from a data file provided on the Linux CD-ROM. A **boot disk** is a floppy disk that can start up your computer and initialize the installation program. Most users can rely on newer computers that have bootable CD-ROM drives. A **bootable CD-ROM drive** is a drive that can launch an operating system (or other program) directly from a CD-ROM.

Most commercial Linux products (including Red Hat Linux 7.3) provide a bootable CD-ROM. To see if your CD-ROM drive is bootable, try inserting the installation or first Linux CD-ROM into the CD-ROM drive and then restarting the computer. If the installation program appears on-screen, your CD-ROM drive is bootable.

 If the installation program does not start from the installation CD-ROM, it's possible that your CD-ROM drive is bootable, but that the BIOS is configured to try to start an operating system from the hard disk before checking the CD-ROM drive. You can change the order in which devices are checked at boot time by reconfiguring the BIOS as described in Chapter 2.

Before you can launch the Linux installation program from a boot disk (also called an **install disk** by some vendors), you often must create that disk yourself. The first Linux CD-ROM in your distribution normally contains a copy of a boot disk in the form of a disk image. A **disk image** is a single file that contains an exact copy of a floppy disk. You can copy the disk image from the CD to a floppy disk by using the rawrite utility in DOS or Windows, or the **dd** utility on an existing Linux system.

Red Hat Linux 7.3 provides three different disk image files from which you can create a boot disk. In the /images subdirectory of CD 1, you will find the following:

- **boot.img**: Used for standard installations from a CD.

- **bootnet.img**: Used when the installation source is located on a network server (such as an NFS server).

- **pcmcia.img**: Used to install Linux on a laptop when the PCMCIA cards must be accessed to complete the installation. This occurs in two situations: when the device containing the installation source (such as a SCSI hard disk) is attached using a PCMCIA expansion card, or when installation is from a network server through a PCMCIA network adapter card. If neither of these situations applies, use the **boot.img** or **bootnet.img** file.

In addition to these three files, you will find four other disk image files in the same subdirectory of CD 1. These four images contain hardware drivers that may be needed during installation to use devices on your computer. For example, if you are using an older computer that has a CD-ROM drive that uses a proprietary interface (rather than IDE or SCSI), you will probably need to create a floppy disk from the **oldcdrom.img** file. You will be prompted to insert a disk containing additional drivers if the installation program cannot locate the devices needed to complete the installation. The files include:

- **drvblock.img**: Additional drivers for block devices such as hard disks.

- **drvnet.img**: Additional drivers for network cards.

- **oldcdrom.img**: Additional drivers for old non-IDE and non-SCSI CD-ROM drives.

- **pcmciadd.img**: Additional drivers for PCMCIA cards.

Few installations require any of these additional drivers, and you can always return to this point in the installation program and create them if it becomes necessary. Each Linux distribution arranges boot disk information differently. On some distributions, you may be required to make two floppy disks for every installation. If you are using a non–Red Hat distribution, check your documentation. The root directory of your Linux CD-ROM often contains enough information to get you started.

Creating Floppy Disks to Start the Installation

Once you have determined which disk images you need for your installation, you can use either Windows or Linux to create those disks.

To complete this task in Microsoft Windows, follow these steps. (Note that these steps should work for any Linux distribution, though the location and names for the disk image files shown here are specific to Red Hat Linux 7.3.)

1. Insert the Red Hat Linux 7.3 CD 1 into a computer running Windows. (Any version of Windows will do.) Insert a blank, formatted floppy disk into the floppy drive.

2. Use the Windows Explorer window to display the contents of the dosutils subdirectory on the CD. Then open the **rawritewin** folder. Note the drive letter associated with the CD-ROM drive (normally D: or E:); you will need this information in Step 5.

3. Double-click the icon for the rawritewin program. The program launches, as shown in Figure 3-1. (Depending on your Windows configuration, you may see this program listed as rawritewin.exe.)

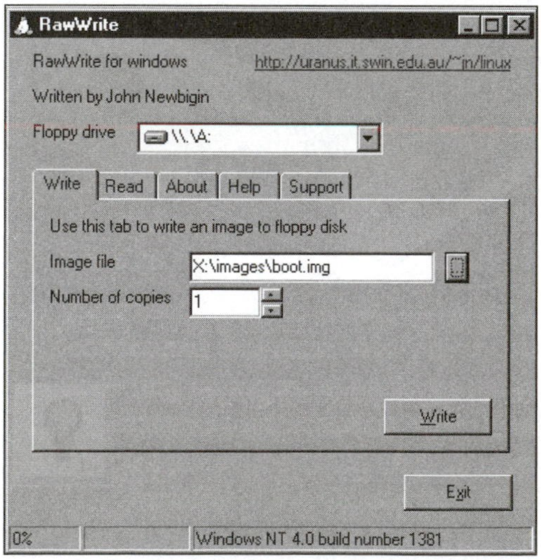

Figure 3-1   The rawritewin program used to create a boot disk

3

4. Use the Floppy drive drop-down list to select the drive letter for the floppy disk drive (this will normally be A:).

5. Within the **Write** tab, enter the full path of the image file you want to use in the Image file field. You can use the button labeled "**...**" to browse through your file system to locate the file if you choose to. As an example, if the CD-ROM drive is drive D: and you need to create the standard boot disk for Red Hat Linux, enter this in the Image file field:

   ```
   D:\images\boot.img
   ```

6. Click the **Write** button. You can watch the progress of disk creation as shown by the percentage in the lower left corner of the window.

7. After the process is completed, a message box appears stating "Image successfully written." Click **OK** to close this message box.

8. Click **Exit** to close the rawwritewin program.

9. Place an appropriate label on the disk you created (for example, "Red Hat Boot Disk") and put it in a safe place until you are ready to install Linux. (Labeling the disk is especially important if you also create one or more supplemental device driver diskettes, as described previously.)

THE INSTALLATION PROCESS

In most cases, installing Linux proceeds to completion without any problems; many users don't even bother to read any documentation before beginning, they simply answer the questions posed on-screen. This section describes what is happening behind the scenes and how your answers to on-screen questions affect the final Linux system.

 Projects 3-1, 3-2, and 3-3, at the end of this chapter, provide step-by-step instructions for installing Red Hat Linux 7.3.

Answering Initial Questions

After you have started the installation program from a bootable CD-ROM or floppy drive, you need to answer questions about how you will interact with the installation program. For example, you must choose a keyboard layout and a language for the installation. Depending on the version of Linux you are using, you might also be asked about your mouse, time zone, video card, or other details before selecting an installation source and target partition.

In many versions of Linux, you can back up to change your answer to previously asked questions until the installation program begins writing data to the hard disk. You can also simply turn off your computer if you choose to abandon the installation before anything is written to the hard disk; any data that was previously stored on your hard disk will remain unaffected.

Preparing Hard Disk Partitions

In Chapter 2 you learned how to divide a hard disk partition containing Microsoft Windows so that Linux could be installed on the same computer. In this section you learn how to use that free space, or free space on any hard disk, to prepare for installing Linux.

Within the Linux installation program, you configure partitions on which Linux is stored. You must set up both a swap partition and a data partition (which will use the `ext2` or `ext3` file system format). To set up partitions, you edit the **partition table**, a small data table stored on the hard disk that defines the size and file system type for each partition on the hard disk.

If you are not creating a dual-boot system, some installation programs (including Red Hat Linux 7.3) will set up partitions for you automatically. This time, to help you learn about Linux, you should perform this task manually.

Most Linux vendors provide a graphical interface in which you can configure partitions. In Chapter 8 you will learn about a powerful text-mode utility called `fdisk` (for *fixed disk*, meaning a hard disk). You can use the `fdisk` utility within some installation programs to create and configure partitions, but in this chapter we focus on using graphical tools.

Hard Disk Specifications

Hard disks in Linux are identified by device names that resemble directory names. In Chapter 4 you will learn more about how devices in Linux are accessed via the same directory structure as normal files. For now, you only need to know that certain names represent hard disk devices and partitions in Linux.

Hard disks that are attached to the computer using an IDE interface are identified as `/dev/hda` for the first hard disk, `/dev/hdb` for the second, `/dev/hdc` for the third, and `/dev/hdd` for the fourth. To refer to one partition, you can add a partition number after the device name. For example, the first partition on the second IDE hard disk is represented as `/dev/hdb1`.

Hard disks that use a SCSI interface use a similar pattern of names, but with the letters *sd* instead of *hd*. For example, the first SCSI hard disk is `/dev/sda`. The second partition on the second SCSI hard disk is `/dev/sdb2`.

You use these same device names to refer to a CD-ROM drive that is attached to the IDE or SCSI controller card on the system. For example, the CD-ROM drive is often the third IDE device (that is, the first device on the second IDE controller). Thus, the CD-ROM can be accessed by referring to `/dev/hdc`. (CD-ROMs do not have multiple partitions as hard disks do.) The Linux installation program normally locates the CD-ROM containing installation files without any input from you.

Deciding on Mount Points

Linux does not use drive letters to refer to storage devices. Instead, different devices are accessed using subdirectories of a single directory structure. For example, in Windows, you might use the designations shown in Table 3-1.

Table 3-1   Typical Drive Letter Assignments in Windows

Drive	Description
A:	Floppy drive
C:	Main Windows hard disk partition
D:	Secondary Windows hard disk partition or second Windows hard disk
E:	CD-ROM drive
F:	Network server home directory

Instead of using drive letters, Linux defines a mount point for different file systems or storage devices. A **mount point** is a subdirectory through which a set of data is accessed. Table 3-2 shows how the devices in Table 3-1 might be represented on a Linux system.

Table 3-2   Typical Subdirectory Mount Points Used to Access File Systems in Linux

Subdirectory (mount point)	Description
/mnt/floppy	Floppy drive
/	Main Linux hard disk partition
/opt	Secondary Linux hard disk partition containing applications
/mnt/cdrom	CD-ROM drive
/remote_home	Network server home directory

The directory names used as mount points are arbitrary, but some standards are normally used, such as /mnt/floppy for the floppy disk drive. You will learn more about configuring mount points in Chapter 8.

To complete the installation, you must specify a mount point for the new Linux file system. That is, you must define which hard disk device will correspond to the directory where Linux will be installed. The beginning point for every Linux file system is called the **root directory**. It is represented by the directory name "/". So, for example, you could specify during your installation that the "/" directory should correspond to the /dev/hda1 partition; the Linux file system would then be created and all Linux files installed on that partition.

Notice that the root directory is represented by a forward slash. Don't use a backward slash (\) for directory names, as you would in Windows.

In Chapter 4 you will learn about the subdirectories that make up a standard Linux file system. One of the standard subdirectories is /home, where the home directory for each user account on the system is normally stored. For example, /home/nwells would be a home directory for the user account nwells. During the installation you can place different subdirectories on different hard disk partitions by defining the subdirectory as a mount point.

When installing Linux on a large server, it is common to store different subdirectories on different partitions. For example, you might decide to store all user home directories and all Linux applications on two partitions of a separate hard disk from the operating system itself. As described previously, you might also need to place some of the operating system files in a separate partition to avoid problems with a hard disk containing over 1024 cylinders. This is normally done by placing the /boot directory on a small separate partition. You could define the configuration described here during the installation by setting mount points as shown in Table 3-3.

Table 3-3   Example Mount Points for a Multiple-Partition Installation

Mount point	Device
/boot	/dev/hda1
/	/dev/hda2
/home	/dev/hdb1
/usr	/dev/hdb2

In addition to the mount points shown in Table 3-3, you would specify the partition to use for swap space (the swap partition).

For your first Linux installation, you should expect to define only a swap partition and a partition for the / directory. All operating system files will then be installed on a single partition. You can experiment with more complex multiple-partition installations after you have learned more about Linux. The bullets that follow outline why files are often divided among multiple partitions:

- Placing the core operating system files on a separate partition allows you to upgrade the operating system without disturbing user data files or applications.

- Placing the core operating system files on a separate partition prevents user data files or applications from using all hard disk space that the operating system needs to continue functioning.

- Storing user data on a separate partition makes it easier to back up that data.

- Separating data onto multiple partitions lets you configure different access and security options for different types of data. (This is described in Chapter 8.)

- Having multiple hard disks working to retrieve data at the same time can improve performance.

Choosing What to Install

As you'll recall from Chapter 1, each Linux distribution includes thousands of different programs, such as the Linux kernel, the Apache Web server, GNU project utilities, programming languages, compilers, graphical systems, games, and so forth. When installing Linux, you must decide which of these components to install. The amount of flexibility you have in deciding what you install varies by distribution.

Some distributions group the many possible components into a few different installation types. The **installation type** you choose determines which Linux software is installed; the right installation type for your system depends on how the system will be used. For example, you might have a choice of installing a minimal system (which includes only the most basic components), installing a standard system (which includes the components the average user would be likely to use), or installing everything from the CD. Often, however, you will have more options regarding which software components you want to install.

Most Linux systems (including Red Hat, SuSE, Caldera, and Debian) gather many related files into a single software package. For example, all Linux products provide the Apache Web server, which is made up of dozens of files, as a software package. A **software package** is a single file that contains all the files needed to install and use an application or group of related applications. Special data formats are used to store many files in a software package. The **Red Hat Package Manager** (abbreviated as **rpm**) is the most popular data storage format for creating software packages; it is used by many different distributions. Another well-known software package format comes from the Debian distribution. Packages stored using this format use a `.deb` file extension and are managed using the `dpkg` utility.

You will learn more about the **rpm** format in Chapter 4. Typical Linux products include between 400 and 2500 software packages. To simplify matters, these packages are grouped into functional categories such as text processing, networking utilities, or software development tools. Some Linux installations employ further generalizations based on a broad usage category for the Linux system. For example, a single selection such as Web server installation or Desktop system might define all of the categories, software packages, and files to install. During the installation you can specify which sets of packages or which type of system you want to install. Different Linux distributions allow different levels of detail in this selection process. Figure 3-2 illustrates conceptually the variety of groupings, from general installation types to specific files. Figure 3-3 shows the screen from the Red Hat Linux 7.3 installation program in which you can specify a high-level installation type.

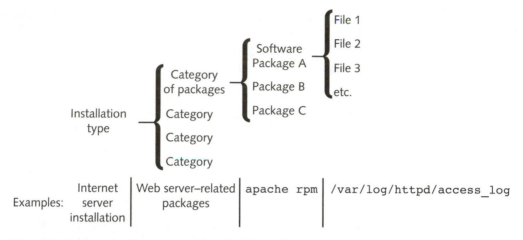

Figure 3-2   Levels of categorization for Linux files and packages

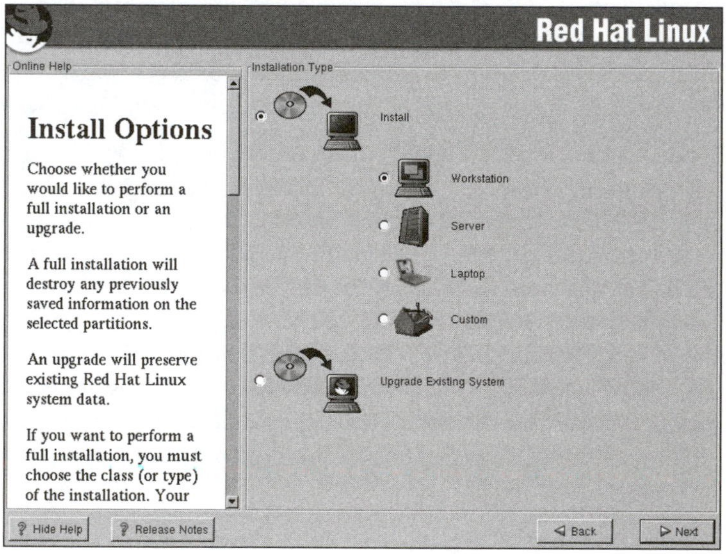

Figure 3-3   Selecting an installation type in Red Hat Linux 7.3

Red Hat Linux 7.3 provides about 30 high-level groupings from which you can select. Examples include software development, graphical desktop, and text processing tools. In addition, Red Hat Linux 7.3 provides a Custom option that lets you select various categories of software packages according to your needs. The Custom option requires you to make decisions about different categories of software packages. For each category, you need to decide whether to include or exclude it from the installation. Although it entails more work on your part, the Custom installation type is recommended for two reasons. First, it allows you to see the many options provided by the distribution you are installing. Second, it allows you to customize your installation to fit your needs.

Table 3-4 shows the categories of packages (called Package Groups) that Red Hat Linux provides during a Custom server installation. Those shown in the left column as bold text are selected by default when you choose the Custom installation option as directed in Project 3-3.

Table 3-4   Package Groups in Red Hat Linux

Package Group	Description
Printing Support	Standard Linux printing programs let you send documents to local or remote printers.
Classic X Window System	Classic UNIX-style graphical interfaces for Linux; built on the core X Window System components.
X Window System	The foundation for all graphical applications in Linux. Required for the Gnome or KDE option.
Laptop Support	PCMCIA and related hardware support for laptop computers.
Gnome	The Gnome graphical desktop interface.
KDE	The KDE graphical desktop interface.
Sound and Multimedia Support	Sound card drivers, sound processing utilities, multimedia utilities for audio and video file playback.
Network Support	System-level components and utilities to let Linux operate on a network (such as an Ethernet or Token Ring network).
Dialup Support	Utilities to let Linux connect to a network over a modem.
Messaging and Web Tools	Client programs for instant messaging and enhanced browser capabilities.
Graphics and Image Manipulation	Tools to edit, create, and view graphics files in numerous formats.
News Server	Usenet newsgroup server.
NFS File Server	A shared network file server using the Network File System protocol.
Windows File Server	A shared network file and print server using the Server Message Block protocol, effectively making Linux a clone of a Windows file and print server.
Anonymous FTP Server	A network server using File Transfer Protocol (FTP).
SQL Database Server	A complete client/server database capability using the Postgres program.
Web Server	The complete Apache Web server.
Router/Firewall	Utilities to make Linux a strong router and firewall.
DNS Name Server	A server providing domain name services for converting domain names to IP addresses and vice versa.

Table 3-4   Package Groups in Red Hat Linux (continued)

Package Group	Description
Network Managed Workstation	Utilities to let network management consoles manage a Linux system using the Simple Network Management Protocol.
Authoring and Publishing	UNIX-style text-processing tools such as TeX.
Emacs	The large and powerful Emacs environment for text editing and much more.
Utilities	Many additional command-line and graphical utilities for system administrators.
Legacy Application Support	Tools to let Linux run older UNIX applications.
Software Development	Software components needed to develop new Linux software or compile Linux source code files.
Kernel Development	Software components needed to change the Linux kernel after installation.
Windows Compatibility/Interoperability	Programs to interact with Windows (or even DOS) systems.
Games and Entertainment	A variety of graphical games and simple entertainment toys.
Everything	Installs the majority of the contents of Red Hat Linux 7.3 (not all packages, however, since some are mutually exclusive). Total space required for this option is 3.6 GB.

 Red Hat Linux also allows you to select individual packages to install, but choosing among hundreds of packages takes more effort than most people want to invest during the installation process. You'll find it easier to install package groups when installing Linux. Then you can easily add or remove individual software packages after completing the installation.

User Accounts

The Linux installation process creates an administrative user account named root. The **root** account is the system administration account. Whoever has access to this account can control the entire system. During installation, you must specify a password for the root account. Choose this password carefully and guard against anyone discovering it. Because the root account is so powerful, you should only use it to complete system administration work.

The **root** account is created automatically during installation, but you also create a regular user account for non–system administration work. You need to choose a brief username (such as thomasj, jane, or rms). You also enter the user's full name and a password for that user account. You can use the commands described in Chapter 8 to change or add information to this user account (and create additional user accounts) after you complete the installation.

Configuring the Boot Manager

During the Linux installation you have the option of installing the Linux boot manager in one of several locations. The option you select depends on how you have configured any other operating systems on the computer. A generally safe choice is to accept the option that is presented as a default by the installation program. This option is selected based on what the installation program finds on your hard disks. The following list explains some reasons for choosing each of the possible locations for the boot manager:

- *The Master Boot Record*: Placing the boot manager on the MBR ensures that Linux boots correctly after a new installation because control passes directly from the BIOS to the Linux boot manager. If you have other operating systems installed on the same computer, however, you must configure the Linux boot manager to launch them. In some cases this is problematic.

- *The boot sector of the partition on which Linux is being installed*: This is the preferred location for the Linux boot manager. Control passes from the BIOS to the MBR, then to the Linux boot manager, so long as the Linux partition is marked as the active partition (this is done by the installation program). The Linux boot manager can pass control to a boot manager on a different partition to launch other operating systems as needed.

- *A floppy disk*: This allows you to keep the MBR intact and leave another partition (such as one containing Windows) as the active partition. To launch Linux, you must insert the floppy disk on which you have installed the Linux boot manager. This can add a small measure of security or ease of use, depending on who will be using your system. But it also takes much longer to boot the system, which is an issue if you are rebooting regularly in a testing environment.

STARTING LINUX

After you have installed Linux, you can reboot your computer and begin using the operating system.

When you turn on your Linux system, you see a series of messages as the Linux kernel identifies and initializes hardware components. The kernel then launches different system services, displaying a message on-screen for each one. After a couple of minutes, you see a login message. The login message can be on a text-mode screen, as shown in Figure 3-4. On most systems, however, the login prompt appears as a graphical screen.

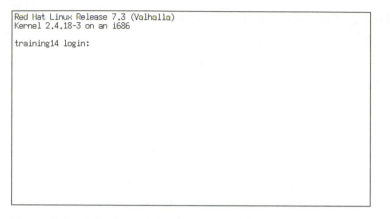

```
Red Hat Linux Release 7.3 (Valhalla)
Kernel 2.4.18-3 on an i686

training14 login:
```

Figure 3-4   A text-mode login screen

You will learn later how to switch between these two possible login screens. If you log in using a text-based login screen, you see a command-line interface after you log in. After logging in, you can launch a graphical interface if you have configured your video card. This is normally done during installation, but as Chapter 5 explains, you can also configure it later. To launch the graphical interface, use this command:

    startx

If you used the graphical login screen, you see a graphical desktop interface immediately after you log in.

To log in, you must enter a username. The system then prompts you for the password corresponding to that user account. You cannot do anything on a Linux system until you have logged in using a valid username and password. The term **logging in** refers to the process of identifying yourself as a valid user who has been assigned a certain set of access rights. **Authentication** is another, more precise, term for logging in. Authentication also refers to entering a valid username and password, but it implies that the system has verified the identity of a user based on specific rules.

You can log in as root, but you should not use this administrative account for normal work. Instead, enter the name of the regular user account that you created during the installation, followed by the password for that user.

Virtually all modern Linux distributions use either the Gnome or KDE desktop as a default graphical interface. Red Hat Linux 7.3 uses the Gnome desktop, as shown in Figure 3-5. Chapter 5 describes the graphical system in detail and explains how to configure it.

The name Gnome is associated with the GNU project mentioned in Chapter 1. For this reason, Gnome is pronounced with an initial hard-G sound, like gnu (an African grazing animal), and not like gnome (a small mythological character from Scandinavia).

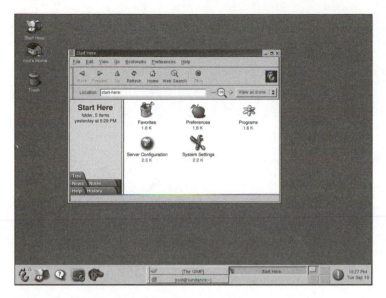

Figure 3-5   The Gnome Desktop interface

If you are using a commercial Linux product such as Red Hat Linux, you may decide to register your product after completing the installation. Registering your product provides you with access to online technical support. (The publisher's edition of Red Hat Linux included with this book does not entitle the reader to technical support, however.) Support services are part of the value that vendors add to free software. As a system administrator, you should become familiar with the services that your Linux vendor provides.

One excellent example of these services is the Red Hat Network. Some versions of Red Hat Linux include an annual subscription to this service; other customers can purchase a subscription. The Red Hat Network allows your system to be automatically updated any time a security issue arises or a software package is upgraded. You can configure the service to control which parts of your system are subject to this remote control feature. To learn more about this service, visit *http://rhn.redhat.com*. Figure 3-6 shows a configuration window for the Red Hat Network service. This dialog box is available by selecting Programs, then System, then Update Agent Configuration from the main menu on the Gnome graphical desktop interface.

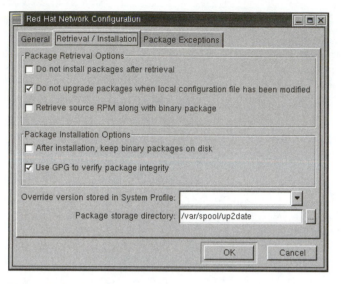

Figure 3-6   Configuring the Red Hat Network service

TROUBLESHOOTING A NEW INSTALLATION

Linux installation *can* be trouble free, completed in about 15 minutes plus the time it takes to copy files from the CD-ROM to your hard disk. But that doesn't always happen. The following sections provide ideas on solving some common problems you might encounter during a difficult Linux installation.

The System Won't Boot

The Linux Installation Program Won't Start

If the Linux installation program will not start, the following are likely causes:

- The boot disk was created incorrectly. Try using a new disk and recreating the boot disk using the rawwritewin or **dd** programs. The **dd** program is more likely to cause trouble if you are unfamiliar with Linux utilities.

- The BIOS is configured to start the operating system from the hard disk without first checking the floppy disk or CD-ROM (whichever you are trying to use). This is a handy security feature that some systems implement by default; it also saves time since most people boot their systems from a hard disk. Edit the BIOS settings as directed in Chapter 2 and try again.

- If the installation program launched but then appears to crash, the installation program may not be able to detect your video card. Try starting the installation by entering the word "text" at the first screenful of text.

3

After Linux Is Installed, the System Won't Boot

Once you install Linux, the system sometimes will not boot into the newly installed Linux system. Here are some likely causes:

- You may have installed the boot manager on the active partition (as selected by default) but another boot manager installed in the MBR causes control to pass to another partition (not the active partition). Use the boot disk you created at the end of the installation to boot into your new Linux system—the boot disk "knows" which partition on your system contains Linux. You can also reinstall Linux, placing the Linux boot manager on the MBR.

- The system may have trouble identifying hardware on your system that was not detected during the installation process. In this case it may help to specify information about the hardware via a boot parameter. A **boot parameter** is a piece of information that you can supply to the boot manager. The boot manager launches the Linux kernel with this parameter attached. These parameters are used both to affect how Linux recognizes hardware devices, and to alter the enabled features of the operating system.

The Graphical Interface Doesn't Work

If the Installation Program Detected the Video Hardware

Sometimes the graphical interface won't work even though the installation program appeared to detect your video hardware without a complaint. In this case, you probably selected a color depth or resolution that is not supported by the Linux driver. This can be true even if higher resolutions are supported on Windows—the Linux driver may still be in development or the developers lack critical technical information to make the video card perform to its capabilities.

If the Installation Program Did Not Detect the Video Hardware

Some video cards that are not supported by XFree86 (the foundation for all Linux graphical installations) are supported by commercial X Window System products that you can purchase and add to your Linux system after installing Linux. These products are available from Xi Graphics (see *www.xig.com*) and MetroLink (see *www.metrolink.com*). In the rare case that your card is not supported by any of these products, you will only be able to use Linux in text mode. This is typical for many server installations, but if you want to use a graphical desktop, you will need to invest in a different video card.

Chapter 5 provides more explanation about how the graphical system works and how to configure the X Window System.

A Device or Part of Memory Isn't Available

Sometimes hardware that is included on the list of supported hardware on the Linux vendor's Web site is nevertheless not available after starting Linux. This is often because the hardware is not correctly configured. As with a system that won't boot, the configuration can sometimes be corrected by adding a boot parameter when starting Linux. For example, some computers running Linux will not access the CD-ROM drive correctly unless the device name is added as a boot parameter, like this:

```
linux cdrom=/dev/hdc
```

Or Linux may not access all of the available system RAM because of limitations in the computer's BIOS. (The `free` command displays the amount of memory available to Linux.) You can tell Linux the amount of RAM on the system using this format:

```
linux mem=<<amount of memory>>M
```

So to indicate 512 MB of RAM, you would use the following command:

```
linux mem=512M
```

Be sure to use the correct value for the amount of RAM on your computer, or Linux will crash as it tries to work with nonexistent memory.

You can also combine multiple boot parameters on a single line separated by spaces. For example:

```
linux cdrom=/dev/hdc mem=512M
```

The Boot Parameters HOWTO document provides details about how to add these parameters to make your computer function correctly in Linux. (Chapter 1 describes how to access HOWTO documents on the Red Hat Linux CD or via the Internet.)

Testing Network Connections

The Red Hat Linux 7.3 installation program includes a window that configures networking. Many users want to begin using a network connection immediately after installation, in order to send e-mail, browse the Web, or share data with other users on the network. If you experience problems when you launch a Web browser or try other Internet access, use the `ping` command as shown below to test the network connection and make sure it is correctly configured.

1. To test your connection, enter the following:

   ```
   ping 127.0.0.1
   ```

   You should see lines appear on-screen once every second. Press **Ctrl+C** to stop the command. If no lines appear, networking is not configured or activated on your system. You should contact your system administrator to ask for assistance in reconfiguring networking.

3

2. If the first `ping` command worked, execute another `ping` command using the IP address that you entered for your system during the installation. (If you used DHCP during the installation, skip this step, since you weren't given an IP address to enter.)

   `ping <IP address>`

   If you see lines appear once every second, your network adapter card has been correctly configured. Press **Ctrl+C** to stop the command. If the system pauses without displaying anything, you can run the `neat` utility in Red Hat Linux to configure your networking card, or contact your instructor or system administrator. (See also *Guide to Linux Networking and Security* for detailed information on configuring Linux networking.)

3. If the first two `ping` commands worked, next try to contact a remote site using an IP address. (You can use any IP address that corresponds to a real server on your local network or on the Internet, if you have an Internet connection.) For example, you might try the following command:

   `ping 207.49.12.1`

   If lines appear once every second, you have established a connection with another computer. Press **Ctrl+C** to stop the command. If the system pauses without displaying anything, your connection to the remote site (perhaps on the Internet) is not functioning or else you have selected a site that does not respond to `ping` commands. Try another site. If that is not successful, ask your instructor, system administrator, or Internet Service Provider to verify that your network is correctly configured to permit Internet access.

4. Finally, if the first three `ping` commands are successful, try using a domain name with the `ping` command. (Note that some computers on the Internet won't respond to `ping`; school names are usually better than commercial servers). Here's an example:

   `ping www.slcc.edu`

   If lines appear once every second, you are ready to use the network. If this last test fails (that is, if no lines appear), you need to ask for assistance to configure your DNS server information.

To access the Internet using a Web browser, you may also need to configure your Web browser to use different server names or addresses for security purposes. Ask your system administrator or ISP if any configuration changes are required.

The preceding information outlines only the most basic network information. Complete details on configuring and using networking are covered in *Guide to Linux Networking and Security*.

CHAPTER SUMMARY

❒ Many Linux distributions are available, each with a slightly different technical focus and often with different end-users as its primary customers. Vendors of commercial distributions try to distinguish their products by offering documentation, technical support, additional software packages, or related services.

❒ Red Hat Linux 7.3 was selected for this book because of its large market share and customer support reputation. Learning Linux on Red Hat will prepare you for any Linux certification examination.

❒ Linux installations are started by a boot disk or bootable CD-ROM. A user defines the source of the Linux files and the target partition where they will be stored. The user also answers a number of questions during the installation process to define exactly what software will be installed and how it will be configured.

❒ Attractive graphical installation programs are standard in commercial versions of Linux such as SuSE Linux, Caldera OpenLinux, Red Hat Linux and others. On many systems a complete Linux installation takes only about 15 minutes plus the time required to copy files to your hard disk.

❒ Linux can share a computer with another operating system via a boot manager program. This program controls, via user selections, which operating system is launched each time the computer is booted. This is called a dual-boot system.

❒ You can install Linux from a CD-ROM, from files stored on a hard disk, across a network connection, or even from floppy disk, in some cases. The CD-ROM option is most widely used except when Linux is installed on a large number of systems at the same time, in which case a network install is most likely.

❒ Linux accesses file systems via mount points—directories designated for accessing a particular set of data. Devices such as CD-ROM drives are also accessed in this way. Linux does not use drive letters.

❒ The various components of Linux are sometimes arranged on different hard disk partitions to make system administration tasks easier. You can configure these partitions within the Linux installation program.

❒ Linux relies on a swap partition as virtual memory—magnetic storage space that acts like additional system memory. You must define a swap partition when you install Linux.

❒ Installation programs generally provide multiple installation types that let you define the sorts of programs you want to install as part of Linux. For example, Server, Graphical Workstation, or Software Development Station might define different sets of applications that are installed with the basic operating system.

❒ Software packages are managed using special file formats such as the Red Hat Package Manager format (**rpm**).

❐ When you start a Linux-based computer, you must log in before you can use its resources. The login screen can be in text mode or graphical mode. Text mode is more often seen on servers, since they often do not need any graphical interface.

❐ Problems with installing Linux are usually related to incorrectly recognized hardware. You can often correct this by using boot parameters or by otherwise adjusting system configurations.

3

KEY TERMS

authentication — The process of identifying a user to a computer system via some type of login procedure.

boot disk — A floppy disk that can launch an operating system, especially one that launches a Linux installation program.

boot parameter — A piece of information passed directly to the Linux kernel as the system is being booted. These parameters are normally used to affect how Linux recognizes hardware devices or to enable certain features of the operating system.

bootable CD-ROM drive — A CD-ROM drive that can launch an operating system (or other program) directly from a CD without accessing the hard disk. (This feature of the CD-ROM drive must be enabled by the BIOS.)

disk image — A single file that contains an exact copy of a floppy disk.

fdisk — A utility used to create hard disk partitions and configure how they are used.

install disk — A disk used to start the Linux installation program on some distributions of Linux. *See* boot disk.

installation source — The set of files from which Linux is installed. These files are normally stored on a Linux CD-ROM.

installation type — A specification indicating which Linux software to install; the appropriate installation type depends on how the Linux system is to be used.

logging in — The process of identifying yourself as a valid user who has been assigned a certain set of access rights.

mount point — A subdirectory through which a set of data such as a hard disk partition is accessed.

partition table — Information on a hard disk that defines the size and file system type of each partition on that hard disk.

ping — A command used to test a network connection.

Red Hat Package Manager (rpm) — A data storage format for software packages.

root — The administrative user account; the superuser. Whoever has access to this account can control the entire system.

root directory — The beginning point for every Linux file system.

software package — A single file that contains all the files needed to install and use an application or group of related applications. Special data formats are used to store many files in a single software package.

target hard disk partition — The location on the system's hard disk where Linux will be installed. Also known as the *target partition*.

REVIEW QUESTIONS

1. How do the various commercial Linux products differ?

   a. Only in packaging, promotion, training, and support programs

   b. Use of development versions of the Linux kernel to give the market the latest Linux features

   c. Different file locations, graphical interfaces, and included applications, as well as packaging, promotion, training, and support programs

   d. Focus on different geographic areas that they can best serve because of language or cultural understanding

2. The installation program included with a Linux distribution is usually created by:

   a. The company, or vendor, that sells the Linux distribution

   b. The team of developers that created the kernel

   c. The GNU project of the Free Software Foundation

   d. Linus Torvalds

3. Name two technical differences and two non-technical (marketing related) differences between various Linux products.

4. Explain why installing a new Linux system is different from installing an application such as a spreadsheet or a database package.

5. The target hard disk partition is where:

   a. A dual-boot Windows system resides

   b. The Linux operating system will be installed

   c. Backup data must be stored for Linux to access it

   d. The Linux installation program is stored

6. Possible locations for the installation source data do *not* include which of the following:

   a. The target hard disk partition

   b. A local CD-ROM

   c. A local hard disk

   d. A networked server using the SMB protocol

7. To start a networked installation you should contact:

   a. Red Hat software to obtain a different boot disk

   b. Your system administrator to obtain the target partition for the installation

   c. Your system administrator to determine whether your hard disk supports a network-based installation

   d. The network administrator of the server containing the installation source

8. When you turn on a computer, _____ sends control to the MBR of the first hard disk, or to another device such as a bootable CD-ROM drive or a floppy drive.

    a. Linux

    b. the `fdisk` utility

    c. the boot manager

    d. the BIOS

9. The boot disk is not needed if:

    a. You are using DHCP for the Linux installation

    b. You have a bootable CD-ROM drive

    c. You are using a network-based installation

    d. You have already created two partitions using FIPS

10. In which circumstance would you need a boot disk to start the Linux installation program?

    a. When the computer does not have a bootable CD-ROM drive

    b. When installing on a laptop

    c. When the hard disk has become corrupted

    d. When installing from a network installation source

11. Name the tool used in Windows to copy a disk image to a floppy disk

12. The `fdisk` utility is used to:

    a. Prepare partitions on a hard disk

    b. Create a boot disk from a disk image

    c. Start a Linux installation program from a boot disk

    d. Launch Linux from a hard disk containing Windows

13. The device name `/dev/hda3` would refer to:

    a. The third partition on the first IDE hard disk

    b. The third partition on the first SCSI hard disk

    c. The third IDE hard disk

    d. The swap partition stored on a boot disk

14. Name three reasons why you might place different parts of the Linux file system on different hard disk partitions.

15. _____ is like a mini–database that holds the size and location on the hard disk of each partition.

    a. MBR

    b. `fdisk`

    c. The partition table

    d. `rpm`

16. Two formats used for software packages are:

    a. Red Hat and Debian

    b. Red Hat and TurboLinux

    c. Debian and SuSE

    d. `rpm` and `ping`

17. Explain why you might choose to select groups of software packages rather than individual software packages during an installation.

18. The _____ user account is created as part of every Linux installation process.

    a. GRUB

    b. installation source

    c. `useradd`

    d. `root`

19. Boot parameters let the boot manager:

    a. Send additional information to the Linux kernel as it is launched

    b. Define which operating system is the default

    c. Alter the partition table when necessary

    d. Automatically create a boot disk on Windows systems

20. The _____ command normally starts the graphical system when working in a text-based Linux system.

    a. `startx`

    b. `GNOME`

    c. `KDE`

    d. `gnome`

21. The `ping` command is used to:

    a. Test a network connection

    b. Test the sound card configuration

    c. Test the integrity of a hard disk connector

    d. Send a small e-mail message to another system

22. The partition table is located on the hard disk and contains:

    a. A list of Linux device names for everything on the system

    b. Boot parameters to help Linux locate and correctly use the different hardware

    c. A copy of the boot manager

    d. A data table with the size and type of each partition on the hard disk

23. Name three reasons why a Linux installation program may not start up correctly.

24. Which of the following is *not* likely to cause hardware problems in Linux?

    a. The correct module supporting that hardware is not yet installed.

    b. A parameter identifying the hardware was not entered correctly.

    c. Windows has disabled the hardware for use under Linux.

    d. The hardware is not supported by Linux.

25. The surest way to have the Linux boot manager correctly start Linux is to install it on:

    a. The MBR

    b. The boot sector of the active partition

    c. A networked server

    d. The installation source partition

HANDS-ON PROJECTS

Project 3-1

In this activity you use a Windows computer to create a boot disk for installing Red Hat Linux 7.3. To complete this activity you should have a computer with any version of Windows installed and both a CD-ROM drive and a 3½ inch floppy disk drive. You should also have a Red Hat Linux 7.3 CD-ROM like the one included in this book and a blank floppy disk.

If you have a bootable CD-ROM drive on your computer, you do not need to create a boot disk before installing Linux using Project 3-3.

1. Start Windows.

2. Insert Red Hat Linux 7.3 CD 1 in the CD-ROM drive and a blank floppy disk in the floppy disk drive.

3. Double-click the **My Computer** icon on the Windows Desktop. A window opens showing you the contents of your computer.

4. Double-click the icon for the CD-ROM drive within the My Computer window. A window appears showing you the contents of the Red Hat Linux CD.

5. Double-click the **dosutils** folder within the CD-ROM drive window. A window appears showing you the contents of the Images folder.

6. Double-click the **rawwritewin** folder, then double-click the **rawwritewin** program within the rawwritewin folder window. (Depending on your Windows configuration, you may see this program listed as rawwritewin.exe.) The rawwritewin program appears as shown previously in Figure 3-1.

7. Make certain that the Floppy drive field contains the drive letter corresponding to your floppy drive. Normally this is A:.

8. In the Image file field, enter the name of the disk image that you want to copy to a floppy disk to create the boot disk. The standard image file to use is called `boot.img`. You should include the drive letter of your CD-ROM and the path to the image file. For example, if your CD-ROM is in drive E:, enter this text:

    `E:\images\boot.img`

    If you are installing Linux on a laptop computer, use the image file name `pcmcia.img` instead of `boot.img`. If you are installing Linux across a network connection, use the image file name `bootnet.img`.

9. Click the **Write** button to create the boot disk from the image file that you specified.

10. When the disk image has been copied from the CD-ROM to the floppy disk, a message window informs you of successful completion. Click **OK** to close that message box.

11. Click **Exit** to close the rawwritewin program.

12. Eject the CD-ROM and newly created boot disk.

13. Label the boot disk appropriately.

Project 3-2

In this activity you use a computer that is already running Linux to create a boot disk for installing Red Hat Linux 7.3 on another computer. To complete this activity you should have a computer with any standard version of Linux, and both a CD-ROM drive and a 3½ inch floppy disk drive. You should also have a Red Hat Linux 7.3 CD like the one included in this book and a blank floppy disk.

If you have a bootable CD-ROM drive on your computer, you do not need to create a boot disk before installing Linux using Project 3-3.

1. Start Linux and log in. Depending on how the Linux system has been configured, you probably have to log in as root to use the CD-ROM and floppy drives in this project.

3

2. Insert Red Hat Linux 7.3 CD 1 in the CD-ROM drive and a blank floppy disk in the floppy disk drive.

3. If you are working at a Linux graphical desktop, the CD-ROM is probably automatically mounted (prepared for use). If any graphical windows appear, close them by clicking **No** or clicking the small X icon in the upper-right corner of the window. If you are using the Gnome interface, click **No** when asked if you want to execute the autorun program.

4. If you are working in a graphical environment, open a Linux command-line window based on instructions from your system administrator or instructor. If you are using Gnome, click the Foot icon, then **Programs**, then **System**, then **GNOME Terminal**.

5. At the Linux command line, enter the following command to make the CD-ROM drive accessible. If you see an error message that the drive appears already to be mounted, go on to the next step.

   ```
   mount /mnt/cdrom
   ```

   (This command should work on most Linux systems, including Red Hat Linux 7.3.)

6. Enter the following command to copy the boot disk image file from the CD-ROM to the floppy disk. After you enter this command, you must wait several minutes for the operation to complete.

   ```
   dd if=/mnt/cdrom/images/boot.img of=/dev/fd0
   ```

   If you plan to install Linux on a laptop, use the image file name `pcmcia.img`. If you plan to install Linux across a network connection, use the image file name `bootnet.img`.

7. Remove the floppy disk after the floppy drive light turns off.

8. Enter the following command, then remove the CD-ROM from the drive.

   ```
   umount /mnt/cdrom
   ```

9. Label the boot disk appropriately.

Project 3-3

In this project you install Red Hat Linux 7.3. To complete this activity you should have an Intel- or compatible-based computer with either a bootable CD-ROM drive or a CD-ROM drive and a floppy disk drive. The computer should have a minimum of 32 MB of memory and about 1.5 GB of free hard disk space. You can choose to install fewer software packages than those described in the steps that follow, in which case less disk space is required. Part or all of the disk space intended for installing Linux can be an empty Windows partition that you created using FIPS (see Project 2-2).

If your CD-ROM drive is not bootable, you should have completed either Project 3-1 or Project 3-2 to create the boot disk used in this project. For this project you also need a second blank floppy disk labeled Red Hat Final Boot Disk.

Installing Linux is the most involved project in this book. Because so many variations exist in available computer hardware, the steps you have to follow may vary slightly from the steps given in this project. Every effort has been made to alert you to important variations and prepare you to answer any questions that come up.

These steps assume that you are installing Linux on a desktop computer (not a laptop), on an IDE hard disk, and that you do not need additional special hardware drivers (though comments are provided regarding such drivers).

1. Insert the Red Hat Linux 7.3 CD 1 in your CD-ROM drive and the boot disk in your floppy drive (if applicable). Turn on your computer.

2. After a few moments, a full screen of text appears on a black background with the title `Welcome to Red Hat Linux 7.3!` at the top of the screen.

   a. If you do nothing, the installation will continue in graphics mode after about 30 seconds.

   b. You can press **Enter** to immediately start the installation in graphics mode.

   c. If you have previously had trouble with the graphics mode, type the word **text** and press **Enter**.

   d. If you have special hardware for which you created a driver diskette (as mentioned in the chapter text), type `linux dd` and press **Enter**.

   e. If you tried this procedure previously and the system appeared to crash during the start-up phase, you can try typing `linux noprobe` and pressing **Enter**. This prevents the installation program from probing hardware, which causes problems on a few systems.

3. Assuming that you pressed Enter without typing any text or simply waited, you see dozens of lines of text scroll down the screen as your hardware components are examined by the Linux kernel. After a few moments, the graphical installation program begins and you see a splash screen with the Red Hat Linux logo and the Welcome title. (This loading process may take as much as four full minutes, depending on your computer's speed.)

   On the left side of the screen you see a help screen. You can review these screens at any time during the installation to see detailed information on the choices presented at that point in the installation. A Release Notes button also has late-breaking information from Red Hat Software and is worth reviewing.

   On the bottom right side of the screen are two buttons labeled Back and Next. You use these buttons to navigate through the installation program, choosing Next to proceed to the following screen or Back if you wish to return to a previous screen to make a change or review something.

   If you are using the text mode installation program instead of the graphical installation (which is the focus of these steps), you see Back and Next buttons. You can navigate between buttons using the Tab key.

If you are using the graphical installation program but your mouse does not work (it normally works immediately), you can use the Tab and Enter keys to choose the Next button; the fourth screen of the Installation program will let you configure your mouse correctly.

4. Choose the **Next** button to continue past the Welcome screen.

5. The Language Selection window appears with a list of language options. Click on a different language than U.S. English if appropriate and then choose **Next**. The language changes immediately to match your selection.

6. The Keyboard Configuration window appears. If you are using a non-U.S. keyboard or a special keyboard such as a Microsoft Natural keyboard, select the appropriate items in the Model and Layout lists.

   The Dead Keys list indicates whether you want to use key combinations to enter foreign characters. For most users, the default settings on the Keyboard Configuration window are acceptable, and you simply choose **Next** to continue.

7. The Mouse Configuration window appears. Your mouse is probably already working, but you can select your model from the list shown if it was not correctly auto-detected and highlighted. If the mouse model you select uses a serial port interface, you can then select the appropriate serial port in the box below the list of mouse models. The list includes both the Linux device name (on the right) and the better known port name (on the left). Click on the appropriate line to select it.

   You may want also to select the Emulate 3 Buttons checkbox at the bottom of this window. Some functions in Linux use the middle button of a three-button mouse. If you are using a two-button mouse, checking this box causes Linux to act as if you pressed a middle mouse button anytime you press both mouse buttons at the same time. Click **Next** to continue.

   If your mouse was not working when you first saw the Mouse Configuration window, it should begin working when you click Next. If it does not, use the Back button on the following screen to return to the Mouse Configuration screen and re-configure your mouse.

8. The Installation Type window appears. Because you are completing a new installation for this project, click the button to the left of the **Install** icon (as opposed to the Upgrade icon at the bottom of the window).

   The simplest installation would result from selecting one of the first three Install options: Workstation, Server, or Laptop (which is simply Workstation with PCMCIA support). For this project, choose **Custom**, then click **Next** to continue.

9. The Disk Partitioning Setup window appears. This window describes the disk partitioning tools you can use. The `fdisk` program mentioned on-screen is challenging to use and is described in Chapter 8. Click the button to the left of the second item to use the **Disk Druid** utility. Then click **Next** to continue.

If you are installing Linux on a computer with no other operating systems, where you are not concerned about erasing other data on your hard disk, you could choose automatic partitioning, the first option. But for this project, you will learn more by using the Disk Druid partitioning tool.

10. The Disk Setup window appears. The top part of the screen shows a representation of your hard disk as a horizontal bar divided into labeled partitions. The bottom part of the screen lists partitions by their Linux device names (such as /dev/hda1) and also gives their sizes, partition types, and other information. Between these two areas of the window are buttons you can use to set up partitions.

   a. If you feel at any time that you have become confused or selected the wrong thing, click the Reset button. The partition table will be re-read from the hard disk. Nothing is written to the hard disk until you click the Next button and confirm your partition changes.

   b. If you have an empty Windows partition that you intend to use for Linux, click on that partition in the list and click **Delete** to remove it from the partition table.

   c. Once you have sufficient free space on your hard disk, click the **New** button. A dialog box appears in which you define the partition. Choose **Swap** from the File System Type drop-down list. In the Size field, enter a size in megabytes for the swap partition (this should be from 64 to 256 MB). Make certain that **Fixed** size is selected in the Additional Size Options section of the dialog box. Click **OK** to add this partition to the new partition table you are defining.

   d. Click **New** again. A dialog box appears. Type **/** in the Mount Point field or select it from the drop-down list. Choose **ext3** from the File System Type drop-down list. You can enter a size if you prefer, but you may want just to choose Fill to maximum allowable size in the Additional Size Options section. Click **OK** to add this partition.

   e. If you want to make a change in your new partition structure, use the Edit or Delete buttons, then use New again to re-create the partition definition. The diagram at the top of the window illustrates the partitions as you create them. Click **Next** to continue.

   f. Depending on your pre-existing hard disk configuration, you are likely to see a dialog box listing the partitions that will be formatted during the installation of Linux. Verify that these partitions are *not* partitions that contain information you want to retain (such as on an existing Windows partition). Then click **Yes** to confirm use of the partitions.

11. The Boot Loader Configuration window appears. You should accept the default selections in this window unless told differently by an instructor or system administrator. In this window you can select either LILO or GRUB as your boot manager (GRUB is the default), where to install the boot manager (the installation program selects the MBR or Linux partition based on your system's pre-existing configuration), and what

3

other operating systems the boot manager will offer to launch at boot time (based on what data it discovers on your other partitions). After reviewing these options, click **Next** to continue.

12. The Boot Loader Password Configuration window appears. If you want to add a boot password to your system, you can select the checkbox on this window and enter the password you have selected (twice). Having a password means that the boot loader will not start Linux without your entering a password. This is a helpful security feature, but is often an annoyance in a lab or classroom setting and is not recommended here. Click **Next** to continue.

13. The Network Configuration window appears. If you are using networking (and have a network card installed) check the Activate on boot checkbox. If you have a DHCP server on your network, check the Configure using DHCP checkbox as well. Otherwise, uncheck this second checkbox and enter the network information in the fields below the checkboxes according to the addresses and names that your instructor, system administrator, or ISP has provided to you. In the Hostname field, enter your FQDN. Some fields on this window may be left blank, even if you are not using DHCP. Click **Next** to continue.

14. The Firewall Configuration window appears. The items on this window are important but are beyond the scope of this book. This project assumes you are working in a lab environment, but for safety's sake, select the **High** option at the top of the window, then click **Next** to continue.

15. The Additional Language Support window appears. In this window you can choose to install documentation and interface text (for dialog boxes and menus) for a number of languages beyond the English that is installed by default. Check the box next to any of these that you wish to install, but note that each one takes up many megabytes of hard disk space. If you do select additional languages, you should also select the default language for your installation from the drop-down list at the top of the window (it only lists languages that you have checked below). Click **Next** to continue.

16. The Time Zone Selection window appears with the Location tab selected. In this window you define your time options. Begin by selecting the time zone where you are located, either by locating it in the list at the bottom half of the Location tab or by clicking on your location in the map. You can select different maps from the drop-down list labeled View. If you are running only Linux on your computer, you should select the checkbox labeled System Clock Uses UTC. Computers that also have Windows installed should not use this option.

If you cannot find your correct time zone on the Location tab, you can select the UTC Offset tab and select your time zone relative to Universal Coordinated Time (also called Greenwich Mean Time, equivalent to the time in Greenwich, England). On that tab you can also check boxes at the bottom of the window to enable daylight savings time and choose whether to set the system clock to UTC or local time. Then click **Next** to continue.

17. The Account Configuration window appears. In this window you set the root password and also define at least one regular user account. Enter the root password you have selected in both the Root Password and Confirm fields.

    Create a regular user account by clicking the **Add** button. In the dialog box that appears, enter a username for the account in the User Name field (for example, jthomas or jamest); enter your complete name in the Full Name field (for example, James Thomas); and enter a password for this account in the Password and Confirm fields. Click **OK** to close this dialog box and add the user account definition to the list in the Account Configuration window.

    You can create other user accounts here if you wish, but most system administrators choose to create them later. Click **Next** to continue.

18. The Authentication Configuration window appears. The default system security options shown on this window are appropriate for nearly all Linux systems. Your system administrator will inform you during installation if you should select additional options in any of the tabs shown. (You can also configure these services after installation as well.) Click **Next** to continue.

19. A message appears: "Reading package information…" The Package Group Selection window then appears. This window appears as the result of selecting Custom for your installation choice. Package groups are listed as shown in Table 3-4. In addition to those selected by default (which are indicated by bold type in Table 3-4), select the following packages by clicking on the checkbox to the left of each:

    ❐ Graphics and Image Manipulation

    ❐ Utilities

    This gives a total size required for the installation of 1,133 MB. (If you have the required 3.6 GB of disk space, you can choose to install everything using the last item on the list.) Click **Next** to continue.

20. A message appears that states "Checking dependencies in packages selected for installation…" Then the Graphical Interface (X) Configuration window appears. Your video card and video memory have been auto-detected at this point and your video card is selected in the list of cards. Don't change this unless you have attempted the installation previously and you know the auto-detection is incorrect. (You can also check the box at the bottom of the window to skip this graphical configuration step, then try it later if you choose.) The Restore Original Values button will re-probe your system to establish the auto-detected selections. Click **Next** to continue.

21. The About to Install window appears. This window simply warns you that you are about to install Linux based on the selections you have made in the installation program.

 If you fear you may have made a selection during the installation that will erase existing data on your computer, you can simply turn your computer off at this point. Nothing has been changed on your hard disk until you press Next on the About to Install window.

3

The Kickstart file `/root/anaconda-ks.cfg` that is mentioned on the About to Install window is a resource for system administrators who install Linux on numerous identical systems, or re-install Linux many times on the same system. That file saves all your choices in the installation program and lets you apply them automatically to a future installation. See Red Hat's documentation on the `anaconda` program to use this feature.

22. Click **Next** to begin the installation of Linux files on your hard disk. The Installing Packages window appears. On this window you can see the progress of the installation as the packages you selected are copied to your hard disk. If you selected the packages as recommended, you will be prompted to remove the CD and insert CD 2. This copying process takes from 3 to 30 minutes depending on the speed of your system components.

23. The Boot Disk Creation window appears. Insert the second blank floppy disk that you labeled Red Hat Final Boot Disk into the floppy drive and click **Next** to create a floppy that you can use to boot your Linux system if your hard drive experiences problems. If you don't have a second floppy disk, you can check the box to skip this step before clicking **Next**.

24. The Monitor Configuration window appears. Although the installation program attempts to auto-detect your monitor, most monitors cannot be auto-detected. Select your monitor manufacturer and model from the list shown. Click **Next** to continue.

25. The Graphical Interface Configuration window appears. Choose a color depth and resolution from the corresponding drop-down lists. Then click **Test these settings** to view the desktop interface as it will appear with these settings. If you see a clear image of the desktop after a couple of moments, click **Yes** in the dialog box that appears to close the test image. You can then click **Next** to continue. If the desktop image did not appear, the Graphical Interface Configuration window will appear again automatically after a few moments. You can then try different color or resolution settings.

The default desktop interface shown on this window is Gnome (assuming you selected the recommended packages in previous steps). You cannot change that default here, but you can change it after completing the installation and restarting Linux.

On any system where you are using the graphical installation program, the program assumes you would prefer a graphical login prompt as well. If you prefer a text login prompt, select Text from the options at the bottom of this window before clicking Next.

26. The Congratulations window appears. Remove any floppy disk that is still inserted and click **Exit** to end the installation program and launch the newly installed copy of Linux. (The CD-ROM will be ejected automatically as part of this launch process.)

Project 3-4

In this activity you begin to use the new Linux system that you installed in Project 3-3. To complete this activity you should have completed Project 3-3 and be ready to work on your newly installed Red Hat Linux 7.3 system.

1. Remove any CDs and floppy disks from the computer.

2. If you are starting this project directly after completing Project 3-3, the computer is already loading Red Hat Linux. Otherwise, turn your computer on.

3. The boot manager splash screen appears with a Red Hat logo and a listing of the operating systems that the boot loader can launch. This list includes Linux and possibly other operating systems depending on the configuration of your system. (If you have Windows installed and created a dual-boot computer, a second line labeled DOS appears in this window.)

4. Use the up and down arrow keys to select the operating system that you want to boot. By default, Linux is listed first, so you should be able to simply press **Enter**. If you do not press Enter, Linux, as the default operating system, will launch automatically after 10 seconds.

5. You see many messages display on the screen as Linux boots up. After a few moments, a login screen appears. (This is probably a graphical login screen, but may be a text-mode login screen depending on the selections you made near the end of Project 3-3.) Enter the username that you created as a regular user account during the installation.

6. Enter the wrong password. What happens? Can you use the system without entering one of the valid usernames and the corresponding password?

7. Enter the correct username of the regular user account, then press **Enter**. Enter the correct password and press **Enter** to log in to the system.

8. After a moment you see the desktop interface that you were able to preview during the installation. The desktop interface includes icons and a menu that you can view by clicking the icon in the lower left corner of the screen. Study the items on the desktop. Click on the menu and review the items that it contains, including items on any submenus that look interesting to you.

9. Exit the desktop interface by clicking on the menu icon and choosing **Log out**. Click **Yes** with the Log out option selected in the dialog box that appears. After a moment you see the graphical login screen again.

10. The graphical login screen includes a dialog box in which you entered the username and password to log in in steps 5–7. Now choose **Halt** from the System menu in this dialog box, then click **Yes**.

If you are using a text-based login, you can shut down the system after you log out by pressing Ctrl+Alt+Del or entering the halt command.

CASE PROJECTS

New project proposals have arrived on your desk at McKinney & Co. consulting:

1. One potential client manages a group of resorts known collectively as Lakewood Resorts. Lakewood Resorts have recently started to expand their operations by promoting their resorts to vacationers around the country. To support this expansion, it has installed a call center with about 100 computers to handle incoming requests for information and reservations. Each computer will be staffed by a representative who can answer questions and make reservations or send out a resort brochure. You propose that all of the computers run Linux and be connected to a large reservations computer located in another office. You and your technical staff will install Linux on all of the systems. Based on the options you learned in this chapter, would you use a local CD-ROM drive to install each system or place the installation source files on a networked server? Explain the reasons for your choice. Describe in detail the additional features (beyond those discussed explicitly in the chapter) you would like to see in a Linux distribution or installation program to support your work on this project. Visit the Web sites of several Linux vendors, and see what features you can find that fit your criteria. How important would having these features be for a project like this? What if you had to install Linux on 2500 computers?

2. You are also trying to decide which Linux distribution you would use for the Lakewood Resorts project. What technical or non-technical features would be important to you as you prepare your plan to install Linux on the call center's computers? Given the standard cost range of Linux distributions mentioned in the previous chapter, how important is the cost of the Linux product in making your decision?

3. Suppose all the call center's computers already have Microsoft Windows installed. You have been asked to make each one a dual-boot system, so that representatives can use Windows software occasionally if they need to. Does this change the Linux product you would choose? Conduct research on the Internet or through Linux vendors to locate commercial Windows software to help you install (or prepare to install) the Linux systems. Assuming that the Linux systems were already installed and you were later asked to add Windows to each system, how would your arrangement of the Linux partitions (and possibly multiple mount points) affect your ability to make the requested change to the systems? Are some possible future needs too costly to prepare for now?

4

RUNNING A LINUX SYSTEM

After reading this chapter and completing the exercises, you will be able to:

♦ Manage files and directories on a Linux system using basic commands

♦ Launch programs and manage corresponding software packages

♦ Add and remove features from the Linux kernel

♦ Review and change the initialization process that starts a Linux-based computer

♦ Shut down a Linux system in an orderly way

In the previous chapter you learned about installing a new Linux system from a CD. You learned how to set up Linux hard disk partitions, how to answer configuration questions, and how to log in to a newly installed Linux system.

In this chapter you learn how to work with key parts of your Linux system, including files, directories, software packages, and the Linux kernel. You also learn more about how Linux is organized and the processes used to start the operating system, launch programs, and interact with devices and data files. In addition, you learn about many commands that system administrators rely on. Graphical tools are often available for administrative tasks, and these are presented as well.

WORKING WITH LINUX FILES AND DIRECTORIES

Manipulating files and directories is a large part of what you do on a computer, whether as a regular user or as a system administrator. For example, you search directories for a file, you open that file to review or change its contents, and you save an updated version of the file. This section describes some basic concepts and tools (both text-based and graphical) that enable you to access files on a Linux system.

Information stored on your computer is organized into files, each with a name and other attributes such as size and date created. To make it easier to keep track of thousands of files, they are organized into directories, which are like file folders that arrange files into groups. Multiple levels of directories are arranged in a branching treelike structure, in which one directory leads to other directories. Each directory can contain both files and other directories. When one directory contains another directory, that relationship is expressed by calling the first a **parent directory** and the second a subdirectory, or **child directory**. The subdirectory may also be the parent directory to another directory—a subdirectory—that it contains.

As you learned in Chapter 3, every file, directory, and device in Linux is accessed as part of a single directory structure. The parent directory for all of these is the root directory and is represented by a forward slash: "/". All Linux configuration files are located in subdirectories of the root directory. All devices are also associated with a filename located in a subdirectory of the root directory. (You may remember examples such as `/dev/hda1` from Chapter 3.) As a system administrator, much of your work consists of managing the status, contents, and location of files and directories.

 The `/root` subdirectory is the home directory of the root user account. Don't confuse this with the root directory, /. For clarity, it's helpful to refer to the `/root` subdirectory as "slash-root," or "root's home directory."

By default, Linux includes a standard set of subdirectories when first installed. Table 4-1 lists these subdirectories. Some versions of Linux may contain subdirectories of the root directory that are not listed here. For example, several versions of Linux use an `/opt` directory for storing optional applications, though Red Hat Linux 7.3 does not.

On newly installed Linux systems, the directory from Table 4-1 that contains the greatest number of files and subdirectories is the `/usr` subdirectory. This subdirectory contains system utilities, the files for the graphical system, documentation files, and much more.

The names of standard Linux subdirectories are not intuitive, but each has a distinct purpose that has been refined through years of UNIX and Linux development. This well-known directory structure ensures that programs can interact with each other because they can locate files in customary locations on any Linux system. You will become familiar with the arrangement and purpose of standard Linux files and directories as you explore your system using the command-line and graphical tools described in the following sections.

Table 4-1   Standard Linux Subdirectories of the Root Directory

Directory	Contents
/bin	Executable programs, typically including system utilities.
/boot	Files used to initialize Linux when the system is booted, such as the Linux kernel.
/dev	Filenames that are linked to hardware resources (devices).
/etc	Configuration files, especially those used by system utilities and network services like e-mail, Web, and FTP.
/home	Home directories for all regular user accounts.
/lib	System libraries (described later in this chapter) used by many Linux programs, especially system utilities and the Linux kernel.
/root	Files used by the root user (the superuser account). This is the home directory of that user account. It is separate from the /home directory so that actions taken on /home (as described later) do not affect the root user's files.
/sbin	Executable programs used only by the root user.
/tmp	Temporary files created by any user or program on the system.
/usr	Files used by all regular users on the system, including data, programs, and documentation.
/var	Variable (changing) information created by system utilities and network services. Examples include system log files, e-mail messages, and files waiting to be sent to a printer.

4

Working at a Command Line

If you logged in to Linux at a text-mode console, you are immediately placed in a command-line environment as shown in Figure 4-1. (This environment is sometimes called character-mode or character-cell mode.)

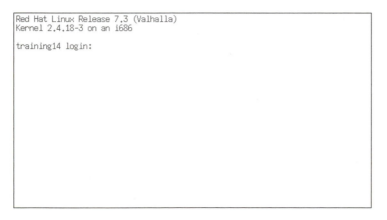

```
Red Hat Linux Release 7.3 (Valhalla)
Kernel 2.4.18-3 on an i686

training14 login:
```

Figure 4-1   A text-mode console environment

If you logged in to Linux using a graphical login prompt, your system launches a graphical environment, normally the Gnome or KDE Desktop. (These graphical environments are discussed in Chapter 5.) Within a graphical environment, you can open a **command-line window** in which you can enter commands at your keyboard. The command-line window is also called a **terminal emulator window** (or terminal window) because it resembles an old-fashioned dumb terminal connection. Within a graphical environment, a program call **xterm** (pronounced "ex-term") is often used to provide a command-line window. Figure 4-2 shows a Gnome desktop with a command-line window.

Figure 4-2   A command-line window in a graphical environment

To open a command-line window, you click an appropriate icon on your desktop or select an appropriate menu item within the graphical environment. For example, within the Gnome Desktop, you can click on the footprint icon in the lower left corner of the window, click on Programs, then System, then GNOME Terminal. Within the KDE Desktop, click on the K icon in the lower left corner of the window, click on Utilities, and then click Terminal.

At a command-line prompt, either in text mode or in a command-line window, you can explore the Linux directory structure and use Linux command-line utilities like those described in the next section.

An ongoing debate pits those who prefer the efficiency of a command line against those who prefer the ease of use of a graphical environment. Each has its advantages and disadvantages, but as a system administrator you should know how to work effectively in both environments. It is true that working at the command line requires you to memorize commands. But many tasks cannot be done, or cannot be done as effectively, using a graphical tool. Throughout this book you learn about both command-line utilities and graphical tools.

4

Managing Files with Command-Line Utilities

Your personal working area in Linux is your home directory. A **home directory** is the subdirectory where all of your personal files are stored, as well as configuration information and program settings specific to your user account. For the root user account, the home directory is `/root`. For regular users, the home directory is a subdirectory of the `/home` directory that matches the user account name. For example, if a person named Chris Rangit logs in as user crangit, his home directory will be `/home/crangit`. On some larger Linux systems, a different location is used for home directories, but this is rare. Within a command-line environment, you can look within different directories besides your home directory.

The command-line environment is provided by the shell. The **shell** is the program that accepts and acts upon the commands that you enter. (In Chapter 6 you learn about the shell in detail.)

When you enter the **pwd** command, the shell displays your **current working directory** (that is, the directory in which you are working). The command name **pwd** stands for *print working directory*. Immediately after you log in, the **pwd** command will display your home directory.

 Linux is case sensitive. Virtually all Linux commands—including all of the commands presented in this chapter—must be entered in lowercase letters. Entering the command PWD will generate an error message.

The **cd** command changes the current working directory to a directory you specify. For example, if you are working in your home directory and want to change your current working directory to the `/tmp` directory, you would use this command:

```
cd /tmp
```

When using the **cd** command, remember the following tips:

- You can specify the full name of the directory that you want to make your current working directory, including a preceding forward slash. This is called the **absolute path**: it is a complete description in absolute terms of which directory you are referring to.

- You can also specify only the name of a subdirectory to which you want to change. To do this, do not include a forward slash at the beginning of the directory name. When you do not include a forward slash, you are specifying a **relative path**: a partial description of the directory you are referring to, which only has meaning relative to another location (your current working directory in this case). For example, if you are working in the directory `/usr` and want to change to the directory `/usr/share`, enter this command with the relative path `share`:

```
cd share
```

- Entering `cd` without any directory name will change your current working directory to your home directory.

- To change to the parent directory of your current directory (one level closer to the root directory, /), use the directory name `..` (two periods). For example, if you are currently in the `/usr/share` directory, use this command to change to the `/usr` directory:

```
cd ..
```

 In DOS and Windows systems you can use the command `cd..` (without a space between `cd` and `..`) to switch to the parent directory. This command does not work in Linux. You must always include a space after the `cd` command.

To manage Linux directories you can use the `mkdir` and `rmdir` commands. **mkdir** creates a new directory in the location you specify. For example, if you are in the directory `/tmp`, you can create a new subdirectory `/tmp/my_dir` using this command:

```
mkdir my_dir
```

If you are working in the `/usr` directory, you can create the `/tmp/my_dir` directory using this command:

```
mkdir /tmp/my_dir
```

The **rmdir** command removes (deletes) an empty directory. If you try to delete a directory that contains files, you receive an error message. To remove entire directory trees, you can use the `rm  -r` command, which recursively removes everything inside a directory, including subdirectories. (Use this command with care!)

The **ls** command lists the files in a directory. The `ls` command has dozens of options for displaying information about files and directories. One commonly used option is `-l` (a hyphen followed by lowercase letter "l"). Entering the command ls -l prints a long list of details about each file, such as when the file was created and how many bytes it contains.

You can include information on the command line after most Linux commands. Some pieces of information define what the command will operate on, such as a file name or directory name. These are called **parameters**. Some pieces of information alter how the command operates. These are called **options**, or command options. You will find in Linux documentation, however, that these two terms are used interchangeably. To understand the difference, consider two examples that apply to the `ls` command: The −l option (mentioned in the previous paragraph) controls what information the command displays. You can also include a parameter that controls which files the command operates on. For example, the following command displays detailed information (via the −l option) on all files that end with html (via the *html parameter).

```
ls −l *html
```

Information about the date and time when an event occurred is stored in the form of a **timestamp**. Linux maintains a set of timestamps for each file and directory that define when the file was created, when it was last modified, and when it was last accessed. The **touch** command updates a file's last accessed timestamp (that is, the date and time when the file was last accessed). If the file does not exist, it is created as an empty file.

To make a copy of a file, use the **cp** command. You can use **cp** to copy a file within the same directory using a different filename, for example:

```
cp report.doc report.backup
```

You can also copy a file to another directory using the same name. For example, the following command makes a copy of the **report.doc** file in the **/tmp** directory:

```
cp report.doc /tmp
```

To delete a file, use the **rm** command (for *remove*). Be very careful using the **rm** command. When you delete a file using **rm**, the file cannot be undeleted like files placed in a trash can or recycle bin on a graphical desktop. (Linux graphical desktops provide a trash can, but the **rm** command does not use the trash can—it permanently deletes files.)

In Linux the operations of moving and renaming a file are combined in one command, the **mv** command. The name **mv** is short for *move*; in essence, renaming a file is the same as *moving* it to a different filename. For example, if you have a file named **test** located in the **/tmp** directory, you can move it to a home directory with this command:

```
mv /tmp/report /home/anjali/
```

You can rename the file at the same time using a command like this, which includes a new filename:

```
mv /tmp/report /home/anjali/report.backup
```

Using the **mv** command without a directory name as a parameter places the renamed file in the same directory as the original file. To move a file to a different directory, include the directory name and, optionally, a different filename.

Linux provides several utilities for viewing the contents of a file. The simplest of these is the **cat** command, which displays the contents of a file to the screen. For example, the following command displays the contents of the **test** file:

```
cat test
```

(The **cat** command is also used to concatenate, or combine, multiple files into one larger file.) The **zcat** command displays the contents of a compressed text file to the screen. If a file ends with the letters **gz**, it has been compressed using the **gzip** command. In this case, you can use the **zcat** command to view the contents of the file without first uncompressing it.

Most files do not fit on one screen, in which case the **cat** command works too quickly—you will only see the last 20 or so lines of text in a file. To view a larger file, use the **less** command, which displays the contents of a file one screenful at a time. You can use the arrow keys or Page Up and Page Down keys to move to different areas of the file. To move to the next screenful of text, press the spacebar. For example, the following command displays a large configuration file one screen at a time:

```
less /etc/termcap
```

Press q to exit the **less** command. The **less** command is similar to the **more** command, which is also used to display the contents of a file one screenful at a time. The **less** command has more features than the **more** command, but you can use either one to view the contents of files. The **less** and **more** commands are intended to display text files (with human-readable content).

You can use the **file** command to determine what a file contains. The **file** command displays the type of data contained in a file. If you are not familiar with a particular file, use the **file** command to see what it contains before using the **less** or **more** command. For example, the following command shows the type of the indicated file:

```
$ file /etc/printcap
/etc/printcap: ASCII text
```

 In the previous example, the $ character shows the command prompt, followed by bold characters showing the command example. The resulting output is shown on the next line. If you are logged in as root, the command prompt is # rather than $. This format is used throughout this book to show commands that you enter and the resulting output.

This section has described a few Linux commands you can use to manage files and directories via a command line. Table 4-2 summarizes these commands. In the projects at the end of this chapter you can practice using these commands.

Table 4-2   Commands for Managing Files and Directories

Command	Description	Example
cat	Displays the contents of a file on-screen.	cat /etc/printcap
cd	Changes to a different directory.	cd /usr/share
cp	Copies a file to a new location or filename.	cp report.doc report.backup
file	Displays a description of what a file contains or is used for.	file /sbin/lilo
less	Displays the contents of a file on-screen, one screenful at a time.	less /etc/termcap
ls	Lists the contents of a directory.	ls -l
mkdir	Makes (creates) a new directory.	mkdir /usr/share/new_dir

Table 4-2 Commands for Managing Files and Directories (continued)

Command	Description	Example
`more`	Displays the contents of a file on-screen, one screenful at a time.	`more /etc/termcap`
`mv`	Renames a file or move a file to a new location (possibly under a new name as well).	`mv testfile testfile.old`
`pwd`	Displays the current working directory.	`pwd`
`rm`	Removes (deletes) a file.	`rm report.old`
`rmdir`	Removes (erases) an empty directory.	`rmdir /usr/share/old_dir`
`touch`	Creates a new, empty file, or updates the timestamp of an existing file.	`touch test`
`zcat`	Displays the contents of a compressed file on-screen.	`zcat /tmp/report.gz`

Note the following points about Linux filenames and directory names:

- All filenames are case sensitive. If you name a file or directory using upper-case letters, you must use uppercase the next time you refer to that file or directory: The filenames `test`, `Test`, and `TEST` are all distinct.

- Filenames can be long—up to 256 characters—and can contain multiple periods, numbers, spaces, and punctuation marks in addition to upper- and lowercase letters. You should not, however, try to use a forward or backward slash within a filename. For clarity, if a filename contains unusual characters (especially spaces), you can enclose the filename in quotation marks when you refer to the file.

- Filenames in Linux can include file extensions, but they don't have the same importance as in Windows. For example, a Linux configuration file may not have an extension, or it may end with `.conf`, or some other file extension. (A **file extension** is the last part of the filename after a period.) The names of Linux program files don't include any file extensions (such as .exe or .com in Windows).

Managing Files with Graphical Utilities

Your Linux desktop includes a file manager that makes it easy to manage files and directories. The **file manager** on your desktop is a graphical program that displays the contents of a directory as a collection of icons or filenames and lets you manage files and directories using menus, mouse clicks, and dialog boxes.

 The descriptions here refer to the Gnome Desktop interface, but the KDE Desktop provides almost identical functionality.

The file manager in Red Hat Linux 7.3 is called Nautilus. To open a Nautilus window, click on the icon immediately to the right of the footprint that opens the main menu. (You can also open the main menu, then click Programs, Applications, Nautilus.) Figure 4-3 shows a sample Nautilus window. (On the KDE desktop, choose Home Directory from the KDE main menu.)

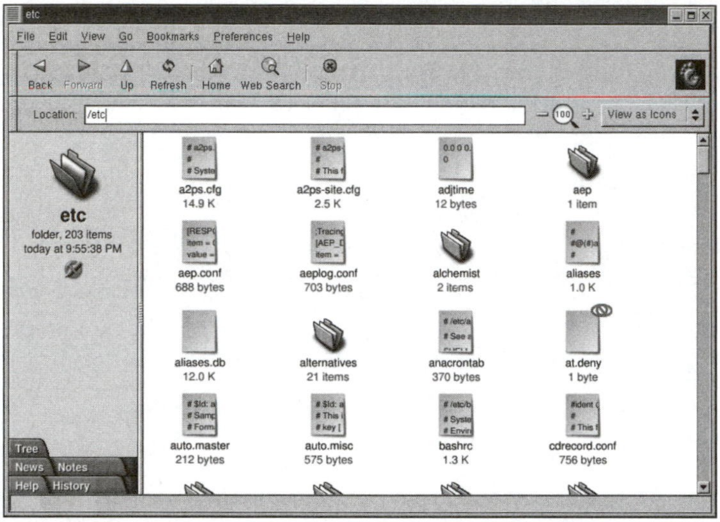

Figure 4-3   The Nautilus file manager window

File managers help you interact with many parts of Linux. They often resemble (and can act as) Web browsers as well. To view files and directories in Nautilus, enter "/" in the Location field, then press Enter. The contents of the root directory are listed on the left side of the window and in the main part of the window. You can change to a new directory or see the contents of many types of files by double-clicking on any icon. To perform an operation on a file or directory, you can:

- Click on an icon and choose an item from the menus.

- Right-click on an icon and choose an item from the pop-up menu that appears.

- Drag and drop an icon to a new location (to move, copy, or delete a file or directory)

Dragging and dropping file icons is an easy way to perform basic file management tasks. Many of the more advanced functions are performed through the Properties dialog box associated with each file and directory. To open this dialog box, right-click on an icon and choose Show Properties. For example, the Properties dialog box for the **fstab** file is shown in Figure 4-4. You learn about the tabs in this dialog box later in this chapter.

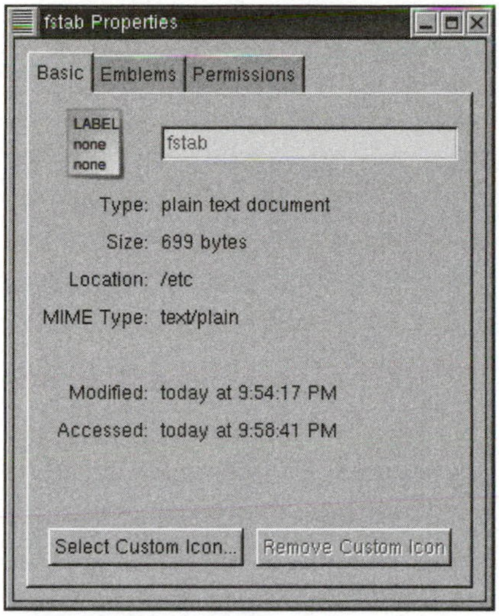

Figure 4-4   The Properties dialog box

File Properties

Several properties are associated with each file in Linux. You learned previously about the timestamp values associated with a file, such as the date when the file was created and last accessed. You can view other basic properties of a file or a directory in the Properties dialog box or by using the `ls -l` command. The output of this command for two sample files is shown here:

```
-rwxr-xr-x  1 thomas users    121024 Nov 18 14:36 newprogram
-rw-rw-rw-  1 thomas users         0 Nov 18 15:22 test
```

The output shown here includes the following fields, from left to right:

- The type indicator, which is the first character of the line. The "-" indicates a regular file. The type might also be **d** for directory, or a few other types as described later.

- The permissions granted to access the file or directory. These are the next nine characters (**rwxr-xr-x** in the first example) and are described shortly.

- The number of hard links to this file or directory (**1** in both examples). Links are explained in Chapter 6.

- The owner of the file (**thomas** in the examples). This is normally the user that created the file or directory.

- The group assigned to the file or directory (**users** in the examples). A **group** is a named account that consists of a collection of users. Each member of a group has access to files assigned to (or "owned by") that group. (Chapter 8 describes users and groups in detail.)

- The size of the file in bytes. (Directories have a number in this position but you can ignore it.)
- The date and time the file or directory was created.
- The name of the file or directory.

File Permissions

The owner of a file or directory determines who can access it. **File permissions** define the access that an owner has granted to others on the Linux system. Linux file permissions provide adequate security to control access to files and directories, but they are not as detailed as those provided by other operating systems. Three different permissions can be assigned, each represented by a single letter as indicated: read (**r**), write (**w**), and execute (**x**).

- **Read permission (r)**: Can read the contents of a file.
- **Write permission (w)**: Can add or change information in a file or create new files in a directory.
- **Execute permission (x)**: Can launch a file as a program or see a file in a directory. For files, this permission is used only on programs or scripts that can be run as programs (as described in Chapter 11).

 Notice this unusual feature of the permissions assigned to directories: You can't see what files are in a directory (using the `ls` command), nor can you access any of those files—even if the file itself grants you permission—unless you have execute permission on the parent directory.

Each of these three permissions can be assigned in three different ways:

- **User permissions** apply to the owner of a file or directory.
- **Group permissions** apply to members of the group assigned to a file or directory.
- **Other permissions** apply to all users on the Linux system who are not the owner of the file or directory in question and are not members of the group assigned to the file or directory.

Three permissions assigned to three sets of users create a total of nine permissions that can be assigned to any file or directory in Linux. These nine permissions are shown on the left side of the output of the `ls -l` command, as you saw previously. (Remember that the far left character of the output is the type indicator, not a permission.)

Although this list of characters can seem cryptic at first, only a few arrangements of permissions are commonly used. Table 4-3 describes the permission settings you are likely to see throughout Linux.

Table 4-3   Commonly Used File Permission Settings

Permissions	Description	Use
rwxr-xr-x	The owner can read, write (change), or execute the program; everyone else can read or execute it.	For program files that everyone should be able to use, such as system utilities.
rw-rw-r--	The owner and group members can alter the file, everyone (including the owner) can read the file.	For data files that everyone on the system should have access to. These are the default permissions granted to a file that you create.
r-x------	The owner can read and execute the program.	For system utilities that only the owner (typically root) is permitted to execute.
rw-r-r--	The owner can read and change the file; everyone else can read it.	For configuration files. root can change the files, but all users need to read the configuration information.

You can change the user and group listed as the owners of a file or directory by using the **chown** command. But you can only use this command when logged in as root; regular users can't change ownership, even of files that they own. To use **chown**, type **chown**, followed by the username and group (separated by a period) that you want to assign to the file or directory, followed by the name of the file or directory. For example, the following command changes the owner of the file **report.doc** to **jtaylor** and the group assigned to that file to **managers**:

        chown jtaylor.managers report.doc

You can also change just the owner of a file by leaving off the period and group name. The user and group that you assign to a file must already exist on the Linux system, as described in Chapter 8.

You can change file permissions using the **chmod** command. As a regular user, you can alter the permissions assigned to any file or directory that you own. If you are logged in as root, you can use **chmod** to change the permissions of any file or directory on the system.

To use the **chmod** command, include the type of permissions you want to change (user, group, or other, entered as **u**, **g**, or **o**), followed by a plus or minus sign to add or remove permissions, followed by the permissions you want to add or remove (**r**, **w**, or **x** for read, write, or execute). For example, to add the write permission for other users to the file **report.doc**, use this command:

        chmod o+w report.doc

Using a plus or minus sign in a **chmod** command adds or removes permissions from what is already assigned, but you can also set specific permissions (overriding any previously assigned) using an equals sign. For example, suppose the `report.doc` file had `r-x` permissions set for the group. The following command would change those permissions to `rwx`:

```
chmod g+w report.doc
```

The following command would change the group permissions to be only `rw`, negating the `x` permission:

```
chmod g=rw report.doc
```

System administrators normally use a shortcut syntax with the `chmod` command. This alternative syntax is easier to use once you are familiar with it, but it's more challenging to learn. In this alternative syntax, each of the sets of three permissions (for user, group, and other) is represented by a number from 0 to 7. The three possible permissions (read, write, and execute) are assigned values of 4, 2, and 1, respectively. Now suppose that a system administrator wanted to grant read (4) and write (2) permission for the user, read (4) permission to the group, and no permissions to other users. The first digit used in `chmod` is 6, the sum of 4 and 2; the second digit is 4; the third digit is 0 (no permissions are granted). So the command would look like this:

```
chmod 640 report.doc
```

Using the same method, if the system administrator wanted to assign read (4), write (2), and execute (1) permissions to the user, and read (4) and execute (1) permissions to the group and to other users for a program file, the command would look like this:

```
chmod 755 program_file
```

Although this method may appear strange at first, you should become familiar with it; you will see it used often by experienced system administrators on all UNIX systems. You will also discover that only a few combinations of file permissions are commonly used. Once you are familiar with the three-digit code for those commonly used sets of permissions, using the three digits is easier than entering all the letters with a plus, minus, or equal sign.

Until those codes become familiar, a graphical environment like Gnome or KDE provides an easy method of setting file permissions. Within the Properties dialog box described previously, the Permissions tab includes checkboxes in which you can activate or remove any of the nine permissions described in this section. Figure 4-5 shows the Permissions tab in the Properties dialog box of the Gnome file manager.

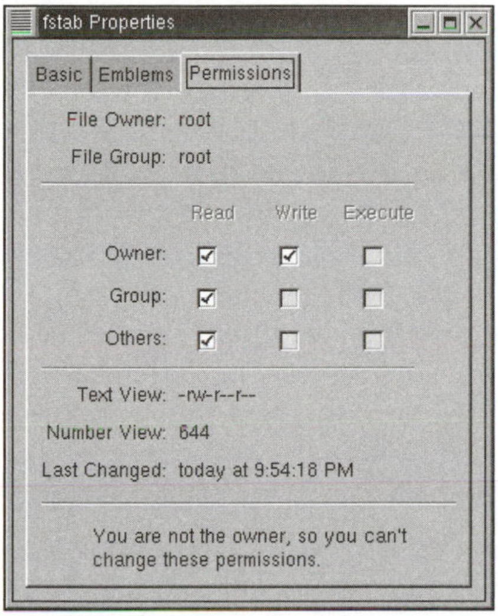

Figure 4-5   The Permissions tab of the Properties dialog box

The **umask** command determines the file permissions assigned when you create a new file. The umask command is executed automatically when you log in to Linux. You can alter the default permissions assigned to a new file by executing the **umask** command again at any time. The **umask** command uses the same three-digit permission codes as the **chmod** command (4 for read, 2 for write, and 1 for execute).

The value you give as a parameter to the **umask** command disables one or more of the existing default permissions. Thus, this **umask** command disables the original write permission for the group:

```
rw-rw-r--
umask 020
```

and results in the following default file permissions:

```
rw-r--r--
```

RUNNING AND MANAGING SOFTWARE

To run any program in Linux—whether system utility or word processor—you enter the program name at a command-line prompt or choose the program icon or menu item in a graphical environment. The shell or desktop then loads and executes the program.

To execute a program, Linux must be able to locate it within the Linux directory structure. For example, when you enter the command cp, Linux must be able to locate the cp program file in the directory where it is stored. To do this, Linux uses the PATH environment variable, which includes a list of all the directories where programs on the system are located. Common entries in the PATH variable are /bin (where cp and many other system utilities are stored), /usr/local/bin, and others. A **variable** is a memory location used by a program to store a value, such as a number or a word. Each variable is assigned a name so that the program can access the value by referring to the name. **Environment variables** are variables that are defined by the Linux shell so that all programs can access their values.

When you enter the name of a program to be executed, the shell searches each of the directories listed in the PATH environment variable until the program name is found. Then the program is loaded and executed. If the program cannot be found in any of the directories listed in PATH, the shell returns an error message. For example, attempting to execute a nonexistent program called makedir (the real command is mkdir) causes the shell to print the following error message:

```
bash: makedir: command not found
```

You can view the value of the PATH environment variable (and thus see where all the programs on your system are stored) by using the **echo** command. The **echo** command displays on the screen whatever text you specify after the command. For example, the command echo This is a test displays on the screen:

```
This is a test
```

Whenever the shell detects the name of an environment variable preceded by a dollar sign, such as $PATH, the shell replaces the name of the environment variable with the numbers or letters stored in memory under that variable's name. Using the **echo** command, you can display on the screen the numbers or letters stored in an environment variable. For example:

```
$ echo $PATH
/usr/bin:/bin:/usr/local/bin:/usr/bin/X11:/usr/X11R6/bin:/home/nwells/bin
```

The directories listed as part of the PATH environment variable differ slightly based on which version of Linux you are using, though the values will always be similar to the preceding output. Notice in the output above that each of the directories where programs are stored is separated by a colon (:).

To run a program stored in a directory that is not named in the PATH environment variable, use the full pathname of the program. For example, if you have a new program called kpacman stored in /tmp/games (which is not part of the PATH variable), use a command like this to start the program:

```
/tmp/games/kpacman
```

You can also use a single period to refer to the current directory. (Remember, use two periods to refer to the parent directory.) So to run a program called **kpacman** that is stored in your current directory (whatever directory you happen to be working in), the command would look like this:

```
./kpacman
```

In Chapter 6 you learn more about creating and using **PATH** and other environment variables.

4

Function Libraries

Many Linux programs require the same underlying functionality to complete tasks. For example, most programs need to open files on the hard disk, read information from the keyboard, and write results to the screen. Each of these tasks is called a function in computer programming jargon. A **function** is a small task that a computer program performs.

To make writing programs more efficient, programmers use a library of prewritten functions to accomplish common tasks. A **function library** (also called a system library or just a library) is a file that contains commonly used functions. Any program can choose to use these functions as it runs. Because many Linux programs run at the same time, using common libraries allows Linux programs to make more efficient use of system resources. Dozens of library files are installed as part of Linux.

The directories **/lib** and **/usr/lib** contain most of the libraries used by Linux programs. If you explore these directories, you will notice that the library files all begin with the name **lib** and end with the file extension **.so**, followed by a version number. The file extension **.so** stands for *shared object*, because the libraries can be shared among many programs. When you install new libraries on your system, they are normally placed in the **/usr/lib** directory. Some parts of the Linux system, however, such as the KDE Desktop or the X Window System, have separate directories for dedicated library files. For example, the X Window System places library files in **/usr/X11R6/lib**.

The **ldd** command lists the libraries that a program requires. If any of the required library files are not installed on your system, the program will not run. For example, to view the libraries used by the **ls** command, use this command (you must use the complete pathname to a file with the **ldd** command):

```
$ ldd /bin/ls
libtermcap.so.2 => /lib/libtermcap.so.2 (0x4001e000)
libc.so.6 => /lib/i686/libc.so.6 (0x42000000)
/lib/ld-linux.so.2 => /lib/ld-linux.so.2 (0x40000000)
```

Larger, more complex programs (such as graphical programs) will use many more libraries.

Using `rpm` to Manage Software Packages

In Chapter 3 you learned that a single software package file normally contains all of the files and configuration information needed to set up a new application or collection of utilities. You also learned that the Red Hat Package Manager (rpm) data format is the most popular type of software package for Linux. After Linux installation is completed, you can use the **rpm** command to manage all of the rpm software packages that were installed from your Linux CD-ROM.

The **rpm** command maintains a database of all the software installed on the Linux system. You can query this database to learn about what software is installed, what version of a software package you are using, and other information. You can also use the **rpm** command to install new software packages or erase software packages from the system.

The name of a package file as you see it on your CD-ROM includes version information. An example filename would be **gedit-0.9.7-8.i386.rpm**. After the package is installed on your system, however, you should refer to it by the package name, without the version information. The corresponding package name for the previous example would be **gedit**. You will see both of these used in the subsequent examples.

The hundreds of options supported by the **rpm** command fall into several categories:

- Use the —q option to query the database and learn about packages (either installed packages or those not yet installed).

- Use the —i or —U option to install or upgrade a package when you have a new rpm file you want to add to your system.

- Use the —e option to erase (uninstall) an rpm package from your system.

These options can be used in combination. For example, to query the rpm database for a list of all files included in a package, you combine the —q option with the —l option:

```
rpm —ql packagename
```

To see a list of all the packages installed on your system, use the —q and —a options:

```
rpm —qa
```

You can install new rpm files from your Linux CD-ROM or that you have downloaded from the Internet. Suppose that you have copied the new rpm file **gedit-0.9.7-8.i386.rpm** to the **/tmp** directory and want to install it on your system. This command would do that:

```
rpm —Uvh /tmp/gedit-0.9.7-8.i386.rpm
```

The options in the previous example upgrade the package (this is a safer way of installing packages, in case you already have a newer version of the package installed); display detailed messages in case of problems (using the —v option, for verbose); and display a series of hash marks (#####) as installation progresses.

An rpm file is a collection of many files. When you install Linux, the data from the rpm files is copied from your Linux CD-ROM or other installation media to your Linux-based hard disk. The rpm package files themselves are not copied; if they were you would actually have two copies of each package: the installed files and the uninstalled package.

This means that if you erase a package from your system, you must locate the rpm file again on your Linux CD or on a Web site in order to reinstall that package. An example of the **-e** (erase) option is shown here:

```
rpm —e gedit
```

The **rpm** command includes dozens of more complex options, which you can review by entering the **rpm** command alone.

Using Graphical Tools to Manage Software Packages

Both Gnome and KDE include graphical programs that you can use to manage software packages. These programs use the **rpm** command in the background as you select menu items and work in dialog boxes.

The GnoRPM package management utility is included with Gnome. To open it from the Gnome Desktop, open the main menu and choose Programs, then System, then GnoRPM. If you are not logged in as root, enter the root passsword when prompted. The main window of GnoRPM is shown in Figure 4-6.

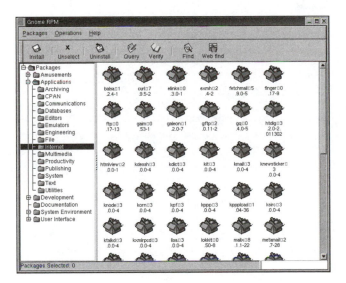

Figure 4-6   The main window of the GnoRPM utility

The left side of the GnoRPM window shows a list of categories into which packages have been divided for reference. The right side of the window displays an icon for each software package included in the category that you select. You can right-click on a package icon to display a list of options related to that package.

The KDE Desktop also includes a package management tool called kPackage. You can start this program from the System menu on most KDE Desktops. If you are not logged in as root, enter the root password when prompted. Within kPackage, categories are displayed on the left. Click on a category to open a list (also on the left side of the window) of the packages in that category. Click a package name to display information about that package in the right side of the window. A description of the package and a list of every file contained in the package are available on two tabs on the right side of the window. Figure 4-7 shows the kPackage utility displaying information for a software package.

Figure 4-7   Using kPackage to display software package information

Both GnoRPM and kPackage provide menu items that you can use to search for a package with a certain name, to search for a package containing a certain file on the system, or to install and uninstall software packages. They do not provide access to all the features of the `rpm` command, but they handle most tasks that you are likely to need as a system administrator. The kPackage utility also lets you manage different types of software packages, such as those in the `.deb` format (used by the Debian Linux distribution).

 Both GnoRPM and kPackage can be started from the command line. Within a terminal window, enter the command `gnorpm` or `kpackage`, respectively.

Using tar Archive Files

Although many Linux systems use rpm software packages, another common format for transferring a group of files is called the tar archive. A **tar archive** is a single file that can contain other files, as well as the directory structure in which those files should be reassembled. You can create a tar archive (also called a tarball) using the `tar` command. You typically give a tar archive a `.tar` file extension; when you include the compression options with the `tar` command, you typically use a `.tgz` or `.tar.gz` file extension. The resulting file is sometimes called a gzipped tarball.

The tar archive is simply a collection of many files stored in a single file. It does not create a database of information about applications on your system as rpm does. One advantage of tar archives, however, is that they are supported on virtually every UNIX and Linux system in the world, so they provide a convenient method of sharing files across the Internet. As you explore Internet sites containing Linux programs, you will see many tar archives.

After you have downloaded a tar archive, you can extract its contents using the `tar` command. For example, to extract the contents of an archive file named `program.tgz`, use this command (note that options for the `tar` command do not use a hyphen):

```
tar xvzf program.tgz
```

The `tar` command is used extensively in Linux for creating backups of files on the system. The name `tar` comes from *tape archive*, because tape drives were traditionally the most popular type of data backup device. (Now other devices such as writeable CD drives are also used.) Chapter 13 describes how to use the `tar` command to create and manage backups on Linux.

It's common to compress files in a tar archive, but you can also compress any file in Linux using the **gzip** command. For example, to compress the file `large.doc`, use this command:

```
gzip large.doc
```

The preceding command transforms the file `large.doc` into a compressed file called `large.doc.gz`. The **gunzip** command uncompresses a file that you have compressed using `gzip`. For example, to uncompress the `large.doc.gz` file, use the command `gunzip large.doc.gz`. The resulting file is named `large.doc`.

 When you use the `tar` command to extract the contents of a tar archive, the tar archive remains intact. When you use the `gzip` or `gunzip` command to compress or uncompress a file, the original file is altered (compressed or uncompressed), and its name is changed accordingly.

How much the `gzip` program compresses a file depends on the type of data contained in the file. Text files and some types of graphics files may be compressed by 70 to 90%. That is, a file of 1 MB may be compressed to only 100 KB to 300 KB. Other types of data such as JPG graphics files or program files may only be compressed by 5 to 10% or less.

The `gzip` utility is the most commonly used compression tool on Linux systems, but it is not the only one available. Table 4-4 lists popular Linux compression utilities.

Table 4-4   Compression Utilities in Linux

Compress/uncompress utility	Description
`gzip` and `gunzip`	Provides good compression ratios. Use this tool for most cases; it is the most commonly used compression tool on Linux. Compressed files have the extension `.gz`.
`zip` and `unzip`	Compresses multiple files into one file, much like a compressed tar archive. Compatible with pkzip and WinZip on other operating systems. Use this program to share files with users on non-Linux systems. Compressed files have the file extension `.zip`.
`compress` and `uncompress`	Provides poor compression compared to `gzip` (files are not as small when compressed with the `compress` command). It is an older utility supported on almost all UNIX systems. Compressed files have the extension `.z`.
`bzip` and `bunzip`	Provides excellent compression (creates very small files), but it is a newer utility that is not widely used yet. Limit your use to sharing files with those you know have `bzip`. Compressed files have the extension `.bz2`.

THE LINUX KERNEL

In Chapter 1 you learned about the role of an operating system kernel. In this section you learn how to manage the Linux kernel.

New features are added regularly to the Linux kernel. The latest stable version of the kernel is integrated into new versions of Linux products such as SuSE Linux, TurboLinux, and Red Hat Linux. You can view the current status of Linux kernel development by visiting *www.linuxhq.com*.

Learning about Your Kernel

The **uname** command with the **−r** option (for *release*) displays the version of your Linux kernel followed by the release number. A **release number** is a number assigned by the company that prepared the Linux product. The release number allows the company to track how many times the kernel has been adjusted before shipping their product. The output on Red Hat Linux 7.3 looks like this:

```
$ uname −r
2.4.18−3
```

Here the kernel version is 2.4.18; the release number is 3.

Each kernel also has a timestamp that indicates the date and time when the kernel was created. When you create your own Linux kernels (you learn how in Chapter 11), you can use the `uname -v` command to check the timestamp of the kernel that is currently running. On Red Hat Linux 7.3 you see the following:

```
$ uname -v
#1 Thu Apr 18 07:37:53 EDT 2002
```

 You can also use the command `cat /proc/version` to display the kernel version and timestamp. You will learn more about this section of the file system in Chapter 10.

4

Kernel Modules

One of the most useful features of Linux is its ability to add and remove features of the kernel without restarting the computer. Linux **kernel modules** are files containing computer code that can be loaded into the kernel or removed from the kernel as needed. Many features of Linux can be created either as built-in parts of the kernel or as modules that can be inserted on-the-fly. Examples include:

- Support for a network adapter card
- Support for a SCSI hard disk controller card
- Networking features such as special firewall capability
- The ability to access other types of file systems, such as data stored in Windows NT
- Support for a sound card

Kernel modules can be automatically loaded based on the configuration you set up during the Linux installation. The **lsmod** command lists the modules that are installed in the Linux kernel. The names of most modules are not very helpful, but some are recognizable. For example, the **sound** module is used for sound card support, and the **scsi** module is part of the support for SCSI hard disk controllers (multiple modules are required for SCSI support). Sample output of the **lsmod** command from a Linux-based laptop computer is shown here:

```
Module                  Size      Used by
nfsd                    150936    8  (autoclean)
lockd                   30856     1  (autoclean) [nfsd]
sunrpc                  52356     1  (autoclean) [nfsd lockd]
pcnet_cs                7456      1
8390                    5920      0  [pcnet_cs]
ds                      5740      2  [pcnet_cs]
i82365                  21956     2
pcmcia_core             39720     0  [pcnet_cs ds i82365]
```

Each kernel module is stored as a file on the hard disk. When the module is added to the kernel, it is copied from the hard disk to memory as part of the kernel.

Adding and Removing Modules

In most cases, the kernel modules needed to communicate with your computer hardware are loaded automatically. But as you explore more advanced Linux functions, you may need to add a module manually. You can do this using the **modprobe** command, which loads a module with any required supporting modules. For example, if you use the command **modprobe sb** to load the SoundBlaster module, other modules will be automatically loaded as well so that the sound card will function correctly.

 You can also use the **insmod** command to insert (add) modules to the running Linux kernel. But the **insmod** command doesn't automatically load dependent modules, so you must know exactly what additional modules to load and the order in which to load them.

The **rmmod** command removes a module from the kernel. The module remains available on the hard disk so that you can load it again later.

Some modules require specific hardware information in order to function correctly. For example, when you add a module to support a network adapter card, you may need to include information about the card's IRQ (interrupt request line). **Module parameters** provide information needed by a module to locate system resources. When using the **insmod** or **modprobe** command, you add module parameters after the module name. For example, to support an NE2000 network adapter, you must load the **ne2** module. The following command includes the hardware's IRQ and I/O port address:

```
modprobe ne2 irq=11 io_port=0x330
```

 The **0x** at the beginning of the last number in the preceding example indicates a hexadecimal value.

When you execute the **insmod** or **modprobe** command, the module attempts to communicate with any related system hardware as it is being loaded. If the module loads successfully, you see no feedback on the screen. If a problem occurs, you see a message stating that the module could not be loaded or could not be initialized. Such a message means that you selected the wrong module for your hardware or that the module parameters were incorrect or inadequate.

Locating Modules

When you see a module name (something like **sb** or **aic7xxx**), it's difficult to know which devices or kernel features that module provides support for. In addition, the parameters supported by each module are difficult to find. You can experiment with different modules until you finally locate the correct module for hardware that is not working correctly. But it is more efficient to contact the vendor of your Linux system or your hardware vendor and ask the technical support representative which module and parameters to use. (You will still need to determine the values for the required parameters based on your computer's hardware configuration.)

 The comments in the source code for each module contain detailed information about what devices and parameters that module supports. To explore the source code, install the kernel-source package, as described in Chapter 11.

4

The module files are stored in `/lib/modules/`*version*`/kernel`, where *version* is the version number of the Linux kernel on the system (for example, `/lib/modules/ 2.4.18-3/kernel`). Within this directory are subdirectories for networking-related modules, device drivers, and other module types. For example, the subdirectory `net/ipv4/netfilter` contains 33 modules devoted to the firewall features of the Linux kernel. The subdirectory `drivers/ieee1394` contains six modules to support Firewire (IEEE 1394) video devices.

When you enter an `insmod` or `modprobe` command, the command searches all the module subdirectories for the module name you have entered. The `−t` option of `modprobe` even lets you specify a subdirectory that `modprobe` should refer to, trying all modules in that subdirectory until one loads without an error.

 In most situations, the Red Hat Linux kernel will load any necessary kernel modules without help from a system administrator. (Chapter 11 describes the kernel in more detail.) Although you should understand modules so you can set up complex devices manually, you will rarely need to use the `modprobe` command.

THE INITIALIZATION PROCESS

When you turn on your computer, many things must occur before the operating system is loaded and ready to accept your commands from the keyboard. The following sections describe the main steps that Red Hat Linux takes to initialize the system each time you turn it on. Some details vary among Linux distributions, but every Linux system uses a process similar to the one described in the steps below and the sections that follow.

1. A boot manager loads and starts the Linux kernel.

2. The Linux kernel initializes hardware and then launches the `init` program.

3. The `init` program launches a script based on the run level in which Linux is to operate.

4. The script started by `init` typically runs many other scripts to launch and manage system services.

Booting the Kernel

When you turn on your computer, the boot manager receives control from the BIOS. The boot manager can be GRUB, LILO, or another commercial product you have installed. Typically the boot manager displays a prompt listing the available operating systems to launch.

At the boot manager selection prompt, you can add boot parameters to control how Linux is started. Boot parameters are codes similar to module parameters that instruct the Linux kernel how to operate or how to access parts of the computer system's hardware. (Chapter 3 mentioned boot parameters briefly in relation to helping Linux work with hardware components that could not be recognized.)

If you are using the GRUB boot manager, press the **a** key when presented with a list of operating system choices. This lets you append a boot parameter before launching Linux. If you are using LILO as your boot manager, enter the name for the system you want to launch, then a space, then the boot parameter(s) to pass to the Linux kernel.

In LILO you can press the Tab key to see a list of names for the available operating systems. GRUB lists the choices for you automatically.

You can use boot parameters to activate features of Linux. For example, by using the boot parameter **S**, you start Linux in a special single-user maintenance mode:

```
linux S
```

The Linux kernel supports dozens of boot parameters. Most are used either to help Linux find hardware or to assist with troubleshooting and system administration work.

The BootPrompt-HOWTO document describes all available boot parameters. See *www.linuxdocs.org/HOWTOs/BootPrompt-HOWTO.html*.

Configuring the Boot Manager

You can update the configuration of a boot manager after the installation is completed. As with other system administration tasks, you must be logged in as root to update the boot manager configuration.

The configuration file for the LILO boot manager is `/etc/lilo.conf.anaconda`. The configuration file for GRUB (the default boot manager in Red Hat Linux) is `/boot/grub/grub.conf`. (Only root can view or edit the GRUB configuration file.)

The two files are quite similar in layout and syntax. A sample GRUB configuration file for a dual-boot Linux system is shown here (without comments that the file includes):

```
default=0
timeout=10
splashimage=(hd0,1)/boot/grub/splash.xpm.gz
title Red Hat Linux (2.4.18-3)
        root (hd0,1)
        kernel /boot/vmlinuz-2.4.18-3 ro root=/dev/hda2
        initrd /boot/initrd-2.4.18-3.img
title DOS
        rootnoverify (hd0,0)
        chainloader +1
```

The `grub.conf` file includes global configuration details as well as a configuration for one or more operating systems. Without going into exhaustive detail on the syntax of this example file, note that two operating systems are defined, each beginning with a title section followed by options that define how to launch that operating system. In the case of Linux, the filename of the kernel is given along with the location of the Linux file system. For the DOS operating system, GRUB simply passes control to another boot manager located on the partition holding the non-Linux operating system. (The DOS label is assigned by default because of the file system type, though this file refers to a dual-boot Windows system.)

Although you can alter the GRUB configuration file directly, the easiest method is often to wait until you need to reboot the Linux system, then press the **c** key while viewing the GRUB splash screen listing operating systems that can be launched. This opens a configuration mode for GRUB in which you can alter the boot manager setup. (This feature is not available in the LILO boot manager.)

Initializing System Services

After the boot manager starts the kernel, the kernel initializes all of the computer's hardware. You see messages scroll by as each piece of hardware is located and initialized. When this process is complete and you have logged in to Linux, you can execute the **dmesg** command to view the messages stored by the kernel during the boot process.

The `dmesg` command displays the contents of the **kernel ring buffer**, an area of memory where messages from the kernel are stored. If the memory space fills up, the oldest messages are discarded. If you don't use the `dmesg` command right after you boot the computer, the `dmesg` command may display messages that the kernel has generated after the hardware was initialized.

After the kernel has initialized the hardware, it launches a program called `init`. The **init program** is a master control program that starts many other programs, such as the program that provides a login prompt. The `init` program also runs many scripts that initialize the system services you have installed. (A **script** is a collection of commands, similar to a macro, that are stored in a text file and executed without user intervention.)

The `init` program is controlled by the `/etc/inittab` configuration file. This file contains pointers to the scripts that `init` will run to initialize the Linux system each time it is turned on. The `/etc/inittab` file is different in each version of Linux, but after reviewing the file on one system, you should be able to recognize features on other Linux systems. Most of the files referred to in `/etc/inittab` are in the `/etc/rc.d` subdirectory. Three main configuration files located in `/etc/rc.d` are listed here.

- `rc.sysinit`: The main system initialization script for Red Hat Linux. It includes commands for setting up how the keyboard is used, which environment variables are needed, and many other hardware-specific configuration details that are not handled by the Linux kernel.

- `rc`: Script that starts system services such as networking, printing, automated script execution, and many others. The specific services that are started depend on how the system is configured. The `rc` script is used to set up run level-related services, as described in the next section.

- `rc.local`: Script executed after other initialization scripts. It is initially empty (it has only a few comments but no commands). You can place commands in `rc.local` that you want to have executed each time the system is turned on.

Reviewing Run Level Services

A **run level** is a mode of operation in which a preconfigured set of services is activated. Table 4-5 shows the run levels used by Red Hat and many other versions of Linux, with a brief description of how each is used.

Table 4-5   Run Levels in Linux

Run level	Name	Description
0	Halt	Shuts down all services when the system will not be rebooted.
1	Single-user mode	Used for system maintenance. Does not provide networking capabilities.
2	Multiuser mode without networking enabled	Rarely used except for system maintenance or testing.
3	Regular multiuser networking mode	Standard multiuser text-mode operation. Non-graphical systems (such as network servers) use this mode for normal operation.
4	-	Not used.
5	Graphical login	Identical to run level 3 except a graphical login is used.
6	Reboot	Shuts down all services when the system will be rebooted.

The run level that the `init` program starts when Linux is booted is defined in the `/etc/inittab` file. The `init` program launches the `rc` script located in the `/etc/rc.d` directory with a parameter that includes the run level to use. The `rc` script then starts the appropriate system services based on the selected run level.

Each run level is associated with a subdirectory. These subdirectories are located in the `/etc/rc.d` directory. For example, the directories `/etc/rc.d/rc5.d` and `/etc/rc.d/rc6.d` include files that control which system services are used in run levels 5 and 6, respectively. The run level subdirectories contain files that indicate which services are to be started or stopped when operating Linux in that run level.

Each file in the run level directories begins with a `K` or an `S`, followed by a two-digit number. The number indicates the order in which services are started or stopped. Services that begin with a `K` are stopped (*killed*); services that begin with an `S` are started. The files included in the run level directories depend on which services you have installed on your Linux system. A typical listing for the `/etc/rc.d/rc5.d` directory is shown here:

```
K20nfs            S10network        S56xinetd
K46radvd          S12syslog         S60lpd
K50snmpd          S13portmap        S80sendmail
K50snmptrapd      S14nfslock        S85gpm
K65identd         S17keytable       S90crond
K74ntpd           S20random         S90xfs
S05kudzu          S25netfs          S95anacron
S08ipchains       S26apmd           S95atd
S08iptables       S28autofs         S97rhnsd
S09isdn           S56rawdevices     S99local
```

Notice that the first `S` item (in the left column, with the lowest number, 05) is for the **kudzu** service. When Linux is booted and instructed to use run level 5 (by `/etc/inittab`), it first starts **kudzu** (which checks for new hardware on the system); next, it starts **ipchains** and **iptables** (both numbered 08). Many other services are started as well, ending with the **local** service, which runs the `rc.local` script. The `/etc/rc.d/rc0.d` directory contains a similar list of services, but with `K` instead of `S` before each filename, because run level 0 is used to shut down the system. For run levels 0 and 6 (shutdown and reboot, respectively), the numbers are in approximately the reverse order: The first services (network access, for example) form a foundation for the entire system and are therefore the last services to be stopped.

The initialization of services in each run level includes another complication. The files you see in the run level subdirectories are not regular files—they are pointers to scripts that stop and start the services. Looking at an example should clarify the point. If you use the `ls  -l` command to see a long listing of the network services in the `/etc/rc.d/rc5.d` subdirectory, you see that the `S10network` file is actually a pointer to another file: `/etc/rc.d/init.d/network`. Because the file (the pointer) in the `/etc/rc.d/rc5.d` subdirectory contains a leading `S`, the `rc` script executes this script with the word `start` after it. Thus, the `rc` script is actually executing this command to start the network service:

```
/etc/rc.d/init.d/network start
```

 The pointers described here are called symbolic links. A symbolic link allows one file to refer to another file on the system. You'll learn more about symbolic links in Chapter 6.

Figure 4-8 shows how the initialization components described in this section relate to each other. Each file in the various run level directories operates in the same manner as the `S10network` pointer just described. All of them point to scripts stored in the `/etc/rc.d/init.d` directory. The scripts in this directory provide an organized method of starting and stopping system services.

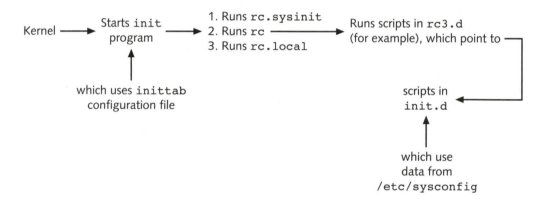

Figure 4-8   The Linux initialization process

 The system initialization process described in this section is known as System V ("system five") initialization. It is based on the model used for years by the System V version of UNIX.

Starting and Stopping System Services

Many of the services listed in the run level directories relate to networking, which is not discussed in this book. But the concept of system initialization is important because these scripts make it easy for you to change almost anything on a Linux system (short of using a new Linux kernel) without restarting the computer. For example, suppose you had reconfigured your printing system (as described in Chapter 12). Rather than restart the system, you could execute these two commands to reinitialize printing:

```
/etc/rc.d/init.d/lpd stop
/etc/rc.d/init.d/lpd start
```

Red Hat Linux and a few other Linux systems support this combined command:

```
/etc/rc.d/init.d/lpd restart
```

Virtually all Linux network services—and many others—use this system.

You can configure which services are started by default when you boot Linux using the **chkconfig** program. With this program you specify the run levels and service you want to configure and specify on or off to indicate that the service should be activated or not activated as part of the run levels you specify. For example, if you do not want the lpd print service to be activated as part of run level 5, you would use this command:

```
chkconfig —level 5 lpd off
```

You must know the name of the service you want to configure as it appears in the /etc/rc.d/init.d subdirectory in order to use chkconfig.

You can also use a graphical utility to configure system services. Red Hat Linux includes a program called **serviceconf**. You can launch this program from the command line by entering **serviceconf** or from the Gnome main menu by choosing Programs, then System, then Service Configuration. The main window of this program lists the services that are available on your system (as determined by the contents of /etc/rc.d/init.d). You can select any service listed, then click the Start or Stop button to activate or stop that service immediately. You can also check the box next to a service to make it activate each time the system is booted. Figure 4-9 shows the Service Configuration utility.

Root access is required to run serviceconf, chkconfig, and ksysv. If you launch any of these from a KDE or Gnome menu, you will be prompted to enter the root password.

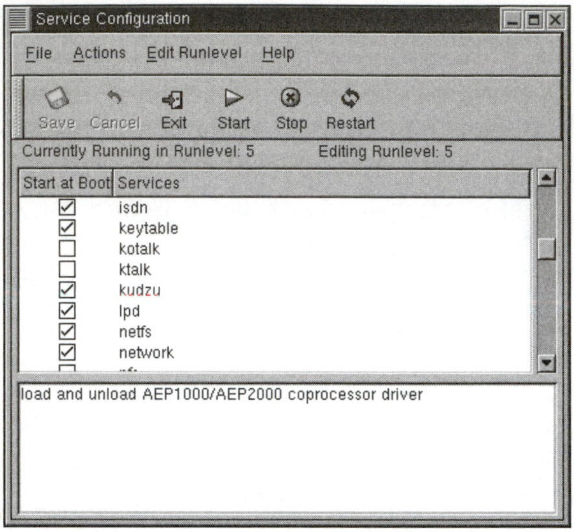

Figure 4-9   The Service Configuration utility

The KDE Desktop includes a similar graphical utility called `ksysv` (though it is not included with every version of Linux that provides KDE). In this utility, all available services are shown on the left of the main window. You can drag and drop icons representing services to either the "Start" list or the "Stop" list for any run level. Figure 4-10 shows the `ksysv` utility.

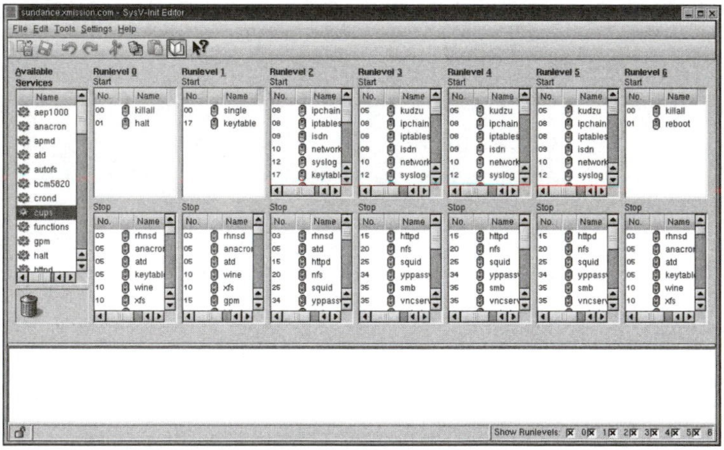

Figure 4-10   The `ksysv` graphical services configuration utility

Configuring System Services

The initialization scripts in `/etc/rc.d/init.d` are provided when you install Linux. If you install a new rpm software package, a script is typically placed in the correct directory and configured to activate the service at boot time.

The initialization scripts in `/etc/rc.d/init.d` use configuration information located in the `/etc/sysconfig` directory and its subdirectories. The files in `/etc/sysconfig` are named for services, with each file containing name-value pairs that define configuration options for that service. For example, the `/etc/sysconfig/network` file on a Red Hat Linux 7.3 system might look like this:

```
NETWORKING=yes
HOSTNAME="incline.xmission.com"
GATEWAY=192.168.100.5
```

These lines are used by the script `/etc/rc.d/init.d/network` to control how networking is set up. (Information on specific network device configurations, such as IP addresses for Ethernet cards, is located in the `network-scripts` subdirectory of `/etc/sysconfig`.)

You can edit the files in `/etc/sysconfig` directly, but because the content of these files is not intuitive, you might avoid configuration problems by relying on utilities designed to configure specific services, as described in other areas of this book. (For example, the `lokkit` program will alter the `/etc/sysconfig/ipchains` file based on your firewall selections.)

Although a file in `/etc/sysconfig` may configure the system service script in `/etc/rc.d/init.d`, the service itself often has another set of configuration files in the `/etc` directory. For example, a file called `/etc/sysconfig/httpd` may define parameters for starting up a Web server using the `/etc/rc.d/init.d/httpd` script, but the Web server itself is configured using the file `/etc/httpd/conf/httpd.conf`. You learn about these other configuration files as you explore specific services in detail (for example, Chapter 12 describes Linux printing, which is configured using several files in `/etc`).

SHUTTING DOWN LINUX

You now know about the Linux initialization process; you also need to know how to shut down a Linux system properly. Because Linux caches hard disk data in memory (as all modern operating systems do), turning off a Linux computer without shutting it down in an orderly way can cause data loss. **Caching** is the process of storing data from the hard disk in RAM so that it can be accessed more rapidly (because RAM is much faster than a hard disk). But caching data in RAM instead of writing it immediately to the hard disk entails a risk: if you turn off the computer suddenly, data in RAM may never be written to the hard disk and will then be lost.

An orderly or methodical shutdown of Linux is also called a **graceful shutdown**. This means that all Linux services are stopped and all data is written to disk. You can then safely reboot or turn off the computer. You can shut down Linux gracefully by:

- Entering the command `reboot`. This will shut down all services and then restart the computer.

- Entering the command `halt`. This will shut down all services and then stop the computer with the message "System halted." When you see this message on-screen, you can safely turn off the computer.

- Using the `shutdown` command with a parameter to indicate how long to wait before shutting down the system and a parameter to indicate whether the system should be rebooted or halted. For example, to halt the system, beginning in five minutes, use the command `shutdown -h 5`.

- Pressing `Ctrl+Alt+Del`. This executes a `shutdown` command immediately. (The command the system will execute when you press Ctrl+Alt+Del is configured in the `/etc/inittab` file.)

- Entering the command `telinit 0` to halt the system, or the command `telinit 6` to reboot the system (shutting down all services first in both cases). The `telinit` command switches the system to a different runlevel: 0 or 6 in this case. (An equivalent command is `init`.)

If you are working in a graphical desktop, you can use the Log out item on the main menu of Gnome or KDE. This item opens a dialog box in which you can choose to log out, shut down the system, or reboot the system. If you choose Log out, the graphical login screen appears after a few moments so that the system is secure and you (or another user) can log in.

Although it's important to know how to shut down Linux, many Linux systems are left running for weeks or months (or years) between reboots. Unless you are working on a machine in a computer lab, or you need to change to a new kernel, or install new hardware, you can leave the system running a very long time without any fear of the system crashing or requiring a reboot. (Ask your instructor or lab manager if systems should be turned off before you leave each day.)

On servers or multiuser Linux systems, only the system administrator should be allowed to shut down the system. By using boot parameters or starting the system from a floppy disk, a user could disrupt the system's security during a reboot. A system administrator should watch for evidence of unauthorized reboots to be certain that nothing improper has been done to the system. In Chapter 10 you learn how to read system log files where information is stored about system reboots.

CHAPTER SUMMARY

❑ Information in Linux is stored in a directory structure that begins with the root directory, /. Subdirectories and parent directories help organize large numbers of files. Commands such as `pwd`, `cd`, `mkdir`, and `rmdir` manage directories.

❑ Standard Linux directory structures define where different types of files are placed. These standards, though cryptic, help Linux programs find needed components.

❑ You can launch command-line utilities in a command-line environment, or shell. Linux commands are case sensitive, and can generally include options and parameters.

❑ Basic file management is done with the `ls`, `cp`, `rm`, `mv`, `cat`, `less`, and `more` commands. Files can also be compressed using `tar`, `zip`, `gzip`, and other utilities.

❑ Linux files can include file extensions, but few Linux programs rely on file extensions to define what the file contains.

❑ Graphical desktops like Gnome include powerful file management utilities. These let you drag and drop files and control properties of a file or directory in a dialog box using checkboxes and menu options.

❑ Linux file permissions control which users or groups can access a file or directory. Read, Write, and Execute permissions for a file or directory can be assigned to the owner, to the assigned group, or to all other users on the system.

❑ You can alter file ownership and file permissions using a graphical file manager or using command-line utilities such as `chown` and `chmod`. The `chmod` command uses letters or numeric codes to define the file permissions being assigned to a file or directory.

❑ Environment variables help the Linux shell locate programs that you execute. Many such variables are defined on a typical Linux system.

❑ Many Linux programs use library files, stored collections of common functions. This makes program execution more efficient.

❑ The `rpm` command gives you access to a database defining many details about the software that is installed on a Linux system. You can use the `rpm` command to query the software package database or to install or erase software packages from the system. Graphical tools such as GnoRPM and kPackage make managing hundreds of software packages much easier.

❑ The `tar` command manages tar archives: combinations of many files within a single file. Any file can be compressed using one of several Linux compression utilities.

❑ The Linux kernel supports loadable modules, which are managed using the `lsmod`, `insmod`, `rmmod`, and `modprobe` commands. Module parameters define information to help modules load and operate correctly.

❑ You can provide boot parameters to the Linux kernel as it is being launched by a boot manager.

❐ The boot manager is configured using a simple text file. You can reconfigure it as needed by altering this file or (for GRUB) entering the configuration mode before Linux is launched.

❐ The Linux kernel starts the `init` program, which in turn runs several scripts. These scripts launch services based on information stored in the run level directories. Different run levels define different sets of functionality that Linux activates.

❐ Linux lets you configure nearly anything on the system and activate that new configuration without restarting the system. Configuration details for system services scripts are located in `/etc/sysconfig`.

❐ You can set up which services are activated at boot time using the `chkconfig` command or using various graphical utilities.

❐ To avoid data loss, you must gracefully shut down Linux using a command such as `reboot`, `halt`, or `shutdown`.

KEY TERMS

absolute path — A complete description of a directory, beginning with a forward slash and including all subdirectories up to the named directory. An absolute path is unambiguous, without needing to reference another directory name to give it a complete meaning.

caching — The process of storing data from the hard disk in RAM so that it can be accessed more rapidly (because RAM is much faster than a hard disk).

cat — Command used to display the contents of a file to the screen.

cd — Command used to change the directory you are working in (the current working directory).

child directory — A subdirectory within another directory. The directory closer to the root directory, /, is the parent; the directory deeper in the directory structure is the child.

chkconfig — Command used to configure which services are started by default when you boot Linux; modifies the contents of run level directories such as `/etc/rc.d/rc5.d`.

chmod — Command used to change the file permissions assigned to a file or directory.

chown — Command used to change the ownership of a file or directory.

command-line window — A window within a graphical environment that permits you to enter commands at the keyboard.

cp — Command used to copy a file or directory from one location or name to another.

current working directory — The directory in which you are working.

dmesg — Command used to view the messages stored by the kernel during the boot process.

echo — Command used to display text to the screen, converting variable names to their corresponding values.

environment variables —Variables that are defined by the Linux shell so that all programs can access their values.

execute permission — A file permission that allows a user to launch a file as a program or see a file within a directory. Represented by a letter **x**.

file — Command used to display a summary of the type of data contained in a file.

file extension — The last part of a filename after a period.

file manager — A graphical window that displays the contents of a directory (usually as a collection of icons) and lets you work with the files and directories using menus, mouse clicks, and dialog boxes.

file permissions — Codes that define the type of access that a user has to a file or directory on the Linux system.

function — A small task that a computer program performs.

function library — A file containing a collection of commonly used functions that any program can use as it runs.

graceful shutdown — The technique used to stop all Linux services and shut down all file access in an orderly way before turning off or rebooting the computer.

group — A named account that consists of a collection of users. Each member of a group has access to files owned by that group.

group permissions — A set of three file permissions (**r**, **w**, and **x**) that apply to members of the group assigned to a file or directory.

gunzip — Command used to uncompress a file that has been compressed using `gzip`.

gzip — Command used to compress any file on a Linux system.

halt — Command used to shut down all services and then stop the computer with the message "System halted."

home directory — The location where all of a user's personal files are stored.

init — Command used to switch the system to a different run level.

init program — A master control program that starts many other processes on the system, such as those providing a login prompt.

insmod — Command used to copy a module file from the hard disk and add it to the Linux kernel running in memory.

kernel modules — Files containing computer code that can be loaded into the kernel or removed from the kernel as needed.

ldd — Command used to list the function libraries that a program uses.

less — Command used to display the contents of a file one screenful at a time. Permits moving around in the file and otherwise controlling the view using the keyboard.

ls — Command used to list the files in a directory.

lsmod — Command used to list the modules that are installed in the Linux kernel.

mkdir — Command used to create a new directory.

modprobe — Command used to load a module with all of its required supporting modules.

module parameters — Information needed by a module to locate system resources. The parameters are added after the module name when using the `insmod` or `modprobe` command.

more — Command used to display the contents of a file one screenful at a time. The `more` command is similar to the `less` command but with fewer keyboard control options.

mv — Command used to rename a file or move it to a new location.

option — Information added to a command that determines how the command operates.

other permissions — A set of three file permissions (`r`, `w`, and `x`) that apply to all users on the Linux system who are not the owner of the file or directory in question and are not members of the group assigned to the file or directory.

parameter — Information added to a command that defines what the command will operate on, such as a filename or directory name.

parent directory — The directory that is one level above the current directory.

pwd — Command that displays the current working directory.

read permission — A file permission that allows a user to read the contents of a file or browse the files in a directory. Represented by a letter `r`.

reboot — Command used to shut down all services and then restart the computer.

relative path — The name of a directory that is only meaningful (and only sufficiently specific) in relation to another directory. A relative path does not include a forward slash.

release number — A number assigned by the company that prepares a Linux product. It allows the company to track how many times the kernel file has been altered before the final product is shipped.

rm — Command used to delete a file.

rmdir — Command used to remove (delete) an empty directory.

rmmod — Command used to remove a module from the kernel.

root directory — The starting point for all access to Linux resources. It is indicated by a single forward slash: `/`.

rpm — Command used to manage all of the rpm software packages on a Linux system.

run level — A mode of operation that defines which Linux system services are activated.

script — A collection of commands, similar to a macro, that are stored in a text file and executed without user intervention.

shell — The program in Linux that captures and handles commands entered in a command-line environment.

shutdown — Command used to shut down Linux gracefully.

tar — Command used to create a single file that contains many other files, often compressed to save space.

tar archive — A file created by the `tar` command.

telinit — Command used to switch the system to a different run level.

terminal emulator window — A command-line window (also called a terminal window) within a graphical environment.

timestamp — A record of the date and time when an event occurred.

touch — Command used to create a new file with no data in it or update the access timestamp of an existing file.

umask — Command used to set the file permissions assigned when you create a new file.

uname — Command used to provide information about the operating system, including the kernel version.

user permissions — A set of three file permissions (**r**, **w**, and **x**) that apply to the owner of a file or directory.

variable — A memory location used by a program to store a value, such as a number or a word. Each variable is assigned a name so that the program can access the value by referring to the name.

write permission — A file permission that allows a user to add or change information in a file or create files within a directory. Represented by a letter **w**.

xterm — A program within a graphical environment that provides a command-line window.

zcat — Command used to display the contents of a compressed file to the screen.

REVIEW QUESTIONS

1. The _____ directory is the beginning of the Linux directory structure.

   a. `/`

   b. `/root`

   c. `/home`

   d. `/dev/hda`

2. The **pwd** command is used to:

   a. Process writeable domains on the network

   b. Control power used by a Linux system

   c. Display the current working directory on the screen

   d. List a summary of the writeable devices on the system

3. Valid Linux commands presented in this chapter include:

   a. `rm, rmdir, rmmod`

   b. `mv, move, rm`

   c. `more, less, some`

   d. `tar, tellinit, touch`

4. Name three commands that can be used to view the contents of text files.

5. The command `Ls -l` is invalid because:

   a. Linux commands cannot contain hyphens.

   b. Linux commands are case sensitive.

   c. `ls` is a script name, not a command.

   d. The `-l` option is not supported by the `ls` command.

6. The command `chmod 744 report.doc` grants _____ execute permission to the report.doc file.

   a. user (the file's owner)

   b. group (member of the assigned group)

   c. other users

   d. all users on the system

7. The owner and group assigned to a file are shown by which of the following commands?

   a. `chown`

   b. `ls -l`

   c. `modprobe`

   d. `useradd`

8. Execute permission on a file is required to:

   a. Launch that file as a program

   b. Create a directory with a matching name

   c. Allow other users to read the file

   d. Use the `insmod` command to add the file as a module

9. Describe the purpose of function libraries and name two directories where they are commonly located.

10. The command `rpm -q packagename` does the following:

    a. Determines whether `packagename` is installed on the system

    b. Locates `packagename` on a CD-ROM

    c. Erases `packagename` if it is currently installed

    d. Summarizes the disk quota for users of `packagename`

11. The `tar` command creates archive files that are commonly compressed by the _____ command.

    a. `bzip`

    b. `compress`

    c. `zip`

    d. `gzip`

4

12. Contrast the advantages of `rpm` and `tar` formats.

13. Which feature is part of GRUB but not LILO?

    a. Including non-Linux operating systems in the list of bootable systems

    b. Altering the boot manager configuration at boot time, while the boot manager is actually running

    c. Handling boot parameters to alter Linux kernel functions

    d. Providing a text configuration file that a system administrator can review within the Linux file system

14. Name two methods of determining the version and timestamp of the kernel currently running on a Linux system.

15. The module files loaded by the `modprobe` command are located in a subdirectory of:

    a. `/etc/modules`

    b. `/lib/modules`

    c. `/usr/lib/modules`

    d. `/boot/modules`

16. The GRUB boot manager can be reconfigured directly as you boot your system, but is also controlled by this configuration file:

    a. `/boot/grub.conf`

    b. `/etc/bootconf`

    c. `/boot.conf`

    d. `/boot/grub/grub.conf`

17. Name four commands used to work with kernel modules.

18. The scripts in `/etc/rc.d/init.d` are provided by:

    a. The system administrator who installs Linux

    b. The `rc` script, which runs before any of the `init.d` scripts

    c. The rpm that installs the service that the script controls

    d. The kernel itself

19. Explain the difference between the configuration data stored in files within the `/etc/sysconfig` directory and service-specific configuration data stored in other subdirectories of `/etc`.

20. Name three commands that can be used to begin a graceful shutdown of Linux.

21. The _____ program displays kernel hardware configuration messages from the system boot process.

    a. `init`

    b. `chmod`

    c. `dmesg`

    d. `uname`

22. Why is `modprobe` preferred over `insmod` as a tool for adding modules to the kernel?

23. The `init` program uses the following configuration file:

    a. `/etc/lilo.conf`

    b. `/etc/inittab`

    c. `/etc/modules/inittab`

    d. `/etc/rc.d/rc`

24. Name the two run levels normally used to run a Linux-based computer, and describe the difference between those two run levels.

25. The files in `/etc/rc.d/init.d` can be used to:

    a. Automatically insert kernel modules

    b. Stop and restart most standard services in Linux

    c. Reconfigure the boot manager

    d. Set default file permissions for the `root` user

HANDS-ON PROJECTS

Project 4-1

In this project you use Linux commands to manage files and directories. To complete this activity you should have an installed Linux system with a valid user account.

1. Log in to Linux using your user account name and password.

2. If you logged in using a graphical login screen, open a terminal window by clicking on the icon third from the left on the Gnome Desktop.

3. Enter the **pwd** command to display your current working directory. Because you have just logged in, this should display your home directory.

4. Create a new subdirectory within your home directory using the command **mkdir archive**.

5. Change to the new subdirectory you just created by entering **cd archive**.

6. Create a new file named **report** using this command: **touch report**.

7. Enter `ls -l` to view a long-format listing of the files in the `archive` subdirectory. Can you identify your username in the command output as the owner of the file `report`?

8. Notice the file permissions in the output of the `ls -l` command from the previous step. What default file permissions were assigned? Use this command to remove all permissions for the group and other users: **chmod go-rwx report**. How could you reset the file permissions using a three-digit code in the `chmod` command?

9. Enter `ls -l` again to review the file permissions with your changes.

10. Change the name of the `report` file to `oldreport` using this command:
mv report oldreport

11. Use the `ls` command to verify that the file `report` is no longer there—it has been renamed as `oldreport`.

12. Copy a system file from the /etc directory by entering: **cp /etc/termcap .** (Remember to include the period to indicate that you want to copy the file to your current directory.) Do you see any feedback when a command is successful?

13. Use the following command to view the contents of the file that you copied in the previous step: **cat termcap**. Can you read the contents?

14. Use the following command to view the contents of the file: **less termcap**. Use the Page Up and Page Down keys to scroll through the file. Press **q** to exit the `less` command.

15. Enter the `ls -l` command. Note the size of the `termcap` file.

16. Compress the `termcap` file using the command **gzip termcap**.

17. Use the `ls -l` command to view the directory contents. How has the filename changed? How has the size of the file changed?

18. Use the following command to display the type of data contained in the `termcap.gz` file: **file termcap.gz**.

19. Erase the `termcap.gz` file using the command **rm termcap.gz**.

20. Change back to your home directory by entering **cd ..** (don't forget the space before the two periods).

21. Erase the `archive` directory using the command **rmdir archive**. Why won't the command work? How could you make it work?

Project 4-2

In this project you learn about the Linux kernel running on your computer. To complete this project you should have an installed Linux system with root access.

1. Log in to Linux as root.

2. If you logged in using a graphical login screen, open a terminal window by clicking on the icon third from the left on the Gnome Desktop.

3. Enter the command **uname -r** to see which version of the Linux kernel is running on the computer. Do you see a release number in the output?

4. Enter the command **uname -v** to see the timestamp of the Linux kernel.

5. Enter the command **cat /proc/version**. How does the information displayed compare to the output of the **uname** command?

6. Review the contents of the **grub.conf** file by entering the command **less /boot/grub/grub.conf**.

7. Locate the indented line in the file that begins with "kernel" and note the directory and filename that it refers to.

8. Press **q** to exit the **less** command.

9. Change to the directory indicated on the kernel line in /boot/grub/grub.conf: **cd /boot**.

10. Enter the **ls -l** command to see the files in the **boot** directory. Can you locate the file named in the kernel line **grub.conf**? That file is the Linux kernel. How large is the file? Why? What is the real kernel size? Where else will you find something like this?

11. Enter the command **dmesg | less** to review the kernel boot messages. What parts of the system hardware do you recognize in the output? How might this output help you manage the system's hardware?

Project 4-3

In this project you review the initialization process for your Linux system. To complete this activity you should have an installed Linux system with a valid user account (one for which you know the password).

1. Log in to Linux using your user account name and password (not the **root** account).

2. If you logged in using a graphical login screen, open a terminal window by clicking on the icon third from the left on the Gnome Desktop.

3. Enter the command **cat /etc/sysconfig/network**. What configuration options do you recognize in the output?

4. Change to the **rc.d** initialization directory: **cd /etc/rc.d**.

5. Enter the **ls** command. What filenames do you recognize from the discussion in the chapter?

6. List the files in the **init.d** subdirectory: **ls init.d**. Can you recognize any network or other services that match the names of the files in this directory?

7. List the files in the **rc5.d** subdirectory: **ls rc5.d**. How do the files in this directory correspond to those in the **init.d** subdirectory?

8. Change to the **init.d** subdirectory: **cd init.d**.

9. View the **syslog** script using the following command: **ls -l syslog**. Notice the file permissions assigned to the script. Who is permitted to read the script? (The **syslog** script controls the system logging programs described in Chapter 10.)

10. Execute the **syslog** script using the command **./syslog restart** (don't forget the **./** at the beginning to indicate that the file is located in the current directory). Wait a few moments for all of the messages to appear on-screen and the command prompt to return. What can you conclude about the file permissions allowing everyone to read the script?

11. Use the following command to look at the contents of the script: **less syslog**. You can learn about creating scripts by reviewing existing scripts on the system. (Chapter 11 describes how to create your own scripts.) Press **q** to exit the **less** command.

12. Change back to your home directory using the command **cd** with no parameters. (This always returns you to your home directory.)

13. Enter **pwd** to verify that you are in fact in your home directory.

CASE PROJECTS

Your most recent McKinney & Co. consulting project involves archiving large quantities of data in compressed form and granting certain users access to the archived data. You need to do some research to answer questions that have come up.

1. Review the list of compression tools available in Linux (see Table 4-4). Install any of these that are not part of your system (using the **rpm** command). Test each of these utilities by compressing a set of text files, program files, and image files. Determine the average compression ratio for each (what percentage of the original size the compressed file occupies). Also note the speed of compression by entering the **date** command immediately before and after each test. (You may need to work with large files to make the timing data reasonably easy to gather.)

2. Experiment with the **touch** and **umask** commands to determine what you think are the optimal default file permissions to be granted on newly created archive files in different circumstances. Create a grid outlining different settings and the default permissions to be used, with the **umask** command to implement each one.

3. During the project planning phase, you learned about a potential security problem with the **ls** command. Launch the GnoRPM utility from the Programs, System menu of Gnome and use the Find feature to determine which package the **/bin/ls** program is a part of. Then query for package details to see when the package was built (assembled into an rpm file) and who or what organization built it. This information will help you determine if your copy of the utility is at risk.

USING LINUX GRAPHICAL ENVIRONMENTS

After reading this chapter and completing the exercises, you will be able to:

♦ Understand how the X Window System functions

♦ Review the installation and settings of the X Window System

♦ Use popular graphical desktop interfaces

In the previous chapter you learned commands to manage files and directories, including file permissions. You also learned how to manage software packages, kernel modules, and system initialization options through both command-line and graphical utilities.

In this chapter you learn much more about how the graphical environment is configured and how you can manage certain graphical resources and options. This environment includes the X Window System as the underlying technology, and a graphical desktop interface such as Gnome or KDE that provides convenient interface components such as a main menu, file manager program, and desktop icons. You learn how to explore your preferred desktop interface and begin using some of the tools that it provides.

UNDERSTANDING THE X WINDOW SYSTEM

When you installed Linux in Chapter 3, the installation program tried automatically to detect your graphical hardware (your video card) and configure the graphical environment. The foundation of that environment is the software that communicates with the video card and makes all other graphical interaction possible: this software is called the X Window System. Later in this section, you will see how other graphical tools, including desktop interfaces such as Gnome, work with the X Window System.

The X Window System is sometimes called *X Windows* (which is often considered an incorrect name) or just *X* (which is commonly used).

A Brief History of X

Graphical environments began to appear on computer systems in the early 1980s. The seeds of this trend were planted at the Palo Alto Research Center, part of Xerox Corporation, where researchers did the earliest work on graphical user interfaces (GUIs) and devices for interacting with them (including the mouse). But Xerox was not the company that made GUIs popular. That honor fell to three different groups, each working independently toward the goal of making its computer system easier to use.

The first GUI to be made widely available was an early version of Windows from Microsoft—Windows 1.0. However, this version and the later version, Windows 2.0, were not functional enough to be anything more than technological curiosities. Conversely, the Apple Macintosh made full and effective use of GUI technology such as menus and dialog boxes when it began shipping in 1984. At Microsoft, developers continued working on versions of Windows until, by the 3.1 release, the product was functional and stable enough to gather a strong following in the market. Because of the dominance of IBM PC and compatible hardware, the early technology lead of Macintosh was soon overwhelmed numerically by Microsoft Windows-based computers.

The third group working on graphical environments was comprised of developers bent on creating a useful GUI for UNIX. As Microsoft Windows was establishing its place in the market during the mid-1980s, UNIX had already been in widespread use for years. It was extremely stable—millions of businesses around the world used UNIX. But it wasn't considered easy to use, or user-friendly. A group working at the Massachusetts Institute of Technology (MIT) and Digital Equipment Corporation (DEC, now part of Hewlett-Packard through its acquisition of Compaq Computer Corporation) began working together on a graphical environment for UNIX. Their goals included making UNIX easier to use and encouraging the development of graphical standards among competing commercial versions of UNIX. This development process was dubbed **Project Athena**.

The work of Project Athena was eventually called the X Window System, with the assumption that *X* would be replaced with something more descriptive. But the X appellation stuck and is used to this day.

The X Window System was released as public domain software in 1985. This allowed many UNIX vendors to begin creating products based on X, and it rapidly became the default graphical system for the entire UNIX market. The GPL (the license under which Linux was released) was not developed by Richard Stallman of the Free Software Foundation until 1992, so X was released under a different legal arrangement. By placing the software in the public domain, the developers (MIT and DEC) gave up their copyright to the software, leaving others free to create derivative works and copyright them. The result was a fragmented market, in which users could choose from various graphical systems based on the original work of Project Athena. Because the UNIX market was already fragmented and did not rely on the mass-market economies that are associated with Microsoft Windows, the availability of many varieties of X was not considered problematic.

In 1988 the Open Software Foundation, or OSF, took over work on Project Athena and continued working on newer, better versions of X. The not-for-profit OSF (now called the Open Group) continues to maintain X. Because X is public domain software, however, the source code is available to anyone. Figure 5-1 shows the Open Group's Web site, at *www.opengroup.org*, where you can find more information about X. For additional background details, visit *www.x.org*.

Figure 5-1   The Open Group Web site

Although the Open Group managed development of the X Window System as public domain software, no version of X was freely available; it was included only as part of expensive UNIX systems from vendors such as IBM and Hewlett-Packard. These versions of X typically ran on expensive minicomputers such as the IBM RS/6000 and Hewlett-Packard PA-RISC-based systems.

The XFree86 Project was started as a nonprofit organization dedicated to creating a version of X for Intel-based versions of UNIX. The XFree86 Project software was welcomed by Linux developers because it provided the foundation for a graphical interface similar to that used by all other UNIX-like operating systems. X was soon incorporated into every mainstream Linux distribution. You can read more about the XFree86 Project at *www.xfree86.org*.

Technical Concepts behind X

Both the Macintosh and Microsoft Windows graphical environments are successful because they run on widely available computer hardware. In particular, the developers of Microsoft Windows worked to ensure that Windows could use any popular video card; as Windows itself became hugely popular, video card manufacturers scrambled to make sure they created software to help Microsoft Windows function with their hardware.

Coming from UNIX roots, the developers of X took a different approach. Instead of embedding video card specifications in a driver, they designed a text-based configuration file that lets the user basically write the driver for any video card that comes on the market. For all this potential technological power, the result was that X was very difficult to configure on Linux.

Fortunately, recent developments by the XFree86 Project and by Linux vendors such as Caldera (now The SCO Group) and Red Hat mean that most video cards are easily configured by the installation program, without any special knowledge on your part. Later in this chapter you learn about using configuration utilities to set up or refine the graphical configuration if you didn't choose to configure it during Linux installation.

Components of the X Window System

The developers of X used a clever design that has allowed X to continue as a viable technology more than 15 years after it was first released. This design separates control of the video card (sending signals to the computer hardware) from management of program information on the screen. The following list of components shows the modular nature of the X Window System design:

- **X server**: The program that communicates with the video card, sending the most basic instructions on what images should appear on screen. It is similar to a video card driver, but an X server also interacts with the keyboard and mouse used in a graphical environment. The X server relies on other components to tell it what to display and to process keyboard and mouse input.

- **X client**: Any graphical application, such as a graphical word processor, graphical configuration utility, or graphical game program. A graphical application in Linux does not directly control the screen display. Instead, the application (the X client) requests that the X server display something or collect keyboard and mouse input. The X server sends instructions on to the video card and collects keyboard and mouse input. By separating X server and X client functions, every X client doesn't need to know how to interact with every type of video card, keyboard, and mouse. The windows and dialog boxes associated with a graphical application are the output of the X server, as requested by the X client. X clients do not communicate directly with the video card, keyboard, or mouse.

- **Window manager**: A special-purpose graphical application (that is, a special-purpose X client). It controls the position and manipulation of the windows in a GUI. The window manager functions between regular user applications and the X server; each application doesn't need to implement window drawing and management features because the window manager takes care of those things. Virtually every graphical application uses the functionality provided by a window manager.

- **Graphical libraries**: Collections of programming functions that an X client can use to manage the elements of a graphical environment more efficiently. Some libraries are tied to a specific environment, such as KDE or Gnome; others are more general.

- **Desktop environment**: A graphical application that provides a comprehensive user interface, including menus, desktop icons, and usually several integrated applications. Also known as a **desktop interface**. A desktop environment allows applications to work together better because they can make assumptions about the functionality of other programs. This permits features such as drag and drop, and copy and paste operations. Gnome and KDE are examples of desktop environments that are installed by default as part of many Linux products. Several other desktop environments are available for Linux.

Figure 5-2 shows how the components of X can be arranged conceptually. The next section explains how these components are actually used in Linux.

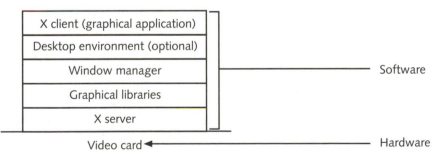

Figure 5-2   Components of the X Window System

Exploring X Components

As part of the Linux installation process, the XFree86 X server program is installed. In Red Hat Linux 7.3 and in other Linux distributions, the X Window System consists of hundreds of different files. The packages installed as part of Red Hat Linux 7.3 are shown in Table 5–1.

Table 5-1   X Window Packages Installed with Red Hat Linux 7.3

Package	Description
XFree86-font-utils-4.2.0-8	Utilities for managing graphical fonts.
XFree86-base-fonts-4.2.0-8	A core set of graphical fonts.
XFree86-ISO8859-15-75dpi-fonts-4.2.0-8	Additional graphical fonts.
XFree86-100dpi-fonts-4.2.0-8	Additional graphical fonts.
XFree86-75dpi-fonts-4.2.0-8	Additional graphical fonts.
XFree86-ISO8859-15-100dpi-fonts-4.2.0-8	Additional graphical fonts.
XFree86-tools-4.2.0-8	Utilities for managing aspects of the graphical environment.
XFree86-xdm-4.2.0-8	A graphical login program.
Xconfigurator-4.10.7-1	Utility for configuring the X Window System.
XFree86-twm-4.2.0-8	A minimal window manager.
XFree86-libs-4.2.0-8	Graphical programming libraries that other graphical programs can use.
XFree86-xfs-4.2.0-8	The X font server, which provides graphical fonts for other graphical programs.
XFree86-4.2.0-8	The X server.
XFree86-devel-4.2.0-8	Tools and libraries for compiling graphical programs.

You can use the **rpm** command with the **-qi** or **-ql** options to see information or a file list for any of these packages (or use the GnoRPM or kPackage utilities). Commercial servers from companies such as Xi Graphics (*www.xig.com*) and MetroLink (*www.metrolink.com*) can be used in place of these XFree86 packages. They may support different video cards or operate more efficiently with some cards.

Unlike with Macintosh and Microsoft Windows systems, each user of the X Window System is free to select the interface type that he or she prefers. Each user can select a window manager, desktop interface, and configuration options for that desktop.

A basic Linux window manager that was formerly very popular is **fvwm**, shown in Figure 5–3. This window manager is similar to the **tvm** window manager that is installed as part of Red Hat Linux. When only the **fvwm** window manager is running, you see a blank screen with a color pattern and a mouse pointer. A window manager alone doesn't provide much of a display; its purpose is to provide services to other programs. Pressing a mouse button opens a menu from which you can start programs or execute other functions to control the graphical environment.

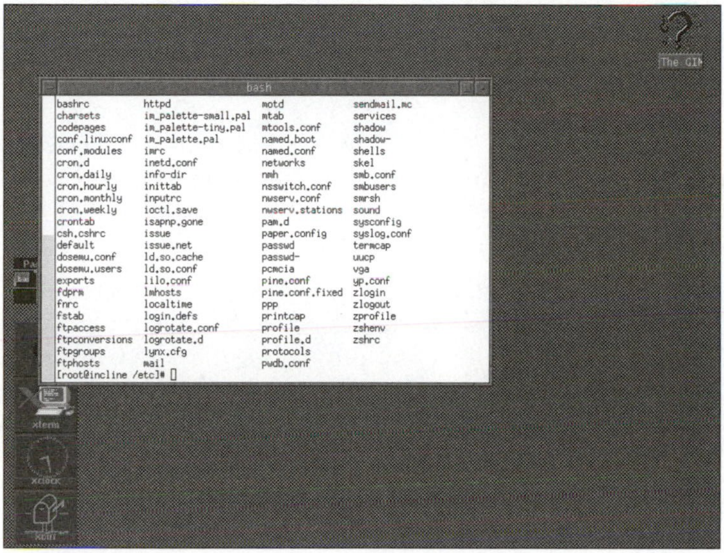

Figure 5-3   The `fvwm` window manager

Several window managers available for Linux are described in the following list.

- **twm** (Tab Window Manager): A classic UNIX window manager that has been used for many years, installed as part of Red Hat Linux 7.3.

- **fvwm** (Feeble Virtual Window Manager): Developed by Robert Nation, this program was the most common window manager for Linux until desktop environments became popular. It includes many of the same characteristics as **twm**, but requires only about half the memory required to run **twm**. The latest version of **fvwm** is called **fvwm2**. You can find more information about **fvwm** at *www.fvwm.org*.

- **AMIwm** (Amiga Window Manager): A window manager that emulates the look and feel of the Amiga computers of the late 1980s, specifically the Amiga Workbench.

- **wm2**: A minimal window manager requiring little memory and allowing little configuration.

- **Window Maker** and **AfterStep**: Window managers that simulate the interface of the NeXT computer, though without the many applications that were included with the NeXT operating system.

- **mwm** (Motif Window Manager): A commercial window manager commonly included with commercial UNIX workstations. Before Linux desktops were popular, many window managers attempted to emulate this commercial window manager.

- **Enlightenment**: A window manager, sometimes called simply **E**, based on **fwvm2**.

- **olwm** (OpenLook Window Manager): A window manager that emulates the OpenLook interface style created by Sun Microsystems; used on Linux primarily by developers who want to emulate the look and feel of a Sun UNIX workstation.

- **Sawfish**: The window manager used by Gnome. It is very flexible in its configuration options, but it is typically tied to the Gnome Desktop. You can view configuration options for **Sawfish** by opening the Gnome main menu and selecting Programs, Settings, **Sawfish** window manager, and then one of the items listed in that submenu. One of the **Sawfish** configuration windows is shown in Figure 5-4.

- **kwm**: The window manager used by KDE. Unlike **Sawfish**, **kwm** is rarely referred to by name in KDE; its many configuration options are integrated with the KDE preferences that control the desktop and the graphical login. (These options are shown on the Preference submenu of the KDE main menu.)

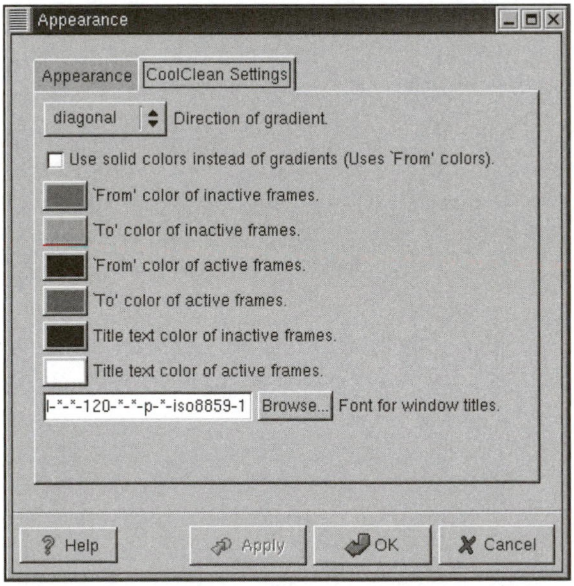

Figure 5-4   A **Sawfish** configuration window in Gnome

Many graphical libraries are also available for X. A graphical library consists of a few files containing programming commands that graphical applications can access. For the most part, each of these libraries was originally created to simplify the development of a specific application. Some libraries were later used by developers of other applications. A graphical library is installed on a Linux system just like any other application (using an `rpm` command, for example). But a graphical library is not launched directly—it only provides tools for other applications. Two graphical libraries you should know about are the libraries associated with the Gnome and KDE Desktops:

- The Qt library is the foundation of the KDE Desktop, which is the most popular graphical environment used on Linux. (See *www.kde.org* for more information.) KDE is described in more detail later in this chapter.

- The GTK+ library was developed by Spencer Kimball and Peter Mattis at the University of California at Berkeley as the foundation of the Gimp graphics application. (Gimp is a program similar to Adobe Photoshop.) Subsequently, GTK+ was used to create the Gnome Desktop. (See *www.gnome.org* for more information.) Gnome is described in more detail later in this chapter.

The default desktop choice in Red Hat Linux 7.3 is Gnome. You can run the `switchdesk` command at any time to select among all the graphical environments that you have installed. For example, the `switchdesk` window (shown in Figure 5-5) might list Gnome, KDE, and `twm` as options. When you choose one, log out, and log in again, your selection is activated. If you select the checkbox to have your action apply only to the current session, the desktop returns to your previous default setting after the *second* time you log out and log in again.

Figure 5-5 The `switchdesk` utility

Displaying X Clients Remotely

You can use any X server to display the window for an X client running on any computer on a network. For example, suppose you have StarOffice (the X client) installed on one computer (call it computer A). Many different users on other computers (B, C, and D in the example) can log in to computer A over the network and start a copy of StarOffice. All of the copies of StarOffice are actually running on computer A, but the X server program on computers B, C, and D, where all of the users are physically located, displays the X client application on those computers as shown in Figure 5-6. The X server on computers B, C, and D receives requests from the X client (StarOffice) on computer A to display windows and collect keyboard and mouse input.

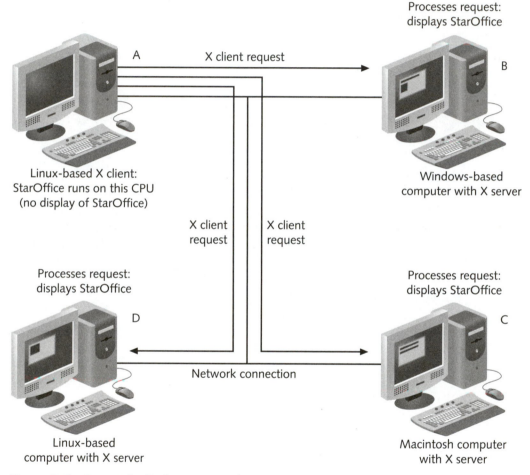

Figure 5-6   Remotely displaying an X client

Any type of computer can run the X server that displays windows and collects input for an X client. For example, by installing an X server on a Microsoft Windows computer, you can launch an application on a Linux computer and use that application while sitting at the Windows computer, as shown in Figure 5-7. Two examples of X servers for Windows are X-Win (*www.starnet.com*) and Exceed (*www.hummingbird.com*).

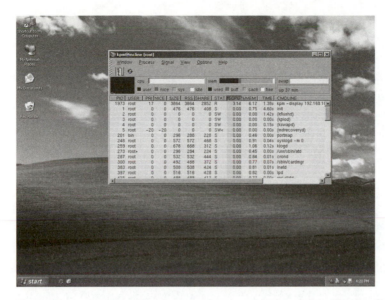

Figure 5-7   Using a Linux program via an X server on Microsoft Windows

Each time you start a graphical application, the application decides which X server to use—that is, it decides where to display its windows and collect keyboard and mouse input. By default, it uses the X server on the same computer where the X client is executed. But you can specify a different X server in two ways:

- Set the **DISPLAY** environment variable to the name of the computer whose X server you want the X client to use. The format of the computer name includes a special code that all Linux systems use to determine X server behavior: **:0.0**. For example, the commands to set this variable to display graphical applications on host nevada are:

```
DISPLAY=nevada:0.0
export DISPLAY
```

- Add the **display** option to the command you are executing. For example, the following command will start the **gimp** application and display it on host oregon:

```
gimp display oregon:0.0
```

Use the **set** command to list all current environment variables. Some environment variables are configured automatically during the Linux start-up process. You can use the **export** command to make an environment variable available to other applications, as shown in the DISPLAY example.

Each user on a system has a different set of environment variables, so all users can log in and have the programs they run displayed on different remote hosts. The `display` option overrides the `DISPLAY` environment variable.

Before an X client can display its windows on a remote host, the remote host must be configured to allow other computers to use its X server. You can do this in two ways: one easy and insecure, the other more work but more secure. The easy method is to execute the **xhost** command on the remote host. This command specifies the name of a remote computer that is permitted to use the local X server. Any user on the remote computer can then display an application on the computer where **xhost** was executed. For example, if this command is executed on host idaho, any user on host oregon can launch an application and display it on idaho:

```
xhost +oregon
```

Some users even use this highly insecure command to permit *anyone* to use their X server:

```
xhost +
```

A more secure system uses the **xauth** command. With this system you can restrict access to those users on a remote system who have a specific token (a long number) in order to use the X server. This token is commonly called a **cookie**. The cookie used by the **xauth** command is also called an **MIT Magic Cookie**.

To use the **xauth** program, follow this process:

1. Suppose you start a program on host oregon that is to be displayed on host nevada (the X server on nevada will be used). The program you execute on oregon examines the `.Xauthority` file in your home directory on oregon to see whether a token is given for the remote host nevada.

2. Assuming that a token is available (you must put it there yourself, as we'll show you next), it is sent to nevada over the network as oregon tries to initiate a connection to use the X server on nevada.

3. The X server on nevada looks in *its* `.Xauthority` file for a token that corresponds to host oregon. If it finds one, it allows the connection to proceed. If not, the connection is refused and the program on oregon will not run (because it has been instructed to use nevada for its display and nevada won't allow that).

The .`Xauthority` files mentioned in this process are stored in a user's home directory. So each user must have the necessary tokens to use another user's X server. Of course, the most common situation is that you have accounts on two systems and you copy the token between your home directories so that you can run and display programs on any of the systems to which you have access. In any case, **xauth** is designed to be a user-to-user security system, rather than a host-to-host security system.

You can see the `.Xauthority` file in your home directory using the `ls -a` command (it's a hidden file). To view or alter the file's contents, you use the `xauth` program, which you can start from any command line. From the `xauth` prompt, you enter commands to manage the tokens stored for your use on the X server. A few helpful commands include `help` to show all the `xauth` commands, `list` to list all the tokens currently stored, and `add` to place a token into the authority file for use by a remote host. For example, if the `add` command shown here is executed on oregon, it will permit oregon to use the X server on nevada (the information in the command was first obtained from nevada):

```
add nevada:0  MIT-MAGIC-COOKIE1 6da29c0a7399aa179c90cba39426dd5f
```

The `.Xauthority` file should always include a token for the host where you are working. A new token is generated each time you log in to X. If your file doesn't include a token for your local host, use the `generate` command within `xauth` to create one. Below, you see `xauth` launched, followed by the `list` command to show all the known tokens on host nevada:

```
[thomasj@nevada thomasj]# xauth
Using authority file /home/thomasj/.Xauthority
xauth> list
nevada/unix:0  MIT-MAGIC-COOKIE-1 da29c0a7399aa179c90cba39426dd5f
nevada:0  MIT-MAGIC-COOKIE-1 6da29c0a7399aa179c90cba39426dd5f
xauth>
```

If you have a file like this one and you want host oregon to be able to use nevada as an X server (that is, to display programs on it), you must get the information from this file into your `.Xauthority` file on oregon. Once you have done this, oregon will have a valid token to send to nevada so that nevada will allow oregon to connect for remote program display.

You can transfer an `xauth` cookie between systems in several ways. Typically, you would use a networking program such as `telnet`, `rlogin`, or `ssh` to connect to a remote computer over the network, then copy and paste the information between two windows. You will learn about using graphical environments later in this chapter, but networking tools are not covered in this book.

Don't be surprised if remote display of graphical applications doesn't work correctly on your first attempt. The many components of X can make it difficult to configure. If you are having problems, be certain that your `DISPLAY` variable is correctly set. Check with your system administrator to see if X was started with the `-nolisten tcp` argument, which stops it from listening for remote connections. Make certain that the hostname you have specified is reachable on the network (try `ping`, for example). Check again that the tokens in the two `.Xauthority` files match and that a problem such as an expired token is not interfering with your efforts. Finally, review the man pages (for X, `xauth`, etc.) and HOWTO documents related to X to see what else might be preventing your setup from functioning as expected.

RUNNING THE X WINDOW SYSTEM

Though the flexibility and features of X are impressive, the X Window System can be difficult to configure if your Linux installation program didn't take care of this for you. The following sections provide some guidance on configuring X after you have Linux installed and running.

Configuring X

When you installed Linux, the XFree86 X server was probably installed on your hard disk. In addition, you probably have many supporting XFree86 packages as listed in the previous section, plus a window manager, and perhaps a desktop interface. Before you can use any of these, the X server software must be configured to use your video card and monitor correctly.

You can learn about configuration options for X by reviewing the X online manual page (enter the command man X). This man page, however, presents a steep learning curve.

Some specialized Linux distributions, such as the Linux Router Project (see *www.linuxrouter.org*), do not include X. On any Linux system, you can choose not to run X to save system resources (both memory and CPU processing time).

After the X server is configured, the window manager or desktop environment that you use will work without additional configuration. You can also make changes in the configuration of a window manager or desktop environment. These changes are relatively simple because they do not require that you know anything about the computer's hardware. But before these components can function, you must properly configure the X server. There are several utilities you can use to configure X. The installation program presents the easiest method of configuration, but it doesn't always succeed.

As you experiment with different configuration settings, launching X may not display anything at all. If the display is garbled or blank when you launch X (using the commands given later in this chapter), try pressing the key combination Ctrl+Alt+Backspace to exit X and return to character mode.

The Configuration File

The X software is normally located in the directory `/usr/X11R6`. This directory is sometimes called the X-root directory. The filename `X11R6` refers to X version 11, release 6. You will hear people who work with many types of Linux and UNIX systems refer to "ex-eleven-R-five" or "ex-eleven-R-six" when describing their version of X. The developers of X have stopped advancing the version number (it stays at 11), but the release number may change every few years.

The configuration file for XFree86 is located either in the /etc directory, in the /etc/X11 directory, or in the /usr/X11R6/lib/X11 directory. The configuration file for the XFree86 X server is called **XF86Config-4**. (Note the use of uppercase and lowercase.) On Red Hat Linux 7.3, the configuration file is /etc/X11/XF86Config-4. A sample configuration file from Red Hat Linux 7.3 is shown here for review—you should not expect to understand all that you see in this file, but reviewing it will help you understand the type of information that the X server uses to interact with system resources.

The "-4" in the name of the configuration file refers to XFree86 version 4. Previous versions of XFree86 used the XF86Config file (without "-4"), and you will see a "fallback" file of that name in the /etc/X11/ directory on Red Hat Linux. XFree86 version 3 relied on a much less robust and flexible X server architecture. Most of the discussion in this section applies to both version 3 and version 4 of XFree86, but you can expect all Linux distributions produced in the past two to three years to include XFree86 version 4 and use it by default.

```
# File generated by anaconda.

Section "ServerLayout"
        Identifier      "Anaconda Configured"
        Screen       0  "Screen0" 0 0
        InputDevice     "Mouse0" "CorePointer"
        InputDevice     "Keyboard0" "CoreKeyboard"
EndSection

Section "Files"

# The location of the RGB database. Note, this is the name of the
# file minus the extension (like ".txt" or ".db").  There is
# normally no need to change the default.

    RgbPath "/usr/X11R6/lib/X11/rgb"

# Multiple FontPath entries are allowed (they are
# concatenated together)
# By default, Red Hat 6.0 and later now use a font server
# independent of the X server to render fonts.

    FontPath    "unix/:7100"

EndSection

Section "Module"
        Load  "GLcore"
        Load  "dbe"
```

```
                Load    "extmod"
                Load    "fbdevhw"
                Load    "dri"
                Load    "glx"
                Load    "record"
                Load    "freetype"
                Load    "type1"
EndSection

Section "InputDevice"
        Identifier   "Keyboard0"
        Driver       "keyboard"

# Option      "AutoRepeat"       "500 5"

# when using XQUEUE, comment out the above line, and uncomment the
# following line
# Option      "Protocol"       "Xqueue"

# Specify which keyboard LEDs can be user-controlled
# (eg, with xset(1))
# Option      "Xleds"             "1 2 3"

# To disable the XKEYBOARD extension, uncomment XkbDisable.
# Option      "XkbDisable"

# To customise the XKB settings to suit your keyboard, modify the
# lines below (which are the defaults).  For example, for a
# non-U.S. keyboard, you will probably want to use:
# Option      "XkbModel"       "pc102"
# If you have a US Microsoft Natural keyboard, you can use:
# Option      "XkbModel"       "microsoft"
#
# Then to change the language, change the Layout setting.
# For example, a german layout can be obtained with:
# Option      "XkbLayout"       "de"
# or:
# Option      "XkbLayout"       "de"
# Option      "XkbVariant"     "nodeadkeys"
#
# If you'd like to switch the positions of your capslock and
# control keys, use:
# Option      "XkbOptions"        "ctrl:nocaps"
Option        "XkbRules"          "xfree86"
Option        "XkbModel"          "pc105"
Option        "XkbLayout"         "us"
#Option       "XkbVariant"        ""
#Option       "XkbOptions"        ""
EndSection
```

```
Section "InputDevice"
        Identifier   "Mouse0"
        Driver       "mouse"
        Option       "Protocol" "PS/2"
        Option       "Device" "/dev/psaux"
        Option       "ZAxisMapping" "4 5"
        Option       "Emulate3Buttons" "no"
EndSection

Section "Monitor"
        Identifier   "Monitor0"
        VendorName   "Monitor Vendor"
        ModelName    "Monitor Model"
        HorizSync    31.5-48.5
        VertRefresh  50-70
        Option "dpms"

        # — 1400x1050 —
        # 1400x1050 @ 60Hz, 65.8 kHz hsync
        Modeline "1400x1050"  129   1400 1464 1656 1960
                              1050 1051 1054 1100 +HSync +VSync

        # 1400x1050 @ 70Hz, 76.8 kHz hsync
        Modeline "1400x1050"  151   1400 1464 1656 1960
                              1050 1051 1054 1100 +HSync +VSync

        # 1400x1050 @ 75Hz, 82.3 kHz hsync
        Modeline "1400x1050"  162   1400 1464 1656 1960
                              1050 1051 1054 1100 +HSync +VSync

        # 1400x1050 @ 85Hz, 93.2 kHz hsync
        Modeline "1400x1050"  184   1400 1464 1656 1960
                              1050 1051 1054 1100 +HSync +VSync

EndSection

Section "Device"
        # no known options
        Identifier   "Intel 740 (generic)"
        Driver       "i740"
        VendorName   "Intel 740 (generic)"
        BoardName    "Intel 740 (generic)"

        #BusID
EndSection

Section "Screen"
Identifier   "Screen0"
```

```
Device          "Intel 740 (generic)"
Monitor         "Monitor0"
DefaultDepth       16

Subsection "Display"
            Depth        16
            Modes        "1024x768" "800x600" "640x480"
EndSubsection

EndSection

Section "DRI"
    Mode 0666
EndSection
```

Each configuration file differs because each refers to specific hardware resources on your computer (notice the reference to an Intel i740 video card in the previous example file). The **XF86Config-4** file defines where to find graphical font information, how to interact with the keyboard and mouse, details about monitor and video card capabilities, and information on combining the video card and monitor details to create a specific view (such as 1024×768 resolution with 256 colors).

Hand-editing an X configuration file to fix a jumbled graphical display is very challenging. Guided by the comments in the file, you might decide you need to edit some X features. But this is rarely done. Instead, system administrators rely on graphical utilities to manage this configuration file. Also, they rarely make any changes after the file is set up correctly on a Linux system.

Commercial X servers do not rely on the **XF86Config-4** file. Each uses a different configuration file with a different format. For example, the Accelerated-X server from Xi Graphics uses the configuration file **/etc/Xaccel.ini**. Commercial X servers include graphical configuration tools similar to what you saw when you installed Linux. When working with a commercial X server, you should review the documentation accompanying the product to learn how to use the product's configuration utility to prepare a configuration file.

Using Xconfigurator

The **Xconfigurator** program creates an **XF86Config-4** file for your XFree86 X server using a menu-driven text-based interface. This program was developed by Red Hat Software. It is not as easy to use as the installation program's X configuration screen, but **Xconfigurator** may successfully configure some video cards that the installation program fails to configure. To run this program from any command line, use this command (note the capital **X**):

```
# Xconfigurator
```

Xconfigurator probes your hardware and lets you select choices from lists of options. Figure 5-8 shows a sample screen from **Xconfigurator**. The program prompts you for the information it needs, although it tries to answer most of the difficult questions automatically, simply asking for confirmation.

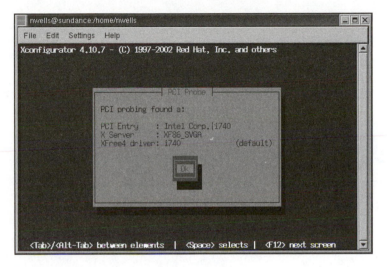

Figure 5-8   The **Xconfigurator** utility

Using **xf86config**

If you are using XFree86 on a non–Red Hat version of Linux and are having trouble getting X configured, you can try the **xf86config** command-line configuration utility (note that the name is all lowercase). After launching this utility you must read lengthy, detailed questions and then answer them as best you can. The **xf86config** utility provides complete flexibility in configuring the XFree86 software, something that other programs (including Linux installation programs) do not provide. If you take the time to read the information presented on-screen and you know the hardware details of your video card (such as the video chipset and the amount of video RAM), **xf86config** is very likely to configure correctly any video card supported by XFree86.

Any version of Linux that includes XFree86 should also include this utility. To launch **xf86config**, enter the utility name at any Linux command line (note again that it is all lowercase):

```
xf86config
```

Figure 5-9 shows one of the questions asked by **xf86config**, along with a list of options to choose from and detailed instructions about how to select the correct option.

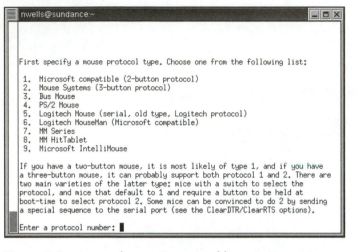

First specify a mouse protocol type. Choose one from the following list:

1. Microsoft compatible (2-button protocol)
2. Mouse Systems (3-button protocol)
3. Bus Mouse
4. PS/2 Mouse
5. Logitech Mouse (serial, old type, Logitech protocol)
6. Logitech MouseMan (Microsoft compatible)
7. MM Series
8. MM HitTablet
9. Microsoft IntelliMouse

If you have a two-button mouse, it is most likely of type 1, and if you have
a three-button mouse, it can probably support both protocol 1 and 2. There are
two main varieties of the latter type: mice with a switch to select the
protocol, and mice that default to 1 and require a button to be held at
boot-time to select protocol 2. Some mice can be convinced to do 2 by sending
a special sequence to the serial port (see the ClearDTR/ClearRTS options).

Enter a protocol number: █

Figure 5-9   A sample question posed by `xf86config`

Configuring X Using Other Resources

Just as you may have consulted your system administrator or Internet Service Provider when gathering information about your network, you may need to contact knowledgeable people to help you set up a problematic video card. For help configuring X, try the following:

- Ask another person who has successfully installed Linux several times to help you configure X. Sometimes options that are unfamiliar to you will be well-known to a person who has already configured a similar system.

- Use other specialized software provided by your Linux vendor. For example, Caldera OpenLinux includes the `lizardx` program and SuSE Linux includes the `SaX` program.

- Visit the XFree86 Web site and search for information about the video card you are trying to configure.

- Visit the Web site of your Linux vendor and search for information about configuring X.

- Buy a commercial X server (after checking that support for the troublesome video card is included). Contact the vendor for support if you have trouble installing the product.

- Visit Web sites dedicated to using Linux. In particular, try the Linux on Laptops page at *www.linux-laptop.net*. This page has links for hundreds of laptop models, where owners of those laptops have posted suggestions (and often sample `XF86Config-4` files) for making X work with specific models of laptops.

- Visit the Web site of the computer vendor and search for information in the technical support database. As more vendors add support for Linux, you are more likely to find helpful information from computer system vendors.

If you have easy access to any of these resources, you might choose to consult them before trying the different programs outlined earlier in this chapter.

 Once you have X configured, you can run the xvidtune program to adjust display parameters. This is not a utility you are likely to need unless your Linux graphical display is not correctly centered on your monitor. It is an interesting tool to study, however, as you learn about X.

5

Launching X

If you configured X while installing Linux and used the default settings for a graphical login prompt, the X Window System starts automatically every time you log in at the graphical prompt.

If you are not using a graphical login prompt, the standard method of starting X is to log in to Linux on a character-mode console and then execute the **startx** command. This command automatically executes a number of other commands that launch the X server and run the programs that make up the graphical environment. In this section, you learn how those programs interact.

The **startx** program is actually a script located in **/usr/X11R6/bin**. This script launches another program called **xinit**, which looks for several scripts in various locations in the Linux directory structure, including **~/.xinitrc**, **~/.Xclients**, **/etc/X11/xinit/xinitrc**, and **/etc/X11/xinit/Xclients**. A system administrator can place scripts in a user's home directory (**~/.xinitrc** and **~/.Xclients**) to define a unique graphical configuration for that user. All of the scripts listed here specify which programs should start along with X. For the most part, these programs are X clients. (As explained earlier in this chapter, an X client is an application that runs in X.)

Each X client is started as a background application. A **background application** is an application that does not prevent the program that started it (the **xinit** program in this case) from going on to other tasks (launching other X clients). In this case, the **xinit** scripts can start an X client and then go on to start another (and another, and another, and so on) without waiting for the first one to finish execution. The X clients that **xinit** starts from the initialization scripts include the window manager, and desktop applications such as a file manager and a toolbar that includes the main menu for the desktop.

The window manager is the last X client that the **xinit** program launches. The window manager is responsible for controlling the graphical screen, and its features are used by all of the X applications that are started before the window manager; the other X applications wait until the window manager is started before trying to display information on-screen.

A very simple script that `xinit` could use to launch one X client and a window manager might look like this:

```
xterm &
fvwm
```

If this script were used by `xinit` to start X, a single `xterm` (command-line window) would appear on a blank background. (The background is provided by `fvwm`, which also manages the keyboard and mouse, as described previously.)

In practice, Linux vendors create complex scripts that check for the availability of default window managers, look at a variety of configuration files, and start numerous X clients to provide a convenient working environment for users. The standard startup process is outlined in the following list and illustrated in Figure 5-10. Details about the last few items in the list are provided later in this section.

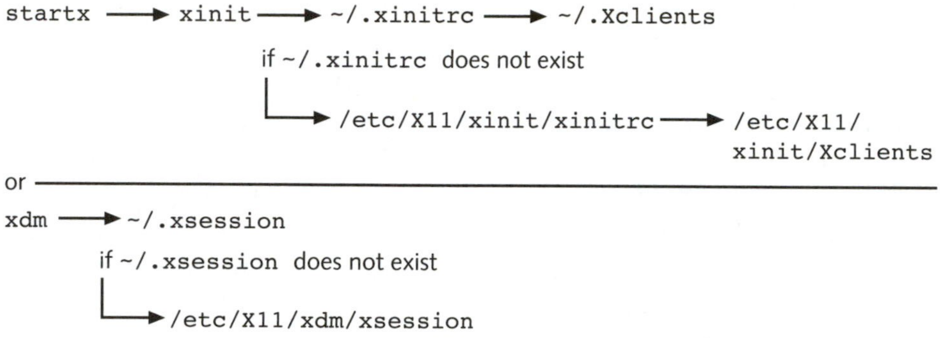

```
startx ──────▶ xinit ──────▶ ~/.xinitrc ──────▶ ~/.Xclients

                    if ~/.xinitrc  does not exist

                    └──────▶ /etc/X11/xinit/xinitrc ──────▶ /etc/X11/
                                                             xinit/Xclients

or ────────────────────────────────────────────────────────────────

xdm ──────▶ ~/.xsession

         if ~/.xsession  does not exist

         └──────▶ /etc/X11/xdm/xsession
```

Figure 5-10   The start-up process for the X Window System

1. The user logs in at a graphical login prompt or executes the `startx` command.

2. The `startx` command or the graphical login prompt initiates the `xinit` command.

3. The `xinit` command starts the X server program.

4. The `xinit` command attempts to launch a script called `.xinitrc` located in the user's home directory.

5. If the file is found, the commands in `.xinitrc` are executed by `xinit`. This script normally executes commands in other scripts, particularly the `.Xclients` script, which can also be located in each user's home directory, if the system administrator implements a different graphical configuration for each user.

6. If the `.xinitrc` file is not found in the user's home directory, the `xinit` program looks for the file `/etc/X11/xinit/xinitrc`. (Notice that this filename does not begin with a period as do those in a user's home directory.)

7. If the `/etc/X11/xinit/xinitrc` file mentioned in Step 6 is found, the commands in it are executed by `xinit`. The `/etc/X11/xinit/xinitrc` script normally executes commands in other scripts, particularly the `/etc/X11/xinit/Xclients` script. (Again, the filename has no initial period.) These two scripts (located in `/etc/X11/xinit`) are system-wide graphical configuration scripts that are used for any user who does not have files in his or her home directory as described in Steps 4 and 5.

The scripts `xinitrc`, `.xinitrc`, `Xclients`, and `.Xclients` often include calls to execute other scripts, such as `Xclients_default`. The names and arrangement of these additional scripts vary by Linux distribution, but you can learn more about them by reviewing the contents of the `xinitrc` or `.xinitrc` file. All of the standard scripts (such as `xinitrc`), and the additional scripts that may be used by a particular Linux distribution, are shell scripts, which are discussed in Chapter 11.

Notice in the previous steps that you can use a separate configuration file in each user's home directory in order to use a different graphical configuration for each user. One user might choose to use `fvwm` as a window manager; another user might select Gnome or KDE as a graphical environment. A very basic `.xinitrc` configuration file is shown here. Notice that the last item executed is a window manager, `twm`.

```
xrdb -load $HOME/.Xresources
xsetroot -solid gray &
xclock -g 50x50-0+0 -bw 0 &
xload -g 50x50-50+0 -bw 0 &
xterm -g 80x24+0+0 -bw 0 &
xterm -g 80x24+0-0 -bw 0 &
twm
```

In Step 3 of the procedure outlined earlier, the `xinit` program starts the X server. To do this, the `xinit` program looks for the file named `X` in the directory `/usr/X11R6/bin`. This file is a pointer to the actual X server (or a program that chooses an X server). You can see what file it points to by using the `ls` command with the `-l` option:

```
$ ls -l /usr/X11R6/bin/X
lrwxrwxrwx 1 root root     7 Sep 18 17:07 /usr/X11R6/
     bin/X -> XFree86
```

The arrow character, `->`, indicates that the file `X` refers to another file, `XFree86` (the X server). If you use a commercial X server, the file `X` will point to an X server such as `Xaccel` (the Accelerated-X server). This type of pointer is called a symbolic link. (You will learn about symbolic links in Chapter 6.)

A user's home directory can contain a file named `.xserverrc` that defines which X server to start for that user. You will rarely see this file, however; all users on the system rely on the same video card and so will probably use the same X server.

5

Fine Tuning X

Once you have X correctly configured, you can use several utilities that come with the X Window System to adjust how applications are displayed and how X behaves in different situations.

Each graphical application uses a number of separate screen elements, such as scroll bars, text fonts, mouse pointers, and title bars for windows or dialog boxes. Each of these elements is called an **X resource**. This is a term used by programmers, but you should be familiar with it because as a system administrator you can configure the appearance of the X resources used in each application.

A collection of default X resource settings applies to all X applications. These default settings govern how windows in the application are displayed, which colors and fonts are used, and which features of the application are active when the application starts. You can also set up additional X resource settings that apply only when a specific user runs a specific application. These resource settings are compiled into a **resource database** file. Collectively, the information in this file defines how an X resource should appear on-screen.

The main resource database file is called `app-defaults`. It is located at `/usr/X11R6/lib/X11`. In addition to this set of resource information, each user's home directory can contain additional settings that override the default appearance of specific applications. A file named `.Xresources` or `.Xdefaults` contains this information. For example, the following sample lines in an `.Xresources` file define how an `xterm` window appears and what features it includes. These same features can be set or changed once the `xterm` program is running, but when a user creates an X resource database, the application is started with the user's preferences already active.

```
XTerm*cursorColor: gold
XTerm*multiScroll: on
XTerm*jumpScroll: on
XTerm*reverseWrap: on
XTerm*curses: on
XTerm*Font: 6x10
XTerm*scrollBar: on
XTerm*scrollbar*thickness: 5
XTerm*multiClickTime: 500
XTerm*charClass: 33:48,37:48,45-47:48,64:48
XTerm*cutNewline: off
XTerm*cutToBeginningOfLine: off
XTerm*titeInhibit: on
XTerm*ttyModes: intr ^c erase ^? kill ^u XLoad*Background: gold
```

X resource database files are activated within one of the startup scripts such as `.xinitrc` or `.Xclients` by using the command **xrdb**. The **xrdb** command loads an initial X database resource file or adds resource configuration details from files such as `.Xresources`.

An `xrdb` command such as the one shown here is part of the X startup scripts described previously:

```
xrdb -load $HOME/.Xresources
```

When there are additional resource settings to be loaded, the **-merge** option is used instead of the **-load** option. You will rarely need to set up the `xrdb` command, because it is part of the default configuration when you install X. But you may want to add information to an `.Xresources` file to configure the appearance of an application. The online manual page for a graphical application will tell you about options you can configure via X resources.

 Linux desktop environments (such as KDE and Gnome) include an X resource database that is designed to give a standard look and feel to all programs that you launch. The desktop environments do not depend on configuration files such as `.Xresources`. Instead of using an `.Xresources` file to configure the appearance and options of the desktop, these environments use their own configuration tools.

Although the configuration file and scripts described thus far control many aspects of X, you can use the **xset** command to adjust the behavior of X to suit your preferences. Execute **xset** at any command line to see a list of the options that you can use with this command to control X. They include:

- Turn keyclick on or off
- Set the keyclick volume
- Choose keyboard auto-repeat settings
- Activate EnergyStar features of compliant monitors
- Set mouse acceleration levels
- Set font locations and other font settings
- Alter properties of the X screen blanker (this is separate from the screen saver that is part of Gnome or KDE)

For example, suppose you notice that the screen of your system goes completely blank after a few minutes without using the system. To turn off this feature, execute this command:

```
xset s noblank
```

To see the current settings for all the features that **xset** controls, use this command:

```
xset q
```

USING DESKTOP INTERFACES

A desktop interface is a graphical environment that provides a collection of functions and utilities to make using a computer easier for those who do not have many commands memorized. In addition, some types of information may be much easier to work with in a graphical format. You can use a desktop interface to:

- Place icons on the screen's background (where no other windows are visible). Clicking on these icons launches applications or displays data files that the user commonly accesses.

- Manage multiple applications efficiently using multiple independent windows, toolbars, and keyboard controls.

- Use menus to access frequently used utilities and applications. You can customize these menus to meet your specific requirements.

- Use a collection of basic applications provided with the desktop, such as a text editor, calculator, calendar, note-taking application, audio CD player, and so forth.

- Use a convenient, integrated file management utility to view and manipulate files.

- Use applications created specifically for the desktop interface. These applications rely on a common set of functions that create a single look and feel for the environment, reduce the system resources required (because of shared functionality), and interact with other applications via drag-and-drop and cut-and-paste features.

Window managers such as `fvwm` include some, but not all, of the features listed above. If you see all of these features on an `fvwm`-based system, it's because your Linux vendor or system administrator has combined numerous Linux applications into a working graphical environment. But cobbling together pieces does not give you an integrated environment with a common look and feel, nor can you easily share data between applications and manage the interface from a central set of desktop utilities. For these reasons, the strength of Linux desktop interfaces like KDE and Gnome is likely to be a primary reason for increased use of Linux on desktop PCs in the coming years.

The KDE Interface

In 1996 Matthias Ettrich began creating a full-featured graphical environment for Linux. He dubbed the project the **K Desktop Environment (KDE)**. KDE is now the most widely used desktop environment on Linux systems. When you install most Linux distributions, KDE is installed by default with a complete set of KDE applications. KDE applications use the same graphical toolkit as the desktop itself and can thus share functionality such as common dialog boxes and drag-and-drop capability.

KDE includes a suite of applications for Internet access, system maintenance, personal productivity (organizers, calculators, music players), and many other basic tasks. KDE includes a
set of icons at the bottom of the screen called the Panel. You can use the icons in the Panel
to start applications such as a terminal window. Each application that you start in KDE appears
as a button in the taskbar (which is normally at the top of the KDE screen). You can switch
between applications or open a minimized application using the corresponding button on the
taskbar. A few standard icons are included on the KDE default desktop; each user can add others. Figure 5-11 shows a basic KDE Desktop.

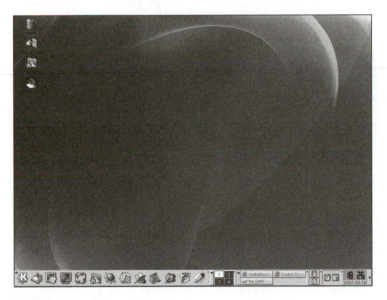

Figure 5-11   The KDE Desktop

KDE includes a powerful file manager that provides several views of files (such as an
icon view and a detailed view) and also acts as a Web browser (much like the Microsoft
Explorer program). The file manager in KDE is designed to assign icons to files automatically, based on the file's type (such as text file, program, or graphics file). Based on
the type of file, the file manager also assigns default capabilities that allow a user to perform appropriate actions. For example, you can click on a text file to view that file. You
can drag and drop a graphics file onto a desktop icon to view that graphics file in the
program represented by the icon. You can right-click on a file and choose Properties from
the pop-up menu to open a dialog box in which you can adjust the file's properties (including the file name and file permissions). Figure 5-12 shows a file manager window with
a dialog box showing properties for one file.

Figure 5-12   The KDE file manager

KDE includes several system administration utilities that are described in more detail in later chapters. KDE also includes a Control Center in which you can configure KDE itself. For example, in the Control Center you can configure color schemes, screen savers, fonts, languages used (KDE supports over 30 languages, including Chinese and Russian), and the position of each part of the KDE screen (such as where the Panel and taskbar are positioned). Advanced options in the Control Center let you decide what information should be included on the title bar of each application window and which keystrokes should switch between applications. Many other options are available. Figure 5-13 shows the KDE Control Center with some of the configuration options for desktop appearance. Each user's configuration choices are stored separately.

The left side of the KDE Control Center window displays a list of sections, such as Look & Feel. By clicking the plus sign next to any section name, you will see a list of items within that section. Clicking on one of these items displays configuration options on the right side of the Control Center window.

You can also configure KDE directly from the Preferences submenus of the KDE main menu without opening the KDE Control Center.

Although a default set of desktop icons is included with KDE, each user can create additional icons, assign icons to applications, and add items to menus as needed. Applications created for the KDE Desktop can interact via drag-and-drop and cut-and-paste. Although non-KDE applications cannot use all KDE features (such as drag-and-drop), you can add any application to a KDE menu or assign it to an icon on the KDE Desktop.

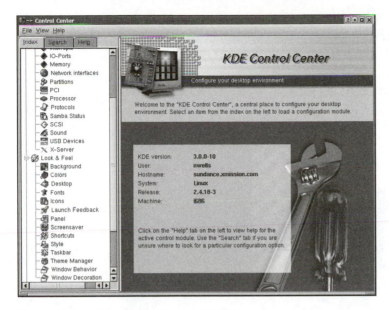

Figure 5-13 The KDE Control Center

New features are added to KDE each year by a worldwide staff of volunteer programmers, designers, writers, and translators. To learn more about the KDE project, visit the Web site *www.kde.org*.

When KDE is installed on a Linux system, the KDE components are integrated into the standard X Window System configuration files, so that the KDE window manager (called `kwm`) and related KDE programs are launched when you log in from a graphical login prompt or execute the `startx` command.

 Remember that you can use the `switchdesk` utility in Red Hat Linux to switch to the KDE Desktop if you have installed KDE on your system. If you are using Gnome as your desktop but have installed KDE, you can still access all KDE applications from the KDE menus item on the Gnome main menu.

The standard KDE installation places all KDE files in the directory `/opt/kde`. Some systems, including Red Hat Linux, place KDE components in a different directory such as `/usr`. In addition, the home directory of each user who runs KDE contains a subdirectory named `.kde`. This subdirectory contains configuration files specific to that user for any KDE applications the user has executed or reconfigured.

The Gnome Desktop

As KDE was first becoming popular, a group of developers within the Linux community became concerned about the fact that KDE was based on a graphical library that was not licensed using the GPL. The entire KDE project now uses an OpenSource license, but because of this concern, a new desktop project based on the GPL was founded: the Gnu Object Model Environment (GNOME, usually written as Gnome).

Gnome is a desktop interface very similar to KDE. It includes a Panel with an integrated taskbar (containing a button for each running application). Icons on the desktop let you launch commonly used applications or data files. A main menu provides quick access to dozens of applications written to take advantage of the look and functionality of Gnome. The applications included with Gnome are similar to those provided with KDE. They include a powerful file manager, personal productivity applications, and system maintenance utilities. Figure 5-14 shows the Gnome Desktop with a file manager window.

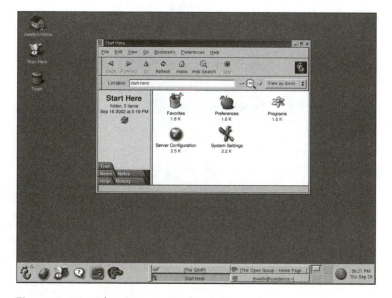

Figure 5-14   The Gnome Desktop

From the beginning, the Gnome project received encouragement and financial support from Red Hat Software. As a result, Red Hat and Mandrake Linux (which is based on Red Hat) are the only major Linux distributions that include Gnome. Because Red Hat is the largest Linux distributor, Gnome enjoys a large following of supporters.

You can configure many features of Gnome by opening the main menu and choosing Programs, Settings, then the item you want to configure (for example, Desktop, then Background). Figure 5-15 shows one of the configuration tools in Gnome.

In later chapters you will learn about many features of KDE and Gnome by exploring various system administration utilities that these desktop environments provide.

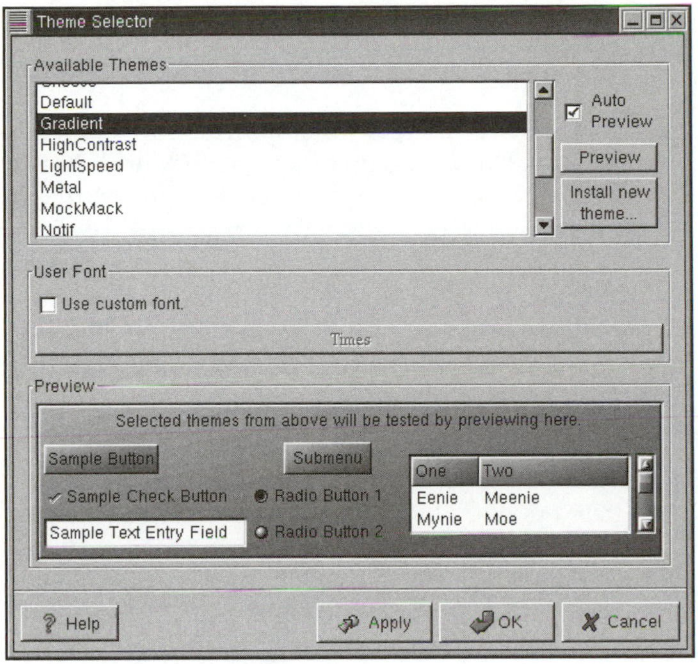

Figure 5-15   Configuring Gnome features

Using a Graphical Login Screen

If the installation of Linux is successful, most Linux distributions will start the system in run level 5 rather than run level 3. As explained in Chapter 4, run level 5 is equivalent to the standard operating mode (run level 3) except that run level 5 always provides a graphical interface. After Linux starts and initializes, it switches immediately to graphics mode and displays a graphical login screen. Once the username and password have been entered, a standard graphical system such as **fvwm**, Gnome, or KDE is launched.

 To change the run level used by default as the Linux system starts, set the value in the `initdefault` line of the `/etc/inittab` file.

The graphical login screen is provided by the X display manager. This program is called **xdm**; versions specific to KDE and Gnome are called **kdm** and **gdm**, respectively. Each operates in much the same way. **xdm** is started by the **init** program as Linux boots. Any time a user exits the graphical environment, **xdm** is restarted automatically to provide a graphical login screen. Thus the user never encounters a character-mode screen—a fact that can make new users much more comfortable with Linux. The **xdm** program is installed as part of the X Window System.

When a user logs in using an **xdm** graphical login screen, **xdm** selects which programs to start based on the session chosen by the user. A **session** defines a set of graphical programs to run when a user logs in.

A configuration file called **xsession** specifies which programs are started by a particular session name. When **xdm** starts X (after a user logs in), it executes the file **/etc/X11/xdm/Xsession** to determine which X clients to launch. The **Xsession** file contains a set of instructions that match the names of sessions defined for **xdm**. For example, if the user selects the **failsafe** session, the **Xsession** script only launches an **xterm** program; if the user selects a KDE session, **Xsession** starts all of the standard KDE components. A per-user configuration file named **.xsession** (all lowercase, beginning with a period) can be placed in a user's home directory to control which sessions that user has available. The available session types are normally common to all users, however, so using an **.xsession** file in a home directory is unusual.

You can configure the features of **xdm** in various text files in the **/etc/X11/xdm** subdirectory. Most users will rely on either **kdm** or **gdm**, both of which you can configure using graphical tools in KDE and Gnome. In KDE, choose Preferences, then System, then Login Manager to set up **kdm**. In Gnome, choose Programs, System, GDM Configurator to set up **gdm**. Figure 5-16 shows a sample configuration screen from the GDM Configurator.

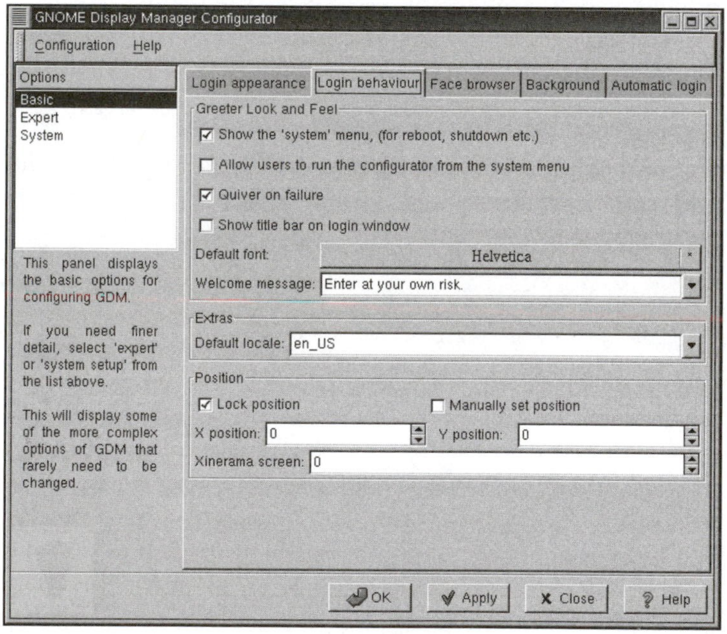

Figure 5-16   The GDM Configurator

CHAPTER SUMMARY

❑ The X Window System is a powerful and flexible graphical environment that was developed by MIT. The XFree86 Project later created a version for Intel-based Linux and UNIX.

❑ Components of X include the X server that interacts with the video card, and the X client, a graphical application that uses the services of the X server. These two components can be located on different computers.

❑ Commercial X servers are available for Linux. They add support for additional video cards and provide higher performance.

❑ A window manager or desktop interface provides the user interface to X. Older, basic window managers like **fvwm** and **twm** are still in use, but most Linux systems rely on a full desktop interface such as KDE or Gnome by default.

❑ Graphical libraries make it easier to create new graphical applications by letting applications share programming code and system resources. Two of the most widely used graphical libraries are Qt (on which KDE is based) and GTK+ (on which Gnome is based).

❑ The **DISPLAY** variable or **display** command-line option controls remote display of X applications. A remote host must permit an application to be displayed by another computer using either **xhost** or **xauth** functionality.

❑ X is often configured during Linux installation, but utilities such as **Xconfigurator**, **xf86config**, and others can help users configure X after installation.

❑ When X is launched, it relies on the **XF86Config-4** configuration file plus a number of scripts that define which X applications should be launched.

❑ Graphical applications include X resources such as windows, scroll bars, and fonts. Default settings control the appearance of these. The default can be altered; many applications also let users alter how resources for that application are displayed.

❑ The **xset** command controls aspects of X such as keyboard repeat rate and screen blanking.

❑ KDE provides a convenient desktop interface with icons, menus, and taskbars. It also includes many graphical applications for configuring the KDE interface.

❑ Gnome provides a similar desktop interface and also provides a set of productivity applications and system administration utilities very similar to those included with KDE.

❑ The graphical login prompt is provided by the **xdm** program, or the **kdm** or **gdm** program if KDE or Gnome is being used. These latter two programs can be graphically configured using utilities in KDE and Gnome.

Key Terms

.Xauthority — A file in a user's home directory that contains cookies defining remote access privileges for X servers and X clients.

background application — An application that does not stop the program that started it from going on to other tasks.

cookie — A numeric token used by a program to identify information about a host or user.

desktop environment — A graphical application that provides a comprehensive interface, including system menus, desktop icons, and the ability to manage files and launch applications easily.

desktop interface — Same as desktop environment.

DISPLAY — An environment variable that defines the host whose X server will be used to display graphical applications.

export — A command-line utility that makes an environment variable available to other applications.

Gnome — A desktop interface similar to KDE; developed in cooperation with Red Hat Software and used principally on Red Hat Linux and distributions derived from that version.

graphical libraries — Collections of programming functions that an X client can use to create and manage the elements of a graphical environment more efficiently.

K Desktop Environment (KDE) — The most widely used desktop environment for Linux systems.

MIT Magic Cookie — A type of cookie used by the **xauth** security system to control remote access to an X server.

Project Athena — The project sponsored by DEC and MIT to create a graphical environment or windowing system for UNIX.

resource database — A file that defines how an X resource should appear on-screen.

session — A configuration that defines a set of graphical programs to run when a user logs in.

set — A command-line utility that lists all currently defined environment variables.

startx — The standard command used to start an X Window System session from a text-mode command line.

window manager — A special-purpose graphical application (X client) that controls the position and manipulation of the windows within a graphical user interface.

X client — A graphical application.

X resource — The separate screen elements of a graphical application, such as scroll bars, text fonts, mouse pointers, and title bars for windows or dialog boxes.

X server — The program that communicates with the video card to create images on the screen.

xauth — A security system that controls remote access to an X server by means of numeric tokens shared between users who are authorized to use a remote X server.

Xconfigurator — A utility in Red Hat Linux for configuring the X Window System.

xf86config — A standard text-based utility for configuring the X Window System.

xhost — A command-line utility that permits users on a host (or all hosts) to use the X server on the computer where the command is executed.

xrdb — A command that loads an initial X database resource file or merges additional resource configuration details.

xset — A command that adjusts the behavior of X by controlling features such as key repeat rate, EnergyStar monitor features, mouse acceleration, and the screen blanker.

5

REVIEW QUESTIONS

1. The historical beginnings of the X Window System originated with:

    a. Project Athena

    b. Early versions of Microsoft Windows

    c. The Apple Macintosh computer

    d. The XFree86 Project

2. Why might a person choose a commercial X server instead of using XFree86?

3. Describe the function of an X server within the X Window System.

4. A(n) _____ is another name for any graphical application running in the X Window System.

    a. window manager

    b. X client

    c. **xinit** program

    d. X resource

5. Name four window managers that can be used with the X Window System on Linux.

6. A window manager is best described as:

    a. A special-purpose X client that provides core graphical functionality for other X clients

    b. The management tool that administers the underlying X server

    c. The program that communicates directly with a video card in order to create windows on a computer's screen

    d. An optional component used to improve the appearance of some graphical applications

7. Name the two graphical libraries used by the two major desktop environments of Linux.

8. A graphical library is best described as:

   a. The functions that control the video card

   b. A collection of functions that any graphical program can use to create a common look and feel

   c. The configuration program used to set up X

   d. The X client that draws all windows and handles mouse and keyboard input

9. To view an X application remotely on a Windows-based computer, you must add a(n) _____ to the Windows computer.

   a. X client

   b. `xinit` program

   c. X server package

   d. Qt library package

10. The X Window System files are normally located in which subdirectory in Linux?

    a. `/etc/X`

    b. `/usr/share`

    c. `/opt/kde`

    d. `/usr/X11R6`

11. Choosing not to run X:

    a. Is pointless because it runs in the background anyway

    b. Can cause configuration problems on server-based systems

    c. Saves the system resources that the X server would have consumed

    d. Would be unreasonable on a Linux system used as an Internet server

12. The `Xconfigurator` program is a standard X configuration tool in which Linux distribution?

    a. SuSE Linux

    b. TurboLinux

    c. Debian Linux

    d. Red Hat Linux

13. Name four programs that you can use to configure the XFree86 X server programs.

14. Explain why configuring the X server can be challenging, but configuring other components of X is fairly straightforward.

15. The _____ program provides an insecure but easy to use method of permitting other computers to use your X server.

    a. `xhost`

    b. `xauth`

    c. `Xsession`

    d. `xinit`

16. Graphical programs use the X server that is:

    a. Defined by the `--display` option of the command, unless a `DISPLAY` variable defines a different X server

    b. Always on the same system as the program is running

    c. Defined by the `DISPLAY` environment variable, or the `--display` option if it is included with the command

    d. Listed in the `xinitrc` script file

17. Besides the standard configuration programs available for Linux, describe four other methods of obtaining information to help you configure X.

18. The _____ command normally used to launch the X Window System is:

    a. `xinit`

    b. `startx`

    c. `xdm`

    d. `xinitrc`

19. The `xinit` program searches for a variety of configuration files, including which of the following?

    a. `/etc/startx`

    b. `/etc/X11/xinit/xinitrc`

    c. `/opt/kde/share/config/kdmrc`

    d. `/tmp/xsession`

20. Name four configuration files that `xinit` checks for as it launches X.

21. To function correctly, the `startx` and `xinit` programs require that:

    a. A symbolic link named `/usr/X11R6/bin/X` is created to point to an X server program

    b. The `xdm` program has been properly configured

    c. All of the X client scripts have the 644 file permission assigned

    d. X resources have not been modified by the root user

22. Name three features associated with a modern desktop environment.

23. An `xdm` session is normally defined by information in:

    a. An `Xsession` file

    b. The resource database

    c. The KDE login manager screen

    d. An `Xclients` file

5

24. The **xrdb** command is used to manage:

    a. X resources using X resource database files

    b. Automatic execution of X applications

    c. The configuration of a screen saver application

    d. The display manager **xdm**

25. The **xdm** program is started by the _____ program (or script).

    a. **init**

    b. **startx**

    c. **xinit**

    d. **xrdb**

HANDS-ON PROJECTS

Project 5-1

In this project you experiment with other desktop interfaces. To complete this project you should have Red Hat Linux 7.3 installed, including both the Gnome and KDE options as described in Chapter 3.

1. Log in to Red Hat Linux. The Gnome Desktop appears by default.

2. Open the main menu of Gnome by clicking on the footprint button in the lower left corner of the screen. Click on **Programs**, then **System**, then **Desktop Switching Tool**.

3. If you prefer, you can open a command-line window in Gnome by clicking on the third icon from the left and then enter the command **switchdesk**.

4. Choose the **KDE** item in the Desktop Switcher window.

5. Click **OK**.

6. A message box informs you that the change has been made but that you must restart the X Window System. Choose **OK** to close that message box.

7. Choose **Log out** on the main menu of Gnome.

8. A confirmation dialog box appears. Make sure that Logout is selected (rather than Reboot or Shut down). Choose **Yes**.

9. When the graphical login prompt appears, log in normally.

10. If necessary, click **No** when asked to make KDE the default desktop. After a moment, a Kpersonalizer window appears. Choose the **Skip Wizard** button in the lower left corner of the window. Choose **Quit and Keep** to confirm that you want to exit the Wizard. (If you have used KDE previously on this computer, the KDE desktop appears without pausing to display this window; if you wish, you can go through the wizard screens to personalize your KDE settings.)

11. If necessary, click **Close** in the Kandalf's Useful-Tip's Window. After the KDE desktop appears, review its icons and main menu items. Notice the ways that KDE differs from Gnome. (If a "Tip" window appears as you work in KDE, click on the title bar of the window and drag it out of your way, or click in the upper right corner of the window to close it.)

12. Open a command-line window by clicking on the third icon from the bottom left corner. If necessary, close the Tip Window.

13. In the command-line window, enter the command `ls ~/.Xclients*`. One of the files that appears ends with the host name of your computer.

14. Use the **cat** command to view the contents of the .Xclients file that ends with your hostname. Notice that the file includes the command to launch KDE.

15. Use the **rm** command to remove the .Xclients file that ends with your hostname.

16. Choose **OK**, then choose **OK** to close the message box that appears.

17. Choose **Logout** from the KDE main menu, then choose **Logout** in the message box that appears to confirm this action.

18. When the graphical login prompt appears, log in normally.

Project 5-2

In this project you work with another student to run a graphical program remotely. To complete this project you should work with another student and have two Linux-based computers; the steps here assume that both systems have the graphical environment configured, though to run an application remotely, only the system providing the X server needs to have a graphical environment configured. The two computers should be connected via a correctly configured network.

1. Both you and your fellow student should log in to your respective systems.

2. Choose one system to be the X client system. Open a command-line window in the graphical environment on this system.

3. On the X client system, enter the command **hostname** and write down the results that are displayed. This is the name of the X client computer on the network.

4. The other system is the X server system. Open a command-line window in the graphical environment on the X server system and execute the **hostname** command. Write down the name of the X server system.

5. On the X server system, enter this command, substituting the name of the X client system for the word *hostname* in the command:

   xhost +*hostname*

6. You have given permission for the X client to display an application on the X server. Now go to the X client system.

5

7. Enter this command on the X client system, substituting the name of the X server system where *hostname* is shown here:

```
gedit --display hostname:0.0
```

8. You see the `gedit` text editor on the X server system. Press **Ctrl+C** on the X client system. The `gedit` window on the X server disappears as the program exits.

9. Enter these commands on the X client, using the name of the X server system for the *hostname*:

```
DISPLAY=hostname:0.0
```

```
export DISPLAY
```

```
gedit
```

10. The `gedit` program appears on the X server system. Because your `DISPLAY` variable is set, you don't need to include the `display` option, but *all* programs executed on the X client system will now appear on the X server system. Press **Ctrl+C** on the X client system to end the `gedit` program.

11. Execute this command on the X client system to restore the `DISPLAY` variable to its previous value, so that applications executed on the X client system will be displayed on that system:

```
DISPLAY=:0.0
```

```
export DISPLAY
```

12. Execute this command on the X server system so that no other computers have permission to display applications on the X server system:

```
xhost —
```

Project 5-3

In this project you change settings for the graphical login prompt used by Gnome—the `gdm` program. To complete this project you must have an installed Linux system with root access.

1. Log in to the Linux system using a regular username and password.

2. At the Gnome Desktop, open the main menu and choose **Programs**, then **System**, then **GDM Configurator**.

3. You are prompted to enter the root password before this utility runs. Enter the root password and choose **OK**.

4. When the GDM Configurator window appears, make sure the Options list on the left side of the window has the word **Basic** selected.

5. Select the **Login Behaviour** tab and find the Welcome message field.

6. In this field, type the following welcome message that will be displayed as part of the graphical login prompt:

Enter at your own risk

7. Choose **OK** on the bottom of the GDM Configurator window.

8. In the confirmation message box that appears, choose **Restart after logout**.

9. Log out of Gnome.

10. Notice the new message that appears in the graphical login prompt based on the text you entered.

CASE PROJECTS

5

1. Your latest consulting client is the Starwood movie studio. The studio has decided to create a movie using computer animation and wants to use Linux-based computers to help with some of the graphical work required. Because this project will use some of the more unusual features of the planned video card, you decide to experiment with `xf86config` program to see what features it will help you configure. Use the `mv` command to rename your `/etc/X11/XF86Config-4` file to some other name, then run the `xf86config` command, study the questions it asks, and give your best responses based on what you know about your system. When you are done experimenting, use a text editor to compare the configuration file created by `xf86config` with the file you were already using. Then use the `rm` command to delete the configuration file created by `xf86config`. Use the `mv` command to restore the `XF86Config-4` file to its correct location and filename so the X server can find it.

2. After you have installed Linux and configured the new high-performance video cards successfully, the studio asks you to adjust the system to display a nonstandard resolution of 1420 × 865 pixels to meet some special film requirements. You know that X is flexible enough to do this, but the configuration tools don't provide this screen resolution as an option. How will you learn more about the video card capabilities and X configuration in order to grant this odd request?

3. As the movie winds down production, and all the graphics work is done, the studio asks you to prepare the Linux systems to be used as regular desktop workstations in the studio. How will you configure the graphical portion of Linux to be used by the inexperienced workers in that section of the studio? Which desktop interface will you use and why? What components of that desktop help you make your decision?

USING THE SHELL AND TEXT FILES

After reading this chapter and completing the exercises, you will be able to:

♦ Describe how a Linux shell operates

♦ Customize your shell environment

♦ Use common text editors to create or modify text files

♦ Describe popular text-processing methods and tools used on Linux

In the previous chapter you learned about using a graphical system on Linux. You learned how to locate and configure X Window System programs using a variety of utilities. You also learned about the scripts that control how the X Window System is launched. The KDE and Gnome desktop environments were introduced, including descriptions of some basic features of those desktops, such as file managers and graphical login prompts.

In this chapter you learn about how a Linux command-line environment—a shell—operates and how you can customize it to fit your preferences or those of other users on a Linux system. Most Linux system administrators spend a lot of time working in the shell environment; the better you can customize and navigate in the shell, the more efficiently you can use system administration utilities. One of the most-used utilities is a text editor. Although many graphical configuration tools are available, every system administrator needs to become skilled at using at least a couple of popular text editors, like those described in this chapter. More advanced system administrators also use text processing tools to modify text files automatically. Several popular text processing utilities are described in the last part of this chapter.

UNDERSTANDING THE SHELL

In previous chapters you learned that the shell is the command interpreter, or command-line environment, for Linux. You learned a few basic commands such as `ls` to list files and `rm` to delete files. In the first part of this chapter you learn more about how the shell operates and how it interacts with the Linux kernel.

In many operating systems, a command interpreter is a foundation or fundamental application. A **command interpreter** is a program that accepts input from the keyboard and uses that input to launch commands or otherwise control the computer system. The most well-known command interpreter is probably the `COMMAND.COM` program, which was part of every system based on older operating systems such as DOS or Windows 98. This command interpreter can provide a C:> prompt where a user can enter commands via the keyboard.

In Linux (or any UNIX-like system), the command interpreter (called the shell) has a very different relationship with the kernel and with users compared to the DOS/Windows model. In Linux:

- The shell is only loaded when a user logs in at a text-mode login prompt or in some other way specifically requests that a shell be launched.

- The shell is like any other program running on Linux. It has no special privileges, no special relationship with the Linux kernel, and no special capabilities.

- Different types of shells are available for Linux. A user can choose which shell best suits his or her preferences or environment.

As you learned in Chapter 4, when you first boot a Linux-based computer, the kernel starts the `init` program, which launches all of the system services that have been configured by the installation process or by the system administrator. The `init` program displays a login prompt (text-based or graphical), but does not start a shell. Two reasons for the initial lack of a shell are:

- Linux is often used as a network server. Because no user is directly using the system (entering commands to launch programs), a shell is not needed. Instead, network services such as a Web server watch for incoming network requests and handle those requests appropriately.

- Linux security requires that no one can access the system until a valid username and password have been entered. Because a user cannot enter any commands until first logging in, no shell is required until a user has logged in.

Network services such as Web servers access files on Linux through a regular user account. This means that a network service is governed by the permissions assigned to its user account. For example, suppose you are using a Web browser to request a particular file from the Web server. The Web server can only retrieve the requested file if its user account has permission to access that file. As a result, the Web server controls what the Web browser can access; you are not free to explore the files on the server as if you were logged in to the server.

When a user logs in from a text-mode login prompt, a default shell is started, which in turn provides a shell prompt where the user can enter commands. After the user logs in from a graphical login prompt, the user does *not* see a shell prompt, because it is not strictly necessary. Instead, the user can manipulate the graphical environment (such as KDE or Gnome), which in turn can launch programs as needed. If you want to access the shell from a graphical environment, you can start one.

Working in a shell has the advantage of great flexibility: you can interact with any file that you have permission to access, you can launch any program on the system, and you can use special features of the shell (described shortly) to work more efficiently. Some users don't care about these advantages; they prefer a graphical environment that requires less training to use. However, the capabilities that are immediately accessible in a graphical environment are limited. For example, users of a graphical desktop can only launch the programs that are included in menus and submenus, and they do not have immediate access to every file on the system. Whether you use a shell or another way of interacting with the Linux kernel depends on the tasks you want to perform and the desktop environment you prefer.

The Shell Prompt

Figure 6-1 shows a standard shell prompt that appears after logging in to Linux using a text-mode login prompt or after starting a shell within a graphical environment. The **shell prompt** is a set of words or characters indicating that the shell is ready to accept commands that you enter. The default shell prompt includes four components:

- The user account name that you used to log in (the first **nwells** in Figure 6-1).

- The hostname of the computer that you logged in to (**sundance** in Figure 6-1).

- The last part of the full directory path for your current working directory (the second **nwells** in Figure 6-1, which is the last part of the full directory path **/home/nwells**).

- A prompt character (the ending **$** in Figure 6-1).

Figure 6-1   A standard shell prompt

Although you can alter the information provided in the shell prompt, the default setting shown here is usually an appropriate choice. The username and hostname help you keep track of your location within a networked environment where you might connect to multiple computers. The last part of your current working directory helps you keep track of your location within the directory structure. Although seeing the full path would be helpful in some cases, a long directory path would be unwieldy, so only the last part of the path is included in the default shell prompt.

The prompt character used in the standard Linux shell is a dollar sign, $. Other shells use different prompt characters, such as a percent sign, %. On all shells, when you log in as root (the superuser), the prompt character changes to a hash mark, #. This makes it easier for you to determine as you work whether you have root permission or not. Remember that you should not use the root account unless you are completing system administration tasks.

 Sometimes a command that you have executed provides its own prompt where you can enter commands similar to a shell environment. When you exit that program you return to the shell itself. Programs that provide their own prompt use a different character so you can tell that you are not working in the Linux shell. For example, when you run the at command (described in Chapter 11), the prompt changes to a > character.

The Functions of a Shell

The purpose of a shell is to make it easy for users to launch programs and work with files in Linux. That simple definition doesn't entirely capture the features of the shells you use in Linux, but it explains the basic rationale behind their design.

A shell's primary purpose is to launch programs. When you use the `ls` command to view the files in a directory, or use the `mv` command to rename a file, or use the `more` command to view a file, you are actually launching a program that performs those tasks. The shell processes the information entered at the keyboard and uses it to launch the program. In many cases, the information you enter on a command line includes parameters, such as the name of the file to copy and the location to copy it to. The shell passes these parameters to the program being launched. For example, entering the following command line at a shell prompt causes the shell to launch the `cp` command, handing it the two parameters `report.doc` and `report.doc.bak`. In this command, the `cp` command must decide what to do with the parameters, or return an error message if it cannot determine how to process the parameters.

```
$ cp report.doc report.doc.bak
$
```

> **Tip** If a standard Linux command is completed without any errors, the shell prompt returns with no feedback at all. This is confusing at first, but it works well when you are creating automatically executed commands (described in Chapter 11).

If you enter the following command at a shell prompt, the shell tries to start a program called `report.doc` and hand that program the parameters `report.doc.bak` and `cp`. Because no program named `report.doc` exists, the shell (bash) returns an error message stating that it could not locate the requested command.

```
$ report.doc report.doc.bak cp
bash: report.doc: command not found
$
```

Besides the ability to start programs, the shell has many built-in features that help you work with files and commands on a Linux system. For example, from the shell, you can use keyboard shortcuts to enter long commands quickly, and you can control multiple programs that you have started from the shell prompt. In addition, you can define variables (assign numbers or strings to a name) to make your shell environment easier to use or to provide information (the values of variables) that other programs can access when needed.

A particularly important feature of a Linux shell is that it gives users the ability to write scripts that the shell can execute. A **script** is like a program or a macro. (A **macro** is a set of commands that can be executed by referring to the name of the macro.) You have already seen several scripts, such as those executed during system start-up (in Chapter 4) and those executed when X starts up (in Chapter 5). A script is essentially a list of commands stored in a text file. Instead of entering each of these commands one by one at the command line, you can use a script to execute a series of commands automatically. You learn how to create your own shell scripts in Chapter 11.

Different Types of Shells

When UNIX was first created, its developers decided that the shell should be separate from the operating system. This meant that the shell could be changed later without affecting the operating system. As described in the previous section, the shell is just a regular program whose purpose is to launch other programs. The original shell for UNIX, written by Stephen Bourne, is called the **Bourne shell**. The Bourne shell program is called `sh` (for *shell*). Although the Bourne shell is standard on all UNIX and Linux systems, it is an old program with limited functionality (it was first written nearly 30 years ago).

True to the foresight of the developers of UNIX, other developers started with the Bourne shell and altered or enhanced it to provide new functionality. These later-generation shells are used on UNIX and Linux systems today. Table 6-1 shows the commonly available shells for Linux.

Table 6-1   Linux Shells

Shell name	Program name	Description
Bourne Again shell (`bash`)	`bash`	An enhanced and extended version of the Bourne shell created by the GNU project for use on many UNIX-like operating systems. Commonly referred to as the `bash` shell, rather than by its full name. `bash` is the default Linux shell.
Bourne shell	`sh`	The original UNIX shell. The `sh` program on Linux usually refers to the `bash` program. `bash` contains all `sh` functionality, plus interactive features such as history and tab completion (described later in this chapter) and shell programming via shell script files.
C shell	`csh`	A shell developed by Bill Joy in the 1970s. He focused on adding easy-to-use features for interactive work at the shell prompt. The C shell was the first to contain features similar to history and tab completion; these features were later added to the `bash` shell and other shells as well. The C shell uses a more complex syntax for shell programming than the Bourne and `bash` shells. Because of this, it is not popular for shell programming, though its interactive features make it popular with users who are not creating shell programs.
TENEX/TOPS C shell (also called the TC shell)	`tcsh`	An enhancement of the C shell. This is the version of the C shell that is commonly used on Linux systems.
Korn shell	`ksh`	A proprietary (not freely available) shell written by David Korn. The Korn shell is a revision of the Bourne shell that includes the interactive features of the C shell but maintains the Bourne shell programming syntax, which is considered easier to use than C shell programming syntax.

Table 6-1 Linux Shells (continued)

Shell name	Program name	Description
Public Domain Korn shell	`pdksh`	A version of the Korn shell that is freely available. (This shell is often accessed using the program named `ksh` on Linux systems.)
Z shell	`zsh`	A recently developed shell that combines Korn shell interactive features with the C shell programming syle (for those who prefer the more complex syntax of the C shell).

The default shell for all Linux systems is **bash** (pronounced as the word looks, "bash"). Users on a Linux system are normally content to use only the **bash** shell. Some experienced UNIX users, those who write a lot of shell scripts, or who need the features of another shell may use other shell programs. (The C shell and TC shell both use different shell programming methods than **bash**.)

Shells can be roughly divided into two groups based on the type of shell programming commands used. The two groups are:

- Those that follow the Bourne shell programming style (which is based on a very old programming language called ALGOL).

- Those that follow the C shell programming style (which is based on the widely used C programming language).

Further shell derivatives have combined features from different shells to make this grouping less distinct. For example, the Z shell includes many popular features of the **bash** shell but uses C shell-style programming. But the overall distinction between these two groups is still valid.

 Not all of the shells in Table 6-1 are installed by default or even included on the CD for all Linux distributions. Contact your Linux vendor or an Internet download site such as *www.linuxberg.com* or *rpmfind.net* to obtain a particular shell that is not included on your Linux CD.

In Linux, the shell started for each user is determined by the settings in the user account configuration file. Chapter 8 describes how you can set up or modify this configuration file. If the shell you want to use is installed on the Linux system, changing to a new default shell is very easy using the **usermod** command described in Chapter 8. Each user on the system can select a preferred shell independent of all other users.

To immediately run a different shell that is installed on the Linux system you are using, enter the name of that shell program. For example, if you are working in the standard **bash** shell but you want to run the C shell instead, enter this command:

```
$ csh
```

Entering Commands

Modern shells like `bash` and the Korn shell include features designed to simplify the process of entering commands and command parameters. Two of the most useful features are tab completion and history.

Using Tab Completion

Tab completion is a shell feature that lets you enter part of a file or directory name, press the Tab key, and have the shell fill in the remainder of the name. Using tab completion makes it easier to enter long or complex directory paths and filenames. This is helpful because Linux filenames can be very long, and they sometimes include punctuation, multiple digits or periods, and mixed upper- and lowercase. Because tab completion is a feature of the shell, it works whenever you are entering text at a shell prompt, no matter which command you are entering. Anytime the shell determines that you are trying to enter a command name, a filename, or a directory name, you can use tab completion.

For example, suppose you want to use the `rpm` command to install a new software package that you have downloaded and placed in the `/tmp` directory. The filename of the package is shown here:

```
desktop-backgrounds-1.1.2-6.noarch.rpm
```

To install this package, you enter the `rpm` command followed by the path and filename of the package. But for this example, suppose you just enter the following:

```
# rpm -Uvh /tmp/deskt
```

To use tab completion at this point, you press the Tab key. The shell looks at the contents of the `/tmp` directory for a file or subdirectory matching the first few letters you typed (`deskt`). Once the shell finds the package name, it fills in the remaining filename. Immediately after pressing Tab, you see this at the command line:

```
# rpm -Uvh /tmp/desktop-backgrounds-1.1.2-6.noarch.rpm
```

Now suppose the `/tmp` directory contains another file named `desktop`. Instead of filling in the full filename when you press Tab, the shell beeps to indicate that a unique matching name is not available. You can then press Tab a second time to have the shell fill in to the point where the filenames differ, then display all of the matching names, like this:

```
# rpm -Uvh /tmp/desktop
desktop    desktop-backgrounds-1.1.2-6.noarch.rpm
```

Depending on the situation in which you use tab completion, the shell will try to judge which items you want to access. For example, in some cases only program files (or script files with the `x` file permission set) will be compared to the text that you enter.

After reviewing this list of available files with similar names, you can type enough of the name to make it unique, and then press Tab again to fill in the complete filename. In this case, because the hyphen is the first character that distinguishes the two filenames, you would enter the following:

```
# rpm -Uvh /tmp/desktop-
```

When you first use tab completion, you may think it's more work than it's worth to keep pressing Tab and entering a few more letters if the filename is not unique. But after some practice, using tab completion to enter long filenames or paths becomes an automatic response—much easier than typing the complete file or directory name.

> When the first part of the name that you enter is a directory, tab completion fills in the directory name, ending with a forward slash. This means you can immediately begin typing the name of a subdirectory or file within that directory.

Using the History Feature

A second time-saving shell feature is the command history. The **command history** records each command that you enter at the shell prompt. You can quickly call up and repeat any command from this list without typing the command again. The list of recently entered commands is called the **history list**.

The simplest way to access the most recently executed command is to press the Up arrow key. To execute the command after it is displayed, press Enter. Pressing the Up arrow key repeatedly displays in turn each of the previously entered commands (the commands in the history list). Hold down the Up arrow key to see dozens of commands flash by at the shell prompt (the full contents of the history list). Press the Down arrow key to display commands farther down in the history list (those more recently entered).

When the command you want to repeat was entered some time ago, using the Up arrow key to locate it in a large history list can be tedious. In this situation, the `history` command is useful. The **history** command displays the entire history list, which normally includes at least 100 commands. The following shows the last few lines of a history list. (Of course, the commands and numbers in the history list on your system will differ from this sample output.)

```
33   who
34   vi /etc/passwd
35   gimp
36   cd /etc
37   cd X11/
38   cd xdm
39   more Xsession
40   rpm -qa |grep XFree
41   mount -t ext2 /dev/hda3 /mnt/openlinux/
42   mcopy /mnt/openlinux/etc/XF86Config-4 A:
43   file Xwrapper
```

```
44    umount /mnt/cdrom
45    type fvwm
46    exit
47    clear
48    mv ch05/ch04fig.zip ch04/
49    mv ch04/ch04fig.zip course_ch04/
50    cd course_ch04/
```

The length of the history list can make it difficult to locate quickly the command you want to reuse. You can use one of the following three methods to locate a previously executed command:

- Use the history number.

- Use the beginning of a command.

- Search the history list.

The term *history number* refers to the number to the left of each item in the history list. For example, in the history list above, the first item has a history number 33.

You can execute any of the commands in the history list by entering the number of that command prefixed by an exclamation point. An exclamation point is sometimes called a **bang** in UNIX and Linux. So to execute the most recent **mount** command, you would enter !41 (pronounced "bang-forty-one").

The shell displays the command matching that number and immediately executes it. You don't need to view the history list before using this technique if you already know the number of the command you want to execute. But be aware that the numbers change as you enter new commands.

To use the command name to repeat a command, use an exclamation point followed by the first part of the command you want to repeat. In the sample **history** output shown, you could execute the most recent **mount** command using this command:

```
#  !mou
```

When you execute this command, the shell searches for the most recent command that begins with the letters "mou" and executes it.

 When executing a command from the history list using any of the three methods described, remember that the commands are executed from your current working directory, which may be different from the directory where they were originally executed. If a command does not include a full pathname, you might see unexpected results. Be especially careful when using the partial command name method to reexecute a command without checking the full text of the command.

You can also search the history list without reexecuting a command to see what the command parameters were or how you completed a task. This method requires the use of a pipe symbol and the `grep` command, both of which are discussed in detail in Chapter 7. To use this method, enter the `history` command followed by the `grep` command and the command name you want to locate. For example, in the sample `history` output shown previously, suppose you want to search for a `mount` command to see what parameters it contains. The following command displays all items in the history list that contain the `mount` command. You can then review the displayed output to learn about the previously executed command.

```
# history | grep mount
```

The `bash` shell supports additional techniques for executing commands. But the examples shown here for using tab completion and the `history` command should help you enter commands much more efficiently in Linux. To learn more about these features, review the online manual page for the `bash` shell by entering `man bash`.

The Shell Start-up Process

You learned in Chapter 5 that certain scripts are executed each time the X Window System is launched. In a similar manner, several scripts are executed when you log in to Linux or start a new shell. These scripts initialize (or configure) various parts of your environment.

When a user first logs in to a Linux system, the script `/etc/profile` is executed. The `/etc/profile` script contains configuration information that applies to every user on the system. Each user's home directory can contain another start-up script called `.profile` (with an initial period). The `.profile` script in a user's home directory is also executed when the user logs in, but the `.profile` script is specific to a single user. Each user's home directory can contain a different `.profile` script. Only the root user can change the `/etc/profile` script; any user can change the `.profile` script in his or her home directory.

On some systems, additional scripts are executed when a user logs in. For example, on Red Hat Linux, a set of scripts located in the `/etc/profile.d` directory is started by the `/etc/profile` script. The scripts in `/etc/profile.d` add specific configuration information for KDE, a language selection, or other system features set up by the installation program. Red Hat Linux also uses a file called `.bash_profile` rather than the standard `.profile` script in each user's home directory.

The profile scripts are executed when a user logs in; additional scripts are executed when a user starts a shell. Because a shell is started immediately when a user logs in at a text-mode screen, these additional scripts are generally executed immediately after the profile scripts. A user working in a graphical environment can start multiple `bash` shells without logging in to Linux again. When a new shell is started by a user who is already logged in, the additional scripts described next (such as `/etc/bashrc`) are executed; however, the profile scripts are not executed again.

Some Linux distributions, including Red Hat Linux, provide an `/etc/bashrc` script that is executed for all users on the system each time a `bash` shell is started. Other Linux distributions rely on the `/etc/profile` script for configuration settings that should apply to all users, though this script is only executed at the time a user logs in.

Each user's home directory contains a script called `.bashrc`. The **`.bashrc`** script is executed each time the user starts a **bash** shell. Any configuration information that a user wants to add to his or her environment can be placed in the **`.bashrc`** file. Additional scripts with similar names are sometimes used on a Linux distribution. Examples include the following:

- **`.bash_default`**, which is executed each time a **bash** shell is started.
- **`.bash_login`**, which is executed each time a **bash** shell is started.
- **`.bash_logout`**, which is executed each time a user closes a **bash** shell.

You may find other scripts with similar names on your Linux distribution. In general, the names of these files describe when they are used. Consult your Linux vendor or try placing test commands in each file (see Chapter 11 for directions) if you are unsure of how the files are used. Figure 6-2 shows how a typical start-up script works when a user logs in to Linux.

```
/etc/profile ──▶ ~/.profile ──▶ /etc/bashrc ──▶ ~/.bashrc
                      or
               ~/.bash_profile
```

Figure 6-2   Shell scripts used at login and when launching a shell

 When a user logs in or starts a shell, the systemwide script file is executed, *followed by* the corresponding file in the user's home directory. When starting the X Window System (see Chapter 5), the system default file `/etc/X11/xinit/xinitrc` is executed *only* if the **xinit** program does not find a `.xinitrc` file in the user's home directory.

The scripts described here apply when a **bash** shell is started. Similar files are executed when a user chooses to work with a C shell, Korn shell, or other shell. For example, a user's home directory may contain a file called `.cshrc` or `.kshrc`. These scripts would be executed each time a C shell or Korn shell was started, respectively. Because the script format is different for each type of shell, different script files are needed to initialize each shell. These configuration scripts can coexist in a user's home directory (and in the `/etc` directory, for systemwide configuration files), each one being executed only when the corresponding shell is launched.

CUSTOMIZING THE SHELL

The configuration scripts that Linux executes when a user logs in, or that **bash** executes when a shell is launched, provide a place where users can customize the Linux environment in which they work. The following sections describe several methods of customizing the shell environment. These features are separate from any customization that a user or system administrator may choose to do within a graphical environment.

Using Aliases

An **alias** is a string of characters that is substituted for another string of characters at the shell prompt. The **alias** command lets you define an alias for text you enter at a shell prompt. The general format of the **alias** command looks like this:

```
alias <string entered by user>=<string substituted by the shell>
```

For example, suppose that you are continually mistyping the `mount` command as `muont`. You could create an alias that corrects your typing error automatically:

```
alias muont=mount
```

With this alias in effect, each time you enter the string `muont` at the shell prompt, the shell replaces it with the string `mount`.

After you create an alias, each time you enter aliased text at a command prompt, the shell substitutes one string of characters for the other that you defined. You must be careful when you create an alias that uses an existing command name. For example, entering the command `alias more=less` would render the `more` command inoperative, because every time you entered `more`, the shell would substitute the string `less`. Many Linux distributions include a few aliases as part of the default configuration by placing them in the `/etc/profile` or `/etc/bashrc` script.

To see a list of aliases that are in effect, enter the `alias` command without any text after it.

When the string substituted by the shell contains a space, it must be enclosed in quotation marks. For example:

```
alias ll="ls -la"
alias rm="rm -i"
alias cp="cp -i"
```

The `alias` command is useful in several circumstances, including those listed here:

- Aliases can shorten long commands. For example, if you regularly enter a command with many options, create an alias so you can enter that command with just two or three characters.

- Aliases can correct typing or spelling mistakes. For example, if you always enter `sl` instead of `ls`, you can create an alias that makes `sl=ls`. Aliases can help people new to Linux use the system without knowing all of the commands perfectly.

- Aliases can protect you from erasing or damaging files by automatically inserting options with commands that are used to delete files. For example, the `alias` command shown previously for the `cp` command (`alias cp="cp -i"`) causes the shell always to execute the `cp` command with the `-i` option, which prevents overwriting files when copying.

- Aliases can add command names that you prefer to use, but that are not part of Linux by default. For example, you can use an alias to substitute the string `mv` for `rename`.

Of course, using aliases for these purposes won't help you master Linux commands, nor will it improve your typing skills. But used wisely, aliases can make tasks proceed more quickly as you work at a Linux command line.

 Entering the `alias` command causes that alias to be active only as part of the current shell. If you decide on additional `alias` commands that you want to use regularly, add them to the `.bashrc` file in your home directory so that they are executed each time you start a shell.

Symbolic Links

Symbolic links are a feature of the Linux file system. They are not part of the shell, but they can make working in the shell easier. Symbolic links are also sometimes confused with aliases in the shell, so they are described here to avoid that confusion. Chapter 9 describes symbolic links in more technical detail.

A **symbolic link** is a file that refers to another file or directory, rather than containing data itself. For example, suppose several employees in a company want to work on the same file. The system administrator can place the file in a directory and then create a symbolic link in each user's home directory to access the real file. If the real file is `/tmp/report.doc`, the symbolic links might be `/home/nwells/report.doc`, `/home/davis/newreport.doc`, and `/home/laura/report.doc`.

Assuming the real file, `/tmp/report.doc`, has sufficient file permissions, all three users can access it by opening the respective files in their home directories. The file system follows the symbolic link to the file that it points to and opens that file. When users make changes after opening the file in their home directory, they are all changing the same file. Figure 6-3 illustrates a symbolic link.

Symbolic links are used when the same data must be accessed from two locations in the directory structure, or by two (or more) different names. Using a symbolic link takes only a few bytes of hard disk space—enough to store the filename that the link refers to. Symbolic links are commonly used in directories such as `/lib` and `/usr/lib`, where a system file must be referred to by several names in order for programs to find it.

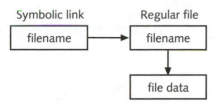

Figure 6-3   A symbolic link

You can identify symbolic links by using the `ls -l` command. For example, part of the output from the command `ls -l /lib` is shown below. In the far left column, a symbolic link is indicated by the letter *l*. In the last column, the filename after the arrow (`->`) is the file to which the symbolic link points.

```
-rwxr-xr-x     1 root       root        5177 Apr 15 09:27 libBrokenLocale-2.2.5.so
lrwxrwxrwx     1 root       root          24 Sep 18 16:55 libBrokenLocale.so.1 ->
   libBroken Locale-2.2.5.so
-rwxr-xr-x     1 root       root     1260480 Apr 15 09:44 libc-2.2.5.so
lrwxrwxrwx     1 root       root          11 Sep 18 17:35 libcap.so -> libcap.so.1
lrwxrwxrwx     1 root       root          14 Sep 18 17:00 libcap.so.1 -> libcap.so.1.10
-rw-r--r--     1 root       root       39215 Feb 28  2002 libcap.so.1.10
```

Graphical file manager windows indicate a symbolic link using a special icon. Figure 6-4 shows a Gnome file manager window with the contents of the `/lib` directory. The small arrow in the upper right corner of the file's icon marks a file as a symbolic link.

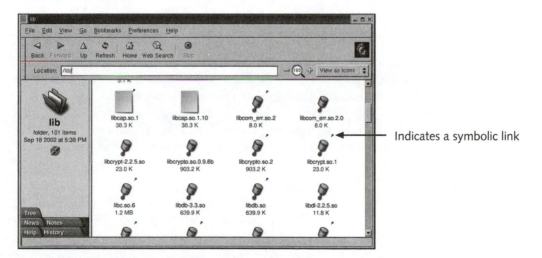

Figure 6-4   Viewing a symbolic link in a graphical file manager

To create a symbolic link, use the `ln` command with the `-s` option. The syntax of this command is:

```
ln -s <existing file> <symbolic link to be created>
```

For example, if you have a file called `report-8-10-03.doc` in your home directory and you want to create a symbolic link in the `/tmp` directory named `report.doc`, you would use the following command:

```
ln -s /home/nwells/report-8-10-03.doc /tmp/report.doc
```

In the command above, you could use relative pathnames depending on your current working directory.

 Don't confuse shell aliases and symbolic links. An alias causes the shell to substitute a different string in text that you enter. A symbolic link causes the file system to pass a request for one file to a different file in the directory structure.

Environment Variables

As you learned in Chapter 4, environment variables are settings, or values, available to any program launched by a particular user. Each user has a separate set of environment variables available to programs launched by that user. Each environment variable is assigned a value. For example, the value of the `HOME` environment variable is the path to a user's home directory. The `USER` environment variable has the value of the current user account name. The `OSTYPE` environment variable holds the string `Linux`.

Many programs use environment variables to obtain information about your environment or about how a particular program should function. For example, a program might use the `HOME` variable to determine where to look for a user's data files. A program might also expect that certain environment variables have been set up specifically for the use of that program. For example, the documentation for a database program may state that before launching the program, you must define an environment variable named `DB_DIR` that defines the directory where the database files are located. If you execute the database program without first setting this environment variable, the program will not function correctly. (The program would normally display an error message indicating the problem.) When programs need certain environment variables set, you should include a command to set those variables either in the systemwide start-up scripts or in a specific user's start-up scripts (if only one user runs the program in question).

The initialization scripts or start-up scripts that are run when Linux is booted or when a user logs in create many environment variables and assign values to them. Each time a user starts a program, the environment of that new program is taken from (inherited from) the program that launched it. When you open a shell within a graphical environment, the shell inherits all the environment variables of that graphical environment. If you launch a program from the shell, that program inherits all of the environment variables from the shell.

The **set** command displays a list of all environment variables defined in your current environment. The output of the **set** command for a regular user (not root) on Red Hat Linux 7.3 is shown below. Many variables listed by **set** are used by system processes with which you are not yet familiar, but you will recognize some of them. For example, the PWD variable contains the value of the current working directory. When you execute the **pwd** command, the value of this environment variable is dispalyed on the screen. When you use the **cd** command, the value of this variable is updated.

```
$ set
BASH=/bin/bash
BASH_VERSINFO=([0]="2" [1]="05a" [2]="0" [3]="1" [4]="release"
[5]="i686-pc-linux-gnu")
BASH_VERSION='2.05a.0(1)-release'
COLORS=/etc/DIR_COLORS
COLORTERM=gnome-terminal
COLUMNS=80
DIRSTACK=()
DISPLAY=:0
EUID=500
GDMSESSION=Default
GDM_LANG=en_US.iso885915
GNOME_SESSION_NAME=Default
GROUPS=()
HISTFILE=/home/nwells/.bash_history
HISTFILESIZE=1000
HISTSIZE=1000
HOME=/home/nwells
HOSTNAME=sundance.xmission.com
HOSTTYPE=i686
IFS=$' \t\n'
INPUTRC=/etc/inputrc
LANG=en_US.iso885915
LESSOPEN='|/usr/bin/lesspipe.sh %s'
LINES=24
LOGNAME=nwells
LS_COLORS='no=00:fi=00:di=01;34:ln=01;36:pi=40;33:so=01;35:bd=40;3
3;01:cd=40;33;01:or=01;05;37;41:mi=01;05;37;41:ex=01;32:*.cmd=01;3
2:*.exe=01;32:*.com=01;32:*.btm=01;32:*.bat=01;32:*.sh=01;32:*.csh
=01;32:*.tar=01;31:*.tgz=01;31:*.arj=01;31:*.taz=01;31:*.lzh=01;31
:*.zip=01;31:*.z=01;31:*.Z=01;31:*.gz=01;31:*.bz2=01;31:*.bz=01;31
:*.tz=01;31:*.rpm=01;31:*.cpio=01;31:*.jpg=01;35:*.gif=01;35:*.bmp
=01;35:*.xbm=01;35:*.xpm=01;35:*.png=01;35:*.tif=01;35:'
MACHTYPE=i686-pc-linux-gnu
MAIL=/var/spool/mail/nwells
MAILCHECK=60
OLDPWD=/etc/profile.d
OPTERR=1
OPTIND=1
OSTYPE=linux-gnu
PATH=/bin:/usr/bin:/usr/bin/X11:/usr/local/bin:/usr/bin:/usr/X11R6
/bin:/home/nwells/bin:/home/nwells/bin
PIPESTATUS=([0]="0")
```

```
PPID=10596
PROMPT_COMMAND='echo -ne
 "\033]0;${USER}@${HOSTNAME%%.*}:${PWD/$HOME/~}\007"'
PS1='[\u@\h \W]\$ '
PS2='> '
PS4='+ '
PWD=/home/nwells
QTDIR=/usr/lib/qt3-gcc2.96
SESSION_MANAGER=local/sundance.xmission.com:/tmp/.ICE-unix/10328
SHELL=/bin/bash
SHELLOPTS=braceexpand:hashall:histexpand:monitor:history:
interactive-comments:emacs
SHLVL=3
SSH_ASKPASS=/usr/libexec/openssh/gnome-ssh-askpass
SUPPORTED=en_US.iso885915:en_US:en
TERM=xterm
TESTVAR='this is a test'
UID=500
USER=nwells
WINDOWID=37748875
XAUTHORITY=/home/nwells/.Xauthority
XMODIFIERS=@im=none
_=set
i=/etc/profile.d/which-2.sh
langfile=/home/nwells/.i18n
mc ()
{
    mkdir -p $HOME/.mc/tmp 2>/dev/null;
    chmod 700 $HOME/.mc/tmp;
    MC=$HOME/.mc/tmp/mc-$$;
    /usr/bin/mc -P "$@" >"$MC";
    cd "`cat $MC`";
    /bin/rm -f "$MC";
    unset MC
}
```

You can view the value of a single environment variable using the **echo** command. The echo command prints text to the screen. To see the value of an environment variable, execute echo followed by the environment variable name preceded by a dollar sign. The dollar sign indicates that the shell should substitute the value of the variable at that point. For example, to print the value of the HOME variable to the screen, use the following command:

```
$ echo $HOME
```

The **export** command makes a newly created environment variable available to other programs launched from that environment. For example, to define a new environment variable for the **db_data** database program, and then make that variable available to other programs (including the database program), use these two commands:

```
$ DB_DIR=/usr/local/db_data
$ export DB_DIR
```

 By convention, environment variables use all uppercase letters. But they are case sensitive. If a program requires that you set up an environment variable, follow the format given in the program's documentation.

The shell itself relies on many environment variables. The online manual page for the **bash** shell lists dozens of variables that the shell uses (or can use, if you set them) to control or select features of the shell. Two of these variables are described here as examples.

The **PATH** environment variable contains a list of directories on the Linux system that the shell searches each time a command is executed. When you enter a program name to be launched at the shell prompt, the shell searches in each directory listed in the value of the **PATH** variable. If the program is not found in the first directory, the second is searched, and so forth. The command to view the value of **PATH** is **echo $PATH**. Sample output of this command on Red Hat Linux 7.3 is shown here. (The value of **PATH** varies depending on whether you are logged in as root or as a regular user. The output here is for a regular user account.)

```
$ echo $PATH
/bin:/usr/bin:/usr/bin/X11:/usr/local/bin:/usr/bin:/usr/X11R6/bin:
/home/nwells/bin:/home/nwells/bin
```

Suppose you want to execute a program, but the directory in which the program is located is not part of the **PATH** variable. You must provide the shell with the file's complete pathname. For example:

```
$ /tmp/downloads/screensaver-sample
```

If you simply enter **screensaver-sample** alone, the shell will look in the **PATH** directories and be unable to find the program. An interesting exercise is to press the Tab key twice on an empty shell prompt line. The shell attempts to use tab completion, but because you have entered no characters, the list of possible matches is very large, and the shell requests confirmation with a message like this one:

```
Display all 2597 possibilities? (y or n)
```

Pressing the Y key for "yes" causes the shell to list all of the executable programs that it can find in the **PATH** directories.

Another environment variable used by the shell is **PS1**. This variable defines the shell prompt for **bash**. Note the default value:

```
$ echo $PS1
[\u@\h \W]\$
```

The \u, \h, and \W parameters refer to the username, hostname, and working directory, respectively. You can alter the shell prompt by changing the value of this variable. This is presented as Project 6-1 at the end of this chapter.

Using Text Editors

The most versatile tool for any system administrator is a text editor. As you may have already noticed, most of what happens on a Linux system is controlled by text configuration files. Graphical configuration utilities are sometimes available to assist with configuration, but a competent Linux system administrator can also modify the configuration files using any text editor. This provides the flexibility to update or repair a Linux system when special configuration utilities are unavailable.

The Variety of Linux Text Editors

Many different text editors are available for Linux; at least two are included with every popular version of Linux. (Red Hat Linux 7.3 includes six.) Some text editors are graphical, such as the **gedit** program in Gnome (see Figure 6-5), or the **kedit** and **kate** programs in KDE. You don't need special training to use a graphical text editor because a menu bar and dialog boxes guide you through any editing tasks you need to perform. The disadvantage of a graphical editor is that you must be using the X Window System. X may not be available either because the configuration of X is damaged, or you are working across a slow network connection, or you have chosen not to install X on an Internet server. Whenever a graphical environment is not available, you can use a text-mode editor.

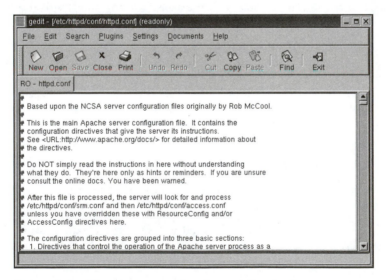

Figure 6-5   The gedit graphical text editor in Gnome

Some widely used text-mode editors are listed here. Not all of them are included with every version of Linux, but several are probably available on the Linux system you are using.

- **vi**: The name stands for *visual editor*, though you may wonder if this title is appropriate the first time you interact with **vi**: it doesn't provide any visual clues about how to use the editor's functions. This is the most widely used editor on UNIX and Linux systems. It is discussed in detail in the next section. Different versions of **vi**, such as **vim** and **elvis**, are usually launched with the command **vi**.

- **emacs**: This powerful editor provides macros, programming tools, customization, and hundreds of keyboard shortcuts. A graphical version called **xemacs** is available. **emacs** has a strong following among UNIX and Linux enthusiasts, but it is not as universally popular among system administrators as **vi**. **emacs** requires a large amount of hard disk space and was not included in the list of recommended packages to install in Chapter 3.

- **pico**: This simple editor includes on-screen information about the Control key sequences used to perform editing functions. It is installed by default in Red Hat Linux 7.3.

- **joe**: This is another simple text editor with on-screen command help.

Figure 6-6 shows the **pico** editor with a text file loaded for editing. Notice the commands at the bottom of the screen. Each item indicates a control character that you can use to control the editor. For example, the text **^X Exit** indicates that you can press Ctrl+X to exit **pico**.

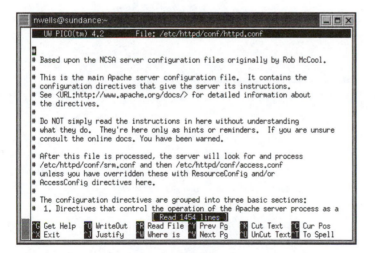

Figure 6-6   The pico text editor

Using the vi Editor

vi is a very powerful program that is available on virtually every Linux system. Although vi is not easy to use, you must learn to use at least the basic features of vi in order to work as a Linux system administrator. This means you must memorize many keystroke sequences and work without any on-screen prompts to guide you. Once you have learned a few commands, however, the patterns used in vi commands start to emerge, and learning new commands becomes easier.

To launch vi, enter the command vi at any Linux shell prompt. You can include the name of a file you want to edit after the program name, such as vi /etc/profile, or just enter vi to begin creating a new file. When you open a new file (or a small file), you see tilde characters (~) down the left side of the screen. These indicate lines that are not part of the file (because a new file is empty). Figure 6-7 shows vi after starting it with a small file to edit.

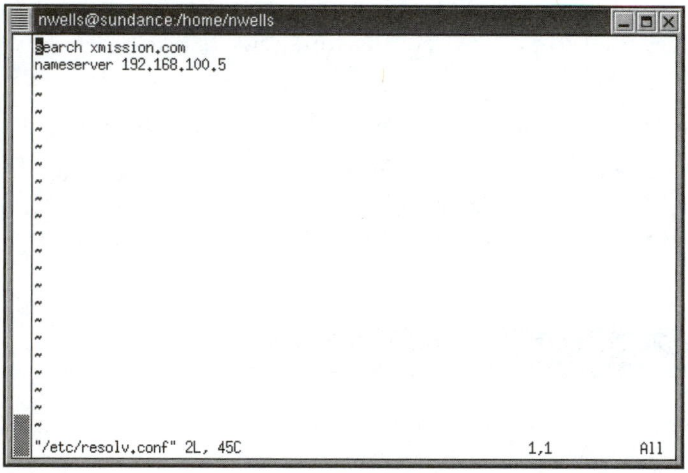

Figure 6-7   Using vi to edit a small file

vi is a modal editor. In a **modal editor**, your keystrokes are interpreted differently depending on the mode you are working in. For example, if you are in command mode and press a key, the key is interpreted as a command; if you are in edit mode and press a key, the key is interpreted as data entry and is added to the document. vi has several modes. The most important ones are:

- *Command mode*: Keystrokes are interpreted as commands to edit the file, such as deleting lines or searching for text.

- *Insert mode*: Keystrokes are inserted into the document you are editing.

- *Replace mode*: Keystrokes are added into the document you are editing, over-writing any existing text at the place where you begin typing.

When you open `vi`, you begin in command mode. You can always return to command mode by pressing the Esc key. When you are in command mode, `vi` displays only the document you are editing. When you are in insert mode or replace mode, you see a message line at the bottom of the screen with the text `--INSERT--` or `--REPLACE--`. (You'll learn how to switch between modes later in this section.)

> For many commands in `vi` you must enter multiple keystrokes. The following tables use the notation "Ctrl+X" to indicate "hold down the Ctrl key while pressing the X key." The notation "1, Ctrl+g" indicates "press the 1 key, then hold down the Ctrl key while pressing the g key." All `vi` commands are case sensitive. The notation "Ctrl+g" indicates a lowercase *g*. The notation "Ctrl+Shift+G" indicates an uppercase *G*.

You can use the arrow keys and the Page Up and Page Down keys to move around the screen as you edit a document. These keys normally work if you are in insert mode or replace mode. Table 6-2 shows additional commands you can use to move around a large document while you are in command mode.

Table 6-2   `vi` Commands Used for Moving around a Document in Command Mode

Keystroke	Description
j	Move the cursor one line down.
k	Move the cursor one line up.
h	Move the cursor one character left.
w	Move the cursor one word forward.
b	Move the cursor one word backward.
Shift+G	Move to the last line of the file.
1, Shift+G	Move to the first line of the file.
10, Shift+G	Move to the tenth line of the file.
Ctrl+g	Display a status line at the bottom of the screen to indicate the line number where the cursor is positioned and the name of the file being edited.

> If you are working on Linux over a network connection (for example, with a Microsoft Windows Telnet program), `vi` may not display text correctly. The first indication of a problem is usually that the arrow keys do not work correctly. You can still use the commands in Table 6-2 to move around the document, but you may want to investigate getting a different terminal program for the Windows system, such as PowerTerm Pro. (See *www.powerterm.com*.)

You can enter the insert or replace mode using several different commands, depending on where you want to begin entering text. Table 6-3 shows the most commonly used commands of this type. When you enter any of these commands (in command mode) you see the `--INSERT--` or `--REPLACE--` indicator at the bottom of the `vi` screen.

Table 6-3 vi Commands to Enter Insert or Replace Mode

Keystroke	Description
i	Begin inserting text to the left of the current cursor position.
a	Begin inserting text to the right of the current cursor position.
I	Begin inserting text at the beginning of the current line.
A	Begin inserting text at the end of the current line.
o	Insert a blank line after the line that the cursor is on, place the cursor on the new line, and begin inserting text.
O	Insert a blank line above the line that the cursor is on, place the cursor on the new line, and begin inserting text.
r	Replace one character with the next character entered.
R	Enter replace mode; all text entered will overwrite existing text beginning at the current cursor position.

Table 6-4 shows a few common editing commands that you can use in vi's command mode. From the commands given here, you can deduce other similar commands. For example, if the command 10,y,y copies 10 lines into the clipboard, the command 20,y,y will copy 20 lines into the clipboard.

Table 6-4 Standard vi Editing Commands

Keystroke	Description
x	Delete one character to the right of the cursor.
5,x	Delete five characters to the right of the cursor.
d,w	Delete one word to the right of the cursor.
5,d,w	Delete five words to the right of the cursor.
d,d	Delete the current line.
D	Delete from the cursor position to the end of the current line.
u	Undo the previous command (use repeatedly to undo several commands).
y,y	Copy the current line into a buffer. (A vi buffer is like the Windows clipboard, but vi has many different buffers; this command uses a standard buffer.)
p	Paste the line(s) from the standard buffer below the current line.
J	Join the next line to the end of the current line (remove the end-of-line character at the end of the current line).

All of the commands shown so far affect the document you are editing but do not display anything as you enter the command characters. Many vi commands do display the text that you enter, making it easier to enter these commands. Table 6-5 shows a few of these commands, most of which begin with a colon or a forward slash. After you enter the colon or forward slash, you see the remaining characters in the command at the bottom of the screen. For most of these commands, you must press Enter to indicate that you have finished entering the command.

Table 6-5   Additional `vi` Commands

Command	Description	Example
:, w, Enter	Save the current document.	:w
:, w, *filename*, Enter	Save the current document as *filename*.	:w report
:, q, Enter	Exit `vi`.	:q
:, q, !, Enter	Exit `vi`, discarding any changes to the current document.	:q!
:, w, q, Enter	Save the current document and exit `vi`.	:wq
/, *searchtext*, Enter	Search for *searchtext*.	/annual
/, Enter	Search again for the most recent *searchtext*.	/
n	Search again for the most recent *searchtext*.	*no on-screen display*
:, !, *commandname*, Enter	Execute *commandname* and return to `vi`.	:!ls

Although the commands in the preceding tables may seem too numerous to memorize, you will quickly become familiar with at least the basic commands required to add or delete text and then save your changes and exit from `vi`.

Use the command `:h` to see help within `vi`. After reading help, use the command `:q` to exit help and return to your document.

TEXT PROCESSING

The editors presented in the previous section are used only to create or edit text files. Most of the text files you work with as a system administrator contain only regular characters, spaces, tabs, and some punctuation. They do not contain formatting such as bold text, italic text, different fonts, tables, and graphic images. To create documents with such elements, you must use different utilities.

You can use two methods to create formatted documents:

- Graphical, or **WYSIWYG** (what-you-see-is-what-you-get, pronounced "whiz-ee-wig") programs that show documents on the computer screen much as they will look when printed on paper or in a Web browser.

- Programs that rely on **markup languages** to define special codes that indicate how you want a document formatted. You can create a document using a markup language in any text editor, but you see the results (the effect of the codes you entered) only when you view the document in another program or print it on paper.

Markup Languages

Most users are familiar with WYSIWYG programs; most word processors, photo editing tools, and Web page creation programs display information on-screen just as it will appear on paper or in a Web browser—you never see the "codes" that are used to define formatting and other features of the documents. The markup method of creating documents is actually much older than the graphical programs that are now available, and markup languages are still popular with many Linux and UNIX enthusiasts. Although graphical programs are easier to learn, they require more system resources and may lack the flexibility and precision of a good markup language. For example, if part of a document created with a markup language is incorrect, it is usually easy to repair or add the markup code that makes the document correct; in graphical systems, the user must locate a menu option that performs the needed alteration of the appropriate hidden document codes.

The best-known markup language is HTML (hypertext markup language). HTML is used on the Web as the format for documents downloaded for viewing on a browser. You can choose from many different graphical programs for creating HTML documents, but you can also use a text editor like **vi** to create an HTML document. Figure 6-8 shows an HTML document in a text editor. The figure shows the format of the markup codes, with each enclosed in angle brackets—for example, **<TITLE>** and **<P>**.

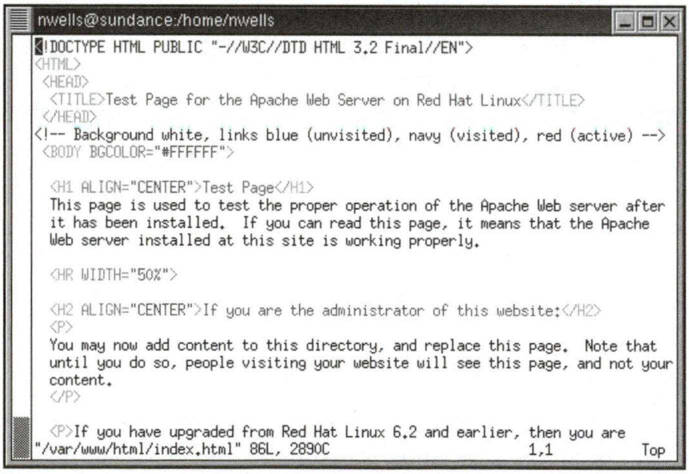

Figure 6-8   An HTML document viewed in `vi`

Many other formats are supported by modern Web browsers, especially the XML (extensible markup language) format. Markup languages such as XML use codes very similar in format to HTML codes. They can all be created in a text editor, though the more complex the document, the more helpful it can be to use a specialized program that keeps track of the codes for you. Numerous HTML and XML editors are available for Linux; search on *www.linuxapps.com* for examples.

A widely used markup language in the UNIX and Linux world is called TeX (pronounced "tek"). **TeX** is a document-processing system that writers use to create documents—or even books—on UNIX or Linux systems. TeX is complex and requires training to use effectively, but it has a long list of features that allow it to be used effectively for projects as complex as creating scientific textbooks and software manuals.

TeX includes the capability to create macros. To make their work with TeX easier, writers often prefer to use a version (or package) that includes many macros. The most popular of these versions are **LaTeX** and **TeTeX**. Because of the popularity of TeX, you will often find it included on a Linux system. If you don't intend to do text processing, you can remove TeX-related packages.

Although LaTeX is a popular format for creating books and reports on UNIX and Linux systems, it is rarely used to format text for display on a computer screen. Another markup language called roff (rhymes with "cough") is commonly used for online documents such as the online manual pages. You can use the **troff** and **groff** programs to format and display documents that are created with roff markup codes. (**Troff** is pronounced "t-roff" and **groff** is pronounced "g-roff.") Figure 6-9 shows an online Linux manual page for the **ls** command as it appears in a text editor. Notice that the roff markup codes begin with a period; they are different from HTML codes. The **man** command converts the roff codes to on-screen formatting, such as indented lines and bold text, when a manual page is displayed on-screen.

Controlling Fonts

The X Window System is typically installed with many different fonts. You see the names of these fonts when you list all software packages installed on your system that relate to XFree86 (using the command **rpm -qa | grep XFree86**). Each font used by the X Window System is stored in one of the font directories named in the **XF86Config-4** configuration file. The common location for the font files is **/usr/X11R6/lib/X11/fonts**. This directory contains subdirectories for different types of fonts, such as Type1 for PostScript fonts. You can review the fonts available on the system by using the **xfontsel** program. **xfontsel** is a graphical program that lets you choose each aspect of a font definition (such as the font family and typeface). It then displays the corresponding font for your review. Figure 6-10 shows the **xfontsel** program with a font selected and displayed in the bottom portion of the program window.

6

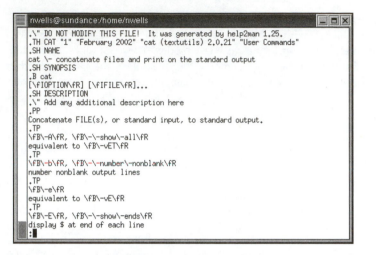

Figure 6-9   ls man page

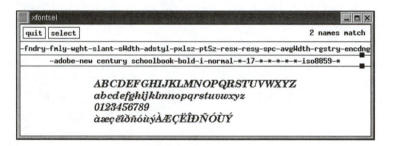

Figure 6-10   The xfontsel program

You can use the **xfontsel** program to select a font for a graphical program. The font that you choose can be added to a resource database file such as **.Xdefaults** (see Chapter 5), or it can be selected within the graphical program itself (if that option is provided by the program). Not all X fonts are appropriate for all displays. Some are very small and cannot be enlarged; others are poorer quality, suitable only for older computer systems with limited video display capabilities.

Within both Gnome and KDE you can select the font for most applications; you can also select a default font for the desktop itself. Both Gnome and KDE provide a standard font selection dialog box in which you can explore fonts available on your system. (Within KDE, choose Preferences, Look and Feel, Fonts. Within Gnome, choose Programs, Utilities, Font Selector.) Many graphical applications allow you to select fonts using the same standard dialog box. The font selection dialog box for the Gnome Control Center is shown in Figure 6-11.

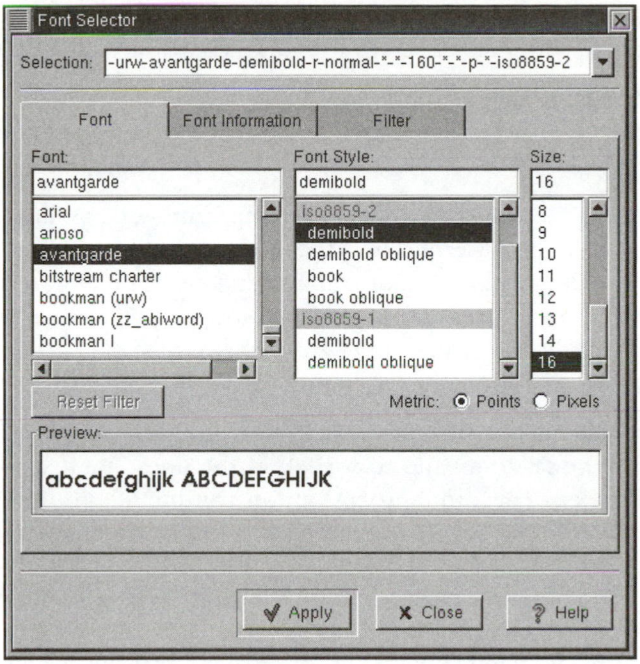

Figure 6-11   The Font Selector dialog box in Gnome

X typically uses a font server called **xfs** to process requests for font information from applications and return the requested font in the desired size. You can add new fonts to a Linux system so that the font server can process them for all graphical applications. To add fonts, follow these steps:

1. Obtain the file for a new font from an Internet site of a font vendor such as Adobe. The preferred file format is **pcf**, but other formats such as **snf**, **pfa**, **pfb**, **spd**, and **bdf** are also supported by XFree86. Check the file extension of the font file to be certain that the format of the font is supported.

2. Go to the font directory specified in the **XF86Config-4** file, which is normally **/usr/X11R6/lib/X11/fonts**. Copy the font file into the correct subdirectory based on its type (such as **Type1**, **Speedo**, or **100dpi**). Ask the font vendor for this information if it is not apparent from the font's name.

3. Within the subdirectory where you copied the font file, locate the **fonts.scale** file. Load it into a text editor and add the font file that you copied into this directory, following the format of the other lines in the **fonts.scale** file. Increase the number on the first line of the file by one (this is the number of fonts in the file). If the font you have installed is not scalable, you can skip this step.

4. Activate the new font immediately by using the following command. (The font will also be activated automatically if you exit and restart the X Window System.)

```
xset fp rehash
```

Manipulating Text Files

At times you'll want to modify part of a text file by adding, removing, or altering data in the file based on complex rules or patterns. This kind of modification is called **filtering**. While some powerful text editors such as **vi** or **emacs** can perform many filtering operations, many system administration tasks are easier if you use command-line programs to filter text files. This is especially true when you want to automate a filtering operation using a shell script, in which case an interactive text editor is inappropriate.

Linux provides many commands for filtering text files. A simple example is the **sort** command. You can use the **sort** command to sort all of the lines in a text file, writing them out in alphabetical order or according to an option you provide to the command. The simple example here prints a list of all users on a Linux system, sorted by the username:

```
sort /etc/passwd
```

Other options for the **sort** command allow you to merge and sort the contents of multiple files, sort based on different fields within each line of a file, or check whether a file is already sorted.

More complex commands for altering text include a complete programming syntax to define how to filter a text file. An example of these complex filtering programs is **sed**. The **sed** command (for *stream editor*) processes each line in a text file according to a series of command-line options (the options can be stored in a separate file if they are lengthy). The following command prints to the screen all lines of the **/tmp/names** file that contain the text **lincoln**:

```
sed -n '/lincoln/p' /tmp/names
```

The pattern between the two forward slashes (**lincoln** in the above example) can be very complex. In Chapter 7 you will learn about regular expressions, which you can use in a **sed** command to match complex patterns. As another **sed** example, the following command prints to the screen all lines of the **/tmp/names** file except those containing **lincoln**. (The **d** after **lincoln** indicates "delete matching lines from the output.")

```
sed '/lincoln/d' /tmp/names
```

A final example shows how to replace all occurrences of the pattern **lincoln** in the file **/tmp/names** with the string **Abraham Lincoln**:

```
sed 's/lincoln/Abraham Lincoln/' /tmp/names
```

The syntax of **sed** commands can become very complex. Developers often use full-blown programming languages such as **awk** and **perl** to create scripts for filtering and performing other tasks on text files. (Both awk and perl are also used for many other types of tasks besides filtering text files.)

Another set of filtering commands treats each line of a text file as a collection of fields separated by spaces, commas, or any character you specify. For example, suppose you have a text file in which each line has a name, address, phone number, and e-mail address, all separated by semicolons. You could use a single Linux command to extract the name and phone number from each line and place them in a separate file. Table 6-6 describes some useful text-filtering commands in Linux. You can learn more about a specific command by reviewing its man page.

Table 6-6 Linux Text-filtering Commands

Command	Description
cut	Remove sections from each line of a file.
expand	Convert tabs to spaces.
fmt	Format text files (standardize spaces, set line width, indent lines, etc.).
head	Display the first 10 lines of a file (or the number of lines indicated).
join	Merge lines from two different files based on a matching field within the files.
nl	Add line numbers to each line of a file.
od	Display the contents of a file in numeric formats such as hexadecimal.
paste	Merge lines from two files.
split	Split a single file into two or more smaller files.
tac	Reverse the lines in a file (last line first).
tail	Display the last 10 lines of a file (or the number of lines indicated); can be run continuously to show updates to a changing file.
tr	Transpose the occurrences of a character with another character.
unexpand	Convert spaces to tabs.
uniq	Remove duplicate lines in a sorted file.
wc	Display the number of lines, words, and characters in a file.

CHAPTER SUMMARY

◻ The Linux shell operates like any other program on a Linux system. It has no special relationship with the Linux kernel. The shell is not always running.

◻ Many shells are available, such as **bash**, the Korn shell, and the C shell. All shells are used primarily for launching other programs, including system administration utilities.

◻ The shell prompt tells you whether you are working as a regular user or as root; it also provides information such as your current working directory. The prompt is configurable.

❐ Tab completion helps you quickly enter long file and directory names.

❐ The command history lets you quickly re-enter a command that you have previously entered. The history is accessible by using the arrow keys, the `history` command, or the ! character at the command prompt.

❐ When a user logs in, certain shell scripts are executed; other scripts are executed each time a shell is launched.

❐ Aliases within a shell cause the shell to replace text on a command-line entry with different text before trying to execute the command.

❐ Symbolic links are filenames that refer not to a "real" file containing data, but to another filename (which in turn refers to a "real" file containing data).

❐ Environment variables store values that any program can access. You can view the value of an environment variable or set up a new environment variable from the shell prompt.

❐ Linux supports numerous text editors. The most widely available is `vi`, a powerful tool that requires you to memorize commands. Graphical editors are included on modern Linux desktops, but knowledge of `vi` remains a critical system administrator skill.

❐ `vi` is a modal editor—keystrokes are interpreted differently depending on the mode you are working in. Command mode and insert mode are the most-used modes for new users of `vi`.

❐ Some programs such as word processors format text using a WYSIWYG display; markup languages such as LaTeX and roff use codes to define formatting features that are not visible on-screen.

❐ Files that use a markup language can be created in any text editor. To see the effect of the markup codes, you must use another program or print the file to paper.

❐ Fonts are managed in X using a font server. You can add fonts to the system at any time. Graphical desktops such as Gnome provide a dialog box in which you can select the font to use for graphical programs.

❐ Filtering text files can be done within some text editors, but also can be accomplished using many different command-line utilities. Some commands provide a single function, such as `wc` and `tail`; others support a complex syntax (such as `sed`) or are complete programming languages in themselves (such as awk and perl).

Key Terms

`.bashrc` — A configuration script that is executed each time the user starts a `bash` shell.

`.profile` — A configuration script that can be located in each user's home directory. A script that is executed each time any user on the system starts a `bash` shell. This script is not included by default on all Linux distributions, but can be created if needed.

`/etc/profile` — A script containing configuration information that applies to every user on the Linux system.

alias — A string of characters that the shell substitutes for another string of characters when a command is entered. Created in the shell using the `alias` command.

`alias` — A command within a shell that assigns a string of characters to a substitute string of characters.

awk — A programming language that developers use to create scripts for working on text files and completing other complex tasks.

bang — In Linux jargon, an exclamation point character.

bash — Short for Bourne Again shell, an enhanced and extended version of the Bourne shell created by the GNU project for use on many UNIX-like operating systems. `bash` is the default Linux shell.

Bourne shell — The original shell for UNIX, written by Stephen Bourne.

C shell — A shell developed by Bill Joy in the 1970s. He focused on adding easy-to-use features for interactive work at the shell prompt. (Most of these features were later added to the `bash` shell as well.) The C shell is not popular for shell programming because its syntax is more complex than that of the Bourne, `bash`, and Korn shells.

command history — A feature of the shell that records in a list (the history list) each of the commands that you enter at the shell prompt.

command interpreter — A program that accepts input from the keyboard and uses that input to launch commands or otherwise control the computer system.

`echo` — Command used to print text to the screen.

`export` — Command used to make a newly created environment variable available to other programs running in the same environment.

filtering — The process of adding, removing, or altering data in the text file based on complex rules or patterns.

`groff` — A command used to format and display documents that are created using roff markup codes.

`history` — A command used to display all of the stored commands in the history list.

history list — A list that contains the most recently executed commands. (Normally at least 100 commands are included in the history list.)

Korn shell — A revision of the Bourne shell that includes the interactive features of the C shell but that maintains the Bourne shell programming style. The Korn shell was written by David Korn.

LaTeX — A version of the markup language TeX that includes numerous macros for easy document creation.

ln — Command used to create a symbolic link.

macro — A set of commands that can be executed at one time by referring to the name of the macro.

markup languages — Computer languages that define a series of codes indicating how to format a document.

modal editor — A text editor that uses multiple modes for editing text and entering commands to apply to that text.

PATH — An environment variable containing a list of directories on the Linux system that the shell searches each time a command is executed.

perl — A programming language that developers use to create scripts for working on text files and completing other complex tasks.

pico — A simple text editor that includes on-screen information about the Control key sequences used to perform editing functions.

script — A list of commands stored in a text file. Instead of entering each command one by one, at the command line, a script automates the execution of a series of commands.

sed — A command used to process each line in a text file according to a series of commands provided by the user.

set — Command used to display a list of all environment variables defined in the current environment.

shell prompt — A set of words or characters indicating that the shell is ready to accept commands at the keyboard.

sort — A command used to sort all of the lines in a text file, writing them out in alphabetical order or according to options provided to the command.

symbolic link — A file that refers to another filename rather than to data in a file.

tab completion — A feature of the shell that lets you enter part of a file or directory name and have the shell fill in the remainder of the name.

TENEX/TOPS C shell (TC shell) — An enhancement of the C shell. This is the version of the C shell that is commonly used on Linux systems.

TeTeX — A version of the markup language TeX that includes numerous macros for technical document creation.

TeX — A document processing system that writers use to create large and complex documents on UNIX or Linux systems.

troff — A command used to format and display documents that are created using roff markup codes.

vi — (stands for *visual editor*) The most widely used text editor on UNIX and Linux systems. Different versions of **vi**, such as **vim** and **elvis**, are usually launched with the command **vi**.

WYSIWYG — A characteristic of programs that show documents on the computer screen much as they will look when printed on paper or in a Web browser (stands for what-you-see-is-what-you-get; pronounced "whiz-ee-wig").

xfontsel — Program that lets the user choose each aspect of a font definition (such as the font family and typeface) and then displays the corresponding font for review.

xfs — The font server typically used by X to process requests for font information from applications and return the requested font in the desired size.

REVIEW QUESTIONS

1. The default shell used by Linux is:
   a. The Bourne Shell
   b. The Bourne Again Shell (**bash**)
   c. The TC Shell
   d. The Z Shell

2. When logged in as root, the shell prompt normally changes to display:
   a. A **%** character
   b. A **#** character
   c. The root directory
   d. A **$** character

3. The main function of a shell is to:
   a. Track kernel resources for **root**
   b. Provide a convenient programming environment
   c. Complement desktop interfaces
   d. Launch programs

4. Name four different shells and briefly describe the differences between them.

5. Tab completion is useful when you need to:
   a. Repeat a previously used command
   b. Reinitialize the X Window System font list
   c. Enter long filenames or directory names at the shell prompt
   d. Create a brief shell program

6. The **history** command is used to:
   a. Display a list of previously entered commands
   b. Execute a previously used command
   c. Change the environment variable controlling tab completion
   d. Edit an existing text file

6

7. Entering the command `!fr` would do the following in the `bash` shell:

   a. Cause an error because the command name is incomplete

   b. Execute the most recently executed command that began with `fr`

   c. Execute the `free` command to display system memory

   d. Search for the pattern `fr` in the `vi` editor

8. To have a command executed each time any user logged in to the Linux system, you would place the command in which one of these files:

   a. `/etc/profile`

   b. `/etc/.profile`

   c. `~/.profile`

   d. `/etc/bashrc`

9. If a `.bashrc` file is found in a user's home directory, the systemwide `/etc/bashrc` script is not executed. True or False?

10. If a directory contains the filenames `micron` and `microscope`, and you enter `micro` and press Tab once, what happens?

    a. The shell prints all matching names, `micron` and `microscope`.

    b. The shell fills in the first alphabetical match, `micron`.

    c. The shell beeps.

    d. The `micron` command is executed.

11. Describe the difference between an alias and a symbolic link.

12. Which of the following is a correctly formed alias for executing the `mv` command?

    a. `alias ren mv`

    b. `alias ren=mv -i`

    c. `alias mv=ren`

    d. `alias ren="mv -i"`

13. Which command is used to create a symbolic link?

    a. `sh`

    b. `ln`

    c. `set`

    d. `sed`

14. The command `echo $HOME` will display:

    a. The word `HOME`

    b. The current user's default shell

    c. The value of the `HOME` environment variable

    d. A prompt requesting a home directory path

15. Describe the contents of the **PATH** environment variable.

16. When the **export** command is used, an environment variable:

    a. Will be available to other programs launched in the same shell where export was executed

    b. Will be available only to the shell itself

    c. Will not be available to any program run by the same user

    d. Will be available to all users on the system

17. Name at least three nongraphical text editors that may be included with a Linux distribution.

18. Knowledge of the **vi** editor is considered an essential skill because:

    a. Memorized **vi** commands correspond to other Linux command options

    b. The **vi** editor is virtually always available to complete system administration tasks

    c. Other editors are not as reliable or easy to use

    d. The developer of **vi** also developed part of Linux

19. Suppose you enter the command **vi file1** and then press the following keys.

    `itest<Esc>yyp:wq<Enter>`

    Describe the result.

20. Man pages in Linux are created using a markup language that is a derivative of:

    a. HTML

    b. **roff**

    c. **LaTeX**

    d. XML

21. Describe the difference between a WYSIWYG program and a document containing markup codes.

22. X uses _____ to supply font information to graphical applications.

    a. an X resources file

    b. a text-based configuration script in each user's home directory

    c. a font server, **xfs**

    d. the **xset** command

23. Fonts for the X Window System are normally stored in which directory?

    a. `/usr/X11/xdm/fonts`

    b. `/usr/X11R6/fonts`

    c. `/etc/X11/xinit/fonts`

    d. `/usr/X11R6/lib/X11/fonts`

24. The **wc** command displays:

    a. The number of lines, words, and characters in a file

    b. The owner of a file

    c. A specific field within each line of a file

    d. Text matching a search string within a file

25. Name five programs that can be used to filter text files in Linux.

HANDS-ON PROJECTS

Project 6-1

In this project you use tab completion to explore the Linux file system and alter an environment variable within the shell. To complete this activity you should have a working Linux system with a valid user account. The filenames described in this activity are taken from Red Hat Linux 7.3, but the steps should work on other Linux versions as well.

1. Log in to Linux using your username and password.

2. If you are using a graphical environment, open a terminal window so you have a shell prompt.

3. Change to the directory /bin using the command **cd /bin**.

4. List the shells that are installed on the system using the command **ls *sh**. Can you recognize all of the shells listed?

5. Change to the directory /etc using the command **cd /etc**.

6. Type the command **ls -l host** but don't press Enter.

7. Press the **Tab** key twice. The first time you press Tab the shell beeps. The second time it displays a list of files in /etc that begin with **host**.

8. Type **s.** (including the period, so that the command line contains **ls -l hosts.**), but don't press Enter.

9. Press the **Tab** key twice. The shell beeps and then displays all the files in /etc that begin with **hosts.** (including the period). The list is shorter than the output of Step 7 because you added more characters to search for.

10. Type **a** and press **Tab**. The shell fills in the full filename so that the line reads **ls -l hosts.allow**.

11. Press **Enter** to complete the **ls** command that the Tab key finished filling in.

12. Change to your home directory by entering the command **cd**.

13. Enter the command **!ls** to execute the most recently used **ls** command, which you entered in Step 11. Why does the command display an error now?

14. Enter the command **echo $PS1** to display the format of the standard shell prompt.

15. Enter the command **man bash** to view the manual page for the **bash** shell.

16. Enter the text **/\\W** to search for the string **\W**, which is part of the **PS1** value you saw in Step 14.

17. Use the arrow keys to review the list of parameters that you can use to redefine the **PS1** environment variable. Locate the **\d** option.

18. Press **q** to exit the man page viewer.

19. Enter the command **export PS1="\d$PS1"**. What happened? What does the **$PS1** at the end of the command indicate?

20. Enter the command **bash** to start a new shell. How does the shell prompt change? Why?

21. Enter the **exit** command to leave the new shell you started in Step 20. How does the shell prompt change? Can you explain this?

Project 6-2

In this project you work with the **vi** editor to make a change to a shell start-up script. To complete this project you should have a working Linux system with a valid user account.

1. Log in to Linux using your username and password.

2. If you are using a graphical environment, open a terminal window so you have a shell prompt.

3. Enter the **pwd** command and check to make certain you are in your home directory.

4. Enter **vi .bashrc** to display the **.bashrc** file in the text editor window.

5. Press **Shift+G** on the keyboard to move to the end of the file.

6. Press the **o** key to start inserting a new line of text.

7. Type the text **TEST_VAR="This is a test"** and press **Enter**.

8. On the next line type the text **export TEST_VAR** and press **Enter**.

9. On the next line type the text **alias tv="echo $TEST_VAR"**.

10. Press **Esc** to return **vi** to command mode.

11. Enter **:wq**, then press **Enter** to save the file and exit **vi**.

12. Type **tv** and press **Enter**. What is the result?

13. Start a new shell by entering the command **bash**.

14. Type **tv** and press **Enter**. What is the result? Why?

15. Enter the **exit** command to exit the additional copy of **bash** that you started in Step 13.

16. Enter the command **vi .bashrc** to begin editing the same file as in previous steps.

17. If necessary, press the **j** key repeatedly until the cursor is located on the line containing TEST_VAR="This is a test".

18. Type **3**, then press **d** twice to delete the three lines that you entered.

If you make an error in editing this file, press u repeatedly to undo your editing changes.

19. Enter **:wq** to save the file and exit.

Project 6-3

In this project you explore various font issues on the Linux system. To complete this project you should have a working Linux system with a valid user account and the X Window System running (using any window manager or desktop interface). The commands described in this activity are included in Red Hat Linux 7.3; other versions of Linux may not have all of the same utilities installed by default.

1. Log in to Linux using your username and password.

2. If you are using a graphical environment, open a terminal window so you have a shell prompt.

3. Change to the X **fonts** directory using the command
   cd /usr/X11R6/lib/X11/fonts.

4. Use the **ls** command to list the subdirectories within the **fonts** directory.

5. Change to the **75dpi** subdirectory using the command **cd 75dpi**.

6. Review the list of fonts included in this directory using the command
   less fonts.dir. Press the **spacebar** or use the **down arrow key** to advance the list of fonts. Study briefly the format of each font name. Press **q** to exit the listing.

7. Start the **xfontsel** program by entering **xfontsel**.

8. Explore the buttons and drop-down lists provided in **xfontsel**. How do the categories listed on the drop-down lists correspond to the fields in the font listing you saw in Step 6?

9. Within Gnome, open a Start Here window (one may be open already on your desktop, or you can open one using the second button from the left on the Panel or the top menu item on the main menu). Notice the appearance of the words "Start Here" in the left side of the window.

10. Choose Preferences, Edit Preferences in the Start Here window. Click **Appearances** in the menu on the left side of the window.

11. In the Default smooth font field, click and select a font that sounds interesting. (You can't review the font appearance in this dialog box.)

12. Click **OK**. Notice how the words Start Here have changed to the new font. (The original font is called Helvetica Default, Normal if you want to change back to it.)

13. Now launch the **gedit** graphical text editor within Gnome by entering **gedit** at a command prompt or choosing **Programs**, **Applications**, **gedit** from the Gnome main menu.

14. Within **gedit**, choose **Settings**, **Preferences** on the menu bar.

15. In the dialog box that appears, choose the **Fonts/Colors** tab.

16. Explore the fonts available. Notice how you can see the appearance of a font that you select in the bottom part of the dialog box. Click **Close** to close the dialog box, then exit **gedit**.

Project 6-4

In this project you use several basic filtering commands to modify a text file. To complete this project you should have a working Linux system with a valid user account. This project should work on any version of Linux with a standard utility set.

1. Log in to Linux using your username and password.

2. If you are using a graphical environment, open a terminal window so you have a shell prompt.

3. Copy the **/etc/passwd** file to your home directory as a test file named **data1** (we use this file because it has lines that are separated into fields).

```
cp /etc/passwd ~/data1
```

4. Make sure you are working in your home directory.

```
cd
```

5. Look at your working file to see how it is organized and formatted. (You will explore the **/etc/passwd** file further in Chapter 8—for now just review it briefly.)

```
less data1
```

6. Each line in this file is divided into fields using a colon. Use the **cut** command to extract from each line the first and seventh fields (the username and associated default shell).

```
cut –d : –f  1,7 data1 > data2
```

The > character causes the shell to store the output of one command in a new filename (**data2** in the above command). You will learn more about using this feature in Chapter 7.

7. Review the contents of **data2** using the **less** command. Then convert the : character between the remaining two fields of each line of **data2** to a tab character using the **tr** command and store the result in **data3**.

```
tr ":" "\t" < data2 > data3
```

8. Sort the lines in the `data3` file into alphabetical order and store the result in `data4`.

   sort data3 > data4

9. Add a line number to the beginning of each line in the `data4` file and store the result in `data5`.

   nl data4 > data5

10. You decide that you should have sorted the file in the opposite order. Reverse all the lines in the `data5` file using the `tac` command, and store the results in `data6`.

    tac data5 > data6

11. Use the `less` command to review the results of these commands.

    less data6

In Chapter 7 you will learn how you can do all of these tasks on a single command line without creating intermediate files.

CASE PROJECTS

McKinney & Co. has sent you to Las Vegas to consult on a project with a large travel agency, Global Worldwide Vistas. Global has Linux workstations for about 70 employees. The employees use the workstations to access several types of text-mode reservations systems. They also use a browser on the Linux systems to review Web sites related to travel and travel destinations, and to exchange e-mail with clients.

1. Jill, one of the more technically minded travel agents, approaches you with some requests and recommendations. It seems some of the programs used by the employees require that certain environment variables be set. Jill has been teaching employees how to set a variable at the command line before launching the programs in question, but she would like to have them set automatically so that users don't have to enter the values each time they start the program. How would you do this? Would it be more difficult or easier if every employee is running the program in question from a single central Linux server?

2. Thor, another travel agent, has taught himself how to use basic `vi` commands to create text files. He asks if you could install another text editor with better functionality. How do you respond? Do you see any reason not to grant this request? What factors play into your decision? What text editors or other programs might you consider setting up for Thor and the other employees?

3. As you study the set-up at the travel agency, you notice that several databases are being used in an uncoordinated way.

   ❑ One database contains a list of customers with name and contact information.

   ❑ A second database contains lists of customer names with a location code and trip description for all trips taken in the last 18 months.

   ❑ A third database contains lists of tour operators (with their contact information) who are interested in offering special discounts to Global's customers who have previously traveled in areas where they offer tours.

   Global employees have been culling bits of information from the lists manually in order to send announcements to former customers. They would like to implement a full-fledged database solution, but they worry it will take you quite a while to have things up and running. It wouldn't take you long of course, but to show them how well-placed their confidence in you is, you decide to produce some lists for them using basic text-filtering commands.

   Assume that all database information is stored as text files and that each record contains all information on a single line.

   Describe the commands you will use to combine data from three databases into a list of customer names (with contact information) for a destination that a tour operator would like to target with a special offer.

6

CHAPTER

7

THE ROLE OF THE SYSTEM ADMINISTRATOR

> **After reading this chapter and completing the exercises, you will be able to:**
>
> ♦ Explain the role of a system administrator
> ♦ Discuss the responsibilities of a system administrator
> ♦ Use basic system administration commands in Linux

In the previous chapter you learned about the Linux command–line environment (the shell) and how to use different text editors and text-processing tools to work effectively at the command line.

In this chapter you learn about the responsibilities of working as a Linux system administrator within an organization. You also learn about the design goals of Linux system administration utilities, which will help you to use the utilities more efficiently. You learn how to use multiple utilities together to complete more complex administration tasks, and additional utilities are introduced in this chapter to illustrate this point. The topics in this chapter lay the foundation for the rest of the book, which covers in detail the different tasks performed by a system administrator.

WORKING AS A SYSTEM ADMINISTRATOR

The role of a system administrator within any organization is simple: make technology work and continue to work for those who do the "real work" of the organization. The term "real work" isn't meant to downplay what the system administrator does—to the contrary, all the powerful technology that an organization invests in will be useless without the knowledge that a system administrator brings. Your goal as system administrator is to enable others to use the benefits that technology can provide.

Imagine any type of organization: an architectural firm, a children's health charity, an auto manufacturer, even a computer software company. Each has reasons for existing, but none of those goals revolves around their computer systems. For example, the architectural firm wants to design buildings. Their computers facilitate that process as long as they are up and running. When they stop running, the firm stops achieving its goals. The architects depend on the computers all day long, but they don't think about them until something goes wrong. Your role is to let them do their work without thinking about the computers.

While others develop software programs or hardware devices with great potential, the system administrator ties hardware and software into complete, operational systems that can increase productivity, lower costs, or otherwise benefit those who use technology.

The system administrator keeps these systems running efficiently as new pieces are added, changes occur, and reconfigurations and failures alter the face of the original systems. The job of the system administrator is primarily practical. It requires perseverance, patience, curiosity, creativity, problem-solving skills, and technical knowledge. To be truly successful as a system administrator, you must continue to increase both the breadth (number of subjects) and depth (expertise in a subject) of your technical knowledge. If you don't, new problems will come along that you won't know how to solve. At the same time, you will lack the ability to integrate new technologies into your systems or to determine how they apply to your environment.

 A term you will often hear is **MIS: Management of Information Systems**, or **Manager of Information Systems** if applied to an employee.

A system administrator generally works as part of the **Information Systems (IS)** or **Information Technology (IT)** department of an organization. In a large organization, this group reports to a **chief information officer (CIO)**. In smaller organizations, a group of system administrators might consult other company officers to make decisions about information technology. The IS or IT department is typically concerned with two areas:

- Internal information systems: The computers on each employee's desk, the software they have installed, the networks that connect them together, and the user accounts that employees log in to. Internal systems normally include telephones as well, which are often computer-based and integrated with other computer systems.

- Organizational information viewed by the public over the Internet: Web servers, FTP download servers, e-mail servers, and similar public services.

In technology organizations (such as companies that develop software or sell computers or telecommunications equipment), the team that develops software and hardware for sale to others is not part of the IS or IT department. Figure 7-1 shows the position of a system administrator in a typical small or large company.

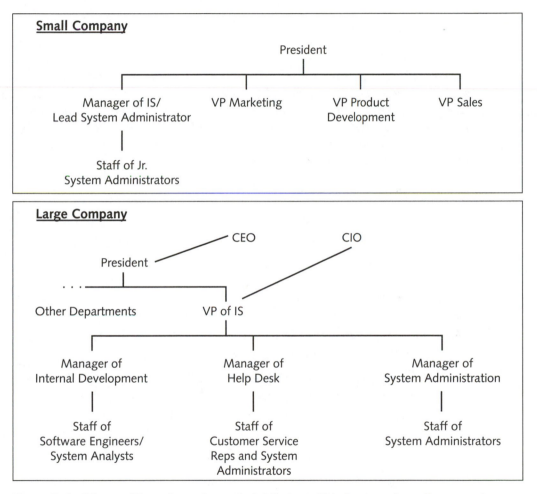

Figure 7-1 The position of a system administrator within large and small companies

System administrators typically have two- or four-year college degrees with specialization in computer science, information technology, or a related field. A few junior system administrators are self-taught or have completed a single program of technical training (such as a month-long Red Hat Certification course). But most employers prefer the longer training that a two- or four-year degree provides, especially when hiring someone without previous work experience. Such a degree also improves your opportunity for promotion within an organization, either to more responsible system administrator positions or to related work such as programming, systems analysis, or management.

Most system administrators work with people as much as they work with technology. They may work primarily with a group of technical colleagues in the IT department, but they also are likely to interact with most of the organization as they answer questions, solve technical problems, train users, install software, and so forth. The employees of the organization are the clients or customers of the system administrator.

In larger organizations, the tasks of working with end users and maintaining the systems are divided into different areas. For example, an IS team may manage internal servers, while a Web team maintains Internet sites, and the **help desk** team directly solves problems for **end users** (those who use computer systems to accomplish their daily work). In such an environment, you, as a system administrator, can focus on the particular area that best suits your interests and skills, be it networking, server software, graphical productivity applications, or different types of computer hardware. Many of the same technical skills and problem-solving abilities are required for all of these areas.

Tasks of a System Administrator

As a system administrator, the tasks for which you are responsible can vary considerably based on factors such as:

- Your expertise and specific job position
- Your seniority in an organization
- The size of the organization

The following list shows some of the tasks that would be part of a system administrator's job description in many organizations.

- Create new user accounts and make changes in existing user accounts, such as granting new access permissions as assignments change.
- Maintain system hardware, including installing new hardware to increase system capacity, replacing damaged systems, or upgrading obsolete components.
- Train end users to use new systems, software, or procedures effectively.
- Perform occasional or recurring tasks that keep the system running smoothly. Some of these are routine, such as backing up files; others require more creativity, such as determining why system response time has slowed, or tracking down an intruder from the Internet.
- Document the system so that other system administrators can understand how it is configured and operated. This might include informing others of how applications are configured, where backup files are stored, and which users have had specific problems with certain hardware or applications. This task is often related to the next one.

- Define procedures and policies related to how systems are administered at your site. Among other things, a system administrator might need to define backup procedures, privacy and security policies, user guidelines, or a disaster plan. (Some of these topics are discussed in later chapters; others are discussed in *Guide to Linux Networking and Security*.)

- Recover from emergencies. Get the system running again after a power outage, hardware failure, employee problem, or natural disaster.

- Plan systems. When working within small organizations or departments, or as you gain experience in a large organization, you may be asked to decide on new hardware purchases or plan for future system components or designs to meet anticipated needs.

In addition to the core tasks listed above, you may be asked to:

- Inform management of potential technical needs for upgrades.

- Watch for security threats and implement remedies when possible.

- Keep yourself up-to-date regarding new developments in your field. Staying current allows you to take advantage of new developments that could benefit the employer's information technology strategy (and thus employee productivity). Keeping up-to-date with technical developments also increases your value as an employee and improves your chances for promotion.

Ethics and the System Administrator

Working as a system administrator involves many ethical issues that may not be evident at first. As a system administrator you have control—full or partial—over an organization's computer systems. Implicit in this responsibility is a great deal of trust on the part of both the company (its officers, managers, and owners) and the individual employees who use the systems that you manage. The way you view this trust will determine how effective you are as a system administrator. For example, if you cheat on school tests or certification exams, or pirate software (make unauthorized copies), you show your disregard for the legal and ethical norms that make employers comfortable trusting you. A professional reputation lost by such acts is very hard to regain.

Employers pay you to maintain their systems in a way that contributes to the success of their organization. Your role also has an important effect on individual users. Although you may be working behind the scenes most of the time (and probably should be if things are running smoothly), remember that your fellow employees count on your work in order to do theirs. A lack of preparation or accuracy on your part can lead to companywide downtime, corrupted or lost files, malfunctioning printers, and so forth. As a result, other employees may not be able to be productive. Everyone in a modern office relies on the work of a good system administrator every workday.

With this influence over the work of others comes the potential for abuse. For example, as the system administrator with root privileges on the Linux server, you have the ability to:

- Read users' e-mail and the files in their home directories

- Alter company or personal files

- Send falsified messages as if they came from other users

- Erase ("lose") files on the system

- Delay fixing a system problem or helping an employee with a simple question

- Neglect security measures that would protect sensitive data

These actions are unethical because they invade others' privacy and impede the work of your employer. Most are also illegal and would make an unscrupulous system administrator subject to criminal prosecution. But as you might suspect, some unethical actions are likely to go undetected, especially if you are the sole person in a company with expertise in Linux.

For information on laws regarding computer-related fraud and abuse, visit the FBI's National Infrastructure Protection Center at *www.nipc.gov*, then click on the Legal Issues link.

To have a successful career as a system administrator, you should decide at the outset on a few guidelines for your relationships with employers and the fellow employees whose systems you manage. Your self-made guidelines might include statements like these:

- I realize that I know more about the systems I manage than others, but I also realize that they know more about their job functions and what they need from their computer systems.

- I understand that other employees and managers trust me to handle their technology needs so they can be productive.

- I know I can never read files that do not belong to me personally unless I am required to do so as part of a legal proceeding or to comply with a publicly acknowledged company policy.

- I must treat other employees as my clients. My success as a system administrator depends on their satisfaction with my work, not on how much I know about technology.

Occasionally, a rogue system administrator decides to configure systems so that no one else can figure out how everything is put together. This is sometimes done in the name of job security: "They can't fire me," this kind of system administrator reasons, "or the entire company will have to shut down."

In fact, however, your best route to success as a system administrator (not to mention peace of mind) will come through making your employer successful. This allows you to grow professionally, with additional responsibility and technical opportunities. If you train yourself well, you need never feel compelled to make implied threats of holding your employer "hostage" because you are the only person who can maintain the computer systems. Remember these two rules:

- Good jobs are always available for well-trained technical people; don't base ideas of job security on working at a single company. Instead, build a reputation as both a technical expert and a personable employee so that potential future employers will be eager to hire you and past employers will be sorry they lost you.

- If you haven't trained yourself well, you're not worth keeping as an employee. Your employer can then replace you with someone who is not being territorial under the guise of "job security." The true expert will always be able to set up efficient, standardized, well-documented systems and have a solid career based on managing those systems.

To read more about working as a system administrator, visit the **System Administrators Guild (SAGE)** at *www.sage.org*. SAGE is part of the USENIX group, an organization for people who work with advanced computing systems (see *www.usenix.org*). USENIX and SAGE have tremendous resources for system administrators. The SAGE Web site contains information about:

- Jobs and salary profiles

- Local user groups

- Technical information

- Events where system administrators gather for technical conferences

In relation to the topics in this section, consider reviewing the SAGE Code of Ethics at *http://sageweb.sage.org/resources/publications/code_of_ethics.html*.

PRINCIPLES OF MAINTAINING A LINUX SYSTEM

Compared to the other types of technical work demanded of a system administrator, learning about Linux is especially rewarding. Whereas some technical topics relate to mastering a specific graphical tool or proprietary method, knowledge that you gain about Linux is applicable to a wide range of systems and situations. Although learning Linux well can be a challenge, that knowledge carries over to other systems. For example, if you learn about the Domain Name Service (DNS) on Linux, you will find that the knowledge applies to DNS servers on practically any system in the world.

Knowledge of Linux also forms a strong foundation for learning about related topics such as TCP/IP routing or NIS+; learning about Apache Web servers on Linux will apply to Web server concepts on nearly every computing platform.

Linux **utilities** (programs used for system administration) differ in fundamental ways from utilities on non–UNIX-like operating systems such as Microsoft Windows or Novell NetWare. The history of UNIX (and thus of Linux) followed a very different path from the Microsoft operating systems. Specialized methods of solving problems have been developed for Linux and UNIX systems. As you learn about these methods, you can better use the utilities that Linux provides to keep your Linux systems running efficiently with the least amount of work and the fewest headaches.

Many of the principles outlined in this chapter have been developed over the 30-year history of UNIX and Linux technology. Thirty years ago, computers were slower, more expensive, and more difficult to use (no graphical interfaces were available until fairly recently). Linux was designed with these constraints in mind. As a result, Linux is generally more efficient in using limited system resources.

For example, special files known as shared libraries allowed multiple programs to use the same set of functions stored in memory. The goal of efficiency in Linux is reflected in the way system administration tasks are organized:

- Each program or system service relies on a separate plain-text configuration file.
- Everything on the Linux system is accessed as if it were a file, including devices and remote computer systems.
- The entire system was designed to be used by multiple users.
- Most Linux command-line utilities are designed to do one task very well. You can connect them together, however, to complete more complex tasks.

The sections that follow describe some of these traits in more detail.

Linux Configuration Files

A Linux system may support hundreds of users and have thousands of programs installed. Many of these programs are system or network services, such as a Web server, an e-mail server, or a Samba server (to allow clients like Windows 2000XP to connect to Linux). Other programs might include a graphical utility on a Linux desktop such as Gnome or KDE, or an end-user program such as the StarOffice office suite or the `gimp` image editing program.

Each of these programs and system services creates and maintains its own configuration information. The configuration files for programs managed by the system administrator, such as a Web server, are normally stored in the `/etc` directory. Configuration files for programs that are used by only a single user are stored in that user's home directory. Programs that are used by all users on a system often include default configuration information that is applied when any user runs the program, plus user-specific options that are stored in a user's home directory.

The names of Linux configuration files do not follow a well-defined pattern or naming convention. Some configuration files end with the word conf, for *configuration*. Others end with rc, for *run control*. The names of some configuration files show no indication of what the file is used for—as the system administrator, you must simply know which file to look for. There are historical reasons for each of the names, but that won't help you memorize the filenames you'll need to know to manage the system. A collection of Linux configuration files is shown in Table 7-1. The exact location of these files may vary depending on the version of Linux that you use—nearly all are located in the /etc directory or one of its subdirectories.

Table 7-1   Some Configuration Files Used by Linux

Filename	What the file configures
XF86Config-4	XFree86 graphical system
smb.conf	Samba server (which provides Windows-compatible file & print services)
httpd.conf	Web server
resolv.conf	DNS name resolver (selects a name server to access for translating domain names to network IP addresses)
hosts	Hostnames and corresponding IP addresses used for networking access
xinitrc	Programs that start when the graphical system is launched from a command line
ftpaccess	FTP server core configuration
grub.conf	GRUB boot loader configuration
bashrc	Configuration script that runs when starting a bash shell
passwd	User account names and configuration information
shadow	Encrypted passwords for each user account

You can learn about the content and format of most of the configuration files in Table 7-1 by entering the command man 5 *filename*.

Advantages of Multiple Plain-Text Configuration Files

The historical forces that have made Linux so powerful have also resulted in many configuration methods: software developers are not required by any authority to follow a specific pattern. UNIX systems have always used text-based configuration files. Using **plain-text configuration files** has several advantages:

- You can easily write a program to manipulate the configuration of a program or service, because this involves basic text string manipulation.

- Each configuration file is small and independent, leading to more efficient use of resources to update or query the configuration of a program.

- If one configuration file becomes corrupted, other configuration information is not affected—Linux configuration has no single point of failure or vulnerability.

- Developers creating programs can create new configuration designs to meet their needs, without being constrained to fit an existing configuration architecture.

- You can configure the most complex features of any program or system service with any text editor that you choose.

For all this flexibility, however, not everyone prefers text-based configuration files. They can be complex, and a Linux system administrator often must learn many different formats to configure a system.

Many efforts have been made to create graphical utilities to configure Linux. Some of these efforts focus on creating a configuration tool for a single complex service, such as the Apache Web server or the Samba server. One graphical tool for configuring networking is shown in Figure 7-2.

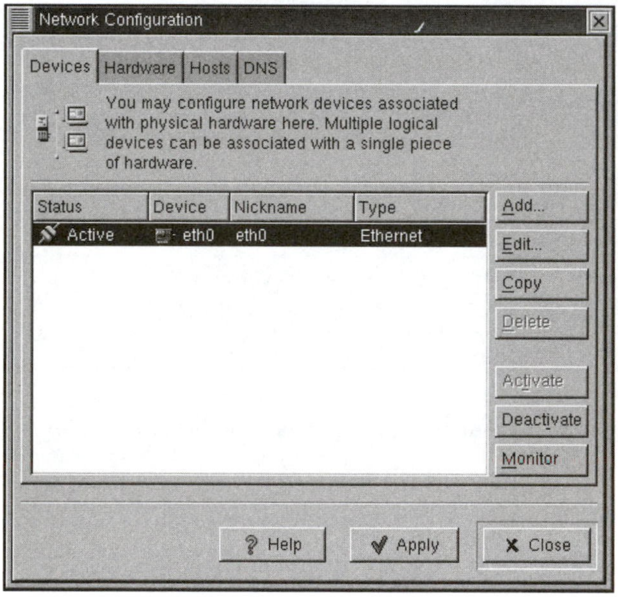

Figure 7-2 Configuring a program with a graphical utility

Other utilities were designed to provide a framework for configuring all (or nearly all) Linux programs. Obviously, this isn't a task for those who think small. A few projects serve as examples:

- KDE: The developers of the KDE Desktop have created dozens of utilities to manage system administration tasks. Many of these are integrated into a single Control Center (shown in Figure 7-3), which you can access by choosing

Control Center from the KDE main menu. KDE utilities have a common look and feel as part of a well-designed desktop environment, but the KDE utilities do not yet have the uniformity that system administrators would like to see.

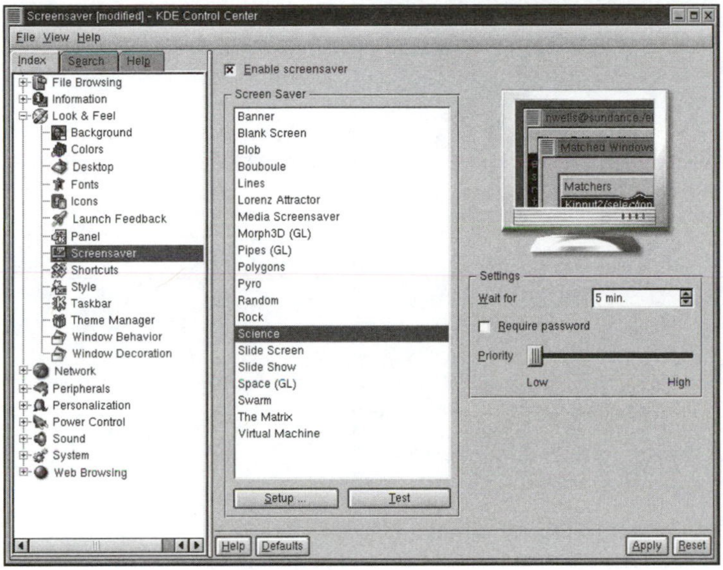

Figure 7-3   The KDE Control Center

- Gnome: The developers of the Gnome Desktop have also created dozens of utilities to manage system administration tasks. These utilities are generally more uniform in design and appearance than the collection of KDE utilities as a whole, but there are fewer Gnome utilities. An example of a Gnome utility is shown in Figure 7-4.

- **Webmin**: This browser-based administration tool lets you add modules to configure additional programs as the need arises. Dozens of Webmin modules are available in addition to the core modules for tasks such as managing file systems and user accounts. (Webmin functionality is described in detail as part of the discussion in several later chapters.) Webmin's browser interface is not as attractive or versatile as KDE's or Gnome's, but it has several advantages such as its modularity, the ease of creating new modules, and the ability to use it across a network. For information, visit *www.webmin.com*.

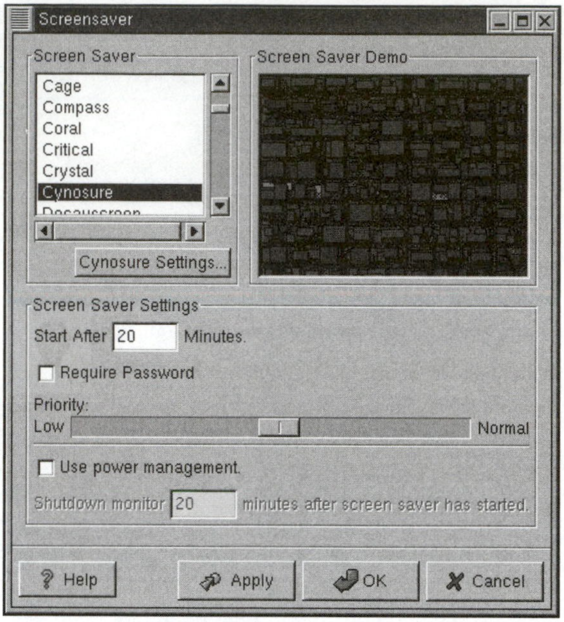

Figure 7-4   A Gnome configuration utility

Many versions of Linux have graphical configuration tools developed by the vendor of that version. For example, Caldera OpenLinux includes the Caldera Open Administration System (COAS) graphical utility; SuSE Linux includes the YAST configuration tool; Red Hat Linux includes a network configuration tool, `neat`, and many others.

Efforts to create comprehensive graphical configuration tools face many technical challenges because of the complex, changing nature of Linux utilities. A simplistic tool would be easy to develop but would ignore the requirements of day-to-day system administration; more complete tools require substantial development time, yet cannot keep pace with all the developers creating new features for hundreds of Linux programs.

Many Linux system administrators prefer to work directly in text files instead of using graphical interfaces to configure their systems. They often feel that they have more control over the configuration and can avoid the system overhead of a graphical interface.

Commercial UNIX systems have long had the **Common Desktop Environment (CDE),** which provides a large set of system administration tools in addition to a common desktop look and feel for all applications. But even CDE, with commercial support from huge companies like Hewlett-Packard, IBM, and Sun Microsystems, has had difficulty keeping up with new requirements and maintaining commonality across multiple UNIX platforms. (See *www.opengroup.org* for information about CDE.) CDE is also available for Linux under the product name Dextop. Visit *www.xig.com* for details.

With the growing availability of graphical utilities in Gnome and KDE, plus the many application-specific graphical utilities, you may wonder why so many command-line utilities and text-based configuration files are introduced in this book.

The answer is more philosophical than practical at this stage: because someone has to know how the system *really* works. As the system administrator for a Linux-based server or network, you will often face problems that cannot be solved by even the most advanced graphical tools. These problems may cross boundaries between different programs; they may involve networking activity over which you have no direct control; they may require that you make minor adjustments to configuration files that would not be possible in a graphical tool. If you can't get "under the hood" of the system to explore and adjust everything, your ability to keep a system running smoothly is much reduced. You are left instead clicking buttons, wondering what is really happening on a system that continues to have a problem you cannot effectively diagnose or repair.

 Linux and most Linux programs provide the added benefit of allowing you to review the program source code. Using this admittedly challenging method of troubleshooting, you can fix anything, given enough time. But before you can take advantage of this option, you must start by learning *how* things work, not simply which buttons to click in order to complete rote or simple tasks.

The numerous plain-text configuration files in Linux provide access to all features of Linux programs.

Understanding Files, Devices, and Processes

Managing a Linux system includes managing all of the resources of the system: the file systems stored on hard disks, tape drives, and CD-ROM or DVD discs; other hardware devices; user accounts; and individual programs. As you learned in Chapter 4, the default Linux file system is large and complex, with predefined locations for most types of files. The task of locating, creating, moving, and deleting files is part of every system administrator's day. The section "Using Basic System Administration Tools" later in this chapter describes additional utilities you can use to manage the Linux file system. The following sections define the terms *devices*, *processes*, *programs*, *daemons*, and *threads*.

Devices

As you have seen during Linux installation and in Chapter 4, you communicate with all types of hardware devices attached to your Linux server by referring to filenames in the /dev subdirectory. A **device** is a hardware peripheral like a printer, scanner, mouse, or hard disk; in Linux a device can also be a part of the system software, such as the devices associated with virtual consoles (tty1 through tty6).

Later chapters, such as Chapter 13, describe more utilities that let you inter-act with devices via the /dev subdirectory.

Some devices are accessed directly through a filename in /dev. For example, when you configure a local printer as described in Chapter 12, you can refer to the /dev/lp0 device name. This name refers to your computer's first parallel port.

Other devices are accessed indirectly—you create an association between a name in the /dev subdirectory and another system resource, then refer to the other resource to read the device. For example, to access files on a hard disk, you must first configure access to the hard disk by referring to a device such as /dev/hda1. You create an association between the device name (such as /dev/hda1) and a standard directory path that is not part of /dev, such as /usr or /home. Then you can access the device by referring to the other resource—the directory that you have associated with the /dev/hda1 device.

Chapter 8 contains detailed information on managing file systems.

Processes

Processes are the individual programs running on a Linux system. Because Linux is a multitasking operating system, many programs are normally running on Linux at the same time. Chapter 8 and Chapter 10 both describe different methods of managing multiple processes to make efficient use of system resources. The section "Using Basic System Administration Tools," later in this chapter, describes a few common utilities that provide information about the processes running on Linux at any moment.

Although process is a precise term used to describe a task that the Linux kernel is running, several other terms are commonly used to refer to various types of processes, as described in the following sections.

Program

The word **program** is a vague term for a piece of software that executes on the Linux system. A program may be composed of many different processes that Linux manages together to accomplish an overall goal; a program may also include just one process. The terms program, utility, tool, and software package are all used interchangeably when discussing software that runs on Linux. All of these terms are imprecise compared to using the term process, but they work fine for casual conversation among system administrators.

Daemon

A **daemon** is a background process. It normally runs continuously, but it does not have any visible output. An example of a daemon is an FTP server. It processes incoming requests, sending back files as needed, but it never displays anything on the Linux screen. Instead, information on the activities of a daemon is normally recorded in a log file (`/var/log/xferlog` in the case of the FTP daemon). On a standard Linux system, many daemons are running all the time. The name of a daemon often ends with the letter *d*. Some of the daemons you may see running on your Linux system after a default installation include those listed in Table 7-2.

 Daemons often provide network services—they listen for requests coming from network connections and respond with data according to how they are configured. Because of this, daemons are sometimes called servers. The two terms are sometimes used interchangeably. To be more precise, a server is nearly always a daemon and many daemons act as servers.

Table 7-2   Daemons Running on Linux

Daemon name	Description
`crond`	Runs scripts at scheduled times (as described in Chapter 11).
`httpd`	Responds to Web browser requests and returns Web pages or other requested information (using the HTTP protocol).
`inetd` or `xinetd`	Watches for incoming requests of many types and starts the appropriate daemon to respond to the request. (Requests to Internet services such as FTP, Telnet, Finger, Talk, and Gopher are normally handled through `inetd` or `xinetd`.)
`syslogd`	Records information from running programs to the system log file `/var/log/messages`.

Thread

A **thread** is a part of a process (or a part of a daemon, since a daemon is a type of process). A thread is sometimes called a subprocess because it is a piece of a larger task that a program is working to accomplish. A single task normally performed by a process in sequential fashion can be split into multiple threads, or subtasks, that can be accomplished in parallel, sometimes by multiple CPUs (on a multiprocessor system). A more precise distinction between processes and threads is not important for most system administration work. The term process is used in most cases that don't involve programmers developing software based on threads.

Multiple Users, Multiple Processes

Linux was designed to be a multiuser operating system. As you have already seen, you must create user accounts before anyone can log in and use the system. No one can enter commands at a Linux command line without first logging in with a valid username and password.

Each user account can execute multiple programs (start many processes), and each of these processes is associated with the user that started it. The system administrator, while logged in as root, can manage all processes on the system. For example, in Chapter 10 you will learn how to assign a higher priority to all of a user's processes so that they are executed more quickly than other users' processes. You will also learn how to stop (kill) a single process that might be consuming too many system resources or that has stopped working correctly.

Because a Linux system often supports many users and each user runs many processes, managing users and processes is an important part of good system administration.

Using Small, Efficient Utilities

The design goal for most Linux utilities is to perform a single task, offer flexibility in how to perform the task, and perform it quickly (that is, with the most efficient use of system resources such as CPU time and memory space).

To provide flexibility, most Linux commands have numerous options that let you modify the basic operation of the command. But all of these options are focused on a single type of task. For example, the Linux utility ls is designed to list files, not manage all aspects of your file system. To give you flexibility in listing files, the ls command supports over 50 options. You can use any of these options by including them after the command name when executing ls.

Most Linux commands use the same format for including options on a command line. Each option is represented by either a hyphen followed by a single letter or two hyphens followed by a word describing the option. If single letters are used to select options, they can be combined after a single hyphen. If full-word descriptions are used to select options, each must be written out separately. In both cases, the options are listed before any filenames or other parameters to the command. Sometimes a command option requires a value after the option, such as a filename.

Some Linux utilities, such as `ps` and `tar`, described later in this chapter, use single-letter options without a hyphen preceding them.

Table 7–3 lists 10 common `ls` command options.

Table 7-3   Common Options of the `ls` Command

Single-letter format	Full-word format	Description
`-a`	`--all`	Lists all files in a directory, including hidden files (files that start with ".").
`-l` Note: Use a lowercase letter *L* for this option.	`--format=long`	Prints not only the names of items in a directory, but also their sizes, owners, dates of creation, and so forth.
`-C`	`--format` `=vertical`	Displays items in sorted columns.
`-r`	`--reverse`	Reverses the sorting order of the items being listed.
`-t`	`--sort=time`	Sorts items being listed by their timestamp rather than alphabetically.
`-S`	`--sort=size`	Sorts items being listed by their size rather than alphabetically.
none	`--color`	Displays files color coded according to type.
none	`--help`	Displays help text with an abbreviated options list.
`-I pattern`	`--ignore` `pattern`	Does not display items matching the pattern given.
`-R`	`--recursive`	Lists the contents of all subdirectories as well as the current directory, showing the entire directory tree.
`-i`	`--inode`	Prints the index number for each file to the left of the filename.

Both the names of Linux commands and their options are case sensitive. The `-r` option and the `-R` option are both valid and have very different meanings.

7

You can combine options in several ways, as the examples in Table 7-4 show. The best way to see how options can be combined is to experiment.

Table 7-4   Combining Command Options

Command example	Description of results
`ls -laSr`	Lists the contents of the current directory, including all files (`-a`), in long format (`-l`), sorted by size (`-S`), in reverse order (`-r`).
`ls -l -a -S -r`	Same as the previous example.
`ls -R --color`	Lists the contents of all subdirectories (`-R`), color coding each item shown (`--color`). In this example, no single character option for `--color` is supported, so the two options cannot be combined.
`ls --format=vertical --sort=time -ai`	Lists all files (`-a`), including their index numbers (`-i`), in a vertical column, sorting them by their creation time and date.

Standard Input and Output

Most input and output in Linux is done using standardized channels. Input normally comes from the keyboard and output normally goes to the screen. Channels of communication in Linux can be redirected, however, using **redirection** operators. The redirection feature gives you great flexibility in using Linux utilities.

When a program expects input such as a line of text, it reads that information from the **standard input** channel (abbreviated **STDIN**). Normally, the STDIN data provided by the kernel comes from the keyboard. But you can redirect input so that the kernel hands the program data from a file or from another program instead of the keyboard.

Similarly, when a program generates output, it normally sends it to the **standard output** channel (abbreviated **STDOUT**) whenever it wants to display that information on-screen. The system normally writes anything sent to STDOUT on your console screen in the window where the program was launched. The STDOUT data can be redirected, however, so that anything a program sends to STDOUT is written directly to a file or sent to another program.

A third standard channel is called **standard error** (abbreviated **STDERR**). Error messages are written to standard error separately from STDOUT, in case STDOUT has been redirected. Of course, the output of STDERR can also be redirected to a new location such as an error log file.

A special tool for redirecting communication between programs is called a pipe. A **pipe** connects the output channel of one command to the input channel of another command. Pipes are used to connect the output of one application to the input of another application. Figure 7-5 shows how this works conceptually.

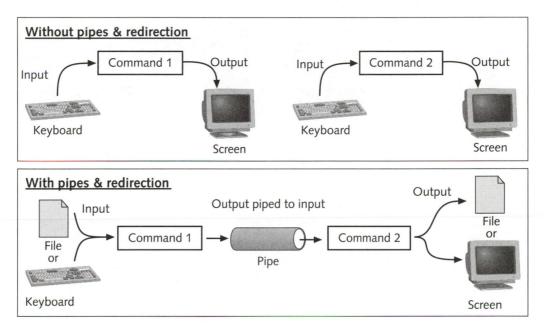

Figure 7-5   Creating a pipe between two applications

To see a pipe in action, consider two commands: `ls`, which lists the contents of a directory; and `sort`, which sorts all the lines in a file. The `ls` command normally writes output to the screen, whereas `sort` normally requires a filename as a parameter. But you can combine the `ls` and `sort` commands by entering the following at a Linux command prompt:

```
$ ls -l | sort
```

The output of this `ls` command is not written to the screen. Instead, it is sent (piped) to the `sort` command. Although the `sort` command normally requires a filename, in this case it receives the names of the items it needs to sort from the `ls` command. The result is that `sort` writes to the screen the lines from `ls`, sorted according to the first word in each line.

By combining the features of STDIN, STDOUT, and STDERR with the ability to redirect these communication channels and use pipes, each Linux utility can interact with other utilities and files to handle complex tasks for users and system administrators. Table 7-5 shows the special characters used on the Linux command line to instruct the shell to redirect communication between programs.

Table 7-5   Redirecting Input and Output

Symbol to use in a command statement	Description	Command-line example
`> filename`	Writes STDOUT output to the given filename.	`ls -l > savelisting`
`>> filename`	Appends STDOUT output to the given filename (adding it to the end of any existing file contents).	`cat newfile >> existing_file`
`< filename`	Sends data from the given filename as the STDIN, rather than reading from the keyboard.	`my_script < input_codes`

`<< word`
`    text lines`
`word`
	Sends text lines as standard input, ending when *word* occurs. (EOF is a typical example of the code word chosen). This is called a "here document" and is used in shell scripts to feed specific text to a program that reads from STDIN. See the bash man page for more details.	`program << EOF`
		`   input line 1`
		`   input line 2`
		`   input line 3`
		`EOF`

`|`	Creates a pipe between two programs, so that the STDOUT output from the command on the left of the pipe symbol is used as the STDIN input for the command on the right of the pipe symbol.	`ls -l	sort`

A savvy system administrator knows command options and is comfortable combining basic utilities to provide all sorts of useful information by entering a single string of connected commands. The next section describes some of these basic utilities and suggests how to combine them using redirection.

USING BASIC SYSTEM ADMINISTRATION TOOLS

A good system administrator has a mental "toolbox" of methods for solving problems. A large part of this toolbox is knowing about a number of basic Linux utilities and the options supported by those utilities. Although a single utility usually has a simple function, multiple utilities combined together can be powerful and extremely useful.

In later chapters you learn about other utilities that are devoted to more specialized system administration tasks, such as backing up files or formatting new hard disks. This section focuses on tools that are useful in many circumstances. If you have worked at a command line in another operating system, some of these tools will be familiar to you. Others are unique to Linux and UNIX environments.

Case Sensitivity in Linux

Nearly everything in Linux is case sensitive. This can be a big change for those accustomed to other operating systems. It means, for example, that typing a command in all capital letters is different from using all lowercase. In fact, each of the items in this list could be a different, distinct command in Linux (in fact, only the first one is a standard Linux command):

- `find`

- `FIND`

- `Find`

- `FiNd`

Linux commands are all lowercase and must be entered without capital letters.

You may accidentally try to enter your password during login with Caps Lock activated on your keyboard. Passwords are case sensitive and are usually mostly lowercase letters. You can't see on-screen what you are typing when entering a password, so the reason your password fails is not obvious. Check the Caps Lock key.

Filenames and File Extensions

Some operating systems use the last part of a filename as an indication of what type of data the file contains. For example, a file ending in `.tif` is a certain type of graphics file; a file ending in `.pdf` is a certain type of document file. The ending part of a filename is often called the file extension, from the days when personal computers used filenames consisting of a maximum of eight letters and a three-character extension.

Linux does not use file extensions in this way. Instead, it examines the contents of a file to determine its type. A file may have an extension that indicates its type, but this information should be regarded as a convenience for the user, not a requirement for the operating system. For example, if you downloaded a graphics file called `hubble15.jpg`, you could change the filename to `hubble15` (dropping the `.jpg` file extension). A graphics program like `gimp` could still display the file.

Some programs in Linux *do* rely on file extensions, though this is rare. One example is a Web server, which may decide on rules for processing files based on file extensions such as .html, .gif, or others.

Another point: filenames in Linux can be very long—up to 256 characters. They can also contain nearly any character except a forward slash (/). Avoid making filenames too long, however, because when many long filenames are combined into a full pathname, the pathname may exceed the length limit imposed by the shell for pathnames. If you use characters besides letters and digits in a filename, such as a space or punctuation marks, you should enclose the filename in quotation marks so that the characters are not interpreted as special commands by the shell.

Learning about Linux Commands

In the following sections (and in future chapters), you will learn about many Linux commands. Because most of these commands have numerous options and sometimes complex **syntax** (formatting) rules, you should develop a habit of reviewing the online documentation for commands to refresh your memory or learn about new options as you work. Methods of accomplishing this include the following:

- Use the online manual page (man page). Each man page contains a description of the command's syntax and all options supported by the command, along with descriptions of how the command can be used, related commands, and additional information. The man pages rarely contain examples, however. To view a man page, enter `man` followed by the command you want to learn about. For example, to learn about the `ls` command, enter `man ls`.

- Use a command's `--help` option. Most commands will print a summary of options and syntax when you enter the command with `--help` or `-h` as a parameter. This information is less complete than the man page, but it provides a quick summary of the command. This is especially useful when you are already familiar with the command and only need a quick reminder about options. For example, to learn about the `ls` command, enter `ls --help`.

- Use the `info` command. For some commands, the man page is not updated regularly. Instead, documentation in another format is provided through the `info` command. For example, to learn about the `ls` command, enter `info ls`.

Nearly every Linux command has a corresponding man page, so they are a good place to start. Sometimes the man page will say "see the info page for complete documentation," in which case the man page will tell you little and you can use the `info` command instead.

- Use the `apropos` command when you don't know the name of a command to complete a certain task. The `apropos` command displays a list of man pages that contain the keyword you enter. For example, to see a list of all man pages that contain information about the GRUB boot manager, enter `apropos grub`. On some systems you must generate a keyword database before using the `apropos` command. On Red Hat Linux 7.3 systems, the command `/usr/sbin/makewhatis` will create such a database, but this is done for you automatically.

You must already know the name of the appropriate command before you can use man or the help options. If you don't know which command to use to solve a problem, use the apropos command or try to find a related word in the index of this book and see which commands are mentioned in that section of the book.

Using Regular Expressions

System administration tasks frequently involve patterns of information. These patterns might apply to filenames, information on a Web server, information within database files, or in many other locations and situations. Linux uses a system of expressing patterns called regular expressions. A **regular expression** provides a flexible way to encode many types of complex patterns. You can use a regular expression as a parameter to almost every Linux command. You also use regular expressions when writing shell scripts and other types of programs that provide system administration functionality.

By way of example, a single regular expression can describe each of the patterns in the following sentences:

- Lines containing the word *President* or *president* (upper- or lowercase *P*)

- Filenames with the digits 18 followed by any other digits

- Text at the beginning of a line that starts with *Cruise* or *cruise* and includes the word *ship* later in the same line

- Filenames that end with TIFF, TIF, Tif, Tiff, tif, or tiff

You may already have experience using wildcards to describe filenames. For example, you can refer to all files ending with the .doc extension by using the wildcard expression *.doc. The * character has special meaning as a wildcard. Regular expressions operate in the same way; they can be as simple as *.doc, but they can also include more complicated statements because they can include many characters that have special meanings. Table 7-6 lists some special characters that you can include in a regular expression. It would take many pages to describe the nuances of creating regular expressions, but mastering the items listed here will let you use regular expressions effectively for many system administration tasks.

Table 7-6 Common Regular Expressions in Linux

Expression syntax	Meaning of syntax
*	Match zero or more characters
? or . (a period)	Match one character
^	Match text at the beginning of a line
$	Match text at the end of a line
[abc]	Match one of the characters in brackets
[^abc]	Exclude all of the characters in brackets

The acceptable syntax for a regular expression varies in small but important ways depending on where you are using the expression. Within a shell script, as a parameter to some utilities, within a `vi` editing command, and in other places, you must watch for slight variations in meaning.

More complex still, the basic information provided in Table 7-6 does not show how the same character can have different meanings in different positions. For example, the ^ character generally means "tie this pattern to the beginning of a line," but when placed inside brackets as in the last example of Table 7-6, the ^ means "not" and serves to exclude all characters within the brackets.

To understand the syntax of regular expressions better, study the examples in Table 7-7.

Table 7-7   Example Regular Expressions

Example regular expression	What it matches
`[iI]tal*`	Any word starting with *I* or *i* followed by *tal*, such as Italy, italy, Italian, italian, Italianate, italianate, and so forth.
`^[mM]us??m`	Text at the beginning of a line that begins with *m* or *M*, followed by *us*, two characters, and *m*. (The two characters are intended to allow misspelled versions of the word *museum* to be found, but note how this pattern will also match *Muslim*.)
`180[0..9]$`	A word at the end of a line that begins with 180 and ends with a digit from 0 to 9 (any of the years from 1800 to 1809 will match).

Deleting Files in Linux

To delete files in many popular operating systems, you transfer them to a trashcan or recycle bin. The deleted file remains on your system until you "empty" the trashcan or recycle bin. In effect, when you delete a file in this way, you are not really erasing the file, but simply marking it for deletion when the trashcan is emptied. This serves as a protective system against accidentally deleting files that you discover you need soon after you delete them.

In many cases, even after you have emptied the trashcan or recycle bin, you can use special utilities to "undelete" the erased file, reassembling the contents of the file from your hard disk so that it is a complete file again.

Linux desktop interfaces also provide a trashcan icon that you can use to discard files you no longer need. But when you work at the command line, you don't have access to the trashcan—instead you use the `rm` command.

The `rm` command in Linux is permanent. Files can almost never be recovered after using `rm`, and no convenient system utility will help you make the attempt. When you use the `rm` command to delete a file, the file is immediately deleted from your hard disk. Because of the way Linux arranges file information on the hard disk, recovering a deleted file is rarely successful. To protect yourself and users on your system from accidentally erasing files that are later needed, consider these methods used by some system administrators:

- Use the `rm` command with the `-i` option, which prompts you for confirmation before deleting a file. This reminds you to reconsider any need for the file you are about to erase.

- Use the **`safedelete`** utility, which compresses and stores files in a hidden directory when they are "deleted." From this directory, they can be undeleted later if needed. Using this type of utility requires additional maintenance and disk space for the compressed files, but it provides a backup copy in case deleted files are needed. (This utility is not installed by default; you can find it at *rpmfind.net*.)

 If you install `safedelete`, consider creating an alias in `/etc/profile` from the `rm` command to the `safedelete` command so that everyone on the system will be using `safedelete` automatically.

- Use the trashcan on the KDE or Gnome Desktop so that files are not actually deleted until you empty the trash.

- Use a low-level disk editing tool that attempts to reassemble the pieces of a deleted file. Using such tools is rarely a complete success, but can often recover at least part of an important file that was accidentally deleted. (One disk editing tool is `lde`, the Linux Disk Editor, available at *lde.sourceforge.net*.)

A separate concern you may have is making sure deleted data is *really* deleted. Although the structure of Linux files makes it hard to undelete a file, a dedicated soul could find important information by checking every sector of your hard disk. As on other systems, the `rm` command does not write over a file's data; it simply makes the file's disk space available for other files. To actually overwrite a file's data as you delete the file, look for the `shred` utility on *rpmfind.net*.

Finding What You Need

Beyond the basic file system utilities like `cd`, `mkdir`, `cp`, and `ls`, Linux provides more complex tools to help you locate specific files and search within files. This section describes three such tools: `locate`, `find`, and `grep`.

Using `locate`

Use the **`locate`** command to search an index of all files on your Linux system. If Linux finds any directory or filename that matches your query, it displays the full pathname of that item. For example, suppose you need to locate the Web server configuration file on a Linux system and can't remember where it is stored. The following command lists all occurrences of `httpd.conf` in the Linux file system:

```
locate httpd.conf
```

The `locate` command does not examine the contents of files, only the filenames. Using `locate` is like searching the output of an `ls` command of the entire file system.

If you are not certain of the complete name of the file you need, you can use part of it with `locate`. If that partial name occurs anywhere in a directory or filename, the `locate` command lists it on-screen. For example, the following command will also print out all occurrences of `httpd.conf`, in addition to other file and directory names containing `http`:

```
# locate http
```

The `locate` command is very fast because it searches an index of your file system rather than creating a new list of files each time you make a query. Using `locate` has two disadvantages, however. First, if you haven't updated the index since you changed your file system, you may not see the results you need (the item you're looking for may not be listed). To update the `locate` index, run the **updatedb** command. This command is run automatically at regular intervals on most Linux systems, including Red Hat Linux 7.3.

A second problem is that you must know what you're looking for fairly precisely, or else `locate` will display a list of files and directories so long as to be useless. (Try executing `locate bin` to see an example of this problem.) This is especially true because you can't use regular expressions to define your `locate` query.

Using `find`

The **find** command can also display a list of files that match a query string, but it provides many more options than `locate`, so it can be used for much more in-depth and powerful system administration work. The **find** command doesn't use a pre-built index; it examines your file system at the time you run a command, so it may work more slowly than `locate`.

The simplest use of **find** is to search for files that match a specific pattern and display them on-screen. In the following example, the path where the search should begin is `/home;` the name of the file to search for is `report.doc`, and the action to take with each matching filename is to display (print) the name on-screen:

```
# find /home -name "report.doc" -print
```

The **find** command uses full words as options, but preceded by only a single hyphen instead of two.

The **find** options let you perform complex searches for information on your Linux system. For example, using a single (complex) **find** command, you could do any of the following tasks:

- Create an archive file of all the files that have been modified in the last 24 hours.
- Delete all files owned by a certain user on the Linux system.
- Create a list of all files that are larger than a certain size.
- Create a list of all files that have specific access permissions.
- Create a list of all files that do not have a valid owner.

In later chapters you will see **find** used in examples for specific tasks like those listed here. For the moment, consider one more example of **find**. The following command searches the **/tmp** directory (and all its subdirectories) for files owned by user wilsonr that have the **.jpg** file extension and are larger than 50 KB. All matching filenames are displayed on-screen and the files are immediately deleted.

```
# find /tmp —name "*jpg" —size 50k —user wilsonr —print
  —exec rm \{\} \;
```

Using grep

The **locate** and **find** commands help you locate a file with specific characteristics. To search the contents of files, use the **grep** command. **grep** can rapidly scan files for a pattern that you specify, printing out the lines of text that contain text matching the pattern. You can then take further action on these matching lines of text by using a pipe to connect **grep** with other filtering commands.

As a simple example of **grep**, suppose you want to see the shell used by a certain user account. Rather than open a user management tool or look at the **/etc/passwd** file in a text editor, you can enter this command and immediately see the line of **/etc/passwd** that contains the information you need:

```
# grep wilson /etc/passwd
wilsonr:x:564:564::/home/wilsonr:/bin/csh
```

The last item in the output line indicates that the current default shell for user wilsonr is the C shell (**csh**). Note that the **grep** command searched only for wilson, not for wilsonr. If multiple usernames on the system included the string wilson, **grep** would have displayed a matching line for each one. As a system administrator, you learn when to take shortcuts—on a system with few users, the search pattern wil might have worked as well as wilson.

Use the `grep` command to search within text files, not within binary-format data such as program executables and image files.

Consider another example: suppose you have a directory full of text files and you want to see all occurrences of a string pattern that includes **ThomasCorp**. The following command lists all of those occurrences, showing the filename containing the string and the complete line of text containing the string:

```
$ grep Thomas[cC]orp  *txt
```

The first parameter—**Thomas[cC]orp**—is a regular expression defining what text to look for. When using the **grep** command, an asterisk is never needed at the beginning or end of the string pattern (such as **ThomasCorp***), because **grep** will locate the string wherever it occurs. The above example of **grep** would find instances of the following strings:

- `Thomascorp`

- `ThomasCorporation`

- `ThomasCorps`

But these strings would not be included:

- `Thomas Corporation`

- `Thomas corporation`

- `Thomas Nast`

The second parameter to **grep** is also a regular expression. It defines which files to search. The asterisk in the command indicates that all files in the current directory that end with **txt** should be searched.

The results of the **grep** command might include lines like these:

- `Annual_report.txt: As news of ThomasCorporation`
  `reaches customers around the world, we are pleased to…`

- `memo0518.txt: that Rachel and I think Thomascorp`
  `should be looking seriously at acquiring an interest in…`

- `meetingsummary.txt: Discussed needs of ThomasCorp to`
  `diversify plastics manufacturing capacity for…`

The **grep** command is often used at the end of a pipe, so that **grep** is searching the output of another command instead of a file. For example, you could pipe the output of the **locate** command through **grep** to refine a search. Suppose you wanted to search among all `.tif` graphics files on the system for your airframe image, but you can't remember the exact filename you used (perhaps `airframe.tif`, `airframes.tif`, `old_air_frame.tif`, or something similar). You might use a command like this:

```
$ locate tif | grep frame
```

In cases like this, `grep` uses only a single parameter—the pattern to search for. Rather than include a filename to define the text to be searched, the output of the `locate` command is searched. The results are printed to STDOUT—the screen.

Reviewing System Processes

Linux includes many utilities for managing processes running on your system. Two of these commands are introduced here. These and others are covered in detail in Chapter 10.

The `ps` command lists the processes that are currently running on your Linux system. The process list can be brief, or it can contain a great deal of information. Selecting various options for the `ps` command lets you control which pieces of information are included in a listing of processes and how that information is organized. The basic format of the `ps` command uses no parameters and produces a listing of programs that you have started in your current session (this is generally a short list, as shown here):

```
$ ps
PID         TTY         TIME         CMD
576         tty1        00:00:00     login
584         tty1        00:00:00     bash
741         tty1        00:00:00     ps
```

In this list, you see a **PID (process ID)** number (a unique number identifying a process); the terminal that the process is using for output (`tty1` is the first text-mode console screen); the CPU time that the process has used so far; and the command that started the process.

Adding options to `ps` causes it to include information such as the user that started the process (the process owner), the process priority, current status (such as paused or running), and the PID number of the parent process (the process that started this one).

You can use the `kill` command to end a process. Chapter 9 explains more about how this occurs within the Linux kernel, but the simplest example of `kill` is shown here (the **–9** option indicates that you want to force a process to end, and the second number is the PID of the process to be ended):

```
kill -9 873
```

CHAPTER SUMMARY

- ❑ The role of a Linux system administrator is to keep Linux-based computer systems running efficiently so that co-workers, managers, or the public can rely on the services provided by technology.

❏ System administrators work with IS, IT, or MIS departments; they may be part of a group reporting to a CIO, or they may work alone; they may focus on maintaining end-user systems, Internet systems, or other aspects of an organization's technical requirements.

❏ System administrators may spend as much time working with people as with technology. They help users solve problems, train users, and inform management of technical developments.

❏ System administrators are trusted employees who have access to valuable personal and business data. Legal and ethical rules control what can be done with that data.

❏ Each program in Linux is configured using one or more plain-text configuration files. The formats used in these files are not consistent between programs.

❏ Plain-text configuration files have the advantage of allowing complex configurations and permitting modifications using any text editor. But they create a learning curve for new users and can be poorly documented.

❏ Many graphical configuration utilities are available for Linux; some configure a single program, others attempt to manage configuration of many or most aspects of Linux system administration.

❏ Devices are accessed via the `/dev` directory, either directly or by creating an association with another system resource.

❏ Processes are the programs running on Linux. Some processes run in the background and are called daemons. The `ps` command is the core utility used to view and manage processes.

❏ Linux supports multiple users working at the same time. Each user can run many processes at the same time.

❏ Linux utilities have standard formats for including options on a command line: single characters with a hyphen or full words with two hyphens. Variations in this standard are not uncommon, however.

❏ Communication to and from programs is managed through standardized channels called STDIN, STDOUT, and STDERR. These channels normally use the keyboard and screen for input and output, respectively. You can redirect where input comes from and where output goes.

❏ Program names in Linux are usually all lowercase and must be entered that way: Linux is case sensitive.

❏ Linux supports very long filenames that can include most special characters, such as spaces and punctuation.

❏ File extensions can be used for convenience in Linux, but they do not have the same importance as in many other operating systems.

❑ To learn about Linux commands, use the `--help` option or view the man or `info` page for the command. The `apropos` command can help you locate an appropriate command based on a keyword search of man pages.

❑ Regular expressions let you define a pattern to use as a parameter for a Linux command. They are similar to wildcard characters in filenames, but are much more flexible and powerful.

❑ Deleting files in Linux using `rm` is permanent. Do not expect to be able to recover a file that has been deleted.

❑ The `locate` and `find` commands help you locate files within Linux. The `find` command is more powerful and lets you specify properties of the files to match.

❑ The `grep` command searches within text files for patterns you specify using regular expressions.

❑ The `ps` command provides a PID and other information about each process running on Linux. Any process can be ended using the `kill` command.

7

KEY TERMS

apropos — A command used to show all man pages that contain a keyword.

chief information officer (CIO) — The executive in an organization who determines how information systems are used within the organization to further its goals or mission effectively.

Common Desktop Environment (CDE) — A graphical desktop interface with accompanying system administration utilities. Provides a common look and feel for many commercial UNIX systems.

daemon — A background process that handles tasks such as responding to network traffic without any visible screen output.

device — A hardware peripheral such as a printer, scanner, mouse, or hard disk; also some specialized parts of Linux system software, such as the devices associated with virtual consoles (tty1 through tty6).

end user — An individual who uses the computer systems in an organization to accomplish assigned tasks, but who often relies on a system administrator to keep those systems running smoothly.

find — A command that searches the file system for files matching certain characteristics.

grep — A command that searches the contents of text files for lines containing a given regular expression.

help desk — A service in many organizations that assists end users in solving problems related to information technology.

info — A command that displays online command reference information. *See also* man.

Information Systems (IS) department — A department within many organizations. IS staff are responsible for maintaining computer and information systems for other employees. (IS is called the IT department in some organizations.)

Information Technology (IT) department — *See* Information Systems (IS) department.

kill — A command that can stop a process.

locate — A command that searches an index of the file system for items matching a word.

MIS (Management of Information Systems or **Manager of Information Systems)** — Another term for the IS or IT department or the staff who work in or manage that department.

pipe — A connection between two commands (indicated by the | character) that causes the output of one command to be used as the input of a second command.

plain-text configuration file — A file containing human-readable instructions that are used by a program to define its configuration.

process — A task or program running on a Linux operating system, managed by the Linux kernel.

process ID (PID) — A number from 1 to 65,000 that is associated uniquely with a process running on a Linux system.

program — An imprecise term used to refer to any process running on a Linux system.

ps — A command that provides information about processes running on Linux.

redirection — The act of changing where a Linux program receives its input or sends its output.

regular expression — A system of expressing patterns using special characters that can be interpreted by many Linux programs.

safedelete — A utility that makes files appear to have been deleted but actually saves a compressed copy of each one in case it is needed later.

SAGE (System Administrators Guild) — A professional organization for system administrators.

standard error (STDERR) — The communication channel used by most Linux programs to send information about errors in program execution.

standard input (STDIN) — The communication channel used by most Linux programs to collect input (normally from the keyboard).

standard output (STDOUT) — The communication channel used by most Linux programs to write output (normally to the screen).

syntax — A formalized arrangement of information to allow a Linux command to understand parameters, options, or configuration files.

thread — A part of a process.

utility — An imprecise term referring to a program used to administer a computer system rather than do work for an end user.

Webmin — A browser-based graphical system administration tool to which you can add modules to configure additional programs as the need arises.

REVIEW QUESTIONS

1. What nontechnical skills are important when working as a system administrator?

2. One advantage of using multiple plain-text configuration files in Linux is that:

   a. They are compatible with configuration files from other operating systems

   b. Several system administrators can access the same configuration file at the same time

   c. If one configuration file becomes corrupted, none of the other system services are affected

   d. Special utilities are required to change system configuration settings

3. Which task is not likely to be assigned to you as a system administrator?

   a. Develop a new cash register system using C programming.

   b. Install new hard disks in Linux servers.

   c. Teach new users how to access their e-mail accounts.

   d. Attend a conference on improving system security.

4. A _____ runs a subtask as part of a larger task.

   a. daemon

   b. process

   c. thread

   d. utility

5. Describe the function of the help desk within an organization.

6. Name three graphical tools that are used either for general system administration or for administration of a specific service (such as a Web server).

7. Given that `ls` uses options in standard format, which of the following does not have correctly formed options?

   a. `ls --help`

   b. `ls --color -R`

   c. `ls -il -aX --reverse`

   d. `ls -sort=time`

8. A pipe is a method of connecting:

   a. Processes with daemons

   b. The output channel of one process with the input channel of another process

   c. Threads

   d. A deleted filename with that file's data as it resides on the hard disk

9. The command `ls | sort` causes which of the following to occur?

a. The output of the `ls` command is sent to the `sort` command. The results are printed to the screen.

b. It cannot be determined without information about the next command to be executed.

c. The output of the `ls` command is written to a file named `sort`.

d. The output of the `ls` command is filtered based on the regular expression contained in the file `sort`.

10. A regular expression is used to:

a. Define a list of threads that a process can execute

b. Assign values to variables

c. Define a potentially complex pattern used for searching

d. Build filenames with specialized file extensions

11. When you run a program called `gather_data`, it normally reads lines entered at the keyboard. If you use the command `gather_data < input_text` to run the program, which of the following occurs?

a. The `gather_data` command is executed followed by the `input_text` command.

b. The input that the `gather_data` program would normally read from the keyboard is taken from the `input_text` file instead.

c. The `input_text` program runs first, collecting data, which is then passed through a pipe to the `gather_data` program.

d. Both `gather_data` and `input_text` run as concurrent processes reading from the keyboard as STDIN.

12. Describe the difference between `find` and `locate`.

13. The regular expression `[cC]hapter0[12345]*` will *not* match which of the following files?

a. `chapter01`

b. `Chapter03.doc`

c. `Chapter1.doc`

d. `Chapter02`

14. The `find` command should be used instead of the `locate` command when:

a. Your `locate` index has not been updated recently

b. The number of processes on the system is large

c. You prefer to use `grep` at the same time

d. The file system appears to be unstable

15. The `grep` command is *not* useful for which of the following?

    a. Searching for all filenames that match a pattern

    b. Determining which directories are currently in use

    c. Finding lines of text that contain a certain word

    d. Locating specific information in the output of another command

16. Some devices are accessed directly through `/dev`; for others, access is provided by:

    a. Switching to a new virtual console

    b. Contacting the vendor for Linux driver information

    c. Associating a device in `/dev` with another system resource such as a different directory name

    d. Graphical utilities

17. Describe the difference between `ps` and `kill`.

18. Linux filenames can include:

    a. Letters and digits, but not punctuation, or any special characters

    b. Letters and digits, plus spaces

    c. Letters, digits, with some punctuation, but no spaces

    d. Letters, digits, punctuation, and many special characters

19. The `rm` command is used in Linux to:

    a. Remove special characters from a filename

    b. Delete files from a hard disk

    c. Remove case-sensitivity settings

    d. Manage regular expressions

20. CDE for UNIX would be equivalent to _____ on Linux.

    a. Gnome

    b. A Web server

    c. the `ps` command

    d. the `man` command

21. Name three methods of learning about Linux commands as you work at a command line.

22. A trashcan facility on a Linux graphical desktop differs from the **rm** command in that:

    a. Files placed in the trashcan are not deleted until the trashcan is emptied, but files deleted by **rm** are deleted immediately

    b. Files placed in the trashcan are deleted immediately, but files deleted by **rm** are not truly erased until the system is restarted

    c. The **rm** command overwrites data when files are deleted, but the trashcan facility simply marks parts of the hard disk as available when the file stored in that space is deleted

    d. Files can be placed in the trashcan by any user, but only root can use the **rm** command

23. Describe the errors in this command: **Ls   /help**

24. The **ps** command does *not* provide information about:

    a. Who started a process

    b. The number assigned to a process

    c. The current status of the process

    d. When the threads of the process expire

25. The **kill** command is used to end:

    a. A process

    b. Redirection

    c. A user account

    d. A **locate** query

HANDS-ON PROJECTS

Project 7-1

In this project you use a graphical system administration tool to change a configuration option and see how the graphical tool has altered a plain text configuration file. To complete this project you should have a Linux system running Gnome.

1. Log in so that the Gnome Desktop is visible.

2. Click the Foot icon in the Panel, choose **Programs**, then **System**. Each item on this menu modifies one or more plain text configuration files.

3. Click the Foot icon in the Panel, choose **Programs**, then **Settings**, then **Desktop**, then **Screensaver**. A dialog box appears in which you can select a screensaver.

4. Select the **Ripples** screensaver from the list.

5. Choose **OK** to close the dialog box.

6. Open a command-line window.

7. From your home directory, change to the subdirectory `.gnome`.

   `cd .gnome`

   Note that other hidden directories with similar names may also be present, such as `.gnome-desktop` and `.gnome_private`.

8. Search the contents of all the files in this directory for the name of the screen-saver you selected. This is based on the assumption that the name of the program that runs the screensaver will resemble the term you picked in the graphical interface. It's true in this project but will not always be so.

   `grep ripple *`

9. Notice that the output of the `grep` command includes the filename where the pattern (`ripple`) was found, along with the line containing the matching text.

10. The file containing `ripple` is called Screensaver. Use the `ls` command to list the files in this directory and locate the Screensaver file.

    `ls`

11. Look at the contents of the Screensaver file.

    `less Screensaver`

12. You see that the command line contains the name of the screensaver program, `xscreensaver`, and a parameter defining the screensaver to use as ripples. The graphical utility updated this text file for you.

Project 7-2

In this project you explore man and `info` pages and learn how to use a few navigation commands within man pages. To complete this project, you need a Linux system.

1. Log in and open a command-line window.

2. View the man page for the `ls` command.

   `man ls`

3. Use the spacebar, down arrow, or Page Down keys to look through the man page and review the options supported by `ls`.

4. Find the SEE ALSO section of the man page and note the reference to the `info` page.

5. Press **q** to close the man page.

6. Open the `info` page for `ls`.

   `info ls`

7. Explore the `info` page. Sometimes the man or `info` page simply refers to the other without containing any substantive information. In this case, both the man and `info` pages contain a fair description of the utility. Do you have a preference for man or `info` based on the navigation utility? What major differences do you see?

8. Press **Ctrl+C** to end viewing the ls info page.

9. View the man page for the shell, bash. This man page may take a moment to open on some systems because it is very large.

   man bash

10. Scroll down in the man page, exploring some of the sections.

11. Go back to the top of the man page by pressing **1** then **G** (uppercase G).

12. Search the man page for the string PROMPT_COMMAND by pressing **/** and then typing **PROMPT_COMMAND** and pressing **Enter**.

13. Within the PROMPT_COMMAND section, review the description of the PS1 environment variable that you learned about in Chapter 6.

14. Search for occurrences of PS1 by pressing **/** and entering **PS1**.

15. After the first occurrence is highlighted, press the **n** key to move to the next occurrence.

16. Press **q** to exit the man page.

17. Man pages are divided into groups called sections. Section 1 is user commands; section 5 is configuration files; section 8 is system administration commands (used only by root). View the man page for **passwd**.

   man passwd

18. Notice that the top line of the man page describes it as PASSWD(1). This is the man page for the **passwd** command, which is used to change passwords (you learn about this in Chapter 8). Press **q** to exit the man page.

19. There is also a configuration file called **passwd**. Force man to display the **passwd** man page from section 5 instead of section 1.

   man 5 passwd

20. Press **q** when you have finished reviewing this man page. What program do the commands you have used in man remind you of?

Project 7-3

In this project you practice using regular expressions and redirecting input and output in various ways. To complete this project, you need a Linux system. The file location given for the sample file (linux.words) is specific to Red Hat Linux 7.3, but you can use locate to find that file on most other versions of Linux.

1. Log in and open a command-line window.

2. Linux uses a dictionary of about 45,000 words to check new passwords against, refusing them if they are in the dictionary. Copy this dictionary file to your home directory.

   cp /usr/share/dict/linux.words ~/words

3. Each word is on a separate line in the `words` file. Use `grep` to search for all words that begin with w.

   ```
   grep ^w words
   ```

4. Pipe the result through `less` so you can page through it.

   ```
   grep ^w words | less
   ```

5. Press **q** to exit `less`.

6. Find all words that end with w.

   ```
   grep w$ words
   ```

7. Find all words that begin with w and end with w. In this pattern, the . matches any single character, the ★ means to match the previous character zero or more times.

   ```
   grep ^w.*w$ words
   ```

8. Use the **-c** option to count how many words begin with s. How many are there? (This actually displays the number of lines matching the pattern; because each line contains a single word, the result here shows you the number of matching words.)

   ```
   grep -c ^s words
   ```

9. How many words start with either st or sm? (Use a single command to determine the answer.)

10. If the `grep` command you enter does not find a file to search listed on the command line, it tries to search STDIN. You can enter data directly at the keyboard or pipe another source of data to `grep`. Use the following command to send the output of the `cat` command as STDIN. No filename is specified for `grep`, so it reads the STDIN provided by `cat`.

    ```
    cat words | grep ^w | less
    ```

11. You can also specify a file to use as STDIN without using `cat`.

    ```
    grep w$ < words
    ```

12. In this case, the command looks very similar to the command without redirection (`grep w$ words`), because `grep` tries to use a filename first, then relies on STDIN. Some programs always look to STDIN for their input, so you could only use the `< words` method to pass that data as input to the program.

13. Refer back to Project 6-4 in Chapter 6. With what you have learned about redirection, write a single string of commands to accomplish the same set of tasks without creating any intermediate files.

7

CASE PROJECTS

This month McKinney & Co. has given you a difficult assignment. You've been asked to visit Tyson VisualWare, a software company that is struggling financially. (They had already paid for your consulting services when financial trouble hit.) When you arrive, the first thing you notice is that the atmosphere in the office is tense and uneasy, as if everyone is expecting to be laid off the next day.

1. One of your first steps is to work with the system administrators to see if productivity can be improved through simple adjustments to the company's information systems.

   One of the product managers soon approaches you with a belligerent tone and insists that you improve the system response time so he can download large e-mail messages faster. You realize that increasing the speed of the company's Internet connection involves a substantial cost. How could you respond to the product manager's request while maintaining a good relationship with the company and other employees? Describe the probable effects on your relationships if you were to retaliate against the belligerent manager by slowing down his connection or creating other technical problems on his account. What if your actions were discovered?

2. The CIO of Tyson is concerned that some employees are discussing the company's financial troubles with colleagues in other companies (often to look for new jobs, it seems). He asks you to collect all the e-mail messages sent by two particular employees who are under the most suspicion so that these e-mails can be reviewed by management. The messages are archived and available to you; you also have the ability to capture new messages as they are sent. The company has a policy stating that e-mail is subject to review, but no one really expects that others will read their mail. What is your reaction to the demand of the CIO? Do you feel you have an ethical obligation to remind employees of the corporate policy so they are more careful in their use of company resources? If the company didn't have a policy about reading employees' e-mail and you left the company because of an incident such as this, what would you tell your manager at McKinney & Co.? If you got fired, what would you tell your next potential employer about what happened?

   Suppose now that all employees are well aware of the policy permitting the company to read e-mail. All e-mail messages are stored in files, one per mailbox, as plain text. Review the man pages for the `find` and `grep` commands. Assemble two or three sample commands using `find` and/or `grep` to help you locate any offensive messages among the employees' e-mail.

3. While checking the available free hard disk space on one Linux server, you notice that one employee uses an inordinate amount of disk space. You suspect that the employee is storing offensive material. What regular expressions will you use to search the employee's command history and the filenames in his home directory for potentially prohibited materials? What action might you take towards this employee? How will the company's stated policies regarding employee privacy and use of company resources affect your actions?

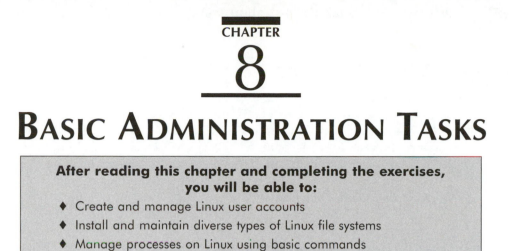

CHAPTER
8

BASIC ADMINISTRATION TASKS

After reading this chapter and completing the exercises, you will be able to:

♦ Create and manage Linux user accounts

♦ Install and maintain diverse types of Linux file systems

♦ Manage processes on Linux using basic commands

In the previous chapter you learned what it means to be a system administrator. You also learned the role that ethics and nontechnical skills play in a system administrator's daily duties. In addition, you learned about some basic concepts of Linux system administration.

In this chapter you look at three important system administration tasks. First, you learn how to create, modify, and delete user accounts using several different utilities. Next, you learn about managing Linux file systems, including creating new file systems and maintaining the integrity of existing file systems. Finally, you learn about managing multiple processes started from a single shell.

MANAGING USER ACCOUNTS

To complete any operation in Linux, a person must first log in using a valid user account name and password. Setting up and maintaining these user accounts is an important part of the work of a system administrator. In Chapter 6 you learned how to manage the initialization files for a user account, such as `.profile` and `.bashrc`. In this section you learn how to configure and manage user accounts. In general, the more user accounts you have on your Linux system, the more work is required to keep them all running smoothly. More users also means more security risks—thus proper management and tracking of user accounts is crucial to keeping the system running securely and efficiently.

 When a remote user accesses your system through certain network services such as a Web server, they do not need to have a user account on your system. Instead, they use a Web browser to ask the Web server to perform a task. The Web server then completes the task via a user account designated for the use of the Web server daemon.

Types of User Accounts

You have used your own user account and the root account on Linux. But Linux has many other preconfigured user accounts with strange names. These accounts serve special purposes on the system and have different characteristics compared to regular user accounts. The following sections discuss different types of user accounts in more detail.

The root Account

The administrative account (the **superuser**) on a Linux system is named root. This account is created when you install Linux. The root user can perform any operation on a Linux system. The root user on Linux is similar to the admin user on a NetWare server.

 The Linux root account is similar to the Administrator user account on Windows 2000/XP. However, the Windows Administrator account does not have unrestricted access to all system files and resources; Windows 2000/XP does not have a user account that is truly equivalent to the Linux root user.

Because the root user can perform any task on the system, you should not log in as root for your normal work. Even though you are the system administrator, root is not intended to be your main account. Always create a separate account (normally based on your name) and log in using this account for normal work. When you need to do administrative tasks that require superuser privileges (such as creating new user accounts), change temporarily to the root user. When you have finished the task, return to your normal user account.

To temporarily change to the root user, use the **su** utility. The **su** utility (for substitute user) temporarily changes your access rights to those of another user. Unless you are already logged in as root, you must enter the password of the user whose access rights you want to assume.

If you type **su** without any parameters, you change to the root account. If you type **su** followed by a username, you change to that user's access rights. This utility is sometimes used to assume the rights of another regular user, but more commonly it is used for the system administrator to become root for a time. (Normally, users should not have the password for any other user.) A hyphen after the **su** command causes the command to run login scripts and places you in the login directory of the user whose rights you are assuming. For example, to change to root access, you would use this command, entering the password when prompted:

```
$ su -
Password:
#
```

If you omit the hyphen, you are not placed in the user's home directory. If you are logged in as root and use **su** to assume the access rights of another user (for example, to create files that have that user as owner), you are not prompted for a password when using **su**.

If you are logged in as a regular user and launch a graphical system administration utility, the Gnome or KDE Desktop prompts you for the root password before launching the program. Figure 8-1 shows this dialog box in Gnome.

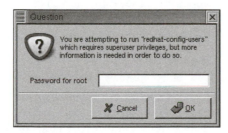

Figure 8-1   Entering the root password to execute a utility in Gnome

Regular Users

Regular user accounts are for users (actual people) who log in at a keyboard and use the Linux system. Although a regular account can be associated with a role in an organization (such as "manager" or "designer"), user accounts are commonly associated with named individuals. Regular user account names typically use a combination of first name or initial and last name or initial. User account names can be long (e.g. "Franklin Delano Roosevelt"), but shorter names ("franklinr") are much more convenient.

It's common to define a standard method of converting real names to usernames within an organization. This helps employees "guess" a person's e-mail address based on their name (if your e-mail address is your username). For example, an administrator might consistently use a user's first name and last initial to create a username. (Duplicate usernames may require variations from any organizational standards you define.)

Special Users

In addition to the root user and the regular user accounts, Linux includes several default user accounts that Linux programs use. By using a special user account, these programs can control file permissions and ensure system security. Most special user accounts are created during the installation of Linux; others may be created by programs that you install.

The special user accounts on your system vary depending on the services you have installed. For example, if you have installed the PostgreSQL database package, your system contains a `postgres` user; otherwise your system will not include this user. Although these user accounts are useful to specific programs, they do not have passwords or default shells defined. This means that a person cannot log in using these accounts.

Linux Groups

Linux lets you organize user accounts into groups. A **group** is a collection of user accounts that can be collectively granted access to files and directories (recall that each file and directory has a set of file permissions for the group assigned to that file or directory). Assigning users to groups makes it easier to manage access to different areas of the system.

Each user in Linux is assigned to a primary group. The name of the user's primary group is stored with the user's account information as described in the next section. Users can also be members of many other groups. The members of each defined group are listed in the `/etc/group` file.

Some Linux systems employ User Private Groups to increase system security. A **User Private Group** system creates a group with a single member for each new user account that is created. The new user is the only member of the group. When a user creates a file or directory, that user's private group is assigned as the group for that file or directory; no other users have access to the file or directory by virtue of belonging to the same group as the user that created it. This prevents inadvertent security mishaps from making a user's files accessible to others that are part of the group assigned to a file.

To understand the nature of groups, suppose you have created a new user account called `chrislee`. Because your system employs User Private Groups, the primary group for this user is the group named `chrislee`. User `chrislee` is also assigned to the following groups: `projectleads`, `salesteam`, and `hrcommittee`. (See Figure 8-2.) Now suppose you want to give all members of the sales team access to a particular directory or group of files. You can just make `salesteam` the group assigned to the directory or files and grant group permissions according to the access that group members should have.

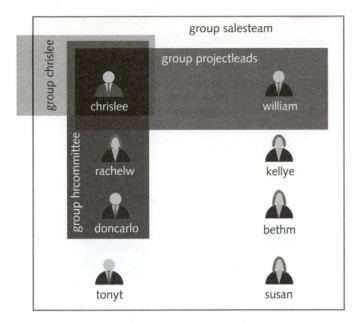

Figure 8-2   A user as a member of multiple groups

 The user account system described in this chapter is the default system for Linux. You can also enable shared user account data between multiple systems using NIS+. See the NIS+ HOWTO document at *www.linuxdocs.org/HOWTOs/NIS-HOWTO* for detailed information. Other less-common user account systems are described as part of the Pluggable Authentication Modules (PAM) security architecture. See *Guide to Linux Networking and Security* (Course Technology 2002, ISBN 0-619-00094-5), Chapter 9, and the PAM HOWTO document at *www.linuxdocs.org/HOWTOs/Security-HOWTO.html* under section 6.5. If you are using Red Hat Linux 7.3, you can also review PAM documentation by pointing your browser to the local file `/usr/share/doc/pam-0.75/html/index.html`.

User and Group Files

User account information is stored in the file **/etc/passwd**. In earlier releases of Linux, password information for each user was also stored in this file, hence the file's name. Because of security problems in the past, password information is no longer stored in this file. Other information about each user is contained in the file, however. A sample **/etc/passwd** file from a new Red Hat Linux 7.3 installation is shown here, followed by a description of each of the file's colon-separated fields.

The exact list of users created on a new Linux system depends on which version of Linux you are using and which features you have selected to install or activate.

```
root:x:0:0:root:/root:/bin/bash
bin:x:1:1:bin:/bin:/sbin/nologin
daemon:x:2:2:daemon:/sbin:/sbin/nologin
adm:x:3:4:adm:/var/adm:/sbin/nologin
lp:x:4:7:lp:/var/spool/lpd:/sbin/nologin
sync:x:5:0:sync:/sbin:/bin/sync
shutdown:x:6:0:shutdown:/sbin:/sbin/shutdown
halt:x:7:0:halt:/sbin:/sbin/halt
mail:x:8:12:mail:/var/spool/mail:/sbin/nologin
news:x:9:13:news:/var/spool/news:
uucp:x:10:14:uucp:/var/spool/uucp:/sbin/nologin
operator:x:11:0:operator:/root:/sbin/nologin
games:x:12:100:games:/usr/games:/sbin/nologin
gopher:x:13:30:gopher:/var/gopher:/sbin/nologin
ftp:x:14:50:FTP User:/var/ftp:/sbin/nologin
nobody:x:99:99:Nobody:/:/sbin/nologin
vcsa:x:69:69:virtual console memory owner:/dev:/sbin/nologin
mailnull:x:47:47::/var/spool/mqueue:/dev/null
rpm:x:37:37::/var/lib/rpm:/bin/bash
ntp:x:38:38::/etc/ntp:/sbin/nologin
rpc:x:32:32:Portmapper RPC user:/:/sbin/nologin
xfs:x:43:43:X Font Server:/etc/X11/fs:/bin/false
gdm:x:42:42::/var/gdm:/sbin/nologin
rpcuser:x:29:29:RPC Service User:/var/lib/nfs:/sbin/nologin
nfsnobody:x:65534:65534:Anonymous NFS
 User:/var/lib/nfs:/sbin/nologin
nscd:x:28:28:NSCD Daemon:/:/bin/false
ident:x:98:98:pident user:/:/sbin/nologin
radvd:x:75:75:radvd user:/:/bin/false
apache:x:48:48:Apache:/var/www:/bin/false
squid:x:23:23::/var/spool/squid:/dev/null
johnl:x:500:500:John Lim:/home/johnl:/bin/bash
```

The following list describes the fields in this list. The last line of the file (the user `johnl`) is used as an example.

- User account name (`johnl`): The name used by a person to log in to Linux.

- Password (`x`): The encrypted password for each user was formerly stored in this field. An `x` in this field indicates that the Shadow Password Suite is in use, in which case the encrypted password is stored in `/etc/shadow`. You will learn more about shadow passwords later in this chapter.

- User ID number, or UID (the first **500**): A number that uniquely identifies this user on this Linux system. The number is arbitrary and normally is automatically assigned by the utility used to create a new user account.

- Group ID number, or GID (the second **500**): A number from 0 to 65,535 that uniquely identifies the primary group for this user account. The GID must correspond to a group defined in the **/etc/group** file (described below).

- The user's real name (**John Lim**): A complete name (or a comment for special users). Spaces are permitted in this field. If the user account was created for a certain role in the organization, other text can be placed here instead, such as "Database Administrator."

- Home directory (**/home/john1**): The location in the Linux file system that is used as the current working directory when the user first logs in.

- Default shell (**/bin/bash**): The program that runs automatically when the user logs in. The default setting for this field is **/bin/bash**, which runs the **bash** shell. If a user prefers a different shell (such as the Korn shell or C shell described in Chapter 6), this field can be changed to accommodate that. This field can also be used to start a non-shell program to restrict the user's actions in the system.

Although you can edit the /etc/passwd file directly in a text editor, this is not a good idea if more than one system administrator might be working on the file over the network. In addition, small typing errors can make one or more user accounts inaccessible. Instead of a text editor, use the programs described in the following sections to update /etc/passwd. If you need to use a text editor to correct a problem in the file, use the special editing program **vipw**.

Groups on a Linux system are defined in the **/etc/group** file. You can edit this file if necessary using the command **vigr**. A part of the file in Red Hat Linux 7.3 is shown here, with the fields in the file (again separated by colons on each line) described in the following list.

```
root:x:0:root
bin:x:1:root,bin,daemon
daemon:x:2:root,bin,daemon
sys:x:3:root,bin,adm
adm:x:4:root,adm,daemon
tty:x:5:
disk:x:6:root
lp:x:7:daemon,lp
. . .
ident:x:98:
radvd:x:75:
apache:x:48:
squid:x:23:
wine:x:66:
```

8

```
nwells:x:500:
rsolomon:x:501:
authors:x:502:rsolomon,nwells
```

- The name of the group: This field cannot contain spaces. As with usernames, shorter is often better; avoid names more than 10 or 12 letters long.

- Group password: This field is either blank or contains **x** (meaning the password is stored in another location). Group passwords allow a person who knows that group's password to assume that group's access rights temporarily; these are rarely used.

- Group ID (GID) number: This number uniquely identifies the group. Group numbers are automatically assigned when you create a new group, though you can specify a number if you prefer.

- Members of the group: This field identifies members of the group. Note in the sample file that many groups do not have member users defined. A program may be able to assume the permissions of the group using system calls (programming instructions), but no user is part of the group by virtue of logging in. Some of the groups (such as **sys** and **adm**) have a comma-separated list of users as the last field. In addition to the two User Private Group items (for **nwells** and **rsolomon** in this sample file), a group named **authors** has been added to this default installation.

 Some UNIX and Linux systems employ a special group called wheel, which has special administrative powers; it is essentially a reduced version of the root account. On some systems a user must be a member of the **wheel** group in order to use the **su** command to change to the root account permissions. Although Linux includes a **wheel** group by default (with root as the only member), no special features or privileges apply to the **wheel** group in Linux.

Shadow Passwords

All programs and users may need to access the list of users stored in **/etc/passwd**. However, if the encrypted password were readable by many users, it would be subject to security breaches, allowing unauthorized use of an account.

To protect against this problem, encrypted passwords are rarely stored in the **/etc/passwd** file. Instead, they are commonly stored in a file called **/etc/shadow**. Systems that use this file rely on the **Shadow Password Suite**, a collection of password-related programs that have been modified to recognize the **/etc/shadow** file. This file can only be read by the root user and special utilities like the **login** program.

Part of a sample **/etc/shadow** file follows. Fields on each line are separated by colons, as in the **/etc/passwd** file. The first field is a user account name that must correspond to a user account in **/etc/passwd**. The second field is the encrypted password text. Additional fields configure password security information for that user. For the many special user accounts, an asterisk in the second field indicates that the account has no password; no one can log in using that account.

```
ftp:*:10815:0:99999:7:::
nobody:*:10815:0:99999:7:::
gdm:!!:10815:0:99999:7:::
xfs:!!:10815:0:99999:7:::
nwells:$1$3gWKUouQ$L7XUsJWpIwtqLUoWlmVvN1:10816:0:99999:
    7:-1:   -1:134538436
rsolomon: lJ42Wuip3dYAh8$1pvNMAVK$UsrD6O90:10817:0:99999:
    7:-1:   -1:134538412
```

Linux supports many password security features beyond shadow passwords. For more information, see *Guide to Linux Networking and Security*, Chapter 9.

Creating New User Accounts

8

You can create new user accounts using several different utilities. If you are working in a graphical desktop, you might prefer using a graphical tool; if you need to create many user accounts, a command-line utility can be much more efficient.

Although many utilities are available to create and manage user accounts, few utilities let you access all possible user account configuration options. Become familiar with the limitations of the tools you use so you know when to use something else to complete a complex or unusual task.

Most commercial versions of Linux include at least one utility for creating and managing user accounts. In KDE systems, the **Kuser** program is normally available on the System menu. In Red Hat Linux 7.3, you can open a similar utility from the Gnome main menu by choosing Programs, then System, then User Manager. Figure 8-3 shows this program with its User Properties dialog box. You can also launch this utility from a command line by entering **redhat-config-users**.

In this Red Hat utility, you can create a new user by clicking the New User button and filling in the fields displayed in the Create New User dialog box. You can also modify any user account by selecting it and clicking the Properties button. By default, only regular users are listed. You can uncheck the item "Filter system users and groups" on the Preferences menu to see all users, including the root and special user accounts.

The basic command-line utility for creating new users is **useradd**. With this utility you can create new accounts using many different options, and even automate user creation in scripts.

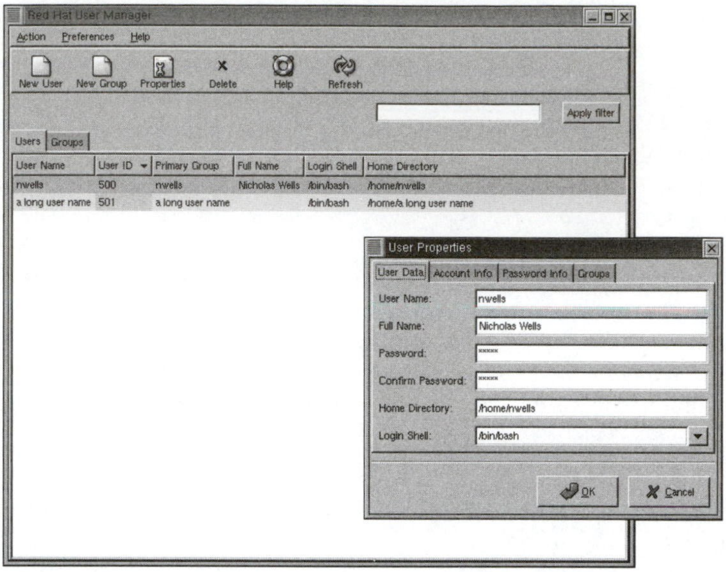

Figure 8-3   Configuring users graphically in Red Hat Linux 7.3

On some Linux systems, a script named `adduser` is available. Using a script to create new users is less secure than the `useradd` command. On more recent Linux systems (such as Red Hat Linux 7.3), the `adduser` command merely points to the `useradd` command.

To add a user with `useradd`, you must be logged in as root. You provide the name of the new user account as a parameter. For example, to add a new account called `rsolomon`, you would use this command:

```
useradd rsolomon
```

System defaults are used to create the account and a home directory. These system defaults are stored in the `/etc/login.defs` file and in the `/etc/default/useradd` file.

You can add options to the `useradd` command to override the system default settings or include more user information as part of the account configuration. For example, if you want to include the user's full name in the comment field (generally a good idea), you can use the `–c` option. The `–g` option defines a primary group for the new user. A command incorporating these two options would look like this:

```
useradd –g sales –c "Raley Solomon" rsolomon
```

Values that include spaces, such as Raley Solomon in the above example, must be enclosed in quotation marks so the `useradd` command does not interpret the part after the space (`Solomon`) as a command parameter.

Table 8-1 shows options you can use when executing `useradd`.

Table 8-1   `useradd` Command Options

Option	Description	Example
-c	Defines a user's full name or other comment for this account	`useradd -c "Jose Carrera" josec`
-d	Specifies the home directory path (useful mostly for special user accounts that use a nonstandard home directory location)	`useradd -d /usr/home/josec`
-e	Specifies the date this user account will expire (and be disabled automatically); used for temporary accounts	`useradd -e 03/15/01 josec`
-f	Specifies the number of days after the password expires until the account is disabled	`useradd -f 7 josec`
-g	Specifies the primary group for the new user (either the group's name or its unique GID number can be used)	`useradd -g ops josec`
-G	Adds a list of additional groups that the new user should be made a member of (this information is stored in the /etc/group file, not in /etc/passwd)	`useradd -G teamlead,party,emt josec`
-m	Forces creation of the user's home directory, even if the default settings do not include creating a home directory	`useradd -m josec`
-M	Does not create a home directory, even if the default is set to include one	`useradd -M josec`
-n	Disables the User Private Group feature so that a group matching the new username is not created	`useradd -n josec`
-s	Sets the user's login shell. The default shell in Linux is bash. The complete path to another shell program can be used with this option	`useradd -s /bin/zsh josec`

Table 8-1   `useradd` Command Options (continued)

Option	Description	Example
-u	Sets a specific numeric value for the user ID of the new user (normally a UID is selected automatically—use this option if you need to force the use of a specific UID number)	`useradd -u 509 josec`

To display the default settings for the `useradd` command, use the `-D` option. Typical output of the `-D` option is shown here:

```
# useradd -D
GROUP=100
HOME=/home
INACTIVE=-1
EXPIRE=
SHELL=/bin/bash
SKEL=/etc/skel
```

The information returned by the `-D` option is described in the following list:

- **GROUP**: The group ID number for the group that all new users will be placed in (as a primary group) if no other is indicated when the user is created.

- **HOME**: The path in which home directories for new users will be created.

- **INACTIVE**: The number of days after a user's password expires that the account will be disabled. Using a value of `-1` for this field disables this option (passwords will not expire).

- **EXPIRE**: The expiration date for a new user account.

- **SHELL**: The path and program name for the default shell (command-line interpreter) to be used by each new user account.

- **SKEL**: The path to the skeleton directory used to fill a new home directory with basic files (this directory is discussed later in this section).

You can change the defaults for `useradd` by editing the file `/etc/default/useradd`. You can also change them with the `useradd -D` option. For example, to change the default shell so that all new users will use the C shell instead of the `bash` shell, use this command:

```
# useradd -D -s /bin/csh
```

 Password expiration settings are not discussed in detail here but are described in the file `/etc/login.defs` and in the `useradd` man page.

Changing User Passwords

Before anyone can log in using a newly created account, the account must be assigned a password. A password is not defined by `useradd` when a new user account is created.

 Graphical utilities for creating users include fields for defining a password. You can include a password by using the `-p` option of `useradd`, but you may prefer not to reveal the password on a command line.

Use the `passwd` command to define or change a user's password. (This command has the same name as the `/etc/passwd` file.) When using this command as root, include the name of the user account whose password you want to define. You must enter the new password twice to be certain you have not made a typing error.

Suppose you have already created a new user named `lizw`, and you want to define her initial password or change her user's password. For either task, do the following:

1. Make sure you're logged in as root.

2. Enter the command **passwd lizw**. The following text then appears on the screen:

   ```
   Changing password for user lizw
   New password:
   ```

3. Type the new password for the Linux user account and press **Enter**. Nothing appears on screen as you type, so work carefully. The following text appears after you press Enter:

   ```
   Retype new password:
   ```

4. Type the new password a second time, exactly as you typed it the first time. This verifies that the password was entered as you intended to type it. When you press Enter the second time, the following text appears:

   ```
   passwd: all authentication tokens updated successfully
   ```

If you enter a password that is a poor choice (such as *password*, the username, or a simple word from the dictionary), you see a message stating BAD PASSWORD. Although this message should cause you to reconsider the password, the password is still changed. For a temporary password on new accounts, almost anything will do. Popular choices include the user's account name (`lizw` in this example), the word *password*, *change.me*, or something similar.

The standard procedure is for a system administrator to assign an initial password to a new account using the steps just given (or with a graphical user management utility). The administrator communicates the password to the new user, who should then immediately select a new password that is unknown to the root user or any other users.

The user can change his or her password using `passwd` without any parameters:

```
$ passwd
```

The root user can change any user's password; when a regular user changes his or her own password, different rules apply:

- The user must enter the current password for the account before entering a new password (twice).

- If a "bad password" is entered (such as a dictionary word), a warning message is displayed and the password is *not* changed.

As the system administrator, you must explain to users the importance of changing their passwords immediately after a new account is created for them. Most system administrators feel that passwords should be changed monthly, even if the Linux system does not enforce frequent changes. This reduces the danger that someone will discover a user's password and be able to continue using it. Good passwords have these characteristics:

- They are at least 5 characters long, though a 7- to 10-character password is *much* more secure.

- They include digits or punctuation marks.

- They mix upper- and lowercase letters in nonstandard ways.

- They are easy for the account owner to remember, but hard for anyone else to guess—even someone who knows the account owner well.

- They are not created from a simple manipulation of a word found in a dictionary or the name of a person or place.

A password that is hard to remember is probably hard for someone else to discover, but it doesn't help security much if the password is written on a note taped to the computer monitor.

As system administrator, you will deal with many different passwords. These include the root password, a personal account password, passwords for special administrative utilities, and passwords for other parts of your life, such as bank accounts, Web pages, and voice mail codes. If these passwords and codes are identical or similar, discovery of one of your passwords could jeopardize the security of many different areas of your work and personal life.

You can alter the password security system used by Red Hat Linux 7.3 by running the `authconf` utility. This advanced security tool is described in *Guide to Linux Networking and Security*.

Creating New Groups

Although modifying the `/etc/group` file in a text editor does not pose as great a danger as editing `/etc/passwd`, the preferred method for adding a new group is to use the **groupadd** command. This command is used much like the **useradd** command, but it supports fewer options.

Graphical tools designed for creating users often allow you to create groups as well. These tools are useful if you prefer to work in a graphical environment. However, you should learn about the `groupadd` command as a backup and for troubleshooting, because the graphical tools rarely allow you to do much besides simply creating and deleting groups.

To add a new group, include the group name as a parameter, as follows:

```
# groupadd managers
```

If you need to use a specific GID number for the new group, you can include it with the −g option. For example:

```
# groupadd -g 919 managers
```

Modifying User and Group Accounts

Shortly after setting up user and group accounts, you will probably need to modify account information. To do this, use the **usermod** (for *user modify*) command or groupmod (for *group modify*) command. The **usermod** command uses the same options as the **useradd** command, but it operates on an existing user account. To use the usermod command to update a user's account information, type **usermod** followed by one of the **usermod** parameters and a value for that parameter. For example, suppose lizw gets married and wishes to have her full name changed from Liz Walters to Liz Osowski on her employment records and user account. Using the −c option, as with the useradd command to change the comment field of the user account, the command to update the lizw account to include the new name would be:

```
# usermod -c "Liz Osowski" lizw
```

You can change the user's login name from lizw to lizo with the −l option:

```
# usermod -l lizo -d /home/lizo lizw
```

Using the −l option alone leaves the home directory as it was before (/home/lizw). By using the −d option shown above, the home directory path in /etc/passwd is updated as well (to /home/lizo). Note that the usermod command does not change the actual directory name. After using the usermod −d command, you must change the actual directory name as follows:

```
# mv /home/lizw /home/lizo
```

As another example, suppose you created an account for a new employee, using the default settings, and then discovered that the new employee prefers to use a different login shell and needs to be part of several additional groups to accommodate his job responsibilities. The command to update his account might look like this:

```
# usermod -G taskforce,marketing -s /bin/tcsh srubenst
```

8

Automating Home Directory Creation

You often want to include basic configuration files in the home directory of each new user that you create. This information might include:

- Company document templates and calendars.

- Environment variable settings to access department printers and servers.

- Terminal settings to make Linux work well with desktop PCs.

- Commands (scripts) to automate basic tasks and set up the user's system each time the user logs in.

Files contained in **/etc/skel** are automatically copied into each user's home directory at the time you create the account. As system administrator, you should place files in /etc/skel when you first install Linux so that those files are automatically placed in each user's home directory that you create with **useradd**. Many of the files in /etc/skel are hidden configuration files. Use the `ls  -la` command to list the contents of /etc/skel. Here is one version:

```
$ ls -la /etc/skel
total 28
drwxr-xr-x  3 root root   4096 Sep 18 17:11 .
drwxr-xr-x 58 root root   4096 Oct 17 08:07 ..
-rw-r-r-   1 root root     24 Apr 12 2002 .bash_logout
-rw-r-r-   1 root root    191 Apr 12 2002 .bash_profile
-rw-r-r-   1 root root    124 Apr 12 2002 .bashrc
-rw-r-r-   1 root root    118 Apr 15 2002 .gtkrc
drwxr-xr-x  3 root root   4096 Sep 18 17:08 .kde
```

The files shown here are used for graphical interfaces such as KDE and the **bash** default shell. If you want to have other files included in each user's home directory, simply copy those files to /etc/skel.

When you add files to /etc/skel, they are not added to the home directories of *existing* user accounts; they are only copied to the home directories of user accounts created *after* the new files are added. For existing accounts, you must use **cp** to copy additional files manually to each home directory.

Disabling User Accounts

You can temporarily or permanently disable a user account. You might need to do this because:

- An employee has left the organization (permanent deletion of the account).

- An employee is on vacation (temporary disabling as a security precaution).

- A guest user has not paid for the account or for computer time (temporary, perhaps permanent later on).

- An employee is under disciplinary action and is not allowed to access company information (temporary, perhaps permanent later on).

To temporarily disable a user's account, change the password with the **passwd** command so the user can no longer log in.

If you are concerned about having an active account with only a new password as security, you can use the command **passwd -l** *username* to lock the account. Then use **passwd -u** *username* to unlock the account so the user can log in again. Similarly, you can edit the **/etc/shadow** file in a text editor and place an asterisk before the encrypted password. This saves the password (because you can simply remove the asterisk later to re-enable the account). But while the asterisk is part of the password, Linux will not allow anyone to log in to the user account. The line in **/etc/shadow** before the edit might look like this:

```
nwells:$12$tJhxVO2kUgVU2/o0434jj0:10799:0:99999:7:-1:-1:134538468
```

And after the edit it looks like this:

```
nwells:*$12$tJhxVO2kUgVU2/o0434jj0:10799:0:99999:7:-1:-1:134538468
```

To delete a user account permanently, use the **userdel** command with the user account name. For example:

```
# userdel lizo
```

This command removes the user named **lizo** from **/etc/passwd**. The user can no longer log in because the user account no longer exists. But **userdel** does *not* remove the user's home directory or its contents. You will typically want to review and archive the home directory for a deleted user account. (If an employee is leaving the organization, friends or coworkers may be able to access part of the former employee's home directory because of common group membership, for example.)

Some system administrators maintain that user accounts should never be deleted. The fear is that files owned by a user that no longer exists on the system may be unexpectedly assigned to a new user account that is given the UID of the previously deleted account. To protect against such dangers, you can use the **find** command with the **-user** option to find all files owned by the user you are about to delete. Use this list to review, archive, and delete the user's files, then use **userdel** to remove the user account.

8

MAINTAINING FILE SYSTEMS

When you install Linux, you create the root file system in which the operating system is stored. The term **file system** refers to an organized set of data that can be accessed via the standard Linux directory structure. The command-line instructions (such as **cd /usr/share**) that refer to the directory paths in Linux provide access to data stored in an underlying file system located on a hard disk or other physical device.

The root file system is normally located on one of the computer's hard disks. Even a basic Linux system uses many other file systems, however. Each provides access to a different set of information. In some operating systems, file systems are accessed using drive letters or special network access tools, but as you have seen in previous chapters, all Linux file systems are accessed as part of a single directory tree, starting with the root directory. The root directory is always indicated by a forward slash /.

To access a file system in Linux, it must first be mounted into the root directory structure. Even the root file system must be mounted—this occurs during the initialization of Linux at boot time. Other special file systems are also mounted during initialization (see Table 8-2). You can configure other file systems that you want mounted during initialization, or you can mount file systems manually after the system has booted. The sample configuration in Figure 8-4 shows how different parts of a Linux directory structure can be located on different physical devices.

Table 8-2   Automatically Mounted File Systems

File system type	Mount point	Description
swap	No mount point; a special file system used by the Linux kernel	Used to create virtual memory, allowing the Linux kernel to work as if the amount of system memory available is the sum of RAM and the swap space
proc	/proc	Provides up-to-date information about the kernel and all processes running on Linux
auto	/auto	Automatically mounts a device when a request is made to the device (this is called the automounting file system or the automount daemon—amd; it is installed automatically with most Linux system
root	/	Serves as the base of a running Linux system; the root file system cannot be unmounted unless you first shut down Linux
usbdevfs	/proc/bus/usb	File system used to access USB devices
devpts	/dev/pts	File system used by the kernel to interact with pseudo-terminals (programs running in graphical environments and certain other situations)
tmpfs	/dev/shm	File system used by programs for accessing shared memory resources
binfmt_misc	/proc/sys/fs/ binfmt_misc	File system used to register different types of programs (older Linux, newer Linux, Java, DOS, Windows) so that the Linux kernel can automatically execute them when a program of that type is given on the command line

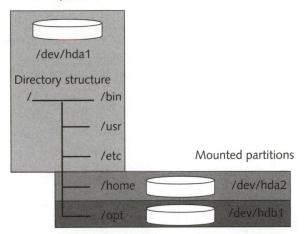

Figure 8-4   File systems mounted in a Linux directory structure

8

A **mount point** is the path in the directory structure where you access the data in a file system. You use the `mount` command to make a new file system accessible via a mount point; you also use `mount` to list all of the file systems currently available to the system. Using the `mount` command without any parameters displays a list of the currently mounted file systems. Here is one example:

```
$ mount
/dev/hda2 on / type ext3 (rw)
none on /proc type proc (rw)
usbdevfs on /proc/bus/usb type usbdevfs (rw)
none on /dev/pts type devpts (rw,gid=5,mode=620)
none on /dev/shm type tmpfs (rw)
/dev/hdb2 on /usr type ext3 (rw)
none on /proc/sys/fs/binfmt_misc type binfmt_misc (rw)
/dev/fd0 on /mnt/floppy type vfat (rw,nosuid,nodev)
```

You learn how to use the `mount` command to access a new file system later in this section. On many Linux systems, inserting a CD-ROM when using a graphical desktop causes the CD-ROM to be mounted automatically, sometimes with a corresponding pop-up message box.

The output of the `mount` command includes fields, from left to right, as described in the following list:

- The device where the file system is located (such as `/dev/hda2` on the first line of the output above, which refers to a hard disk partition).

- The mount point for the file system (the path in the directory structure where the file system can be accessed, such as / on the first line of the output above).

- The type of the file system. This indicates the format of data stored on the file system (**ext3** is the type on the first line above).

- The options that apply to the file system. These are described in detail later in the chapter. The options on the first line of the output above are **rw**, indicating that the file system is mounted for both reading and writing of data.

Managing Linux file systems is critical to running an efficient Linux system. Although file systems as a rule don't require much day-to-day maintenance, the more people using a Linux system and the more crucial the data stored on that system, the more important it becomes to watch over and maintain the file systems.

Checking File System Status

One of the very rare times when the Linux kernel crashes is when the root file system becomes full. Likewise, if the space where users' files are stored becomes full, users will not be able to complete their work.

The **df** command displays space usage information for each file system that is currently mounted. (**df** only displays information for regular file systems, not the special file systems like the swap partition and **/proc**.) In the following sample output from **df**, the first two file systems are dangerously full.

```
$ df
File system   1k-blocks    Used       Available    Use%    Mounted on
/dev/hda4     956173       895614     11160        99%     /
/dev/hda3     1018329      901074     64643        93%     /opt
sundance:/a   2017438      1210459    806979       60%     /a
```

The fields output by the **df** command, from left to right, are described in the following list:

- The device where the file system is stored. This is normally either a hard disk device name or a networked location (as in the last line of the sample output, which indicates a remote file system on the host named sundance).

- The number of 1 KB blocks on the device. This indicates the file system's overall size. For example, in the sample output, the size of the three devices currently mounted are approximately 1 GB, 1 GB, and 2 GB, respectively.

- The number of 1 KB blocks that are used on the device.

- The number of 1 KB blocks that are free on the device.

- The percentage of capacity reached so far (percentage full) for the device.

- The mount point for this device.

If a file system is becoming full, you probably won't have the luxury of shutting down the Linux system while you figure out what to do. The busier your Linux system, the quicker a file system can fill up as multiple users download files, create new documents, and so forth.

Executing the **df** command on a major ISP server looks like the following example. After reviewing this output, you should be able to see why larger systems require more careful maintenance procedures to keep them running smoothly.

```
File system           1024-blocks   Used      Available  Capacity  Mounted on
/dev/dsk/c0t3d0s0       229610     110187      119423      48%      /
/dev/dsk/c0t3d0s6       306954     245175       61779      80%      /usr
/dev/dsk/c0t0d0s0      5783718    3378119     2405599      58%      /var
/dev/dsk/c0t1d0s7      2663048    1983612      679436      75%      /space1
/dev/dsk/c0t1d0s6       533992     232744      301248      44%      /usr/local
nfs.isp.com:/home     69837128   42182931    27654197      60%      /home
mail.isp.com:/var/mail 10766840   8172635     2594205      76%      /var/mail
```

If you see that a file system is nearing 100% of capacity, you can immediately free space by performing one of the actions in the following list. Remember, however, that you must free space in the directories where the file system is mounted. For example, if you have a separate partition mounted as the **/home** directory and that partition is almost full, you must free space in **/home** or its subdirectories. Freeing space in **/tmp** won't help.

- Look for large or numerous files in the **/tmp** directory that can be deleted (if it's part of the file system that is becoming full).

- Look for large or numerous files in the **/var** subdirectories, especially in **tmp/** and **spool/**.

- Move the system log file (**/var/log/messages**) to another file system that isn't as full.

- See if any of the user subdirectories are using an unusually large amount of disk space.

- Consider deleting unused archive files that are backed up or even applications that you can reinstall later when space is not critically short.

Although you need to be very careful as you delete files, you may have to act quickly to respond to an overly full file system. The **du** (disk usage) utility can be a big help. The **du** utility lists the size of a directory and all its subdirectories. A few sample lines from the output of **du** are shown here:

```
# du /home/lizo
22     ./public_html
2228   ./Public/shell_programming
2229   ./Public
2       ./Desktop/Autostart
2       ./Desktop/Trash
8       ./Desktop/Templates
```

```
13      /Desktop
1       /.kde/share/apps/kfm/tmp
1       /.kde/share/apps/kfm/bookmarks
6       /.kde/share/apps/kfm
1       /.kde/share/apps/kppp/Rules
1       /.kde/share/apps/kppp/Log
3       /.kde/share/apps/kppp
10      /.kde/share/apps
15      /.kde/share/config
1       /.kde/share/icons/mini
2       /.kde/share/icons
1       /.kde/share/applnk
1       /.kde/share/mimelnk
30      /.kde/share
31      /.kde
1       /archive
2337    /home/lizo
```

The number at the far left indicates how many 1 KB blocks are used by the subdirectory. Every subdirectory is shown separately, with totals for the parent directory. For example, the line showing 13 KB for the /Desktop directory includes the sum of the /Desktop/Autostart directory, the /Desktop/Trash directory, and the /Desktop/ Templates directory, as well as any files located in the Desktop directory itself. By looking at the last line (the period indicates the current directory), you can see how much space is used by the entire directory tree. More importantly, if you need to manage how space is used on a file system, you can see which subdirectories are consuming space, even if they are buried deep in the directory structure.

Suppose you wanted to see if any single home directory consumed more than 100 MB of space. The output of the du command is given in KB, so we calculate that 100 MB is equal to roughly 100,000 KB of space. The following commands would change you to the /home subdirectory and then list any directories containing over 100 MB of data:

```
# cd /home
# du | grep ^.....[0-9]
```

If any line of the output of du starts with a number with more than five digits, grep will display that line, showing you the oversized subdirectory. The output of the above command might look like this:

```
172529    ./nwells/images/NASA_mars/
110218    ./nwells/database/archive/
121749    ./rsolomon/doc/HTML/
```

Running du on the root directory of a large system can take some time (and slow down everyone else's work). Any directory that contains thousands of files or hundreds of subdirectories requires some time for the du command to process.

To avoid drains on the system, consider using the du command in the middle of the night to update a file containing the output of du. Then you can quickly search that file for overly large directories—directories that may require your attention if space becomes scarce.

In addition to the df and du commands, you can use various graphical tools and system administration scripts to check the status of file systems. In Chapter 11, for example, you will learn how to schedule tasks (such as running du) so they run automatically whenever you choose.

 Red Hat Linux 7.3 provides a basic graphical utility for reviewing hardware information, including hard disk status information similar to that provided by df. To start this utility, enter hwbrowser or open the Gnome main menu and choose Programs, then System, then Hardware Browser.

Creating New File Systems

As a Linux system grows, it may require additional storage space. As you will learn in Chapter 13, you can use archive systems to remove unused information and store it on compact disc, streaming tape, or other devices. Nevertheless, the amount of "live" storage needed often grows to exceed an administrator's original expectations. In fact, part of planning a Linux system in an organization is knowing in advance what steps will be taken when the system must be expanded. If these steps are outlined in advance, a system administrator is less likely to make choices that create obstacles to efficient system upgrades later on.

Adding a file system generally means adding a hard disk device to your system and making that hard disk available to Linux by formatting and mounting it. This is done for the root file system as part of the Linux installation process. But in that case, the installation utility takes care of most of the details. In this section you will learn how to set up additional file systems stored on a hard disk, CD-ROM, or other devices.

You can install new file systems that are permanent (loaded each time you boot Linux) or temporary (loaded only occasionally, as needed). File systems can be stored on a device with removable media (such as a cartridge) or fixed media (such as a hard disk).

 Linux can use the Network File System (NFS) to mount and access file systems located on remote hosts. Many techniques described in this section apply to managing remote file systems. Details about setting up NFS network shared file systems are included in Chapter 5 of *Guide to Linux Networking and Security*.

To install a new hard disk or other peripheral device, consult your hardware manual. Once the hard disk or other device is installed, you can use the Linux **fdisk** command described in the next section to examine its partitions, creating new Linux partitions as needed. Before any hard disk can be used as a native Linux file system, it must have Linux partitions defined.

8

Using the `fdisk` Utility

Almost all file system devices use either an IDE or SCSI interface to communicate with your computer. Devices connected to these interfaces use standardized device names in Linux. As you recall, `hda` refers to the first IDE device, on which partitions are numbered starting with 1. So, for example, `/dev/hda3` is the third partition on the first IDE device. SCSI devices use the same naming system except the device names begin with `sd`. So, for example, `/dev/sdb4` is the fourth partition on the second SCSI device.

To manage partitions in Linux after the operating system is installed, you typically must use the `fdisk` utility. This text-mode utility is not hard to use, but it can make new users nervous because it modifies hard disk partitions, and a small error can make everything on the hard disk inaccessible. Just remember that nothing you do in `fdisk` is written to the partition table until you exit `fdisk`. Your modifications to the partition table are only effective when you write the changes to disk with the `w` command to exit `fdisk`.

Suppose you had just installed a second IDE hard disk on your Linux system. You could begin using `fdisk` to set up partitions on that hard disk with the following command (notice that no partition number is given; `fdisk` is operating on the entire hard disk device):

```
# /sbin/fdisk /dev/hdb
```

Table 8-3 lists the single-character commands in `fdisk` that you are most likely to need.

Table 8-3   `fdisk` Commands

Command	Description
m	Lists all `fdisk` commands
p	Displays the current partition table
n	Begins defining a new partition
t	Defines the file system type marker on an existing partition
d	Deletes a partition currently extant in the partition table
b	Sets a selected partition as active (bootable)
w	Writes to disk any changes made to the partition table within `fdisk`, then exits `fdisk`
q	Quits `fdisk`, abandoning any edits to the partition table

Figure 8-5 shows sample output from the `p` command in `fdisk`, showing how partition information appears onscreen. The steps that follow show how you can define a Linux partition on a newly installed hard disk.

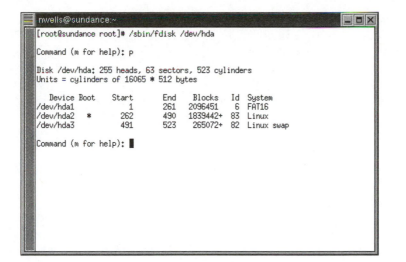

```
nwells@sundance:~
[root@sundance root]# /sbin/fdisk /dev/hda

Command (m for help): p

Disk /dev/hda: 255 heads, 63 sectors, 523 cylinders
Units = cylinders of 16065 * 512 bytes

   Device Boot    Start     End    Blocks   Id  System
/dev/hda1            1      261   2096451    6  FAT16
/dev/hda2    *     262      490   1839442+  83  Linux
/dev/hda3         491      523    265072+  82  Linux swap

Command (m for help):
```

Figure 8-5 Sample output of the `p` command in `fdisk`

8

1. Launch **fdisk** with the device name of the new hard disk.

   ```
   # /sbin/fdisk /dev/hdb
   ```

2. Type **p** to list the partitions currently defined on the hard disk. (On a new hard disk there may be none.)

3. If you are using an old hard disk that contains existing partition data, enter **d**, followed by the partition number when prompted, to delete each partition on the hard disk. (Remember, you're only deleting the definition from a memory copy of the partition table; you can press Ctrl+C to exit **fdisk** if you become uncertain of what you're doing.)

4. Enter **n** to begin creating a new partition.

5. Enter **p** for primary partition. (You can create more than four partitions on a hard disk using extended, or logical, partitions, but you shouldn't need to do this.)

6. Enter a partition number for the partition you are creating. For this value, enter the next free partition on the hard disk. On a brand new hard disk, the number you enter should be 1.

7. Begin to define the size of the new partition by entering its first cylinder as requested. The range of available cylinders on the hard disk is listed in parentheses, like this:

   ```
   First cylinder (201-526, default 201):
   ```

8. Finish defining the size of the partition. To do this you can enter either a size, or a cylinder number. Example sizes you could enter are +900M for a 900 MB partition, or +4G for a 4 GB partition. To use the entire hard disk as a single partition, enter the last cylinder number displayed in the **fdisk** prompt.

If you specify a cylinder number rather than a size to finish defining a partition, you can determine the size of the partition only by using the **p** command to list the partitions and the size of each.

9. Specify the partition type by entering **t**. The partition type informs any operating system that looks at the partition table what format the data stored on the partition is in.

10. When prompted, enter the partition number for the partition you just created.

11. Enter the type code for a Linux native partition, which is **83**. (At this point you can enter **l**, for list, to see a listing of partition type codes, which is quite interesting to review.)

If you were creating a new Linux system using a Linux installation program, you would want to create a partition of type 82 for the Linux swap partition. You would also want to use the **a** command to define one of the partitions as active (bootable). The bootable partition is shown with an asterisk in the output of the **p** command.

12. Use the **p** command to see how the partitions are now defined.

13. If you are satisfied with the partition configuration, write the partition table to the hard disk and exit **fdisk** by entering **w** for write.

If you do not want to write the new partition table to the hard disk (you prefer to abandon your work within **fdisk**), enter **q** to quit **fdisk**.

Formatting File Systems

Once you have marked a partition as containing a certain type of data (Linux, type 83), you must format the partition with a corresponding file system. As an analogy, think of a file cabinet. Marking a partition is like placing a label on a file drawer. Formatting a partition is like filling the drawer with labeled file folders. The drawer is then ready to have data filed in a useful way.

The native file system used by Linux is **ext2**, the extended file system, version 2, or **ext3**, version 3. These two file systems are very similar except that version 3 adds journaling. File system **journaling** is a feature that protects against data corruption by tracking each "write" to the hard disk in a special way so that it will either be completely finished or left completely undone. Red Hat Linux 7.3 uses **ext3**; some versions of Linux still prefer **ext2** to avoid the overhead of journaling.

To create a new **ext2** or **ext3** file system, use **mke2fs** (for *make* **ext2** *file system*). This command formats the partition, erasing all information on it, and organizes space for data to be recorded so that the partition can be used by Linux. The command is as simple to use as adding the device name as a parameter:

```
# /sbin/mke2fs /dev/sdb2
```

Another way to access this program is to use the **mkfs** program with an appropriate "extension" or option. Both of these are equivalent to the previous example:

```
# /sbin/mkfs -t ext2 /dev/sdb2
# /sbin/mkfs.ext2 /dev/sdb2
```

Many options are supported when you format a file system, especially if you are creating an **ext3** file system. Most are not needed unless you have special concerns about high performance or security. You can review available options by entering **man mke2fs** or by visiting *www.linuxdocs.org/HOWTOs/Filesystems-HOWTO.html*.

When you format an **ext2** or **ext3** file system, you see many lines of output on the screen as the program lists all of the structure information that is being written to the device. In any case, formatting even a large hard disk is quite fast. On a fast Pentium system, using **mke2fs** on a 40 GB partition takes only a couple of minutes.

You can use the **fdformat** command to format floppy disks. This command is rarely used, however, because all floppy disks are preformatted. Most users discard as defective any floppy disk that appears to need reformatting.

Mounting File Systems

After you have formatted a file system, you can mount it as part of the Linux directory structure and begin storing data on it. To access a file system, you use the **mount** command, indicating the device on which the file system is stored and a directory (a mount point) where the file system should be made accessible in the directory structure.

For example, if you formatted a new hard disk as a document archive for your office, you could create a directory called **/archive**, then mount the new file system so it is accessible at that point. These two example commands would accomplish that:

```
# mkdir /archive
# mount -t ext2 /dev/sdb2 /archive
```

This **mount** command says: mount a file system of type **ext3** located on the device **/dev/sdb2**, and make it accessible at the directory **/archive**.

Now when you go to the **/archive** directory, you see a subdirectory called **lost+found**. The **lost+found** directory is placed in the beginning of all new **ext2** and **ext3** file systems. This directory is initially empty, but when you use disk-checking utilities (described in Chapter 9), files may be created in the **lost+found** directory. You very rarely see anything in this directory, but nevertheless don't delete the directory. The presence of the `lost+found` directory indicates that the new file system has been mounted successfully.

The standard devices that are included when you install Linux generally have a mount point directory already created for them. For example, the floppy disk drive and CD-ROM drive are normally mounted to `/mnt/floppy` and `/mnt/cdrom`, respectively. These directories are created when Linux is installed. CD-ROMs are sometimes mounted automatically when you insert them, but you can also mount a CD-ROM using this command, including the mount point as a parameter:

```
$ mount /mnt/cdrom
```

You can mount a floppy disk with this command:

```
$ mount /mnt/floppy
```

Why don't these commands include the information in the `mount` command given previously, such as a file system type and device name? You'll learn the answer shortly, in the section "Automating File System Mounting."

Once you have mounted a floppy disk or CD-ROM, you should not eject the disk or CD-ROM until you have first unmounted the file system as described in the next section.

Unmounting File Systems

To unmount a file system, use the **umount** command with the device name or mount point. For example, to unmount a floppy disk, you might use this command (depending on the mount point defined on your Linux system):

```
$ umount /mnt/floppy
```

To unmount a CD-ROM, the command would typically be:

```
$ umount /mnt/cdrom
```

Similarly, to unmount a hard disk partition such as the one described in the previous section, the command would be:

```
# umount /archive
```

 The command name is `umount`, not `unmount`. If you see errors when you attempt to unmount a file system, look for an extra "n" in the command.

A file system cannot be in use when you unmount it. If any users on the Linux system are working with a file on the file system, or if any user's current working directory is located within that file system, the `umount` command will fail, indicating that the file system is busy. The Linux kernel stores information about each mounted file system that includes the number of files currently being accessed. All users must stop using files on the file system and change their current working directory to a location outside the file system before you can unmount that file system.

 When removable media such as a CD-ROM is mounted, the Eject function of the drive is disabled until the device is unmounted. This is not true of floppy disk drives, which means it is possible for a user to eject a floppy disk while it is still mounted. This can cause minor problems, or even result in lost data. For example, files will still be marked as open even though they cannot be accessed.

Automating File System Mounting

As a system administrator, you'll want to automate everything that you can so that your time is free for tasks that require new analysis and problem-solving skills. As you saw earlier, several types of file systems are mounted automatically when you start Linux, such as the swap partition. The new file systems that you create from additional hard disks or other devices can also be automatically mounted at boot time.

The key to automounting file systems is the **/etc/fstab** configuration file. This file contains one line for each file system that you want to have automounted when Linux boots. It also contains a line for file systems that you want to mount after booting Linux without providing all of the file system information in the **mount** command. A typical default **fstab** configuration file is shown here:

```
LABEL=/         /            ext3     defaults               1 1
none            /dev/pts     devpts   gid=5,mode=620         0 0
none            /proc        proc     defaults               0 0
none            /dev/shm     tmpfs    defaults               0 0
LABEL=/usr      /usr         ext3     defaults               1 2
/dev/hda3       swap         swap     defaults               0 0
/dev/cdrom      /mnt/cdrom   iso9660  noauto,owner,kudzu,ro  0 0
/dev/cdrom1     /mnt/cdrom1  iso9660  noauto,owner,kudzu,ro  0 0
/dev/fd0        /mnt/floppy  auto     noauto,owner,kudzu     0 0
```

The fields of this configuration file, from left to right, are described in the following list:

- The device where the file system is located or, if LABEL is used, the volume label on the hard disk to use for this file system. The label can provide a shortcut reference to a partition; you can have the label point to a different partition without needing to edit the **fstab** file.

- The mount point in the directory structure where the device will be accessed after being mounted. Each file system has a mount point directory except the **swap** space, which is used only by the Linux kernel.

- The file system type. **iso9660** is the CD-ROM standard; **proc** and **swap** are examples of special file system types.

8

- Options that apply when this file system is mounted. You will learn more about these options later in this section.

- Whether the file system can respond to the **dump** command (this command is called **dumpe2fs** in Linux). A **1** in this field indicates that the **dumpe2fs** command can be used to print information on the structure of the file system. Only **ext2** or **ext3** partitions should have this field set to **1**.

- The order used to check file systems when Linux is booted. Each time Linux starts, it checks the status of file systems in **fstab** before mounting them. The root file system should be numbered **1**; other **ext2** or **ext3** file systems should be numbered **2**. If **0** is used, the file system is not checked. All file systems that are not automounted can have **0** in this field.

The options used to mount file systems are an effective way to increase security and ease system administration work. The options that you can use on a line within **/etc/fstab** depend on the type of file system being mounted. For example, many options can be used for NFS (network-mounted) file systems that are not applicable to other types of file systems. Key options are described in Table 8-4.

Table 8-4   Option Field Settings for the **mount** Command

Mount option	Description
async	Specifies that all reads and writes to the file system should be asynchronous—in other words, that information will be buffered (stored in memory) to improve access speed
auto	Specifies that the file system should be automatically mounted at boot time or when the mount command is used with the -a option
dev	Designates the file system as a special device in the /dev directory
exec	Permits programs stored on the file system to be executed
noauto	Indicates that this file system should not be automatically mounted; instead, the file system must be mounted by an explicit mount command
noexec	Indicates that programs stored on the file system cannot be executed
nouser	Specifies that no regular users can mount the file system; instead, only root can mount it
ro	Mounts the file system as read-only, which means no data can be written to it
rw	Mounts the file system as read/write—the standard mode in which data can be written to the file system
suid	Allows special user ID permissions to be used on this file system
user	Allows a regular user to mount the file system; this is useful if you are running a desktop Linux system and don't want to switch to the root user account to mount a floppy or CD-ROM
users	Functions the same as the user option except that any user can unmount the device
defaults	Includes the options rw, suid, dev, exec, auto, nouser, and async

Additional options are described in the man page for the mount command.

You can add options when executing a mount command, rather than relying on the options within /etc/fstab. If you do, as shown in this example command, the options given on the command line override any listed in /etc/fstab.

```
# mount -t ext3 -o defaults /dev/sdb2 /archive
```

Consider two examples when you would add a line to /etc/fstab to automate file system mounting. Suppose you had set up a large SCSI hard disk to hold a database application. You want the database file system to be mounted automatically when you start Linux. Users should not be able to run programs off the database file system or modify the file system configuration. For this situation, the fstab line might look like:

```
/dev/sdb2  /opt/db  ext3  defaults,noexec,nosuid  1  2
```

As a second example, suppose you are using Linux as your desktop workstation and have installed a new DVD drive. The device shouldn't be mounted at boot time because you don't normally keep a DVD disk in the drive, but you want to be able to mount the device without changing to the root user account. You also want to protect any write-able DVD disks from having any data damaged. You might use this line in the fstab file:

```
/dev/hdd /mnt/dvd  iso9660  ro,noauto,user  0 0
```

Once you have the fstab file set up, you can use the mount command with only the device name or mount point. The mount command looks in the fstab file for all of the additional information needed to mount the file system. For example, the CD-ROM device is normally configured in fstab after a Linux installation. The CD-ROM can thus be mounted with this command:

```
# mount /mnt/cdrom
```

No additional information is needed on the command line because mount retrieves everything else from the fstab file. If you use the mount command without sufficient information (and the information is not contained in the fstab file), mount displays an error message and the file system is not mounted.

Linux supports many different file systems. File system types that you may want to mount within Linux include msdos (older DOS and Microsoft Windows 3.1), hpfs (OS/2), vfat (newer Windows products), and ntfs (Windows NT, Windows 2000, and Windows XP). All these file system types assume the hard disk is located on the same computer as Linux is running on.

Linux or UNIX file systems accessed across a network are typically mounted using NFS. Networked Windows file systems (called shares in the world of Windows Networking) are accessed using the smbmount command, which is part of the Samba suite. See

8

Chapter 5 of *Guide to Linux Networking and Security* for information on these networked file systems.

Managing Swap Space

The swap space (also called the swap partition) is a special partition type used by the Linux kernel for virtual memory. Recall that virtual memory is hard disk space that is used by the kernel as if it were RAM. A program that is not in active use is moved to virtual memory (stored on the swap partition) so other active programs can use the "real" memory. When the inactive program is needed again, it can quickly be moved from virtual memory back to RAM.

The swap space is set up during Linux installation and activated (via the `fstab` file) each time Linux boots. The swap space is normally located on a separate partition. (It's also possible to define a single large file as the kernel's swap space, but this is very inefficient compared to using a separate partition.)

A swap partition can be several GB in size. The appropriate size depends on factors such as how many users are working on the system, how many programs are running at the same time, which of them are active versus inactive, and the amount of RAM installed. If you have a large, busy Linux server, having the swap partition on a separate hard disk (even a separate disk controller) from the main data partitions will improve performance. Such an arrangement means the kernel's requests for data from swap space don't compete with other programs' requests for data from other partitions. You can also establish multiple swap partitions on multiple disk drives if needed.

You can use the **mkswap** command to format a swap partition. This is similar to using the `mke2fs` command to format an `ext2` or `ext3` partition. After you have created partition and marked it as type 82 (Linux `swap`), use a command such as this one to format the partition as swap space:

```
# mkswap /dev/hda2
```

Once you have formatted a partition as swap space, you can add a line to `/etc/fstab` to tell Linux how to activate the swap space at boot time. The example file shown previously includes this line:

```
/dev/hda3    swap    swap    defaults    0 0
```

Swap space is activated by the **swapon** command within the system initialization scripts described in Chapter 4. You can view the status of swap space (virtual memory) using the **free** command. Here is typical output from this command:

```
                    total     used     free   shared  buffers   cached
        Mem:       191260   187480     3780        0    11232    55124
-/+ buffers/cache:          121124    70136
        Swap:      265064        0   265064
```

Note the `total` and `free` columns. The `Mem` row refers to RAM memory; `Swap` refers to swap space. On the system shown here, a total of about 192 MB of RAM and 256 MB of swap space are available on the system. None of the swap space is used, but most of the RAM is in use (187 MB) as memory buffers to hold disk files (121 MB).

Because swap space is located on a hard disk, it is significantly slower to access than the RAM on your system board. Because of this, you may think it best to avoid using it by installing enough RAM so that the Linux kernel never needs to save information in the swap space. In truth, both RAM and swap space are useful. A typical system should have at least as much swap space as RAM. The reason for this is that the Linux kernel will attempt to cache (store) in RAM as many files and programs as possible in order to increase the system speed. But if many users on a system are working with many programs, it's likely that not all programs will be active at the same time. Rather than have these programs use RAM, they can be placed in the swap space while they are inactive. On a well-tuned system, the kernel can quickly bring these programs back into memory when a user needs them—so quickly that most users won't notice any delay.

Another reason to make wise use of swap space is cost. Hard disk space is much cheaper than RAM. While swap space is an important part of your system, however, its advantages diminish on systems with insufficient RAM. On systems with too little RAM, the swap space will be overused. This means that a single program might be moved to the swap space and back into system memory several times per second, as it competes with other programs for processor time. The time required to move an active program to and from the swap space greatly reduces the efficiency of the system. This problem is called **thrashing**. To solve this problem you need to reduce the system load or add more system RAM.

To see detailed information about how the swap space is used, run the **vmstat** command (for *virtual memory statistics*). The output of **vmstat** describes which processes are using swap space, how much space they are using, what processes are waiting for RAM to become available, and more.

Setting Quotas on Disk Usage

Another way you can manage file systems is by imposing a limit on the amount of hard disk space that any user or group can use. These limits are called **disk quotas**. For example, if you have defined a quota of 100 MB for a user and that user tries to create a new file (of which he is the owner) after using 100 MB of disk space, the system will not permit him to create that file.

Setting up quotas requires four steps:

1. Enable quotas on a file system by including the `usrquota` or `grpquota` option when the file system is mounted (for example, include it within the `/etc/fstab` file).

8

2. Use the `edquota` command to establish a quota for one or more users or groups.

3. Activate the quota system using the `quotaon` command.

4. Review current disk usage for a file system using the `quotacheck` command, or for a particular user or group using the `quota` command.

Quotas are not often used in business offices, but may be very helpful in schools or other institutions where many users share a Linux system. You can learn more about disk quotas by reviewing the man pages for the commands described in this list.

SIMPLE TASK MANAGEMENT

In Chapter 7 you learned about using the `ps` command to list the processes running on Linux. In the sections that follow, you learn more about controlling processes within a shell. More information on managing processes is provided in Chapter 10.

Job Control in the Shell

Often you will want to start multiple programs at the same time. For example, you might launch an editor, a Web browser, an audio CD player, and then want to test a script you have written. You can start multiple programs from graphical menus on your desktop, or from a command line. Linux shells include many tools for managing processes that you have started from a command line.

 Because the default shell for Linux is bash, commands described in this section apply to the `bash` shell. Similar features are supported by other shells such as `ksh`, `csh`, `tcsh`, and `zsh`.

Processes

When you start a program, that program takes control of the command line where you are working. For example, if you enter the command

```
$ man ps
```

the man page for `ps` appears, and you no longer see a prompt where you can enter additional commands. Some commands don't display screen output like the man page viewer, but they still leave you without an active prompt to enter additional commands. The shell is effectively "busy" running the command you entered.

If you type an ampersand (&) after the name of a command, the shell places the process in the background—in other words, the process runs, but it doesn't control the command line—the shell is not "busy" running it any longer. You can then start another command immediately. For example, if you are working in a graphical command-line window and enter the command

```
$ gedit &
```

the `gedit` text editor window appears, but you can also enter other commands in the same shell where you launched `gedit`. Compare this with entering `gedit` without the ampersand, in which case you cannot enter other commands at the shell prompt. Multiple processes started from a single shell are called jobs.

Jobs

A job is a process that is associated with a shell. The **jobs** command lists all jobs or processes that are running from the current shell.

You can use the Ctrl+Z key combination to suspend a job that the shell is busy running. For example, if you had launched **gedit** without an ampersand, you could press Ctrl+Z to suspend **gedit**, returning you to an active shell prompt. Then you use the **bg** command to run the suspended program in the background.

A suspended job is not ended, but it stops running normally. It waits for further instructions before beginning normal execution again. The **jobs** command lists processes that are currently suspended, as in the following output:

```
$ jobs
[1]+   Stopped (signal)    gedit
```

The output of the **jobs** command shown above includes a job number at the left of the line (1 in the output above). The process ID number is not shown by the **jobs** command. When a job is suspended, you can either place it in the background (restart it without displaying output to the current console) or place it in the foreground (allow it to take control of the screen again). To place a job in the foreground, use the **fg** command. You specify a job number (given by the **jobs** command) in order to recall a job to the foreground.

The following procedure illustrates how to use **bg** and **fg**:

1. Open a Linux command line within a graphical environment.

2. Launch the **gedit** command:

   gedit

   This command runs in the foreground and occupies the command line so you can't enter other commands.

3 Press **Ctrl+Z** to pause the foreground command (**gedit**).

4. Enter the **jobs** command. You see **gedit** listed, probably as job number 1.

5. `gedit` is currently paused or suspended. Resume it as a background process by entering this command:

   bg %1

   The command line is now free to run other programs.

6. Enter the command **man ls**. The man page for the `ls` command appears.

7. Press **Ctrl+Z** to pause the `man` command.

8. Enter the command **man ps**. The man page for the `ps` command appears.

9. Press **Ctrl+Z** to pause the second `man` command.

10. Enter the command **jobs**. You see output showing both `man` commands and the `gedit` command.

11. Note the job number of the first `man` command. Enter the command **fg %2**. (Use the number for the first `man` command in place of 2 if necessary.) The `ls` man page appears again.

12. Press **q** to end the `man ls` command.

13. Enter the **jobs** command again. You see that the `man ls` command is no longer listed.

Some commands (including the `man` command) are only used to display information. Using `bg` while viewing a man page automatically suspends the command. It only runs when in the foreground.

You can use the process ID (PID) number instead of the job number when executing `fg` or `bg`. Just include the PID without the percentage sign that you use with the job number. For example, suppose a process you have started is job number 3 in the current shell and has a PID of 725. You can bring the process to the foreground with either of these commands:

```
fg %3
fg 725
```

Using Virtual Consoles

As you learned in Chapter 4, you can open multiple command-line windows within a graphical environment. You can also use virtual consoles in Linux to work in multiple text-mode sessions at the same time. A **virtual console** is a separate login screen that you access by pressing a combination of keys on your keyboard. A virtual console allows you to start multiple text-based login sessions on the same computer.

Networked Linux systems allow many users to log in using a network connection. Virtual consoles provide the same type of login functionality without a network connection—from a single keyboard.

The virtual consoles are assigned to the function keys, typically F1 through F6. (Some systems may have more than six consoles, but six is standard.) The graphical environment (X) operates on virtual console 7.

When you are viewing a text-mode screen, you start working in the first virtual console. You access the second virtual console by pressing Alt+F2. This displays a new login prompt, where you can log in using any valid username and password. Any commands that you start from this virtual console run independently of those on other virtual consoles. Each console starts a separate copy of the **bash** shell, so the **jobs** command will only list jobs started in one virtual console, even if you have logged in using the same username.

When you are viewing a graphical desktop, you access a text-mode virtual console by pressing Ctrl+Alt+F1 for the first virtual console, Ctrl+Alt+F2 for the second, and so on, to Ctrl+Alt+F6 for the sixth virtual console.

To switch back to your first virtual console, press Alt+F1. If you were working in a graphical desktop, switch back to that environment by pressing Alt+F7.

Learning about Processes

The **ps** command (introduced in Chapter 7) includes many options that show the status of processes on your Linux system. A simple **ps** command shows you only the commands that you have started in the current command-line environment (also called the current terminal):

```
$ ps
PID TTY      TIME CMD
 576 tty1    00:00:00 login
 584 tty1    00:00:00 bash
 951 tty1    00:00:00 ps
```

This is useful, but provides little more than the **jobs** command. As a system administrator, you'll want to use **ps** options. For example, the **a** and **x** options show you the processes started by all users, and those started by the system at boot time or other processes that have no controlling terminal (**tty**).

The output of **ps** with the **a** and **x** options is much longer than the output of **ps** alone. It includes all of the daemons that are running in the background as you work on Linux. For example, multiple **login** commands running on other virtual consoles, the Web server (called **httpd**), the system logging daemon, and possibly many other daemons and components of a graphical desktop are all included in a typical listing. By adding the **u** option, you

8

can see information about how each process is using your Linux system. The first few lines of `ps` with these three options are shown here:

```
$ ps aux | less
USER       PID  %CPU %MEM SIZE   RSS TTY STAT START   TIME COMMAND
bin        381  0.0  0.9   840   300  ?  S     13:32   0:00 rpc.portmap
daemon     451  0.0  1.9  1156   596  ?  S     13:32   0:00 lpd
daemon     471  0.0  1.0   828   324  ?  S     13:32   0:00 atd
nobody     845  0.0  2.5  1384   784  ?  S     13:32   0:00 httpd -f
nobody     846  0.0  2.5  1384   784  ?  S     13:32   0:00 httpd -f
root         1  0.0  1.0   828   332  ?  S     13:31   0:04 init
root         2  0.0  0.0     0     0  ?  SW    13:31   0:00 (kflushd)
root         3  0.0  0.0     0     0  ?  SW    13:31   0:00 (kpiod)
```

The first line of the output contains column headings that indicate which user started the process, the percentage of CPU time and memory used by the process, the terminal that the process is running on, current status, and other information. To manage a process, you'll want to note the PID of the process in the second column from the left.

You can use the `f` option to display the relationship between different processes, showing which processes start other processes. A partial listing based on the `a`, `x`, and `f` options is shown here:

```
$ ps axf
PID TTY     STAT TIME COMMAND
  1 ?        S    0:04 init
  2 ?        SW   0:00 [kflushd]
  3 ?        SW   0:00 [kpiod]
535          S    0:00 sendmail: accepting connections: p
550 ?        S    0:00 gpm -t ps/2
564 ?        S    0:00 httpd
568 ?        S    0:00 \_ httpd
571 ?        S    0:00 \_ httpd
577 ?        S    0:00 \_ httpd
594 ?        S    0:00 xfs
638 tty2     S    0:00 login - root
664 tty2     S    0:00 \_ -bash
676 tty2     T    0:00   \_ man ls
677 tty2     T    0:00     | \_ sh -c /bin/gunzip
678 tty2     T    0:00     |   \_ /bin/gunzip
679 tty2     T    0:00     |   \_ /usr/bin/less -is
680 tty2     T    0:00   \_ top
686 tty2     R    0:00   \_ ps axf
639 tty3     S    0:00 /sbin/mingetty tty3
642 tty6     S    0:00 /sbin/mingetty tty6
644 ?        S    0:00 update (bdflush)
```

The processes are presented in a tree diagram. For example, process ID (PID) 638 (see the left column of the output above) is the `login` command, where a user has logged in as root. The login process started a `bash` shell (the next line in the output, process 664). The root user started several commands within the shell, including `man ls` (PID 676), `top` (PID 680), and the `ps` command (PID 686). The `man` command started other commands to uncompress the man page file. Many processes were started by the Linux kernel when the system was booted. These processes appear without any tree structure.

Each process has a parent process—that is, the process that started it. A parent process can have many child processes. As stated in Chapter 4, the first process started on a Linux system is called `init`. This process is the parent to all processes and has a PID number of 1.

Controlling Processes

You can use the `jobs`, `fg`, and `bg` commands to control processes (jobs) that were started within a single shell. Using the `kill` command, you can control any process on the system. The name of this command is somewhat unfortunate: although it is often used to kill, or end, processes, it actually sends signals to processes. Some of those signals end the process; others serve different purposes, such as suspending a process or causing a program to reread its configuration file.

You must be logged in as root to control processes that you didn't start.

Signals are messages that can be sent between processes. About 30 different signals are available, but most of these are not used regularly. Each signal has a name and a number associated with it. To see a list of all the signals, use the `kill` command with the `-l` option (for list):

```
$ kill -l
```

When writing a program, a developer decides which signals the program will respond to. Some programs only respond to one or two signals. Others may respond to more signals, depending on the purpose of the program. For example, a program designed to control your computer in the event of a power failure will respond to the signal from a power supply indicating that the main power is out. Other programs wouldn't respond to this signal.

Almost all programs respond to the SIGTERM signal (signal number 15). This signal requests that the program end. Another special signal is SIGKILL (signal number 9). The SIGKILL signal is not handled by the program itself. Instead, if you send a SIGKILL using the `kill` command, the signal is handled by the Linux kernel, which shuts down the indicated process. Any unsaved data in a program will be lost when SIGKILL is used to end a process. You should use SIGTERM (rather than SIGKILL) to shut down processes, because SIGTERM requests that a program close itself, giving the program a chance to clean up its work, close any open files, and so forth, before ending. When you use SIGKILL, the process is cut off before it can do any of those things. SIGKILL is very useful, however, when a process is not responding to SIGTERM.

As an example of using the `kill` command to send a signal, suppose a user on your Linux system had started a program called **myeditor**. The program has stopped responding to user commands (it is "locked up"). But it still appears on-screen. You could use **ps** to see the state of the process:

```
# ps ax | grep myeditor
```

The output of this command shows you the PID number for the **myeditor** program. Using this information, you can send a signal to the process. (Here we assumed you are logged in as root; the user that started **myeditor** could also use the `kill` command to send a signal):

```
# kill -15 1482
```

This command sends a request to **myeditor** to close. The command could also be written using the name of the signal:

```
# kill -SIGTERM 1482
```

If the program does not respond to the request to terminate (it still appears in the output of **ps ax** and on-screen), you can send a SIGKILL signal that will cause the Linux kernel to end the process immediately:

```
# kill -9 1482
```

A special form of the `kill` command is **killall**. This command sends a signal to all processes started by a given command. This is particularly useful when a program is starting copies of itself faster than you can locate the PIDs and use `kill` to shut them down. For example, if the **myeditor** program were doing this, you could use this command:

```
# killall -9 myeditor
```

 Be careful not to use `killall` when multiple copies of a program are running and you only want to end one of them. In that case, use `kill` with the appropriate PID.

In Chapter 10 you will learn more about managing processes in Linux, including how to allocate time and disk space to processes and track how busy your Linux system is.

CHAPTER SUMMARY

- ❏ Types of user accounts include root, regular accounts, and special accounts. Special accounts cannot be used to log in, but instead are used by programs running on Linux.

❏ To work as root after logging in as a regular user, use the **su** command.

❏ Groups include users as members. User Private Groups have only a single user as a member. A user can be a member of multiple groups, but can only have one primary group, as listed in **/etc/passwd**. Groups are defined in **/etc/group**.

❏ The **/etc/passwd** file defines user accounts. It contains user IDs, full names, and a default shell. Encrypted passwords are stored in **/etc/shadow** so that regular users cannot read them.

❏ New user accounts can be created with the **useradd** command or with various graphical utilities. Default settings apply when using **useradd**; these can be modified on the command line or by editing a configuration file for **useradd**.

❏ New groups can be created with the **groupadd** command.

❏ The **groupmod** command lets you modify membership of a group. The **usermod** command lets you modify user account parameters stored in **/etc/passwd** or **/etc/shadow**.

❏ The **passwd** command changes a user's password. Accounts can be deleted using **userdel**.

❏ Whenever a user account is created, the contents of **/etc/skel** are copied into the new user's home directory.

❏ File systems are accessed by using the **mount** command to specify a device and a mount point (a directory). Entries in **/etc/fstab** can simplify the **mount** command or even automatically mount file systems at boot time.

❏ The **df** and **du** commands display status and size information about file systems. Similar graphical tools are available within KDE and Gnome.

❏ The **fdisk** utility can configure partition data on a hard disk. New partitions must be formatting using **mke2fs** or **mkswap** before they can be used.

❏ Virtual memory resides in swap space, which can be created on multiple partitions. The **vmstat** command displays current status details for how virtual memory is being used.

❏ You can use disk quotas to restrict how much disk space a user is permitted to consume.

❏ Multiple processes can be started from a single shell. Within a shell, the **jobs** command manages these processes, placing them in the foreground or background using the **fg** and **bg** commands.

❏ Virtual consoles let you log in at multiple independent text-mode screens.

❏ Options to the **ps** command let you display all processes running on Linux, with many details about each one, including parent-child relationships between processes.

8

❑ The `kill` command sends signals to processes or to the Linux kernel when necessary to end a process.

KEY TERMS

`/etc/fstab` — A configuration file that contains a file system table with devices, mount points, file system types, and options. Used by the `mount` command.

`/etc/group` — A configuration file in which group information (group names and membership lists) is stored.

`/etc/passwd` — A configuration file in which user account information is stored.

`/etc/shadow` — A configuration file in which encrypted user passwords and password configuration data are stored.

`/etc/skel` — A directory containing files that are copied to a new user's home directory at the time a new user account is created.

`bg` — A command used to place a job (process) in the background (either by suspending it or by preventing its output from appearing in the current shell's terminal window), thus allowing the shell prompt to become active again.

`df` — Short for display file systems. A command used to display file system summary information such as device, mount point, percentage used, and total capacity.

`disk quotas` — Limits assigned to each user that restrict the total amount of space that the user can consume on a file system.

`du` — Short for disk usage. A command used to display disk space used by a directory and each of its subdirectories.

`fdformat` — A command used to format a floppy disk.

`fg` — A command used to bring a job (process) running in a shell to the foreground so that the job controls the shell's terminal window.

`free` — A command used to display the amount of free and used memory, both RAM and swap space.

`group` — A collection of user accounts that can be collectively granted access to a system resource.

`groupadd` — A command used to add a new group to a Linux system.

`groupmod` — A command used to modify group information.

`jobs` — A command used to list jobs (processes) started in the current shell environment.

`journaling` — A feature of `ext3` file systems that protects against data corruption by tracking each "write" to the hard disk in a special way so that it will either be completely finished or left completely undone.

`kill` — A command used to send signals to processes, often to end them via a SIGTERM or SIGKILL signal.

killall — A command used to send signals to all processes that match a command name rather than a PID (as used with **kill**).

mke2fs — A command used to format a device such as a hard disk partition with an **ext2** file system.

mkfs — A command used to format devices using various file system types. The **ext2** or **ext3** type for Linux file systems can be indicated as an option. *See also* **mke2fs**.

mkswap — A command used to format a partition as swap space for the Linux kernel.

mount — A command used to make a logical or physical device available as a file system in the Linux directory structure.

mount point — The place or path in the Linux directory structure where a file system is accessed.

root — The superuser account name in Linux.

Shadow Password Suite — A set of password-related utilities that implement a security system used to restrict access to encrypted password text in **/etc/shadow**.

signal — A message (one of a fixed set determined by the Linux kernel) that can be sent to any process and responded to according to how that program is written.

su — (Short for substitute user) A command used to take on the identity of a different user account.

superuser — The root user account, which has supervisory privileges throughout the Linux system.

swapon — A command used by Linux initialization scripts to activate the swap partition defined in the **/etc/fstab** file.

thrashing — Excessive movement of processes between RAM and swap space, resulting in reduced system performance and excessive wear on the hard disk.

umount — A command used to unmount a file system that is currently accessible as part of the Linux directory structure.

User Private Group — A security system that creates a new group containing one user when that user is first created.

useradd — A command used to create (add) a new user account in Linux.

usermod — A command used to modify or update an existing user account.

vigr — A command used to edit **/etc/group**.

vipw — A command used to edit **/etc/passwd**.

virtual console — A separate login screen that you access by pressing a combination of keys on your keyboard. It allows you to start multiple text-based login sessions on the same computer.

vmstat — A command used to display detailed usage information for the swap file system (plus basic information about RAM usage).

wheel — A special system administrative group, not used officially in Linux.

8

REVIEW QUESTIONS

1. Describe the effect of including a hyphen when executing the `su` command.

2. A user's primary group can be a User Private Group. True or False?

3. The `/etc/passwd` file does *not* contain which of the following fields:

    a. The name of the user account

    b. The file privileges for the user

    c. The user's default shell

    d. A UID and GID for the user

4. Explain the meaning of this line in the `/etc/group` file:
   `webmasters:x:710:rthomas,cyang`

5. To create or change a password on any user account, the following is used:

    a. The `useradd` utility

    b. The file `/etc/shadow` with a text editor

    c. The `passwd` command

    d. The UID and GID of the user

6. Name the command and corresponding file that control defaults used by the `useradd` command.

7. When you add a file to the `/etc/skel` directory, the file is added to the home directory of users:

    a. When you create new users after that time

    b. Immediately

    c. When the next `usermod` command is executed

    d. Based on the options set in the `/etc/shadow` file for each user

8. What does the fourth field in `/etc/passwd` contain?

9. The Linux command used to format a Linux `ext3` hard disk partition is:

    a. `mke2fs`

    b. `fdisk`

    c. `fsck`

    d. Linux does not use formatted partitions

10. Why should you not use a standard text editor to add users to `/etc/passwd`?

11. If you enter a new password for a user account that can be easily guessed, the message `BAD PASSWORD` appears and the password is:

    a. Not updated unless you are root

    b. Updated unless you are root

c. Only updated if you are logged in as a regular user

d. Updated if the password is not part of the dictionary of common words

12. Disk quotas let you manage how much disk space a user consumes, but they must be first enabled:

a. On a group-by-group basis using standard file permission settings

b. Within the startup scripts in a user's home directory

c. On the file system where you want the quota to apply

d. By adding an option to the `/etc/passwd` file for each affected user

13. Describe one simple method of temporarily disabling a user account without using a graphical utility.

14. A mounted file system is one that:

a. Has been included as part of the Linux directory structure

b. Has been correctly formatted for use in Linux

c. Allows any user to run programs located on it

d. Includes at least a root user account

15. How can you switch between multiple virtual consoles in text and graphical environments?

16. The Shadow Password Suite enhances Linux security by:

a. Validating members of the `wheel` group as they log in

b. Hiding encrypted passwords in a file that only root can read

c. Checking that new passwords entered for users are not easily guessed

d. Stopping unauthorized users from accessing the root account

17. Which of the following is an acceptable way to create a new user account?

a. Use a user creation script.

b. Use the redhat-config-users utility in Red Hat Linux.

c. Use an editor to add a line to `/etc/passwd` with appropriate information.

d. Start the Shadow Password Suite with the `/sbin/shadow` command.

18. The `fdisk` utility is used to:

a. Format Linux partitions

b. Configure the boot loader

c. Establish partitions of the correct type to hold a Linux file system

d. Configure swap space

8

19. The **df** utility provides information about which one of the following?

    a. Which users have mounted a file system

    b. The virtual memory usage as stored on all mounted file systems

    c. File system capacity, device name, and percentage used status

    d. Per-directory usage and file system mount point

20. Describe the effect of the **defaults** option in a configuration line of the **/etc/fstab** file.

21. Describe at least four fields of information provided by the command **ps auxf**.

22. Describe the main advantage of having swap space located on a hard disk separate from the Linux data partitions.

23. List two reasons why a user account might need to be disabled.

24. If you attempt to unmount a mounted file system and receive an error message, the most likely cause is:

    a. The file system was not mounted correctly in the first place

    b. The **df** command is in the process of computing file system statistics

    c. An error on the physical media that Linux cannot interpret

    d. One or more users are working in the file system

25. By starting multiple jobs from one shell, you can:

    a. Conserve resources for each process you start

    b. Prevent the swap space from thrashing

    c. Manage those jobs with the **jobs**, **fg**, and **bg** commands

    d. Kill any unneeded process quickly

HANDS-ON PROJECTS

Project 8-1

In this project you practice managing user and group accounts. To complete this project you need an installed Linux system with root access. This procedure should work on any version of Linux, though the defaults assume you are working on Red Hat Linux 7.3.

1. Log in as root and open a command-line window.

2. Create a new group named webmasters:

       groupadd webmasters

3. Display the group file and review the new group on the last line of the output:

       cat /etc/group

4. Review the default settings for `useradd`:

   `useradd -D`

   Notice the SHELL= setting refers to the `bash` shell.

5. Change the default for all users created after this point:

   `useradd -D -s /bin/tcsh`

6. Review the contents of the `/etc/skel` directory:

   `ls /etc/skel`

   Why is nothing listed?

7. Review the contents of the `/etc/skel` directory again:

   `ls -a /etc/skel`

8. Examine the default `.bash_profile` script where you could place environment variables or aliases that were to be part of users' environments:

   `cat /etc/skel/.bash_profile`

9. Create a new user account with a primary group assignment, an expiration date, and a full name in the comment field:

   `useradd -g webmasters -e 12/31/03 -c "Hailey Mendez" hmendez`

10. Display the user account file and review the new user account information in the last line of the output:

    `cat /etc/passwd`

11. Review the contents of the new user's home directory and compare it with what you viewed in `/etc/skel`:

    `ls -a /home/hmendez`

12. Set a password for the new user account:

    `passwd hmendez`

13. Enter a new password twice, as prompted.

14. Change to the new user account using the substitute user command:

    `su - hmendez`

    No password is required because you are logged in as root.

15. Display the aliases that are in effect for the new user:

    `alias`

16. Check which shell you are currently using:

    `echo $SHELL`

17. Return to the root account:

    `exit`

8

18. Change the shell used by the `lmendez` account with the following `usermod` command:

    `usermod -s /bin/bash hmendez`

19. Change the default shell used when creating new user accounts:

    `useradd -D -s /bin/bash`

20. Change to another virtual console by pressing **Ctrl+Alt+F2** if you are working in a graphical environment or **Alt+F2** if you are working in a text-mode console.

21. Log in using the new account you created and the password you assigned.

22. Change back to your previous virtual console by pressing **Alt+F7** for graphical mode or **Alt+F1** for the first text-mode console.

Project 8-2

In this project you practice accessing file systems in Linux. To complete this project you should have an installed Linux system with root access and a formatted floppy disk. The configuration of directories in the project is based on Red Hat Linux 7.3, but most Linux systems will be identical to what is described here.

1. Log in to Linux and open a command-line window.

2. Insert a floppy disk in the floppy drive of your computer.

3. Mount the floppy disk:

   `mount /mnt/floppy`

4. Copy a file to the floppy disk:

   `cp /etc/login.defs /mnt/floppy`

5. List the contents of the floppy disk:

   `ls /mnt./floppy`

6. Unmount the floppy disk:

   `umount /mnt/floppy`

7. Try to list the contents of the floppy disk again:

   `ls /mnt/floppy`

   Why doesn't the file appear?

8. Review the line in `/etc/fstab` that lets you mount this file system without specifying a device name:

   `grep floppy /etc/fstab`

9. Create a file full of zeros in the root directory to use as an experimental 64 MB swap file.

   `dd if=/dev/zero of=/swap bs=1024 count=65536`

10. Format the swap file you just created:

    mkswap /swap

11. Edit the /etc/fstab file in a text editor:

    vi /etc/fstab

12. Add this line to the end of the /etc/fstab file:

    /swap   swap   swap   defaults   0 0

13. Save the file and exit the text editor.

14. Activate all swap space listed in the /etc/fstab file:

    swapon –a

15. Your original swap partition and the experimental swap file are now both available to the kernel as swap space. To see evidence of this, display the kernel's swap space table using this command:

    cat /proc/swaps

16. Edit the /etc/fstab file again and remove the extra line you added to the swap file.

17. Would you expect this step to immediately affect the current state of the swap space?

18. Turn off the experimental swap file:

    swapoff /swap

19. Delete the swap file, confirming the deletion when prompted:

    rm /swap

Project 8-3

In this project you explore how signals sent with the **kill** command interact with running processes. To complete this project you should have an installed Linux system with root access.

1. Log in as root and open a command-line window.

2. Switch to the third virtual console by pressing **Ctrl+Alt+F3** if you are working in a graphical environment or **Alt+F3** if you are working in text mode.

3. Log in to virtual console 3 using a regular user account.

4. View a man page in virtual console 3:

    man mount

5. Switch back to where you logged in for Step 1 by pressing either **Alt+F1** or **Alt+F7**.

6. Review a structured list of processes running on Linux and locate the processes running on `tty3` (look under the TTY column for tty3):

    ps axf | less

7. For each, note the PID (on the far left) and the command name (on the far right). Also notice the tree structure they are shown in.

8. Use the `kill` command with the appropriate PID to request that the `man` command running on the third virtual console close (the PID you use depends on what you observed in the previous step):

    kill -15 1114

9. Switch to virtual console 3. What result do you see?

10. Start a new `man` command:

    man mount

11. Switch back to your original console.

12. Execute the same `ps` command and note the same information for tty3:

    ps axf | less

13. Has the PID of the `man` command changed?

14. Within the output of the previous `ps` command, find the `login` command that appears to be the parent of the processes running on `tty3` (it probably lists ? as its TTY). Note the PID of that `login` process.

15. Kill the `login` process on that terminal:

    kill -SIGTERM [PID]

16. Switch to virtual console 3. What result do you see and what do you conclude?

CASE PROJECTS

McKinney & Co. has been awarded a contract to help with a foreign assistance project. You have been asked to lead the project and, hearing that it was near some beautiful beaches, you have graciously turned over your current project to a colleague and accepted this challenging new assignment. Your task is to help the Ministry of Justice of the Government of Cylonica place all of their supreme court cases and various other legal materials online. One of the first technical aspects of the project is designing the file systems on which the data will reside.

1. The legal data consists of statutes (laws) and court cases, and is never altered once it is loaded. Several hundred GB of data are anticipated as part of the final project. Legal researchers can add their own notes to cases, creating a personal database of

study items. Several applications also run to manage the databases, execute searches, index newly loaded material, and interact with users (chat, e-mail to the Minister's office, etc.). Several hundred users are expected to begin using the system as soon as it is completed; usage will increase as more people become aware of it.

Design the layout of the file systems for the Linux server on which this system will reside. Show how you would set up partitions or separate hard disks and devices to accommodate each of the needs mentioned above. Prepare sample entries for an `fstab` file showing the options that you would likely use for each mounted file system. Include information about how you would configure the swap space on the devices you choose to use.

2. An international conference in England had generated substantially more interest in the legal research site than was expected. You notice one day that the `df` command shows one file system at more than 95% capacity. Describe some steps you might take to remedy this problem. How would your actions vary depending on which of the file systems was at 95%?

3. After completing this project and returning home, you learn that a typhoon has raged through Cylonica. The resulting power fluctuations caused one of the hard disks to crash. Your plan included regular backups, of course. What factors in the file system arrangement you designed make it easier to get the system running again?

8

PREPARING FOR EMERGENCIES

After reading this chapter and completing the exercises, you will be able to:

♦ Understand your system's vulnerabilities and plan to protect data and ensure minimum downtime

♦ Manage the power supply to your Linux computer

♦ Check the integrity of your Linux file systems

♦ Understand how redundant disk systems can protect data

In the previous chapter you learned how to perform basic administrative tasks including creating and managing user accounts, mounting and examining file systems, and using the `fdisk` utility. You also learned how to view and manage processes in a Linux shell.

In this chapter you learn how to protect the data on your Linux system and minimize downtime caused by various types of emergencies—power outages, disk drive failures, and other hardware problems. Protecting your Linux system involves planning for potential trouble before it occurs and understanding how to configure parts of your Linux-based computer to avoid downtime.

UNDERSTANDING A SYSTEM'S VULNERABILITIES

As you probably know by now, computer systems are not infallible. For all the dependence society places on computers, they continue to break down, leading to crises for customers, managers, and system administrators. These crises loom largest for system administrators, the people everyone else looks to for immediate guidance and resolution when an organization's computer systems malfunction. These are the times when a system administrator who has prepared for emergencies really shines. Although handling crises is part of the system administrator's job description, those who excel in this area are on the path to promotions or raises when the proverbial sky falls. Conversely, those who have not prepared to handle difficult situations are likely to be looking for work elsewhere.

Creating a Disaster Plan

The first step in preparing for emergencies is to do everything possible to avoid them. A "disaster" somewhere else doesn't have to mean an emergency for your systems. Rather than sending out a distress call, how much better to send the following message to your management team: "You may have heard that a tornado ripped through downtown Salt Lake City last night—I just wanted you to know that our systems are all backed up, with full power, running smoothly and without interruption." The preparation that allows you to send such a message begins with a **disaster plan**—a written document stating how you have prepared your systems and what you will do in the event that various problems occur. A disaster plan should cover a wide range of potential problems. Your plan may include guidelines regarding some of the following problems:

- A hard disk crash.

- A power supply failure.

- A cyberattack that attempts to block all network access to the system.

- An employee or intruder destroying data on the system or attempting to crash it.

- A fire in the server room.

- A terrorist attack that affects your system.

- A natural disaster that wipes out all backups in the office, destroys the server, and blocks anyone from getting near the office.

Some parts of a disaster plan are closely tied to a security plan. A security plan (or security policy) is another important document that describes how your organization prevents security breaches and handles them when they do occur. The purpose of both documents is to safeguard the integrity of your computer systems. A security plan deals more with purposeful attacks to steal, manipulate, or destroy data, often over a network connection and often caused by employees. A disaster plan deals more with random events not directed at your computer systems, but which have a wider impact that threatens their stability and usefulness.

For more information on creating and implementing a security plan, see *Guide to Linux Networking and Security* (Course Technology 2002, ISBN 0-619-00094-5), Chapter 7.

Disaster planning is all about risk management. To create an effective disaster plan you must accurately analyze what potential risks threaten your computer systems, how costly each of these would be to recover from, and what steps would prevent or lessen the effect of each risk. Many companies and government agencies specialize in helping organizations analyze and prepare for risks. To understand how risk analysis works, consider these example scenarios that different organizations might think through while creating a disaster plan.

A small charity in Salt Lake City evaluates the need to protect its mailing list from fire, theft, and water damage. They decide to keep one backup copy in a bank safe deposit box, updating it monthly, for a total cost of about $35 per month. The American Express processing center down the street spends thousands of dollars each day to archive customer data at a secure off-site location in another state. A company located in New Orleans might include hurricane, major flooding, and fire in their risk assessment. Volcanic eruptions are part of the plan for a company located in Seattle.

Government agencies can provide statistics regarding natural disasters. For example, areas near bodies of water are categorized by how often, statistically, they will experience a flood. If your property lies in a 50-year flood plain, it will flood on average once every 50 years. Using statistics like these can help you gauge the likelihood of different threats and weigh them against the value of your information and the value of keeping systems running continuously.

A disaster plan should outline policies and procedures to guide the actions of the system administrator and other staff members in preparing for and reacting to many types of emergencies. Information in a disaster plan should include the following:

- Detailed system specifications for all hardware.
- A list of software installed on the server.
- Location of software masters, manuals, and licensing information for each application.
- Information about the server's power supply.
- Steps required to start the server using a boot or rescue disk (described later in this chapter).
- Steps required to reinstall critical applications and data archives for those applications.
- Names and contact information for those to be informed of server emergencies.
- Names and contact information for those who can be called to help in case of emergencies (including key technical support numbers for hardware and software vendors).

The exact steps outlined in the plan depend on the nature of your organization. For example, a company that provides credit card services to customers around the world wants to keep providing service even if an entire data center is shut down because of a major disaster. Millions of dollars are at stake for the company, so it will spend millions to prepare its systems for disasters. A study done by Oracle, the largest database software company, estimated that for their key customers, every *hour* of system downtime resulted in a loss of $80,000 to $300,000.

On the other hand, a small company with a server or two is not subject to such losses, though it may be just as dependent on its computer systems. Small firms can take some simple precautions that will greatly help in nearly all situations. A critical difference is the amount of time that the organization is willing to be without data.

By performing all the tasks on the following checklist, you could get any office up and running again in a few hours after most emergencies, at much less cost than keeping duplicate networked servers in cities around the country.

- Keep a replacement hard disk and possibly other parts (power supply, network cards) in storage.

- Back up the system each night to a rotating set of archive media (as described in Chapter 13).

- Take copies of the backup media off-site once per week (to another office, a bank vault, or even someone's home in the case of a small company).

As you draft a disaster plan in consultation with management teams and others involved with the information systems at your organization, consider the monetary value of time. Can you calculate the dollar value of each minute that data is inaccessible to employees or customers? Many companies can; they should then spend accordingly to keep systems up and running.

Depending on your organization's requirements, you should consider all of the following components as potential points of failure, setting up redundant systems when possible:

- Hard disks.

- Memory chips.

- Network cards.

- Power supplies (within a computer).

- Incoming AC power (wall socket).

- Software failure (kernel or application crash).

Preventing Downtime

Downtime refers to occasions when an organization's computer systems cannot respond to requests for information. For example, a Web server that doesn't respond to browser requests, a database server that can't respond to queries, or a print server that can't accept print jobs are all experiencing downtime. In computer parlance, these services are down. A computer can be down without being powered off. If software or hardware problems prevent a computer from responding as intended, it is effectively down because users can't perform the tasks they need to. The rest of this chapter describes techniques that you can use to protect your Linux system from excessive downtime. Below are some key concepts related to preventing downtime:

- **Redundancy:** A state of readiness in which a duplicate component can take over if the primary component fails. A completely redundant system is a replicated system. Most computer systems are not completely redundant. Because of cost considerations, only those components that are most likely to fail or that cause the greatest problems if they fail are supported by redundant systems.

- **Fault tolerance:** The ability of a system to deal effectively with problems (also known as faults). Faults can include hardware failure, power failure, stolen data, and many others. The more fault-tolerant a system is, the more unexpected problems it can handle without going down.

- **Points of failure:** Weakness or vulnerability in an information system. Looking for possible points of failure is a good way to strengthen the fault tolerance of your system. Your goal is to eliminate any single point of failure—a single highly vulnerable part of a system whose failure will bring down the entire system. If a single (or most dangerous) point of failure cannot be eliminated entirely, try to make that part of the system redundant.

Understanding High Availability

Fault-tolerant computer systems that run continuously are said to provide **high availability**. A high availability computer system is able to run nearly continuously without going down as often as computers typically do. The availability of a system may be measured as a percentage. For example, a system may have a statistical availability (**uptime**) of 99.999%.

In reading about high availability systems, 99.999% availability is also referred to as **five-nines** availability. Reaching this challenging technical goal equates to about 5 minutes of unplanned downtime per year.

Most standard Pentium-class systems running Linux have a statistical availability of 95% or higher, depending on the environment in which they are running. (For example, if the municipal power supply was subject to frequent outages, the availability might be lower.) But improving system availability becomes increasingly difficult as you approach 100%. To achieve 100%, all possible causes of downtime must be eliminated.

Although achieving 100% uptime is an admirable goal, it is only a theoretical goal. All systems will necessarily experience some degree of downtime. Companies need to set practical availability goals, based on both the amount of downtime the organization can realistically tolerate and the amount they are willing to spend to avoid that downtime.

One way a company can accommodate unavoidable downtime is to schedule it in the form of maintenance or upgrades. A network that is carefully maintained and upgraded in this way is far less likely to experience costly, unexpected downtime.

Downtime, like availability, is generally measured as a percentage. For example, suppose your organization can tolerate one hour of downtime per year. In other words, out of the 8760 hours in a year, 1 can be allocated to downtime (scheduled, if all goes well). Dividing 1 by 8760 gives a value of 0.0001142. Multiplying by 100 gives the percentage of downtime: 0.01142%. Subtracting that allowed downtime figure from the theoretical goal of 100% uptime, this organization requires 99.989% uptime. Once you have calculated this goal, you can more easily determine the amount of time and resources required to achieve it.

On a system with high availability, a **resource group** refers to an application, the data that it requires to operate, and any other resources the application requires to complete its computing tasks. For example, one resource group could be a Web server, plus all the Web pages and server-related scripts that the server uses. A **high availability cluster** is a group of servers that have high availability features and are dedicated to handling a common set of tasks. Each high availability cluster is devoted to handling a set of tasks or resource groups. Several methods are used to control how the servers in a cluster respond to problems. The two most widely used of these methods are:

- One or more servers in a cluster sit idle, waiting to take over a resource group (a task) in the event that a working server fails. When the failed server is restored to activity, the backup server becomes idle again. This method requires additional hardware equivalent to the working server to provide redundancy, and thus is expensive.

- Every server in a cluster handles various tasks. If one server goes down, the other servers take over the resource groups of that server. This doesn't require costly hardware to sit idle waiting for a failure, but performance may be seriously degraded if all servers are already busy when one fails.

Linux supports some high availability features. These include UPS devices and both hardware and software RAID (these subjects are discussed later in this chapter). However, Linux does not support other high availability features, such as software control of high availability clusters and applications that monitor high availability features. Many Linux developers are working on such software tools and hardware components. In the future these will allow Linux to compete better with UNIX vendors that have been working on high availability systems for decades. These high availability systems, from vendors like Oracle, IBM, and Hewlett-Packard, can cost millions of dollars. They include all of the redundancy features described in this chapter, as well as others that Linux does not yet support. By increasing its high availability features, Linux can be used in more business-critical computing environments.

Creating Rescue Disks

A fairly common system failure is a hard disk problem. Sometimes this takes the form of a complete crash, in which case you may have to restore all of the data to a new hard disk from a backup archive. In other cases, part of the disk is corrupted so that the system cannot boot. Sometimes a hard disk problem can even be caused by something that the system administrator has done to the system. In the case of many hard drive failures, you cannot boot the Linux system normally from the hard disk; you must boot from a floppy disk or bootable CD-ROM before you can access the hard disk and solve the problem.

A **rescue disk** is a floppy disk that you can use to boot a Linux-based computer. It may have only a boot manager and enough information to locate the Linux partition on your hard disk. Often, it includes a minimal version of Linux and enough system utilities to diagnose and repair problems in hard disk files. After booting the system from a rescue disk, you can mount the hard disks of your system (as described in Chapter 8) and edit files to correct problems.

 When the floppy disk only has enough information to launch a functioning Linux partition on the hard disk (without including system utilities or the Linux kernel), the disk is often called a **boot disk**.

Some system administrators always boot their servers from a boot disk. This takes more time than booting from a hard drive, but because a server is rarely rebooted, speed of booting is not really a concern. By using a boot disk, the system administrator can control how the system boots and easily maintain a backup of the boot disk in case of problems. A separate rescue disk is used when the boot disk or hard disk fails.

Ideally, you create a boot disk for your system when installing Linux. This guarantees that the boot disk and the boot manager information on the computer's hard disk are compatible.

For example, when you installed Red Hat Linux 7.3 in Chapter 3, you were asked to insert a blank floppy disk near the end of the installation process. You can use that disk to boot your system if your boot manager experiences problems. If you have the boot disk you created for installing Red Hat Linux, you can use that disk and Red Hat Linux 7.3 CD 1 as a rescue disk. To do this, boot from the floppy disk or CD-ROM and enter `linux rescue` at the prompt that appears. This takes you into **rescue mode**, in which you can examine the system and make repairs.

Other Linux distributions use similar techniques to create a boot disk or rescue disk. Many installation programs also provide multiple virtual consoles that you can use to diagnose or repair problems after booting the system from an installation disk. By switching from one virtual console to another, you may be able to mount a hard disk and diagnose or repair a problem. Press the Alt key and then a function key (F1 to F6) to switch between virtual consoles. When using an installation disk rather than a rescue disk for this task, keep in mind that the installation disk may not have the tools you need to diagnose and fix a problem.

Chapter 3 mentioned one specialized rescue disk, Tom's Boot disk. This rescue disk contains a Linux kernel and dozens of useful utilities. Having such a rescue disk handy when a disaster strikes can be a huge time-saver. You can download a copy by visiting *www.toms.net/rb* and try this disk in the Hands-on Projects at the end of this chapter.

Maintaining Software Masters

As you will learn in Chapter 13, most backup strategies focus on backing up user data: the information created by your organization, for use only within your organization. System administrators are often careless about backing up the software tools and operating system files used to create and work with that data because they think these items can be purchased in any computer store. But this is not always the case. Consider the following problems that can occur after a system failure, when you attempt to repair a disk by installing your company's preferred application software:

- The vendor that created the software may no longer be in business. This is a particular problem when the software is specific to one industry, such as a credit union software package, chemical plant software, or medical office software. In this case, an equivalent replacement is harder to find, compared to a simple accounting or word processing package.

- The particular version used by your company may no longer be available from the vendor. A costly upgrade would then be required, with new training for all employees.

- The vendor may not be able to ship the replacement application software immediately. For instance, if your system goes down on a Friday, the vendor probably wouldn't be able to ship the software until Monday, for delivery on Tuesday. Thus, the process of reconstructing the system data from backups could not begin until five days after the initial failure.

In all of these situations, a system administrator would be better served if he or she had carefully and securely stored the **software masters** (such as the installation CD) originally provided by the vendor. Unfortunately, software masters are often discarded along with the unread user manuals as soon as the products are installed. Instead, they should be stored along with backups of other system data and mentioned prominently in your disaster plan. When using complex applications such as large database management systems or customized business software, application data sometimes cannot be restored properly until the application is first installed. If you can immediately locate software masters for important applications used on your server, you can then rebuild a system as follows:

- Rebuild or repair hardware components such as hard disks.
- Install the operating system and applications used by the company.
- Restore user data files.

If you can afford the additional capacity, it's a good idea occasionally to back up the operating system and applications as well as user data. This safeguards your custom configurations as well as the applications themselves. But keep track of the software masters and documentation nevertheless. You may need them to retrieve license information or activation keys for your applications.

MANAGING THE COMPUTER'S POWER SUPPLY

The power supply is one of the easier components to protect within a Linux server. This component converts the **AC power** from a wall socket to the low-voltage DC power used by computer chips, disk drives, and other peripherals. As shown in Figure 9-1, the **power supply** is usually the single largest component inside your computer. It rarely fails if it is properly cooled by an internal fan or room air conditioner. For occasions when the power supply does fail, two remedies can be part of your disaster planning:

- Keep a second power supply on hand. If the power supply inside a computer fails, you should be able to replace the part and have the system running again within an hour. Spare power supplies are not overly expensive.

- Purchase a server with a built-in backup power supply. This is similar to having an uninterruptible power supply (described in the next section) within the computer. It allows you to schedule a time to shut the server down when it is not being used so you can replace the failed power supply. Servers with dual power supplies are generally quite expensive because of the circuitry required to switch to the backup supply in case of a failure.

9

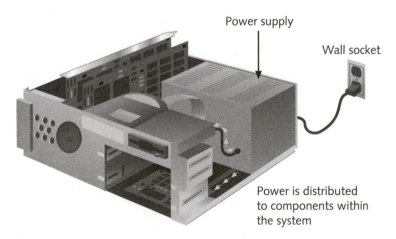

Figure 9-1   A computer's power supply

A power supply is a single component in your computer. Don't ever try to disassemble and repair it, or you risk receiving a powerful electric shock. Replace it as a complete unit. Opening a power supply unit is very dangerous. A power supply contains components such as capacitors that can hold a large electric charge even when the power to the system is shut off.

Providing Consistent Power to a Linux System

Power outages or unexpected irregularity in the AC (wall socket) power are both much more likely than a failure of the computer's power supply. You can limit the damage done by irregular power by using a surge suppressor. **Surge suppressors** protect the computer's power supply by removing the voltage spikes and minor power irregularities that don't affect your refrigerator or office lights, but can damage sensitive electronic equipment. Figure 9-2 illustrates how a surge suppressor removes voltage spikes in the computer's power supply.

Figure 9-2 A surge suppressor removes voltage spikes

When the power actually fails, however, a surge suppressor doesn't help. For these cases, an **uninterruptible power supply (UPS)** is needed. A UPS contains batteries that are continually charged by the main AC power when it is active. During a power outage, the batteries in the UPS take over, delivering power to the computer as if the outage had not occurred. Figure 9-3 shows a computer connected to a UPS.

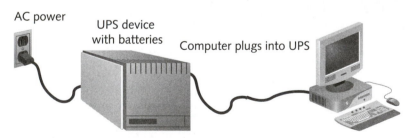
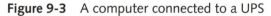

Figure 9-3 A computer connected to a UPS

 A UPS also includes surge suppressor features, so that power from a UPS is always free from voltage spikes, brownouts, and other problems. A separate surge suppressor is not necessary.

Because batteries are expensive, a low-cost UPS typically provides only 5 to 30 minutes of battery power to a computer. Systems that require high availability may have a UPS costing thousands of dollars that provides power for up to several days. Such high-end UPS systems may be integrated with gas-powered generators that recharge the UPS batteries. For most situations, however, a UPS is intended to provide power during momentary power outages, which generally last less than five minutes. In the event of a long-term outage due to weather or utility company problems, a UPS allows you to shut down your computer systems gracefully. (If your Linux system shuts down "ungracefully," the system may require a few minutes—or several hours—at restart to check the integrity of the hard disk.)

Automating Linux Shutdown

Although a UPS allows time for a system administrator to shut down a Linux system gracefully, the system administrator may not be present when the power outage occurs. For this reason, UPS devices typically have a serial communications port (similar to the connection used by an external modem) that signals the Linux system in the event of a power outage. The Linux system then executes simple scripts to determine what actions to take. UPS devices can generally recognize three events, as described in Table 9-1.

9

Table 9-1   Events Tracked by a UPS Device via a Serial Port

Event recognized by UPS	Linux system response	Notes
Power failure	Begin a system shutdown.	The shutdown process may take 5 to 30 minutes, depending on the capacity of the UPS device and the type of work and number of users supported by the Linux server.
Power is out and the UPS battery is low	Shut down quickly.	In this situation, Linux usually executes an immediate halt command to write cached data to files and unmount file systems before the UPS battery fails. Users logged in to the system may have very little warning about closing their files, but typically no data is lost.
Power has been restored	Cancel any pending shutdown.	When a nonemergency shutdown (taking 5 to 30 minutes) is in process, the shutdown can be canceled before any services are shut down.

Each item in Table 9-1 corresponds to a signal number (recall the discussion of signals in Chapter 8). When a UPS is connected to a computer running Linux, the system administrator also installs a software package that monitors the serial cable that the UPS uses to communicate with the computer. Figure 9-4 shows a UPS connected to a Linux system via a serial cable.

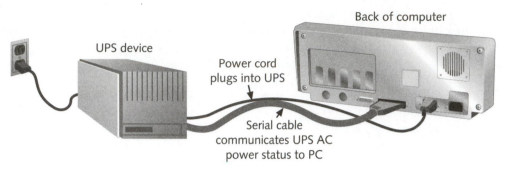

Figure 9-4 A serial connection between a UPS and a Linux system

Many different programs are available to monitor a UPS. One popular UPS manufacturer, American Power Conversion (APC), has Linux-specific programs designed to provide access to special control features of its UPS devices. (See *www.apcc.com* for more information.) Because most UPS devices use similar methods to communicate with a server, you can use standardized UPS management tools to manage many different UPS products.

The Network UPS Tools package provides a number of software utilities to let you manage multiple computers or UPS devices. This package, available at *www.exploits.org/nut*, supports UPS devices from APC, Belkin, BestFort, and other vendors. A graphical interface to manage the Network UPS Tools software is available for the Gnome Desktop. This package is available at *www.stud.ifi.uio.no/~hennikul/gupsc* and is shown in Figure 9-5.

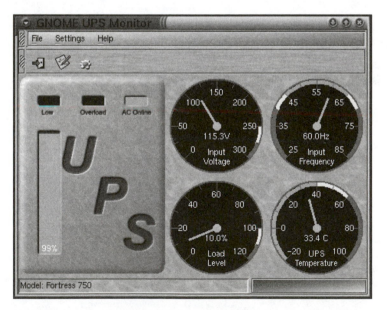

Figure 9-5 A Gnome-based graphical interface to the Network UPS Tools package

Several other UPS monitoring utilities are available:

- Power Daemon can monitor a UPS and alert other systems on a network that the power is out. It automatically determines UPS and cable configurations. See *power.sourceforge.net*.

- `bpowerd` is a daemon for interacting with Best Power UPS devices. See *bpowerd.sourceforge.net*.

- `inpowerd` is a UPS utility designed to run as a network service. It can alert other servers on the network of power problems. See *goliat.eik.bme.hu/~balaton/inet*.

Responding to a Power Outage

In most cases, a UPS utility does not directly shut down your Linux system. Instead, when the utility receives a signal from the UPS indicating a power problem, it sends a signal to the `init` control program.

The `init` program is configured by the file `/etc/inittab`. When a UPS utility sends a signal to the `init` daemon, `init` checks the `/etc/inittab` configuration file to determine what action to take. The file `/etc/inittab` normally includes two or three lines indicating how Linux should respond when a power outage occurs, the UPS battery is low, or the power is restored. The exact action indicated depends on your Linux vendor and version, but these lines taken from Red Hat Linux 7.3 are good examples:

```
pf::powerfail:/sbin/shutdown -f -h +2 "Power Failure;
   System Shutting Down"
pr:12345:powerokwait:/sbin/shutdown -c "Power Restored;
   Shutdown Cancelled"
```

The first part of the line (`pf` or `pr` in these two example lines) is a label chosen by Red Hat. The second part, `powerfail` and `powerokwait`, indicates to the `init` daemon what is being configured: either power failure or power restored. Only two possible signals are represented here. (Testing for a low battery condition is not part of the `/etc/inittab` configuration in Red Hat Linux 7.3.) In another distribution, the configuration line for a low battery would look something like this:

```
p1:powerfailnow:/sbin/shutdown –h now "Battery Low…"
```

All three of these signals cause `init` to use the `shutdown` command. In each case, different parameters are included with the `shutdown` command to determine how `shutdown` operates. (The message in quotation marks appears immediately on the screen of every user who is logged in to the Linux system.)

- `shutdown –f –h +2 "Power Failure; System Shutting Down"`: Initiates a timed shutdown that warns all users on the system that the server will be halted (shut down and not automatically rebooted, using the `–h` option) in two minutes. No system services are actually shut down until the end of the two minutes. If your UPS can supply power for a longer time, you could change the +2 parameter to another number—for example, to +10 for 10 minutes.

- `shutdown -c "Power Restored; Shutdown Cancelled"`: Cancels an existing shutdown. This command is useful after a timed shutdown has been announced to users but before the time has expired. If power is restored, there is no need to shut down the system, so another announcement is sent to all users that the shutdown has been canceled and they can continue working normally. This would be used if a short power outage causes the `init` program to announce a shutdown in 2 to 10 minutes (or more, depending on your UPS), but the power was restored before the given time had expired.

- `shutdown -h now "Battery Low"`: Initiates an immediate shutdown (halt and do not automatically reboot, using the `-h` parameter with `now`) because the UPS battery is about to fail. This command disconnects any networked users and closes all applications. This is unpleasant for users because it ends their Linux session without warning, but it is necessary to preserve file system integrity. As a rule, you can avoid low battery shutdowns by careful planning. Ideally, your UPS device would be adequate for your Linux system, which means this command would never be necessary.

You can update the information in the `/etc/inittab` file so that the `init` daemon executes any command that meets the needs of your system. The `shutdown` command is effective for unmounting file systems and preventing data loss, but you might also want to create a script (see Chapter 11) that completes a set of tasks related to shutting down the system. These tasks might include:

- Writing an incident to a log file.
- Sending an e-mail message to another system.
- Signaling a backup server to take over a critical task.
- Writing information to a networked hard disk so it can still be accessed.
- Starting the `shutdown` command to halt the system.

CHECKING FILE SYSTEM INTEGRITY

Maintaining the integrity of file systems is a key part of protecting data on your Linux systems. The main utility for routinely testing file system integrity is called `fsck`. This utility is described in the next section. The concepts and definitions that follow apply to all Linux `ext2` and `ext3` file systems and will help you understand how to maintain Linux file systems.

The **superblock** is a collection of information about a file system. It includes items such as the following:

- Maximum number of times the file system can be mounted between complete file system checks (using the **fsck** utility described in the next section).

- Size of the file system in blocks (the standard block size is 1024 bytes).

- Number of free blocks on the file system.

- Number of reserved blocks (reserved blocks can only be used by the root user or another user or group that the root user specifies).

- Amount of time since a complete integrity check was performed on the file system.

If the superblock is corrupted, the entire file system is unusable. Copies of the superblock are stored in multiple locations across the hard disk during the formatting of the file system to protect against a superblock problem rendering the system unusable. Some parameters stored in the superblock, such as the maximum number of times the file system can be mounted between integrity checks, can be configured during formatting or reset using the **tune2fs** utility described later in "Tuning a Linux File System." Some features of the file system, such as the size of a data block, cannot be changed without reformatting the entire file system.

An **inode** (pronounced eye-node) is a file information record. Each inode contains all of the information about a single file except the file's name. The inode information includes:

- The file access permissions.

- The owner and group of the file (noted as a user ID and group ID number).

- The time and date of the last access, last modification, and file creation.

- The number of blocks used by the file on disk and the precise size of the file in bytes.

- A pointer to the blocks of data in which the file's contents are stored.

A **file record** contains a filename and the inode number for that file; the file record is an indirect pointer to the file's data, through the inode. Every subdirectory is just a list of file records. Specifically, a **directory record** is a file that contains a list of files with corresponding inode numbers.

Because of the way inodes are arranged on an **ext2** or **ext3** file system, each file system can contain only a limited number of inodes and thus a limited number of files. The number is large, and you're never likely to run out of inodes for creating new files. But you will notice as you use the **fsck** utility in the next section that the utility indicates the maximum number of files that the file system can hold. For example, when you see output from **fsck** such as **43686/247808 files**, you know that of 247,808 possible files on this file system, 43,686 have been created.

A **link** allows two or more file records to refer to the same physical data stored in a file system. For example, a link makes it possible for two users to have two different filenames listed in their home directories, but actually be working with the same data when they edit those two files. Links are of two types: symbolic and hard. You learned briefly about symbolic links in Chapter 6. You can now understand a more technical definition: A **symbolic link** (also called a soft link) is a file record that includes a path and filename, but not an inode number. When a user refers to a symbolic link, Linux looks at the path and filename given in the symbolic link's file record. The file record for *that* path and filename includes an inode, which is used to access the file data for the symbolic link.

A **hard link** is a file record that includes a filename and inode, just like a regular file record. But a hard link refers to an inode that already has a file record pointing to it. The hard link is a second file record pointing to the same physical data. A single inode can have numerous file records (hard links) pointing to it. After a hard link is created, it is equal to the first file record that points to the same inode. If the first file record is deleted, the second file record (created as a hard link) is unaffected—it still refers to the same file data.

Both symbolic and hard links are used often in a Linux file system. Whenever you use the `ls -l` command, any symbolic links are indicated as extra filenames in the right column of the output. An example of a symbolic link in Red Hat Linux is the `view` command. This output illustrates how you can use the `ls -l` command to show the `view` command:

```
$ ls -l /bin/view
lrwxrwxrwx   1  root root 2 Aug 12 13:36   /bin/view  ->  vi
```

The arrow in the right column indicates that the file named `view` is a symbolic link to the file named `vi` (located in the same directory, because no pathname is included). The letter `l` in the far left column of the screen output also indicates that the file is a symbolic link.

The number in the second column from the left (in this case, 1) indicates the number of file records that refer to the same inode as this file record.

The `zcat` filename (also in Red Hat Linux) is an example of a hard link. The `zcat` file record refers to an inode that two other file records also refer to. The `ls -l` command again shows this:

```
$ ls -l /bin/zcat
-rwx-r-xr-x   3  root root  63555   Mar 25 13:28 /binzcat
```

In this sample screen output, the number 3 in the second column from the left indicates that the file record holding the filename `zcat` refers to an inode that two other file records also refer to (for a total of three).

Figure 9-6 illustrates the difference between a symbolic link and a hard link. In this figure, a programming language named perl is stored in a file called **perl5.6.1**, where the **5.6.1** indicates a precise version number. Other file records also point to the same information (inode) using different filenames. This allows users who might not know the precise version number to access the perl programming language file.

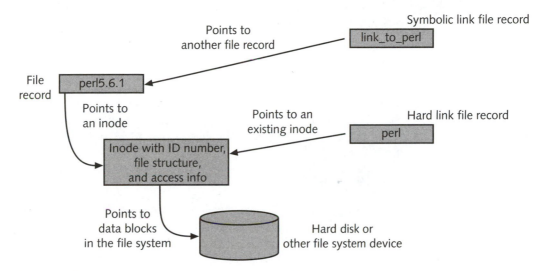

Figure 9-6   Hard and symbolic links in a Linux file system

To see the inode numbers associated with the filenames in a directory, use the **–i** option of the **ls** command. (The numbers shown for a file vary on each system.) For example:

```
$ ls -i /bin
```

Using the `fsck` Utility

You can run the **fsck** utility at any time to check the integrity of a Linux file system. The **fsck** utility determines whether any file system problems are evident. If none are apparent, **fsck** runs very quickly. You can, however, force **fsck** to execute a full suite of file system tests even when the utility would otherwise exit quickly because no errors are apparent. This is called forcing the **fsck** utility.

Each time you boot Linux, the **fsck** program runs automatically to check all mounted file systems. Under normal circumstances, this automatic check takes only a few seconds. Two situations cause the **fsck** utility to spend more time checking the file systems:

- Linux was not shut down gracefully (all system services were not shut down in an orderly way).

- The file system has been mounted numerous times. After a certain number of mounts, Linux forces the **fsck** utility to go through a complete check of the file system even if no problems are evident.

When the second condition occurs, Linux displays a message like the following as you boot the system:

```
Maximal mount count reached: check forced.
```

By default, Red Hat Linux 7.3 does not force an `fsck` check after a fixed number of mounts. You can change this setting using the `tune2fs` utility described in the next section.

Performing a complete file system check is a good idea before doing any disk-intensive operations, such as a complete system backup.

To force a complete check of a file system, use the `fsck` command with the `-f` option, followed by the name of the device on which the file system is located. The following example of the `fsck` command checks the file system located on the first partition of the second IDE hard disk:

```
fsck -f /dev/hdb1
```

You can only use the `fsck` command on file systems that are *not* mounted. Using it on a mounted file system will damage the file system. To check the root partition of Linux, boot your system from a floppy disk that includes the `fsck` utility.

You can also run `fsck` using the mount point in the directory structure. For example, if the first partition of the second IDE hard disk (`/dev/hdb1`) is mounted as `/database`, you could use this command:

```
fsck -f /database
```

Multiple file systems can be checked at the same time by listing them. For example:

```
fsck -f /dev/hdb2 /dev/hdb3 /dev/hdc1
```

The `fsck` program runs all the file system checks at the same time, querying you as questions arise about file system information. If a file system you are checking is fine, you see only a brief output after running `fsck`, as follows:

```
# fsck /dev/hdb1
Parallelizing fsck version 1.27 (8-Mar-2002)
e2fsck 1.27, 8-Mar-2002 for EXT2 FS 0.5b, 95/08/09
/dev/hdb1: clean, 43686/247808 files, 906478/987997 blocks.
```

Launching `fsck` with the `-f` option provides more detailed information. Sample output is shown here:

```
# fsck -f /dev/hdb1
Parallelizing fsck version 1.27 (8-Mar-2002)
e2fsck 1.27, 8-Mar-2002 for EXT2 FS 0.5b, 95/08/09
Pass 1: Checking inodes, blocks and sizes
```

```
Pass 2: Checking directory structure
Pass 3: Checking directory connectivity
Pass 4: Checking reference counts
Pass 5: Checking group summary information
/dev/hdb1: clean, 43686/247808 files (0.3% non-contiguous),
    906478/987997 blocks.
```

Running a complete file system check using the **-f** option takes some time. Checking a full file system containing 20 GB of data may take 30 minutes; if **fsck** must attempt to repair file system errors, the process can take several hours. The need to perform such checks is greatly reduced when you are using the **ext3** file system instead of **ext2**. An **ext3** file system saves file system changes in a "journal" and can undo partially completed disk operations that might have corrupted data. This **journaling** feature makes Linux file systems much more robust, even if the power to a Linux system is cut off without a graceful shutdown.

The output of a forced **fsck** shows five complete passes through the file system. The **fsck** utility automatically corrects any problems detected during each of the five passes. If an automatic correction is not possible, a query appears on-screen. These queries are simple questions asking you whether to save or delete unidentified pieces of information, or to provide some other piece of information that the file system requires. It is rare to have **fsck** ask a question during a file system check unless a serious disk-related problem occurred, such as the power to the Linux system being cut off during a complex disk operation.

Defragmenting a File System

All file systems are divided into units of storage called **blocks**. A standard block contains 1024 characters (bytes). All of the files stored in a file system are broken into pieces and stored in file system blocks. On many operating systems, the information stored in a file system becomes fragmented. That is, the blocks that make up an individual file are spread all over a hard disk or other device. Reading such a file requires much more time than reading a file whose data is stored in sequential blocks of the hard disk.

When managing some operating systems you must regularly defragment the file system to move the pieces of files next to each other. Defragmenting is also called **disk optimization** because it optimizes access time to files and reduces wear on the hard disk.

Fortunately, the **ext2** and **ext3** file systems used by Linux are not subject to much file fragmentation, as Windows operating systems are. When new files are written to a Linux hard disk, the files are stored at locations spread across the entire hard disk. This allows space for each file to grow in size without becoming fragmented. The output of **fsck** displays the percentage of files on each file system that are fragmented. This percentage is normally less than 3%.

Hard disks that are close to being full, however, may have more fragmented files. Because defragmenting a hard disk is so rarely needed in Linux, an appropriate utility is not included with most Linux products. You can search for **defrag** on sites such as *rpmfind.net* or *freshmeat.net*.

Tuning a Linux File System

The **dumpe2fs** command provides information about the superblock and data blocks of a Linux **ext2** or **ext3** file system. This command only reads information; you cannot change settings with **dumpe2fs**. Because of this, you can use it to examine a mounted file system.

```
# /sbin/dumpe2fs /dev/hda3 | less
```

You can use the **tune2fs** utility both to read and to change file system parameters (most of which are stored in the superblock). When you format an **ext2** or **ext3** file system, the **mke2fs** command described in Chapter 8 uses default options for the items described in this section. You can add parameters to the **mke2fs** command to set those options as you format a new file system, or you can alter many of them using the **tune2fs** command after the file system is formatted.

 Do not use tune2fs on a mounted file system. Unmount the file system that you need to tune; boot Linux from a floppy if you need to tune the root file system.

The tunable file system parameters affect stability and, to a lesser degree, performance. Some configuration options, such as the block size, cannot be changed without reformatting the file system and using a parameter with the **mke2fs** command. The more useful options of the **tune2fs** command are described in the following paragraphs.

Using **tune2fs**, you can set the maximum number of times the file system can be mounted without having a complete **fsck** integrity check. A lower number will check for errors more often, but will also slow down system startup more often as the system is being checked. You can use **dumpe2fs** to see what the current maximum mount count value is set to. (In Red Hat Linux 7.3, this value is −1, meaning that a check is never forced based on the number of times the file system has been mounted.) This sample command sets the maximum mount count value to 25:

```
# /sbin/tune2fs -c 25 /dev/hda3
```

The superblock also records the number of times the file system has been mounted since the last time it was checked. Each time the file system is mounted, this number is incremented. You can change this value using the **-C** option. By lowering or raising this number in relation to the maximum mount count parameter, you can control when the next forced automatic integrity check will occur.

You can determine the Linux system's response when a file system error is detected. The response is normally to **continue**. However, you can choose to stop the Linux kernel when an error is detected, or remount the file system as read-only instead of read/write.

(Note that mounting the file system as read-only may make the operating system unusable, although safe for examination and repairs.) A sample command is shown here:

```
# /sbin/tune2fs -e remount-ro /dev/hda3
```

Part of each Linux file system is set aside as reserved space that can only be used by root or users that root has indicated, as described below. This reserved space allows root to continue to operate the system when the hard disk becomes too full for regular users to log in.

The space reserved for root is normally 5% of the total file system space. However, you can configure this amount as a percentage of the total file system size or as a number of data blocks on the file system. You configure these options using the **-m** or **-r** option of `tune2fs`. The root user can always access this reserved space, but you can also allow another user ID number or group ID number to access it by using the **-g** and **-u** options of `tune2fs`. For example, on a file system used with a database server you could allow the database administrator's group to access the reserved space.

In addition to the `dumpe2fs` command, you can use the **-l** option of `tune2fs` to list the contents of the superblock.

A useful set of utilities for working with floppy disks is the `mtools` package, which is installed by default on Red Hat Linux 7.3. This package includes programs such as `mdir` and `mcopy` that mimic DOS/Windows command-line programs, including the use of A:. For example, to see the contents of a floppy disk in Linux without mounting it, use `mdir A:`.

UNDERSTANDING REDUNDANT DISK SYSTEMS

One of the most vulnerable parts of a computer system is the hard disk. It contains many moving parts, and is often subjected to constant heavy use. If the data on your hard disks becomes unavailable because of a failure, the rest of the computer system is useless. For these reasons, a lot of effort has gone into making hard disks redundant. Although specialized redundant hard disks have been available for mainframe computers for decades, most users now rely on groups of hard disks, known as **redundant arrays of inexpensive disks**, commonly called **RAID** subsystems or RAID arrays.

The idea behind RAID is simple: instead of trying to create a single hard disk that never fails (an expensive proposition), we use a group, or array, of inexpensive hard disks. The assumption is that if one disk fails, the others can take over until the failed disk is replaced. RAID takes advantage of the statistical fact that multiple hard disks are unlikely to fail at the same time.

You can add RAID to your system using a separate hardware device, as described later, or by relying only on features within the Linux kernel. It can contain as many disks as necessary to reach the storage capacity needed. A RAID system does not have a specific number of hard disks, a specific storage capacity, or even a specific platform.

RAID systems are used by all operating systems. Instead, the different forms, or levels, of RAID are distinguished by the techniques used to store data, as explained in the following sections.

Within the Linux kernel, RAID capability is implemented as a device called `/dev/md0` (meta-disk). `/dev/md0` may be comprised of several actual hard disk partitions, as described in the sections that follow. The Linux kernel processes requests to `/dev/md0` so that they reach the correct physical hard disk partition.

On Red Hat Linux 7.3, RAID is implemented in the default installation through the raidtools package. This package includes a sample configuration file and utilities such as the following, each of which has an associated man page:

- `mkraid`: Creates a RAID `/dev/md0` device based on the information in `/etc/raidtab`.
- `lsraid`: Lists information about all RAID devices on the system.
- `raidstart`: Initializes/activates the specified RAID devices.
- `raidstop`: Stops/shuts down the specified RAID devices.

Setting up RAID in Linux is not difficult. The Disk Druid utility (described in Chapter 3) even lets you define a RAID array during installation of Red Hat Linux 7.3. Besides the man pages for the above utilities, the Software-RAID-HOWTO provides a good overview, though it has not been revised recently. It is available at *www.linuxdocs.org/HOWTOs/Software-RAID-0.4x-HOWTO.html*. Sample configuration files are included in Red Hat Linux 7.3 in `/usr/share/doc/raidtools-1.00.2`.

Defining RAID Levels

RAID can be implemented in many forms, or levels. The levels differ in the amount of fault tolerance they provide, the speed of reading or writing data, and the cost of implementation. The next sections introduce the different RAID levels and define the terms and techniques associated with RAID.

 Vendors occasionally differ in the features they associate with the different RAID levels. When reviewing RAID technologies or products, look for specific features rather than just a RAID level.

RAID-Linear

RAID-Linear lets you combine multiple physical devices into a single logical device. This allows one logical Linux file system to span multiple disk drives or partitions, which is useful when you want a file system to be larger than a single hard disk. For example, suppose you need a huge file system for the `/home` directory. By storing this file system on multiple disk drives, you avoid buying one very large (expensive) hard disk. Instead, you can purchase multiple disks of a more common size. But the `/home` directory can still be managed as a single file system because of RAID-Linear.

RAID-Linear is not truly a RAID level because it does not provide any redundancy or fault tolerance, nor does it improve system performance, as some RAID levels do. In fact, RAID-Linear reduces fault tolerance: if any disk in a RAID-Linear array fails, the entire file system is unusable. RAID-Linear is illustrated in Figure 9-7.

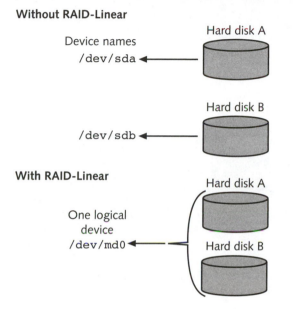

Figure 9-7   RAID-Linear

RAID-0 (Striping)

RAID-0 uses a data storage technique called **striping**, in which a single block of data is divided into pieces and stored on more than one hard disk. This allows faster access, because two disk drives work together to gather parts of any requested information at the same time. The performance gain is increased if each hard disk uses a separate hard disk controller (for example, using two SCSI cards); multiple hard disk controllers prevent a bottleneck in communicating from the hard disk to the CPU. However, if either hard disk fails in a RAID-0 setup, the entire file system is unusable. Hence, using RAID-0 without other measures described in this chapter reduces fault tolerance significantly. Figure 9-8 illustrates striping.

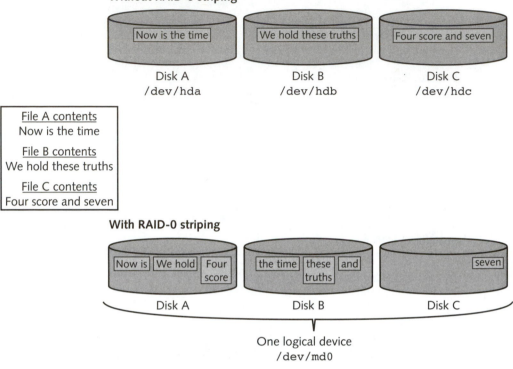

Figure 9-8 RAID-0, or data striping

RAID-1 (Disk Mirroring and Duplexing)

RAID-1 mirrors data across multiple hard disks. **Mirroring** refers to a system with two or more hard disks that contain identical information. Each time one hard disk is updated, the copy or copies (the mirrors) are also updated. If one hard disk fails, the mirrored hard disks continue to respond to data requests without interruption. **Duplexing** refers to mirrored hard disks that are on separate controller cards, which increases performance and reduces vulnerability to a hardware failure.

Mirrored and duplexed hard disks increase performance when reading from a hard disk because multiple hard disks respond to data requests at the same time. This technique also increases fault tolerance: if one hard disk fails, the duplicate disks continue to respond without interruption. But using mirroring or duplexing has two downsides. First, the time required to write files to a hard disk is increased because data must be written to each disk instead of just one. Second, these techniques require extra hard disks that are used only for mirroring—they don't provide extra storage capacity. For example, if you want 120 GB of mirrored hard disk storage, you must pay for 240 GB of hard disk space. With the low price of hard disks today, this may be a very good investment, but it can be a limiting factor when planning a system with large amounts of storage (e.g., thousands of GB of data). Figure 9-9 shows a mirrored hard disk system.

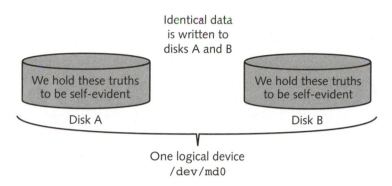

Figure 9-9 RAID-1 with mirrored hard disks

RAID-3 (Striping with Parity)

RAID-0 (striping) improves performance but makes a system more vulnerable to failure. **RAID-3** combines the performance advantages of striping data across multiple hard disks but provides additional protection against the failure of one of the hard disks by using parity. **Parity** is a technique that allows corrupted data to be reconstructed using an extra piece of information that is created as the data is stored. The parity information provides redundancy to the piece of data. In RAID-3, this extra information is stored in a **parity stripe**. If one of the hard disks fails, the system can use the parity information to reconstruct the data stored on that disk. Figure 9-10 illustrates a RAID-3 system.

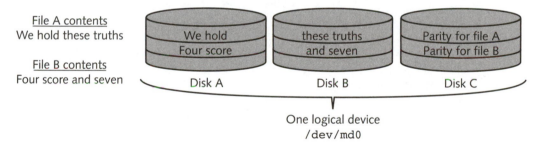

Figure 9-10 RAID-3, striping with parity

RAID-3 provides good fault tolerance because of the parity stripe. If a hard disk fails, data is still usable; when the failed hard disk is replaced, the data is automatically rebuilt on the new hard disk. RAID-3 also improves performance on systems that perform a lot of disk reads. All the hard disks in a RAID-3 array can work in parallel to respond to multiple requests at the same time. Instead of waiting for a single disk, the chances are good that a hard disk that is not busy can immediately begin to service a read request. Also, unlike disk mirroring, with RAID-3 only one hard disk (the one containing the parity information) is unavailable for data storage. For example, to have 200 GB of usable storage space in a RAID-3 system, you might only need to purchase 250 GB of hard disks. One disadvantage of RAID-3 is that the write performance suffers because parity information must be computed and several hard disks must store information for each write operation.

 Although RAID-2 and RAID-4 are listed in some definitions of RAID, they are not used in production systems and so are not presented here. These two RAID levels simply use different combinations of the techniques implemented by other RAID levels.

RAID-5 (Striping and Parity)

RAID-5 is similar to RAID-3 except that with RAID-5 both the parity information and the stored data are striped across multiple hard disks. This has the advantage of making read performance better, but it makes write performance even worse than RAID-3. As with RAID-3, if a hard disk fails, the parity information allows the information to be reconstructed once the disk is replaced. In the meantime, data remains available. Figure 9-11 illustrates how RAID-5 spreads information across multiple hard disks. Many vendors who sell RAID-5 hardware systems (see the next section) use built-in **write caching** to store new information in memory until it can be written to the multiple hard disks without degrading performance overall.

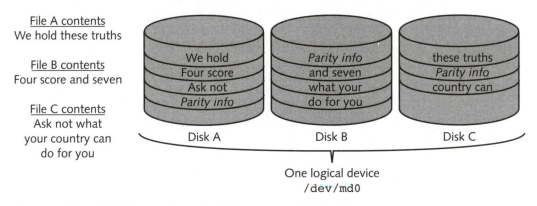

Figure 9-11   RAID-5, parity and striping over multiple disks

Using Hardware-Based RAID

A RAID system can be implemented as a separate device that connects to your Linux computer, like an external printer or CD-ROM drive. This is called **hardware-based RAID** because the control and management of the disk array depends on a separate hardware system (called a **RAID subsystem**). Hardware-based RAID devices include RAM, a CPU, and other components besides the array of hard disks; it is practically a separate computer with the sole purpose of providing data redundancy to your main system. The main advantage of using a hardware-based RAID system is that all of the special technology is contained in the RAID device. For example, a huge RAID subsystem connected to your Linux server by a SCSI controller appears to Linux as a single SCSI disk drive. No special utilities or management are needed on Linux.

Another advantage of hardware-based RAID systems is that they often allow **hot-swapping** disks, meaning that you can pull out and replace a failed hard disk without turning off the RAID subsystem. A system administrator would normally keep one or two "spares" on a shelf and swap them with a failed hard disk when necessary. Hot-swapping is an expensive feature; it is also available as part of high-end Linux-based servers from companies like Hewlett-Packard and IBM.

 A hardware-based RAID system may include utilities that run on the host operating system and that are designed to manage or configure the RAID device. Check whether such utilities can be used on a Linux platform.

The main disadvantage of hardware-based RAID is its cost. Because the RAID system includes a CPU and other electronics to manage the hard disks, plus a separate case and software utilities, hardware-based RAID is much more expensive than simply using the RAID capabilities of the Linux kernel.

9

CHAPTER SUMMARY

❐ A disaster plan describes how an organization will respond to various threats to its information systems. It is based on an evaluation of different risk levels and the value of having systems up and their data available.

❐ A disaster plan includes information about your computer systems, immediate steps that you will take to reduce their vulnerability, and the steps required to get them running again when various problems occur.

❐ Fault tolerance is achieved by removing single points of failure and making vulnerable components redundant.

❐ High availability systems use special hardware and software to improve statistical uptime, sometimes reaching 99.999% uptime or more. A high availability cluster uses a resource group to handle computing tasks.

❐ A rescue disk or boot disk lets you start your Linux system when the hard disk or boot manager has been damaged.

❐ Software masters and manuals should be carefully stored and maintained to allow recovery after a disaster.

❐ Surge suppressors and UPS devices provide clean power to a computer system. A UPS can inform a Linux system of power outages via a serial cable, while supplying power from its batteries until the system can be gracefully shut down.

❐ Utilities that manage a UPS typically interact with the `init` program to send signals for a power outage, a low battery on the UPS, or restored power.

❏ Each Linux `ext2` or `ext3` file system includes a superblock where parameters about the file system are stored. These can be viewed using `dumpe2fs` and viewed or altered using `tune2fs`.

❏ The `fsck` utility checks the integrity of a Linux file system at boot time or whenever the `fsck` utility is run from a command line. `fsck` attempts to repair file system errors.

❏ `ext3` file systems include file system journaling, which tracks disk operations to prevent data corruption if an operation cannot be completed normally.

❏ An inode contains parameters that describe each file in a file system. File records hold a file's name and point to an inode. Directory records are files that contain a list of filenames and corresponding inode numbers.

❏ Symbolic links and hard links let a file name refer either to another file record or to an inode that already has a file record referring to it.

❏ Linux hard disks rarely need to be defragmented.

❏ RAID systems let you improve speed, fault tolerance, or both, depending on the configuration you choose. Hardware-based RAID systems let you use RAID without configuring RAID as part of the Linux kernel, but they are expensive.

❏ RAID levels include features such as mirroring and duplexing to make data redundant, striping to make data access faster, and parity information to reconstruct data when one disk in the array fails.

Key Terms

AC power — The standard alternating current power coming into a building from a public utility; the power from a wall socket.

block — A unit of storage on a file system. A standard block contains 1024 characters (bytes).

boot disk — A disk used to launch the Linux operating system stored on your hard disk. It can be used in normal operating situations to start the Linux system.

defrag — A utility used to defragment a Linux partition.

directory record — A special type of file that contains a list of the names and inode numbers of other files.

disaster plan — An organized written plan that describes how to respond to various threats to information systems.

disk optimization — The same as defragmenting a hard disk.

downtime — Occasions when an organization's computer systems cannot respond to requests for information.

dumpe2fs — A utility used to display technical statistics and parameters about a Linux `ext2` or `ext3` file system.

duplexing — A redundancy technique in which hard disks are accessed via different hard disk controllers. Compare to "mirroring," a technique that provides identical information on two file systems but without redundant disk controllers.

fault tolerance — The condition of being able to tolerate errors or events that might otherwise cause system failure.

file record — A record within a Linux file system that contains a filename and an inode number or else, if a symbolic link, a filename and another filename that the link refers to.

five-nines — High availability at a statistical level of 99.999% uptime.

fsck — A utility used to check the integrity of an **ext2** or **ext3** file system.

hard link — A file record that points to an inode that is already pointed to by at least one other file record.

hardware-based RAID — A RAID array that is contained in a separate hardware device (a RAID subsystem) and is controlled by a CPU and other components separate from the CPU of the Linux system.

high availability — Processes, products, or programs that ensure that a system experiences as little downtime as possible. The theoretical goal of a high availability system is 100% uptime.

high availability cluster — A group of servers that process the same tasks (resource groups) and take over each others' functionality in the event of an outage or failure.

hot-swapping — Removing and replacing a failed hard drive or other component without turning off the power to the device.

inode — A file information record, identified by a unique number within a file system, which contains detailed information about a block of data commonly called a file.

journaling — A file system feature that saves file system changes in a "journal" and can undo partial changes that might have corrupted data. Part of the **ext3** file system.

link — A special file record that refers to the same physical file data as another file record. *See* symbolic link and hard link.

mirroring — A redundancy technique in which the contents of two file systems contain identical information. Mirroring improves data access speed and provides fault tolerance in the event that one of the file systems fails.

parity — A redundancy technique that allows corrupted data to be reconstructed using an extra piece of information (the parity information) that is created as the data is stored.

parity stripe — Parity information stored as part of a RAID-3 or RAID-5 system.

points of failure — Parts of an information system that are subject to failure.

power supply — The component within a computer system that converts the incoming AC power from a wall socket or UPS device to the correct DC voltage for use by components in a computer.

RAID (redundant arrays of inexpensive disks) — A storage technique using multiple inexpensive hard disks arranged in a predefined pattern (an array) to improve performance, increase fault tolerance, or both.

9

RAID-0 — A RAID level that uses striping to improve disk performance without adding any fault tolerance.

RAID-1 — A RAID level that uses disk mirroring to significantly improve fault tolerance. Disk read performance is also improved, but disk write performance suffers.

RAID-3 — A RAID level that uses striping with parity information to improve performance and increase fault tolerance.

RAID-5 — A RAID level in which striping with parity is spread across all disks in the RAID array (compared to RAID-3, in which the parity information is stored on a single hard disk).

RAID-Linear — A storage technique in which multiple physical devices are combined into a single logical device.

RAID subsystem — A hardware-controlled RAID device containing a CPU and other components to control the array of hard disks.

redundancy — Duplication of a system component or piece of data. Many fault-tolerant systems rely on the use of redundant components or data; in the event of a failure, the duplicate component or copy of the data would still be available.

redundant arrays of inexpensive disks — *See* RAID.

rescue disk — A disk created specifically to boot a Linux system in the event of a system failure. Contains the software tools most likely to be of help in diagnosing and repairing problems with the failed system.

rescue mode — A mode of operation in Red Hat Linux. Used to repair a system failure that blocks normal booting and operation.

resource group — An application or task, along with the data and system resources the task requires, defined within a high availability cluster. Each server in the cluster can take over a complete resource group if the server handling that resource group fails.

software masters — Original copies of an application supplied by a software vendor or manufacturer, usually one or more CDs, tapes, or disks.

striping — A data storage technique in which parts of a file are written to more than one disk in order to improve performance. *See* RAID-3 and RAID-5.

superblock — A part of a Linux file system that contains key parameters about the file system. Numerous copies of the superblock exist on each file system; if the superblock cannot be accessed, the file system is unusable.

surge suppressor — An electronic device that prevents potentially damaging electrical irregularities from reaching a computer system's power supply.

symbolic link — A file record that includes a path and filename, but not an inode number. Also called a soft link.

tune2fs — A utility used to view or adjust parameters within the superblock of a Linux file system.

uninterruptible power supply (UPS) — A device that uses batteries to provide power to a computer when the incoming AC power (wall socket power) fails. A UPS can typically also inform the Linux system of the status of the power via a serial cable.

uptime — The time when a computer is running and available.

write caching — A feature of some storage systems in which information that is to be written to a file system (particularly a RAID file system) is stored in memory temporarily in order to improve the overall read/write performance of the file system.

REVIEW QUESTIONS

1. When creating a disaster plan, you must consider:

    a. How likely various disasters are to occur in your area compared with other areas having companies of a similar size

    b. The maximum cost that you can justify to keep your systems running in the event of all possible disasters

    c. Both the likelihood of various disasters and the costs of having your systems down for different lengths of time

    d. Whether a plan is really needed when most disasters only occur very rarely in your area of the country

2. How does the amount of time that a company can tolerate its systems being down affect the contents of a disaster plan?

3. Why is it important to maintain software masters rather than rely on vendor support?

4. At a minimum, a rescue disk should contain which of the following?

    a. A virtual console option

    b. A text editor and disk repair utilities

    c. High availability features defining the resource group to which your main server belongs

    d. The file system superblock for your root file system

5. Compared to a system without redundant components, a system with redundant components:

    a. Has greater fault tolerance

    b. Typically costs less

    c. Is built around a single point of failure

    d. Will very rarely have write caching

6. Describe the difference between a built-in backup power supply and an uninterruptible power supply.

7. A surge suppressor protects against which of the following?

    a. Power outages

    b. Voltage spikes

    c. Reduced voltage

    d. Brownouts

9

8. Name two utilities that can monitor a UPS and send a signal indicating that Linux should shut down.

9. A `shutdown` command that was initiated by the `init` command based upon a signal received from a UPS control daemon can be canceled if a corresponding signal from that control daemon indicates that the main AC power has been restored. True or False?

10. By adding journaling features via the `ext3` file system, Linux is able to:

    a. Recover deleted files by using hard link and inode information

    b. "Back out" a disk write action that was not completed and may have left corrupted files on the file system

    c. Permit system administrators to run utilities like `fdisk` and `tune2fs` on mounted file systems

    d. Replicate hard disk superblocks to floppy disk in case the superblock becomes unreadable

11. The `init` daemon does which of the following?

    a. Manages all processes and receives signals from a UPS control daemon

    b. Monitors the UPS via a serial cable

    c. Manages the `inpowerd` utility

    d. Creates a high availability server

12. Which condition is normally *not* monitored by a UPS?

    a. Main AC power failure

    b. UPS battery low

    c. Main AC power restored

    d. Telephone power failure

13. Redundant arrays of inexpensive disks (RAID) are used to provide:

    a. Lower-cost systems than single disks

    b. Redundant superblock information

    c. Fault tolerance

    d. Beowulf clusters

14. Striping refers to which of the following?

    a. Spreading a single file across multiple hard disks

    b. Duplicating file information on multiple hard disks

    c. Adding error-correcting codes to a file

    d. Duplicating inode data

15. Define the advantages and disadvantages of using hot-swapped disk drives.

16. The `mdir` command:

    a. Is part of the mtools package, which lets you access floppy disks as you would in DOS or a Windows command line

    b. Displays a directory of `/dev/md0`

    c. Is part of the mtools package, which includes other utilities such as `mkraid`, `lsraid`, and the `raidtab` configuration file

    d. Creates hard and symbolic links based on inode numbers displayed by `ls -i`

17. Which RAID level provides redundancy and fault tolerance at the *highest cost*?

    a. RAID-0

    b. RAID-1

    c. RAID-3

    d. RAID-5

18. When a soft link is deleted:

    a. The link data in the inode that the link referred to is decremented by one

    b. The file that the link referred to is also deleted

    c. The file records of the link and the file referred to are both affected

    d. Only the file record of the link is affected

19. If none of the copies of a file system's superblock can be read, the file system cannot be accessed. True or False?

20. An inode contains information about a file, including all of the following except:

    a. The file's name

    b. The location of the file's data on a hard disk or other device

    c. An inode number

    d. Dates and times of creation and last access

21. Given this output from `ls -l`:

    ```
    -rwx-r-xr-x    3   root root   63555    Mar 25 13:28 zcat
    ```
    which of the following is true?

    a. The filename `zcat` is a symbolic link, though the file it links to is not included in this output.

    b. Three different users have access rights to this file.

    c. The lack of a code letter at the beginning of the output line indicates that neither symbolic nor hard links are associated with this file.

    d. A total of three file records refer to the inode that the `zcat` file record refers to.

22. Describe the purpose of reserving a percentage of the space within a file system for the root or other user account.

9

23. At boot time, the **fsck** utility does the following:
    a. Checks each mounted **ext2** or **ext3** file system for errors
    b. Unmounts any damaged file systems
    c. Reads and resets key superblock parameters
    d. Calls the **tune2fs** utility to manage file system start-up
24. If the output of **dumpe2fs** indicates a maximum mount count of −1, then which of the following is true?
    a. The maximum mount count for this file system has been reached and an **fsck** check will be executed the next time the system is rebooted.
    b. The count of how many times the file system has actually been mounted has been reset using **tune2fs** and is no longer a relevant measure of when the file system needs to be checked.
    c. The superblock may well be corrupted, in which case you must refer to one of the copies of the superblock located elsewhere on the hard disk in order to continue using the system.
    d. No maximum mount count has been set; the system will never automatically force a complete **fsck** check.
25. Disk fragmentation is not a problem in Linux **ext2** or **ext3** file systems because:
    a. New files are created at locations spread around the entire file system
    b. Striping prevents fragmentation
    c. The **fsck** utility defragments the file system each time the system is booted
    d. Fragmentation is not a single point of failure for a high availability system

---

HANDS-ON PROJECTS

Project 9-1

In this project you create a boot disk and start your computer using it. To complete this project you must have a working Linux system with root access, a blank floppy disk, and Internet access.

1. Log in to Linux.
2. Start your Web browser using an icon on the panel or a menu item.
3. Enter **www.toms.net/rb** in the Address bar of the browser and then press **Enter**. The tomsrtbt Web page appears.
4. Click the link to download **tomsrtbt**.
5. Click on one of the mirror sites. After a moment, you see a list of files.
6. Click on the file **tomsrtbt-2.0.103.tar.gz** or whatever the latest version of the file is called. When prompted, save the file on your hard disk and note the location where you saved it. (Using **/tmp** is a good choice.)

7. Uncompress the file you just downloaded. Read the `tomsrtbt.FAQ` file and note the installation instructions.

   ```
   $ tar xvzf /tmp/tomsrtbt-2.0.103.tar.gz
   ```

8. Following the instructions in the `tomsrtbt.FAQ` file, type **./install.s** at a command prompt and follow the on-screen directions to install the program.

9. Shut down your Linux system.

10. With the floppy disk inserted, restart your system. The boot disk should load the operating system and eventually display a login prompt.

11. Log in as root. The on-screen instructions will tell you that a password is needed and what the password is.

12. You are now logged in to a real Linux operating system. Feel free to explore the file system and utilities included with this single-disk version of Linux.

Project 9-2

In this activity you create a floppy disk containing an `ext2` file system and work with that file system using the `fsck` and `tune2fs` commands. This allows you to experiment with concepts explained in this chapter without damaging the data on a hard disk. To complete this project you need a blank disk and an installed Linux system with root access.

1. Insert a blank 3 1/2-inch disk in the disk drive of your Linux computer.

2. Log in to Linux as root and open a command-line window.

3. Format the disk, creating an `ext2` file system:

   ```
   # /sbin/mke2fs /dev/fd0
   ```

   Study the information that appears on-screen during the formatting process to see what items you recognize from the discussion in the chapter (such as inodes, blocks, and the superblock).

4. View information about the floppy file system:

   ```
   # /sbin/dumpe2fs /dev/fd0
   ```

   The listing is short because the floppy is a small file system. Review the information found on the superblock to see which fields you recognize from the chapter discussion. (Other fields are described in the `dumpe2fs` man page.)

5. Change the maximum mount count for the floppy file system:

   ```
   # /sbin/tune2fs -c 5 /dev/fd0
   ```

6. Check that the new value for the maximum mount count is stored on the disk by using the `-l` option of the `tune2fs` command to view the superblock (this is similar to the `dumpe2fs` command but only dumps the superblock parameters):

   ```
   # /sbin/tune2fs -l /dev/fd0
   ```

7. Check the integrity of the floppy file system:

   ```
   # fsck -f /dev/fd0
   ```

8. Mount the floppy disk so you can write a file to it:

    ```
    # mount -t ext2 /dev/fd0 /mnt/floppy
    ```

9. Copy a file to the floppy disk:

    ```
    # cp /etc/termcap /mnt/floppy
    ```

10. Verify that the file is on the floppy:

    ```
    # ls -l /mnt/floppy
    ```

11. Unmount the floppy disk:

    ```
    # umount /dev/fd0
    ```

12. Run the `fsck` command again:

    ```
    # fsck -f /dev/fd0
    ```

    Can you see a difference in the output compared to Step 7?

Project 9-3

In this activity you review information on the root file system. This is similar to the previous activity except that you work directly on your hard disk rather than on a blank floppy disk. Follow the instructions carefully to avoid damaging data on your Linux hard disk. To complete this project you need an installed Linux system with root access.

1. Log in to Linux as root and open a command-line window.

2. Enter the **mount** command with no options to see which device contains your root file system. The first line of the output from the **mount** command includes this information. The line looks like the following sample output except that the first part (the device name) will be different on your system:

    ```
    # mount
    /dev/hda3 on / type ext3 (rw)
    ```

3. Use the `dumpe2fs` command to review information about your root file system. Pipe the results through the `less` command so you can page through them one screen at a time. (Substitute the device name of your root file system where `/dev/hda3` is shown here).

    ```
    # dumpe2fs /dev/hda3 | less
    ```

4. Look for the line containing `Filesystem volume name` in the output of the `dumpe2fs` command. Is a volume name defined on your system?

5. Look for the line containing `Mount count` in the output of the `dumpe2fs` command. What does this number represent? How does this number relate to the line labeled `Maximum mount count`?

6. Use the `tune2fs` command to list information from the superblock of your root file system:

    ```
    # tune2fs -l /dev/hda3
    ```

How does this information compare to the first part of the output from the `dumpe2fs` command?

7. The `tune2fs` command cannot be used to change parameters on a file system that is mounted. Because the root file system is always mounted when you boot your system normally, you must boot from a disk (such as a rescue disk) to change parameters on your root file system, or else use special commands to mount your root file system as read-only. View the man page of the `tune2fs` command to review what parameters can be changed using this command. Can you identify a hard disk parameter that cannot be changed with `tune2fs`?

Project 9-4

In this activity you experiment with hard and symbolic links. To complete this project you must have a working Linux system.

1. Log in to Linux and open a command-line window. Make certain you are in your home directory:

   ```
   $ cd
   ```

2. Copy a file to your home directory to use during this project:

   ```
   $ cp /etc/termcap ~
   ```

3. Examine the file using `ls -l`. Notice the file size, the first character of the output (by the file permissions) and the second column, to the right of the file permissions.

4. Create a symbolic link to the file:

   ```
   $ ln -s termcap termcap-soft
   ```

5. Look at the `termcap-soft` listing using `ls -l`. Notice the same areas mentioned in Step 3. What differences do you see?

6. What do you conclude about the space used by a symbolic link?

7. Create a hard link to the file:

   ```
   $ ln termcap termcap-hard
   ```

8. View the long listing for `termcap-hard` using `ls -l`. What do you notice about the three areas mentioned previously?

9. Since the file size for `termcap-hard` is the same as for `termcap`, how does this hard link differ from a file copy operation? Have you just doubled the amount of disk space used in your home directory?

10. View the inode numbers associated with all three files:

    ```
    $ ls -i termcap*
    ```

11. What do you notice?

12. View the last few lines of the `termcap` file (this is a long file; displaying the last few lines simply tests that the file data is accessible):

    ```
    $ tail termcap
    ```

9

13. View the last few lines of the `termcap-soft` file:

    ```
    $ tail termcap-soft
    ```

14. Delete the `termcap` file (confirm the deletion if prompted):

    ```
    $ rm termcap
    ```

15. Again, view the last few lines of the `termcap-soft` file:

    ```
    $ tail termcap-soft
    ```

16. What results? Why?

17. View the last few lines of the `termcap-hard` file:

    ```
    $ tail termcap-hard
    ```

18. What results? Why?

19. View the long listing of `termcap-hard` using `ls -l`. Can you see a difference since you viewed this information previously?

CASE PROJECTS

The McKinney & Co. project for the Ministry of Justice in Cylonica was a great success, but a few thorny issues remain unsolved. Along with beautiful beaches, Cylonica has a fair number of typhoons, tsunamis, and a high danger of volcanic ash from neighboring islands. In addition, the municipal services of Cylonica have turned out to be worse than expected, with power outages almost weekly and brownouts more days than not.

1. Use your Web browser to visit *www.warehouse.com, www.cdw.com,* or your favorite online computer store. Research at least three UPS devices that have enough power to handle a large Linux server. What wattage do you figure you will need to support the server? Go to the Web site for each of the three products you locate to determine what Linux support they mention.

2. Visit *www.ibm.com, www.hp.com, www.vasoftware.com,* and *www.turbolinux.com* to research high availability systems based on Linux.

3. If you are comfortable installing Linux, had little difficulty with Linux recognizing your hardware, and have a few hours to experiment, do the following. Reinstall Linux, but instead of creating basic swap and root partitions, divide your hard disk into multiple logical partitions using the Disk Druid utility in Red Hat Linux 7.3. In that same utility, define a RAID device. Finish installing Linux and use the RAID utilities mentioned in the chapter (such as `lsraid` and `raidstart`) to learn more about how RAID operates. Now you'll be ready for your next trip to Cylonica.

10

MANAGING SYSTEM RESOURCES

> **After reading this chapter and completing the exercises, you will be able to:**
>
> ◆ Access the /proc file system to manage system status
> ◆ Control how processes use system resources
> ◆ Track physical and virtual memory usage
> ◆ Locate and relieve system bottlenecks
> ◆ Manage system logs

In the previous chapter you learned about safeguarding information on your Linux server by creating a disaster plan for your information systems. You learned about using an uninterruptible power supply and checking the integrity of your file systems using `fsck`. You also learned about fault tolerant capabilities such as RAID.

In this chapter you learn how to manage system resources so that users on your Linux system can complete their work efficiently. The material in this chapter builds on what you have already learned. For example, you learned in Chapter 8 about managing processes in a shell using the `jobs` command. In this chapter you learn much more about managing processes using a variety of utilities. You also learn about managing system memory and using system log files to see how system resources are being used. As you learn about viewing and managing system resources, you will better be able to locate and alleviate bottlenecks that reduce system performance.

Viewing System Status in /proc

As you work at your graphical desktop or command-line interface, the Linux kernel and many other programs are managing the system in the background. For example, the kernel is managing memory and network traffic, one program might be sending files to a printer, and another may be logging many activities for later review.

The **/proc file system** is a specialized file system that lets you view and control system resources such as processes, memory, and kernel networking parameters. /proc is similar to the /dev directory in that you use it to interact with system resources as if they were files. For example, you can read information within /proc or its subdirectories using a command such as cat. But the information you see from /proc is not stored on a hard disk. When you query a filename in /proc, the Linux kernel responds with live information about the status of a process, memory, or other resource. This information can change from moment to moment.

For example, you can query /proc to see the memory capacity of your system and how it is being used:

```
# cat /proc/meminfo
           total:     used:     free:       shared:    buffers:  cached:
Mem:       31559680   30765056  794624      45461504   782336    12251136
Swap:      133885952  1318912   132567040
MemTotal:  30820 kB
MemFree:   776 kB
MemShared: 44396 kB
Buffers:   764 kB
Cached:    11964 kB
SwapTotal: 130748 kB
SwapFree:  129460 kB
```

You can also write information to some filenames in /proc. For example, you can write a value to /proc/sys/fs/file-max to change the number of file handles that can be used at one time in Linux. (A **file handle** is an internal storage mechanism that allows a single file to be opened and used in Linux.) This command displays the number of file handles currently configured in the Linux kernel:

```
# cat /proc/sys/fs/file-max
19660
```

This command changes the number of file handles available in the Linux kernel to 48000:

```
# echo 48000 > /proc/sys/fs/file-max
```

Viewing Device Information

You can query /proc to learn about many parts of your system hardware. This information can be useful as you configure devices or software services. Table 10-1 lists the paths in your Linux directory structure where you can access various hardware information.

Table 10-1   Hardware Information Accessible through /proc

Hardware information	Path
Battery information for systems using advanced power management (APM) software	/proc/apm
CPU information	/proc/cpuinfo
Direct memory access (DMA) channels used by system devices	/proc/dma
Interrupts configured for system devices	/proc/interrupts
Ports (memory addresses) used to communicate with system devices	/proc/ioports
File systems currently available to the Linux kernel	/proc/mounts
Disk partitions known to the Linux kernel	/proc/partitions
Information on all PCI devices in your system, such as video cards and hard disk controllers	/proc/pci
Information on all SCSI devices in your system	/proc/scsi and its subdirectories
Swap device information	/proc/swaps

As one example of viewing hardware information, consider this command:

```
# cat /proc/interrupts
          CPU0
   0:   2555629      XT-PIC timer
   1:       892      XT-PIC keyboard
   2:         0      XT-PIC cascade
   5:         0      XT-PIC Crystal audio controller
   6:        34      XT-PIC floppy
   8:         1      XT-PIC rtc
   9:         0      XT-PIC usb-uhci
  11:    265625      XT-PIC aic7xxx, eth0
  12:     93809      XT-PIC PS/2 Mouse
  14:     61686      XT-PIC ide0
  15:    155476      XT-PIC ide1
 NMI:         0
 ERR:         0
```

10

You can use information such as the interrupts listed by the preceding command to help you avoid conflicts as you configure devices on your system. Of course, you won't find *all* hardware information in `/proc`. For example, if your system includes a PCI video card, `/proc/pci` will tell you about the PCI interface to the video card, but it will not provide details on the video chipset, clock rates, and other details needed to configure X manually.

Many Linux system administration utilities use information from `/proc`. One example is the system information provided in the Control Center within KDE, as shown in Figure 10-1. Notice that the items listed under Information correspond to the list of hardware information described in Table 10-1. Other utilities such as `free` and `ps`, described later in this chapter, also obtain information from `/proc` and present it in a format that is easier to read than the `/proc` files themselves.

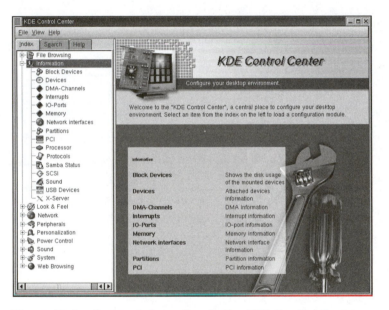

Figure 10-1   System information in the KDE Control Center

Viewing Process Information

The `/proc` file system contains detailed information about each process running on Linux. This information is updated from moment to moment, as the status of a process changes. Before you can access information in `/proc` regarding a specific process, you need to find the process's PID number. (As you learned in Chapter 8, every process running on Linux is assigned a process ID, or PID, number.) To find the PID for a running process (such as a program that you have started), use the `ps` command.

Suppose that, using the **ps** command, you discover the PID for a particular process is 1066. You can then look for information about the process in the directory **/proc/1066**. Most of this information is difficult to use directly because it consists of numbers without explanations—you have to use administrative utilities to display this process data in a meaningful way. One part of the process data that is readable, however, is the **cmdline** file, which tells you the command used to start the process. This command shows the line entered to launch process 1066 (the result indicates that **gedit** is used to start the process):

```
# cat /proc/1066/cmdline
gedit
```

You can explore other subdirectories of a process information directory like **/proc/1066** on your Linux system to see what types of process-related information is available.

MANAGING PROCESSES

In Chapter 7 you learned about using the **ps** command to see a list of processes, and in Chapter 8 you learned about using the **kill** command to send signals to processes. In this section you learn more complex options for **ps** and other utilities that control how processes function. You also learn about several useful graphical utilities for managing processes.

To manage your system effectively, you will often need to display detailed information about specific processes. The **ps** command has many options that let you select which processes are included in the command output. It also has options to let you select what information is displayed about each of those processes. Table 10-2 lists **ps** options for selecting which processes to display.

 It may be helpful to think of a large spreadsheet with every process on a separate row, and every piece of information about the process in a separate column. The **ps** options in Table 10-2 let you choose which rows to display. The **ps** options in Tables 10-3 and 10-4 let you choose which columns to display. You can combine both types of options in one **ps** command to see exactly the information you need.

For example, root could use the following command to list all processes owned by user **jtaylor**:

```
# ps --user jtaylor
```

Table 10-2 ps Options Used to Select Processes

Command-line option	Description
-A	Selects all processes on the system.
T	Selects all processes running in the current terminal.
x	Selects all processes that were not started normally from a terminal (this list includes system initialization scripts and network services).
r	Restricts output to running processes (those that are not sleeping). This option is used in conjunction with another selection option.
-C	Selects processes by the command used to start the process. To use this option, you need to follow it with the name of the command.
-p	Selects processes by PID number. To view information on a single process, enter its PID number as a value after the option.
--user	Selects processes by username. To use this option, type the username after the option.
--group	Selects all processes belonging to users who are members of the group named after the option.

You can select which pieces of information (sometimes called fields) ps displays for each process by adding command-line options like those shown in Table 10-3. Many of the unfamiliar terms in the Description column (such as "nice level") are discussed later in this chapter. A few are used only for special troubleshooting or programming tasks—refer to the ps man page for more information on these.

Table 10-3 Process Information Fields Available from ps

Display code (column heading in ps output)	Description	Command-line option
PID	Process ID	pid
PPID	Process ID of the parent process	ppid
PGID	Process group ID	pgid
SID	Session ID	sess
TTY	Controlling terminal	tty
TPGID	Process group ID of the owner of the terminal running the process	tpgid
USER	Owner of the process	user
PRI	Time left of a possible timeslice allocated to the process	pri
NICE	Nice level	nice
PLCY	Scheduling policy	plcy
RPRI	Real-time priority	rpri

Table 10-3 Process Information Fields Available from ps (continued)

Display code (column heading in ps output)	Description	Command-line option
MAJFLT	Number of major faults loading information from a file system	majflt
MINFLT	Number of minor faults (with no disk access involved)	minflt
TRS	Size of the text used by the program (in KB)	trs
DRS	Size of the data used by the program (in KB)	drs
SIZE	Virtual image size of the process (in KB)	size
SWAP	Space used on swap device by this process (in KB)	swap
RSS	Kilobytes of the program resident in memory	rss
SHARE	Shared memory size in KB	share
DT	Number of pages of information that are dirty (not yet updated to hard disk)	dt
STAT	State of the process	stat
FLAGS	Process flags	f
WCHAN	Kernel function at the point where the process is sleeping	wchan
UID	User ID of the owner of this process	uid
%WCPU	Weighted percentage of CPU time consumed	wpcpu
%CPU	Percentage of CPU used since last update	pcpu
%MEM	Percentage of memory used	pmem
START	Time that the process was started	start
TIME	Total amount of CPU time (cumulative) that the process has used since it was started	time
COMM	Command line that started the process (abbreviated)	comm
CMDLINE	Command line that started the process (complete)	cmd

To specify a field from Table 10-3, use the arguments in the right column of the table with the **o** option. For example, to display processes owned by **jtaylor** and display just the command line and PID for each of those processes (option **comm** in Table 10-3), use this command:

```
# ps –user jtaylor o "comm pid"
```

Instead of listing the exact fields you want, you would normally use one of the options in Table 10-4. These options each define a collection of related fields.

Table 10-4 Combination Process Information Fields Available from `ps`

Command-line option	Description
j	Show fields related to controlling jobs in a shell
s	Show fields related to signals that each process handles
u	Show fields that define how the owner of each process is using system resources
v	Show fields detailing how each process is using virtual memory
l	Show numerous fields considered by system administrators to be of interest in tracking processes but not otherwise related (as the above groupings for job control, virtual memory, and so forth, are groups of related fields)
o or --format	User-defined format (display all of the fields listed after the option; each field to be included in the output is defined by using a code from the right column of Table 10-3)

As a system administrator, you must manage numerous processes started by many users. You need to track how these processes consume system resources—particularly CPU time. The `%CPU` and `TIME` fields of the `ps` command output are especially useful in tracking how processes use CPU time.

The `%CPU` field compares the amount of CPU time used by a process with the total time elapsed since the previous computation of the `%CPU` field, in the form of a percentage. The Linux kernel tracks a small slice of time (such as one second) and then determines for how much of that one second a process was using the CPU. That computation creates a percentage used for the `%CPU` field of the `ps` command output. The `%CPU` field does not show the average amount of CPU time used by the process since it was started. The `%WCPU` field is weighted to show a 30-second average of the percentage of CPU time used by a process. This field is more helpful for showing the overall usage pattern for a process.

The `TIME` field provides a cumulative measure of the amount of CPU time consumed by a process. Processes that have been running since the system was booted may still have a `TIME` value of `0:00` because they are background processes with very little activity to monitor. But some processes that are only recently started may show a large `TIME` value (for example, `5:30` to indicate five and a half minutes), indicating that they are using a lot of the CPU's time. The `START` field tells you when a process began running. When a process has a large `TIME` value after running for only a short time, you may need to change the priority of that process to prevent it from slowing down other processes. The next section describes how to do this.

Changing Process Priorities

Each process is automatically assigned a **priority** when it is started. This priority determines how much CPU time is granted to the process. Normally, all processes have the same priority—that is, all processes are assigned an equal portion of CPU time for processing. Another name for the priority of a process is **nice level**. The idea behind the name "nice" is that if a user on the system decides a certain program is not time sensitive, the user can make the program "nicer" to other users' programs by giving up some of its CPU time. The system administrator can make any process nicer, whether the user who started it is feeling generous or not.

 PRI in the `ps` command output is short for *Priority*, but this field actually indicates how a process is using the CPU time allocated to it. You will notice that this field changes regularly for a given process as the process works, using CPU time at different moments.

The `NICE` or `NI` field in the output of the `ps` command indicates the nice level, or priority level, assigned to a process. The nice level is a fixed value for a process. This value determines whether a process receives extra CPU processing time or less CPU processing time compared to other processes running on the system. You can change the nice level to alter the relative priority of a process.

You can alter the priority of a process using the **nice** and **renice** commands. The standard nice level is 0, which indicates that a process has equal priority with all other processes that have not had their nice level altered. Any user can raise the nice level of a process that he or she has started (and thus owns), making it nicer to other programs. The highest nice level, which makes a program run the slowest, is 20. The root user can make any process nicer, but root can also make programs less nice by lowering their nice level. The root user can lower the nice level of a process to -20, which gives that process a lot of extra CPU time. This may be necessary, for example, if the root user is trying to do an emergency backup of data due to a failing drive. The current nice level of a process is shown as the `NI` or `NICE` field in the output of the `ps` command. (This field is also shown in the output of the `top` command described in the next section.)

You can use the `nice` command to launch a process and assign it nonstandard priority at the same time. You include a nice level and the name of the program to launch. For example, to start a script named `analyze` with a nice level of 10, use this command:

```
# nice -10 analyze
```

The **renice** command changes the nice level of a process that is already running. Regular users can increase the nice level of processes that they own; root can increase or decrease the nice level of any process. To use `renice`, you must know the PID of the process you want to affect. The root user can perform more complex tasks using `renice`. These tasks require additional information such as the user ID (UID) of the owner of a process.

10

As a first example, suppose you start a complex script named `analyze`. After starting the script, you decide you can wait for the results of the script, allowing other programs to run more efficiently. You can change the nice level of the process by using the PID of the running script with the `renice` command. For example, if the PID of the `analyze` script is 1776, this `renice` command will change the running script's priority so that it takes longer to complete.

```
# renice +10 1776
```

Suppose next that as the system administrator you discover that a certain user, `jtaylor`, is running several computationally intensive programs that are slowing down system response for other users. After checking with this user, you learn that the programs are a valid use of the system resources, but they are not time-critical. To make things run more smoothly for other users, you raise the nice level of all processes run by `jtaylor` so they run more slowly. This command changes the priority of all running processes owned by `jtaylor`:

```
# renice +5 -u jtaylor
```

Viewing Processor Usage with `top`

The `top` utility displays a list of running processes arranged by how much CPU time each is using. The process that is consuming the greatest amount of CPU time is shown at the top of the list, and the output of `top` is updated regularly (every five seconds by default, but you can configure the update interval).

You can run `top` and leave it on your screen to watch the activity of different processes and see which are using a lot of CPU time. If one process begins to take more than its fair share of CPU time (in your judgment as system administrator), you can take corrective action by changing the nice level of that process with the `top` command, as explained later in this section.

`top` is normally launched without any options, like this:

```
# top
```

When you launch `top`, it takes over the text window that you are working in. You cannot run `top` in the background (using the symbol & after the command), because `top` sends its output immediately to the screen. You can, however, use redirection (such as the > operator) to send the output of `top` to a file. Figure 10-2 shows `top` in a terminal window.

```
root@sundance:~                                                    _ □ ×

File   Edit   Settings   Help

 5:00pm  up  7:53,  2 users,  load average: 1.46, 1.31, 1.21
73 processes: 69 sleeping, 4 running, 0 zombie, 0 stopped
CPU states: 24.6% user,  7.6% system,  0.0% nice, 67.6% idle
Mem:   191260K av,  185384K used,     5876K free,      0K shrd,    17552K buff
Swap:  265064K av,      28K used,   265036K free                  56192K cached

  PID USER      PRI  NI  SIZE  RSS SHARE STAT %CPU %MEM    TIME COMMAND
10068 root       16   0 13116  12M 10472 S    7.4  6.8  25:44 ksysguard
 1127 root       15   0 28344  19M  3896 R    7.1 10.2   1:47 X
10106 root       15   0  6004 6004  3596 S    4.5  3.1  11:33 gtop
10082 root       15   0   764  764   580 S    3.1  0.3  12:02 ksysguardd
10678 root       15   0  2768 2768  2280 S    2.5  1.4   0:00 screenshot
 9870 root       15   0  4232 4232  2128 S    1.3  2.2   0:09 sawfish
 9923 root       15   0 10792  10M  5316 R    1.3  5.6   3:19 rhn-applet
 1050 xfs        16   0  4092 4092   980 S    0.9  2.1   0:02 xfs
10033 root       15   0  5212 5212  3972 R    0.9  2.7   0:02 gnome-terminal
10677 root       15   0  1040 1040   836 R    0.9  0.5   0:01 top
 9918 root       15   0  4004 4004  3244 S    0.5  2.0   0:02 tasklist_applet
10495 root       15   0 11296  11M  3768 S    0.5  5.9   0:02 gimp
 9920 root       15   0  3880 3880  3208 S    0.3  2.0   0:02 deskguide_apple
 9902 root       15   0  5884 5884  3976 S    0.1  3.0   0:07 panel
    1 root       15   0   476  476   420 S    0.0  0.2   0:06 init
    2 root       15   0     0    0     0 SW   0.0  0.0   0:00 keventd
    3 root       15   0     0    0     0 SW   0.0  0.0   0:00 kapmd
    4 root       34  19     0    0     0 SWN  0.0  0.0   0:00 ksoftirqd_CPU0
    5 root       15   0     0    0     0 SW   0.0  0.0   0:00 kswapd
    6 root       15   0     0    0     0 SW   0.0  0.0   0:00 bdflush
    7 root       15   0     0    0     0 SW   0.0  0.0   0:00 kupdated
    8 root       25   0     0    0     0 SW   0.0  0.0   0:00 mdrecoveryd
   14 root       25   0     0    0     0 SW   0.0  0.0   0:00 scsi_eh_0
```

Figure 10-2   The `top` command

You can use a number of keyboard options to control `top`. One of the most useful is the ability to renice a process, which you can do by pressing the `r` key and entering the PID of the process. For example, suppose the first few lines of the process list in `top` look like this:

```
PID   USER       PRI NI SIZE RSS  SHARE STAT LIB %CPU  %MEM  TIME  COMMAND
1066  jtaylor    17  0  1012 1012 820   R    0   4.7   3.2   0:00  analyze
1     root       0   0  100  52   36    S    0   0.0   0.1   0:04  init
2     root       0   0  0    0    0     SW   0   0.0   0.0   0:00  kflushd
3     root       0   0  0    0    0     SW   0   0.0   0.0   0:00  kpiod
4     root       0   0  0    0    0     SW   0   0.0   0.0   0:00  kswapd
```

To change the nice level of process 1066 (the **analyze** command, as indicated by the far right column), you would follow these steps:

1. Press the `r` key. A message appears above the process list asking you to enter the PID of the process to be reniced.

2. You enter the PID of the process (1066 in this example).

3. A message appears asking you for the new value to assign to this process. For this example, the nice level is being raised to 10; it could also be lowered from 0 to a negative number if you are running as root. Enter 10.

4. Watch the `NI` column of the process listing to see the nice level value change. Because of the higher nice level, the process moves down in the process list after a moment as its CPU usage decreases (unless the system has

nothing else competing for CPU time, in which case the process list may not change much).

 You will often see the `top` command itself in the output of `top`. When the `top` program is listed near the top of the output, you can be sure that the system is not under a heavy load.

As you are viewing the output of the `top` command, you can use the keys listed in Table 10-5 to control `top`. Other command options can also be specified on the command line when you first launch `top`.

Table 10-5 Interactive Commands in `top`

Description	Press this key	Notes
Update the process list display immediately	Spacebar	
Show a help screen with a command listing	h *or* ?	
Kill a process	k	You will be prompted for the PID
Change the number of processes included in the display	n *or* #	You will be prompted for the number of processes to include
Quit the `top` program	q	
Renice a process	r	You will be prompted for the PID and new nice level
Change the automatic update interval	s	You will be prompted for a value (in seconds) for the update interval

Additional options are available for sorting information in `top`, displaying or hiding certain information fields, and changing how some fields (such as `%CPU`) are calculated. See the man page for the `top` command for further details.

Using Graphical Process Management Tools

Several graphical process management tools are available for Linux. This section briefly describes where to find some of those tools and how to use them.

The **KDE System Guard** utility graphically displays a process list and lets you interact with that list to rearrange or kill processes. You can launch this program by selecting System, then KDE System Guard on the main menu of KDE or on the KDE Menus submenu of the Gnome main menu. You can also launch it from a command line within your desktop using the command `kpm` (for KDE process manager, the program's previous name).

Figure 10-3 shows the KDE System Guard window with the status bar activated (by choosing Show Statusbar from the Settings menu). The status bar displays information about RAM and virtual memory. In this figure, the Tree checkbox is also selected to display parent–child relationships among running processes.

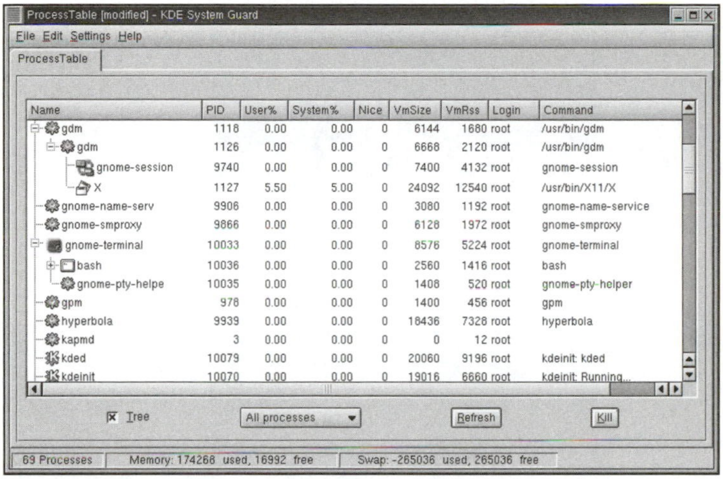

Figure 10-3   The KDE System Guard utility

Within the KDE System Guard, click any column heading to sort the process list using that column.

The process list in the KDE System Guard is similar to the output of the `top` command. Fields of information are shown for each process. The list is updated every few seconds. You can click on the drop-down list below the process list to select which processes are displayed. This is equivalent to using one of the selection options in Table 10-2. You can also click the Refresh button to update the process information if it's not updating quickly enough for you. After you click on a process to select it, you can click the Kill button below the list to end that process. You can also right-click on a process to do any of the following:

- Change which information fields are displayed for all processes.

- Select certain processes from the list.

- Send a signal to a process (remember, SIGTERM and SIGKILL are the signals commonly used to stop a program).

- Renice a process. When you choose this item, a dialog box appears in which you use a slide control to adjust the nice level of the process (moving the slider to the left for a lower nice level yields a higher priority, faster running process).

If you're using the Gnome Desktop, you can use the **Gnome System Monitor** to manage processes graphically. To launch this utility, choose Programs, then System, then System

Monitor on the Gnome main menu, or enter the command `gtop`. Figure 10-4 shows the main window of the Gnome System Monitor.

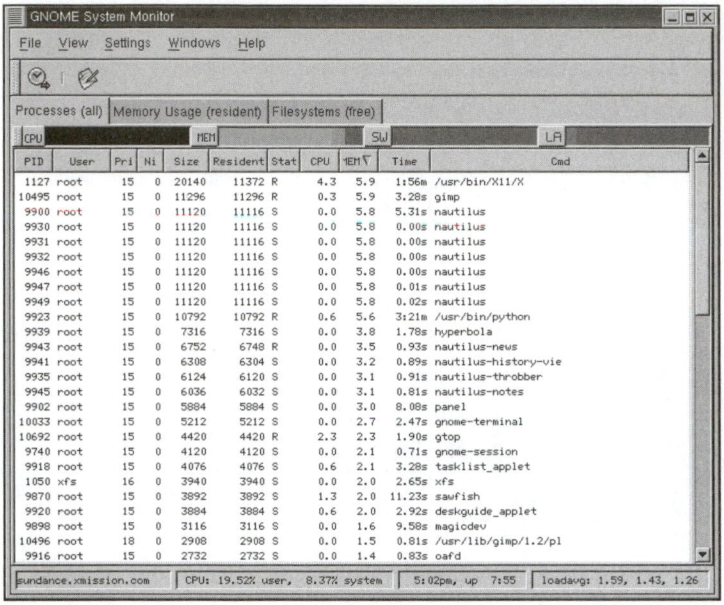

Figure 10-4   The Gnome System Monitor utility

As with the KDE System Guard, the Gnome System Monitor displays a list of processes with graphs and related information. You can click any column heading to sort the processes by that column. (Some of the displays in this program relate to memory status and are discussed in the next section.) The items on the View menu let you choose which processes you want to see in the list. You manage a process by right-clicking on it, then choosing an item from the pop-up menu that appears. The choices include:

- Renice the process (a dialog box appears in which you select the nice level).

- Kill the process nicely (using a SIGTERM, signal 15).

- Kill the process now (using a SIGKILL, signal 9).

- Send another signal to the process.

- See details on the process—all the information fields, including those not shown on-screen.

In addition to the KDE System Guard and Gnome System Monitor, several less ambitious tools display only a graphical representation of the system load—a tall line for a busy CPU and a short line for a CPU that is not loaded down. To try these mini-system monitors in Gnome, choose the following on the main menu: Panel, then Add to panel, then Applet, then Monitors, then CPU/MEM Load, CPULoad, or Load Average. Several other

monitors in this submenu display information about memory, disk usage, and network traffic. After you select a monitor, it appears in the Gnome Panel, as shown in Figure 10-5. To
remove any monitor from the Panel, right-click it and choose Remove from Panel from
the pop-up menu that appears.

Figure 10-5   A CPU load monitor on the Panel in Gnome

Actively Monitoring the CPU Load

You have learned about several tools for viewing process information and updating the
status of one or more processes. But how can you apply that knowledge to manage your
Linux system effectively?

Many system administrators begin by keeping a CPU load monitor visible on their Panel
as they work. When the CPU load is consistently high, you can begin checking for
processes that may need attention. As you start working on a new Linux system, you will
need to judge from user comments what load level on the CPU monitor equates to slow
response times for users based on the programs they are running. A very fast CPU may
tolerate a high load level and still deliver acceptable response times.

When you decide to investigate the cause of a high load, begin by using **top** or one of the
graphical utilities to see if a single process is using a high percentage of CPU time. A "run-
away process" started by a user may be the cause of the heavy load. In this case, you can
change the priority of the process, talk to the user who started the process, and kill the process
if necessary. As you become more familiar with the normal load on your system, you will be
able to tell from a small load graphic on your Panel when a single process has suddenly run
wild (for example, because of incoming network traffic or a programming bug).

When many legitimate processes are causing the heavy CPU load, the **ps** and **top** command options (or the graphical utilities) can help you determine whether one set of programs (such as the Web server), one type of program (such as shell scripts), or one user's
programs are causing the heavy load. In each case, when you know the details, you can
take corrective action by renicing a set of processes based on the command name or the
username.

Even if you can't immediately fix a system with a slow response, consider explaining the
situation to end-users. Leaving end-users uninformed is one of the fastest ways to lose
their support, and most people will be quite accommodating as long as they know you
understand their concerns and are working on the problem.

10

In some situations, everything may appear to be normal, with no processes taking undue CPU time and no troublesome applications, yet the system may nevertheless be very busy. When this situation persists for several days or weeks (depending on the IT strategy of your organization), you may have to begin planning for increased capacity. As a rule, you will always need more of everything in the future. Tracking CPU usage and taking action to correct errant processes simply lets you delay spending money on additional computing power until you really need it. To this end, you can reduce the CPU load in several ways. Here are a few ideas:

- Raise the nice level of numerous user processes so that they are not all competing at the same level. Of course, users will complain about the slowness of the system unless the CPU is fast enough to run their applications adequately. You must determine the importance of various tasks and then judge the performance levels that are allowable for different users and tasks. Maybe your Web server is critical because it generates sales, but users won't notice if their word processors run a bit slower. Or maybe the Web server just provides information, while users run important macros in their word processors. You must determine which processes are most critical.

- On systems with this capability, you can add a second microprocessor. (Linux supports up to four CPUs.) This will significantly reduce the load on your server, but it may be expensive and requires that you upgrade Linux to use a kernel with multiprocessing enabled. (This feature is called SMP—it is included with Red Hat Linux 7.3 and other versions, but is not enabled by default.)

- Move some tasks to a separate computer. You may have an older system that is too slow to handle many user accounts, but will sustain an e-mail server. Removing the e-mail server functions from your main server may reduce the load enough to let users' programs run more quickly. You can use the NFS protocol to access information stored remotely on a second server if necessary.

- Add memory. This will often reduce the CPU load on a busy system because the CPU spends less time moving data to and from the swap space. System administrators accustomed to Linux are proud that it can run well with 32 MB of memory, but a system with 512 MB has distinct advantages.

- Use higher-performance peripherals. As described in Locating System Bottlenecks later in this chapter, many systems are slow because the CPU is waiting on a component such as a network connection or hard disk. Replacing slow components can increase overall system throughput dramatically.

Managing Memory

The previous section described how to track and manage a system's CPU time. This section describes how to manage another key system resource: physical memory (RAM) and virtual memory. More RAM always leads to better performance on a busy system, because the Linux kernel and Linux programs can only interact with information stored in RAM. Information stored on a hard disk (even on a swap partition—in virtual memory) must be loaded into RAM before it can be manipulated or presented to a user.

Understanding Shared Libraries

In Chapter 4 you learned about programming libraries that provide a developer with prewritten functionality as he or she creates a new program. A standard Linux system contains dozens of libraries, each contained in a separate file. When you run a program that was created using a library, the library must either be installed on your system or included within the program itself. These two categories define the relationship between a library and program that uses it:

- **Statically linked applications** include library functions in the main program. They require no additional library files on the Linux system. Each copy of an application loads a duplicate copy of all the library functions it uses.

- **Dynamically linked applications** assume that any needed library files are available on the Linux system. The library functionality is not included with the program itself. Dynamically linked applications use **shared libraries**. This means that several applications can use a single copy of a library that has been loaded into memory. (This also means that if the correct libraries are not loaded on the Linux system, a dynamically linked application cannot run.)

Running multiple applications that are dynamically linked to the same libraries requires less memory than running multiple statically linked applications. If you load one application and its attendant libraries, then load a second application that is dynamically linked to those same libraries, the libraries will not be loaded a second time. Instead, the second application "shares" the libraries with the first application. If 10 applications were using one shared library, the library would still only load into memory once, rather than 10 times. Dynamically linked applications save a great deal of memory in situations where applications use the same libraries.

Most Linux applications are dynamically linked to use a set of shared libraries that are installed on a Linux system by default. For example, if you run numerous Gnome applications at the same time, most of the functionality of each application is contained in libraries shared by all Gnome applications.

Understanding Paged Memory

The natural assumption when you first learn about Linux swap space is that the kernel moves one application at a time to or from swap space. In fact, however, information is transferred to and from swap space in smaller units, known as pages. A **page** of memory is a block of 4 KB of RAM.

10

You will see references to an *application* being swapped; it's fine to use this expression, just understand that the kernel does not swap complete applications; it swaps enough pages from the application's memory to create the amount of free space needed by other programs.

When an application (A) requires additional RAM that is not available, the Linux kernel locates an application (B) that is not actively running. It then moves data from pages of memory in application B's memory space to the swap partition. The kernel moves only enough data to free the amount of memory needed by application A. The copied data might be taken from the middle of the inactive application's memory. The kernel keeps track of which pages of memory are moved to swap space and makes the freed memory available to application A.

When a program that was inactive becomes active again, the kernel moves the swapped data back from swap space to the same memory pages from which they were taken. Because the memory is restored by the kernel, the application cannot tell that its memory was used by another application for a time.

Swapping individual pages of memory (rather than complete applications) dramatically improves the performance of Linux on heavily loaded servers. If Linux swapped complete applications (rather than individual memory pages), system resources might be wasted copying a very large application to swap space when only a small percentage of its memory was needed by another program.

Tracking Memory Usage

The **free** command displays information on both RAM and virtual memory.

```
# free
        total         used      free     shared   buffers cached
Mem:    191260        182144    9116     0        28840   49196
-/+ buffers/cache:    104108    87152
Swap: 265064          0         265064
```

All the information displayed by **free** is in kilobytes. You can use command-line switches to change the display to bytes or megabytes. Each of the columns of information in the output of **free** is described here:

- The **Mem** line refers to physical memory (RAM).

- The **-/+ buffers/cache** line refers to RAM that is allocated to data stored by applications or data cached from the hard disk.

- The **Swap** line refers to swap space (located on your swap partition).

- The **total** column indicates the total amount of memory available to Linux. The sample output shows a system with about 192 MB of RAM and 256 MB of swap space.

- The `used` column indicates how much of the total memory is currently in use for both RAM and swap space.

- The `free` column indicates how much space is free for both RAM and swap space.

- The `shared` column indicates how much of the used space is dedicated to shared libraries. Often this will be the majority of the used space.

- The `buffers` column indicates the amount of memory dedicated to buffers. A **buffer** is memory used by an application for data storage. (For example, an application such as a spreadsheet uses buffers to hold documents as you edit them.)

- The `cached` column indicates memory used to store data from the hard disk, on the assumption that it may be needed by an application. If few applications are running, Linux will use most of the available RAM as a disk cache to improve performance. As more applications are launched, less memory is used for disk caching.

The first few times you see the output of `free`, the numbers won't mean much. With experience, you will come to understand what Linux is doing by reviewing these numbers. Some indicators to watch for in the output of `free` include the following:

10

- If the value in the `shared` column is small on a busy system, you may be able to decrease memory consumption by using more applications that are dynamically linked. Check the documentation for large or critical applications to see if a dynamically linked version is available.

- If the last line of the `free` column (the `Swap` line) is small, you are in danger of running out of both physical and virtual memory. If this happens, the kernel will crash. As you get closer to running out of memory, performance will decrease significantly.

- If many applications are running at the same time on a system without much RAM, the system will be subject to thrashing. As you learned in Chapter 8, thrashing is when applications are regularly paused and part of their data moved to swap space on disk so that another application can run for a moment, even when the first application was not inactive. Thrashing wears out the hard disk and significantly decreases application performance. Thrashing indicates that you need more RAM.

- The first line of the `free` column on the `Mem` line is normally very small. This is because Linux tries to use all available RAM for caching hard disk information. If more applications are launched, less information will be cached. If the `Mem` line of the `free` column shows a value near zero, you may still start several applications without using swap space. Check the value of the `cache` column to see how much memory might be available for additional applications.

Several fields of `ps` command output also provide information about memory usage:

- The `%MEM` field shows the percentage of available system memory that the process is using.

- The `STAT` field (for Status) shows whether the application is sleeping (indicated by an `S`). Pages from a sleeping application can be swapped to hard disk if memory is needed for another process. The `STAT` field shows a `W` if pages from a process have been swapped to hard disk. The command line used to start a process (the `COMMAND` field) is enclosed in square brackets if pages from a process have been swapped to hard disk.

- The `RSS` (Resident Set Size) field shows the amount of RAM currently used by the process. This value is given in kilobytes.

The Gnome System Monitor described in the previous section provides several helpful tools for tracking system memory. After launching the Gnome System Monitor, click the Memory Usage (resident) tab to see how memory is currently allocated (see Figure 10-6).

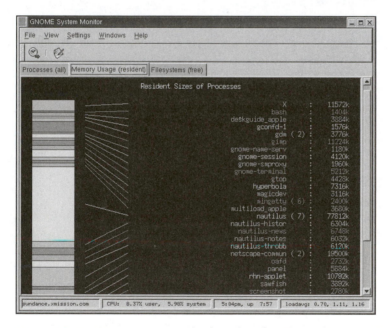

Figure 10-6   Memory usage displayed in the Gnome System Monitor

By default, this window shows the amount of RAM used by each process. You can select other memory statistics to view by choosing File, then New, then Memory Usage on the menu bar. Each of the following memory information pages appears as a separate tab in the Gnome System Monitor when you select it from the Memory Usage submenu:

- Resident Sizes of Processes: The amount of RAM used by each application. This is the default view on the Memory Usage (resident) tab.

- Shared Sizes of Processes: The usage of shared library memory space.

- Virtual Sizes of Processes: The actual size of each process including the sum of all shared libraries the program uses.

- Swapped Sizes of Processes: The amount of space each process currently occupies in swap space.

- Total Sizes of Processes: The total amount of space used by each process.

You can also open a Preferences dialog box via the Settings menu. This dialog box includes eight different tabs that let you control how process and memory information is displayed. Figure 10-7 shows one of these tabs.

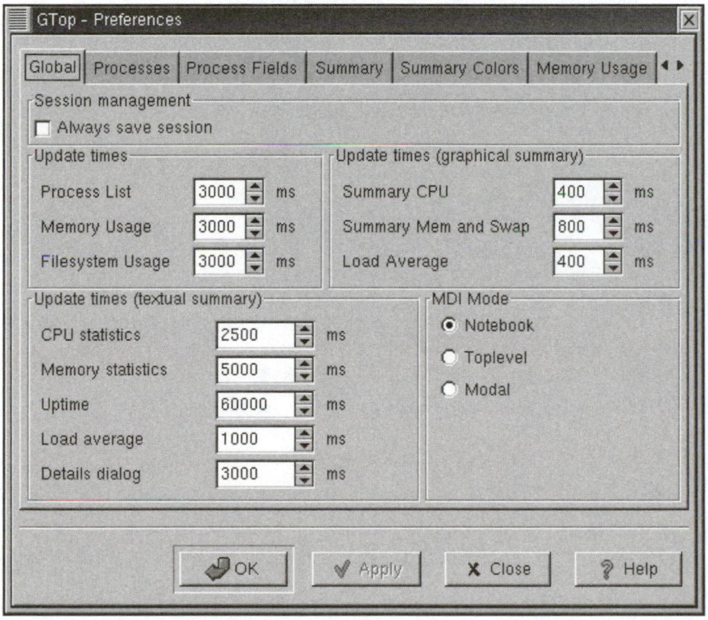

Figure 10-7 The Preferences dialog box in the Gnome System Monitor

Tracking Per-Application Memory Use

You can also use the Gnome System Monitor to view how a single process is using memory. To do this, view the process list by selecting the Processes tab in the System Monitor. Right-click on any process and choose Memory Maps from the pop-up menu. The Memory Maps dialog box appears for the process you selected. This dialog box includes three tabs:

- The Process info tab summarizes process details that you see on the main window of the Gnome System Monitor (or in the output of the **ps** command).

- The Raw memory map tab lists each component of the application—including all libraries that it uses—with memory information about each one. This information is useful to software developers studying the operation of a program.

- The Graphical memory map tab lists the same components as the Raw memory map tab, but shows a graphical representation of the memory used by each so you can immediately see which are consuming the most memory. The listing is color coded for easier reading. Figure 10-8 shows this tab.

Figure 10-8   The Graphical memory map tab for a single process in the Gnome System Monitor

Viewing Virtual Memory Information

The general state of the swap space (the virtual memory) on your system is shown by the **free** command and by both graphs and numeric displays in the utilities described in this section, such as the KDE System Guard and the Gnome System Monitor.

You can also use the **vmstat** command to view detailed information about how swap space is being used. The output of the **vmstat** command is cryptic until you become familiar with the abbreviated labels for the fields that it displays. When **vmstat** is run as a regular command, its output is based on information averaged over time since the system was booted. You can also run **vmstat** as you would **top**, with the display updated every few seconds. In this case the information is computed since the last update rather than since the system was booted. To run **vmstat** as a regular command, simply enter **vmstat**. Sample output is shown here:

```
# vmstat
procs      memory                      swap    io     system    cpu
 r  b  w   swpd   free   buff  cache   si so   bi bo   in  cs   us sy id
 0  0  0   11112  4108   700   11980    1  1    6  1   119 87    3  3 94
```

The fields displayed in the output of `vmstat` are explained in the following lists. Under the `procs` main heading:

- `r`: Number of processes waiting for run time
- `b`: Number of processes in uninterruptible sleep
- `w`: Number of processes swapped out but otherwise runable

Under the `memory` main heading you see fields that mirror the output of `free`:

- `swpd`: Amount of virtual memory used (KB)
- `free`: Amount of free RAM (also called idle memory) (KB)
- `buff`: Amount of RAM used as buffers (KB)
- `cache`: Amount of RAM used to cache hard disk data (KB)

Under the `swap` main heading:

- `si`: Speed as data is swapped into RAM from disk (average, in KB per second)
- `so`: Speed as data is swapped out to disk from RAM (average, in KB per second)

Under the `io` main heading:

- `bi`: Speed as data is sent to a block device (the hard disk), measured in blocks per second
- `bo`: Speed as data is received from a block device (in blocks per second)

Under the `system` main heading:

- `in`: Number of interrupts per second, including the clock
- `cs`: Number of context switches (changes between active processes) per second

Under the `cpu` main heading, each item indicates a percentage of total CPU time for three areas:

- `us`: User time, devoted to functions not within the kernel
- `sy`: System time, devoted to functions within the kernel
- `id`: Idle time, when the CPU is waiting for something to do

To run the `vmstat` command in interactive mode as you would `top`, so that its output is periodically updated, include a number after the command to indicate the delay between updates. For example, the following command displays an updated line of information every two seconds:

```
$ vmstat 2
```

10

The information provided by `vmstat` is useful for locating bottlenecks on your system related to hard disk performance, lack of sufficient memory, or problems with specific applications. The next section discusses these issues in more depth.

LOCATING SYSTEM BOTTLENECKS

A **bottleneck** is the part of a computer system that significantly slows down completion of the task at hand. To understand the bottleneck metaphor, think of holding a bottle of soda pop upside down and trying to pour the contents out as rapidly as possible. Because the neck of the bottle (the bottleneck) is narrow, the liquid is restricted; it can't flow out as rapidly as it would if you cut off the top of the bottle, removing the bottleneck. Computer systems always have a bottleneck—a part that is slower than the other components of the system. Your goal as a system administrator is to configure the system so that the user's actions are the bottleneck—so the computer is always waiting on the user's next request and responding immediately. When you discover that a computer system is not performing adequately, you must identify the bottleneck and improve the situation. Here are several examples:

- Many users on the network are accessing the Internet at the same time over a single dial-up modem connection. They all complain about slow service. The modem-based network connection is a bottleneck. To fix it, you could change to a higher-speed Internet connection using another technology.

- A large database index is created automatically each morning at about the time users arrive for work. You notice that the system response is slow until the database task is completed. The CPU capacity is a bottleneck. You could add a separate CPU for the database to run on, add memory to improve database performance, or schedule the database task to begin earlier, so it does not compete with users' tasks each morning.

- A dedicated server gathers network statistics and stores them on the server's hard disk. Because the server's hard disk is old and slow, and the network is very fast, the server generates statistics from the network faster than they can be written to disk, resulting in lost data. The hard disk speed is a bottleneck. To fix it, upgrade the hard disk to a newer, faster model with a faster interface, such as Ultra-IDE or SCSI.

These three examples illustrate that bottlenecks in your computer systems can be inside your computer or outside—often in the network infrastructure. Depending on the tasks your server performs, just about any part of your Linux server could become a bottleneck. Possible bottlenecks include:

- Physical memory (RAM)

- Swap space (virtual memory)

- CPU time

- Hard disk space

- Hard disk access speed

- Video card speed

- Serial port speed

- Network bandwidth

- Internal bus speed (internal buses such as ISA, EISA, MCA, and PCI determine how rapidly data can be moved between components of a single computer, such as from the system's RAM to its video card)

Identifying and Removing Bottlenecks

You can use the tools described in this chapter to identify and eliminate bottlenecks on your Linux system. Before you start, however, realize that improving system performance is to some degree more art than science. As you develop a better understanding of what is happening on the systems you manage, you will learn to make adjustments that noticeably improve performance.

The only way to master this art is through experience with Linux systems and related technologies. In the beginning, however, you will need to rely on science—that is, using various utilities, testing many programs, and reviewing performance measurements and system status. These sometimes-laborious steps will eventually lead you to a more intuitive understanding of the way events unfold within the system. At that point, you will probably use the commands described in this chapter to verify your own judgments, rather than to locate the source of a problem.

 Most Linux servers operate in a networked environment, and networks are a major source of bottlenecks. You will not be able to fully optimize your system without learning more about Linux networking. (See *Guide to Linux Networking and Security*, Course Technology, 2002, ISBN 0-619-00094-5.)

Using Benchmarks

Another type of utility that can help you identify bottlenecks is a **benchmark program**. Benchmarks provide a numeric measurement of one aspect of system performance. You can use the benchmark value to compare multiple systems that are working on the same task (for example, running the same program or responding to Web requests). A benchmark is also useful for showing you the speed at which events unfold within your

10

system. If that speed is lower than expected, you can look for the bottleneck that is slowing performance. This list describes some benchmarks that you can use to test the performance of your system:

- A good place to start is the Linux Benchmark Web site, which compares different versions of the Linux kernel to show how performance has improved over time. See *http://euclid.nmu.edu/~benchmark*.

- The values given in `/proc/cpuinfo` include a field called `bogomips`, which provides one measure of the speed of your processor. This value is not a highly accurate measure of the CPU speed on your system (hence the name, which is short for "bogus measure of instructions per second speed"). Although viewing this value on a single machine is not very useful, comparing it among multiple machines can help you determine whether the CPU in your Linux system is slower than you thought it was.

- A file system benchmarking tool called `bonnie` provides throughput statistics in megabytes per second for various types of disk transfers, such as random and sequential reads. This program is an excellent way to identify bottlenecks in your system's performance. You can learn more about the `bonnie` package and link to the free download at *www.textuality.com/bonnie*.

- A collection of benchmarking tools for Linux is included in the `lmbench` package for Debian Linux. See *http://packages.debian.org/unstable/admin/lmbench.html*. This page provides only a Debian format package, but developer types can use the source code to run it on other versions of Linux.

- A specialized memory benchmarking tool is `mbench`, available at *www.public.iastate.edu/~mslagell/cs/mbench.html*.

- You can learn about several other benchmarking tools for specific system components or entire systems by visiting *freshmeat.net* or *www.linuxapps.com* and searching on "benchmark."

MANAGING SYSTEM LOGS

On any ship, the captain keeps a log of information about each day, including where the ship has traveled, its cargo, and any noteworthy events. The log serves as a record not only for the captain and crew, but also for others who may need detailed information about the ship.

In much the same way, Linux keeps detailed records of events within the system. These records, known as **log files**, are created by many programs. As the system administrator, you can refer to the log files to determine the status of your system, watch for intruders, or look for data about a particular program or event. Table 10-6 lists some commonly logged events and the location of the corresponding log files. This chapter focuses on the main system log, which is typically located at `/var/log/messages`.

Table 10-6   Commonly Logged Events and Their Log Files

Event	Path and filename of the log
Main system messages	`/var/log/messages`
Web server transfers	`/var/log/httpd/access_log`
FTP server transfers	`/var/log/xferlog`
E-mail server information	`/var/log/maillog`
Automatic script executions	`/var/log/cron`

Many different programs write messages to `/var/log/messages`. A **message** is a description of what is happening within a program. The message may report information (someone has logged in), a warning (someone tried to log in unsuccessfully), or a serious error indicating that a program is about to crash. Several sample messages are shown later in this section. A number of daemons, like the Web server, e-mail server, and login security programs, write to the file, as does the Linux kernel itself. The messages from the kernel tell you about low-level system activities such as when devices are first initialized and when daemons are started by the kernel.

The **messages** file uses a standard format. Each line of the file makes up an individual log message. Each message, in turn, contains the following information:

- The date and time when the event being logged occurred (often called the **timestamp**)

- The hostname (or computer name) of the system on which the event occurred

- The name of the program generating the log message

- The message text itself, which may be more than one line long

A few sample lines from a **messages** log file are shown here. Notice that the hostname for all of these messages is `brighton`, the name of someone's computer. Also notice that several different programs have generated the log messages shown here, including the Linux kernel, the `httpd` daemon (the Web server), the sound system, and other programs.

```
Oct 26 06:42:29 brighton kernel: Installing knfsd (copyright (C) 1996 ok
Oct 26 06:42:29 brighton nfs: rpc.nfsd startup succeeded
Oct 26 06:42:29 brighton keytable: Loading keymap:
Oct 26 06:42:30 brighton keytable: Loading /usr/lib/kbd/keymaps/i386/qwe
Oct 26 06:42:30 brighton keytable: Loading systemffont:
Oct 26 06:42:30 brighton rc: Starting keytable succeeded
Oct 26 06:42:30 brighton gpm: gpm startup succeeded
Oct 26 06:44:57 brighton rpc.statd[451]: gethostbyname error for brighto
Oct 26 06:45:01 brighton httpd: Cannot determine local host name.
Oct 26 06:45:01 brighton httpd: Use the ServerName directive to set it
Oct 26 06:45:01 brighton httpd: httpd startup failed
Oct 26 06:45:01 brighton sound: Starting sound configuration:
```

10

```
Oct 26 06:45:01 brighton sound: sound
Oct 26 06:45:01 brighton rc: Starting sound succeeded
Oct 26 06:45:02 brighton PAM_pwdb[582]: (su) session opened for user xfs
Oct 26 06:45:03 brighton PAM_pwdb[582]: (su) session closed for user xfs
Oct 26 06:45:03 brighton xfs: xfs startup succeeded
Oct 26 06:45:05 brighton rc: Starting local succeeded
Oct 26 06:54:08 brighton PAM_pwdb[629]: check pass; user unknown
Oct 26 06:54:09 brighton login[629]: FAILED LOGIN 1 FROM (null) FOR ro
opt, User not known to the underlying authentication module
```

Right now you don't have to understand everything in the preceding log file lines. But you should become familiar with the format of a log line. Not all messages are written to `/var/log/messages`.

The `syslogd` and `klogd` Daemons

Any program running on Linux can call the shared programming function `syslog` and pass it a message. The `syslog` function writes each message to the `/var/log/messages` file or another configured location, as described shortly. All of the calls to the `syslog` function are managed by **syslogd**, the system logging daemon.

`syslogd` watches for messages submitted by programs; another daemon called `klogd` (kernel logging daemon) watches for messages submitted by the Linux kernel. `klogd` logs kernel messages to `/var/log/messages` (or another configured location). Both `klogd` and `syslogd` write messages to the same log file. Figure 10-9 shows how everything works together to record log messages.

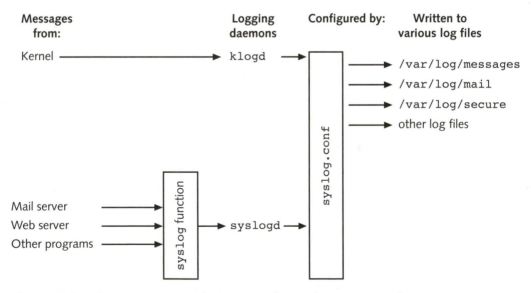

Figure 10-9   How `syslogd` and `klogd` work together to process log messages

The `syslogd` and `klogd` daemons are started by the system initialization scripts in `/etc/rc.d/init.d` each time you boot your Linux system. You should never need to start these programs manually.

Configuring the System Log

You can configure what information you want `syslogd` and `klogd` to store in the main system log (`/var/log/messages` by default) and what information you want stored in other files. Both `syslogd` and `klogd` rely on a single configuration file: `/etc/syslog.conf`. Figure 10-10 shows the format of each line in the `syslog.conf` file. The parts of the figure are described below.

```
facility.priority  ;facility.priority    Action
```
      Selector   Optional additional
                          selectors

Figure 10-10   The format of each line in `/etc/syslog.conf`

 As with most configuration files, lines that begin with a hash mark (#) in `/etc/syslog.conf` are comments and are ignored by the logging daemons.

Each line in the `syslog.conf` file contains two parts:

- A **selector**, a set of code words that selects what events are being logged

- An **action**, a filename or username that determines either the file in which the message describing an event is written or the users on whose screen the message appears (the action can also refer to a remote computer for networked logging, as described later in this section)

Each selector describing an event to be logged is composed of two parts:

- The **facility**, a code word that specifies which type of program is being selected (the category of program providing the log entry)

- The **priority**, a code word that specifies the type of messages being selected for logging

Consider this example log configuration line:

```
daemon.info          /var/log/messages
```

The left part of the line contains a selector: `daemon.info`. The facility of this selector is `daemon`. The priority is `info`. So, messages from any daemon program with a priority of `info` or higher are selected by these code words. On the right, the line contains an action: `/var/log/messages`. This action is a filename, which specifies that messages selected by the `daemon.info` selector will be written to the file `/var/log/messages`.

The Facilities

When a Linux program wants to log a message, it issues a programming call to the `syslog` function. As part of that call, the program indicates its type, or category. For example, when the `login` program records a message about a user logging into the system, the `login` program specifies that the message is coming from an authentication (security-related) program. The `syslogd` daemon uses this category information to determine where to write the message, based on the `syslog.conf` configuration. The actual name of the program (`login`, in this example), rather than the category (authentication in this example), is written to the log file. Table 10-7 lists the different facilities, or types of programs, for which you can separately configure logging.

Table 10-7   Code Words Used to Specify Facilities in `syslog.conf`

Facility description	Facility name
Messages from user authentication utilities such as `login`	auth (formerly called `security`)
Special-purpose (private) user authentication messages	`auth-priv`
Messages from the `cron` program (used to control automated, scheduled tasks)	`cron`
Messages from all standard daemons or servers not otherwise listed by name here	`daemon`
Kernel messages (through `klogd`)	`kern`
Printer server messages	`lpr`
Mail server messages (from the Mail Transfer Agent)	`mail`
News server messages	`news`
Messages about the system logging process itself (such as starting the logging program)	`syslog`
Messages from programs started by end users	`user`
Messages from the `uucp` program (rarely used)	`uucp`
Eight special-purpose categories that a Linux vendor or programmer can define for specific needs not covered by the other categories	`local0` through `local7`

In many cases, multiple programs use the same facility. The `daemon` facility, in particular, is used by many programs.

The Priorities

All Linux programs generate different types of messages. Some messages are informational; they might describe how the program is using system resources, for example. Other messages indicate a potential problem. Still other messages indicate a serious or critical problem that will corrupt data or shut down the program. Each program can generate messages with different priorities, depending on the seriousness of the event. You can configure your system so messages of different priorities are logged in different ways.

Table 10-8 shows the different priorities available in `syslog.conf`, listed from lowest to highest priority.

Table 10-8 Message Priorities Used in `syslog.conf`

Priority description	Priority name
Debugging messages used by programmers or those testing how a program works	debug
Informational messages about what a program is doing	info
Information about noteworthy events occurring as a program executes	notice
Warnings about potential problems with a program	warning (formerly called warn)
Notices about errors occurring within a program	err (formerly called error)
Critical error messages that will likely cause a program to shut down	crit
Error messages that will cause a program to shut down and may also affect other programs	alert
Messages about events serious enough to potentially crash the system	emerg (formerly called panic)

10

As a software developer writes a program, the developer decides which events are associated with which priority levels. For example, the developer might design a program so that a certain event generates a message with the priority of `warning`. Another programmer might decide that the same event would generate a message with the priority of `notice`. Thus, the programs themselves determine what facility they pertain to and what priority individual events or messages should have. As a system administrator, you simply determine where messages are logged based on their facility and priority.

The Actions

Once you set up a selector (consisting of a facility and a priority), you can assign an action to that selector. The action determines what `syslogd` and `klogd` do with the messages defined by the selector. Possible actions are listed here:

- Write the message to a regular file using the given filename. (This is by far the most commonly used action.)

- Write the message to the terminal indicated. This can be a standard virtual terminal name, from `/dev/tty1` to `/dev/tty6`, or the console device, `/dev/console`.

- Write the message to the screen of any users who are logged in, from a given list of users. For example, if the action is `root,lsnow`, the messages in the selector will be written to the screen of users root and `lsnow` if they are logged in. This ensures that root and perhaps other users are immediately informed when a serious error occurs that might cause a program to shut down.

- Write the message to the log file on a remote system. This is done using the symbol @ in the action. For example, you could specify the action as `@incline.xyz.com` to send log messages for the given selector to the `syslogd` daemon running on the system named `incline.xyz.com`.

The option of writing messages to a remote system is useful in several circumstances:

- *To consolidate important messages*: Many systems in an organization can send log messages to a single system so they can be archived and studied as a group.

- *To safeguard information on a failed system*: When a system crashes because of a hardware failure, any system log files stored on the hard disk can be damaged, or at least rendered inaccessible until the system is restored. By storing log files on another system, you ensure that these messages can be reviewed even after the system that generated them fails.

- *To enhance security*: Storing log files remotely makes it more difficult for intruders to delete records of their activities that may be stored in system log files.

Configuration File Syntax

The following sample listing shows lines from a `syslog.conf` file. The comment lines (beginning with the # character) precede and explain the purpose of each configuration line.

```
# Log anything (except mail) of level info or higher.
# Don't log private authentication messages!
*.info;mail.none;authpriv.none                  /var/log/messages

# The authpriv log file has restricted access.
authpriv.*                                      /var/log/secure

# Log all the mail messages in one place.
mail.*                                          /var/log/maillog

# Everybody gets emergency messages
*.emerg                                                    *

# Save boot messages also to boot.log
local7.*                                        /var/log/boot.log
```

Some aspects of the configuration file syntax are not obvious even after reading about facilities and actions:

- An asterisk (*) used as the facility or the priority matches all facilities or all priorities, respectively. For example, the selector `*.emerg` selects all messages with the `emerg` priority from any facility.

- An asterisk (*) used as the action means that all users who are logged in will see matching messages on their screen (if they have a command line available to receive the message). The `*.emerg` selector in the sample lines above uses `*` as the action.

- The facility and the priority are separated by a period.

- Multiple selectors can be included on the same configuration line by separating them with a semicolon (;).

- Multiple facilities or priorities can be specified at the same time using a comma-separated list. For example, `uucp,news.crit` matches messages of priority `crit` for either the `uucp` or `news` facility.

- The keyword `none` as a priority excludes all messages from the named facility. For example, specifying `*.info;mail.none` matches messages of `info` priority or higher from any facility, but all messages from the `mail` facility are excluded.

- For any priority specified in a selector, all messages of that priority and all *higher* priorities (more serious problems) are included.

- The same messages can be logged to more than one place by including the same selector on multiple lines with different actions. For example, critical kernel messages might be displayed on the `/dev/console` device and also logged to a remote machine for later analysis. Configuration lines in `syslog.conf` do not override previous configuration lines; each action configured by a line in `syslog.conf` adds to everything already configured.

10

In addition to these basic rules of syntax for `syslog.conf`, several special symbols are occasionally used to specify facilities or priorities with greater precision. The man page for `syslog.conf` has complete details on these rarely used features.

Table 10-9 describes the effect of several sample `syslog.conf` configuration lines.

Table 10-9   Sample `syslog.conf` Configuration Lines

Sample configuration line	Effect of the configuration line
`#kern.*   /dev/console`	None; this line begins with a comment character
`kern.*   /dev/console`	Log all kernel messages (of any priority) to the console (the computer screen)
`*.info;mail.none;authpriv.none` `    /var/log/messages`	Log all messages from any facility with a priority of `info` or higher to the file `/var/log/messages`, but exclude all messages with a facility of `mail` or `authpriv`, no matter what priority
`authpriv.*    /var/log/secure`	Log all messages from the `authpriv` facility to the file /var/log/secure
`uucp,news.crit /var/log/spooler`	Write any messages of priority `crit` or higher for the facilities `uucp` or `news` to the file `/var/log/spooler`
`*.emerg        *`	Display any messages with a priority of `emerg` on the screen of all users who are logged in
`mail.*     /var/log/maillog`	Log all messages from the `mail` facility to the file `/var/log/maillog`
`*.emerg     @loghost`	Send all messages of priority `emerg` (from all facilities) to the `syslogd` daemon running on the computer named loghost

After changing the **`syslog.conf`** configuration file, you must tell **`syslogd`** and **`klogd`** to reread the configuration file, so that your changes to the file are implemented on your system. This is typically done by sending a "reconfigure" signal to the logging daemons. Several Linux daemons store their PID in files for occasions when you need to send a signal to the process. The following command shows you the PID of **`syslogd`**:

```
# cat /var/run/syslogd.pid
```

The following command shows you the PID of **`klogd`**:

```
# cat /var/run/klogd.pid
```

Use the PID returned by these commands with **`kill`** to send a **SIGHUP** signal to each daemon. This signal tells the daemon to reread its configuration files. You can also use single backward quotation marks to execute the **`cat`** command and insert the resulting text as a parameter for the **`kill`** command. (Be sure to use single backward quotation marks rather than forward marks.) The following command will cause **`syslogd`** to reread the **`syslog.conf`** configuration file:

```
# kill -HUP `cat /var/run/syslogd.pid`
```

Similarly, you can have `klogd` reread the configuration file using this command:

```
# kill -HUP `cat /var/run/klogd.pid`
```

Another acceptable method of restarting the logging daemons is to use the `killall` command with the name of the daemon, as these two commands show:

```
# killall -HUP syslogd
# killall -HUP klogd
```

Using the `logger` Utility

The `logger` utility lets you send a message to the `syslog` function, just as programs do. You can use the `logger` utility from a command line or from a script (as described in Chapter 11). You can use the `logger` command with just a message. For example, suppose you created a script to compress files automatically. The script could include a simple `logger` command like this:

```
$ logger Compression utility started
```

This would log the message using a default selector of **user.notice**. The message would be logged wherever the `syslog.conf` file had configured messages matching that selector (normally in `/var/log/messages`). Because no additional information is specified, the username of the user running the script is included in the log file as the program name providing the log message. The resulting log entry would look something like this (the timestamp, machine name, and username would differ on your system):

```
Oct 26 11:42:25 brighton rajw: Compression utility started
```

You can also specify other selectors with the `logger` command. For example, to log a message to the **mail** facility with a priority of **info** and the name of the compression script as part of the log file, use this command:

```
$ logger -p mail.info -t compressor Mail folders
compressed
```

This would log a message like the following:

```
Oct 26 11:46:13 brighton compressor: Mail folders
compressed
```

Analyzing Log Files

Log files require attention because they contain a valuable record of what has occurred on your Linux system. You can use the information in the log files to check for various problems, watch for intruders, and compute statistics about your system. At the same time, log files can become very large, eventually filling up the hard disk on a busy system.

10

A system administrator should regularly check log files for indications of trouble. By reviewing log files and locating problems before they become critical, you can save a great deal of time and expense troubleshooting and recovering from security breaches and program failures. As you review log files regularly, you become accustomed to what is normal and what is unexpected. Table 10-10 lists some sample log file entries with possible interpretations. For the sake of brevity, only the program name and message text are shown in the table; the timestamp and computer hostname have been removed from the log entries.

Table 10-10   Interpreting Sample Log File Entries

Sample log entry	System administrator considerations
`login: FAILED LOGIN 3 FROM (null) for nwells, Authentication failure`	Someone has tried to log in as user `nwells` and entered the wrong password three times in a row. If this happens repeatedly in a short period of time, someone may be trying to break in using that user account.
`login: ROOT LOGIN ON tty1`	Someone has logged in as root, but the timestamp (not shown here) indicates that the login occurred at 2 a.m. If no one is expected to be working at that time, an intruder may have access to the system.
`syslogd 1.3-3: restart`	The `syslogd` daemon was restarted. If you did not do this as system administrator, someone may have changed the logging configuration to try to circumvent a security check or cover a security break-in.
`kernel: eth0: NE2000 Compatible: port 0x300, irg 5, hw_addr 00:E0:98:05:77:B2`	The kernel successfully located the Ethernet card as the system booted. The parameters used to access the card are shown in the kernel log message.
`named[339]: Ready to answer queries`	The DNS server has successfully started and is able to respond to requests from clients to resolve domain names to IP addresses.
`modprobe: can't locate module block-major-48`	The `modprobe` command was unable to initialize a device. Some device on the system may not be configured properly.
`kernel: cdrom: open failed`	A user has tried to mount or access the CD-ROM device and either used an incorrect `mount` command or has made some other mistake. The user may need instruction in using the CD-ROM device.
`--MARK--`	The `syslogd` program has inserted a marker to indicate that a fixed amount of time has passed (20 minutes by default). This helps you determine how many messages are written to the log file in each period, but not all systems use this feature. (Red Hat, for instance, does not.)

You can use standard Linux tools like **grep** to search for information in the log files. For example, to search for all lines in **/var/log/messages** that contain the program name **login:**, use this command:

```
# grep login: /var/log/messages
```

You can also use special log management utilities that watch your log files for conditions that you specify and notify you via e-mail about problems. One of the better log management tools is LogSentry, a commercial product available from *www.psionic.com*.

Rotating Log Files

Over time, log files become too large to leave on your system. Part of every system administrator's job is to rotate the log files regularly so they can be reviewed and then archived or discarded. The process of **rotating log files** can include:

- Erasing old log files to free up disk space for new log information

- Compressing log files and storing them on an archive medium as a long-term record of system activity

- Renaming and compressing the log files so they can be studied at some future time

A common log rotation system stores log files for a month, with a separate archive file for each week. Your particular circumstances must dictate whether you use a separate file for each day, each week, or each month, and how many of those files you maintain. Log files are normally moved to another directory and often to another file system (another hard disk or hard disk partition) to free up space on the root partition.

For example, suppose you want to maintain four weeks' worth of archived data for the **/var/log/messages** log. Each Monday morning you would rotate the log files using this process:

1. Rename all old log rotation files. For example, **week4** is deleted, **week3** is renamed to **week4**, **week2** is renamed to **week3**, and **week1** is renamed to **week2**.

2. Rename the **/var/log/messages** file to **week1**.

3. Create a new file named **/var/log/messages** using the **touch** command (initially the file is empty).

4. Send the **syslogd** and **klogd** programs a SIGHUP signal so they will begin to use the new **/var/log/messages** file. (This signal causes them to "find" the inode for the new **/var/log/messages** instead of continuing to write to the previously valid inode, which is now your renamed **week1** file.)

10

You can create scripts to complete these tasks, but Red Hat Linux provides a utility called **logrotate** that will do all this (and more) for you. This utility is configured by default when you install Red Hat Linux 7.3 so that it runs weekly. The configuration file **/etc/logrotate.conf** defines how log files are rotated. This utility manages many types of log files, not just the system log. Specific instructions are included in separate files in the **/etc/logrotate.d** directory. Review the man page for **logrotate** if you want to modify the default configuration for your system. Other Linux distributions may not include **logrotate**, but often include similar utilities or scripts.

CHAPTER SUMMARY

- ❑ The **/proc** file system lets you view details about the kernel, running processes, and other system information.

- ❑ You can view process information using **/proc** or using a number of other utilities, such as **ps** and **top**.

- ❑ The **ps** command can display many different fields of information about each process, as determined by command-line options. You can also select which processes to display using command-line options.

- ❑ Each process in Linux is assigned a priority, called a nice level. You can raise the nice level to make a process run slower (be nicer to other processes). The root user can change the priority of any process; other users can raise the nice level of processes they have started.

- ❑ The **nice** and **renice** commands set a process's nice level; other command-line and graphical programs also let you change a process's nice level.

- ❑ The **top** command lists processes according to how much CPU time they are using. The output of **top** is updated every few seconds. **top** can also be used to control processes by sending them signals.

- ❑ KDE System Guard and the Gnome System Monitor are two powerful graphical process management utilities. Each displays many fields of information about each process and can be used to send signals to a process.

- ❑ The Gnome System Monitor also provides many memory management features, including the ability to view exactly how a single application is using RAM.

- ❑ Many system administrators like to display a small CPU load monitor on the Panel of their desktop so they can keep an eye on system load.

- ❑ Shared libraries let many Linux programs access the same programming functionality without loading it into memory multiple times.

- ❑ Dynamically linked applications use shared libraries; statically linked applications have a copy of the programming libraries they need built into the application itself.

- The Linux kernel moves data to and from swap space in pages—4 KB pieces.

- The `free` and `vmstat` commands display information about RAM and virtual memory usage.

- A system without sufficient RAM may experience thrashing as applications are repeatedly moved to and from swap space.

- Bottlenecks reduce system performance when one component, such as a slow network connection or disk drive, can't keep up with the rest of the system. Benchmarks can help identify bottlenecks.

- Log files record the activities of Linux programs. The main system log used by the kernel and many daemons is `/var/log/messages`.

- System and kernel messages are logged by the `syslogd` and `klogd` daemons using the configuration in `/etc/syslog.conf`.

- Each line in `syslog.conf` defines a set of messages and what action to take with those messages. Messages are defined using a selector, which is made up of a facility and a priority. The facility defines the type of program that generated the message; the priority defines the severity or type of message.

- Special characters in `syslog.conf` let you define multiple facilities or priorities, use multiple selectors, or implement other special features.

- The `logger` utility lets you send a message to the system logging daemon from any command line or script.

- Log files must be maintained by rotating them. This is typically done using the `logrotate` command. Analyzing log files can help a system administrator spot problems with security or performance.

10

KEY TERMS

`/proc` file system — A special file system that lets users view what the operating system kernel and other programs are doing.

action — A field in the `syslog.conf` configuration file that determines what to do with messages matching the selector on that line.

benchmark program — A program that provides a numeric measurement of performance for part of a system.

bonnie — A hard disk benchmarking program.

bottleneck — Part of a computer system that slows down completion of the task at hand.

buffer — An area of memory dedicated to holding the working data associated with a running program.

dynamically linked applications — Linux programs that do not include within themselves the library functions that they require to operate. The libraries must be installed (as shared libraries) on the Linux system on which the applications are executed.

facility — A category assigned to a system message, identifying the type of program providing the message. Facilities are used in `syslog.conf`.

file handle — An internal storage mechanism that allows a single file to be opened and used in Linux.

free — Linux command used to display the amount of free and used memory (physical and virtual), with basic information about how that memory is being used.

Gnome System Monitor — A graphical utility for the Gnome Desktop that is used to monitor and control processes running on Linux. Also called `gtop`. Similar to the `kpm` program for KDE.

KDE System Guard — A graphical utility that displays a process list and lets you interact with that list to rearrange or kill processes. Can be launched from the command line with the `kpm` command.

klogd — A daemon used to log kernel messages according to the configuration given in the `syslog.conf` configuration file.

log file — A file that contains detailed records of activity on a Linux system.

logger — A program that lets you send a message to the `syslog` function. Messages are written to the log files according to the configuration in `syslog.conf`.

logrotate — A program that manages the rotation of multiple log files at regular intervals according to the `logrotate.conf` configuration file.

message — A description of what is happening within a program.

messages — The main system log file in Linux, usually stored in the directory `/var/log`.

nice — A command used to set the nice level of a Linux process as it is being launched.

nice level — The priority level assigned to a Linux process.

page — A block of 4 KB of memory. A page is the unit of memory in which the Linux kernel moves data to and from swap space.

priority — (1) A value assigned to a process running on Linux that determines how much CPU time is granted to the process. (2) A label indicating the severity of a message submitted for logging. Priorities are used in `syslog.conf`.

renice — Linux command used to change the nice level of a Linux process that is already running.

rotating log files — The process of moving existing log files to another filename and location for archiving or review.

selector — A field in the `syslog.conf` file that determines what events are being logged. A selector is composed of a facility and a priority.

shared library — A single copy of a function library that has been loaded into memory for use by multiple dynamically linked applications.

SIGHUP — A signal sent to a logging daemon to instruct the daemon to reread its configuration files and the log file it writes to. Sometimes called HUP.

statically linked applications — Linux programs that include library functions in the program itself so that they are not dependent on the libraries loaded on the Linux system.

syslog.conf — The configuration file used to control how and where messages are logged by `syslogd` and `klogd`.

syslogd — The background program (or daemon) that manages all of the calls to the `syslog` function, writing log messages according to the `syslog.conf` configuration.

timestamp — The date and time when an event being logged occurred.

top — A command used to view the most CPU-intensive processes running on Linux at a given moment, along with related information for those processes.

vmstat — A command used to display detailed information about virtual memory usage.

REVIEW QUESTIONS

1. Although the `/proc` file system is not stored on a hard disk, it is called a file system because:

   a. It is accessed via a directory structure using standard commands that are also used for regular files

   b. It contains information about partitions, mount points, and hard disk devices

   c. The information from `/proc` can be stored on a hard disk using standard redirection operators

   d. Special utilities must be used to access the information contained in `/proc`

2. The command `ps -A xo comm` will display the following information:

   a. The command is invalid; it will display an error message.

   b. All processes started by the user who executes the `ps` command, with a standard set of fields pertaining to that user

   c. All processes running on the system; a revised nice value will be requested for each one that matches the string `comm`

   d. All processes running on the system, with the nice level and command-line fields displayed for each one

3. The _____ field in the `ps` command output defines how much cumulative CPU time a process has used since it was launched.

   a. `TIME`

   b. `%CPU`

   c. `RSS`

   d. `START`

10

4. The CMD field of the **ps** command output displays:

    a. The command used to start the **ps** command (including all **ps** command options applied to the current output)

    b. The command used to start the process shown on each line

    c. The last signal sent to control the process on each line

    d. The equivalent output from the **vmstat** command

5. Which of the following commands is invalid if run by a regular user?

    a. `renice -10 1035`

    b. `renice 10 1035`

    c. `vmstat 5`

    d. `renice 5 1035`

6. Which of these programs does not allow you to change the nice level of a running process?

    a. `gtop`

    b. `free`

    c. `kpm`

    d. `top`

7. To update the process data displayed by the **top** command, you would press which key?

    a. r

    b. spacebar

    c. u

    d. n

8. Dynamically linked applications are preferred for their better memory usage unless:

    a. Statically linked applications are also available

    b. Multiple users need to run the same application at the same time

    c. The necessary libraries to run the application are not installed on the Linux system

    d. The **free** command indicates that only virtual memory is available

9. Thrashing occurs when:

    a. An excessive amount of information is moved to and from the swap partition in a short time

    b. The **top** and **ps** commands both try to access process information at the same time

   c. Physical and virtual memory are deadlocked over where program data should be stored

   d. Multiple bottlenecks limit the speed of a Linux system

10. A bottleneck occurs in a Linux system when:

   a. The system administrator is not able to respond to all end-user requests in a timely fashion

   b. The `free` command indicates a shortage of physical memory

   c. One part of the system restricts adequate system performance because it cannot keep up with the demands of other system components and applications

   d. Multiple processes try to access the hard disk at the same time

11. The `bonnie` program is useful for determining which of the following?

   a. Hard disk performance data

   b. CPU speed benchmarks

   c. The balance of virtual and physical memory

   d. The status of information in the `/proc` file system

12. The command `vmstat 4` will do which of the following?

   a. List information on the process with PID of 4 if it is located in virtual memory.

   b. Set the default nice level for virtual memory processes to 4.

   c. Display continuous updates of the virtual memory status on a new line every four seconds.

   d. Start four instances of the virtual memory management module.

13. Log files are generally *not* used for which of the following tasks?

   a. Watching for security problems

   b. Calculating system usage statistics

   c. Calculating memory usage for applications

   d. Determining the cause of system failures

14. Given the log entry,

```
Oct 26 06:45:01 brighton httpd: Cannot determine local
host name
```

the word `httpd` refers to which of the following?

   a. The system name on which the event being logged occurred

   b. The program that generated the event being logged

   c. The daemon handling the logging of the event

   d. The configuration file used to control logging of this event

10

15. Explain the differences between the `syslogd` and the `klogd` logging daemons.

16. The `syslogd` and `klogd` logging daemons depend upon which configuration file?

    a. `logrotate.conf`

    b. `syslog.conf`

    c. They are internally configured and use no configuration file.

    d. The `syslog` function called by individual applications

17. A configuration pair consisting of a facility and a priority is called:

    a. An action

    b. The timestamp

    c. A selector

    d. A SIGHUP signal

18. If `*.info` appears in the log configuration file, the following will be logged:

    a. Messages from all facilities with a priority of `info` or higher

    b. Messages without a facility assigned with a priority of `info`

    c. Messages with a facility of `info` and any priority

    d. Messages from the `info` command that will be posted on the screens of all users who are logged into the system

19. Which of the following is not a valid facility name?

    a. `auth`

    b. `httpd`

    c. `user`

    d. `mail`

20. This configuration line

    `*.emerg   @brighton`

    will cause which of the following to occur?

    a. All messages with a facility of `emerg` are logged to a file matching the system name (the hostname).

    b. All messages with a priority of `emerg` or lower are logged to the file configured as an alias to `brighton`.

    c. All messages with a priority `emerg` are sent to the machine named `brighton` for logging.

    d. All messages of any priority but `emerg` are displayed on the screen of user `brighton`, if that user is logged in.

21. This configuration line

    ```
    *.info:mail,news.none:authpriv.none  -/var/log/messages
    ```

    is invalid because:

    a. A colon cannot be used to separate multiple selectors

    b. Each selector can only include one facility

    c. The `none` keyword cannot be used as a priority

    d. The hyphen can only be used in the action field when associated with a set of usernames

22. Describe why the system logging daemons must be reinitialized using a HUP signal in order to access new configuration files.

23. The `logger` utility does which of the following?

    a. Sends messages to the `syslog` function for logging according to the `syslog.conf` file

    b. Writes messages to `/var/log/messages`

    c. Rotates log files according to a predetermined configuration

    d. Restarts the logging daemons with a SIGHUP signal

24. Which of the following is a valid reason to rotate your log files?

    a. Leaving them open for long periods can cause file corruption.

    b. The files become too large to store permanently on the `root` partition.

    c. System administrators cannot study live log files.

    d. Security-minded individuals feel rotated log files are safer.

25. If you saw the message

    ```
    login: FAILED LOGIN 3 FROM (null) for rajw, Authentication failure
    ```

    you might reasonably assume any of the following *except*:

    a. Someone is trying to break into your system using the `rajw` account.

    b. User `rajw` has forgotten his password.

    c. The `login` program has become corrupted.

    d. A user on your system is trying to break into the files owned by `rajw`.

HANDS-ON PROJECTS

Project 10-1

In this project you use the Gnome System Monitor to explore different ways of viewing process information. The tasks shown in this activity could also be done using the `ps` command on any Linux command line, but the graphical interface provides a good way to interact with a large amount of system information without requiring you to memorize numerous command options. To complete this project you need Red Hat Linux 7.3 installed with the Gnome Desktop.

1. Log in to Linux and start Gnome.

2. Start a program that you can monitor. On the Gnome main menu, choose **Programs**, then **Utilities**, then **Simple Calculator**.

3. Launch the Gnome System Monitor by entering the command `gtop` or selecting the program from the Gnome menu by choosing **Programs**, **System**, **System Monitor**. The main window of the System Monitor utility appears.

4. Click **View** on the menu bar and select **Only TTY Processes**. This limits the list of processes to those associated with one of the Linux terminals. Can you identify some processes that are removed from the list when you choose this option?

5. Click **View** and select **Only TTY Processes** again to deselect that option. Click **View** again, then click **Hide System Processes**. How would you describe the process list now?

6. Deselect the **Hide System Processes** item on the View menu so that all processes are listed.

7. Open the Preferences dialog box by selecting **Preferences** on the Settings menu.

8. Select the **Process Fields** tab in the Preferences dialog box.

9. Check the **NI** field box so that the nice level of each process is shown. Click **OK** to close the Preferences dialog box.

10. The calculator that you started in Step 2 is called `gcalc`. Locate that process in the list and right-click on it.

11. Click **Renice** in the pop-up menu that appears.

12. Raise the nice level of that process to 20 with the slider bar and click **OK**. You see the new nice value in the NI field. The field displays 19 because internally, nice values are represented from -19 to +19.

13. Right click on **gcalc gedit** and choose Memory Maps. In the dialog box that appears, select the Graphical memory map tab.

14. View the components of `gcalc`. What do you notice about them?

15. Close the dialog box and exit the Gnome System Monitor. Close the `gcalc` application and log out.

Project 10-2

In this project you track the status of the virtual memory (swap space) as you work with several applications. Normally you will not track virtual memory this carefully as you personally work with applications. Instead, you will have the easier job of watching the system-monitoring tools while other users are working with the programs. To complete this project you should have an installed Linux system. The Mozilla browser is used in the steps that follow, but you can substitute any large program on your system.

1. Log in to your Linux system and start the graphical system.

2. Open a command-line window.

3. Enter this **vmstat** command in interactive mode to display an updated status line once every two seconds:

   ```
   $ vmstat 2
   ```

4. Open Mozilla. You may also choose to open Netscape Communicator by choosing **Programs**, then **Internet**, then **Netscape Communicator** on the Gnome main menu.

5. Watch the values in the **vmstat** output change as the browser program starts. Which fields do you see changing? Do you see any changes that indicate a potential bottleneck on your system if many copies of this program were started at the same time?

6. Open a second terminal emulator window and enter the following command to see the physical and virtual memory information, updated once every two seconds:

   ```
   # free -s 2
   ```

7. Start another large program, such as a second copy of Mozilla or Netscape, the Gnumeric spreadsheet, or the Abiword word processor (both located under Programs, Applications on the Gnome menu).

8. Watch the values in the output of the **free** command change. Do the values in **vmstat** change as well? What additional information can you see in the **vmstat** output? If you opened a second copy of Mozilla or Netscape, how do the shared libraries used by the two copies of the same program affect the memory usage when you started a second copy?

9. Click on one of the command-line windows (where you are running **vmstat** or **free**) to activate the window. Then press **Ctrl+C** to end the output of the command displayed in that window. Enter the command **top** and review the output to see which processes are currently swapped out (stored on the swap partition). The letter **W** in the **STAT** column indicates that a process is swapped out.

10. As you read the output of these system administration tools, what can you conclude about how these tools affect system performance? What comments would you make about the value of using graphical system-monitoring tools such as those mentioned in this chapter? Close all open windows and log out.

Project 10-3

In this project you watch the system log file as new messages are written to it by the **syslogd** daemon. To complete this project you need a Linux system with a graphical interface.

1. Log in to Linux as root and start the graphical environment.

2. Open two command-line windows.

3. In one of the windows, enter this command to display the last 15 lines of the system log file, updating the display every few seconds.

   ```
   # tail -f /var/log/messages
   ```

4. In the second window, enter this command to restart the `syslogd` daemon:

   ```
   # killall -HUP syslogd
   ```

   Notice that a message is added to the first window stating that the `syslogd` program was restarted.

5. In the second window, enter `killall -HUP crord` to restart the scheduling daemons. Were any messages added? Are any copies of `httpd` running on your system? How can you check?

6. Leave the first window open for a few minutes as you work on your system, opening other applications or browsing the Web. Are additional messages written to `/var/log/messages`? Can you interpret the messages?

7. Close all open windows and log out.

Project 10-4

In this project you use the `logger` command to send a message to `/var/log/messages`. To complete this project you need a Linux system with a graphical interface.

1. Log in as root and start the graphical environment.

2. Open two command-line windows.

3. In one of the windows, enter this command to display the last 15 lines of the system log file, updating the display every few seconds:

   ```
   # tail -f /var/log/messages
   ```

4. In the second window, enter this command:

   ```
   # logger -p user.info -t TESTING This is a logging test.
   ```

5. Notice the message that is added to the `/var/log/messages` file shown in the first window.

6. Using the facility and priority names you have learned, try sending one or two other messages using the `logger` program. In particular, try sending a message with the priority `emerg`. For example, you might use this command:

   ```
   # logger -p user.emerg -t TESTING Emergency message test.
   ```

   What do you notice about how this command is treated compared to the other `logger` commands you entered? Can you explain why, based on the information in the `syslog.conf` file?

7. Close all open windows and log out.

CASE PROJECTS

In your recent project for McKinney & Co. in Cylonica, the Linux servers sometimes slowed down inexplicably. You have decided to do some research back in your office to see if you can determine possible causes.

1. The servers were running Red Hat Linux 7.3 with Gnome. The Nautilus program is the default file manager/browser/document viewer for Gnome. Use the Gnome System Monitor to locate the process or processes for this program. Then use the Memory Map option with the Automatic update option selected while you experiment with Nautilus to see which components of this massive program use the most memory. (If you can identify what aspects of the program are most resource intensive, you may be able to find another tool to use for that task.)

2. You are also concerned that the hard disks you installed are a bottleneck—they can't respond in time to requests from the busy server. What utilities have you learned about that will help you check this theory? Which simple command-line tool includes information related to hard disk data transfer speed? What other programs could you download to test the speed of your hard disks? What will you do if the hard disks are indeed the bottleneck?

3. The Web servers used in your project rely on database programs that feed them information. The data is requested using scripts that you have written to query the databases and return results as Web pages. What technique could you use to track exactly which queries are being used most frequently? You need a technique that doesn't slow down the system by pausing, or require that you sit in front of the computer watching a screen listing of activities. When you decide on the technique, write a few sample command lines that you will use and a sample configuration file line that will enable the commands to work.

10

11

USING ADVANCED
ADMINISTRATION TECHNIQUES

**After reading this chapter and completing the exercises,
you will be able to:**

♦ Create shell scripts using basic shell programming features

♦ Automate one-time and repetitive tasks using at and crontab

♦ Reconfigure the Linux kernel

In the previous chapter you learned about managing processes, memory, and log files using a variety of command-line and graphical tools. You learned how to discover the status of those resources and watch for potential problems that might limit the productivity of end users on your system.

In this chapter you learn about three advanced administration techniques. First, you learn how to create basic Linux programs called shell scripts (you have seen shell scripts mentioned in many previous chapters). Second, you learn how to use the **at** and **crontab** commands to automate repetitive tasks. Your system already uses these utilities to manage several background tasks such as log rotation; now you'll see how to use them for any task you choose. Finally, you learn how to reconfigure the Linux kernel, creating a new kernel from source code using easy-to-use graphical tools.

WRITING SHELL SCRIPTS

As a Linux system administrator, you often enter a series of commands in a shell to accomplish an administrative task. In many cases, the commands you enter are identical—or nearly so—to commands you have recently entered. You can automate the process of entering frequently used commands by creating a shell script. A **shell script** is an executable file containing lines of text as you would enter them at a command line, including special commands to control the order in which lines in the file are executed. To execute the commands in a shell script, you simply execute the shell script.

 A shell script is like a batch file in DOS or Windows. Batch files in DOS or Windows end with the file extension .BAT, for example, AUTOEXEC.BAT. The capabilities of shell scripts, however, go far beyond those of batch files.

Shell scripts are used in every Linux system. The following list describes a few examples of shell scripts discussed in preceding chapters:

- The system initialization scripts in the `/etc/rc.d` subdirectory (such as `rc` and `rc.local`)

- The scripts in `/etc/rc.d/init.d` that start system services (such as a Web server)

- The `/etc/profile` and `/etc/bashrc` scripts that Linux executes each time you log in

- The scripts that the X Window System uses to launch initial graphical programs (for example, `/etc/X11/xinit/xinitrc` and `/etc/X11/xdm/xsession`)

All of these functions could be implemented using standard Linux programs, as described in the next section, rather than using shell scripts. But shell scripts have two advantages for you as a system administrator. First, they let you study what is happening on the Linux system because you can view the contents of the scripts that control various system services. Second, you can change the way anything on the system occurs simply by altering the relevant shell script.

Interpreting and Compiling Programs

Before you can create shell scripts, you need to be familiar with some basic programming concepts. There are two basic types of computer programs: interpreted programs and compiled programs. Both are written using a computer language. A **computer language**, or **programming language**, is a set of words and syntax rules that can be arranged in predefined ways to cause a computer to perform tasks defined by the person using the language. The words used in a computer language are often called **keywords**, because they have special meanings when used within a computer program. For example, later you will learn the keyword `for`, which defines certain actions when used in a shell script.

A software developer or programmer writes a computer program using a computer language, storing the keywords and related programming in a file. This file is called the program's **source code**. The keywords that make up the computer language are human readable, though you must be familiar with the computer language to understand what the program does. The computer cannot act directly on the keywords of the computer language. The keywords must first be converted to numeric codes that the computer's CPU can process. The collection of numeric codes is called the **binary file**, or **executable file**. To use a program, the user runs the appropriate executable file.

The process of converting computer language keywords into computer-readable numeric codes can occur in two ways:

- When the computer language is a compiled language, the source code is converted to a binary file immediately after the programmer writes the source code. The binary file is given to people who want to use the program. (Linux and related programs are unusual in that the source code is *also* available, but few people need to access it.) A **compiled language** is one for which the source code is converted to a binary file before the program is run by users. A **compiler** is a special program that converts the source code of a compiled language into a binary file.

- When the computer language is an **interpreted language**, the source code is converted into numeric codes at the instant a user runs the program. This conversion takes place each time the user runs the program. The source code is given to people who want to use the program. The user running the program must have an **interpreter** to convert the source code of an interpreted language into numeric codes.

Because conversion to numeric codes in an interpreted language takes place during program execution, interpreted languages are much slower than compiled languages.

A shell script is an **interpreted program**, that is, a program written in an interpreted language. The commands that you learn in this chapter are part of the interpreted language for the `bash` shell. The shell is the interpreter that acts on the keywords that you include in shell scripts. All of these keywords can also be used at the shell prompt. Thus, a script is a text file that can be interpreted or executed by another program. (Several interpreters besides the shell are mentioned at the end of this section.)

Understanding Programming Concepts

Writing a shell script, though not overly difficult, is really computer programming. In order to write effective shell scripts, knowledge of a few programming concepts is helpful.

A computer program is executed one command at a time. Execution normally proceeds from the first line of the program to the last. Each command within the program is also called a **statement**. A statement is often a single keyword, but a statement can also be a group

11

of keywords and other elements that the computer language syntax requires or allows to be used together. One such keyword, described later in this chapter, is `if`. You can never use the `if` keyword without also using two other keywords: `then` and `fi`.

The real power of a computer program lies in its ability to decide which parts of the program to execute based on factors that the program itself examines. For example, if you make a shell script that retrieves a stock price from the Web, you could cause the script to execute one set of statements if the stock price is over a certain value, and another set of statements if the price is below that value. This is done with a selection statement. A **selection statement** lets a computer programmer determine which parts of a program will be executed according to values that are determined as the program is executed. Using a selection statement means that all lines in a shell script will not necessarily be executed when the script is run—the results of the tests in the selection statements determine which steps are executed. Figure 11-1 illustrates a selection based on the results of a test.

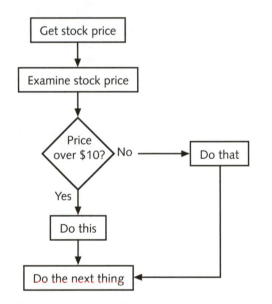

Figure 11-1   A selection statement chooses among alternative actions

Most shell scripts include selection statements. They can be very complex, with many options, or very simple, with only a simple test such as "if this number is 4, do this; otherwise, don't." The tests performed in shell scripts (and in any computer programming language) only have two possible outcomes (values): true or false. You must design your script to respond to these two possible values. Tests used in a shell script usually check the status of a file or the value of an environment variable. They are not designed for mathematical computations, though you can perform math functions using Linux commands within the script.

A selection statement is used to determine whether part of a computer program should be executed. A **loop statement** is used to determine whether part of a computer program should be executed more than once. A loop statement has several parts:

- A counting variable, which is assigned a different value each time the loop is repeated; the counting variable is often called the **index** of the loop, because it tracks how many times the loop has executed a list of statements

- A list of values that should be assigned to the counting variable

- A list of statements to be executed each time through the loop

Figure 11-2 shows an example of a loop in which several files in a list are to be compressed. (This example does not use shell script keywords, only descriptive text to help you understand how a loop operates.) Each of the files is named as part of the loop statement. The counting variable is assigned the value of a different filename each time through the loop.

Collect filenames (`file 1`, `file 2`, `file 3`)
Repeat block once per file

Block ──────▶ | Compress file |

Counting variable updated on each repetition

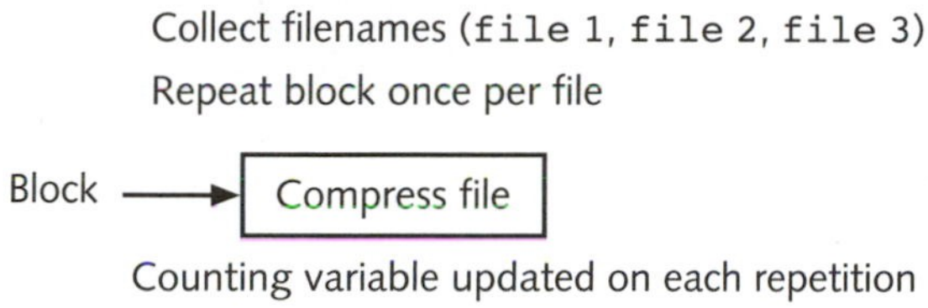

Figure 11-2   A loop repeats a block of statements

With both selection statements and loops, you define a list of statements that are executed once, many times, or not at all depending on what happens when the selection or loop statement is executed. The list of statements controlled by a selection or loop statement is often called a block, or a **statement block**. The statement block in Figure 11-2 is the single item, "Compress file." Statement blocks often contain many statements. They can even contain other selection and loop statements. **Nesting** is a programming method in which one selection or loop statement contains another selection or loop statement.

Components of a Shell Script

You can create a shell script in any text editor, including **vi**, **emacs**, or a graphical editor within KDE or Gnome. Any text file that adheres to three basic rules is considered a shell script:

- The first line of the text file must indicate the name of the shell (or other program) that should be used to interpret the script.

- The text file must have the execute file permission set for the user, group, or other category (whichever you want to be able to run the script, as you learned in Chapter 4).

- The text file must contain valid commands that the interpreter can recognize.

A shell script is sometimes called a shell program. The process of writing a shell script is also called shell programming, because you must adhere to a shell's programming syntax.

When you execute a shell script, you are launching a program. The program just happens to be contained in a human-readable text file rather than a binary file. But to the shell, launching a shell script and launching a program such as StarOffice both require a similar process. In order for the shell to identify a text file as an executable script, the execute file permission must be set. Both of the following example commands allow anyone to execute the script `stock_quote` (remember, you must be the file's owner or root to change file permissions):

```
chmod ugo+x stock_quote
chmod 755 stock_quote
```

After using either of these **chmod** commands, the file permissions for the file look like this, indicating to the shell that the file can be executed as a program:

```
rwxr-xr-x
```

One difference between launching a shell script and launching a program like StarOffice is that the shell must start another program to interpret the shell script. This is why the first line of the shell script must contain the name of the interpreter that will execute the script.

When you execute a shell script by entering the script name at a shell prompt, the shell examines the first line of the file and launches the interpreter named there, with the file you indicated as a parameter. If you are running the **bash** shell and launch a shell script that requires **bash**, the shell starts a second copy of **bash** to execute the shell script.

The format of the first line of a shell script consists of a hash mark (#), followed by an exclamation point, followed by the complete path to the interpreter. For example, the first line of a script written for the **bash** shell looks like this (the path shown is the standard on most Linux systems):

```
#!/bin/bash
```

Conversely, the first line of a shell script written to be executed by the TC shell looks like this:

```
#!/bin/tcsh
```

 If you don't include the name of the interpreter on the first line of a script, your default shell will try to execute the script itself. This can generate unexpected results if you created the script to run under a different shell or programming language.

Many of the script examples in this chapter use the **echo** command. The **echo** command prints the text that you enter after the **echo** command to the STDOUT channel—to the screen unless output has been redirected. For example, to print the message "Hello world" to the screen, you would use the command **echo Hello world**. If the text after the **echo** command includes special characters, such as (or *, you should enclose the text in quotation marks so the shell does not try to give the character a special meaning. Suppose you created a file named **testscript** containing the following lines (you could do this in any text editor):

```
#!/bin/bash
echo This is a sample shell script.
```

 It doesn't matter what filename you use for your shell scripts. You can use any filename and any file extension, so long as you adhere to the three rules listed previously.

To test a new script, enter the name of the file as a command at a Linux command line. Use a period and a backslash (**./**) before the filename to tell the shell that the file is located in the current directory rather than in a directory that is part of the PATH environment variable. For example:

```
$ ./testscript
```

After you enter **./testscript** at the command line, the following steps occur:

1. The shell you are working in looks at the first line of the **testscript** file and sees **#!/bin/bash**.

2. The shell you are working in launches a new **bash** shell with the filename **testscript** as a parameter. In effect, the shell executes this command for you:

```
bash ./testscript
```

3. The new copy of **bash** loads the **testscript** file and executes each of the lines in the file as if they had been entered at a shell prompt, printing output from commands on the screen.

4. When the new copy of **bash** reaches the end of the **testscript** file, it exits, returning control of the screen to the shell from which the shell script was originally launched.

The sections that follow describe how to create shell scripts based on **bash** shell programming syntax. As you will recall from Chapter 6, other shells use different programming syntax rules. **bash** shell programming is more common than other types of shell programming on Linux systems, but note that the shell you are working in and the shell used to execute a script can be different.

Suppose, for example, that you prefer to work in the TC shell because of its interactive shell features, but you want to execute a shell script written for **bash**. This is fine, so long as the first line of the script contains `#!/bin/bash` and `bash` is installed on your system. As in Step 2 above, the TC shell would launch a copy of the `bash` shell in order to execute the shell script. When the shell script finished, the `bash` shell would exit, and you would again be working in the TC shell.

Creating a Simple Shell Script

Some Linux commands are used mostly within shell scripts. This section describes some of these commands and explains how you can use them within simple shell scripts. For example, consider the following sample shell script contained in a file named `clean`:

```
#!/bin/bash
find /home —name core —exec rm {} \;
du /home >/tmp/home_sizes
```

The purpose of the second line of this script is to locate and remove all files named `core` within all users' home directories. In the third line, the `du` command creates a summary of the size of every subdirectory under `/home`, storing that information in a file named `home_sizes`. This script is not long, but the commands are somewhat complicated. By storing these lines in a script, you can execute both complex commands by entering one simple script name, for example:

```
./clean
```

 The files named `core` that the preceding script finds are produced when a Linux program ends unexpectedly. A developer can use the `core` file produced by a program to determine why a program ended. The `core` files can be quite large and are not needed unless someone is troubleshooting a recurring problem, so deleting any `core` files on the system saves disk space.

The script above doesn't produce any output on the screen. All of the commands in the script work directly with files. Other scripts write information to the screen or require input from the keyboard to process the statements in the script. The following script, called `filesize`, uses the `read` command. The `read` command causes the shell to pause for a user to enter information at the keyboard. The information entered is assigned to a variable provided with the `read` command.

```
#!/bin/bash
echo Enter a filename to process:
read THEFILE
echo The number of lines in $THEFILE is:
wc —l $THEFILE
echo The number of words in $THEFILE is:
wc —w $THEFILE
echo End of processing for $THEFILE
```

You have learned previously about environment variables. You can create your own variables to store values within a script. You can define a variable by simply assigning a value to a name that you choose. For example, including this line in a script defines a new variable named MYFILE and assigns it a value of index.html:

```
MYFILE="index.html"
```

The previous script used a variable with the **read** command. This command causes a script to pause for keyboard input. The text that a user enters at the keyboard is assigned as the value of the variable given in the **read** command. Once a value is assigned to a variable using either of these methods (a direct assignment or using a **read** command), the script can refer to the variable in other commands. In the example script just referred to, the script references the variable THEFILE as it executes the **wc** command.

If the above script were stored in a file called **filesize**, any user with execute permission to the file could launch the script using this command:

```
./filesize
```

The output from the **filesize** script is shown here. The script pauses after displaying the first line of this output so that the user can enter a filename. The filename shown (**report.txt**) would be entered by the user running the script.

```
Enter a filename to process:
report.txt
The number of lines in report.txt is:
    453 report.txt
The number of words in report.txt is:
    3215 report.txt
End of processing for report.txt
```

Although the **read** command is useful for collecting input from a user, you should make sure your scripts test the validity of values entered by the user. For example, if the user running the **filesize** script entered a filename that did not exist on the system, the other commands in the script (the **wc** commands in this example) would generate error messages. Later in this chapter, you will learn how to create scripts that can test values entered by the user.

Because scripts use standard Linux commands that write information to the screen, they can also use the Linux redirection operators to change the flow of information to and from commands. As you learned in Chapter 7, you can use redirection operators to change how the standard input and standard output for any command are treated. For example, suppose you start the **filesize** script using this command:

```
./filesize > /tmp/output
```

Because of the > redirection operator, all of the data that would normally be written to the screen is instead written to the file /tmp/output. When you view the contents of the /tmp/output file, you see exactly what you would have seen on-screen if you ran the **filesize** command without a redirection operator.

11

You can use any of the Linux redirection operators (<, >, >>, <<, or |) in conjunction with shell scripts. By using these operators, you can treat a shell script as you would treat any regular Linux command, using pipes to connect scripts with other commands, storing script output to files, and so forth. You will see other examples of using redirection operators later in this chapter.

Using Variables in Scripts

The `filesize` sample script in the previous section used a variable to store information entered by a user. A variable used in a shell script in this way is sometimes called a **shell variable**, though shell variables and environment variables are essentially the same thing. Shell variables are usually defined by a person writing a shell script; environment variables are predefined by scripts that came with the operating system or by programs running on Linux. When you define a variable within a shell script, you will often want to **initialize** the variable by assigning it a value such as zero or "" (an empty string).

As you write shell scripts, you are likely to refer to many variables. For example, a command in your shell script may need to copy a file into the home directory of the user running the shell script. To do this, you can refer to the `HOME` environment variable. The following sample command copies the file `report.txt` to a user's home directory:

```
cp /tmp/report.txt $HOME
```

Instead of the `HOME` environment variable, you could use the following command in the script, but this type of command only works if user `rajw` is running the script.

```
cp /tmp/report.txt /home/rajw/
```

By using the `HOME` environment variable, you ensure that the script works for any user who launches the script. As a system administrator, you should use techniques like this to create shell scripts that are as flexible as possible. This allows the scripts to be used safely by different system administrators and users. Not all users can execute every script, however. Some scripts access parts of the system that only the root user can access. If another user runs such a script, an error will occur; even if the user has execute permission on the script file itself, he or she may not have permission to access the files that the script tries to access.

Shell scripts often use special variables called positional variables. Rather than taking on a value assigned to it within the script, a **positional variable** takes a value based on the information that the user includes on the command line. If the `filesize` script shown earlier incorporated a positional variable, the user could enter the filename at the command line with the command to execute the script. For example, the user would enter the following command to process the file `report.txt`:

```
./filesize report.txt
```

Within a script, you indicate positional variables using a dollar sign and a number. The notation $0 indicates the first item on the command line (the script name: ./filesize in the example above). A $1 indicates the second item on the command line (report.txt in the example above). A $2 indicates the third item on the command line, and so forth. To incorporate a filename entered at the command line as data within a script, you could rewrite the filesize script as shown here. As you compare this script with the previous version, notice that the read command is not used. Instead, the user executing the script must provide a filename on the command line. The shell assigns the filename on the command line to the variable $1 as it starts the script. The $1 positional variable is used in place of the THEFILE variable throughout the script.

```
#!/bin/bash
echo The number of lines in $1 is:
wc -l $1
echo The number of words in $1 is:
wc -w $1
echo End of processing for $1
```

When working with positional variables, it's helpful to know how many items the user running the script has included on the command line. For example, you may want to include commands to verify that the correct number of items is included on the command line before having the script proceed. Each time you execute a script, the shell defines a special variable called $# that contains the number of items on the command line used to execute the script. Later you will learn how to test the value of $# to determine how many items a user provided on the command line when the script was launched. The following version of filesize reports the value of $# but does not alter its action based on that value:

```
#!/bin/bash
echo The script you are running is $0
echo The number of filenames you provided is $#
echo The number of lines in file $1 is:
wc -l $1
echo The number of lines in file $2 is:
wc -l $2
echo The number of lines in file $3 is:
wc -l $3
echo The number of lines in file $4 is:
wc -l $4
```

Suppose you launched the script above with this command:

```
./filesize data1 data2 data3 data4
```

The shell assigns the name of the script—the first item on the command line—to the positional variable $0. The shell also assigns the filenames included on the command line to the positional variables $1, $2, $3, and $4, respectively. Finally, the shell assigns the value of 4 to the $# variable (which you see on the third line of the script) because the command line used to execute this script contains four items besides the name of the script.

11

The output of the script would look like this (depending on the size of the data files):

```
The script you are running is filesize
The number of filenames you provided is 4
The number of lines in file data1 is:
123
The number of lines in file data2 is:
11241
The number of lines in file data3 is:
2321
The number of lines in file data4 is:
3159
```

Positional variables are a useful way to provide information to the commands in a script. But the previous example expected precisely four filenames. We can make a more flexible script by testing the value of a variable and taking action based on the results of the test.

Using `if/then/else` Tests

A **test** is a type of selection statement that lets you determine if a condition is true or false. For example, you could test:

- Whether a filename entered by a user or included on the command line actually exists
- Whether two numeric values are identical
- Whether a file is empty
- Whether the number of parameters on the command line is correct, so the script can function as intended

A test statement uses a rule to examine a file or variable, returning a result of true or false. The script chooses which commands to execute according to the test result. The **if** command introduces a test in a shell script. An **if** command must be followed by a **then** command, which lists the commands to be executed if the test succeeds (returns a value of true). The **fi** command marks the end of the **if** statement. When the **if** test succeeds, all the commands between **then** and **fi** are executed. When the test fails, none of those commands are executed. The **test** command evaluates parameters you provide and returns either true (a value of 1) or false (a value of 0). The results of the **test** command are evaluated by the **if** command. An example of an **if** command used with a **test** command is shown here (the parameters after **test** are described shortly):

```
if test $1 -eq report
```

Instead of the **test** keyword, you can use square brackets around the parameters of the test, followed by a semicolon, like this:

```
if [ $1 -eq report ];
```

Figure 11-3 shows conceptually how an `if/then` statement is organized.

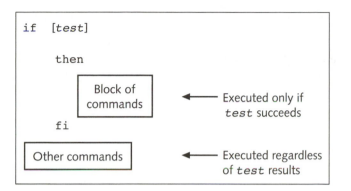

Figure 11-3 Structure of an `if/then` statement

Each test includes either one or two items being tested and a test operator that defines what aspect of the item you want to test. Table 11-1 lists the test operators available in `bash`.

Table 11-1 File-Testing Operators in the `bash` Shell

Test operator	Description
-d	Test whether the item is a directory name
-e	Test whether the filename exists
-f	Test whether the file exists and is a regular file
-h or -L	Test whether the file exists and is a symbolic link
-r	Test whether the file exists and is readable
-w	Test whether the file exists and is writable
-x	Test whether the file exists and is executable
-lt	Test whether the numeric variable on the left (of the operator) is less than the numeric variable or value on the right
-gt	Test whether the numeric variable on the left (of the operator) is greater than the numeric variable or value on the right
-le	Test whether the numeric variable on the left (of the operator) is less than or equal to the numeric variable or value on the right
-ge	Test whether the numeric variable on the left (of the operator) is greater than or equal to the numeric variable or value on the right
-eq	Test whether the numeric variable on the left (of the operator) is equal to the numeric variable or value on the right
-ne	Return a value of true if the numeric variable on the left (of the operator) is not equal to the numeric variable or value on the right

11

An **if/then/else statement** is another kind of selection statement. It specifies that if a test returns a value of true, then one set of commands should be executed; if a test returns a value of false, then another set of commands should be executed.

The **else** command extends the capability of an **if/then** statement by adding a block of commands that are *only* executed if a test returns a value of false (that is, if the test fails). You can use an **else** command only as part of an **if/then** statement. The structure of an **if/then/else** statement is shown in Figure 11-4. Notice especially that the **else** block of commands is skipped if the test returns a value of true.

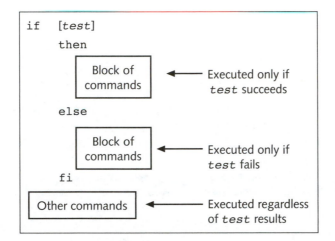

```
if    [test]
    then
        ┌─────────────┐
        │ Block of    │  ◄──── Executed only if
        │ commands    │         test succeeds
        └─────────────┘
    else
        ┌─────────────┐
        │ Block of    │  ◄──── Executed only if
        │ commands    │         test fails
        └─────────────┘
    fi
┌──────────────────┐
│ Other commands   │  ◄──── Executed regardless
└──────────────────┘         of test results
```

Figure 11-4   The structure of an `if/then/else` statement

The following sample statement shows how **if/then/else** is used. As with a simpler **if/then** statement, the **fi** keyword ends the entire statement. The commands between **then** and **else** are executed only if the test succeeds. The commands between **else** and **fi** are executed only if the test fails. Commands after **fi** (none are shown here) are executed regardless of the results of the test.

```
if [ -f /etc/smb.conf ];
    then
            echo The Samba server appears to be configured.
    else
            echo The Samba server cannot be started.
    fi
```

The indentation of lines using tabs and spaces is a convention designed to make the script easier for a person to read. Tabs and spaces included in a program are called **white space**. White space between commands or lines has no effect on a shell script's operation.

The **exit** command stops the execution of a script immediately. The **exit** command is often included within an **if/then/else** statement, but it is executed only if certain conditions exist as determined by the test within the statement. For example, "Test whether file X exists. If it does not exist, print an error message and exit; if it does exist, continue with other commands."

 A **comment** is a line within a script that is not processed by the shell, but is only included to help someone reading the file understand the purpose of the script or how it functions. To include a comment, begin a line with a hash mark, #. (The first line of a script that begins with #! is a special case and is not a comment.)

The following script includes a test using the **–ne** (not equal) operator within an **if/then** statement to determine whether the **$#** variable has a value of 2 or not. This script includes several comment lines. You should include numerous comments to help other system administrators understand the scripts you write (and to remind yourself how and why you created a script when you review it months later).

```
#!/bin/bash
#
#   Script to add a user for database access
#   Requires a username and database table name on the command line
#   Created 20 April 2003; Nicholas Wells; nwells@xyz.org
#
if [ $# -ne 2 ];
then
        echo You must provide a username and a database table name.
        exit
fi
# Begin processing: Store command line parameters in shell variables
DB_USER=$1
DB_TABLE=$2
```

If you review the scripts in /etc/rc.d/init.d, you will see complex test expressions using multiple environment variables. Studying these scripts is a good way to learn about shell scripting, though you may not immediately understand everything you see. Refer to the **bash** man page to learn about more advanced types of tests available for shell scripts.

Adding Loops to a Script

A loop statement causes a block of commands to be repeated a certain number of times or until a condition is met. You can define several types of loops in **bash** shell scripts.

The **for** command creates a **for loop**, which repeats a statement block once for each item in a list. You can include a list of items when you write the script, or you can design the loop so that the list items are provided on the command line when the script is executed.

The syntax of the `for` command is shown here. The keywords `for`, `in`, `do`, and `done` are all part of a `for` loop:

```
for <counting variable> in <list of items>
do
        <statement block>
done
```

The <statement block> is executed once for each item in <list of items>. Each time through the loop is called an **iteration**. The <counting variable> is assigned the value of the next item in the <list of items> each time the <statement block> is executed—each iteration. The **do** and **done** commands are keywords used to begin and end a statement block within a `for` loop (and in other places, as you'll see).

The <list of items> can be, among other things, any of the following (an example of the first line of a `for` loop is shown for each):

- Numbers: `for COUNT in 1 2 3 4 5 6 7`
- Words: `for NAME in george ali maria rupert kim`
- A regular expression used to match filenames: `for db_filename in *c`
- The special variable `$@`, described below: `for db_filename in $@`

When you use a regular expression (like `*c`) as the <list of items> in a `for` loop, the shell replaces the regular expression with all matching filenames. Using the example of `*c`, the shell will substitute all the filenames in the current directory that end with the letter *c*. This substitution occurs before the shell executes the `for` loop.

A special variable used in `for` loops is `$@`. This variable contains all the parameters that were included on the command line when the script was executed. If you include a regular expression on the command line, such as `*txt`, the shell finds all matching filenames and includes them as part of `$@` when the script is executed. By using `$@` as the <list of items> in a `for` loop, you automatically include all items from the command line.

The following example script shows a `for` loop that compresses each filename given on the command line:

```
#!/bin/bash
for i in $@
do
     gzip $i
done
```

Suppose the above script was stored in a file called `squash` and you started the script using the following command line:

```
./squash phoebe.tif charon.tif europa.tif
```

The `for` loop would execute the commands between **do** and **done** (the `gzip` command in this example) three times, once for each filename on the command line. The counting variable $i takes the value of each of the three filenames in turn during the three iterations through the statement block enclosed by do and done.

A second type of loop uses a test like an if/then statement. As long as the test returns a value of true, the statement block within the loop is executed again and again. As soon as the test returns a value of false, the loop exits. You use the **while** command to create such a loop. The syntax of a while loop is shown here. The three keywords while, do, and done must be used together:

```
while <test>
do
        <statement block>
done
```

A while loop uses the same tests as an if/then statement. Consider, for example, the following while loop:

```
DB_FILE=""
while [ ! -f $DB_FILE ];
do
        echo Please enter the database file to archive:
        read DB_FILE
done
```

First, the **DB_FILE** variable is initialized as an empty string. This prevents the **while** loop from behaving unexpectedly the first time the variable is tested. The loop then begins by testing whether the filename defined by **DB_FILE** exists. This test uses the **-f** operator to test whether a file exists, and a **!** character to reverse the result of the test. You could read this test as "while not DB_FILE exists," or "As long as the filename stored in DB_FILE doesn't exist." While this condition is met, the statement block between **do** and **done** is executed, requesting a filename from the user.

The logic behind this loop is that we want to make sure the user enters a valid filename before the script continues and tries to use that file. The loop will repeat the statement block indefinitely until the user enters a valid filename.

   You normally exit any script by pressing Ctrl+C.

Other Scripting Methods

You have learned the basics of creating shell scripts, but many other types of scripts are used in Linux. The statements in a shell script must follow specific syntax rules for tests, loops, and so forth. Other types of scripts are written using different computer languages and interpreted by different interpreters (rather than the **bash** shell). The specific syntax rules a script must follow depend on the interpreter that will execute the script.

Different scripting languages are used for different purposes. As you learn more about the types of scripts available, you can decide which type is best suited for a given programming task.

Table 11-2 lists popular scripting languages used in Linux. An interpreter for each of these languages is included in most Linux distributions. Many books are available to teach you how to write programs using these scripting languages.

Table 11-2   Popular Scripting Languages

Language	Comments
perl	Used extensively to process data on Web servers. Very popular and well-known. See *www.perl.org*.
Awk	Used for system administration work, often processing text files in conjunction with the `sed` program (see Chapter 6). The most widely used version of the `awk` interpreter used on Linux is the `gawk` program from the GNU project. Enter `man awk` to learn more.
Tcl/Tk	A popular language for creating graphical applications. See *www.scriptics.com*.
Python	A more recently developed language, popular for creating graphical programs. Used by Red Hat Software to create many system administration utilities in Red Hat Linux. See *www.python.org*.
PHP	A very popular server side scripting language used for managing dynamic content on a Web site. See *www.linuxdocs.org/HOWTOs/PHP-HOWTO.html* or *www.php.org*.

By convention, scripts often use standardized file extensions to help users identify them. For example, perl scripts often end in `.pl`, Python scripts in `.py`, and Tcl/Tk scripts in `.tcl`. These file extensions are for convenience, however, and don't affect the interpreters' ability to run the script. The next two sections describe some of these scripting languages in more detail.

perl Scripts

perl is a programming language developed by Larry Wall, a famous free software developer. perl is especially well suited to processing text strings and was very popular for years as a tool for managing data submitted by Web page forms. When you submitted information through a Web page, a perl script on the Web server examined your input and returned a new Web page based on it. Although many Web servers now use PHP or specialized Web programs like ColdFusion, perl remains a reliable workhorse in this area.

 The first line of a perl script typically includes the following line, though the exact location of the perl interpreter varies on some Linux distributions:
`#!/usr/ bin/perl`

perl scripts and scripts written in other languages interact with Web servers using a communication standard called the **Common Gateway Interface**, or **CGI.** CGI uses the standard input and standard output channels to permit communications between two programs. These steps outline how a perl script and a Web server interact using CGI:

1. A user running a Web browser enters data in a form, such as the user's name and e-mail address.

2. The browser sends the user's data to a Web server running on Linux.

3. The Web server starts a perl script designed to process the data from the form.

4. The perl script retrieves the form data submitted by the browser and acts on it (perhaps adding it to a file or sending an e-mail to the user).

5. The perl script creates a customized response for the user based on the data that the user entered and writes that response text to standard output.

6. The Web server collects all the output of the perl script and sends it back to the browser as a document.

The interaction between the perl script and the Web server in Steps 5 and 6 unfolds according to the standards of CGI. By using CGI standards, the Web server can rely on standard communication channels as a gateway between two programs. Other methods of processing Web server data can provide higher performance because they do not require launching a separate perl interpreter. But CGI allows a Linux Web server to communicate with any other Linux program.

Scripts for Graphical Programs

Scripting languages like Tcl/Tk and Python let you create graphical programs that include dialog boxes and menus. Creating graphical programs in a scripting language is easier than using a compiled language like C or C++, but interpreted graphical programs execute much more slowly.

Tcl/Tk is a scripting language developed by John Ousterhout. The name Tcl/Tk stands for *tool control language/toolkit*. The word *toolkit* refers to the graphical toolkit, a set of programming functions that you can use within Tcl/Tk scripts to create graphical interfaces. (Tcl/Tk is often referred to as "tickle-tee-kay.")

Scripts written in Tcl/Tk are executed by an interpreter called wish. The first line of a Tcl/Tk script includes a line like this (depending on how your Linux distribution is configured):

```
#!/usr/bin/wish
```

The **Python** scripting language uses the same Tk graphical programming toolkit as Tcl. Python is an object-oriented language, meaning that parts of a Python program can be reused in another program with minimal effort. Python was developed by Guido van Rossum. You can use either Tcl/Tk or Python to create powerful and complex graphical program scripts. Figure 11-5 shows an example of a graphical program written in Python.

11

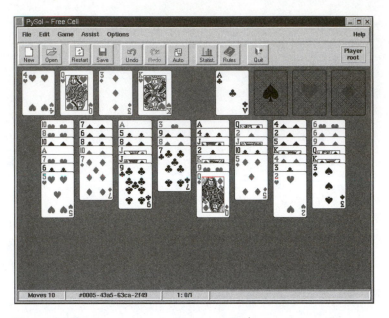

Figure 11-5 A program written as a Python script

AUTOMATING TASKS WITH `at` AND `crontab`

Scripts are not the only way to automate a series of commands in Linux. This section describes other tools that let you define a task and have it execute automatically, either when you are doing other work on the system or when you are away from the system (such as in the middle of the night).

The **at** command lets you define one or more commands to be executed at some future time. The **crontab** command lets you define one or more commands that will be executed repeatedly at intervals that you designate. The **at** command relies on a daemon called `atd`; the `crontab` command relies on a daemon called **crond**. Both of these daemons are started by the standard system initialization scripts located in `/etc/rc.d/init.d`. Each of these programs (`atd` and `crond`) checks once per minute to see whether any scheduled tasks should be executed.

A scheduled task is often called a job. The terms **at job** and **cron job** refer to commands or scripts that you have scheduled to be executed at a specific time using the **at** or **cron** commands, as described in the sections that follow.

Automating One-Time Tasks

Sometimes you would like to perform a task automatically at some future time. For example:

- You need to start a backup operation after all employees have left for the evening.

- You want to start a large database query during lunch, but you need to leave the office early.

- You need to remind several users on the network (and yourself) of a 3:00 meeting.

In each of these cases, you can use the `at` command to schedule the task for future execution.

Using the `at` Command

To automate a task with the `at` command, you can either enter commands directly at the command line, or you can list them in a file. For complex tasks that require several commands, it's best to list them in a file so you can review them carefully before scheduling them using the `at` command.

After you create a list of commands to execute in a file, you can schedule execution using this syntax:

```
at -f <filename> <time specification>
```

For example, suppose you created a file called **usage_report** containing the following lines:

```
logger Starting du to create disk usage report on /home
du /home > /var/log/du_report
logger Completed disk usage report
```

If you want these commands to execute at 11:30 p.m., you would enter this command:

```
at -f usage_report 23:30
```

Note   When you give a filename to the `at` command, the file should not be a shell script (it should not begin with `#!/bin/bash`). Each of the lines in the file will be executed as if you had entered it at the shell prompt.

The `atd` daemon will check once per minute for any jobs that have been scheduled using the `at` command. At 11:30 p.m., the job scheduled by the command above will be executed. Any results from the command (that is, text that would normally be written to the screen) will be e-mailed to the user who scheduled the `at` job. In this example, the commands in **usage_report** do not generate any screen output—it has been redirected to a file.

The time specification in the `at` command is very flexible. You can include a standard 24-hour format, such as 23:30 in the previous example; but you can also include items such as the words `now`, `minutes`, `hours`, `days`, or `months`. You can include the words `today`, `tomorrow`, `noon`, `midnight`, and even `teatime` (4:00 p.m.). Table 11-3 shows several examples of specifying a time with the `at` command.

Table 11-3   Example Time Specifications Using the `at` Command

Time specification	Description
`at -f file now + 5 minutes`	Execute the commands in `file` five minutes after the at command is entered
`at -f file 4pm + 5 days`	Execute the commands in `file` at 4:00 p.m., five days from now
`at -f file noon Jul 31`	Execute the commands in `file` at noon on July 31
`at -f file 10am 08/15/03`	Execute the commands in `file` at 10:00 a.m. on 15 August 2003
`at -f file 5:15 tomorrow`	Execute the commands in `file` at 5:15 a.m. tomorrow

Here are some points to remember about specifying times within the `at` command:

- Each item in the time specification is separated by a space.
- You cannot combine multiple phrases (such as 4 hours and 25 minutes).
- When you use the word `now`, it should be the first word of the time specification.
- When a specific clock time is used (such as 11:00), the command file will be processed the next time the system clock reaches the indicated time. For example, if it is currently 9:00 a.m. and you want to schedule a task for 11:00 a.m. tomorrow, you must indicate `tomorrow` in the time specification or the task will be executed at 11:00 a.m. today (because 11:00 a.m. has not occurred yet today).
- If the `at` command cannot understand the time specification, you see a message stating `Garbled time`, and the command is not accepted for processing.

When you enter an `at` command with a valid filename and a valid time specification, you see a message like the one shown here:

```
warning: commands will be executed using /bin/sh
job 9 at 2003-10-21 05:15
```

The job number and the time displayed depend on the state of your Linux system. This message reminds you that the commands in the file will be executed using the `/bin/sh` program. (On most Linux systems this is another name for the `bash` shell.) It also indicates the exact date and time when the commands will be executed.

Using at Interactively

To use the at command as shown in the preceding section, you must prepare a file containing the commands you want to execute. If you prefer, you can enter commands at the shell prompt instead of preparing a separate file in advance. The only disadvantage of entering commands interactively is that you cannot alter a command after it has been edited; you would have to cancel the at job and re-enter it.

To use the at command interactively, simply omit the **-f filename** portion of the at syntax. For example, you could enter a command such as this:

```
at now + 5 hours
```

When you press Enter after typing such a command, you see a special prompt: at>. At this prompt you enter the command that you want the atd daemon to execute (5 hours from now, in this example). You can enter multiple commands, one after another. You can also enter shell programming commands. For example, you can enter if/then statements or for loops, as described earlier in this chapter. Suppose, for instance, that you entered a for loop that uses the mail command to e-mail a short list of text files. Your screen would look like this after you had entered all of the lines of the for loop:

```
# at now + 5 hours
at> for file in *.txt
at> do
at> mail -s "File $file" tomr < $file
at> done
at>
```

After entering all the commands that you want the atd daemon to execute, you indicate that you have finished by pressing Ctrl+D. This key combination sends a special character that signifies the end of your input. You see <EOT> on the last line containing the at> prompt, followed by a message indicating the job number and time that the atd daemon will execute the command.

When you enter a series of commands at the at> prompt, any results that would have been displayed on-screen when the commands are executed are e-mailed to you, just as they are when you specify a command file using the **-f** parameter. The e-mail message that the atd daemon sends you has a subject such as "Output from your job 11," where the number at the end of the message is the job number assigned by at when you finished entering commands at the at> prompt.

Your Linux system must be turned on at the time an at job is scheduled to run. For example, if you schedule an at job to run in four hours, but your computer is not turned on in four hours, the command will not be executed then (obviously), nor will it be executed when the system is turned on again. The atd daemon does not check for commands that should have been executed previously but were not.

Sometimes you want the output from a command to appear on-screen instead of being e-mailed to you. For example, if you need to send yourself a reminder, having it sent to e-mail won't be much help. If you remember to check for the e-mail message, you'll remember the event you were to be reminded of. As an alternative, you can use the `tty` command to send output from a command to the location where you are currently logged in. The `tty` command returns the name of the terminal device that you are currently working in. For example, if you have logged in on the first virtual console of a Linux system and you enter the command `tty`, you see the device name `/dev/tty1` displayed on-screen. You can use the output of this command to redirect output of a command that you submit to the `at` command. For example, suppose you submitted the following command as an `at` job (notice that the `tty` command at the end of this command is enclosed in single backward quotation marks):

```
echo Go to your 401k meeting in conference room 6! > `tty`
```

When the `atd` daemon processes this line, the `tty` command is executed first, and the output from the `tty` command (such as `/dev/tty1`) is substituted for the `` `tty` `` text. The `echo` command then sends the line of text to the terminal where you are working (such as `/dev/tty1`). Any error messages will still be sent to standard output (and thus e-mailed to you). You can also redirect the Standard Error channel using this format:

```
echo Go to your 401k meeting in conference room 6! 2>&1 > `tty`
```

The Standard Error channel is channel number 2. The above statement redirects channel 2 to channel 1, which is Standard Output. Standard Output is then redirected to the device name given by the `tty` command: the device where you are logged in.

If you are working in multiple graphical terminal windows, the `tty` command may not allow the `atd` daemon to send the output to the precise window in which you are working.

Using the `batch` Command

A command similar to the `at` command, and which also relies on the `atd` daemon, is the `batch` command. Rather than running commands at a specified time, the **batch** command runs your commands when the system load average drops below 0.8. (You can see the system load by using the `top` command.) If you enter multiple commands at the same time using the `batch` command, to avoid overloading the system the `batch` command only starts one command at a time. The `batch` command is useful for times when you want to run a CPU-intensive or time-consuming program but the system is currently very busy with other tasks. In this case, you can use the `batch` command to enter the name of the program you want to run. As soon as the system is no longer so busy, the command will be executed. As with the `at` command, the results of commands run by `batch` are e-mailed to you.

For example, suppose you need to start a time-consuming task such as reconfiguring the Linux kernel using the `make` command (as described in the next section). You could enter the `batch` command as shown below. Notice that no time parameters are included; the commands run as soon as the system load permits. You can include the `-f` option with the `batch` command, or just use the command name and then enter commands at the `at>` prompt, as you would when using the `at` command.

```
# batch
at> cd /usr/src/linux
at> make dep; make clean; make bzImage
at><EOT>
```

As with the `at` command, you press Ctrl+D when you have finished entering the commands you want `batch` to process. As soon as the load on the system is small enough, `batch` executes the commands you entered.

Automating Recurring Tasks

You can use the `crontab` command to execute commands automatically at regular intervals. You might use `crontab` when you need to regularly:

- Create a list of files that have not been accessed in a long time to check whether they can be deleted or archived.

- Create a backup copy of all active files (those recently accessed).

- Compile a list of all directories on the system, sorted by size, to help you identify areas that are using a lot of hard disk space.

- Remove core files or other unused files that are using a lot of hard disk space.

- Delete files in the `/tmp` directory that have not been used recently.

- Rotate log files to keep them from becoming too large.

- Run security scanning software (for example, check e-mail attachments for viruses or search system log files for multiple login failures).

- Store the results of the `ps` or `df` command to make a snapshot of the system's state at different times.

Many Linux distributions include a simple method of automating tasks that doesn't require you to use the `crontab` command. In Red Hat Linux 7.3, the `/etc` directory contains subdirectories named `cron.hourly`, `cron.daily`, `cron.weekly`, and `cron.monthly`. You can place a file in any of these subdirectories. The commands in that file will be executed hourly, daily, weekly, or monthly, depending on which directory you place the script in. This does not let you specify a precise time for your script, but most system administration tasks don't require a precise execution time; often the important thing is not running them during the work day when most systems are busy with other tasks.

11

The files you place in the `cron`-related subdirectories of `/etc` can be either shell scripts (with `#!/bin/bash` as the first line), or lists of commands as you used with the `at` command.

Every Linux system should include an `/etc/crontab` file, which shows the format of a standard entry for the `crontab` command. The `/etc/crontab` file in Red Hat Linux 7.3 is shown here. This example file uses a special script called **run-parts** that is provided with Red Hat Linux 7.3.

```
SHELL=/bin/bash
PATH=/sbin:/bin:/usr/sbin:/usr/bin
MAILTO=root
HOME=/

# run-parts
01 * * * * root run-parts /etc/cron.hourly
02 4 * * * root run-parts /etc/cron.daily
22 4 * * 0 root run-parts /etc/cron.weekly
42 4 1 * * root run-parts /etc/cron.monthly

0-59/5 * * * * root /usr/bin/mrtg /etc/mrtg/mrtg.cfg
```

In this `/etc/crontab` file:

- The **SHELL** variable defines which shell the **crond** daemon will use to execute the commands and scripts listed in the file.

- The **MAILTO** variable defines which user on the Linux system will receive an e-mail message containing the output from all **cron** jobs defined in the file.

- The **HOME** and **PATH** variables define a working directory and the directories where system commands are located. These variables will be used by all commands and scripts listed in this file (and hence by all scripts in the **cron.daily** through **cron.monthly** subdirectories).

- The lines that end with the names of the subdirectories (such as **cron.daily**) include the username root. All of the **cron** jobs that you place in the **cron.daily** and related directories will be executed via the root user account. They are executed by an administrative utility called **run-parts**, which is only used within this file.

If you want to specify an automated task more precisely than just placing a script in a directory such as `/etc/cron.daily`, you can create your own **cron** job similar to those listed in `/etc/crontab`. The flexibility of **crontab** can make it challenging to use, however.

The /etc/crontab file in Red Hat Linux 7.3 includes numbers and asterisks that define when the commands on that line (run-parts for most of /etc/crontab) will be executed. Each crontab specification begins with five fields, described here as they appear on each crontab line from left to right:

- *Minute of the hour:* This field can range from 0 to 59.

- *Hour of the day:* This field can range from 0 to 23.

- *Day of the month:* This field can range from 0 to 31, but be careful about using the days 29, 30, or 31: nothing will happen in the month of February; and nothing will happen in February, April, June, September, or November if you use 31.

- *Month of the year:* This field can range from 0 to 12. You can also use the first three letters of a month's name (in upper- or lowercase).

- *Day of the week:* This field can range from 0 to 7 (0 and 7 are both Sunday; 1 is Monday). You can also use the first three letters of a day's name (in upper- or lowercase).

The crond daemon examines all five of these fields once per minute. If all five fields match the current time, crond executes the command on that line. Using an asterisk in a field means "execute this command no matter what the current value of this field is." In order for the command to be executed, all five fields must match the current time and date. For example, based on the following time specification, crond will run the command on this line at 10 minutes after every hour, every day. The specification is not limited by certain days of the week or month.

```
10 * * * * du /home > /tmp/disk_usage
```

 If you do not include a username after the time specification, crond will execute the command as whichever user submits the cron job. Only root should bother including a username, since regular users can't submit a job to be run as another user.

Based on the following time specification, crond will run the command on this line on the first day of every month at 2:15 in the morning:

```
15 2 1 * * du /home > /tmp/disk_usage
```

Any field can contain multiple values, either separated by commas (without spaces after the commas) or defined by ranges with a hyphen separating them. For example, this time specification will cause cron to execute the command on this line on the 1st, 10th, and 20th of every month at 1:00 a.m.:

```
0  1 1,10,20 * * du /home > /tmp/disk_usage
```

To view examples and learn more about forming complex time specifications for use with `crontab`, view the man page for the `crontab` configuration file by entering `man 5 crontab`.

To use `crontab` to submit your own `cron` jobs, you create a file that has a time specification and a command to execute. Unlike the `at` command, you must create a file containing this information; you cannot enter `cron` job commands interactively. Suppose, for example, that you wanted to run the `du` command on `/home` and sort the results every morning at 1:00 a.m. You would do this by following these steps:

1. Create a text file containing the time specification and the command you want to execute. For this example, the file would contain the following line (you would need to submit this `cron` job as root so that the `du` command could access all home directories):

   `0 1 * * *  du /home | sort > /root/disk_usage`

2. Submit the file to the `crond` daemon using the `crontab` command. If the file you created in Step 1 were called `du_nightly`, the command would look like this:

   # crontab du_nightly

Notice that the file created in Step 1 does not include the `#!/bin/bash` information, as a shell script would. Also, the command shown in Step 1 fits on a single line.

If you need to perform more complex tasks, you can create two files: a shell script and a `cron` job specification. You cannot use multiple command lines within a single `cron` job specification.

Suppose, for example, that you had developed a series of shell scripts that check the security of the Linux system by reviewing log files, checking network activity, and watching user login activity. If the script that performed all of these activities were called `secure_system`, you could run that script every morning at 1:30 a.m. by adding this line to your `du_nightly` file before submitting the file using the `crontab` command:

   `30 1 * * * /sbin/secure_system`

The full pathname of the script is included so that the `crond` daemon is able to locate the script when it attempts to execute this job.

In the `/etc/crontab` file shown previously, you saw environment variables at the beginning of the file. You can also include environment variables in `crontab` specification files that you create. For example, suppose you want the `du_nightly cron` job to be executed via the root user account so that it can access all home directories, but you want an e-mail message sent to your regular user account so you won't have to log in as root to read the message. To do this, you can include a MAILTO variable at the top of the du_nightly file. The du_nightly file now looks like this:

```
MAILTO=nwells
0 1 * * *  du /home | sort > /root/disk_usage
30 1 * * * /sbin/secure_system
```

You can learn about other environment variables supported by the crontab command in the crontab man page. You can also use the –u option to submit a cron job as another user if you are logged in as root. For example, you could submit the du_nightly job as user jtaylor using this command:

```
crontab -u jtaylor du_nightly
```

Managing Automated Tasks

After you have submitted commands for future execution using at or crontab, you can view what commands are waiting to be executed and delete them if necessary. You must be logged in as root to manage at jobs and cron jobs that you did not submit. The root user can submit jobs as any user (using the –u option shown previously) and can also view or modify jobs submitted by any user on the system.

Checking the Status of Jobs

The two daemons atd and crond are started when you boot Linux using standard service scripts in /etc/rc.d/init.d. You can use those scripts to stop and restart the daemons if needed, but because these daemons carefully check the dates on files to see when new cron jobs have been submitted, you should never need to restart the daemons.

All of the commands that you submit using at or crontab are stored in a subdirectory of /var/spool. Jobs submitted using at are stored in the /var/spool/at directory; jobs submitted using crontab are stored in the /var/spool/cron directory. The two types of jobs are stored differently, however. Jobs for the atd daemon contain all the environment variables and related information that the shell needs to execute the at job, independent of any other process. cron jobs store a more limited amount of information because they are executed in an environment that the crond daemon defines for the user who submitted the cron job.

Suppose you enter a single du command using the at command. When you enter this command, it might appear on-screen like this:

```
# at now + 10 minutes
at> du /home > /tmp/du_save
at> <EOT>
```

If you view the contents of the /var/spool/at directory, you see a strange filename such as a0000d00f08407. This filename is generated automatically by the at command. Looking at the contents of this file, you will see a number of environment variables. These

11

variables record the state of the shell in which the command was entered via the `at` command. This allows the same shell environment to be duplicated when the command is executed at a later time. The last line of the file is the command that will actually be executed at the specified time.

The information in the `/var/spool/at` directory does not, however, indicate the time when the command will be executed. Because of the complicated format of these files and their interaction with the `atd` daemon, you should not directly modify files in the `/var/spool/at` directory. Instead, use the `atq` and `atrm` commands to manage `at` jobs that are awaiting execution.

The `atq` command lists all queued `at` jobs—jobs awaiting execution by `atd`. For each job, this command lists a job number and the date and time when the job will be executed:

```
# atq
6     2003-08-15 10:00 a root
9     2003-12-21 05:15 a root
12    2003-12-31 11:45 p root
```

 You can also use the `at` command with the `-1` option (for *list*) to see the same output as the `atq` command.

Use the `atrm` command to cancel a command that you have submitted using `at`. You can also use the `-d` option (delete) with the `at` command to remove a job from the list of pending `at` jobs. To use either `atrm` or `at` `-d`, you must include the job number. You obtain the job number using `atq` or `at` `-1`. For example, to remove job 11, you could use either of these commands:

```
# atrm 11
# at -d 11
```

You can use a similar set of commands to manage `cron` jobs. To begin with, you'll notice that files stored in `/var/spool/cron` are different from files stored in `/var/spool/at`. The `/var/spool/cron` directory contains a single file for each user who has submitted jobs using `crontab`. For example, if you have submitted a job using `crontab` while logged in as root, the file `/var/spool/cron/root` exists. If you submitted a job using `crontab` while logged in as `jtaylor`, the file `/var/spool/cron/jtaylor` exists. The file in `/var/spool/cron` that is named for your username contains a composite of all `cron` jobs that you have submitted. For example, when you have submitted a single `cron` job, the file looks something like this:

```
# DO NOT EDIT THIS FILE - edit the master and reinstall.
# (secure_cron installed on Mon Oct 20 18:12:16 2003)
# (Cron version — $Id: crontab.c,v 2.13 1994/01/17 03:20:37 vixie
  Exp $)
30 1 * * * /sbin/security_scan
```

As with the contents of the `/var/spool/at` directory, you should not directly edit a `crontab` file in `/var/spool/cron`. Instead, use the options provided by the `crontab` command, as summarized here:

- `crontab -l` lists `cron` jobs for your user account.

- `crontab -r` removes your `crontab` file. Use this option carefully, as it removes the entire file; any `cron` jobs you have submitted are lost.

- `crontab -e` opens your `crontab` file in a text editor, so you can make changes in the times or commands defined for your `cron` jobs. It's important that you use the `-e` option on the `crontab` command rather than using a regular editor session (such as `vi /var/spool/cron/jtaylor`) to change your `crontab` file. Using `crontab -e` prevents file locking conflicts that would cause problems with the `crond` daemon.

Controlling Access to at and crontab

The default settings on most Linux systems allow any user to submit commands for future execution using either `at` or `crontab`. You can restrict access to `at` and `crontab` so that only certain users can use these commands. The files that enforce this control are:

- `/etc/cron.allow`: Contains usernames (one per line) that are allowed to use the `crontab` command

- `/etc/cron.deny`: Contains usernames (one per line) that are not allowed to use the `crontab` command

- `/etc/at.allow`: Contains usernames (one per line) that are allowed to use the `at` command

- `/etc/at.deny`: Contains usernames (one per line) that are not allowed to use the `at` command

 On some Linux systems, the files listed above may be located in the `/var/spool/cron` and `/var/spool/at` subdirectories, in which case they will be named simply `allow` and `deny`.

On most Linux systems, none of these four files exists, meaning that any user can use both `at` and `crontab`. (On some systems, however, having none of these files may mean that only root can use `at` and `crontab`.) When you attempt to use the `at` or `crontab` command, the command checks the permission files in the following order:

- If the `/etc/cron.allow` file exists, a user must be listed in that file in order to use the `crontab` command. The same rule applies to `/etc/at.allow` for the `at` command.

- If the `cron.allow` (or `at.allow`) file does not exist, but the `cron.deny` file does exist, any user listed in `cron.deny` (or `at.deny`) cannot use the `crontab` command (or the `at` command).

By controlling access to the `at` and `crontab` commands on a busy Linux system, you can make it more difficult for regular users to consume system resources when you need to do system administration work or schedule business-critical tasks.

MODIFYING THE LINUX KERNEL

A standard Linux kernel such as the one installed as part of Red Hat Linux 7.3 provides many popular features and support for many types of hardware. Red Hat Software and other vendors configure the available features of the kernel to appeal to a broad collection of users. You can add features to the kernel by inserting kernel modules, as you learned in Chapter 4. But some kernel features are not available as modules; you can only use them if they are configured when the kernel is compiled from source code.

It's unusual that you would need to recompile the Linux kernel. Some situations that might require it include:

- You want to activate a feature that the Linux kernel includes but that is not activated in the default kernel from your Linux vendor. For example, you might want to activate experimental networking features that cannot be added as modules.

- You want to disable a feature that is part of the default kernel but which you don't need. For example, knowing that you do not have any SCSI devices, you might decide to remove all support for SCSI devices in order to make your kernel smaller.

- You need to compile support for a hardware device into the kernel rather than loading it as a module.

- You want to use an updated version of the Linux kernel to add new features or fix a security problem that was discovered with your current version.

For any of these reasons, you can recompile the Linux kernel from source code, creating a new kernel. The file **vmlinuz** contains the Linux kernel. It is usually located in the **/** directory or in the **/boot** directory.

Creating a new kernel involves three steps:

1. Make certain the kernel source code and supporting packages are installed on your system.

2. Configure which features you want the new kernel to have.

3. Execute the commands to compile the source code with the features you selected.

Installing Kernel Source Code

Before recompiling the kernel, you must have several packages installed on your system, such as the source code itself, the compiler, and numerous supporting packages. In Red Hat Linux 7.3, the source code is in a single (large) rpm named **kernel-source**. You can use the **rpm** command with the **-q** option to see if this package is installed:

rpm —q kernel-source

If this package is not installed, you can use the **rpm** command to install it, but you will probably see that other supporting packages are needed before you can install the **kernel-source** package. Use the **rpm** command to install those additional packages as directed, then install the **kernel-source** package.

 By far the easiest way to install the kernel source code is by selecting Kernel Development as an option when you install Red Hat Linux 7.3. This option with its supporting packages requires about 600 MB of disk space.

Once the source code is installed, you can explore the source code files in the directory **/usr/src/linux-2.4**. When you recompile the source code to create a new kernel file, you are not changing the version of the kernel. You are only changing the features that are activated in the kernel. After you recompile the kernel, the timestamp on the kernel you create will be different than the kernel that was installed by default on your system.

Configuring Kernel Features

The Linux kernel supports hundreds of different options. The kernel source code package includes several different utilities to help you configure which options you want to include in the kernel you are creating.

Three utilities are available. All of them create or edit the **.config** file in **/usr/src/linux-2.4**. The data in this file is based on your selections in the configuration utilities, as well as information stored in the **configs** subdirectory (**/usr/src/linux-2.4/configs**). Each of the configuration files is used for a different type of system; the configuration utilities detect the type of CPU you have and use the appropriate configuration file. The three utilities are:

- **config**: A text-only question and answer session
- **menuconfig**: A text-mode menu-based program
- **xconfig**: A graphical program

You launch each of these utilities using the **make** command. The **make** command is a programming utility that uses instructions in a configuration file (called **Makefile**) to execute a series of instructions. By using the name of a kernel configuration utility after **make**, you tell **make** which part of the **Makefile** to use for kernel configuration. You

11

must be in the source code directory (`/usr/src/linux-2.4`) before using the `make` command. Then use one of these three commands to launch the configuration utility:

```
# make config
# make menuconfig
# make xconfig
```

After entering any of these commands, you see a number of strange lines of text scroll up your screen as the `make` command starts a compiler to prepare the configuration utility you have requested.

Figure 11-6 shows the text-mode questions presented by `make config`. This mode is useful for advanced users because you can use input redirection (the < operator) to feed configuration options to the configuration program. Most users, however, will not want to use this utility.

Figure 11-6   The `config` utility for setting kernel options

All three kernel configuration utilities provide access to exactly the same options; they simply give you a different interface to those options.

Figure 11-7 shows the text-mode menu-based configuration tool `menuconfig`. Use the arrow keys and other keys as directed in this interface to select kernel features that you want to activate. Over 1,000 options are available in the 2.4 kernel. One advantage of this interface is that you can use it when you don't have the X Window System installed.

Figure 11-7   The `menuconfig` utility for setting kernel options

Figure 11-8 shows the graphical configuration tool `xconfig`. Both `menuconfig` and `xconfig` include help buttons. These buttons next to each option provide a description of that option, with a recommendation for when you might use the option and when you should avoid it. The help text for all three utilities is identical.

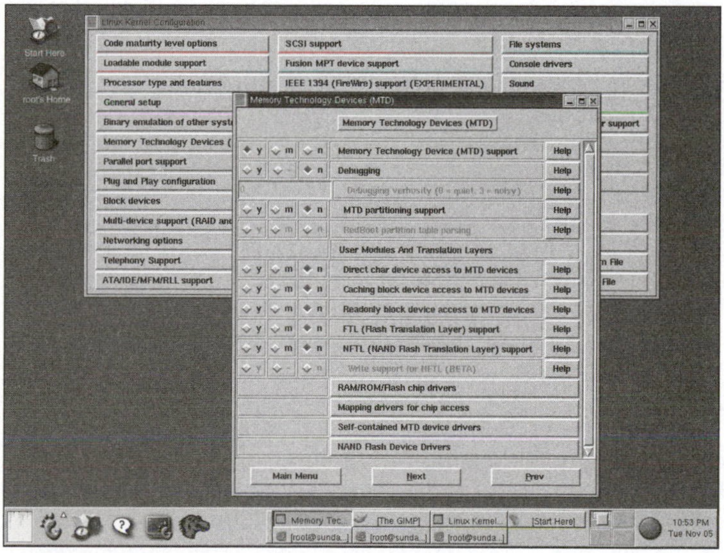

11

Figure 11-8   The `xconfig` utility for setting kernel options

Beyond its appearance, the `xconfig` utility is a good choice for learning about kernel compilation because of how it displays options. Many kernel features can be either built-in (compiled into the kernel itself) or built as modules (which you can load into the kernel at any time). The advantage of modules is that you can have hundreds of features available and only use those you decide you need later on. The advantage of building in features is that you don't have to worry about managing modules to get a feature activated. Beyond that, some features can only be built-in. For example, the `ext3` file system must be compiled into the kernel; it cannot be built as a module. Such relationships between kernel components may be easier to see in the `xconfig` interface.

Even if you do not need to recompile your kernel, exploring the kernel features and reading the help text in the `xconfig` program is an excellent way to learn about Linux capabilities. Many help screens also include Web URLs to direct you to additional information on relevant topics.

When you exit `config`, `menuconfig`, or `xconfig`, the utility saves any changes you have made to the configuration file. If you decide you want to revert back to the original configuration of your current kernel, enter this command from within `/usr/src/linux-2.4`:

```
# make mrproper
```

Compiling a New Kernel

After selecting a new kernel configuration, you are ready to compile the kernel source code into a new kernel file that you can use to boot your system. To do this, you execute a series of `make` commands that prepare all the source code files and then compile them into a kernel image. You also compile and install new modules for the new kernel as a separate operation. Running all of these commands requires between 30 minutes and 3 hours, depending on the speed of your system. They are often placed on the same command line, separated by semicolons, so you can enter one command line and return to your computer after all the commands have completed. A typical command string is:

```
# make dep; make bzImage; make modules; make modules_install
```

You can also use `make bzdisk` in place of `make bzImage` to create a boot disk containing the new Linux kernel. This is a safe way to experiment with new kernels because your original kernel remains intact: you can try the new kernel by booting from a floppy disk, or eject the disk and return to your default kernel. The default configuration of the kernel is too large to fit on a floppy disk, however. You will need to deactivate several features if you want to experiment with boot disks.

The `make bzImage` command creates a compressed kernel image called `bzImage` in the directory `/usr/src/linux-2.4/arch/i386/boot`. To use that kernel, you should make a backup copy of your current kernel in `/boot`, then copy the `bzImage` file to `/boot`. In Red Hat Linux 7.3, the `/boot/vmlinuz` file is a symbolic link to

`/boot/vmlinuz-2.4.18-3`, so you can use the following commands to set up the new kernel:

```
# cd /boot
# cp /usr/src/linux-2.4/arch/i386/boot/bzImage ./vmlinuz-new
# ln —s vmlinuz vmlinuz-new
```

When you reboot your system, the new `vmlinuz` file will be used. After rebooting, execute the `uname —v` command to see the timestamp of the kernel you are running.

> Recompiling the kernel *can* be much more complicated than what we've outlined here. For further study, refer to the README file in `/usr/src/linux-2.4`, the help screens within the configuration utilities, and the copious documentation provided in `/usr/src/linux-2.4/Documentation` and on *www.linuxhq.com*.

CHAPTER SUMMARY

- ❐ Shell scripts let you execute a complex set of commands by entering a single script name. Scripts can include control statements and tests to determine which commands in the script file are executed.

- ❐ Each script uses keywords from a programming language. An interpreter converts the source code of the script to an executable format as you run it. Compilers perform a similar conversion before a program is executed. The `bash` shell interpreter is often used for shell scripts.

- ❐ Each script file must start with a line identifying the interpreter to use for that script; it must have the execute permission set; and it must use only correctly formed statements for the interpreter you are using.

- ❐ Environment and positional variables are often referenced in scripts. You can also create your own variables to hold information the script needs to process.

- ❐ The `if/then/else` statement tests a condition and executes statements if the condition is present.

- ❐ Loops using `for` and `while` repeatedly execute a statement block based on either a fixed number of iterations or a condition being tested.

- ❐ Many scripting languages are used on Linux systems, including perl, PHP, Python, and Tcl/Tk. Some are appropriate for use with Web servers via CGI; some are appropriate for creating graphical programs.

- ❐ The `at` command schedules a task for execution by `atd` at some future point. The task can be defined using a filename containing one or more commands, or by entering the specific commands directly.

11

❐ Tasks scheduled using **at** can be managed using the **atq** and **atrm** commands. The ability to use **at** to schedule tasks can be managed using **at.allow** and **at.deny** files in /etc.

❐ The **crontab** command schedules tasks that are to be executed on a regular basis, such as daily or weekly. A complex but flexible time specification indicates when the task should be executed. The **crontab -e** command lets you edit all tasks for users that have been scheduled for regular execution.

❐ The **batch** command accepts tasks for future execution without a fixed time. They are executed when the system is not busy.

❐ Many administrators place scripts in the **cron**-related directories instead of creating their own **cron** job definitions. For example, they place a script in /etc/cron. daily to have it executed once each day.

❐ You can modify the Linux kernel to activate or deactivate features, including making features built-in instead of loadable modules.

❐ The kernel source code is available as an rpm package or as raw source code from *www.linuxhq.com.* This site also has patches to let you upgrade to a newer version of the kernel, though that is rarely necessary.

❐ Three kernel configuration utilities are supported: **config**, **menuconfig**, and **xconfig**. Each uses the same help text and the same options, but each interface has its own advantages and disadvantages.

❐ Kernel configuration utilities are started using the **make** command, which is also used after configuration is completed to start the actual kernel compilation process. This process can take several hours on a slower machine.

❐ The new kernel is located in /usr/src/linux-2.4/arch/i386/boot. It must be copied to /boot to make it usable. You can also create a boot floppy disk using **make bzdisk**, though the default kernel configuration will not fit on a floppy.

KEY TERMS

$@ — A special shell variable that includes all of the parameters on the command line.

$# — A special shell variable that holds the number of parameters entered on the command line.

at — A command that lets you enter one or more commands to be executed once at some future time.

at job — A command or script that you have scheduled to be executed at a specific time in the future using the **at** command.

atq — A command that lists each of the jobs awaiting execution by **atd**, including a job number and the date and time when the job will be executed.

atrm — A command that deletes (removes) a job from the queue used by **atd** to execute commands.

batch — A command that executes scheduled tasks when the system load average drops below 0.8.

binary file — *See* executable file.

comment — A line in a script that begins with a # character. Comments are not processed by the shell, but are only included to help someone reading the file understand the purpose of the script or how it functions.

Common Gateway Interface (CGI) — A method of communication between two programs using the standard input and standard output channels.

compiled language — A computer language for which the source code is converted to a binary file before the program is executed.

compiler — A program that converts the source code of a compiled language into a binary file.

computer language — A set of words and syntax rules that can be arranged in predefined ways to cause a computer to perform tasks defined by the person using the language.

cron job — A command or script that you have scheduled to be executed repeatedly at specific times in the future.

crontab — A command that lets you enter one or more commands to be executed repeatedly at intervals that you designate.

do — A command used with the **done** command to enclose a statement block as part of a **for** loop or a **while** loop.

done — A command used with the **do** command to enclose a statement block as part of a **for** loop or a **while** loop.

else — A command that extends the capability of an **if/then** statement by adding a statement block that is only executed if the test after "**if**" returns a value of false (that is, if the test fails).

executable file — A file containing numeric codes that a computer can execute. Created from a source code file by a compiler, the executable file is the program that a user can run.

exit — A command that stops the execution of a script immediately.

fi — A command that marks the end of an **if/then** or **if/then/else** statement.

for — A command that repeats a statement block one time for each item in a list.

for loop — A list of commands that is repeatedly executed according to the parameters provided with the **for** command.

if — A command used to introduce a test within a shell script. An **if** command is always followed by a **then** command.

if/then/else statement — A set of commands used to determine whether other commands in a script are executed. An **if/then/else** statement is one kind of selection statement.

index — A counting variable used within a loop statement. The index acts as a marker to count how many times the loop has executed a list of commands.

initialize — To set a variable to a pre-defined value such as zero or "" (an empty string) so a script can use the variable without uncertainty about its initial value.

11

interpreted language — A language for which the source code of a program is converted to numeric codes at the time a user runs the program. This conversion takes place each time the user runs the program.

interpreted program — A computer program that is converted from human-readable form to a format that can be used by a computer (numeric codes) at the moment you execute the program.

interpreter — A program that converts the source code written in an interpreted language into numeric codes that a computer can execute.

iteration — An occurrence of an event or process that can or must be done many times.

keyword — A word used in a computer language to define a specific task or meaning.

loop statement — A statement used to determine whether part of a computer program should be executed more than once.

make — A command that uses information stored in a configuration file to compile source code into a binary program or take other preset actions.

nesting — A programming method in which one selection or loop statement contains another selection or loop statement.

perl — A popular programming language developed by Larry Wall.

positional variable — A variable used within a shell script that contains data included on the command line when the script was launched.

programming language — *See* computer language.

Python — A scripting language developed by Guido van Rossum. Often used for creating graphical programs.

selection statement — A statement that lets a computer programmer determine which parts of a program will be executed according to values that are calculated by testing as the program is executed. The `if/then` statement is a selection statement used in shell scripts.

shell script — An executable file containing lines of text as you would enter them at a command line, with special commands to control the order in which lines in the file are executed.

shell variable — A variable used within a shell script to store information for use by the script.

source code — The file that a programmer writes using the keywords and syntax rules of a computer language.

statement — A command within a computer program. A statement is often a single keyword, but the term may also refer to a group of keywords that the computer language syntax requires or allows to be used together.

statement block — A list of commands (or statements) that are controlled by a selection or loop statement.

Tcl/Tk — A scripting language developed by John Ousterhout; often used to create graphical programs.

test — A command that evaluates the arguments provided after the command name and returns either true (a value of 1) or false (a value of 0).

test — A method of examining data within a shell script and acting according to the result of the examination (or test).

then — A command that identifies the commands to be executed if the test introduced by the `if` command succeeds (returns a value of true).

tty — A command that displays the name of the terminal device you are currently working in.

while — A command that creates a loop based on a test. The loop executes a statement block as long as the test returns true.

white space — Tabs or spaces included in a program or script that make the script easier for a person to read.

REVIEW QUESTIONS

1. Name four shell scripts that are included on a standard Linux system, and describe the use of each one.

2. The first line of a standard shell script must contain:

   a. A comment defining the username of the person creating the script

   b. A valid command as you would enter it from a command line

   c. The path and filename of the shell used to execute the script

   d. A time specification for when the script will be executed

3. In order to be executed by any user (including root), a shell script must have the _____ file permission set.

   a. execute

   b. write

   c. other

   d. owner

4. Which of these statements contains a standard positional variable?

   a. `gzip $file`

   b. `gzip $1`

   c. `gzip /tmp/listing 2>&1`

   d. `gzip HOME`

5. Which two commands involve a test value of true or false?

   a. `if` and `while`

   b. `while` and `for`

   c. `for` and `do`

   d. `crontab` and `at`

11

6. The `test` command is equivalent to using square brackets around a test expression, but the `test` command is less frequently used. True or False?

7. Briefly explain why comments are an important part of any shell script.

8. Describe the difference in control methods between a `for` loop and a `while` loop.

9. A loop beginning with the command "`for i in 2 4 6 8`" will be executed how many times?

   a. Eight

   b. Four

   c. The preset value of `i`

   d. It cannot be determined without knowing what files are in the current working directory.

10. Name three non-shell scripting languages. Include a statement on the use, characteristics, or author of each one.

11. CGI is popular for which of the following purposes?

    a. Creating Web servers

    b. Interfacing between scripts and Web servers

    c. Automating system administration work

    d. Creating graphical programs

12. Briefly explain the difference in time specification formats for the `at` and `crontab` commands.

13. The daemons that manage commands submitted using `at` and `cron` are:

    a. `/etc/cron.allow` and `/etc/cron.deny`

    b. `crond` and `bash`

    c. `atd` and `crond`

    d. `init.d` and `xconfig`

14. When using the `at` command interactively to enter commands scheduled for future execution, you indicate that you have finished entering commands by pressing:

    a. Ctrl+D

    b. Ctrl+C

    c. Esc

    d. Ctrl+X

15. The `batch` command is used to schedule jobs so that:

    a. Jobs from `at` and `crontab` are not executed at the same time

    b. Commands used in a DOS environment can be executed by Linux

    c. The system will not be overloaded with scheduled tasks

    d. Regular users can schedule tasks

16. A simple method for root to schedule recurring system administration tasks is to:

    a. Use the **at** command in interactive mode

    b. Add a script to a directory such as **/etc/cron.daily** or **/etc/cron.weekly**

    c. Create a graphical program using Python with Tk extensions

    d. Debug existing shell scripts on the system

17. The output of a **cron** job is normally sent via _____ to the user who submitted the **cron** job or to the user defined by the _____ variable within the file containing the **cron** job.

    a. e-mail, **MAILTO**

    b. e-mail, **USERLOG**

    c. tty, **MAILTO**

    d. standard output, **USERLOG**

18. Name, in order from left to right, the fields of the **crontab** time specification, giving the range of valid numeric values for each one.

19. Output from a command executed as part of a **cron** job cannot be redirected to a file using standard redirection operators because the environment in which the **cron** job was created is unlikely to exist when the **cron** job is executed. True or False?

20. The _____ file can include a username in order to deny that user access to the **crontab** command.

    a. **/etc/cron.allow**

    b. **/etc/cron.deny**

    c. **/usr/local/bin/deny**

    d. **/etc/at.deny**

21. Name the two separate commands that can be used instead of **at –l** and **at –d**.

22. Name an advantage of using the **make config** kernel configuration utility.

23. The **make** command acts based on:

    a. The contents of a configuration file called **Makefile**

    b. The contents of a configuration file called **.config**

    c. The file permissions of the script that it is executing

    d. The time specification used for the appropriate **cron** job

11

24. The preferred method of installing kernel source code is to include Kernel Development as an option during the initial installation of Linux.

    a. This is true because there are so many dependent packages that it is a lot of work to install them all manually.

    b. This is false because the kernel source code is always installed—the system could not run without it.

    c. This is true because the interpreters used to compile the kernel must also be installed as part of the default Linux system.

    d. This is false because the make command will locate the needed components no matter where they are located on the system.

25. A newly compiled kernel created using the `make bzImage` command is initially stored in which directory?

    a. `/boot`

    b. `/usr/src/linux-2.4`

    c. `/`

    d. `/usr/src/linux-2.4/arch/i386/boot`

HANDS-ON PROJECTS

Project 11-1

In this activity you create a simple shell script, then execute that script at the command line. To complete this activity you should have Linux installed.

1. Log in to Linux using your regular username and password.

2. If you are using a graphical environment, open a command-line window.

3. Start **vi** (or another text editor):

   ```
   $ vi ~fileinfo
   ```

4. If you are using **vi**, press **i** to change to insert mode.

5. Enter the following lines in **vi**:

   ```
   #!/bin/bash
   if [ $# -lt 1 ]; then
           echo You must include a filename on the command line.
           exit
   fi
   echo Beginning to process files.
   for i in $@
   do
   ```

```
        echo Number of lines in $i
        wc -l $i
        echo Number of words in $i
        wc -w $i
done
```

6. Press **Esc** to return to command mode.

7. Type **:wq** and press **Enter** to exit **vi** and save the file. If you are using a different text editor, such as **gedit**, save the file you entered as **fileinfo** and close the text editor.

8. Change the file permissions on **fileinfo** to include the execute permission:

    $ **chmod 755 fileinfo**

9. Enter **./fileinfo** to execute the command without any parameters. What happens? What result is returned by the test in the second line of the script?

10. What other methods could you use to test for the presence of a command-line parameter? What would happen if you removed the **if/then** test but didn't include any filenames on the command line?

11. Enter **./fileinfo /etc/termcap** to execute the command with a parameter. What happens? How many times was the **for** loop executed?

12. Execute the command with the parameter shown here:

    ./fileinfo /etc/m*conf

    What happens? How could you alter the script to test the validity of each file-name that was provided on the command line before using the **wc** command? (*Hint*: Use the **-r** file test from Table 11-1.)

13. Pipe the results of a longer set of output through **less** to see if the script is using STDOUT:

    $ **./fileinfo /etc/*conf | less**

14. (Optional) Revise the script to display the number of words and lines for each file on a single output line. Then add to the script (perhaps using commands you learned in Chapter 6) to display a list of filenames with word counts for each one, sorted by which files have the most words.

Project 11-2

In this project you submit a job for future execution using the **at** command. To complete this project you must have Linux installed with a regular user account.

1. Log in to Linux using your regular username and password.

2. If you are using a graphical environment, open a command-line window.

3. Enter the **at** command with a time designation as follows:

    $ **at now + 15 minutes**

4. At the `at>` prompt, enter this loop command:

```
at> for i in /etc/*conf
```

5. Enter the **do** command at the next `at>` prompt.

6. Enter **wc -w $i** at the next `at>` prompt.

7. Enter **done** at the next `at>` prompt. Your screen should now look like this:

```
$ at now + 15 minutes
at> for i in /etc/*conf
at> do
at> wc -w $i
at> done
at>
```

8. Press **Ctrl+D** to finish entering the commands you want to automate. What message do you see? What time is specified? Is it a relative time or an absolute time based on the time specification that you entered?

9. Enter the **atq** command. What information do you see about the job you just entered? What is the job number?

10. If you wish, use **atrm** to remove the job from the **at** queue, using the job number given by the **atq** command. For example:

```
$ atrm 15
```

11. If you decided not to remove the **at** job you entered, what will happen at the time given by the **at** command (when you finished the entry with Ctrl+D)? Wait 15 minutes and then use a mail reader (such as **mail**, **elm**, **pine**, or Netscape) to view the output of your at job as an e-mail message.

Project 11-3

In this project you submit a job for future execution using **crontab**. To complete this project you must have Linux installed with a regular user account and root access. (If you don't have root access, you won't be able to complete all the steps.

1. Log in to Linux using your regular username and password.

2. If you are using a graphical environment, open a command-line window.

3. Start **vi** or another text editor and create a file in your home directory called **du_job** that contains this single line:

```
30 2 * * * du /home > /tmp/du_output
```

4. Describe the time specification that you entered in the **du_job** file.

5. What problem could occur with the command entered in the **du_job** file because you are working as a regular user?

6. Submit the file you created as a new **cron** job:

```
$ crontab du_job
```

7. Review the contents of the `crontab` file for your regular user account:

    ```
    $ crontab -l
    ```

8. What do you see? How does it relate to the information you entered in the `du_job` file? Can you see an indication of the filename `du_job` and when it was submitted using `crontab`?

9. Enter **su** to change to the root account.

10. Enter the root password when requested.

11. Open a text editor to create a new file called `/etc/cron.deny`.

12. Enter a single line in the new `cron.deny` file that includes the regular user account name that you used to log in, in Step 1. For example, the file might include a single line like this:

    ```
    jtaylor
    ```

13. Save the text you entered and exit the text editor.

14. Switch from the root account back to a regular user account:

    ```
    # exit
    ```

15. Enter `crontab -r` to remove the `crontab` file for your regular user account. What happens? Why?

16. Enter **su** to change back to the root account, entering the root password when prompted.

17. Enter a command such as this one to erase the `crontab` file for the regular user account (substitute your own regular user account name):

    ```
    # crontab -u jtaylor -r
    ```

18. Remove the `cron.deny` file so that in the future all user accounts will have access to the `crontab` command (unless you prefer to restrict it for some reason on this Linux system):

    ```
    # rm /etc/cron.deny
    ```

19. Enter **exit** to log out of the root account.

CASE PROJECTS

The Starwood movie studio, for whom you have previously consulted (see Case Projects in Chapter 5), has asked for your help again. The computer graphics specialists creating their next feature film want to automate some of their CPU-intensive graphics commands so they can schedule them to run during lunch or after hours. You set up the

`/etc/cron.allow` file to permit this, but after a few days, it becomes obvious that your training session was not sufficient:

1. One of the `cron` jobs submitted by a user looks like this:

   `* * * * 1-5 grep html `ls -r /` > ~/Webpages`

   Describe what this command does and explain why it is causing problems for every user on the system.

2. Write a shell script that asks a user to input a single-line command that they want to have executed once each week. Ask the user to input the day of the week on which they want the command to be executed. Submit their command as a correctly formatted `cron` job.

3. After working out some of the automation issues with the Starwood staff, they ask you about using their digital video cameras with Linux. The cameras use a video interface called FireWire, or IEEE 1394. The FireWire interface of the cameras is based on an OHCI-1394 chipset manufactured by NEC. Research whether Linux supports this chipset (you may want to refer to the help screens in the kernel configuration utilities.)

4. The person who manages the systems at Starwood when you are not around would like to be able to manage user accounts in some basic ways (he has root access), but he is nervous about using all the different commands like `useradd`, `usermod`, `groupadd`, `groupmod`, `vipw`, etc. Write a script that asks questions about what the user wants to accomplish and then executes a command with appropriate options to complete that task. For example, you might ask about the username to be modified or created, perhaps selected from a list of available regular user accounts; or which default shell should be used for a user, again perhaps choosing from a list of available shells on the system; or which groups a user should be a member of; or which users are currently members of a certain group; or permit entry of a new full name. In short, write a script that is a text-based replacement for some of the graphical user management tools described in Chapter 8. Make it as complete and error proof as you can, testing input to avoid errors that the person using the script won't know how to respond to.

5. As part of a larger project for several clients, you need to help the Starwood system administrator prepare for possible system failures. Write a script that queries relevant system information from the `proc` file system, the `uname` command, the output of `dmesg`, and possibly other sources on the system. The script should collect this information in variables, format it, then store it in a text file. (System administrators will run this script, then give you the file it creates so you can develop disaster plans for each site.)

6. The director of Starwood has asked that you prepare a special game as a skills–building device for the studio's employees. The game displays a series of random numbers or letters on-screen for a brief time, then clears the screen and asks the user to enter what they saw. The game develops short-term memory and visual acuity. Skilled "players" can view a 12-digit number for 1 second and reenter it accurately. Create a simple script to implement this skills game using the $RANDOM variable (see the **bash** man page), the **sleep** command to pause for a length of time, and the **clear** command to clear the screen after pausing. Format the random string for easy reading, read in the user's response and compare it with the string displayed, then report how the user did. After creating a basic version, you might expand your script to permit the user to define the length of the string (perhaps starting at 3 digits and growing if the user scores well); to include scoring information displayed on-screen and saved to a file for comparison with later progress; to keep track of which types of strings the user does best on; or to select whether to include only digits or both digits and letters, among other features. If you decide the game is useful, you can add features over time to play it over the network with other users and to make it graphical. These last two features can be added by creating the script using Python, Tcl/Tk, or other languages.

PRINTING IN LINUX

After reading this chapter and completing the exercises, you will be able to:

♦ Configure and use the traditional Linux printing architecture

♦ Understand the Common UNIX Printing System (CUPS)

♦ Print files from different applications

♦ Manage networked printing resources

In the previous chapter you learned about creating shell scripts using selection statements, loops, and variables. You learned how to set correct permissions to execute these scripts from a command line and how to schedule a script or other command for later execution using the `at` and `crontab` commands. You also learned how to reconfigure and recompile the Linux kernel using three different utilities.

In this chapter you learn how to print files in Linux. Printing in Linux has undergone major shifts in the last couple of years. You first learn about the traditional methods of printing in Linux, which are straightforward and easy to use if you have a **local printer** (a printer directly attached to your computer) or are working with only Linux systems on your network. Then you learn about the newer Common UNIX Printing System (CUPS), which lets Linux and UNIX systems effectively share printing resources over a network. Both the traditional method and CUPS let users print files using the same commands; you learn to print from both a command line and from graphical applications. Finally, you learn about managing multiple printers and users in a networked environment.

USING TRADITIONAL LINUX PRINTING

Two competing but similar architectures have been developed for the two major variants of UNIX: BSD and System V. The traditional Linux printing system is based on the BSD version and is called LPRng. (The name refers to the "next generation" of the LPR printing system, though LPRng is quite old at this point.) LPRng printing allows multiple users to print files at the same time to either local or networked printers.

The Printing Process

Before a user can print files in Linux, the system administrator must define the printers that the system supports. The administrator creates one or more printer definitions that describe the type of printer and the features to be used when something is printed on it, such as the resolution or color settings and which users can print to it. These printer definitions are also called print queue definitions, and are often referred to simply as **print queues**. When we speak of printing a file, we usually say we're sending it to a certain *printer*, even though we really send it to a print queue, a set of definitions that is in turn associated with a physical printer.

The process of printing a file in the LPRng system includes the following steps:

1. An application submits a file to be printed, as directed by a user. The file submitted for printing is called a **print job**, and can include various options to describe how the printing should be accomplished, such as which printer to use and how many copies to print.

2. The print job is processed by a **print filter**. The print filter converts the information from a Linux application into formatting codes that will produce the desired output on the printer. The printing system chooses which print filter to use based on the information configured for the printer that was specified when the print job was submitted.

3. After sending the print job through a print filter, the printing utility stores the print job in a **print spool directory**, which is a location in the file system set aside to hold files waiting to be printed. The default print spool directory for the LPRng system is /var/spool/lpd. Within this directory, subdirectories are created for each print queue. For example, if you had created a printer definition called hplj, print jobs submitted to that print queue would be stored in /var/spool/lpd/hplj.

4. The print server program, lpd, keeps track of all the print jobs in all the print queues on the system. When a printer is available (for example, it finishes what it was printing or is reactivated), lpd sends the next print job to the printer.

5. At any time after a print job is submitted, the user or system administrator can use various utilities to see what print jobs are waiting to be printed or are being printed, and modify the contents of print queues or the actions of the lpd print server.

The print spool directory, `/var/spool/lpd`, can consume a lot of disk space on a system where many users are printing. Users can submit files for printing much more quickly than printers can process them; be certain you have enough hard disk space to hold print jobs while they wait their turn to be printed.

The correlation between a print queue and a physical printer is not always one-to-one. That is, one print queue might be used to send print jobs to multiple printers. Conversely, several print queues might all specify the same physical printer.

To understand why LPRng printer definitions might not correspond one-to-one to physical printers, consider two examples. In the first, imagine a large network where many users need to print files. By configuring a single print queue that sends print jobs to multiple printers, users can send files to a single location instead of trying to discover which printer isn't busy at the moment. The lpd print server will send print jobs from the single print queue to whichever printer is available. This arrangement is shown in Figure 12-1.

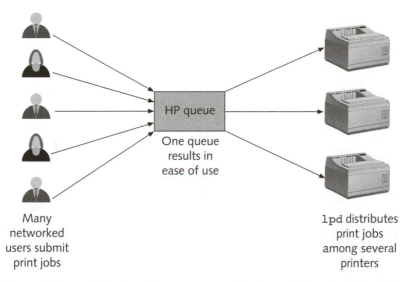

Figure 12-1 A single print queue can refer to multiple physical printers

The arrangement in Figure 12-1 can also be implemented using classes in the Common UNIX Printing System, as described later in this chapter.

As a second example, suppose you have only a single printer. The system administrator on a small office network configures separate print queues for envelopes, color printing, legal-sized documents, and standard printing. Users on the network submit files to the print queues depending on the type of document being printed. The person maintaining the printer would activate the print queue for legal-sized documents (and disable all other print queues) only when legal-sized paper was inserted and ready to print. When envelopes were inserted in the single printer, the envelope queue could be activated, and so forth. This method requires that someone actively maintain the printer unless the printer holds multiple paper trays, and users must wait while each queue is processed in turn. But this may be much more convenient than trying to print an envelope while everyone else is printing out reports. Figure 12-2 shows this arrangement.

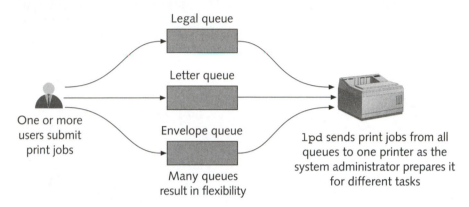

Figure 12-2   Many print queues can refer to a single physical printer

 The arrangement in Figure 12-2 can also be implemented using multiple instances of a single print queue in the Common UNIX Printing System, as described later in this chapter.

Understanding Print Filters and Drivers

To print different types of documents from Linux applications to a variety of printer devices, Linux uses special programs called print filters, as described previously. A Linux print filter is essentially the same as a printer driver in other operating systems: it converts documents or images into a format that the printer can use.

Printer Languages

Each printer uses a page description language to guide what it prints. A **page description language** is a special set of codes that determine the graphics elements, text font, and everything else about what appears on a printed page. The most widely used page description languages are PostScript and Printer Control Language (PCL). If a printer uses PostScript, for example, everything sent to that printer must be written in the PostScript page description language.

The documents you create in text editors, word processors, spreadsheets, and other Linux programs are not written in PostScript, PCL, or any other page description language. The print filter converts each document that you want to print into instructions using the appropriate page description language for the printer you want to use.

PostScript was developed by Adobe and is widely used in many types of printers. PCL, developed by Hewlett-Packard, is supported by most Hewlett-Packard printers and by many others as well. Many printers support multiple page description languages.

If you want to see what PostScript looks like, use the cat or less command to view the file `/usr/share/doc/HTML/en/kdvi/aboutkde.ps` on Red Hat Linux 7.3. Use the command `locate .ps` to see what other PostScript files are on your system.

The Magic Filter

Most Linux distributions use a "super print filter" or "**magic filter**" that can convert documents into formats for many different printers. This makes it convenient to support hundreds of printers on Linux, but it doesn't generally allow Linux to use the specialized features of each printer. For example, if you have used expensive laser printers on Microsoft Windows systems, you have seen graphical configuration utilities that let you access and configure dozens of features for your particular printer. Few manufacturers are yet providing such tools for Linux (one exception from Hewlett-Packard is mentioned in the next section), though the Linux printing architecture makes it easy to use such tools when they appear.

Red Hat Linux 7.3 is a good example of how most Linux distributions handle print filters. When you configure a print queue (as described in the next section), the configuration utility lets you select a printer from a list of supported devices. The printer model that you select is stored in the printer configuration file and used to direct the print filter.

The main print filter in Red Hat Linux 7.3 is a script called `/usr/share/printconf/util/mf_wrapper`. You can view this script in any text editor, but don't alter it! This script starts the `magicfilter-t` program with a parameter describing the printer for which output should be generated. To see some of the details behind `magicfilter-t`, enter this command:

```
$ magicfilter-t --dump
```

The `magicfilter-t` program (sometimes just called the magic filter) accepts many different printing options and produces output for many different printers. You will see the list of printers that the magic filter supports as you configure a printer in the next section. The magic filter uses several other programs such as **gs**, **enscript**, and **nenscript**, to convert documents for various formats.

Another popular tool that manages filtering for multiple printer models is **foomatic**. You can learn more about this program at *www.linuxprinting.org*.

Besides not having access to all printer features, using multiple interpreted programs to convert each print job to the appropriate page description language is much slower than a single dedicated program would be. Later in this chapter you learn about **PostScript Printer Description (PPD)** files, which are a great improvement on the print filter system described here, but which LPRng does not use.

In fact, for many of the printers you are likely to use, the manufacturer has created a filter or driver designed to take advantage of the specific features of that printer. For example, dozens of Lexmark printers are fully supported by special Linux drivers available from *www.lexmark.com*. You can download both the drivers and a 100+-page user guide for UNIX and Linux printing from the Lexmark Web site. Hewlett-Packard has created a separate Web site for Linux-related printing solutions. See *hp.sourceforge.net*, where you can read about HP efforts to improve Linux printing. HP has even created a basic graphical interface that lets you select which available features you want to apply to the job you are submitting. It isn't integrated with graphical applications, but it's certainly a step in the right direction.

With all this progress by the major printer manufacturers, you still must rely on the printing architecture described in this chapter. For example, the impressive user guide from Lexmark still describes how to set up a printer and print files using the same command-line and graphical tools described in the following sections.

Besides Lexmark and HP, several other groups are working on high-quality Linux printer drivers that you can use in place of the all-purpose magic filter. IBM has created a multi-purpose printer driver called Omni; the Gimp graphical program has a graphically oriented driver that supports many printers. Some manufacturers (for example, Canon) have done nothing with Linux, but others, such as Epson, are making a strong effort without providing official support for Linux-related software. Visit *www.epkowa.co.jp/english/index_e.html* and click the Linux link for unofficial drivers supporting several high-end Epson color printers. Additional information on Epson printers, with several useful links for Linux printing, is available at the unofficial site *www.epsondevelopers.com*. Finally, try Xwtools, a set of utilities that permit high-quality color printing on Epson, Canon, and some HP inkjet printers. See *xwtools.automatix.de/*.

Configuring Local Printer Definitions

When you install most Linux systems, the printing system is configured and running. All you need to do is define one or more printers before you can print documents. On some Linux systems, you configure a printer as you install the operating system, but Red Hat Linux 7.3 does not use this method.

Reviewing `printcap`

Each LPRng printer definition is created as a print queue entry in the `/etc/printcap` configuration file. The **`printcap`** (printer capture) file uses a complex format that can include dozens of options for each print queue. For this reason, you rarely configure the **`printcap`** file manually (in a text editor). Instead, you use one of the graphical tools described later in this chapter to set it up.

To use a local printer—one connected to the parallel or serial port of your computer—you must provide the appropriate Linux device name when you configure the printer. Parallel ports use the device name `lp` (`lp` stands for line printer) followed by a device number; serial ports use the name `ttyS` followed by a device number. For example, if your printer were attached to the first parallel port of the Linux computer, you would refer to device `/dev/lp0`. If your printer were attached to the third serial port, you would refer to `/dev/ttyS2`.

Device names accessed as filenames are sometimes called block special files or character special files. A **block special file** is associated with a physical device that transfers data in blocks of characters, such as a hard disk drive. A **character special file** is associated with a physical device that transfers data in single characters, such as a serial port.

The leftmost column of the output of the `ls -l` command indicates a block special file with a `b`, and a character special file with a `c`.

The format of a `printcap` entry consists of a print queue name, followed by a series of two-character option codes that apply to that printer. Each option is separated from the next by two colons. In the example file that follows, one of the colons is at the end of each line, and the second is at the beginning of the next line. Multiple options could be listed on a single line, so that you would see two colons together; you see here a standard formatting method for this file. Many options are followed by specific parameters. For example, the parameter `lp=/dev/lp0` specifies that the physical printer is connected to the first parallel port. For readability, each option is typically placed on a separate line of the file, with a backslash after each option to indicate that the line break should be ignored when processing the file. A basic `printcap` entry taken from Red Hat Linux is shown here:

```
local:\
      :ml=0:\
      :mx=0:\
      :sd=/var/spool/lpd/local:\
      :af=/var/spool/lpd/local/local.acct:\
      :sh:\
      :lp=/dev/lp0:\
      :lpd_bounce=true:\
      :if=/usr/share/printconf/util/mf_wrapper:
```

Table 12-1 lists many of the two-letter codes that can appear in a `printcap` file. Be careful with colons, backslashes, and so forth if you manually edit `printcap`. To see a list of all available `printcap` options, enter `man 5 printcap`.

12

Table 12-1   Useful Option Codes in `/etc/printcap`

Option code	Description	Example
af	The print accounting file	af=/var/adm/lp_acct/hplj_acct
bq	Define a remote system that should receive the print job, but filter the print job before sending it to the remote system	bq=ps@192.168.100.67
ff	The form feed (start a new page) character	ff='\f'
if	The print filter to use when printing to this printer	if=/var/spool/lpd/hplj/filter
lp	The device name to open for printing (the first parallel port is shown in the example)	lp=/dev/lp0
mx	The maximum file size for print jobs submitted to this printer (in 1024-byte blocks); the first example indicates a maximum print job size of about 2 MB, the second example (with #0) indicates that no maximum print job size is enforced	mx=2000 mx#0
pc	Price per page (or foot for plotters) to use for print accounting, in hundredths of a cent; the example shows 15 cents per page	pc=1500
pl	Page length, in lines	pl=66
pw	Page width, in characters	pw=80
rg	Restricted group; only members of the group named may submit print jobs to this printer	rg=eng
rm	Hostname of a remote print server to which print jobs submitted using this printer name should be sent (see the section "Printing Remotely Using lpd" later in this chapter)	rm=ps.xyzcorp.com or rm=192.168.100.67
rp	Remote printer; the queue name to use on the remote print server (defined by rm)	rp=hplj5
rs	Restrict users trying to print from other machines to those with an account (or the same name) on this machine	rs
sb	Use a short banner page of only one line	sb

Table 12-1 Useful Option Codes in /etc/printcap (continued)

Option code	Description	Example
sc	Suppress multiple copies of the same print job even if they are specified in the lpr command submitting the job	sc
sd	The spool directory where submitted print jobs will be stored by lpd	sd=/var/spool/lpd/hplj
sh	Suppress printing of a banner or header page containing the username, filename, and other print job inform-ation; the banner page is helpful when many users use the same printer, but it uses a lot of paper	sh

Configuring printcap Graphically

Several graphical tools can create basic **printcap** entries, but the tools at your disposal depend on which Linux distribution you use. For example, Red Hat Linux has **printconf-gui**; SuSE Linux uses the YAST utility; and Caldera OpenLinux users should rely on Webmin. Most of these tools present similar interfaces, since they all create a printer entry using a limited set of the options in Table 12-1.

In this section you learn about utilities for setting up the **printcap** file so that users can begin to print files. Later in this chapter, in the section "Managing Printing," you learn about graphical utilities used to manage print queues.

To start the Printer Configuration Tool **printconf-gui** in Red Hat Linux 7.3, open the main menu of Gnome and choose Programs, then System, then Printer Configuration. Or, enter **printconf-gui** at a graphical command line. To begin defining a printer, click the New button. A printer definition wizard appears. Click Next in the first screen of the wizard to continue.

 A text-mode version of this program is available. You can launch it from any command line with the command **printconf-tui**.

In the next screen of the wizard, you must enter a name and select a type for the printer you are defining (see Figure 12-3). The name typically refers to the printer model, or sometimes the location in an office area. Examples include canon-downst, hp6, and epson11×17. The printer name can be long (though long names become inconvenient), but it should not contain spaces.

12

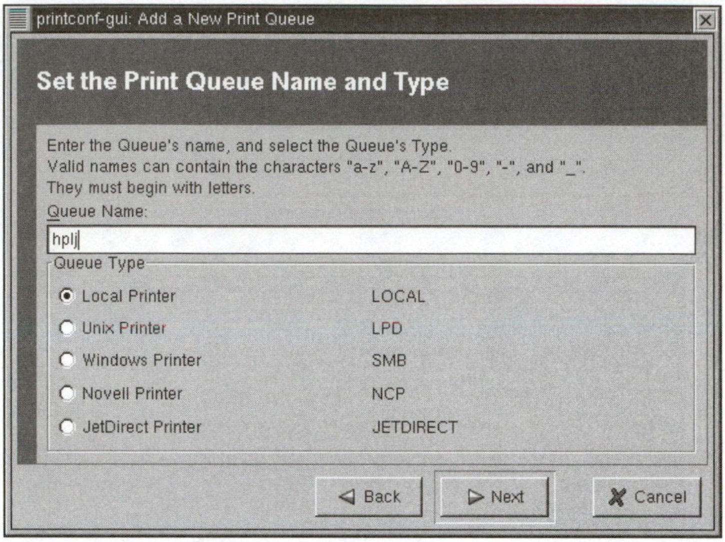

Figure 12-3   Defining the printer name and type in the `printconf-gui` utility

This section concentrates on the Local printer type. The next section discusses different types of networked printers. When you choose Next, a list of Linux devices appears (such as **/dev/lp0**). Here you choose which port the printer is connected to. You can click Custom Device to enter a different device name, such as **/dev/ttyS1** for the second serial port.

After you click Next, a list of printer manufacturers and models appears. You can click on the arrow to the left of a manufacturer name to see a list of printer models for which drivers are available. If you click on the arrow to the left of the printer model, you see a list of printer drivers that support that model. Figure 12-4 shows the listing for a Hewlett-Packard LaserJet printer for which one driver is available. The driver that you select has no effect at the moment; after you select a driver and choose Next, you confirm all the data you have entered so far and click Finish to end the configuration process. The new printer definition appears in the main window of **printconf-gui**, as shown in Figure 12-5. The driver that you select determines which options are recognized when you print a file, as described later in this chapter.

You can select a printer definition and click the Edit button to make changes in it, or click the Delete button to remove it from **printcap**. Save your changes to **printcap** by choosing Save Changes on the File menu. If you have defined multiple printers, select the one you want as the default printer and click the Default button. (The default printer is used when you print a file without specifying a printer by name.) It's a good idea to print a test page after defining a printer by selecting an item on the Test menu. For printers supporting PostScript, choose US Letter PostScript as the test page; for printers that don't support PostScript, choose ASCII Text.

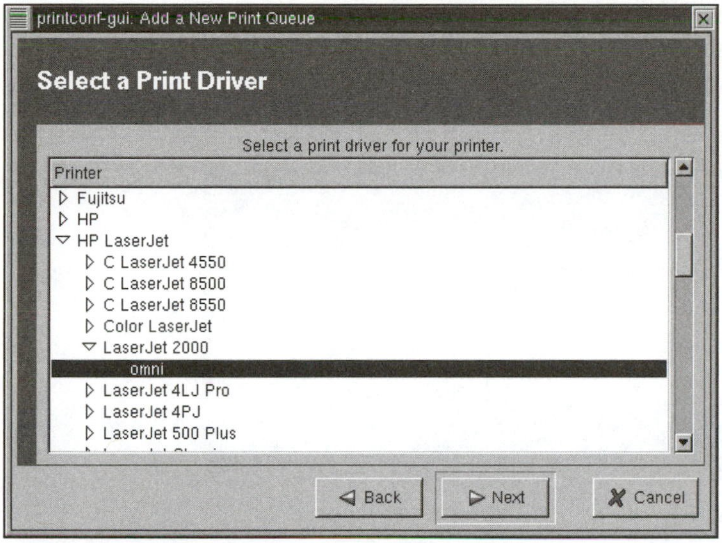

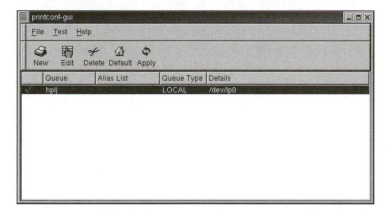

Figure 12-4   Selecting a printer driver in `printconf-gui`

Figure 12-5   The main window of `printconf-gui`

After you have defined a printer, you should restart the **lpd** print server so it reads changes in the **printcap** file. You can do this using the Restart lpd item on the File menu, or from a command line using the **service** command. The **service** command lets you access a script in **/etc/rc.d/init.d**:

```
# service lpd restart
```

You can also use the KDE Control Center to define a **printcap** entry. Open the Control Center from the KDE main menu or from the KDE menus submenu in Gnome. Click the plus sign next to System on the left side of the screen to open a list of options. Click the Printing Manager item to display the print configuration tool on the right side of the Control Center window.

Before you can use this window, you must select the type of printing system that you are configuring. In the lower right corner, click on the drop-down list next to the label "Print system currently used" and select "LPR/LPRng print system." (See Figure 12-6.) Nothing changes on-screen, but this indicates how your selections will be processed.

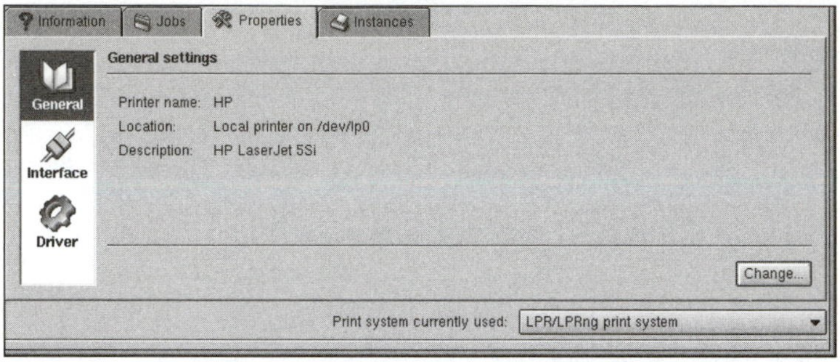

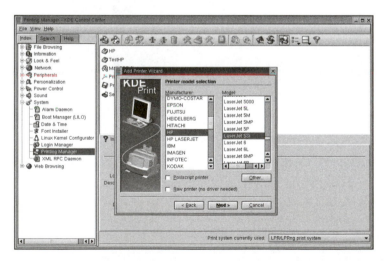

Figure 12-6   Selecting the print system to configure within the KDE Control Center

In the upper part of the right side of the window, click the leftmost icon to create a new printer definition. An Add Printer Wizard appears. Click Next in this window to continue. This wizard is very similar to the selections described for the Red Hat `printconf-gui` tool described previously. In the screen that appears now you select which type of printer you are creating. As before, we focus for the moment on the Local printer type. Select Local printer and choose Next. Then choose the port to which the printer is connected (for example, Parallel Port #1), then choose Next. After a moment, a list appears showing printers that you can configure, as shown in Figure 12-7. Select your manufacturer from the list on the left, then select a model from the list on the right.

Figure 12-7   Selecting a printer in the KDE Printer Manager Wizard

If you have downloaded a file from a manufacturer or other source to support a printer that is not listed, choose Other to specify the location of that additional driver file. When you choose Next, you may see a list of multiple drivers that are available for the printer you selected. For example, some popular Hewlett-Packard printers have drivers from Omni and Gimp, as well as the `ljet` driver. Select the one you prefer or accept the default if you have no reason to prefer one over another. Choose Next to continue.

A Printer test window appears that lists the printer and driver you have selected. You can click the Test button to print a test page, which is generally a good idea if this is the first time you have configured a particular printer. You can also click the Settings button to display the Configure dialog box (see Figure 12-8) that shows how the printer driver you selected is configured. In the Configure dialog box, you can click on an option and select the value you prefer in the bottom part of the screen. Choose OK to close the Configure dialog box and return to the Printer test window, where you can choose Next to continue defining the printer.

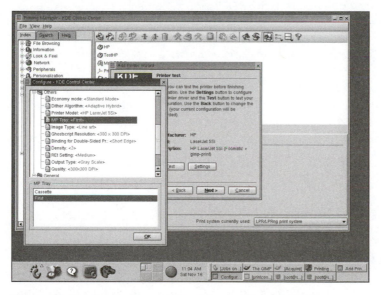

Figure 12-8   Reviewing printer driver settings in KDE

In the General information window that appears, you must enter a printer name in the Name field. As with the `printconf-gui` tool, this should be a descriptive name that isn't too long and doesn't include spaces. You can include more descriptive text in the Location field. For example, you might enter "mainhplj" as a printer name and "Front reception by the break room" as a description. The Description field is filled in automatically based on the model you selected previously. Choose Next to continue. Review your selections in the Confirmation window, then click Finish to complete the configuration process. The printer you defined is listed in the top part of the KDE Control Center on the right side (see Figure 12-9). The other items that are already listed, such as Print To File or Send To Fax, are special methods of printing that don't require defining a print driver.

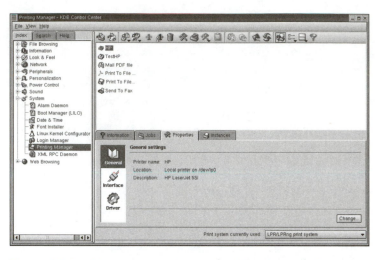

Figure 12-9   Managing printers in the KDE Control Center

After selecting a printer definition in the top part of the KDE Control Center, you can click the Instances tab in the bottom part of the window. Within this tab, click default to make that printer the default, click Test to print a test page, or click Settings to alter how the printer operates. (These settings are different from the driver settings you saw as you configured the printer driver in the previous steps.) The Information and Properties tabs describe the settings you have already defined. The Jobs tab shows what print jobs are waiting to be printed to the selected printer, as described later in this chapter.

Once you have set up printers in the KDE Control Center, choose Quit from the File menu to close the Control Center.

Printing Remotely Using `lpd`

In both of the graphical tools we've explored, "Local" was only one type of printer you could define. A Local printer relies on the `lpd` print server daemon to accept print jobs and send them in turn to the printer. You can also define a **remote printer** so that `lpd` sends print jobs to another computer instead of to a printer connected to your computer.

To do this, you define a printer on your system that refers to the remote computer and a print queue on the remote system. The `lpd` daemon on your computer communicates with the `lpd` program on the remote computer, transferring the print job. This arrangement is shown in Figure 12-10.

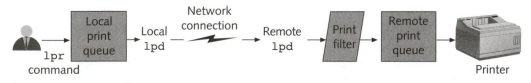

Figure 12-10   Printing to a remote printer using `lpd`

Once a print job has been sent to a remote system using lpd, you have no direct control over it. If you want to see the status of the print job, you must have permission to log in to the remote printer and use the printer management tools on that system.

Within the /etc/printcap file, a simple remote printer definition looks like this:

```
lp:\
      :sd=/var/spool/lpd/lp:\
      :mx#0:\
      :sh:\
      :rm=brighton.xmission.com:\
      :rp=lexmark:
```

The key options to note here are rm, where the remote system is specified, and rp, where the remote print queue is specified.

Within the **printconf-gui** tool, you can select Unix Printer (LPD) in the wizard where you define a printer. Then enter the remote system and queue name. See Figure 12-11.

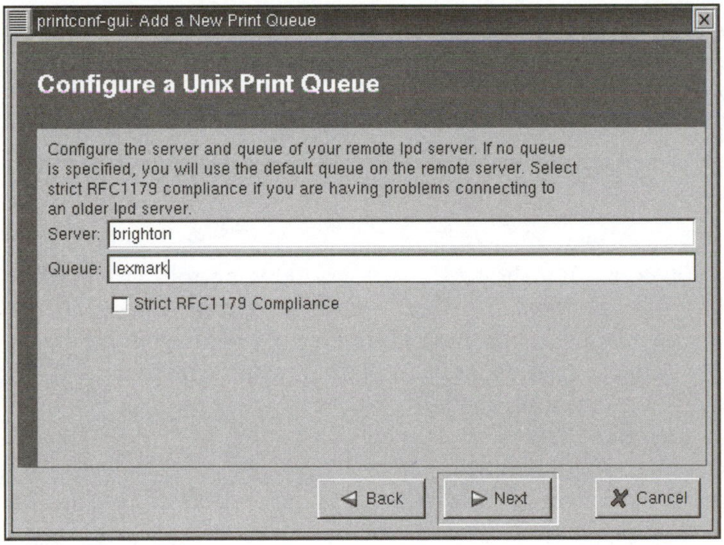

Figure 12-11   Defining a remote lpd-based printer in printconf-gui

Within the KDE Control Center wizard described in the previous section, you can select Remote LPD Queue, then enter the remote host and queue name, as shown in Figure 12-12.

The lpd daemon is configured by options in /etc/lpd.conf. Typically, lpd is not used in an environment where security is a big concern, because it is not considered highly secure. But you can set permissions for numerous lpd functions using /etc/lpd.perms. Both lpd.conf and lpd.perms have complete man pages describing lpd configuration options.

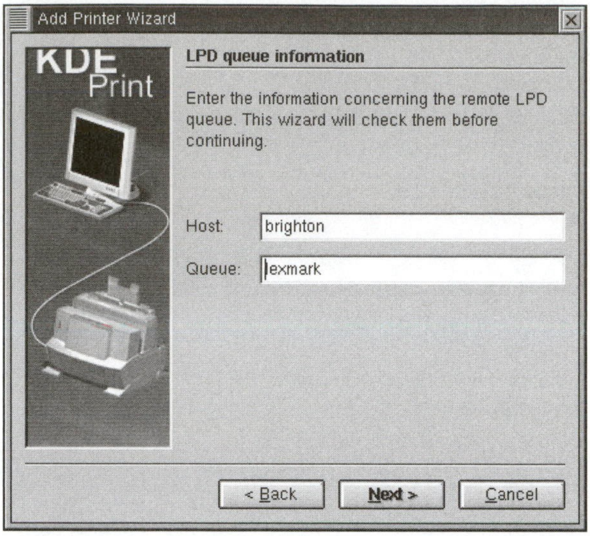

Figure 12-12 Defining a remote `lpd`-based printer in KDE

The `lpd` daemon is generally used only on Linux and UNIX systems, though it is available for other operating systems. Because of this limitation, you would only use `lpd` when sharing a printer between two Linux or UNIX systems. Both the `printconf-gui` and KDE utilities let you define remote printers using other popular protocols besides `lpd`, such as:

- Windows printer using the SMB protocol: This option uses the Samba suite, a networking service that is included with Red Hat Linux 7.3, but which is not configured by default. When you define an SMB printer, users on your system can print from their Linux applications to a printer connected to a Windows system on your network. The Windows system must be configured to permit network users to print.

> The Samba suite is described in detail in *Guide to Linux Networking and Security*, Chapter 5. You can also refer to *www.samba.org*, and to the documentation files included with the Samba software packages. (See, for example, the information in Red Hat Linux 7.3 under `/usr/share/doc/samba-2.2.3a/docs`.)

- NetWare printer using the NCP protocol. This option lets users on your system print directly to a print queue stored on a NetWare server.

- JetDirect. Use this option when you have a printer connected directly to your network instead of to a computer on the network. Print jobs are processed using the appropriate page description language as if they were going to a locally attached printer, but they are sent over the network instead of to a parallel or serial port.

The general term for this type of printer is a **network attached printer**, and refers to any printer that includes a networking interface (such as an Ethernet port) so that the printer is attached directly to a network instead of to a parallel, serial, or other port on a computer. A network attached printer has built-in software that lets it accept print jobs directed to its network address.

Understanding the Common UNIX Printing System

The LPRng printing system and the `lpd` daemon have been used for many years. But they lack key features that system administrators would like to have for a multiuser, network-capable printing system.

To understand what LPRng lacks, consider how some other operating systems manage printing. With Windows and NetWare systems, a user can "browse" the network to see what printers are available. Finding one that is appropriate, a user can send a print job directly to that printer, without first defining a local printer that refers to it. System administrators can use a single print management utility to see and control print jobs on multiple computers. And they can do this from anywhere on the network that has the appropriate utility installed, without needing additional user accounts on each system.

These are the capabilities that the **Common UNIX Printing System (CUPS)** provides to Linux and UNIX. CUPS is a fairly recent development. It provides a new architecture for Linux printing that lets users and system administrators browse the network to find and print to networked printers and other devices. It also lets system administrators manage printer definitions and print jobs across the network.

One of the less obvious problems with LPRng and other `lpd`-based printing systems was that each UNIX vendor produced a slightly different version of the printing software. A system administrator who managed a network with several versions of UNIX and Linux systems faced numerous configuration obstacles to provide convenient printing services for users. Using CUPS overcomes this problem because the same architecture is available for all versions of UNIX and Linux.

CUPS is installed by default in Red Hat Linux 7.3 as a set of six software packages. The main print server daemon is `cupsd`, which is controlled by the `cups` script in `/etc/rc.d/init.d`. A number of configuration files are included in the `/etc/cups` subdirectory. You can use command-line utilities to interact with the CUPS server to submit print jobs, as described in the next section, or to manage the server. Many system administrators will prefer to use the browser-based management interface described in this section.

You can learn more about CUPS at *www.cups.org*. CUPS implements a widely supported printing protocol called the Internet Printing Protocol (IPP), which you can learn about at *www.pwg.org/ipp*. An invaluable resource for information on all aspects of printing within Linux is *www.linuxprinting.org*, which has links to articles and other sites for CUPS, LPRng, numerous printer drivers and filters, and much more.

12

Configuring Printers within CUPS

The `cupsd` print server daemon operates much like a Web server. It uses the same HTTP protocol as Web servers and accepts requests and processes print jobs sent over the network. It also manages printers using a Web browser interface. This interface is configured by default in Red Hat Linux 7.3. On other systems you may have to install the correct software packages and enable networking to use the CUPS features described here.

The CUPS architecture uses network port 631 to communicate between CUPS-enabled print servers. A **port** is like the address of an application on a networked computer. The `cupsd` daemon on one computer sends a message to the `cupsd` daemon on another computer by sending it to the predefined port address of 631, which you indicate by adding ":631" to the name of the CUPS server you want to contact.

You can start the CUPS user interface in Red Hat Linux 7.3 by choosing Programs, then System, then CUPS Printer Configuration on the main menu of Gnome. After a moment, a Web browser appears with the main menu of the CUPS management utility, as shown in Figure 12-13. The URL shown is *http://localhost:631*.

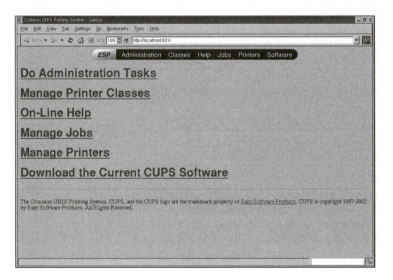

Figure 12-13 The main page of the CUPS browser-based interface

If you want to manage the printers or the print jobs on another system running CUPS anywhere on your network, you enter that system's name with the CUPS port, 631. For example, suppose you are working on host arizona and you want to manage CUPS on host colorado. You simply enter this URL in any browser: *http://colorado:631*.

 Before you can perform any management tasks, such as defining new printers, you should log in as root when prompted. This is true even when you are managing CUPS on your local system.

The `cupsd` program is configured in much the same way as the popular Apache Web server. The file `/etc/cups/cupsd.conf` contains directives that specify a setting for each active server option. Hundreds of comments in this file describe the current options, as well as options that are supported but not activated. For example, this file can configure CUPS to:

- Use a variety of authentication systems for determining which users can configure or manage printing.

- Use encryption techniques to protect your user and password information as you manage networked print servers.

- Manage how hosts can browse the network to see printers on each print server.

- Limit which hosts on the network can use certain printers.

To configure a new printer from the first page of the CUPS interface, choose the Manage Printers link or the Printers item on the bar across the top of the page. The page that appears shows any CUPS printers that you have already defined. These are taken from the `/etc/printcap` file, and CUPS will generate a revised `/etc/printcap` file by default when you make changes using CUPS. (Printer information is also maintained in a separate file, `/etc/cups/printers.conf`.) To define a new printer (add a new printer definition, or print queue), click the Add Printer button at the bottom of the page. On the pages that follow, enter printer information as you did for the `printconf-gui` and the KDE Control Center tools: you enter a name, a location, and a description; you select a port for the printer; you select a manufacturer, model, and print filter. Once you have completed the definition, the printer you defined appears on the Printers page, as shown in Figure 12-14.

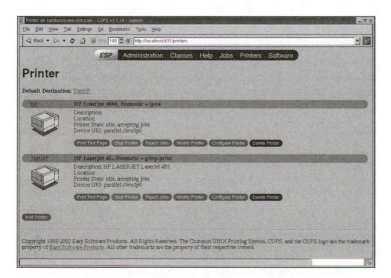

Figure 12-14   The Printers page in the CUPS Web interface

From this page, you can use the buttons below a printer's definition to do any of the following:

- Print a test page. This sends a one-page print job to the printer so you can see that it is working.

- Stop the printer. This doesn't prevent users from submitting print jobs to the print queue, but it stops `cupsd` from sending jobs to the printer itself. Use this when you must fix a paper jam, add paper, check toner, or otherwise adjust the printer. This button is red because you may need it in emergencies, like when a printer is printing one character per page and threatens to go on for hours unless interrupted.

- Reject jobs. This stops `cupsd` from accepting new print jobs for this print queue. Use this when you want to make changes in the printer configuration. You can stop accepting new print jobs, let all the current print jobs finish, then make your changes and begin accepting print jobs again.

- Modify the printer definition. This lets you re-enter the information you entered when first defining the printer, making changes as needed.

- Configure the printer. This lets you configure default settings for how this printer is used. The exact information provided on the Configuration screen—as shown in Figure 12-15—depends on the model of printer you are working with.

- Delete the printer. Use this option to remove the printer definition from CUPS. Any print jobs in the queue will be lost.

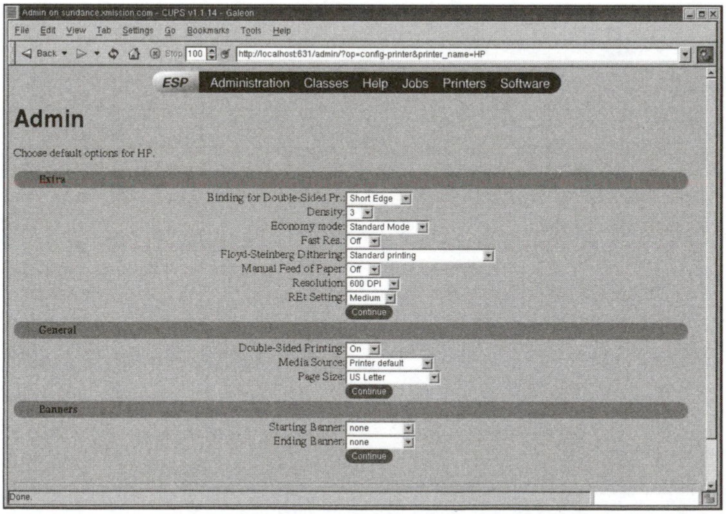

Figure 12-15   Configuring an existing printer in CUPS

To learn more about CUPS, begin by clicking the Help button at the top of the CUPS page in your Web browser. A list of documentation appears. You can click the HTML link for any document and read it immediately. If you are new to printing in Linux, begin with the Software Users Manual, followed by the Software Administrators Manual. Many of the other documents are for developers or system architects. (That is, you can teach yourself to write your own CUPS printer drivers using the documentation on this page.)

Behind the scenes in CUPS, many printers are configured using a PostScript Printer Description (PPD) file. Each PPD file describes the capabilities of a printer using a standardized language. By consulting the PPD file for a printer model, a graphical print configuration utility or a graphical application such as OpenOffice or Gimp can display all supported options for a specific printer. An appropriate graphical dialog box is built "on-the-fly" based on the information in the PPD file. You see an example of this in Project 12-1 using `printconf-gui`. By relying on PPD files, printer manufacturers can easily create a text-based configuration file that permits their printer to be graphically configured using standard utilities.

PPD files are sometimes available from printer manufacturers or from free software sites, in which case the PPD has been created by someone besides the printer manufacturer. Despite the name, PPD files are used for all types of printers, not just PostScript-capable printers.

In addition, some specialized programs will create a PPD file based on information taken from standard print filters. One example is the PPD-O-Matic program.

As a system administrator, you should never need to explore the contents of a PPD file, though you may need to search for a PPD file to support a printer model that is not installed on your Linux system. You can also explore a PPD file to learn more about how they are constructed by viewing one of the files on your system. Red Hat Linux 7.3 has over 1000 PPD files installed by default in `/usr/share/cups/model`. Most of the PPD files are located in subdirectories named for different manufacturers. You can view a sample file using this command:

```
$ zcat /usr/share/cups/model/laserjet.ppd.gz | less
```

Additional information about PPD files is available on the Linux Printing Web site at *www.linuxprinting.org/ppd-doc.html*.

Setting up CUPS Classes

When many users share several printers, they may jockey for position, trying to get their print job completed quickly when another user is printing a very long document. Classes are a more elegant solution to this problem than the LPRng system shown in Figure 12-1. A CUPS class is a group of printers to which a user can submit a print job. Whichever printer within the class is first available will be used to print the job.

12

For example, suppose you manage the printing for a busy office that has three high-capacity laser printers that you have defined as lexmark1, lexmark2, and lexmark3. Without classes, users would try to guess which printer to send their print job to so it wouldn't have to wait for another long job to finish; polite users might send out a department-wide e-mail: "380 page job going to lexmark2." You decide to use CUPS and create a class called lexmarks that includes all three lexmark print queues. Now users send all print jobs to lexmarks. Each time any one of the three printers finishes a print job, CUPS sends the next print job to that printer. Users get the fastest possible service. In exchange, they have to check three different printers to see which one their print job came out on. (Printers within a class are typically located next to each other in an office.)

To create a class in CUPS, click the Classes button at the top of the CUPS page and then click the Add Class button on the Classes page. The page that appears lets you define a name, location, and description. You must include at least a name, such as lexmarks. In a large department with many users or printers, it's also a good idea to enter a location and description, for example "Downstairs by Robin's Cube" and "Main dept. laser printers."

When you choose Continue, you see a listing of all printers defined within CUPS. You select all of the printers that should be included in the class you are defining. Then choose Continue. A confirmation page shows you that the class was successfully completed. If you return to the Classes page by clicking Classes at the top of the page, you see that your class is shown with most of the same options as a regular printer, except that the icon shows multiple printers, and the Configure and Modify buttons differ. Figure 12-16 shows the Classes page.

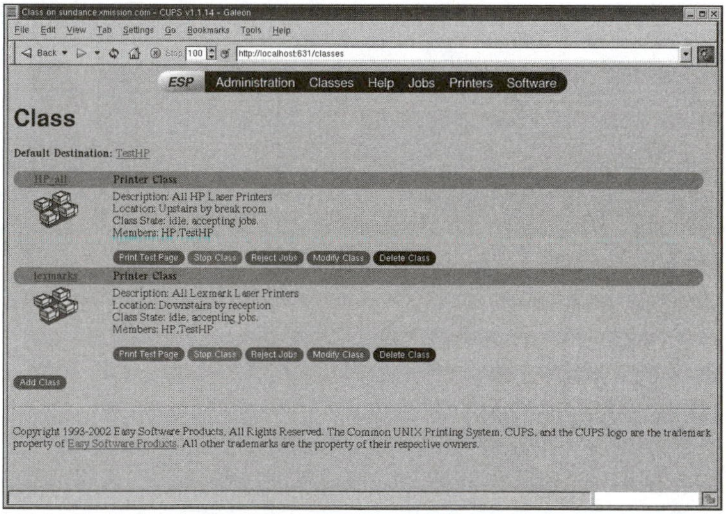

Figure 12-16   The Classes page within the CUPS configuration

Users can still send print jobs to an individual printer that is part of a class (such as lexmark2 in the previous example). But the class provides a more efficient method of distributing print jobs on a busy network with many users and more than one printer.

You can also set up CUPS printers using the KDE Control Center interface described previously. Recall that in the lower right corner of the KDE Printing Manager window you selected LPRng in the previous section, as shown in Figure 12-6. You can also select CUPS and define CUPS printing options using the same basic interface.

PRINTING FILES

Once you have defined at least one printer in either an LPRng-based or CUPS-based print system, printing a file in Linux is straightforward. You can print from a command line, from a specialized graphical tool, or from any graphical application. Because many graphical applications will not let you control printing options precisely, it's a good idea to become familiar with the command-line options.

Printing from a Command Line

The basic printing command is `lpr`. You can print a file to the default printer using this command format:

```
$ lpr filename
```

The `lpr` command is used for printing to both LPRng and CUPS-based printers. However, in Red Hat Linux 7.3, `lpr` is configured to use either the LPRng or the CUPS *version* of the command. In Red Hat, the file `/usr/bin/lpr` is a link to `/etc/alternatives/print`, which is in turn a symbolic link to either `/usr/bin/lpr.LPRng` or `/usr/bin/lpr.cups`. Both versions support the basic options described below, and also support options that are specific to the features of their underlying architectures and the print filters that you have selected for a specific print queue.

The `lpr` command is associated historically with the BSD (Berkeley) version of UNIX. The LPRng printing system supports the `lp` command as well, which is associated with System V versions of UNIX. The `lp` command options differ from the `lpr` options, though the underlying capabilities are very similar. Because you are likely to focus only on one of these commands unless you are coming from a System V UNIX background, we focus here on the `lpr` command and leave you to research the `lp` man page for corresponding options if you need to use that command.

In general terms, the filter that the default printer uses will determine the type of file being printed and process it accordingly. So the same command works for PostScript files, PDF files, images, or plaintext files, among others. The `lpr` command gets much more complicated when you want to control the print job more precisely instead of relying on the system defaults. Table 12-2 shows basic options that you can include with the `lpr` command to process a file in many different ways. These options apply to a specific print job, not to all print jobs sent to the printer. You can use the configuration tools for LPRng or CUPS to set up different default settings for all print jobs.

Table 12-2   Command Options for `lpr`

Option	Description	Example
`-C`	Set a priority class for the print job. Priorities range from `A` to `Z`. The default is `A`. Print jobs of a lower priority are printed after all print jobs of a higher priority.	`lpr -C D stats.txt`
`-h`	Don't use a banner or header page for this print job, even if `printcap` specifies one.	`lpr -h stats.txt`
`-i`	Indent each line of the print job by this many spaces. This feature is not supported on all printers.	`lpr -i 5 stats.txt`
`-J`	Assign a name to this print job. The name appears on the banner page to help a user identify the print job.	`lpr -J "Weekly statistics" stats.txt`
`-#`	Specify the number of copies of the file to be printed. Note that there is no space between the # option and the numeric value.	`lpr -#3 stats.txt`
`-m`	Send an e-mail to the named user account if an error occurs during printing. If the user account is located on the same system, only the user's account name is needed, as in this example.	`lpr -m nwells stats.txt`
`-P`	Specify a nondefault printer using a printer name from the `printcap` file. Don't put a space between the P and the printer name.	`lpr -Phplj5 stats.txt`
`-w`	Specify the page width in characters.	`lpr -w132 stats.txt`

Many additional options are supported by the CUPS version of `lpr`. Some of these are shown in Table 12-3. The PPD you install for your printer allows CUPS to access whichever options your printer supports using the options that you include from this table.

The `lpr` command sends print jobs to the default printer unless instructed differently. The steps that `lpr` uses to determine which printer to send a print job to are shown here:

1. If the `-P` option is included with the `lpr` command, the printer named after `-P` is used.

2. If the `-P` option is not included, but an environment variable named `PRINTER` exists for the user printing the file, the value of the `PRINTER` variable is used.

3. When a `PRINTER` environment variable is not configured, the default printer specified by either the LPRng configuration or the CUPS configuration is used. You can see and alter these defaults in any of the graphical configuration tools described in this chapter.

Table 12-3   `lpr` Options Supported by CUPS

Option	Description	Possible option values
media	Which paper tray to use	letter, legal, A4, COM10 (#10 envelope), DL, transparency, upper, lower, multipurpose, LargeCapacity
sides	Two-sided (duplex) printing	one-sided, two-sided-short-edge, two-sided-long-edge
job-sheets	What text to include on the banner page that begins the print job	none, standard, classified, confidential, secret, topsecret, unclassified
page-set	Which pages to print	odd, even
number-up	How many document pages to print on each page of output	1, 2, 4
page-ranges	Which pages to print; any numeric range can be used or multiple pages or ranges, separated by commas	*Dependent on document pages (e.g., 1,5-10,22)*
brightness	How bright to make the output, given as a percentage from 1 to 100	1-100
prettyprint	Includes a header on each page with the page number, filename, and date printed	*None*
gamma	Gamma correction; values above 1000 lighten the output, values below 1000 darken it	1-5000
cpi	Select the font to print a text file by choosing a characters-per-inch value; the default is 10	10, 12, 17
lpi	Lines per inch; the default is 6	6, 8
columns	How many columns to output on each page; the default is 1	1, 2, 3
page-left	Set a hard left page margin (the value is given in points, or 1/72nds of an inch [0.35 mm]); the default used is the physical minimum of the printer	*Dependent on paper size*
page-right	Hard right margin; see the page-left option	*Dependent on paper size*
page-top	Hard top margin; see the page-left option	*Dependent on paper size*
page-bottom	Hard bottom margin; see the page-left option	*Dependent on paper size*

12

Table 12-3 lpr Options Supported by CUPS (continued)

Option	Description	Possible option values
position	Where to position an image on a page	center, top, left, right, top-left, top-right, bottom, bottom-left, bottom-right
scaling	Percentage size for output of an image	1-800
ppi	Pixels per inch—another method of scaling an image	1-1200
natural-scaling	Another method of scaling an image; the value is the percentage of the image's natural size	1-800
hue	The color value for an image	-360 to 360
saturation	The color saturation for an image	0-200

You can combine multiple lpr options on a single command line with the name of the file you want to print at the end of the command. If you regularly use multiple options, you should use the lpoptions command to "save" them so that each time you use lpr, the same set of options will be applied to the command. For example, to set the media to legal and the banner page to confidential for all future print jobs, use this command:

```
$ lpoptions -P hplj -o media=legal -o job-sheets=confidential
```

You can create distinct instances of a printer that apply certain options, then print to that instance to use the options you have set. An **instance** is like a version of a printer definition with particular options set. For example, you could use the lpoptions command to create an instance of the hplj printer called *briefs*:

```
$ lpoptions -P hplj/briefs -o media=legal -o job-sheets=confidential
```

Then you could print a file to that instance of hplj using this command:

```
$ lpr -P hplj/briefs williams.doc
```

You can also print a file using a pipe symbol (|), so that lpr gathers data from another program's output. For example, this command prints the output of the **sort** command to the default printer:

```
$ sort namelist | lpr
```

Using a pipe symbol to print, however, means that the print job has no distinct filename associated with it.

Printing from Graphical Applications

You typically print from a graphical application by choosing Print from the File menu. You review a few options in the printing dialog box and then choose OK to print the current document or file.

Graphical applications don't have separate printing systems—they rely on the same `lpr` utility that you use to print from the command line. Often you will see the `lpr` command in the printing dialog box. You can add options to the `lpr` command as if you were working at the command line; the graphical application then launches the `lpr` command with those options and the document you are working on as the filename.

 Some advanced Linux applications like WordPerfect for Linux and StarOffice include printing features beyond those described in this chapter. These may include additional filters or graphical tools to configure advanced features of popular printers. Such capabilities are becoming less important, however, as Linux printing becomes more powerful and more widely supported by easy-to-use management tools and vendor-supported driver software.

Within a graphical application, nearly all of the options shown in the printing dialog box relate to how the application formats a document. Few or none relate to how the printer is controlled. For example, in either a Page Setup or Print Document dialog box you might see options to set:

- Page margins (right, left, top, and bottom)

- Which pages to print (all or certain page numbers)

- How many copies of the document to print

- Whether to collate multiple copies

You will also see an option to print to a file. In modern Linux distributions, you can choose to print using any of the following:

- A PostScript filter, which creates a `.ps` file that you can later send to any PostScript printer or view online using a program like `gs` (GhostScript).

- A PDF writer, which creates an Adobe-compatible `.pdf` file (portable document format) that you can exchange with anyone who uses Adobe Acrobat.

- A fax filter that will send the document through your modem using fax software. (The fax software is typically installed by default but may need additional configuration to access your modem.)

- An e-mail filter that will send the document as an e-mail to an address you select.

Gnome and KDE applications build upon a standard dialog box provided by the shared libraries of those desktop interfaces. You can see the similarities by reviewing `gedit` and

Gnumeric (a spreadsheet program), both of which you can launch by choosing Programs, then Applications on the Gnome main menu. Within each program, choose Print from the File menu to view the Print dialog box. The dialog box in Gnumeric includes an option to select how many copies to print, but the dialog boxes are very similar. They both let you select whether to print to a file or to a printer using the `lpr` command. The `lpr` command is shown in the dialog box, and you can add options such as those listed in Table 12-2 or Table 12-3. Figure 12-17 shows the Print dialog box in Gnumeric.

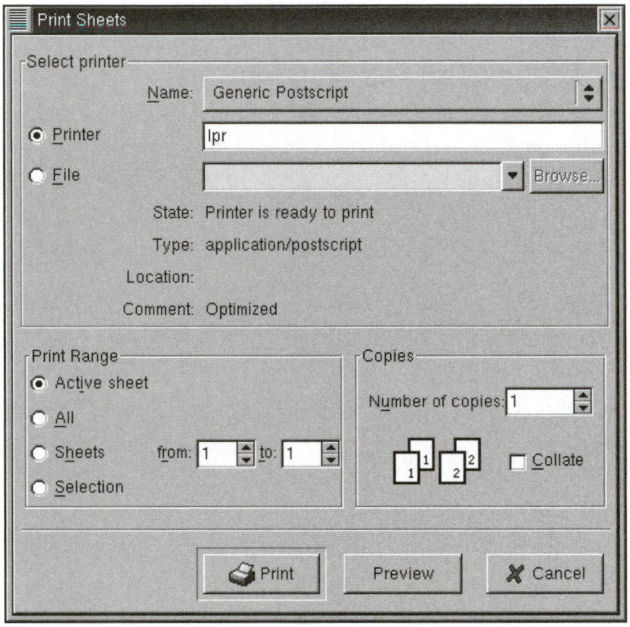

Figure 12-17   The Print dialog box in Gnumeric

You select a printer from the Name drop-down list. The option you select determines whether the Printer or File field is active.

The standard dialog box in KDE applications is more comprehensive. It lets you select between different printing architectures such as LPRng and CUPS, as you could within the KDE Control Center printer definition utility.

To view examples of KDE printing dialog boxes, launch a few applications such as KWord, KSpread, and KOrganizer from the Office or Applications submenu within KDE or under KDE Menus on Gnome (if you have installed both desktops). The basic layout of the KDE and Gnome printing dialog boxes is similar, but KDE includes more graphical configuration options. Figure 12-18 shows the Print dialog box in KWord after clicking the Expand button to show more options. (The Collapse button is shown in the figure; it hides the bottom part of the dialog box.)

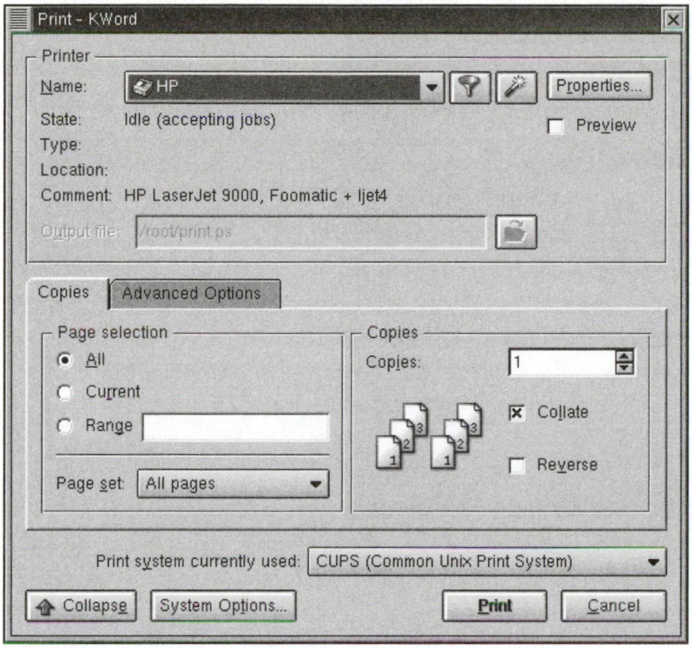

Figure 12-18   The Print dialog box in KWord

In the bottom part of this dialog box you can select which printing system you are using (such as LPRng or CUPS). The printers defined within that system are shown in the Name drop-down list at the top of the dialog box. You can select which printer you want to use, then use the other buttons and fields to refine how the print job will be processed. The Properties button lets you choose the document orientation (portrait or landscape), the number of document pages per printed page, and other options.

KDE applications have integrated the features of the KDE Control Center by including a button (just to the left of Properties) that lets you define a new printer from within the Print dialog box of a KDE application.

Other graphical programs that are not based on KDE or Gnome use similar printing dialog boxes, though typically without as many graphical configuration or selection options. For example, Netscape Communicator lets you select whether to print to a printer or a file, but you cannot select which printer to use. If you don't want to print to the default printer, you must add a `-P` option to the `lpr` command shown in the dialog box to name the printer to use. And you must know the name of the printer, since the options are not shown in the dialog box. A sample Print dialog box, which is a representative of many Linux applications, is shown in Figure 12-19.

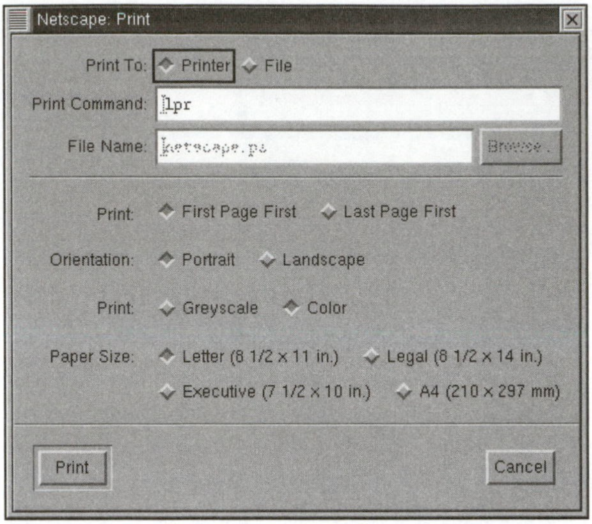

Figure 12-19   The Print dialog box in Netscape Communicator

Some vendors, particularly Hewlett-Packard, are working to make end-user printing easier in Linux. The Enhanced Printing System (EPS) from HP uses PPD files for your printer, which you can download from *hp.sourceforge.net*, to dynamically create a graphical interface that lets you select and control printer features. For example, features like duplex (two-sided) printing, stapling, watermarks, and selecting among paper trays are supported. The graphical printing application in EPS is called `gpr`. You can learn about this system at *hp.sourceforge.net/uhowto/eps-uhowto.php*.

MANAGING THE PRINTING ENVIRONMENT

As a system administrator you are likely to spend a lot of time managing printing. Printers have many moving parts and are more subject to breakdowns than anything inside a computer. Printing also consumes resources such as paper and toner that must be replenished even when the system is working correctly. (Some companies have an employee designated to take care of these things who does not manage other aspects of printing.)

A single large hard disk will meet the storage needs of several dozen users on a standard system. Regular data backups and a redundant system such as disk mirroring provide protection against problems, and once users know where their data is stored and file permissions have been established, the system will generally run a long time without serious problems.

The same users who rely on a single large hard disk probably require several printer devices, depending on the type of work they do. Each printer may cost three times as much as a single hard disk. And supplies for the printers are a continuing cost.

For users who print numerous reports, artwork sheets, or mechanical drawings, the printers become a bottleneck. If many users submit large print jobs at the same time, they must wait for the printer.

The potential problems are compounded because users often try to help themselves with printing issues: they may switch the paper to letterhead or insert envelopes, cause paper jams, or try to bypass other users' print jobs and end up ruining several of them by turning the printer off. The system administrator must physically go to the printer to solve such problems.

Deciding on Printing Policies

For all of these reasons, a printing policy is a helpful document for any organization with more than two or three users who rely on the same printer. A **printing policy** is a brief statement of rules describing how printing resources can be used and how printers will be managed. Having a printing policy that everyone in the organization can review will help a system administrator avoid the headaches that come with multiple hardware failures and demands from users for special treatment. A typical printing policy would include statements about the following issues and might be on a single sheet of paper posted next to a bank of printers:

- Unless the system administrator is specifically authorized by a manager, no one's print jobs will receive priority over other print jobs. (The system administrator can move any print job to the top of the queue, but doing so invariably causes friction among users who have to wait longer because someone received special treatment—you may not want users even to know that you can change print job priorities.)

- Printers are to be used only for projects related to the organization (be it a school, business, or other type of organization). The policy may include a statement about using printers for personal work after certain hours with payment of a fee (such as ten cents per page) to a fund for replenishing paper and toner.

- Each user's printer usage will be tracked and recorded. Anyone who prints an excessive number of sheets may need to explain why. A specific page limit per week or month is sometimes stated. This feature, called **print accounting**, is especially useful for schools.

- No one should alter the printer settings without instructions from the system administrator. This includes changing the default paper size or default paper tray.

- In case of a paper jam or other malfunction, users should contact the system administrator. No one else should open the printer or attempt to make repairs.

Some of these statements might seem severe or inappropriate within your organization. You can decide which will be helpful in maintaining both the printers and the system administrators in good working order.

12

Using the `lpc` Utility

The `lpc` utility is the printer control utility. (The letters `lpc` stand for *line printer control*.) This command-line utility lets you control LPRng or CUPS printing, specifying how print jobs are accepted and processed.

 Many Linux system administrators use one of the graphical utilities described later in this section instead of `lpc`.

As with the `lpr` command, the `lpc` command is a symbolic link, in this case to `/etc/alternatives/print-lpc`, which in turn points to either `/usr/sbin/lpc.LPRng` or `/usr/sbin/lpc.cups`. The link is changed when you use an LPRng or CUPS configuration tool (for example, using the `printconf-gui` tool resets the links to LPRng). The two versions provide the same functionality but act on different underlying systems. Using `lpc` you can:

- Prevent new print jobs from being accepted by a print queue.
- Prevent print jobs from being sent to a printer.
- Cancel a print job that is currently being printed.
- See the status of any printer (such as whether it is enabled, whether the corresponding print queue contains any print jobs, or how much of the current document has been sent to the printer).

You must be root to use `lpc`. You can include an `lpc` command as a parameter on the command line. This command displays the status of the default printer:

```
# lpc status
```

You can also use `lpc` interactively to enter multiple commands. To begin using `lpc` in interactive mode, enter the utility name without any parameters:

```
# lpc
lpc>
```

Table 12-4 lists the commands that you can use at the `lpc` prompt or as parameters to the `lpc` command (if you prefer not to use the interactive mode for some tasks).

For each of the commands shown, `lpc` acts on the default printer (the first one listed in the `printcap` file) unless you specify a printer name. For example, if the first printer in `printcap` is `hp`, using this command will bring down the `hp` printer:

```
# lpc down
```

If the `printcap` file contains a definition of another printer named `stylus`, you can use this command to bring down the `stylus` printer:

```
# lpc down stylus
```

Table 12-4   `lpc` Commands

Command	Description	Example (noninteractive mode)
`help`	Display a list of all `lpc` commands	`lpc help`
`status`	Display status of the `lpd` printer daemon and the print queue indicated (or the default if none is indicated)	`lpc status`
`abort`	Cancel the print job currently being printed (use the `start` command to restart printing)	`lpc abort`
`stop`	Stop sending print jobs to the printer after the current print job has finished printing	`lpc stop`
`start`	Start sending print jobs to the printer (used after `abort` or `stop`)	`lpc start`
`disable`	Prevent users from submitting new print jobs	`lpc disable`
`enable`	Allow users to submit new print jobs	`lpc enable`
`down`	Stop sending print jobs to the printer and prevent new print jobs from being submitted (equivalent to using `stop` and `disable`)	`lpc down`
`up`	Begin sending print jobs to the printer and allow new print jobs to be submitted (equivalent to using `start` and `enable`)	`lpc up`
`exit or quit`	Exit the `lpc` program	Used only in interactive mode
`restart`	Attempt to restart the `lpd` printer daemon (equivalent to using the command `/etc/rc.d/init.d/lpd restart`)	`lpc restart`
`topq`	Move a print job to the top of the named print queue; this command requires a printer name (where the print job will be placed) and the print job number (which you can obtain using the `lpq` command)	`lpc topq hplj 16`

When using any of the `lpc` commands (except `topq`), you can use `all` to refer to all printers. For example, to completely shut down printing, so that no print jobs can be submitted and all printing stops after the current print jobs are finished, use this command:

```
# lpc down all
```

The `lpr` command you learned previously uses a `-P` parameter to define the printer name. For the `lpc` command you simply add the printer name as an additional parameter.

Figure 12-20 illustrates how some key `lpc` commands affect the printing process. The same terms you see in the figure are used in the `lpc` man page and in graphical print management tools.

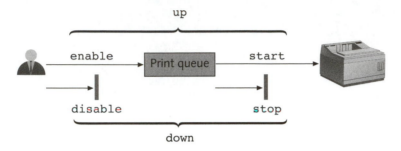

Figure 12-20   Using `lpc` to control the printing process

 You can also use the `lpstat` command to see a quick summary of what each printer is doing.

Tracking Print Jobs

To view the print jobs in the default print queue, enter the command `lpq`. The `lpq` utility lists each of the print jobs in a print queue with the following information:

- Status of the print job, such as active (currently printing), ready, or error
- Owner (the user who submitted the print job)
- Class of the print job (its priority; normally **A**, unless the **-C** option was used with the `lpr` command)
- Job number assigned by the print server
- Size of the file in bytes (characters)
- Time that the print job was submitted

Any user can view the current print jobs using `lpq`. Sample output from the `lpq` command is shown here:

```
$ lpq -P hplj
Printer: hplj@sundance
Queue: 1 printable job
Server: pid 10334 active
Unspooler: pid 10335 active
Status: IF filter 'mf_wrapper' filter msg - '' at 11:14:57.966
Rank    Owner/ID          Class Job Files          Size Time
active  nwells@sundance     A   308 stats.txt      2241 11:09:10
1st     cynthia@brighton    A   312 index.html     9617 11:12:34
2nd     alexv@sundance      A   323 userguide.ps 434898 11:14:41
```

If you are working on a server where the print queue contains many documents, you may either want to use the **-s** option, to display a shorter format for each print job, or add a job ID to the **lpq** command. The job ID refers to the print job number assigned by the print server and displayed under the **Job** field in the sample **lpq** output above. To see a list of all print jobs submitted by user **alexv**, enter this command:

    $ **lpq alexv**

If you have previously used **lpq** to identify the job number of a large print job, use that number to query the status of the job, as in this example:

    $ **lpq 572**

You can delete print jobs from any print queue. If you are logged in as root, you can delete anyone's print jobs, or move a print job to another print queue or to the top of a print queue so that it is printed next. The **lprm** command deletes a print job from a queue. You need a job ID from **lpq** before you can use **lprm** to delete a specific print job. For example, if you decide after viewing the output of **lpq** that print job number 491 should be deleted before it is printed, use this command to remove it from the **hplj** print queue:

    $ **lprm -P hplj 491**

You can remove all of a user's print jobs by referring to a username. Each user can remove his or her own print jobs in this way; root can remove anyone's print jobs:

    # **lprm nwells**

You can also remove all of the print jobs in a queue by using the – (hyphen) parameter:

    # **lprm -P hplj -**

When you are using CUPS, the **cancel** command works just like the **lprm** command.

Using Graphical Print Management Utilities

Instead of **lpc**, **lpq**, and **lprm**, you can use either of two KDE graphical utilities to manage printing. The first of these is KJobViewer. You can launch it by choosing Print Jobs on the Utilities menu of KDE. (On the Gnome main menu, choose KDE Menus, then Utilities, then Print Jobs.)

Figure 12-21 shows the Print Job Viewer. To select which print jobs are shown, open the Filter menu, then choose Select Printer, then click a printer name or All Printers.

12

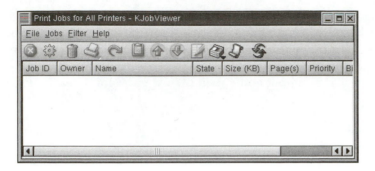

Figure 12-21 The KDE Print Job Viewer

You can select a print job by clicking it, then choosing an action for that job on the Jobs menu:

- *Hold* pauses printing on that print job.

- *Resume* restarts printing for that print job.

- *Remove* deletes the print job from the queue.

- *Move* lets you select another printer from a submenu; the print job is moved to the other print queue.

These same actions are available as buttons on the icon bar just below the menus or by right-clicking a print job in the list.

The Print Job Viewer is also used within the KDE Control Center's printing manager, under the System section. You can select a print queue in the top part of the Control Center window (shown earlier in Figure 12-9), then click the Jobs tab on the bottom right to select which print jobs to view.

Another KDE printing utility that is not integrated with the Control Center is the KLpq program. You can launch it from a command line using the `klpq` command or from the KDE Utilities menu by choosing KLpq. (Some Linux distributions may use a different menu name for this program.)

 When you first launch KLpq, you must specify which printing system you are using. Choose LPRng; CUPS is not listed, but the utility uses the underlying command-line tools that will work with CUPS if the symbolic links have been updated during your printer configuration process.

The main window of KLpq, shown in Figure 12-22, lists all the jobs for the print queue selected in the Printer Name drop-down box. Each defined printer is included in the list. When the Queuing checkbox is checked users can submit new jobs to the print queue—when unchecked, new jobs cannot be submitted. The Printing checkbox determines whether jobs are being sent to the printer or held in the queue. The Queuing checkbox is equivalent to the `lpc` commands **enable** / **disable**; the Printing checkbox is equivalent to the `lpc` commands `start` / `stop`. You must click the Update button after changing one of the checkboxes.

```
┌─────────────────────────────────────────────────────────────┐
│ ▤ Print Queue                                      _ □ ×     │
│ File  Options  Help                                          │
│ ┌─ Printer Configuration ──────────────────────────────────┐ │
│ │                                                          │ │
│ │  Printer name: │local    ▼│      □ Queuing  □ Printing   │ │
│ │ ┌──────┬─────────────┬──────┬────────────────┬────────┬┐ │ │
│ │ │ Rank │ Owner       │ Job  │ Files          │ Size   ││ │ │
│ │ ├──────┴─────────────┴──────┴────────────────┴────────┴┤ │ │
│ │ │       0 root@sunda          0 3    A  333 ERRO...   0 │ │ │
│ │ │       0 root@sunda          0 3    A  913 report.txt 0│ │ │
│ │ │                                                      │ │ │
│ │ │                                                      │ │ │
│ │ │                                                      │ │ │
│ │ │                                                      │ │ │
│ │ └──────────────────────────────────────────────────────┘ │ │
│ │ ┌─────────┐ ┌──────────────────────────┐  ▲  ┌──────────┐│ │
│ │ │ Remove  │ │ Printer: local@sundance  │  ▼  │  Auto    ││ │
│ │ ├─────────┤ │ Queue: 1 printable job   │  ▲  ├──────────┤│ │
│ │ │Make Top │ │ Server: pid 2914 active  │  ▼  │  Update  ││ │
│ │ └─────────┘ └──────────────────────────┘     └──────────┘│ │
│ └──────────────────────────────────────────────────────────┘ │
└─────────────────────────────────────────────────────────────┘
```

Figure 12-22   The KLpq printing manager

If you are logged in as root, you can select any print job listed and remove it by clicking the Remove button, or make it the next job to be printed by clicking Make Top. The list of print jobs is updated automatically every few seconds. You can alter the update interval by choosing Update Frequency on the Options menu.

> The `lpd` daemon can log print job information to track how your printing resources are being used. A basic type of this print accounting capability is enabled by default when you use the `printconf-gui` utility to create a printer definition. The `af` code in `/etc/printcap` defines a file where print job information is logged. The man page for `lpd` describes additional print accounting options.

When you are using CUPS for printing, you can manage print jobs in the same interface where you create and modify printer definitions. After launching a browser with the *localhost:631* address, choose the Jobs link to view print jobs. You can use the options on that page, shown in Figure 12-23, to control each print job as needed.

The design of CUPS allows you to manage print jobs on any networked system where you have been granted permissions in the **cups.conf** configuration file. Compare this to `lpd`, for which you must have a shell account with root access to a system in order to manage print jobs, and then can probably only do so using command-line utilities.

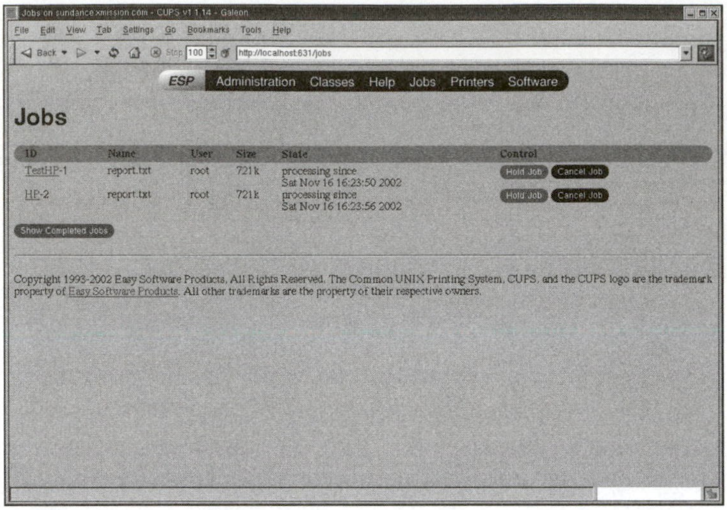

Figure 12-23   Managing CUPS print jobs in a browser

CHAPTER SUMMARY

- ❐ The traditional Linux printing architecture is called LPRng and is based on the system developed for BSD UNIX.

- ❐ More recent developments include the Common UNIX Printing System (CUPS) and the Enhanced Printing System (EPS) from Hewlett-Packard.

- ❐ Both LPRng and CUPS rely on a print server that accepts print jobs and manages the process of sending jobs to printers. A print server can interact with print servers located on other networked computers.

- ❐ The lpd print server can interact with other lpd daemons on the network. The cupsd daemon is more flexible in a networked environment where different types of computers are present and is also easier to manage remotely.

- ❐ Printers are typically connected locally to either a parallel or serial port, both of which are referred to as character special files or devices, as opposed to hard disks, which are block special files or devices.

- ❐ A system administrator creates printer definitions, which act as print queues. Printer definitions are stored in /etc/printcap and can be created using printconf-gui or other text-mode or graphical tools.

- ❐ Users submit print jobs to a named print queue using either the lpr command or a graphical dialog box that typically also relies on the lpr command.

- ❐ Linux can print to Windows-based printers (using the Samba suite), to NetWare-based printers, and to network attached printers that do not rely on another computer to provide a network connection and print management software.

- The data that a user submits as a print job is processed using a print filter or print driver to prepare it to be sent to a certain printer model. The filter or driver software may provide access to special features such as duplex printing or input tray selection, though this is still rare in Linux.

- Filters convert raw document data into a format a printer can understand, such as PCL or PostScript. Some "magic filter programs" can produce output for many types of printers; some vendors provide specific utilities to print to their devices.

- A printing policy informs users of how they can use printing resources and what they can expect from the system administrator who manages the printers.

- The lpc program and several graphical utilities let you manage print jobs currently waiting to be printed.

- Print jobs waiting to be printed on a system using CUPS can be managed using the CUPS browser-based interface.

KEY TERMS

block special file — A type of file (normally located in /dev) referring to a physical device that transfers data in blocks of characters, such as a hard disk drive.

cancel — A command supported by CUPS to delete a print job from a print queue.

character special file — A filename referring to a physical device (such as a serial port) that transfers data in single characters.

Common UNIX Printing System (CUPS) — A printing architecture for Linux and UNIX systems that lets users and system administrators browse the network to find and print to networked printers and other devices. It also lets system administrators manage printer definitions and print jobs across the network using a browser interface.

driver — A software program that provides abstract services for a hardware component, such as opening files or reading character input.

instance — A version of a printer definition with particular options set.

local printer — A printer directly attached to your computer.

lpc — The Linux printer control utility. It stands for *line printer control*.

lpd — The print server used in the LPRng print architecture. It sends files prepared by lpr to the physical printer device or remote print server. It stands for *line printer daemon*.

lpq — A utility that lists each print job in a print queue and includes information such as the owner and size of each job.

lpr — A command that prepares files to be sent to a physical printer device, effectively "printing" files for Linux users.

lprm — A command that deletes a print job from a print queue.

lpstat — A command that displays a brief summary of the status of each printer.

12

magic filter — A print filter program that automatically processes a file into the correct output format based on the file's type.

network attached printer — A printer that includes a networking interface (such as an Ethernet port), so that it is attached directly to a network instead of through a computer (such as through a parallel port).

page description language — A special set of codes that determine the graphics elements, text font, and everything else about how information appears on a printed page. PostScript and PCL are examples of page description languages.

port — A networking parameter that permits one application to communicate with a specific application on a networked computer.

PostScript Printer Description (PPD) file — A file containing a standardized printer description that can be used by several printing architectures on different operating systems. PPD files are used to describe many types of printers, not just PostScript printers.

print accounting — A method of tracking how users are using printing resources based on print job information logged by `lpd`.

print filter — A script that contains instructions for formatting documents using the page description language required by a specific printer. The print filter is used by the `lpr` program to prepare files to be sent to a physical printer.

print job — A file submitted for printing via the `lpr` command or a graphical dialog box.

print queue — A printer definition; also a subdirectory where files are stored to wait for a print server daemon (`lpd` or `cupsd`) to retrieve them one by one and send them to the printer. Also called a print spool directory.

print spool directory — The directory where print jobs submitted to a print queue are stored until they are sent to a printer.

printcap — The printer definition file used by LPRng Linux printing. This file specifies how and where files to be printed are stored and processed by `lpr` and `lpd`. It stands for *printer capture*.

printing policy — A brief document that describes how printing resources can be used and how they will be managed within an organization.

remote printer — A printer attached to another computer on the network or to the network itself, rather than to the computer on which you are working.

service — A command that lets you launch a script in `/etc/rc.d/init.d` to control a system service.

REVIEW QUESTIONS

1. Each time a user prints a file, a _____ is created.

   a. printer definition

   b. print queue

   c. print job

   d. printer instance

2. The two print server daemons described in this chapter are:

   a. `lpd` and `cupsd`

   b. `printconf-gui` and the KDE Control Center

   c. `lpstat` and `lpc`

   d. LPRng and CUPS

3. Printer definitions, or print queue definitions, are stored in the
   _____ file.

   a. `/var/spool/lpd/lp`

   b. `/var/adm/acct`

   c. `/etc/printcap`

   d. `/etc/lpd.conf`

4. The graphical utility provided in Red Hat Linux 7.3 to configure a printer
   definition is:

   a. `printconf-gui`

   b. `lpc`

   c. KLpq

   d. `lpoptions`

5. Print filters are used to:

   a. Convert graphics formats before printing images

   b. Prepare documents in a printer-specific format

   c. Remove unprintable characters from documents

   d. Compress print job files before transfer to a remote print server

6. Describe at least two purposes of having a printer policy in place.

7. Multiple options in the `printcap` file are separated by:

   a. An equal sign

   b. Two colons

   c. A carriage return/new line

   d. A tab

8. Define the meaning of the following option codes as used within the `printcap`
   file: `sh`, `mx`, `sd`, `if`, and `af`.

9. The CUPS printing architecture *does not* allow system administrators to:

   a. Use the same printing system on diverse UNIX and Linux systems

   b. Check the status of print jobs on a remote server using a browser-based interface

   c. Use multiple instances of a printer that include specific sets of printing options

   d. Graphically configure features specific to one model of printer, such as duplex
   printing or dots-per-inch settings

12

10. Explain the difference between the `lpc` commands **up**, **enable**, and **start**.

11. CUPS management is accomplished:

    a. By contacting a Web-server–like server using port 631

    b. Using a browser to reach *linuxprinting.org*

    c. Using port 631 of `printconf-gui` or the KDE Control Center

    d. By using any standard Web server on a system with `cupsd` and the appropriate PPD files installed

12. Graphical tools are *not* helpful for setting up printing when:

    a. You have only root account access

    b. You require advanced printing security or accounting features

    c. You are printing to a remote or non–Linux printer

    d. You are using a standard Linux distribution

13. You can use the `lpr` command to print a file using a redirection pipe, but this has the disadvantage of:

    a. Not formatting the document using the correct print filter

    b. Not being able to control the resulting print job using standard commands like `lpq` and `lprm`

    c. Not permitting use of options with the `lpr` command

    d. Not including a filename in the description of the print job

14. Explain when the **PRINTER** environment variable is used.

15. The _____ utility displays the owner, size, and submission time for print jobs.

    a. `lpq`

    b. `lprm`

    c. `lpc`

    d. `lpd`

16. The command `lprm -a kate` would do the following:

    a. Remove all print jobs from a printer called `kate`

    b. Remove print jobs submitted by user `kate` from all print queues on the system

    c. Remove the print job that will print the file `kate`

    d. Remove the accounting files for printer `kate`

17. A CUPS class lets you:

    a. Aggregate print jobs for multiple printers using a single name for increased end–user convenience

    b. Specify options that apply to a printer definition when you indicate the class name as the selected printer

   c. Specify the features that a model of printer supports, such as duplex printing, color printing options, scaling, or multiple paper trays

   d. Control print jobs that were submitted to a remote printer

18. Printing from graphical applications typically relies on:

   a. The `lpr` command

   b. Separate print filters designed to implement the features of the graphical application

   c. CUPS

   d. LPRng

19. Describe two limitations of the remote printing architecture implemented by Linux using `lpd`.

20. The print server daemons are network services similar to a Web server. True or False?

21. Printing from Linux to a Windows-based computer is accomplished using:

   a. The NCP protocol

   b. A magic filter

   c. The Samba suite and SMB

   d. `lptions` and CUPS

22. Your Linux distribution may include default printing capabilities for all except:

   a. Creating PDF files

   b. PostScript printing

   c. Faxing

   d. Color printing

23. Which `lpc` command will stop the printing of the current print job?

   a. `lpc abort`

   b. `lpc cancel`

   c. `lpc stop`

   d. `lpc disable`

24. Describe how both LPRng and CUPS can be supported by the same commands such as `lpr` and `lpq`.

25. Linux print utilities determine which printer to use by checking:

   a. The `-P` option, then the **PRINTER** environment variable, then the `printcap` file

   b. The **PRINTER** environment variable, then the `-P` option included with the command

   c. The order of print queues in the `printcap` file

   d. The systemwide printer configuration in `/etc/sysconfig`

12

HANDS-ON PROJECTS

Before beginning these projects, you should enable the LPRng printing system on your Linux system using this command: `service lpd start`

Project 12-1

In this project you create a new print queue using a graphical utility and review how it affects the text configuration files. To complete this project you need a working Red Hat Linux 7.3 system with root access.

1. Log in as root.

2. Launch the `printconf-gui` program by entering the command `printconf-gui` or choosing **Programs**, then **System**, then **Printer Configuration** on the Gnome main menu.

3. Click the **New** button to begin creating a new printer definition. The Add a New Print Queue window appears.

4. Click **Next** to continue. The Set the Print Queue Name and Type window appears.

5. Enter **lex** in the Queue Name field and click **Local Printer** in the Queue Type section of the window. Click **Next** to continue. The Configure a Local Printer window appears.

6. Select a device from the list shown. You will normally see `/dev/lp0` and can choose this device. You could also click Custom Device and enter a specific device name, such as `/dev/ttyS1` for the second serial port, but you will not be printing using this queue, so the device you select is not important.

7. Click **Next** to continue. The Select a Print Driver window appears.

8. Scroll down until you see Lexmark. Click the arrow to the left of **Lexmark**.

9. Scroll down until you see 5700. Click the arrow to the left of **5700**.

10. Among the three driver names listed under 5700, click **lex5700**, then click **Next** to continue.

11. The Finish, and Create the New Print Queue window appears. Click **Finish** to complete the printer definition. The printer you defined is listed in the main window of `printconf-gui`.

12. Click on **lex** in the main window of `printconf-gui`.

13. Click the **Edit** button to open the Edit Queue dialog box.

14. In the Name and Aliases tab, use the **Add** button to create an alternate name for this print queue. This is similar to creating an instance in CUPS, but you cannot associate different options with an alias in `printconf-gui`.

15. Click the **Driver Options** tab. After a few moments, a list of options for this printer appears. These options are taken from the lex5700 Linux driver provided by Lexmark and included with Red Hat Linux 7.3.

16. Set the resolution to **1200×1200 dpi**.

17. Choose **OK** to close the Edit Queue dialog box.

18. Choose **Exit** on the **File** menu of `printconf-gui`.

19. When prompted, choose **Yes** to save the changes you made to printer configurations.

20. After a moment, a message box informs you that `lpd` has been restarted. Click **OK** to continue. The utility closes.

21. Open a command-line window if one is not already open.

22. View the `/etc/printcap` file:

    ```
    less /etc/printcap
    ```

23. Can you see the lex print queue that you created? Where is the alias?

24. Refer to Table 12-1 and identify each of the options included by `printconf-gui` in the queue definition.

25. Change to the directory `/var/spool/lpd/lex`:

    ```
    cd /var/spool/lpd/lex
    ```

26. Explore the contents of the two files `mf.cfg` and `lex5700-62016.foo`. Describe what you see.

27. Close all windows and log off.

Project 12-2

In this project you practice managing print jobs in the new print queue that you created in Project 12-1. To complete this project you need a working Red Hat Linux 7.3 system with root access. This project assumes you have already completed Project 12-1.

1. Log in as root and open a command-line window.

2. Stop the print server from sending print jobs to the printer (since this print queue is only for experimentation, this will prevent errors caused by trying to print to a non-existent device):

    ```
    lpc stop lex
    ```

3. Enable the lex queue so it can accept print jobs:

    ```
    lpc enable lex
    ```

4. Print a text file to your lex print queue:

    ```
    lpr -Plex /etc/termcap
    ```

5. Open the `gedit` text editor at the command line:

    ```
    gedit &
    ```

6. Click the **Open** button, type `/etc/inittab` and press **Enter**. The `/etc/inittab` file appears in `gedit`.

12

7. Click the **Print** button in `gedit`.

8. In the Printer field, where you see `lpr`, add the text `-P lex`.

9. Click **Print** to print the document.

10. Choose **Exit** on the **File** menu of `gedit` to close the text editor.

11. Print a third file using redirection at the command line:

    ```
    sort /etc/password | lpr -P lex
    ```

12. View the print jobs awaiting service in the lex print queue:

    ```
    lpq -P lex
    ```

13. Launch the graphical KDE print queue manager:

    ```
    klpq &
    ```

14. When the utility window appears, click the **Printer name** drop-down box and choose **lex** if necessary.

15. If necessary, select the first print job by clicking on the first line in the Rank column.

16. Click **Remove** to delete this job from the queue. Click **Yes** to confirm the removal.

17. Select the last remaining print job by clicking on the last line in the Rank column.

18. Make this job the next to print (assuming you restarted printing and had an actual printer attached), by clicking **Make Top**. Click **Yes** to confirm the move.

19. Choose **Quit** from the **File** menu.

20. Delete all the remaining print jobs from the lex print queue by entering this command:

    ```
    lprm -P lex all
    ```

21. Close all windows and log off.

Project 12-3

In this project you create a remote print queue to access the print queue you created in Project 12-1. To complete this project you need a working Red Hat Linux 7.3 system with root access. In this project you should work as a team with another person working on a second computer. You should have completed Project 12-1 on one computer (referred to in the steps as the server) and have another computer as well (referred to in the steps as the client). Both systems must have networking correctly configured.

1. Log in as root on the server and open a command-line window.

2. On the server computer, display the hostname of the computer.

    ```
    echo $HOSTNAME
    ```

    Note the output from this command.

3. On the client computer, log in as root and open a command-line window.

4. Start `printconf-gui`.

5. Click **New**.

6. Click **Next** to continue.

7. Enter **remote_lex** in the Queue Name field.

8. Choose **Unix Printer** in the Queue Type field.

9. Click **Next** to continue.

10. The Configure a Unix Print Queue window appears. In the Server field, enter the host name you noted in Step 2.

11. In the Queue field, enter **lex**.

12. Click **Next** to continue.

13. In the Select a Print Driver dialog box, click the arrow next to **Lexmark**.

14. Click the arrow next to **5700**.

15. Click **lex5700** and then click **Next** to continue.

16. Click **Finish** to complete the queue creation process.

17. Choose **Restart lpd** from the File menu to activate your new print queue on the client computer.

18. On the client computer, print a file to the remote print queue:

    `lpr -Premote_lex /etc/termcap`

19. On the server computer, review the contents of the lex print queue:

    `lpq -P lex`

20. Are any print jobs stored on the client computer?

21. Remove all print jobs on the server computer:

    `lprm -P lex all`

22. Close all windows and log off.

Project 12-4

In this project you explore the CUPS management interface. To complete this project you need a working Red Hat Linux 7.3 system with root access. This project activates the CUPS printing system. If you later wish to use the LPRng system, refer to the note at the beginning of these projects.

1. Log in as root and open a command-line window.

2. Stop the `lpd` print server:

    `service lpd stop`

3. Start the CUPS print server:

    `service cups start`

12

4. Open the CUPS print management interface by opening the main menu of Gnome and choosing **Programs**, then **System**, then **CUPS Printer Configuration**.

5. Click **Manage Printers**.

6. When the Printer page appears, click the **Add Printer** button.

7. When prompted, enter **root** in the Username field of the message box, and the root password in the Password field. Click **OK** to continue. The CUPS server can be configured to allow different users to access CUPS configuration options.

8. Enter **HP** in the Name field and then click **Continue**. (The Location and Description fields are optional; you can enter information if you choose to.)

9. When you click **Continue**, you may see a message box warning you about submitting data over a network connection. Click **Continue** to close the message box.

10. In the Device field, choose **Parallel Port #1**. Then click **Continue**.

11. In the Make field, choose **HP**. Then click **Continue**.

12. In the Model field, choose **HP LaserJet 9000, Foomatic + ljet4 (en)**. Then click **Continue**.

13. A message informs you that the print queue has been successfully created.

14. Click the **Printers** link at the top of the page. You see an entry for the HP print queue you just created.

15. Click the **Jobs** link. Are any print jobs pending for any print queues?

16 Close all windows and log off.

CASE PROJECTS

Starwood Movie Studios have called you back in for further consulting. They have traditionally used only a couple of standard laser printers in their offices to print word processing documents. Now they would like to be able to render the high-resolution color images from their Linux-based computer graphics terminals. The studio manager would like you to recommend a color printer model that they can connect to their Linux systems.

1. Using the Web resources described in the chapter text, locate the highest-end color printer that has good Linux support. What features make you select one model over another? What level of Linux support can you find for high-end color printers?

2. You select two very nice color printers and install them at Starwood. The management team is very happy with the results, but they call you a month later with a concern: they are spending a small fortune on supplies for the new printers. They have created a set of rules for employees that limits printing, but they want you to

make the rules effective. Review the man page for `lpd` under the ACCOUNTING section. Then review the log files that were generated by the projects for this chapter. Now create a basic script that will extract printing data from the logs and display a summary of each user with the amount each has printed. You may also decide to include time and date information and overall summary statistics.

3. Although the new printing setup at Starwood appears to be working well, they would like to increase your involvement until the users are accustomed to both the technology and the rules. You will need to perform some daily management tasks remotely. Will you use LPRng or CUPS? What factors influence your decision?

12

13

BACKING UP SYSTEM DATA

After reading this chapter and completing the exercises, you will be able to:

♦ Understand data backup strategies

♦ Describe hardware and software used to back up Linux systems

♦ Use popular backup utilities such as `tar`, `cpio`, and graphical backup utilities

In the previous chapter you learned how to configure and manage Linux printing using either the traditional LPRng architecture with the `lpd` print server, or the newer CUPS architecture with its browser-based configuration tools. You learned how to define print queues, submit files for printing, and manage printers using a variety of command-line and graphical utilities.

In this chapter you learn about backing up data stored on a Linux system. The information in this chapter is an extension of what you learned in Chapter 9, Preparing for Emergencies; a sound plan for managing backups of system data is a great way to prepare for emergencies and should be part of every system administrator's work. You learn in the following sections about planning backups for different types of systems and environments, about the hardware components and backup media you rely on to execute your backup strategy, and the software utilities you use for backing up data—both those included with Linux and with other commercial products.

UNDERSTANDING BACKUP STRATEGIES

A **backup** is simply a copy of data on a computer system. Making a backup of critical data is a form of insurance. A system administrator takes on extra expense and effort to back up data with the understanding that systems sometimes fail; the small, regularly occurring cost of backups is better than the exorbitant, when-you-least-expect-it cost of a system failure that wipes out your data.

Backing up thousands of files owned by dozens or hundreds of users can be a complex process. A **backup plan** is a written document that outlines when, how, and perhaps why various files will be backed up, stored, and—when necessary—restored. As you might guess, implementing the backup plan normally falls to the system administrator.

 The information described in this section as part of a backup plan will often be included in broader plans made by an organization, such as a security plan or a disaster plan. The name of the plan is much less important than having steps and rationale written down and then implemented.

Among other things, a backup plan will normally specify the type of backup media that the organization will use. **Backup media** is the item that holds backed-up data, such as a tape cartridge, writeable CD or DVD, or even a floppy disk. The backup plan also specifies how lost data can be restored. To **restore** data is to copy it from backup media (for example, a tape cartridge) back to the file system where that data is normally used, and from which it was lost.

Developing a backup strategy that works well for your organization is an ongoing process. As a system administrator, you can expect to work with many types of computer systems, a variety of applications and data storage needs, and computer users whose preferences and actions are rarely predictable. The following sections address some of the questions that you should consider when formulating a backup plan.

Asking Initial Questions

Some of the initial questions you should consider as you formulate a backup plan include the following:

- *What files should be backed up?* Backing up everything on the system is an admirable goal, but time and cost restrictions might make it impractical. You should evaluate the various parts of your system to determine what data is easily restored from a vendor CD, such as the operating system or an application. If you are short on resources, these items can be re-created (and then reconfigured) from their original sources rather than from a backup that you create.

- *Who will back up files?* As mentioned previously, this task normally falls to the system administrator. You may, however, decide that users on a networked system should take on part of this responsibility themselves. For example, you could inform users that only data placed in a certain directory area will be backed up each night. Multiple system administrators could also share the responsibility for backups, either to reduce the work burden on one person or to make backups more accessible in case they are needed for restoring data.

- *Where are files located?* You probably know offhand where different types of data are located on your Linux system. A more thorough review will let you decide which specific directories on the system are being actively used, which contain data that is easily reconstructed, and which hold temporary files that don't warrant the effort of a regular backup. These are just three examples of the categories you might assign to parts of your system as you review the various file systems and devices that store data.

- *How should backups be performed?* The answer to this question might be determined by the equipment you purchase, as well as by how your organization operates its computer systems. Many system administrators must back up data during non-work hours. This process can be automated in most cases using a `cron` job (see Chapter 11) or other specialized utilities. You might also want certain events to trigger a regular backup, or a different type of backup than would normally occur. For example, you might want to back up the entire system before installing new hardware devices such as SCSI adapters.

- *Must you be able to restore data within a specific period of time?* When a problem occurs (and it will), several factors affect how rapidly you can restore lost data to the system. These factors include the size and location of the lost files and the media format on which the backup data was stored. Your backup plan should reflect the value of time within your organization. In some organizations, the ability to restore lost data immediately is essential. In others, speed is not as critical.

13

Ideally, your backup plan should prevent the headaches associated with having to locate files and figure out how to reconstruct damaged or lost data in the midst of a crisis. A well-designed backup plan will make it easy and convenient for you to regularly back up system data and restore files according to the needs of your organization. It will also help you justify to management the costs of the equipment and time needed to make your backup plan effective.

Determining the Value of Data

Many of the decisions you make as you create a backup strategy should be based on the value of the data you are backing up. The more expensive data is to create, acquire, or refine, the more you should spend to protect its integrity. Some data may only be valuable to one person in an organization, but if that person's time is required to re-create any data that is lost, the data still has value to the entire organization.

For example, a study of the value of data held by an organization might determine that a given set of files required 4,000 hours of work by the employees of the firm to create. A different estimate might state that the data could be re-created given current experience and facts in about 2,000 hours. If the average wage of the employees involved in the project is approximately $40 per hour, the data would have a value of $80,000. But the study doesn't end there.

Cost-of-data calculations involving employee pay should include the benefits paid to the employee. When a company pays an employee a salary of $60,000 per year, the company also pays taxes, insurance, retirement benefits, and other costs that raise the total cost to the company for that employee by 35% to 100%—the $60,000 employee costs the company a total of $81,000 to $120,000. This is called the burdened cost of the employee.

The estimate of 2,000 hours—about one work-year—is based on an experienced employee re-creating the data. If that well-trained employee spends time re-creating lost data, what current work will he or she not be able to do? This is called the opportunity cost. The employee might forgo a project worth many times $80,000 in order to re-create the lost data. Opportunity cost extends even further. How was the data that was lost going to be used? Was it part of a multimillion dollar advertising campaign? Or perhaps a financial merger? A great deal of money may be lost because the data is unavailable when needed. Even if $80,000 can be invested to re-create it, the moment of opportunity when the data was needed may be past.

This discussion doesn't address the anger or low morale of an employee who must re-create a project that was partially or completely finished. These factors can also affect the financial health of an organization and are worth considering as justification for spending money on a solid backup strategy.

The following list summarizes questions to ask when determining the value of data:

- How many hours of effort were spent creating the data?
- How many hours of effort would be required to re-create the data?
- How much inherent value does the data have for the operation of the organization?
- Is the data irreplaceable?
- Is the data time-critical to a current project?

These considerations are similar to those raised in the discussion of hardware redundancy and fault tolerance in Chapter 9. The decisions you make as a system administrator are also similar to those you might make when evaluating your system's hardware: if data is worth millions of dollars to your organization, don't hesitate to spend $50,000 to $100,000 to protect that data. By answering the questions in the preceding list, you may be able to convince company officers or supervisors that the expense is warranted. With the right hardware and software tools, you'll be well prepared to back up the information that you are charged with safeguarding.

Determining When to Back up Data

Once you have created an initial backup or archive of important data, the question of how often to refresh the backup arises—that is, how often to back up the system again to account for changes in the data since you last backed it up. Having at least one backup of data is better than having none at all, but data changes frequently in most organizations. Regularly backing up the latest information stored on the system is a critical part of most system administrators' jobs.

The question of when to back up data is related to how valuable the data is to an organization. You can begin by asking, "How often does the data change?" and "Do changes to the data affect the value of the data?"

The answers to these questions vary by which part of a Linux system you are evaluating. The operating system itself probably changes very little after the initial configuration. Applications installed on the system are also unlikely to change regularly. In contrast, user data, log files, and e-mail archives change daily and are normally the focus of frequent backups. This data constitutes the daily work of users within your organization. By maintaining regular backups, no one is ever likely to lose more than a few hours worth of work, even if the entire system crashes or a hard disk is destroyed.

Several backup strategies are commonly used. You can select a strategy based on how often data on your system changes and how valuable or critical each incremental piece of data is. The following discussion describes a widely used backup strategy for Linux.

13

A Linux Backup Strategy

Different backup strategies balance the desire for a complete backup of data at all times with the need for convenience in creating and maintaining backups. The method described here is a standard used for many Linux and UNIX systems. You can adjust the time frames according to how often the data on your system changes.

Using Backup Levels

This strategy relies on multiple backup levels. A **backup level** defines how much data is to be backed up in comparison with another backup level. A backup operation at a given backup level stores all of the data that has changed since the last backup of the previous level. For example, a backup at level 1 stores all files that have changed since the last level 0 backup; a backup at level 2 stores all files that have changed since the last level 1 backup. A commonly used arrangement operates with three levels, as described here:

- Level 0 is a full backup. Everything on the system is backed up. A level 0 backup might be performed on the first of every month.

- A level 1 backup might be done once per week. Every file that has been modified since the last level 0 backup (on the first of the month) is included in the level 1 backup. Storing only files that have changed since a full backup is called an **incremental backup**.

- A level 2 backup could then be done each day. Every file that has been modified since the first of the week (the last level 1 backup) is included in the level 2 backup. Like a level 1 backup, this is considered an incremental backup.

Figure 13–1 illustrates the three-level backup just described.

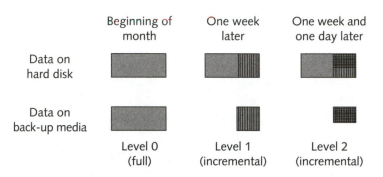

Figure 13-1   Backup levels

The times associated with backup levels are arbitrary. A level 0 backup is normally a full backup in which every file is backed up, but other levels can store incremental data each month, week, day, or hour, as you choose. Each level always records all the changes since a backup of a previous level.

The advantage of using backup levels is that you can back up data frequently, so very little data is lost if a system fails, but you don't have to back up the entire system each time you do a backup.

Restoring a File from a Three-Level Backup

Suppose you had backed up data using the system just described. A user comes to you and needs you to recover a file that was inadvertently deleted. The user can't recall when the file was last modified, but it was "recently." You can follow these steps to locate the file:

1. Check the most recent level 2 backup. If the file is there, it was changed in the last day. This backup probably doesn't include very many files compared to the size of the entire system, so it's easy to search for a file. If the file isn't there, then it wasn't modified in the last 24 hours, so proceed to Step 2.

2. Check the most recent level 1 backup. If the file is there, it was changed sometime after the first of the week, but not in the last 24 hours. This backup contains more files, so it takes a little longer to search. If the file is not found, proceed to Step 3.

3. Check the most recent level 0 backup. The file will always be included on this backup because a full backup includes every file on the system. Searching through this backup may be time-consuming because it is fairly large.

Backup media such as tape drives and optical disks always have directories of their contents to help you locate files as rapidly as possible, but a tape cartridge must be rewound to the place where the file is stored. As a result, restoring a single file from a tape cartridge can be time-consuming.

You might wonder why you shouldn't start searching for the file in the level 0 backup, since it is certain to be part of that backup. You should always start with the most recent backup in order to find the most recent version of a file. If the file had been altered since the first of the month, the most recent copy of the file will not be on the level 0 backup.

If a file was created and deleted on the same day, it wouldn't be part of any backup plan that backed up data each evening. If a user asked for help in this situation, you would need to rely on "undelete" utilities to find the deleted file on the hard disk.

Advantages to the three-level backup method include the following:

- Creating the level 2 daily backups requires little of the system administrator's time because few files are altered on any given day.

- No user will ever lose more than a single day's work because the changes in the file system from each day are recorded in a level 2 backup.

- Files that rarely change are still backed up and available, but don't require daily maintenance by the system administrator.

Some backup utilities explicitly use the term "backup levels" to refer to how data is backed up and how backup media are tracked. The concept can be applied to any utility, however. For the system to work well, you need to keep careful records and label backup media clearly.

In the event that an entire system must be restored using a set of backup media that have been prepared using the three-level method, a system administrator would follow this procedure:

1. Restore everything from the most recent level 0 backup.

2. Restore everything from the most recent level 1 backup.

3. Restore everything from the most recent level 2 backup.

Figure 13-2 illustrates how this procedure results in all of the latest information being included in the restored file system. (Compare the backup levels pictured in Figure 13-1 to the restore operation pictured in Figure 13-2.)

13

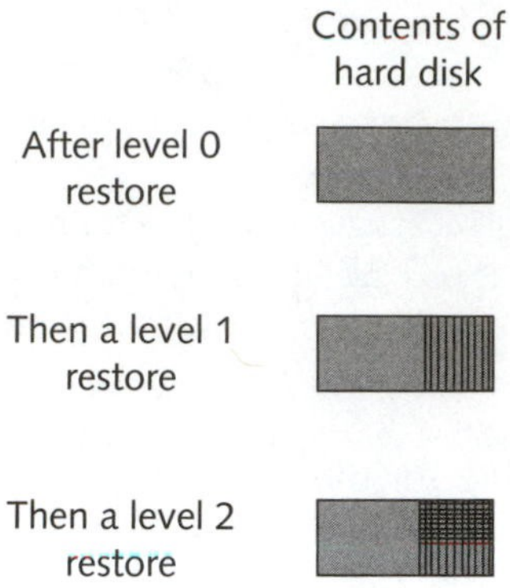

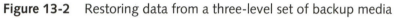

Figure 13-2 caption area:

Contents of
hard disk

After level 0
restore

Then a level 1
restore

Then a level 2
restore

Figure 13-2   Restoring data from a three-level set of backup media

Managing and Storing Backup Media

As you create a backup plan that specifies backup levels and times appropriate to your organization's needs, you must determine how many backup media you will need (disks, tapes, cartridges) for each level. That is, a level 0 full backup may require five tape cartridges, but a typical level 2 backup requires only a single cartridge (because relatively few files are modified each day). As an example, the three-level backup described previously might include the following:

- Three months of level 0 backups; each requires 5 tape cartridges, for a total of 15.

- Five weeks of level 1 backups (some months have five weeks); each requires 3 tape cartridges, for a total of 15.

- Five days of level 2 backups (you might need seven days if your organization runs seven days per week); each requires 1 tape cartridge, for a total of 5.

You would therefore need a total of 35 tape cartridges for this plan. Figure 13-3 illustrates this arrangement. The importance of carefully labeling each tape cartridge cannot be overstated. If you can't identify which backup media is the most recent of any given level, much of your backup effort will be useless when a serious problem arises.

Most organizations would store one set of the monthly (level 0) backup media and perhaps the most recent weekly (level 1) backup media off-site. The strategy for off-site storage depends on how critical data is and how often someone wants to take the responsibility of carrying the backup media to the chosen secure location (such as a bank vault).

Most backup media are designed to be used repeatedly. For example, a rewriteable CD can be used about 1000 times, according to the manufacturer. But you should nevertheless plan on scheduled replacement of backup media to avoid problems with deteriorating, outdated products.

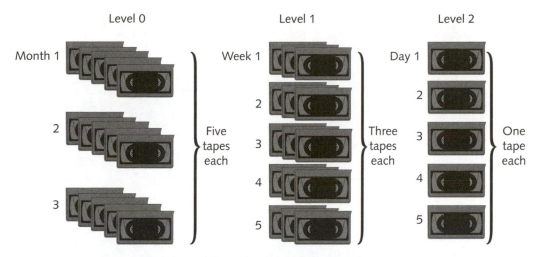

Figure 13-3   Multiple tapes used for a three-level backup plan

Using the plan just outlined, you could reuse the same set of level 1 weekly tape cartridges each month, starting with the oldest one. The same applies to the level 2 tape cartridges. For example, on any Wednesday afternoon, you should have five level 2 tape cartridges containing the following:

- Last Wednesday's backup, which you will overwrite this evening with new data
- Last Thursday's backup, which you will overwrite tomorrow evening with new data
- Last Friday's backup
- Monday's backup (from two days ago)
- Tuesday's backup (from last night)

In addition to being fairly easy to manage, this system provides data redundancy. If you have a problem and need to restore a file on this particular Wednesday, you first check the Tuesday backup that you made last night. If a problem occurs with that tape cartridge, you can also check Monday morning's level 1 backup, Monday evening's level 2 backup, or even last Friday's backup. A single user may lose more work if you cannot use the most recent backup, but the organization won't lose all its data, because many copies of the data exist on different media.

Backing Up the Root File System

The root file system requires special attention in your backup plan because it contains the tools that you normally use to restore damaged data, such as a deleted file or data from a corrupted hard disk partition. You should think about how to respond if the root file system is damaged, either by a hard disk failure or by corrupted configuration files that prevent you from booting the Linux operating system kernel.

Chapter 9 described how to create a rescue floppy or a boot floppy. That disk, which you can use to boot the system in an emergency, should contain the files necessary to restore the contents of the root file system from your backup device. These files might include:

- The kernel modules needed to access the backup device (such as SCSI modules)

- Other kernel modules needed to access the device where the root file system is stored

- Configuration files needed to set up access to the backup device

- Information such as file indexes that are needed to locate the correct data and restore it from backup media

As you prepare a backup plan, you'll want to consider the hardware and software that you'll use to implement that plan. The following section describes some key issues you face in making hardware and software choices.

HARDWARE AND SOFTWARE ISSUES

Once you have determined why, when, and how you want to back up your Linux system, you must determine the best tools to get the job done. Linux includes all the necessary software utilities for many backup tasks. You can also purchase commercial backup software. Both of these options are described later in this chapter.

Many different hardware devices are available for backing up data. The following sections provide a review of the different options available to you.

Choosing Backup Media

The size of hard disks in standard PCs is growing very rapidly. A 500 MB hard disk was considered huge just a few years ago, but today hard disks with 50 to 120 GB are common and can be purchased for a few hundred dollars. Storage space is often measured according to its cost per megabyte or per gigabyte. For example, if an 80 GB hard disk costs $300, the cost per gigabyte is about $3.75 (about 0.375 cents per megabyte). Similarly, if a tape cartridge used to back up a system costs $90 and holds 200 GB, the cost per gigabyte is 45 cents.

You normally have multiple copies of the data on your system, backed up at different times. Backup media such as tape cartridges cost much less than a hard disk, but you use multiple tape cartridges (35 in the previous example) to back up the system.

The following sections review different backup media (and corresponding devices) that you might consider for backing up your Linux system.

Magnetic Media

You can use several types of magnetic media for backing up data:

- *RAID hard disks*: Most of the data that you want to back up is already on a hard disk. It doesn't make sense to rely on long-term data storage located on another hard disk—even a RAID array—if the same vulnerabilities apply to that device as to your main hard disk. On the other hand, storing a backup copy of crucial data from several locations on a centralized RAID array is a useful way to maintain an online backup—that is, a backup of the data that is still available if one of the hard disks becomes unavailable. Just don't plan your entire backup strategy around hard disks. Instead, look to removable media such as tapes and optical formats.

- *Floppy disks*: Floppy disks are a great way to back up small, sensitive pieces of information. For example, a boot disk, a rescue disk, a firewall or other server configuration, or relatively small files can fit on a floppy disk. Floppy disks are inexpensive, easily transported, and easily stored. Just be certain to label the disk and move the write-protection tab over so you don't erase the floppy disk. An important disadvantage of floppy disks is that they are fragile. You should maintain multiple floppy disk copies of any critical data and check the integrity of the disks regularly. A standard floppy disk holds 1.4 MB.

- *Removable magnetic media*: New types of specialized storage devices are introduced regularly. Examples include Floptical disks (high capacity floppy disks holding 20 MB or more), Iomega Zip and Jaz cartridges, and others. The data capacity of these cartridges continues to rise, but the cost per megabyte is usually much higher than for optical or tape cartridge formats. Other potential disadvantages include a lack of history to prove their reliability, and a lack of broad industry support in some cases.

- *Removable hard disks*: Because hard disk storage has become so inexpensive, some administrators use a "pluggable" hard disk slot on their computer and have several high-capacity hard disks that they can remove and secure after backing up data to them. Some may even consider using newer hard disk storage devices that attach to the computer using FireWire or USB ports. These can be convenient because the data transfer rate is high (backups are completed quickly), and they are handy to carry around. Again, the cost per megabyte may be high compared with optical media or tape cartridges, and so may not be appropriate for many systems.

Optical Media

Optical media used by devices such as writeable CD drives and DVD drives are an attractive backup choice. Advantages of optical media include:

- A large storage capacity that is sufficient for many needs. A CD holds up to 700 MB; a DVD-RAM disk holds 4.7 GB.

13

- Storage media are very low cost, with CD blanks selling for a few pennies and DVD-RAM disks for less than $5.

- Storage media are widely available at any office supply store or computer shop.

- Optical media are easily exchanged with vendors, customers, or other organizations. Virtually every system can read a CD-ROM and most new computers have DVD-capable drives.

Standard CDs, in particular, are a valuable method of exchanging data with suppliers and also of easily creating data archives. Because a CD costs so little, it can be a cost-effective way to back up key data files regularly and have a set of backup CDs stored with snapshots at various times. Rewriteable CDs can be used hundreds of times, but these cost more than one-time writeable CDs.

The 700 MB storage capacity of a CD is less appropriate for backing up today's hard disks that offer 40–120 GB of storage or more. But a CD is often sufficient for backing up an entire project directory, graphics archive, programming project, or operating system.

DVD recording devices and media are rapidly dropping in price. For systems with larger amounts of data, DVDs are an alternative worth considering.

Tape Cartridges

Tape drives are the workhorses of most computer backup efforts. Tape drives are fairly inexpensive, as is the media (tape cartridges). Many formats are available, but in general, data capacities have kept pace with that of hard disks. You can purchase a tape drive that will record 20, 40, 80, or even 200 GB on a single tape cartridge. All these cartridges are priced under $100, with the smaller capacities costing much less. If you need to back up large amounts of data (thousands of gigabytes), you should consider a tape cartridge jukebox or one of the high-end digital tape formats available from major device manufacturers such as IBM, Quantum, and Hewlett-Packard. A **jukebox** is a backup device that holds multiple backup media (usually multiple tape cartridges) and can switch between them without assistance from a system administrator.

One thousand gigabytes is a terabyte (TB); one thousand terabytes is a petabyte. References to storage capacities for jukeboxes are often in the terabyte range.

Tape drives are available in a variety of formats, each offering a different combination of cost, reliability, and data capacity. The information that follows provides enough basic details to familiarize you with the formats you're likely to see. As you review the summary of tape formats that follows, note that tape cartridges can accommodate different methods for storing data, depending on the tape drive you use. This is analogous to a regular 3.5-inch floppy disk, which can be formatted with either an MS-DOS, Macintosh, or Linux file system.

When reviewing the variety of tape devices on the market, you may feel overwhelmed by the alphabet soup of formats, companies, and product names. After the following list describes some major tape cartridge device types and data formats, the next section will help you determine what factors to consider when choosing a backup device.

- Digital Linear Tape (DLT) is a half-inch-wide tape inside a cartridge. The tapes typically store about 40 GB and are considered highly reliable. Quantum is considered the leader in DLT technology, but many others, such as HP, IBM, and StorageTek, sell DLT drives. Newer SuperDLT tape drives store up to 320 GB on a single tape cartridge.

- Linear Tape-Open (LTO) is an open tape standard used by Hewlett-Packard, IBM, and Seagate (a prominent hard disk manufacturer). Several companies sell devices based on this high-capacity format. The Ultrium brand name from IBM is a popular version of LTO. The next generation of LTO devices is expected to support capacities of over 200 GB per tape.

- Helical-scan tape drives write data onto a narrow tape—either 4mm or 8mm. This format uses the same storage method used by videotapes for recording movies. Figure 13-4 illustrates how a helical-scan device stores information by writing short, angled strips of data on the tape. Helical-scan tapes are used in several tape formats as described below.

Data tape

Stripes of information
written to tape

Spinning
read/write mechanism

Figure 13-4   The helical scan method is used on 4mm and 8mm tapes

- Advanced Intelligent Tape (AIT) is a format developed by Sony. Each AIT cartridge contains a memory chip that is used to increase the efficiency of data access. Sony plans to release a revised version of AIT every two years, with a doubled storage capacity and data transfer rate in each new version. AIT-3 tapes hold about 130 GB each and can store data at a rate of nearly 1 GB per minute. The S-AIT currently under development is expected to hold 500 GB per tape.

- VXA is a technology developed by the Ecrix company. The VXA format attempts to overcome some of the technical limitations that most other standard formats face. For example, VXA avoids stopping and starting the tape drive while waiting for the computer to send more data by using a variable-speed tape drive and organizing data into packets rather than a single stream, as most formats use.

13

■ Travan tape drives are widely used and are manufactured by many different companies. They do not have the highest capacities—10 to 40 GB is standard—but they have a longer history of reliability than many of the newer formats, and tape drives and cartridges are relatively inexpensive. Travan drives use tapes that may be called Travan, QIC, or SLR format.

Comparing Devices

Choosing a backup system from all of the available devices and technologies is challenging. System administrators who are creating a new system from scratch and need to store large amounts of data may be able to focus on the latest technology for high-capacity, high-speed tape drives. Other system administrators may be more concerned with sharing copies of data between several existing computers using a CD drive, and so may opt for a low-cost CD recorder. Still other administrators may be forced to purchase new devices that use older technologies simply to keep costs low or maintain compatibility with existing systems, even though this means more work to maintain numerous backup media. These are just three examples of the varying requirements that have led manufacturers to develop so many different devices and formats.

In most cases, the cost of the backup device and media is an issue. Although you should keep in mind the discussion at the beginning of this chapter regarding the value of an organization's data, managers who control budgets will still expect you to be as frugal as possible with an organization's money. The cost of the various backup options is affected by several factors, including the following:

■ *What interface is used to connect the device to the computer?* The interface is often SCSI (fast and expensive), IDE (common and inexpensive, but slower), or parallel port (great for special applications and inexpensive, but slow compared to IDE and SCSI). Special interfaces like USB and FireWire are also used for some special applications and can make it easy to move a single backup device between multiple computers.

■ *How recent is the format?* The more recently developed formats like LTO and VXA are more expensive than older formats like Travan. But newer formats hold more data on each cartridge.

■ *How much data can one disk or cartridge hold?* The same media may be able to hold slightly different amounts of data when used in different devices. The difference in storage is unlikely to be more than 10%, however.

■ *Is the device from a name-brand manufacturer?* As with everything else in the computer industry, buying a product from a company such as IBM or Hewlett-Packard generally costs more than buying from a start-up or relatively unknown company. The start-up company may support newer technologies, however, and may actually have better products. You must decide whether the potential benefits of buying from a new company outweigh the risks.

- *Does the device have special features?* The most common of these is an auto-mounting or jukebox feature, which allows you to load a number of disks or cartridges so that the device can create a multivolume archive without user intervention. These devices are always much more expensive than a device supporting a single manually inserted disk or cartridge.

Many factors will influence your decision to use a particular backup device. The following list, though not exhaustive, presents several of these factors. It also will help you understand why so many different devices are available.

- *How much does the hardware device cost to acquire?* A quick survey on a major hardware supplier site such as *www.cdw.com* or *www.warehouse.com* will show you prices ranging from $129 for a basic 40 GB tape drive to more than $20,000 for a high-capacity, name-brand jukebox tape cartridge system with a capacity of several terabytes.

- *What is the data transfer rate of the device?* This figure is the largest factor in determining how fast you can back up a given amount of data. It is less important if you intend to back up using a scheduled `cron` job in the middle of the night. It may suddenly become important again if you need to restore a large amount of data with many people waiting while you do it. Data transfer rates are usually measured in megabytes per second (MB/sec). For example, a tape drive with a capacity of 100 GB might advertise a data transfer rate of 32 MB/sec, meaning that an entire 100 GB tape could be filled in about an hour. Faster transfer rates generally cost more, but the actual rate of backing up data is based on many factors, such as the speed of your CPU, the quality of your system board components, and the type of interface used to connect to the backup device.

- *Is data randomly accessible?* In other words, is it easy to back up a single file or set of files without restoring or going through an entire archive set? Data on CDs and hard disks can be accessed randomly (like selecting a scene on a DVD movie); data on tape cartridges is stored sequentially and can't be accessed without winding the tape to the data you need (like fast-forwarding past the previews on a VHS tape).

- *Can the device you choose perform very large backups using an autoloader or jukebox mechanism?* If it can't, you may always need to be present during system backups to switch media when one is full.

- *How much does media for the device cost?* In the long run, you can expect media to cost more than the backup device. Determine the media costs based on your planned backup strategy, with replacement media purchased regularly as recommended by the manufacturer to avoid storage errors.

13

- *Does the organization already own backup hardware?* Are the cost savings for not purchasing new hardware worth using the existing hardware if it relies on older or obsolete technologies? When dealing with this issue, you must consider **legacy systems**: computer systems that an organization already owns. Working with existing systems is a common concern when organizations plan computer hardware or software acquisitions.

- *How recent is the technology of the device?* Some older devices are still very viable and stable, but it may be difficult to locate media for them. If you have a nine-track tape reel in your office, you may have to work with a special service bureau to read the tape because these devices are rarely used now. On the other hand, very new technologies may not have proven themselves cost-effective or technologically sound. For example, some tape formats had problems when first released to the public because magnetic material flaked off of the storage tapes.

- *Does the device rely on an industry standard that many vendors support, or is it specific to one vendor?* If the device is only supplied by one vendor, can you rely on that vendor to be around in five years? How likely is it that the vendor will change formats or discontinue a product, leaving you with outdated products or the prospect of retooling your backup plans?

- *How long is the media life?* This is not a concern for daily backups, but most organizations should also maintain an archival backup of company financial records, personnel records, computer program source code, and other electronic assets. The media that these assets are stored on should last long enough so that you don't have to make a new copy of massive amounts of data every two years. Table 13-1 shows the anticipated life of some key materials. (Paper and microfilm are included in the table for comparison.) Note that the industry's experience with many of these technologies does not extend past their supposed useful life. We *know* that paper can last 500 years. No one really knows if CDs can last 30 years, because they haven't existed that long.

Table 13-1   Media Life Spans

Media	Approximate useful life (before data loss potentially occurs)
Archive-quality acid-free paper	500 years
Microfilm	100 years
CD-ROM and similar optical media	5–30 years, depending on media quality
Hard disks and similar magnetic media	10–20 years, depending on media quality
Reel-to-reel data tapes	15–25 years, depending on media quality
Tape cartridges (QIC, 4mm, 8mm, etc.)	5–10 years, depending on media quality
3.5 inch disks	2–5 years

■ *How robust is the media?* Can they be dropped? Can they handle the environmental conditions that are part of your working area (heat, humidity, dust)? Most media formats are quite robust, but if you work in a factory or outdoor environment, you should consider these factors. Many device specifications will include the **mean time between failures (MTBF)**. This is an average measure of how long the device can function between breakdowns and is typically measured in hours of operating time. A high-end tape drive costing several thousand dollars might advertise a MTBF of 250,000 at 100% duty cycle. This equates to about 28 years of continuous operation.

■ *Is the media easily transportable (if this is a requirement of your organization)?* Most system administrators keep the majority of backup media near the systems that contain the original data. This makes it convenient to restore data if a problem occurs. But it's also a good idea to take at least one copy to another location in case a fire or other problem destroys the backup media located nearby. Many organizations have a strict policy about regularly taking a data backup to a bank vault or other secure off-site location.

■ *Do you need to exchange data with other organizations?* If so, make certain you are both using the same media format. If that isn't feasible, you can use a service bureau to convert data to a different format when necessary. Consult a service bureau to determine the cost and timelines for the services you anticipate needing. (Service bureaus typically advertise in the back of popular computer magazines. They can extract data from virtually any format, including many crashed hard disks.)

■ *How reliable is the hardware device?* An unreliable or faulty backup device can corrupt backup media so that no device can read them. Even if a hardware problem doesn't corrupt media, a breakdown can interrupt your scheduled backups or delay restoring data when a problem occurs.

Once you have selected a backup device and media format, you are almost ready to implement your backup plan. But a few additional issues still remain to be resolved. These are discussed in the next section.

Verification, Permissions, and Compression

Although problems are rare once you have a backup system up and running, you should verify your backups on a regular basis. Almost all backup utilities create log files that record their actions. This is especially important because they often run in the middle of the night. You should make a habit of checking the backup log each morning after a backup utility has run to see if any problems occurred during the night. You can then take immediate action to back up any files missing from the automated backup operation.

13

Verifying a backup is sometimes done as part of a backup utility, as described later in this chapter, but you can always perform your own verification using steps such as these:

1. Pick a backup tape or disk, either at random or according to a reasonable plan. For example, you might decide to test a randomly chosen level 1 backup tape once per week.

2. Check the file listing on the tape by querying for the contents of the backup media. (This would be equivalent to using the ls command to see the contents of the backup media. With some media you can actually use the ls command, with others you'll need to use a backup utility.)

3. Restore a randomly selected file to the /tmp directory of your Linux system, just to be certain that the data in the file can be retrieved and reassembled without errors. If possible, do this step immediately after backing up data (on your regular schedule), and then compare the file you restored with the original file that you backed up to see that the size and contents match. (Use the **diff** command to compare the contents of two files.)

In addition to verifying the data, you should also know exactly what information is backed up. Does the backup include the contents of each file? What about the owner and file permissions associated with each file? Many times a system administrator will have problems after restoring a large number of files because the owner and group assigned to files and directories, or the file and directory permissions, are not stored as part of the backup. If this information is not backed up and then restored in a consistent way, access to all files may be denied to all users, or granted to all users. Either way, you would need to assign new file permissions to each file manually.

 A backup utility typically must run with root permission because only root can access all users' files on the system and the backup device itself. You must protect access to the backup utility and to the backed up data so that users who are not authorized to see data on the system also cannot access it as part of a backup operation or on backup media. Most system administrators keep all backup media in a locked cabinet or closet.

Backup utilities normally include options to maintain or ignore file ownership and permissions. Normally you want to maintain this information and check it carefully when you verify your backups by restoring selected files.

In most backup utilities, you can also choose whether to use a compression feature for your backed up data. Tape drives typically list a standard capacity and a compressed capacity; backup commands include options to compress data as it's being archived. Should you use these features? Probably, but you should also be aware of their limitations. By definition, when you compress data you remove the redundancy from it. That is, compressed data can be re-created in its original form by adding back the redundant information using an established set of rules.

To understand compression better, consider this example. When you see the words "hllo my nm is Nchlas," you can probably understand their meaning even though part of the information is missing. The missing information is redundant—it's not needed for you to understand the sentence. You can also use standard rules (English grammar and spelling) to reconstruct the original sentence: "Hello my name is Nicholas."

The danger with using compression is that with all the redundancy removed from a set of information, all of the information and rules are needed in order to reconstruct the data. For example, if you don't speak English well, English words with missing letters are difficult to decipher. In the same way, if even a small part of some compressed data is lost, the original cannot be easily reconstructed. By leaving the redundancy in the data that you back up, you might make it easier to fix any problems that occur on backup media.

Most backup media formats are highly reliable, but when age, environmental factors like heat and dust, and regular wear and tear are working against the data you have carefully saved, you should consider whether compression is always necessary.

USING LINUX BACKUP UTILITIES

Many utilities are available to back up data from a Linux system in a secure and organized way. The most widely used of these utilities are the old UNIX standbys `tar` and `cpio`. Sometimes other utilities rely on these programs in the background but use a graphical interface to make configuration and selection of backup options easier. Popular commercial backup utilities include features such as tracking tapes for you, keeping online indexes of each backup that you have performed, and automating schedules for unattended backup (similar to the options provided by the `crontab` command).

The following sections outline basic information about using these backup utilities. Although a complete discussion of `tar`, `cpio`, and commercial tools is not presented here, you should understand enough to use these tools for basic backups and to locate more exhaustive information when needed.

It's common to use Linux backup utilities across a network—a single system equipped with a tape drive or other backup device is used to back up file systems located on machines all over the network. You can do this using many techniques, such as remotely mounting file systems using NFS or Samba software, or downloading files using Linux FTP server software. Most full-featured backup utilities create their own network connections between software components installed on the machine to be backed up and the machine where the tape drive is located. The documentation for specific utilities will describe their networking capabilities; basic Linux utilities such as those described in the next section rely on services such as NFS to access networked data. Networking topics such as NFS, Samba, FTP, and more are all covered in *Guide to Linux Networking and Security*.

13

Using `tar` and `cpio`

The name `tar` stands for *tape archive*; it is the oldest of the backup tools for UNIX. The `cpio` command (for *copy in and out*) is newer and includes additional features compared to `tar`. `cpio` also reads `tar`-formatted files. Both `tar` and `cpio` can create archive files, such as the `.tgz` format files that you may have seen when downloading Linux programs from Internet sites. But `tar` and `cpio` can also create an archive directly on a tape cartridge or other backup device without first creating a file on your hard disk.

> In order to use a tape drive or other backup device, you must first install and configure that device using the information presented in previous chapters. For example, see Chapters 2, 3, and 4 regarding the installation of Linux and the use of kernel modules for adding device support. See also the documentation for your backup device.

The `tar` and `cpio` commands operate differently. With the `tar` command you must specify files to be included in a backup archive on the command line. By contrast, `cpio` always reads from the STDIN channel for the filenames to include in an archive. The `tar` command writes data to a filename or device that you provide; the `cpio` command always writes data back to STDOUT. To compare these two methods of operation, consider the following two examples for creating a full backup of the `/home` directory. You can assume for this example that the device `/dev/tape` is configured as a tape drive. (Notice that you refer directly to a tape drive device; you do not mount it first.)

```
# tar cf /dev/tape /home
```

This command uses the `c` option of `tar` to create a new archive. The `f` option (for *filename*) followed by the device name indicates the location where the archived data will be stored. The last parameter, `/home`, indicates which files are to be archived. Because the parameter is a directory name, `tar` includes all files within that directory. A `cpio` command equivalent to the above `tar` command would be:

```
# find /home -print | cpio -o > /dev/tape
```

This `cpio` command relies on the `find` command to generate a list of files (one filename per line) for `cpio` to back up. Those filenames are sent to `cpio` using a pipe symbol because `cpio` reads the filenames in from STDIN. The `>` redirection operator sends the archived files to the device `/dev/tape`. The `-o` option on `cpio` indicates that the archive is being output—that is, that data is being written out. A simpler example of `cpio` could archive the contents of a single directory to a local file using the `ls` command to generate the list of files to archive:

```
$ ls | cpio -o > /tmp/archive.cpio
```

> You might have noticed that `tar` options do not normally include a preceding hyphen; those of the `cpio` command do.

The **v** option is normally added to both **tar** and **cpio** so that the output of the command is verbose, meaning that the command prints details of what it is doing to the screen. With that option added, the last example would look like this:

```
$ ls | cpio -ov > /tmp/archive.cpio
```

You use a similar command with different options to extract files using **tar** or **cpio**. If you had created an archive on a tape cartridge using **tar**, you could restore the contents of the tape into the current directory using this command (with the **x** option standing for *extract* and the **v** option included to see verbose messages about command progress):

```
# tar xvf /dev/tape
```

The **cpio** command uses the **-i** option for input, again extracting the contents of the backup media into the current directory. The **-d** option is also added here so that **cpio** will create subdirectories that existed in the data as required to re-create the original data organization. When using the **cpio** command with the **-i** option, **cpio** reads the STDIN channel to get the archived data; so the < redirection operator is used with the filename or archive device name.

```
# cpio -idv < /dev/tape
```

These are very basic examples of **tar** and **cpio**. Each command supports dozens of options for features such as compressing files, preserving file attributes, controlling a tape device, setting timestamps on archived data, and many other things. You can review the man and **info** pages for each command to learn more.

Both **tar** and **cpio** rely on other Linux commands to help you create an incremental or multilevel backup. The most useful of these is the **find** command. For example, the following **find** command prints a list of all files in the /home directory (and its subdirectories) that have been modified in the last day by using the **-mtime** parameter with a value of 1:

```
# find /home -mtime 1 -print
```

By using the list of files generated by this command as the archive list for **cpio** or **tar**, you can easily create a level 2 backup, as described earlier in the chapter. The above command would be used on a Tuesday; a different number of days would be used for each day of the week so that data changed since the beginning of the week was included in the backup. The following two commands illustrate how to do this with either **cpio** or **tar**:

```
# find /home -mtime 1 -print | cpio -ov > /dev/tape
# tar cf /dev/tape ` find /home -mtime 1 -print`
```

The options available with the **find** command make it a powerful companion to **tar** and **cpio**. With **find** you can create a list of files owned by certain users, files modified or accessed within certain time limits, files with certain file permissions, or many other criteria.

13

Other Backup Utilities

The `tar` and `cpio` commands can operate either with a tape drive or with backup devices that rely on a standard Linux file system or standard mounting operation, such as an Iomega Jaz drive or a writeable CD drive. When you are using tape drives that are not randomly accessible (as a CD is), you may want to use additional tools to manage tape indexes, tape rewinding and searching, and so forth. If you intend to use a tape drive, the KDE graphical utility `kdat` is worth reviewing. This program is included with the KDE Desktop, on the Utilities submenu under KDE menus in Red Hat Linux when using Gnome. Most other Linux distributions include this program on the Utilities submenu of the KDE main menu.

The `kdat` Tape Back-up Tool provides handy features like the following, all available from the graphical interface (see Figure 13-5):

- Back up and restore files by dragging and dropping them between a list of the tape contents and a list of the hard disk contents.

- Verify tape contents from the menu.

- Manage mounting and unmounting of tape cartridges.

- Create and maintain indexes of multiple tapes.

- Set preferences from a graphical dialog box (see Figure 13-6).

- Format tapes before their first use.

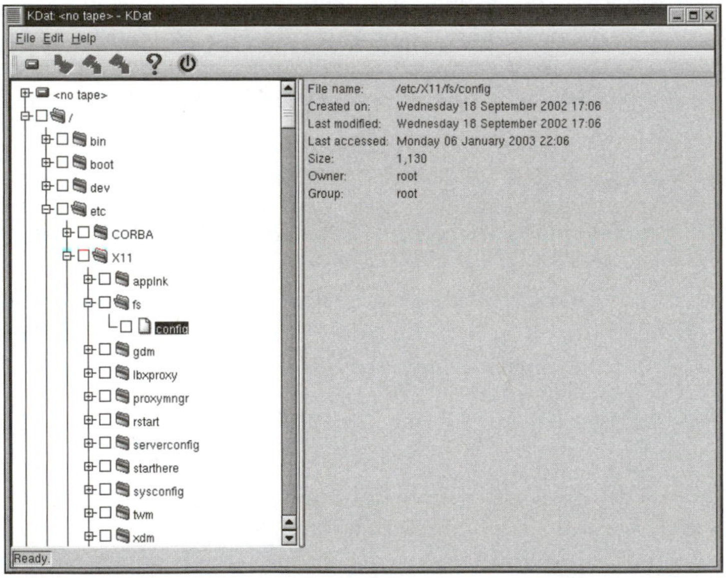

Figure 13-5 The `kdat` utility in KDE

Figure 13-6   Setting preferences in `kdat`

The `kdat` Tape Back-up Tool is not intended to be compatible with all the high-end tape drives that you might consider using for your Linux servers, but it provides an easy-to-use method of tracking backups. It also makes it very simple to access data from a backup tape.

The complexities of maintaining large numbers of backup media for large volumes of data led manufacturers long ago to create specialized software to help with the task. Fortunately, several of these tools have made their way to the Linux platform:

- BRU (Backup and Restore Utility) from Enhanced Software Technologies has been popular among Linux users for many years. It provides multiple levels of data verification, unattended operation with scheduled backups, and support for numerous types of backup devices. See *www.bru.com*.

- Arkeia from Knox Software is another popular Linux backup tool. Arkeia is an enterprise network backup solution that is designed to control backup of multiple remote systems from a single location, saving or restoring data from anywhere on the network. See *www.arkeia.com*. Figure 13-7 shows a sample Arkeia screen.

- Storix provides system backup and disaster recovery designed specifically for IBM AIX and Linux operating systems. You can learn more at *www.storix.com*.

- HyperTape from BridgeHead Software provides automatic unattended backups to local or networked tape drives. See *www.BridgeHeadSoftware.com*.

- Replicator runs on Linux or Solaris-based servers. It automatically sends data over the network to a remote archive. Clients can access the data replicated on the archive to retrieve files as needed. See *replicator.sourceforge.net*.

- AMANDA is a freely available backup system that coordinates data backups from multiple servers on a network to a single master server. See *www.amanda.org*.

13

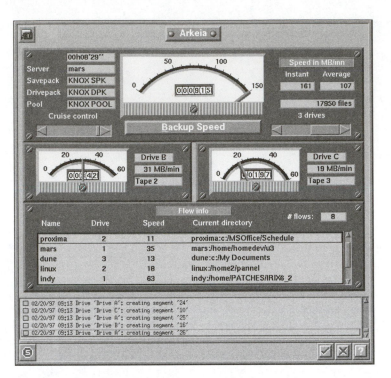

Figure 13-7   The Arkeia commercial backup program

- Legato, a traditionally strong vendor in the UNIX market, now provides its high-end data management and backup/restore software on a variety of Linux platforms. See *www.legato.com*.

- Vendors of tape devices such as Hewlett-Packard, IBM, Quantum, and MTI increasingly include support options for Linux and even Linux software utilities.

Many other backup utilities are available—free and commercial, graphical and command-line. A good place to look for others is *www.linuxapps.com*, which has a separate section listing dozens of backup utilities.

CHAPTER SUMMARY

- A backup plan helps a system administrator create an orderly system for backing up Linux data on a regular basis and restoring lost data as needed.

- A backup plan must address questions such as who is responsible for maintaining backups, which parts of each Linux file system will be backed up at what intervals, and how often backups will be performed.

- The dollar value and time sensitivity of the data stored on your Linux systems determines how much expense you can justify in creating a backup plan. The value of data includes several factors beyond the money paid to an employee to create the data.

◘ A three-level backup method is commonly used. All data is backed up monthly (level 0), and changed files are backed up weekly (level 1) and daily (level 2).

◘ A multilevel backup system provides a reasonable trade-off between convenience and low cost on one side, and protecting data on the other.

◘ Backing up the root file system and preparing to restore critical applications are parts of a backup plan that may require special attention.

◘ Magnetic and optical backup media are available, but tape cartridges continue to be the most popular and cost-effective backup media for most larger systems.

◘ Several different backup tape systems are available. They vary in speed, storage capacity, technologies used, availability, and cost, among other factors.

◘ Backups should be verified regularly to be certain that data is recoverable from the backup media.

◘ File permissions must be part of a valid backup in order to avoid problems when files are restored.

◘ Compression is commonly used when backing up data, but does increase vulnerability in case of corrupted data.

◘ The `tar` and `cpio` command-line utilities are commonly used for simple backups on every Linux system. They are typically used in conjunction with other utilities such as `find`.

◘ Many free and commercial utilities are available to help system administrators manage their backup strategy. Most of these are graphical applications and include facilities for network-wide backup, managing large sets of backup media, and verifying or restoring files from backup media.

13

KEY TERMS

backup — A copy of data on a computer system.

backup level — A description of how much data will be stored in a backup operation. A backup level is only relevant in comparison with another backup level. When performing a backup operation at a given level, all of the data that has changed since the last backup of the previous level is recorded.

backup media — A device on which data can be stored, such as a tape cartridge, write-able CD or DVD, or floppy disk.

backup plan — A written document that outlines when, how, and why various files and file systems will be backed up, stored, and—when necessary—restored to prevent permanent data loss.

cpio — A Linux archiving program. The `cpio` command also reads archive files created by the `tar` command.

diff — A command that compares the contents of two files, displaying any differences between them.

incremental backup — A backup process that stores only files that have changed since a full backup was made.

jukebox — A backup device that holds multiple backup media (such as tape cartridges or writeable CDs) and that can switch between them without assistance from a system administrator.

legacy systems — Computer systems that an organization already owns. This term usually refers to older systems that are no longer widely used.

mean time between failures (MTBF) — A reliability measurement giving the average time a device can function between breakdowns. It is typically measured in hours of operating time.

restore — To copy data from a backup location (for example, a tape cartridge) onto the file system where that data is normally used, and from which it was unintentionally lost.

REVIEW QUESTIONS

1. A backup plan would normally *not* include the following:
   a. A list of tape drive prices
   b. Times when backups are performed
   c. The location of critical files on the system
   d. A recommended time to replace old tape cartridges with new ones

2. Explain how the speed with which files need to be restored affects a backup plan.

3. Why might you back up operating system files as well as user data files?

4. Which of the following is not likely to be a factor in selecting a specific backup device?
   a. The value of a project that cannot be done because data needed for the project was destroyed
   b. The cost of a complete set of backup media to implement a three-level backup plan
   c. The average data transfer rate of the backup device
   d. The average storage capacity of the backup devices

5. Name two parts of a Linux system that are likely to change daily.

6. Explain why a level 1 backup is called an incremental backup.

7. Using backup levels has the advantage of:
   a. Reducing the time required to back up the entire file system
   b. Making it easier to recover a file that has not been changed in several weeks
   c. Allowing a system administrator to spend less time with backups but keep data backed up very frequently
   d. Causing all system backups to be available via a single file index

8. Using a standard three-level backup plan with the time intervals described in the chapter text, a user would expect never to lose more than _____ worth of work.

   a. a week's

   b. a day's

   c. an hour's

   d. 20 MB

9. Explain why a system administrator must use backup media from three backups in order to completely restore a system that used three backup levels.

10. Floppy disks are a useful backup media in cases where:

    a. The cost of writeable CDs is prohibitive

    b. Small amounts of critical data need to be backed up

    c. Extreme durability is a key factor in the choice of media

    d. A high data transfer rate is critical

11. As a rule, tape cartridges can hold much more than optical media. True or False?

12. The burdened cost of an employee includes:

    a. The costs an employee must pay for benefits like health insurance

    b. The costs an employer must pay that are not part of the employee's salary

    c. The value of data that an employee created for an organization but that is lost because of unverified backups

    d. Two to three times the employee's salary

13. Using a SCSI interface to connect a backup device has the advantage of:

    a. Low cost

    b. Being proprietary (controlled by one company)

    c. High data transfer rates

    d. Limited availability

14. Name five factors to consider when selecting a backup device and media type. Explain the circumstances in which each would be a controlling factor in the decision.

15. Name three tape cartridge formats and comment briefly on each.

16. You can expect a CD or other optical media to last about as long as high-quality microfilm. True or False?

13

17. The purpose of verifying your backups is to:

    a. Be certain that files are correctly recorded and can be restored

    b. Determine whether anyone has tampered with data contained in a backup

    c. Secure data from unauthorized use

    d. Compare data transfer rates among competing products

18. Explain how redundancy relates to compressed data and why that is relevant to data backup operations.

19. The `tar` utility differs from the `cpio` utility in that:

    a. `cpio` always reads and writes to STDIN and STDOUT, while `tar` uses command-line parameters

    b. `cpio` is a commercial utility, while `tar` is free software

    c. `cpio` is widely used for Internet archive files, while `tar` is not

    d. `cpio` is an older format that is not compatible with newer `tar` archives

20. The _____ utility is a commercial backup utility from Knox Software.

    a. BRU

    b. `kdat`

    c. Arkeia

    d. `mke2fs`

21. Describe why the `find` command is often used with `tar` or `cpio` for incremental backups.

22. The _____ option causes the `tar` command to extract files from an archive file or device.

    a. `a`

    b. `x`

    c. `c`

    d. `e`

23. Describe the special considerations that must be taken in order to restore the root file system of Linux after a hardware failure.

24. Which of the following formats holds the most data?

    a. SLR

    b. Travan

    c. SuperDLT

    d. AIT-3

25. In the long term, backup media are likely to cost more than the backup device used to access them. True or False?

HANDS-ON PROJECTS

Project 13-1

In this project you experiment with the **tar** command to create a simple data archive file and then extract the contents of that file into another directory. To complete this activity you should have a working Linux system with root access.

1. Log in to Linux as root.

2. If you logged in using a graphical login window, open a command-line window.

3. Enter **cd /etc** to change to the /etc directory.

4. Enter **ls -l | less** and review the filenames and file permissions for the various configuration files in this directory.

5. Create a **tar**-format archive of the configuration files in the /etc directory:

   ```
   # tar cf /tmp/testing.tar /etc
   ```

   Because you are including the pathname to both the **testing.tar** archive file and the directory containing the information you want to archive, you could execute this command from any location on the system.

6. Enter a similar command, this time including the **v** option:

   ```
   # tar cvf /tmp/testing2.tar /etc
   ```

   After you execute this command, you see a list of all the files in the /etc directory appear on the screen as each is added to the archive file.

7. Change to your home directory by entering the **cd** command.

8. Use the **ls** command to examine the contents of your home directory. Make certain you do not have a file called **xinetd.conf** in your home directory. (You shouldn't, but if you do from a previous exercise, rename it to something else to complete this project.)

9. Use the **x** option of the **tar** command to extract a single file from the **tar** archive that you just created:

   ```
   # tar xvf /tmp/testing.tar etc/xinetd.conf
   ```

   The file is placed in your current directory. Because of the **v** option the filename is printed to the screen as it is extracted.

10. Use the **ls** command to review the contents of your home directory. Do you see a file called **xinetd.conf**? Look for an item named **etc**.

11. Enter **cd etc** (without a forward slash) to change to the **etc** subdirectory of your home directory. The **tar** command created the subdirectory in which the requested file was located, starting with your current directory when you issued the command to extract the file from the archive.

12. Use the **ls** command again to see the **xinetd.conf** file in the **etc** subdirectory of your home directory.

13. Close the command-line window and log out.

13

Project 13-2

In this project you experiment with the `cpio` archive utility. To complete this activity you must have a working Linux system with root access. The directory names used as examples assume you are running Red Hat Linux 7.3, but the commands will work on any version of Linux.

1. Log in as root and open a command-line window.

2. Create a `cpio` archive of a small subdirectory using the following command:

   `# find /usr/share/doc/pam-0.75/ -print | cpio -oVH ustar > ~/archive.cpio`

3. Look in the man page for `cpio` to find what the V and H options do.

4. Use the `tar` command to view the contents of the archive you created:

   `# tar tvf ~/archive.cpio | less`

5. Notice that the full directory path for each file is included. What information is included for each file besides the filename?

6. What option could you use to change the ownership stored with each file? (See the `cpio` man page.)

7. Determine the size of the subdirectory you archived using this command:

   `# du /usr/share/doc/p* | grep 75$`

8. View the size of the `cpio` archive file:

   `# ls -l ~/archive.cpio`

9. How do these two compare?

10. Add another directory to the archive file using this command:

    `# find /usr/share/doc/ipchains-1.3.10/ -print | cpio -oAVH ustar -O ~/archive.cpio`

11. View the `cpio` man page again to determine what the A and O options are used for.

12. What is the size of the archive file now?

    `# ls -l ~/archive.cpio`

13. Compress the archive file:

    `# gzip -9 ~/archive.cpio`

14. What is the compressed size of the archive?

15. Uncompress the archive so you can work with it:

    `# gunzip ~/archive.cpio.gz`

    Many tape drives and backup utilities automatically compress data that is not compressed, so storing the `cpio` file to a tape cartridge without using `gzip` would not take up as much space as the uncompressed file takes up on your hard disk.

16. Delete one of the files that you archived from its original location (confirm the deletion when prompted):

    # **rm /usr/share/doc/ipchains-1.3.10/HOWTO.html**

17. Extract the backed-up version of that file from your `cpio` archive:

    # **cpio --extract /usr/share/doc/ipchains-1.3.10/HOWTO.html < ~/archive.cpio**

18. Make certain the file is back:

    # **ls /usr/share/doc/ipchains-1.3.10/HOWTO.html**

19. Delete your archive file (confirm the deletion when prompted):

    # **rm ~/archive.cpio**

20. Close the command-line window and log out.

Project 13-3

In this project you experiment with the KDE graphical archive utility Ark. To complete this activity you must have a working Linux system with KDE installed. The steps used to add files to the archive assume you are running Red Hat Linux 7.3, but any standard version of KDE will include the Ark program.

1. Log in to Linux and open a command-line window.

2. If one is not already on your desktop, open a Start Here window by clicking on the icon just to the right of the footprint on the Gnome Desktop.

3. In the Location field of the window, enter this directory name:

   /usr/share/doc/pam-0.75/txts

4. Now open the KDE archiving utility called Ark by entering **ark** at a command line or opening the Gnome main menu and choosing **KDE menus**, then **Utilities**, then **Ark**.

5. In the txts window, click and drag to select a number of the text files in the directory you specified in Step 3.

6. Click on one of the selected items in the txts window and drag your mouse to the Ark window, then release your mouse button.

7. You are asked whether you want to create a new archive file. Click **OK**.

8. A file browsing window appears in which you can select the directory in which you want your new archive file created. Your home directory is shown by default, which is fine for this project. In the Location field of the Create a New Archive–Ark window, enter **testark.tar**. Then click **Save**.

9. The files you dragged and dropped are listed in the Ark main window. The titlebar also changes to show the name of the archive you created, **testark.tar**.

10. Open the **Action** menu and click **Add Directory** in the Ark window.

13

11. In the Location field, enter **/usr/share/doc/ipchains-1.3.10/** and click **OK**. All the files from that directory are added to the **testark.tar** file and are also listed on-screen.

12. Right-click any filename in the Ark main window. What options are available for any file in the archive?

13. Choose **File**, then **Quit** from the menu of Ark.

14. Delete the archive file you created by entering this command at the command line:

    ```
    # rm ~/testark.tar
    ```

15. Confirm the deletion when prompted, then close the command-line window and log out.

CASE PROJECTS

Choose one of the projects that you have worked on for McKinney & Co. Consultants, such as the Starwood Studio project, the Cyclonica court documents project, or the PixelDust digital photo project. Use your work on that project as the basis for your decisions here.

1. Based on the needs of the project you selected, what basic backup strategy will you use? Specifically, how often will you run a complete backup? How often will you do an incremental (level 2) backup? Will you back up applications and operating system configurations regularly or focus on user data? Provide business justifications for each of your responses.

2. Determine the amount of data that you must back up, making reasonable assumptions about the size of hard disks you have used for the project you selected. Go online to a site like *www.cdw.com* and review tape devices. Based on your answers to the previous question and the business environment of your client, what tape device will you select? What will the total cost be for the device and a full set of media to implement your backup plan? Prepare a backup program budget for the next 12 months with brief but specific justifications based on protecting your client's data.

3. Write a simple set of scripts that you could use as a **cron** job that extracts a list of files based on the timing in your backup plan and writes that data to your backup device. You can assume that the device is accessible as **/dev/tape**. You will need multiple scripts (for example, one each for the monthly, weekly, and daily backups). After you have completed the scripts, what complications can you foresee in using these scripts? Review the Web sites of two or three backup product vendors and describe what additional features they add that you feel might be useful to your clients (making their system administrator more productive). As examples, you could visit *www.legato.com*, *www.mti.com*, *www.arkeia.com*, or *www.bru.com*.

A

LINUX CERTIFICATION OBJECTIVES

This Appendix contains the official testing objectives for the two Linux certification programs that were used in creating this book and its companion volume, *Guide to Linux Networking and Security* (Course Technology, 2003, ISBN 0-619-00094-5):

- SAIR/GNU Linux Certified Administrator, Level 1 (see *www.linuxcertification.com*), which requires that you pass four exams on Installation, Administration, Networking, and Security.

- Linux Professional Institute Level 1 Certification (see *www.lpi.org*), which requires that you pass two exams (numbered 101 and 102).

Other Linux certification programs exist, including more advanced certifications from each of the two organizations above, a Linux+ certification from CompTIA (see *www.comptia.com*) and the Red Hat Certified Engineer program (RHCE, see *www.redhat.com*). The material in this book and its companion volume, while not mapped to the objectives for these other examinations, forms a solid foundation for any additional study and practice that may be required to obtain other certifications. In the descriptions that follow:

- **Book 1** refers to this book, *Guide to Linux Installation and Administration*, 2nd Ed. (ISBN 0-619-13095-4).

- **Book 2** refers to *Guide to Linux Networking and Security* (ISBN 0-619-00094-5).

SAIR/GNU LINUX CERTIFIED ADMINISTRATOR (LCA) LEVEL 1 OBJECTIVES

The SAIR/GNU objectives appear to be in transition as of this writing. Given the comprehensive nature of the objectives as they currently stand, however, any changes will not be likely to leave a reader unprepared for passing the SAIR/GNU exams. Please check the SAIR/GNU Web site to review updates at *www.linuxcertification.com*.

 For each objective, please refer to the Table of Contents and Index of this book and of Book 2 (*Guide to Linux Networking and Security*) for help in locating the desired information. When multiple references are provided for a single objective and one contains the more detailed or precise treatment of the subject, that listing is given in **bold** type.

Exam 1: Linux Installation and Configuration

Theory of Operation

Objective	Book/Chapter/Section
State the definition, origins, cost, and trade-off of free software.	Book 1, Chapter 1, **The World of Linux** *and* The Strengths of Linux
Compare proprietary versus open source software licenses.	Book 1, Chapter 1, The World of Linux
List the GNU public license (GPL) principles.	Book 1, Chapter 1, The World of Linux
Describe how to sell free software.	Book 1, Chapter 1, The World of Linux
Describe the structural components of Linux.	Book 1, Chapter 1, The Strengths of Linux Book 1, Chapter 4, *throughout*
Contrast multiuser multitasking versus single-sequential user multitasking.	Book 1, Chapter 1, Understanding Operating Systems
Contrast command-line interpreters versus graphical user interfaces with trade-offs.	Book 1, Chapter 5, Running the X Window System Book 1, Chapter 6, Understanding the Shell
List PC system architecture configuration issues.	Book 1, Chapter 2, Preparing to Install Linux
Describe hard disk partitioning strategies.	Book 1, Chapter 2, Preparing Your Hard Disk
Contrast video adapter versus monitor capabilities.	Book 1, Chapter 5, Running the X Window System
List the network configuration parameters.	Book 1, Chapter 2, Preparing to Install Linux

Base System

Objective	Book/Chapter/Section
List and give the trade-off of installation media.	Book 1, Chapter 3, Understanding Installation Issues
Explain the Linux device driver lag and give examples.	Book 1, Chapter 3, The Installation Process
List the installation steps common to all distributions.	Book 1, Chapter 3, The Installation Process
Contrast high volume Linux distributions and give trade-offs.	Book 1, Chapter 1, The World of Linux
Install four Linux distributions.	Book 1, Chapter 3, The Installation Process Book 1, Chapter 7, Using Basic System Administration Tools
List the boot up sequence, login, and shut-down sequence.	Book 1, Chapter 4, The Initialization Process
Define "package" and describe how to use it.	Book 1, Chapter 4, Running and Managing Software
Describe basic file system principles.	Book 1, Chapter 4, Working with Linux Files and Directories Book 1, Chapter 8, Maintaining File Systems
Explain the use of mounting versus the use of "mtools" for removable media.	Book 1, Chapter 9, Providing Consistent Power to a Linux System
List and describe the role of common directories.	Book 1, Chapter 4, Working with Linux Files and Directories
List and describe the use of basic system navigation programs ps, kill, w, etc.	Book 1, Chapter 8, **Simple Task Management** Book 1, Chapter 10, Managing Processes
Describe the use and misuse of the superuser account.	Book 1, Chapter 3, **Starting Linux** Book 1, Chapter 8, Managing User Accounts
List the steps in creating a user account.	Book 1, Chapter 8, Managing User Accounts
Install, configure, and navigate two X11 window managers.	Book 1, Chapter 5, Using Desktop Interfaces

Shells and Commands

Objective	Book/Chapter/Section
Describe shell configuration files.	Book 1, Chapter 6, Understanding the Shell
Compare and contrast environmental versus shell variables.	Book 1, Chapter 6, Customizing the Shell
Use commands that pass special characters among programs.	Book 1, Chapter 7, Using Basic System Administration Tools
Use commands that allow programs to communicate.	Book 1, Chapter 7, Using Basic System Administration Tools
Manipulate files and directories.	Book 1, Chapter 4, Working with Linux Files and Directories Book 1, Chapter 6, Using Text Editors *and* **Text Processing**
Use the shell for multitasking.	Book 1, Chapter 8, Simple Task Management
Describe common shell editing commands.	Book 1, Chapter 6, Customizing the Shell
Use the following commands in isolation or in combination with each other: ls, cd, more, less, cp, mv, mkdir, rm, rmdir, ln, head, tail, file, grep, du, df, and zcat.	Book 1, Chapter 4, Working with Linux Files and Directories Book 1, Chapter 7, UsingBasic System Administration Tools
Use the following vi commands: i, ZZ, :w, :w! :q!, dd, x, D, J.	Book 1, Chapter 6, Using Text Editors

System Services

Objective	Book/Chapter/Section
List and describe seven tools that provide information on other tools.	Book 1, Chapter 1, **Learning More About Linux** Book 1, Chapter 7, Using Basic System Administration Tools
Describe and use LILO.	Book 1, Chapter 2, **Preparing Your Hard Disk** Book 1, Chapter 3, The Installation Process Book 1, Chapter 4, The Initialization Process
Install run-time device drivers.	Book 1, Chapter 4, The Linux Kernel
Configure a printer capabilities file.	Book 1, Chapter 12, Using Traditional Linux Printing *and* Understanding the Common UNIX Printing System

Objective	Book/Chapter/Section
Configure a printer filter.	Book 1, Chapter 12, Using Traditional Linux Printing *and* Understanding the Common UNIX Printing System
Use lpr, lpq, lprm, and lpc to control file printing.	Book 1, Chapter 12, Managing the Printing Environment
List the sections of the X server configuration file.	Book 1, Chapter 5, Running the X Window System
Configure the X server video hardware.	Book 1, Chapter 5, Running the X Window System
Contrast xf86config, XF86Setup, Xconfigurator, and SaX.	Book 1, Chapter 5, Running the X Window System
Describe five components of the X Window System architecture.	Book 1, Chapter 5, Running the X Window System
List and give the trade-offs of Afterstep, KDE, Window Maker, FVWM95, Enlightenment, and Blackbox.	Book 1, Chapter 5, Using Desktop Interfaces

Applications

Objective	Book/Chapter/Section
Describe the general control of X11 desktops.	Book 1, Chapter 5, Using Desktop Interfaces
Describe Netscape functions, FTP functions, Telnet functions, and mail functions.	Book 2, Chapter 1, Networking Software Book 2, Chapter 5, Running an FTP Server Book 2, Chapter 3, Web and E-mail Clients Book 2, Chapter 2, Using Basic Networking Utilities
Contrast WYSIWYG versus mark-up word processing.	Book 1, Chapter 6, Using Text Editors

Troubleshooting

Objective	Book/Chapter/Section
Describe the cause and solution to read errors.	Book 1, Chapter 3, Understanding Installation Issues
Explain why FTP keeps missing certain files in group transfers.	Book 2, Chapter 5, Running an FTP Server
Explain the problem and solution when LILO says LI.	Book 1, Chapter 3, Troubleshooting a New Installation
Define rescue disk and describe three reasons for using it.	Book 1, Chapter 9, Understanding a System's Vulnerabilities

Objective	Book/Chapter/Section
Explain how to get around a locked-up program.	Book 1, Chapter 10, Managing Processes
List eight steps to resolve an unresponsive printer.	Book 1, Chapter 12, Using Traditional Linux Printing *and* Understanding the Common UNIX Printing System
Explain why Linux may report the wrong time and describe how to fix the problem.	Book 2, Chapter 4, Using Administrative Services
Describe how to reset the console screen, the keyboard repeat rate, and the num lock key.	Book 1, Chapter 5, Running the X Window System
Describe the role of system logging and how to use it for troubleshooting.	Book 1, Chapter 10, Managing System Logs

Exam 2: Linux System Administration

Theory of Operation

Objective	Book/Chapter/Section
The student will understand file system structure and hierarchy.	Book 1, Chapter 4, Working with Linux Files and Directories
The student will understand file system backup and cron.	Book 1, Chapter 13, Understanding Backup Strategies Book 1, Chapter 11, Automating Tasks with at and crontab
The student will understand printing and system tuning.	Book 1, Chapter 9, Checking File System Integrity Book 1, Chapter 10, Managing Memory Book 1, Chapter 12, Using Traditional Linux Printing *and* Understanding the Common UNIX Printing System
The student will understand troubleshooting and emergency procedures.	Book 1, Chapter 9, Understanding a System's Vulnerabilities
The student will understand system resources.	Book 1, Chapter 10, Managing Processes *and* Managing Memory
The student will understand user profiles.	Book 1, Chapter 8, Managing User Accounts
The student will understand RAID.	Book 1, Chapter 9, Understanding Redundant Disk Systems

A

Base System

Objective	Book/Chapter/Section
The student will understand adding and removing a user.	Book 1, Chapter 8, Managing User Accounts
The student will understand run levels.	Book 1, Chapter 4, The Initialization Process
The student will understand fstab and volume remounting.	Book 1, Chapter 8, Maintaining File Systems
The student will understand recompiling the kernel.	Book 1, Chapter 11, Modifying the Linux Kernel
The student will understand performance and Hard Disk analysis.	Book 1, Chapter 8, Maintaining File Systems Book 1, Chapter 9, Checking File System Integrity
The student will understand system shutdown techniques.	Book 1, Chapter 4, The Initialization Process

Shells and Commands

Objective	Book/Chapter/Section
The student will understand the role of the superuser.	Book 1, Chapter 8, Managing User Accounts
The student will understand motd and the issue with it.	Book 1, Chapter 4, The Initialization Process
The student will understand the MS-DOS tools.	Book 1, Chapter 4, Working with Linux Files and Directories
The student will understand the ARP/Route precedence.	Book 2, Chapter 2, Configuring Networking with Command-Line Utilities
The student will understand Bootp and DHCP.	Book 1, Chapter 3, Understanding Installation Issues Book 2, Chapter 3, Using DHCP
The student will understand make and touch.	Book 1, Chapter 7, Using Basic System Administration Tools
The student will understand CGI scripts.	Book 1, Chapter 11, Writing Shell Scripts
The student will understand system status, system message logging, and performance analysis.	Book 1, Chapter 10, Managing Processes *and* Managing Memory *and* Book 1, Chapter 10, Managing System Logs

System Services

Objective	Book/Chapter/Section
The student will understand basic "user" commands.	Book 1, Chapter 7, Using Basic System Administration Tools
The student will understand the archive utilities.	Book 1, Chapter 13, Using Backup Utilities
The student will understand using fsck and why.	Book 1, Chapter 9, Checking File System Integrity
The student will understand process management.	Book 1, Chapter 10, Managing Processes
The student will understand printer settings and restarting.	Book 1, Chapter 12, Managing the Printing Environment
The student will understand the background line printer daemon and the foreground line printer requester.	Book 1, Chapter 12, Using Traditional Linux Printing *and* Understanding the Common UNIX Printing System
The student will understand software packages.	Book 1, Chapter 4, Running and Managing Software

Applications

Objective	Book/Chapter/Section
The student will understand AMANDA, ORL's VNC, Mail Exchange, News, and the Apache Web server.	Book 1, Chapter 13, Using Backup Utilities Book 2, Chapter 3, Web and Mail Clients Book 2, Chapter 6, Creating a Linux Web Server
The student will understand X Window desktops.	Book 1, Chapter 5, Running the X Window System
The student will understand benchmarks.	Book 1, Chapter 10, Managing Processes

Troubleshooting

Objective	Book/Chapter/Section
The student will understand core dump control.	Book 1, Chapter 11, Writing Shell Scripts

Exam 3: Linux Networking

A

Theory of Operation

Objective	Book/Chapter/Section
The student will understand the basic technology of the Internet, Ethernet, and area networks.	Book 2, Chapter 1, *throughout*
The student will understand addresses and addressing.	Book 2, Chapter 1, Networking Software
The student will understand the protocols.	Book 2, Chapter 1, Networking Software
The student will understand DNS, applications, and Internet access.	Book 2, Chapter 3, Setting up Name Resolution
The student will understand broadcasting, address assignment, and multicast.	Book 2, Chapter 1, Networking Software
The student will understand the UUCP subsystem.	Book 2, Chapter 3, Running Applications Remotely
The student will understand SMB and IPX.	Book 2, Chapter 2, Other Networking Protocols [IPX] Book 2, Chapter 5, Windows File and Print Integration with Samba [SMB]

Base System

Objective	Book/Chapter/Section
The student will understand networking interfaces.	Book 2, Chapter 2, Understanding Network Devices in Linux
The student will understand the ARP and Routing tables.	Book 2, Chapter 2, Configuring Networking with Command-Line Utilities
The student will understand firewalls.	Book 2, Chapter 11, Using Advanced Routing and Firewalls
The student will understand VPN and Proxy Servers.	Book 2, Chapter 11, Using Advanced Routing and Firewalls
The student will understand IP multicast.	Book 2, Chapter 1, Networking Software

Shells and Commands

Objective	Book/Chapter/Section
The student will understand basic network configuration.	Book 2, Chapter 2, Preparing to Configure Networking
The student will understand how to access and the importance of system startup files.	Book 1, Chapter 4, The Initialization Process Book 2, Chapter 2, Configuring Networking with Command-Line Utilities
The student will understand UUCP.	Book 2, Chapter 3, Running Applications Remotely
The student will understand network troubleshooting.	Book 2, Chapters 1, 2, *throughout*

System Services

Objective	Book/Chapter/Section
The student will understand DNS, FTP, and NFS.	Book 2, Chapter 3, Setting up Name Resolution [DNS] Book 2, Chapter 5, Running an FTP Server [FTP] Book 2, Chapter 5, File Sharing with NFS [NFS] Book 2, Chapter 6, Setting up a DNS Name Server [DNS]
The student will understand the Internet superserver.	Book 2, Chapter 4, The Superservers
The student will understand Samba.	Book 2, Chapter 5, Windows File and Print Integration with Samba
The student will understand sendmail, smail, qmail.	Book 2, Chapter 6, Configuring a Basic and E-mail Server
The student will understand POP3 and IMAP.	Book 2, Chapter 3, Web and Mail clients
The student will understand News, mail list servers, and the Apache server.	Book 2, Chapter 4, Understanding Mailing Lists and News Servers Book 2, Chapter 6, Creating a Linux Web Server

Applications

Objective	Book/Chapter/Section
The student will understand mail and pine.	Book 2, Chapter 3, Web and Mail Clients
The student will understand browsers.	Book 2, Chapter 3, Web and Mail Clients

Exam 4: Linux Security, Ethics, and Privacy

A

Theory of Operation

Objective	Book/Chapter/Section
The student will understand daemons as superusers and the buffer overflow problem.	Book 2, Chapter 11, Reviewing Threats to Your Network
The student will understand the protection scheme.	Book 2, Chapter 7, Introducing Computer Security and Privacy
The student will understand the access control list.	Book 2, Chapter 12, Using Intrusion Detection Software
The student will understand Trojan horses, password weakness, and screening IPs.	Book 2, Chapter 11, Reviewing Threats to Your Network
The student will understand CERT advisories, daily system check, and stealth file names.	Book 2, Chapter 7, Security-Focused Organizations
The student will understand cert.org and root-shell.com.	Book 2, Chapter 7, Security-Focused Organizations
The student will understand intruder detection and removal.	Book 2, Chapter 12, Using Intrusion Detection Software
The student will understand user-mode viruses and worms.	Book 2, Chapter 11, Reviewing Threats to Your Network
The student will understand Ken Thompson on trusting trust.	Book 2, Chapter 7, Introducing Computer Security and Privacy

Base System

Objective	Book/Chapter/Section
The student will understand setting the superuser status from a shell script.	Book 1, Chapter 6, Understanding the Shell
The student will understand the importance of classification of user, group, and everybody.	Book 1, Chapter 8, Managing User Accounts
The student will understand UMASK.	Book 1, Chapter 4, Working with Linux Files and Directories
The student will understand shadow passwords, host.allow, and host.deny.	Book 1, Chapter 8, Managing User Accounts
The student will understand the importance of files for logging in as superuser, file transfer as superuser, printer configuration, and system logging.	Book 2, Chapter 10, Reviewing Linux File Permissions Book 1, Chapter 10, Managing System Logs Book 1, Chapter 12, Using Traditional Linux Printing *and* Understanding the Common UNIX Printing System

Shells and Commands

Objective	Book/Chapter/Section
The student will understand the access control list and emulation.	Book 2, Chapter 10, Reviewing Linux File Permissions

System Services

Objective	Book/Chapter/Section
The student will understand checksecurity, rotatelogs, quotaon, quotacheck, and sa.	Book 2, Chapter 10, Using the System Logs for Security Checks
The student will understand pluggable authentication modules.	Book 2, Chapter 9, Using Pluggable Authentication Modules
The student will understand TCP/UDP wrappers.	Book 2, Chapter 4, The Superservers
The student will understand find, its switches, important commands, and their significance.	Book 1, Chapter 7, Using Basic System Administration Tools
The student will understand the importance of daily cron checks.	Book 1, Chapter 11, Automating Tasks with at and crontab

Applications

Objective	Book/Chapter/Section
The student will understand hidden logfile backup.	Book 2, Chapter 12, Using the System Logs for Security Checks

Troubleshooting

Objective	Book/Chapter/Section
The student will understand why setuid shell scripts do not work.	Book 2, Chapter 10, Reviewing Linux File Permissions

OBJECTIVES FOR THE LINUX PROFESSIONAL INSTITUTE (LPI) CERTIFICATION EXAMS

A

The objectives covered here are for LPI Level 1 certification, encompassing two exams:

- 101, General Linux, Part 1
- 102, General Linux, Part 2

The LPI Level 2 certification includes two additional exams:

- 201, Advanced Linux Administration
- 202, Linux Networking Administration

Although the objectives for the Level 2 exams are not given here and are not the focus of this book (or Book 2), you will find that many of the topics addressed in the Level 2 exams are addressed in the two books. See *www.lpi.org* for more information about Level 2 certification.

A revised version of the LPI objectives was released in August 2002. The revision had little effect on the content of the objectives, but the numbering was redone to account for additions and deletions that had occurred since the LPI objectives were first published.

A weight is assigned to each objective. The weights range from 1 to 10; a higher weight indicates that the topic will be covered by more exam questions. As of this writing, the revised objectives do not yet have weights assigned. The weight shown for the objectives is taken from the previous version of the LPI objectives and may not match the weight actually assigned for the revised objectives. The Web site *www.lpi.org* includes details about the LPI Certification Program.

In the tables that follow, **Book 1** refers to this book, *Guide to Linux Installation and Administration*, 2nd Ed. (ISBN 0-619-13095-4). **Book 2** refers to *Guide to Linux Networking and Security* (ISBN 0-619-00094-5). Please refer to the Table of Contents and Index of each volume for more precise information.

OBJECTIVES FOR EXAM 101 (REVISED AUGUST 2002)

Topic 101 Hardware & Architecture

1.101.1 Configure Fundamental BIOS Settings

Weight	Description	Book/Chapter/Section
3	Candidates should be able to configure fundamental system hardware by making the correct settings in the system BIOS. This objective includes a proper understanding of BIOS configuration issues such as the use of LBA on IDE hard disks larger than 1024 cylinders, enabling or disabling integrated peripherals, as well as configuring systems with (or without) external peripherals such as keyboards. It also includes the correct setting for IRQ, DMA and I/O addresses for all BIOS administrated ports and settings for error handling. Key files, terms, and utilities include: /proc/ioports, /proc/interrupts, /proc/dma, /proc/pci	Book 1, Chapter 2, Preparing to Install Linux Book 1, Chapter 3, Understanding Installation Issues

1.101.3 Configure Modem and Sound Cards

Weight	Description	Book/Chapter/Section
4	Candidates should ensure devices meet compatibility requirements (particularly that the modem is NOT a win-modem), verify that both the modem and sound card are using unique and correct IRQs, I/O, and DMA addresses, if the sound card is PnP install and run sndconfig and isapnp, configure modem for outbound dial-up, configure modem for outbound PPP	SLIP	CSLIP connection, set serial port for 115.2 Kbps.	Book 1, Chapter 2, Preparing to Install Linux Book 1, Chapter 3,Understanding Installation Issues

1.101.4 Set up SCSI Devices

Weight	Description	Book/Chapter/Section
4	Candidates should be able to configure SCSI devices using the SCSI BIOS as well as the necessary Linux tools. They also should be able to differentiate between the various types of SCSI. This objective includes manipulating the SCSI BIOS to detect used and available SCSI IDs and setting the correct ID number for different devices, especially the boot device. It also includes managing the settings in the computer's BIOS to determine the desired boot sequence if both SCSI and IDE drives are used. Key files, terms, and utilities include: SCSI ID, /proc/scsi/, scsi_info.	Book 1, Chapter 2, Preparing to Install Linux Book 1, Chapter 3, Understanding Installation Issues

1.101.5 Set up Different PC Expansion Cards

Weight	Description	Book/Chapter/Section
4	Candidates should be able to configure various cards for the various expansion slots. They should know the differences between ISA and PCI cards with respect to configuration issues. This objective includes the correct settings of IRQs, DMAs, and I/O ports of the cards, especially to avoid conflicts between devices. It also includes using isapnp if the card is an ISA PnP device. Key files, terms, and utilities include: /proc/dma, /proc/interrupts, /proc/ioports, /proc/pci, pnpdump(8), isapnp(8), lspci(8).	Book 1, Chapter 2, Preparing to Install Linux Book 1, Chapter 3, Understanding Installation Issues

1.101.6 Configure Communication Devices

Weight	Description	Book/Chapter/Section
4	Candidates should be able to install and configure different internal and external communication devices like modems, ISDN adapters, and DSL switches. This objective includes verification of compatibility requirements (especially important if the modem is a winmodem), necessary hardware settings for internal devices (IRQs, DMAs, I/O ports), and loading and configuring suitable device drivers. It also includes communication device and interface configuration requirements, such as the right serial port for 115.2 Kbps, and the correct modem settings for outbound PPP connection(s). Key files, terms, and utilities include: /proc/dma, /proc/interrupts, /proc/ioports, setserial(8).	Book 1, Chapter 2, Preparing to Install Linux Book 1, Chapter 3, Understanding Installation Issues

1.101.7 Configure USB devices

Weight	Description	Book/Chapter/Section
4	Candidates should be able to activate USB support, and use and configure different USB devices. This objective includes the correct selection of the USB chipset and the corresponding module. It also includes the knowledge of the basic architecture of the layer model of USB as well as the different modules used in the different layers. Key files, terms, and utilities include: lspci(8), usb-uhci.o, usb-ohci.o, /etc/usbmgr/, usbmodules, /etc/hotplug.	Book 1, Chapter 2, Preparing to Install Linux Book 1, Chapter 3, Understanding Installation Issues

Topic 102 Linux Installation & Package Management

1.102.1 Design Hard Disk Layout

Weight	Description	Book/Chapter/Section
Unknown	Candidates should be able to design a disk partitioning scheme for a Linux system. This objective includes allocating filesystems or swap space to separate partitions or disks, and tailoring the design to the intended use of the system. It also includes placing /boot on a partition that conforms with the BIOS' requirements for booting. Key files, terms, and utilities include: / (root) filesystem, /var filesystem, /home filesystem, swap space, mount points, partitions, cylinder 1024.	Book 1, Chapter 2, Preparing Your Hard Disk

1.102.2 Install a Boot Manager

Weight	Description	Book/Chapter/Section
3	Candidates should be able to select, install, and configure a boot manager. This objective includes providing alternative boot locations and backup boot options (for example, using a boot floppy). Key files, terms, and utilities include: /etc/lilo.conf , /boot/grub/grub.conf, lilo, grub-install, MBR, superblock, first stage boot loader.	Book 1, Chapter 3, The Installation Process

1.102.3 Make and Install Programs from Source

Weight	Description	Book/Chapter/Section
5	Candidates should be able to build and install an executable program from source. This objective includes being able to unpack a file of sources. Candidates should be able to make simple customizations to the Makefile, for example changing paths or adding extra include directories. Key files, terms, and utilities include: gunzip, gzip, bzip2, tar, configure, make.	Book 1, Chapter 11, Writing Shell Scripts

1.102.4 Manage Shared Libraries

Weight	Description	Book/Chapter/Section
3	Candidates should be able to determine the shared libraries that executable programs depend on and install them when necessary. Candidates should be able to state where system libraries are kept. Key files, terms, and utilities include: ldd, ldconfig, /etc/ld.so.conf, LD_LIBRARY_PATH.	Book 1, Chapter 4, Running and Managing Software

1.102.5 Use Debian Package Management

Weight	Description	Book/Chapter/Section
5	Candidates should be able to perform Debian package management. This objective includes being able to use command-line and interactive tools to install, upgrade, or uninstall packages, as well as find packages containing specific files or software (such packages might or might not be installed). This objective also includes being able to obtain package information like version, content, dependencies, package integrity and installation status (whether or not the package is installed). Key files, terms, and utilities include: unpack, configure, /etc/dpkg/dpkg.cfg, /var/lib/dpkg/*, /etc/apt/apt.conf, /etc/apt/sources.list, dpkg, dselect, dpkg-reconfigure, apt-get, alien.	Book 1, Chapter 4, Running and Managing Software

1.102.6 Use Red Hat Package Manager (RPM)

Weight	Description	Book/Chapter/Section
6	Candidates should be able to perform package management under Linux distributions that use RPMs for package distribution. This objective includes being able to install, re-install, upgrade, and remove packages, as well as obtain status and version information on packages. This objective also includes obtaining package information such as version, status, dependencies, integrity, and signatures. Candidates should be able to determine what files a package provides, as well as find which package a specific file comes from. Key files, terms, and utilities include: /etc/rpmrc, /usr/lib/rpm/*, rpm, grep.	Book 1, Chapter 4, Running and Managing Software Book 2, Chapter 7, Other Security Applications

Topic 103 GNU & Unix Commands

1.103.1 Work on the Command Line

Weight	Description	Book/Chapter/Section
4	Candidates should be able to interact with shells and commands using the command line. This includes typing valid commands and command sequences, defining, referencing and exporting environment variables, using command history and editing facilities, invoking commands in the path and outside the path, using command substitution, applying commands recursively through a directory tree and using man to find out about commands. Key files, terms, and utilities include: . , bash, echo, env, exec, export, man, pwd, set, unset, ~/.bash_history, ~/.profile.	Book 1, Chapter 4, Working with Linux Files and Directories

1.103.2 Process Text Streams Using Filters

Weight	Description	Book/Chapter/Section
7	Candidates should be able to apply filters to text streams. Tasks include sending text files and output streams through text utility filters to modify the output, and using standard UNIX commands found in the GNU textutils package. Key files, terms, and utilities include: cat, cut, expand, fmt, head, join, nl, od, paste, pr, sed, sort, split, tac, tail, tr, unexpand, uniq, wc.	Book 1, Chapter 6, Text Processing

1.103.3 Perform Basic File Management

Weight	Description	Book/Chapter/Section
2	Candidates should be able to use the basic UNIX commands to copy, move, and remove files and directories. Tasks include advanced file management operations such as copying multiple files recursively, removing directories recursively, and moving files that meet a wildcard pattern. This includes using simple and advanced wildcard specifications to refer to files, as well as using find to locate and act on files based on type, size, or time. Key files, terms, and utilities include: cp, find, mkdir, mv, ls, rm, rmdir, touch, file globbing.	Book 1, Chapter 4, Working with Linux Files and Directories

1.103.4 Use Streams, Pipes, and Redirects

Weight	Description	Book/Chapter/Section
3	Candidates should be able to redirect streams and connect them in order to process textual data efficiently. Tasks include redirecting standard input, standard output, and standard error, piping the output of one command to the input of another command, using the output of one command as arguments to another command, and sending output to both stdout and a file. Key files, terms, and utilities include: tee, xargs, <, <<, >, >>, |, ` `.	Book 1, Chapter 6, Understanding the Shell

A

1.103.5 Create, Monitor, and Kill Processes

Weight	Description	Book/Chapter/Section
5	Candidates should be able to manage processes. This includes knowing how to run jobs in the foreground and background, bring a job from the background to the foreground and vice versa, start a process that will run without being connected to a terminal, and signal a program to continue running after logout. Tasks also include monitoring active processes, selecting and sorting processes for display, sending signals to processes, killing processes and identifying and killing X applications that did not terminate after the X session closed. Key files, terms, and utilities include: &, bg, fg, jobs, kill, nohup, ps, top.	Book 1, Chapter 10, Managing Processes

1.103.6 Modify Process Execution Priorities

Weight	Description	Book/Chapter/Section
2	Candidates should be able to manage process execution priorities. Tasks include running a program with higher or lower priority, determining the priority of a process, and changing the priority of a running process. Key files, terms, and utilities include: nice, ps, renice, top.	Book 1, Chapter 10, Managing Processes

1.103.7 Search Text Files Using Regular Expressions

Weight	Description	Book/Chapter/Section
3	Candidates should be able to manipulate files and text data using regular expressions. This objective includes creating simple regular expressions containing several notational elements. It also includes using regular expression tools to perform searches through a file system or file content. Key files, terms, and utilities include: grep, regexp, sed.	Book 1, Chapter 7, Using Basic System Administration Tools

1.103.8 Perform Basic File Editing Operations Using vi

Weight	Description	Book/Chapter/Section
2	Candidates must be able to edit text files using vi. This objective includes vi navigation, basic vi nodes, inserting, editing, deleting, copying, and finding text. Key files, terms, and utilities include: vi, /, ?, h, j, k, l, G, H, L, i, c, d, dd, p, o, a, ZZ, :w!, :q!, :e!, :!.	Book 1, Chapter 6, Using Text Editors

Topic 104 Devices, Linux File Systems, File System Hierarchy Standard

1.104.1 Create Partitions and File Systems

Weight	Description	Book/Chapter/Section
3	Candidates should be able to configure disk partitions and then create file systems on media such as hard disks. This objective includes using various mkfs commands to set up partitions to various file systems, including ext2, ext3, reiserfs, vfat, and xfs. Key files, terms, and utilities include: fdisk, mkfs.	Book 1, Chapter 2, Preparing Your Hard Disk Book 1, Chapter 8, Maintaining File Systems

1.104.2 Maintain the Integrity of File Systems

Weight	Description	Book/Chapter/Section
5	Candidates should be able to verify the integrity of file systems, monitor free space and inodes, and repair simple file system problems. This objective includes the commands required to maintain a standard file system, as well as the extra data associated with a journaling file system. Key files, terms, and utilities include: du, df, fsck, e2fsck, mke2fs, debugfs, dumpe2fs, tune2fs.	Book 1, Chapter 8, Maintaining File Systems Book 1, Chapter 9, Checking File System Integrity

1.104.3 Control Mounting and Unmounting File Systems

Weight	Description	Book/Chapter/Section
3	Candidates should be able to configure the mounting of a file system. This objective includes the ability to manually mount and unmount file systems, configure file system mounting on bootup, and configure user mountable removeable file systems such as tape drives, floppies, and CDs. Key files, terms, and utilities include: /etc/fstab, mount, umount.	Book 1, Chapter 8, Maintaining File Systems

1.104.4 Managing Disk Quotas

Weight	Description	Book/Chapter/Section
1	Candidates should be able to manage disk quotas for users. This objective includes setting up a disk quota for a file system, editing, checking, and generating user quota reports. Key files, terms, and utilities include: quota, edquota, repquota, quotaon.	Book 1, Chapter 8, Maintaining File Systems

1.104.5 Use File Permissions to Control Access to Files

Weight	Description	Book/Chapter/Section
3	Candidates should be able to control file access through permissions. This objective includes access permissions on regular and special files as well as directories. Also included are access modes such as suid, sgid, and the sticky bit, the use of the group field to grant file access to workgroups, the immutable flag, and the default file creation mode. Key files, terms, and utilities include: chmod, umask, chattr.	Book 1, Chapter 4, Working with Linux Files and Directories

1.104.6 Manage File Ownership

Weight	Description	Book/Chapter/Section
2	Candidates should be able to control user and group ownership of files. This objective includes the ability to change the user and group owner of a file as well as the default group owner for new files. Key files, terms, and utilities include: chmod, chown, chgrp.	Book 1, Chapter 4, Working with Linux Files and Directories

1.104.7 Create and Change Hard and Symbolic Links

Weight	Description	Book/Chapter/Section
2	Candidates should be able to create and manage hard and symbolic links to a file. This objective includes the ability to create and identify links, copy files through links, and use linked files to support system administration tasks. Key files, terms, and utilities include: ln.	Book 1, Chapter 4, Working with Linux Files and Directories

1.104.8 Find System Files and Place Files in the Correct Location

Weight	Description	Book/Chapter/Section
2	Candidates should be thoroughly familiar with the File System Hierarchy Standard, including typical file locations and directory classifications. This objective includes the ability to find files and commands on a Linux system. Key files, terms, and utilities include: find, locate, slocate, updatedb, whereis, which, /etc/updatedb.conf.	Book 1, Chapter 7, Using Basic System Administration Tools

Topic 110 X

1.110.1 Install and Configure XFree86

Weight	Description	Book/Chapter/Section
4	Candidates should be able to configure and install X and an X font server. This objective includes verifying that the video card and monitor are supported by an X server, as well as customizing and tuning X for the video card and monitor. It also includes installing an X font server, installing fonts, and configuring X to use the font server (may require a manual edit of /etc/X11/XF86Config in the "Files" section). Key files, terms, and utilities include: XF86Setup, xf86config, xvidtune, /etc/X11/XF86Config, .Xresources.	Book 1, Chapter 5, Running the X Window System

A

1.110.2 Set up a Display Manager

Weight	Description	Book/Chapter/Section
1	Candidates should be able set up and customize a display manager. This objective includes turning the display manager on or off and changing the display manager greeting. This objective includes changing default bitplanes for the display manager. It also includes configuring display managers for use by X-stations. This objective covers the display managers XDM (X Display Manager), GDM (Gnome Display Manager), and KDM (KDE Display Manager). Key files, terms, and utilities include: /etc/inittab, /etc/X11/xdm/*, /etc/X11/kdm/*, /etc/X11/gdm/*.	Book 1, Chapter 5, Running the X Window System Book 2, Chapter 3, Running Applications Remotely

1.110.4 Install and Customize a Window Manager Environment

Weight	Description	Book/Chapter/Section
4	Candidates should be able to customize a system-wide desktop environment and/or window manager, to demonstrate an understanding of customization procedures for window manager menus and/or desktop panel menus. This objective includes selecting and configuring the desired X-terminal (xterm, rxvt, aterm etc.), verifying and resolving library dependency issues for X applications, and exporting X-display to a client workstation. Key files, terms, and utilities include: .xinitrc, .Xdefaults, xhost, DISPLAY environment variable.	Book 1, Chapter 5, Running the X Window System *and* Using Desktop Interfaces

EXAM DETAILS FOR EXAM 102 (REVISED AUGUST 2002)

Topic 105 Kernel

1.105.1 Manage/Query Kernel and Kernel Modules at Runtime

Weight	Description	Book/Chapter/Section
3	Candidates should be able to manage and/or query a kernel and kernel loadable modules. This objective includes using command-line utilities to get information about the currently running kernel and kernel modules. It also includes manually loading and unloading modules as appropriate. It also includes being able to determine when modules can be unloaded and what parameters a module accepts. Candidates should be able to configure the system to load modules by names other than their file name. Key files, terms, and utilities include: /lib/modules/kernel-version/modules.dep, /etc/modules.conf & /etc/conf.modules, depmod, insmod, lsmod, rmmod, modinfo, modprobe, uname.	Book 1, Chapter 4, The Linux Kernel

1.105.2 Reconfigure, Build, and Install a Custom Kernel and Kernel Modules

Weight	Description	Book/Chapter/Section
4	Candidates should be able to customize, build, and install a kernel and kernel loadable modules from source This objective includes customizing the current kernel configuration, building a new kernel, and building kernel modules as appropriate. It also includes installing the new kernel as well as any modules, and ensuring that the boot manager can locate the new kernel and associated files (generally located under /boot, see objective 1.102.2 for more details about boot manager configuration). Key files, terms, and utilities include: /usr/src/linux/*, /usr/src/linux/.config, /lib/modules/kernel-version/*, /boot/*; make, make targets: config, menuconfig, xconfig, oldconfig, modules, install, modules_install, depmod.	Book 1, Chapter 10, Managing the Linux Kernel

Topic 106 Boot, Initialization, Shutdown and Run Levels

1.106.1 Boot the System

Weight	Description	Book/Chapter/Section
3	Candidates should be able to guide the system through the booting process. This includes giving commands to the boot loader and giving options to the kernel at boot time, and checking the events in the log files. Key files, terms, and utilities include: dmesg, /var/log/messages, /etc/conf.modules or /etc/modules.conf, LILO, GRUB.	Book 1, Chapter 4, The Initialization Process

1.106.2 Change Run Levels and Shutdown or Reboot System

Weight	Description	Book/Chapter/Section
3	Candidates should be able to manage the run level of the system. This objective includes changing to single user mode, shutdown, or rebooting the system. Candidates should be able to alert users before switching run level, and properly terminate processes. This objective also includes setting the default run level. Key files, terms, and utilities include: shutdown, init, /etc/inittab.	Book 1, Chapter 4, The Initialization Process

Topic 107 Printing

1.107.2 Manage Printers and Print Queues

Weight	Description	Book/Chapter/Section
2	The candidates should be able to manage print queues and user print jobs. This objective includes monitoring print server and user print queues and troubleshooting general printing problems. Key files, terms, and utilities include: lpc, lpq, lprm, lpr, /etc/printcap.	Book 1, Chapter 12, Using Traditional Linux Printing Book 1, Chapter 12, Understanding the Common UNIX Printing System

1.107.3 Print Files

Weight	Description	Book/Chapter/Section
1	Candidates should be able to manage print queues and manipulate print jobs. This objective includes adding and removing jobs from configured printer queues and converting text files to PostScript for printing. Key files, terms, and utilities include: lpr, lpq, mpage.	Book 1, Chapter 12, Printing Files

1.107.4 Install and Configure Local and Remote Printers

Weight	Description	Book/Chapter/Section
3	Candidates should be able to install a printer daemon, and install and configure a print filter (e.g., apsfilter, magicfilter). This objective includes making local and remote printers accessible for a Linux system, including PostScript, non-PostScript, and Samba printers. Key files, terms, and utilities include: lpd, /etc/printcap, /etc/apsfilter/*, /var/lib/apsfilter/*/, /etc/magicfilter/*/, /var/spool/lpd/*/.	Book 1, Chapter 12, Using Traditional Linux Printing Book 1, Chapter 12, Understanding the Common UNIX Printing System Book 2, Chapter 4, Using Administrative Services [lpd]

Topic 108 Documentation

1.108.1 Use and Manage Local System Documentation

Weight	Description	Book/Chapter/Section
5	Candidates should be able to use and administer the man facility and the material in /usr/share/doc/. This objective includes finding relevant man pages, searching man page sections, finding commands and man pages related to them, and configuring access to man sources and the man system. It also includes using system documentation stored in /usr/share/doc/ and determining what documentation to keep in /usr/share/doc/. Key commands and terms: man, apropos, whatis, MANPATH.	Book 1, Chapter 1, Learning More about Linux

1.108.2 Find Linux Documentation on the Internet

Weight	Description	Book/Chapter/Section
2	Candidates should be able to find and use Linux documentation. This objective includes using Linux documentation at sources such as the Linux Documentation Project (LDP), vendor and third-party Web sites, newsgroups, newsgroup archives, and mailing lists.	Book 1, Chapter 1, Learning More about Linux

1.108.5 Notify Users on System-Related Issues

Weight	Description	Book/Chapter/Section
Unknown	Candidates should be able to notify users about current issues related to the system. This objective includes automating the communication process, e.g., through login messages. Key files, terms, and utilities include: /etc/issue, /etc/issue.net, /etc/motd.	Book 1, Chapter 8, Managing User Accounts

Topic 109 Shells, Scripting, Programming, & Compiling

1.109.1 Customize and Use the Shell Environment

Weight	Description	Book/Chapter/Section
4	Candidates should be able to customize shell environments to meet users' needs. This objective includes setting environment variables (e.g., PATH) at login or when spawning a new shell. It also includes writing bash functions for frequently used sequences of commands. Key files, terms, and utilities include: ~/.bash_profile, ~/.bash_login, ~/.profile, ~/.bashrc, ~/.bash_logout, ~/.inputrc, function (Bash built-in command), export, env, set (Bash built-in command), unset (Bash built-in command).	Book 1, Chapter 6, Customizing the Shell

1.109.2 Customize or Write Simple Scripts

Weight	Description	Book/Chapter/Section
5	Candidates should be able to customize existing scripts, or write simple new (ba)sh scripts. This objective includes using standard sh syntax (loops, tests), using command substitution, testing command return values, testing of file status, and conditional mailing to the superuser. This objective also includes making sure the correct interpreter is called on the first (#!) line of scripts. This objective also includes managing location, ownership, execution, and suid-rights of scripts. Key files, terms, and utilities include: while, for, test, chmod.	Book 1, Chapter 11, Writing Shell Scripts

Topic 111 Administrative Tasks

1.111.1 Manage Users and Group Accounts and Related System Files

Weight	Description	Book/Chapter/Section
7	Candidates should be able to add, remove, suspend, and change user accounts. Tasks include to add and remove groups, and to change user/group info in passwd/group databases. This objective also includes creating special purpose and limited accounts. Key files, terms, and utilities include: chage, gpasswd, groupadd, groupdel, groupmod, grpconv, grpunconv, passwd, pwconv, pwunconv, useradd, userdel, usermod, /etc/passwd, /etc/shadow, /etc/group, /etc/gshadow.	Book 1, Chapter 8, Managing User Accounts

A

1.111.2 Tune the User Environment and System Environment Variables

Weight	Description	Book/Chapter/Section
4	Candidates should be able to modify global and user profiles. This includes setting environment variables, maintaining skel directories for new user accounts, and setting the command search path with the proper directory. Key files, terms, and utilities include: env, export, set, unset, /etc/profile, /etc/skel.	Book 1, Chapter 6, Customizing the Shell Book 1, Chapter 8, Managing User Accounts

1.111.3 Configure and Use System Log Files to Meet Administrative and Security Needs

Weight	Description	Book/Chapter/Section
3	Candidates should be able to configure system logs. This objective includes managing the type and level of information logged, manually scanning log files for notable activity, monitoring log files, arranging for automatic rotation and archiving of logs, and tracking down problems noted in logs. Key files, terms, and utilities include: logrotate, tail -f, /etc/syslog.conf, /var/log/*.	Book 1, Chapter 10, Managing System Logs

1.111.4 Automate System Administration Tasks by Scheduling Jobs to Run in the Future

Weight	Description	Book/Chapter/Section
4	Candidates should be able to use cron or anacron to run jobs at regular intervals and to use at to run jobs at a specific time. Tasks include managing cron and at jobs and configuring user access to cron and at services. Key files, terms, and utilities include: at, atq, atrm, crontab, /etc/anacrontab, /etc/at.deny, /etc/at.allow, /etc/crontab, /etc/cron.allow, /etc/cron.deny, /var/spool/cron/*.	Book 1, Chapter 11, Automating Tasks with at and crontab

1.111.5 Maintain an Effective Data Backup Strategy

Weight	Description	Book/Chapter/Section
3	Candidates should be able to plan a backup strategy and backup filesystems automatically to various media. Tasks include dumping a raw device to a file or vice versa, performing partial and manual backups, verifying the integrity of backup files and partially or fully restoring backups. Key files, terms, and utilities include: cpio, dd, dump, restore, tar.	Book 1, Chapter 13, Backup Strategies

1.111.6 Maintain System Time

Weight	Description	Book/Chapter/Section
3	Candidates should be able to properly maintain the system time and synchronize the clock over NTP. Tasks include setting the system date and time, setting the BIOS clock to the correct time in UTC, configuring the correct timezone for the system and configuring the system to correct clock drift to match NTP clock. Key files, terms, and utilities include: date, hwclock, ntpd, ntpdate, /usr/share/zoneinfo, /etc/timezone, /etc/localtime, /etc/ntp.conf, /etc/ntp.drift.	Book 2, Chapter 4, Using Administrative Services

Topic 112 Networking Fundamentals

A

1.112.1 Fundamentals of TCP/IP

Weight	Description	Book/Chapter/Section
4	Candidates should demonstrate a proper understanding of network fundamentals. This objective includes the understanding of IP addresses, network masks, and what they mean (i.e., determine a network and broadcast address for a host based on its subnet mask in "dotted quad" or abbreviated notation or determine the network address, broadcast address, and netmask when given an IP address and number of bits). It also covers the understanding of the network classes and classless subnets (CIDR) and the reserved addresses for private network use. It includes the understanding of the function and application of a default route. It also includes the understanding of basic Internet protocols (IP, ICMP, TCP, UDP) and the more common TCP and UDP ports (20, 21, 23, 25, 53, 80, 110, 119, 139, 143, 161). Key files, terms, and utilities include: /etc/services, ftp, telnet, host, ping, dig, traceroute, whois.	Book 2, Chapter 1, Networking Software Book 2, Chapter 2, Configuring Networking Using Command-Line Utilities *and* Using Basic Networking Utilities

1.112.3 TCP/IP Configuration and Troubleshooting

Weight	Description	Book/Chapter/Section
10	Candidates should be able to view, change, and verify configuration settings and operational status for various network interfaces. This objective includes manual and automatic configuration of interfaces and routing tables. This especially means to add, start, stop, restart, delete, or reconfigure network interfaces. It also means to change, view, or configure the routing table and to correct an improperly set default route manually. Candidates should be able to configure Linux as a DHCP client and a TCP/IP host and to debug problems associated with the network configuration. Key files, terms, and utilities include: /etc/HOSTNAME or /etc/hostname, /etc/hosts, /etc/networks, /etc/host.conf, /etc/resolv.conf, /etc/nsswitch.conf, ifconfig, route, dhcpcd, dhcpclient, pump, host, hostname (domainname, dnsdomainname), netstat, ping, traceroute, tcpdump, the network scripts run during system initialization.	Book 2, Chapter 2, Configuring Networking with Command-Line Utilities

1.112.4 Configure Linux as a PPP client

Weight	Description	Book/Chapter/Section
4	Candidates should understand the basics of the PPP protocol and be able to configure and use PPP for outbound connections. This objective includes the definition of the chat sequence to connect (given a login example) and the setup commands to be run automatically when a PPP connection is made. It also includes initialization and termination of a PPP connection, with a modem, ISDN, or ADSL and setting PPP to reconnect automatically if disconnected. Key files, terms, and utilities include: /etc/ppp/options.*, /etc/ppp/peers/*, /etc/wvdial.conf, /etc/ppp/ip-up, /etc/ppp/ip-down, wvdial, pppd.	Book 2, Chapter 3, Dial-Up Network Access Using PPP

A

Topic 113 Networking Services

1.113.1 Configure and Manage inetd, xinetd, and Related Services

Weight	Description	Book/Chapter/Section
5	Candidates should be able to configure which services are available through inetd, use tcpwrappers to allow or deny services on a host-by-host basis, manually start, stop, and restart Internet services, and configure basic network services including Telnet and FTP. Set a service to run as another user instead of the default in inetd.conf. Key files, terms, and utilities include: /etc/inetd.conf, /etc/hosts.allow, /etc/hosts.deny, /etc/services, /etc/xinetd.conf, /etc/xinetd.log.	Book 2, Chapter 4, The Superservers

1.113.2 Operate and Perform Basic Configuration of sendmail

Weight	Description	Book/Chapter/Section
5	Candidates should be able to modify simple parameters in sendmail configuration files (including the "Smart Host" parameter, if necessary), create mail aliases, manage the mail queue, start and stop sendmail, configure mail forwarding, and perform basic troubleshooting of sendmail. This objective includes checking for and closing open relays on the mailserver. It does not include advanced custom configuration of sendmail. Key files, terms, and utilities include: /etc/sendmail.cf, /etc/aliases or /etc/mail/aliases, /etc/mail/*, ~/.forward, mailq, sendmail, newaliases.	Book 2, Chapter 6, Configuring a Basic E-mail Server

1.113.3 Operate and Perform Basic Configuration of Apache

Weight	Description	Book/Chapter/Section
3	Candidates should be able to modify simple parameters in Apache configuration files, start, stop, and restart httpd, and arrange for automatic restarting of httpd upon boot. Does not include advanced custom configuration of Apache. Key files, terms, and utilities include: apachectl, httpd, httpd.conf.	Book 2, Chapter 6, Creating a Linux Web Server

1.113.4 Properly Manage the NFS, smb, and nmb Daemons

Weight	Description	Book/Chapter/Section
4	Candidates should know how to mount remote file systems using NFS, configure NFS for exporting local file systems, start, stop, and restart the NFS server. Install and configure Samba using the included GUI tools or direct edit of the /etc/smb.conf file (Note: this deliberately excludes advanced NT domain issues but includes simple sharing of home directories and printers, as well as correctly setting the nmbd as a WINS client). Key files, terms, and utilities include: /etc/exports, /etc/fstab, /etc/smb.conf, mount, umount.	Book 2, Chapter 5, File Sharing with NFS [NFS] *and* Windows File and Print Integration with Samba [smb and nmb]

1.113.5 Set up and Configure Basic DNS Services

Weight	Description	Book/Chapter/Section
3	Candidates should be able to configure hostname lookups and troubleshoot problems with local caching-only name server. Requires an understanding of the domain registration and DNS translation process. Requires understanding key differences in configuration files for bind 4 and bind 8. Key files, terms, and utilities include: /etc/hosts, /etc/resolv.conf, /etc/nsswitch.conf, /etc/named.boot (v.4) or /etc/named.conf (v.8), named.	Book 2, Chapter 3, Setting up Name Resolution [client] Book 2, Chapter 6, Setting up a DNS Name Server [server]

A

1.113.7 Set up Secure Shell (OpenSSH)

Weight	Description	Book/Chapter/Section
Unknown	Candidates should be able to obtain and configure OpenSSH. This objective includes basic OpenSSH installation and trouble-shooting, as well as configuring sshd to start at system boot. Key files, terms, and utilities include: /etc/hosts.allow, /etc/hosts.deny, /etc/nologin, /etc/ssh/sshd_config, /etc/ssh_known_hosts, /etc/sshrc, sshd, ssh-keygen.	Book 2, Chapter 11, Encrypting Network Traffic

Topic 114 Security

1.114.1 Perform Security Administration Tasks

Weight	Description	Book/Chapter/Section
4	Candidates should know how to review system configuration to ensure host security in accordance with local security policies. This objective includes how to configure TCP wrappers, find files with SUID/SGID bit set, verify packages, set or change user passwords and password aging information, and update binaries as recommended by CERT, BUGTRAQ, and/or distribution's security alerts. Includes basic knowledge of ipchains and iptables. Key files, terms, and utilities include: /proc/net/ip_fwchains, /proc/net/ip_fwnames, /proc/net/ip_masquerade, find, ipchains, passwd socket, iptables.	Book 2, Chapter 4, The Superservers Book 2, Chapter 10, Reviewing Linux File Permissions

1.114.2 Set up Host Security

Weight	Description	Book/Chapter/Section
4	Candidates should know how to set up a basic level of host security. Tasks include syslog configuration, shadowed passwords, setup of a mail alias for root's mail, and turning off all network services not in use. Key files, terms, and utilities include: /etc/inetd.conf or /etc/inet.d/*, /etc/nologin, /etc/passwd, /etc/shadow, /ets/syslog.conf.	Book 1, Chapter 10, Managing System Logs Book 2, Chapter 4, The Superservers

1.114.3 Set up User Level Security

Weight	Description	Book/Chapter/Section
2	Candidates should be able to configure user level security. Tasks include limits on user logins, processes, and memory usage. Key files, terms, and utilities include: quota, usermod.	Book 2, Chapter 9, Using Pluggable Authentication Modules

B

COMMAND SUMMARY

This appendix lists alphabetically all commands referred to in this book and in the companion volume, *Guide to Linux Networking and Security* (Course Technology, 2003, ISBN 0-619-00094-5). Table B-1 includes:

- Standard command-line utilities
- Server daemons
- Many specialized utilities that are part of software packages described in the chapter text
- Graphical utilities (using their program name, as they would be launched from a graphical command line)

Configuration files are not included in this table. To learn about any of the server daemons or command-line utilities, use the `man` or `info` command followed by the name of the program. (In some cases, the `man` command will refer you to the `info` command for more complete information.) Most graphical programs do not have man pages. For graphical programs, and for many specialized command-line utilities, you can learn more by reviewing the documentation that accompanies the utility. For example, in Red Hat Linux 7.3, the documentation for each package is stored as a subdirectory within `/usr/share/doc`.

Table B-1 Command-Line Utilities, Server Daemons, and Graphical Configuration Programs

Command name	Description
alias	Assign a new name to a command.
apropos	See a list of man pages that contain a given keyword.
arp	Display stored MAC to IP address mappings that were collected using the Address Resolution Protocol.
at	Set up a one-time task for later execution by the atd daemon.
atd	Daemon that processes tasks submitted by at.
atq	See the list of jobs submitted to atd using the at command.
atrm	Remove a scheduled job from the queue of jobs to be executed by the atd daemon.
authconfig	Text-mode menu-based configuration tool for setting authentication options in Red Hat Linux.
authconfig-gtk	Graphical configuration tool for setting authentication options in Red Hat Linux.
awk	Scripting language often used for text processing.
balsa	Graphical e-mail client (message reader) for Gnome Desktops.
bash	The default Linux shell.
batch	Set up a scheduled task for future execution by the atd daemon when the processor load falls below a certain level.
bg	Make the current process a background process within the current shell.
bindconf	Graphical tool for setting up zone information files for the named DNS name server daemon.
bunzip	Uncompress a file that was compressed using bzip.
busybox	A miniature version of dozens of standard Linux utilities in a single compact binary file.
bzip	Compress a file.
cancel	Cancel a print job within the CUPS printing system.
cat	Print the contents of a file or files to STDOUT.
cd	Change the current working directory.
chattr	Change the file attributes of one or more files.
chgrp	Change the group assigned to a file or directory.
chkconfig	Turn a system service on or off in a particular run level, so that the service will be activated or not activated when the system boots.
chkrootkit	Check system for signs of a rootkit, much like a virus checker.
chmod	Change the permissions assigned to a file or directory.
chown	Change the user (owner) assigned to a file or directory.
clear	Clear the screen.
coas	Collection of administration utilities included with Caldera OpenLinux.

Table B-1   Command-Line Utilities, Server Daemons, and Graphical Configuration
Programs (continued)

Command name	Description
compress	Compress a file. See also `zip`, `gzip`, `bzip`.
cp	Copy files or directories from one location or filename to another.
cpio	Backup utility, similar to `tar`.
crond	Daemon that processes tasks submitted using `crontab`.
crontab	Submit a script with assigned times for repeated future execution by the `crond` daemon.
csh	The C shell.
cut	Remove specified fields from each line of text within a file.
date	Display the system date and current time.
dd	Data dump—copy raw data from one device to another.
df	Display file system information for all mounted standard file systems (not `swap` and `proc`).
dhcpcd	A DHCP client daemon. Used to lease network addresses from a DHCP server.
dhcpd	The DHCP server.
diald	Daemon that manages dial-up connections (PPP connections), establishing or dropping them as determined by network traffic.
dig	Query a name server for any data the name server maintains in its zone information files.
dmesg	Display the contents of the kernel ring buffer, where certain kernel messages are stored.
do	Begin a statement block in a *for* loop or *while* loop.
done	End a statement block in a *for* loop or *while* loop.
dpkg	Manage software packages in the Debian package format.
du	Display usage information about the size of a directory and its subdirectories.
dump	Back up data in a file system.
dumpe2fs	Dump superblock and related inode information from an `ext2` or `ext3` file system.
echo	Display text to STDOUT.
elm	A text-based e-mail client with a menu-style interface.
else	Begin a statement block within an *if/then/else* structure; the `else` statements are executed only if the "if" test fails.
emacs	A powerful text-mode editor.
ethereal	Powerful graphical utility for analyzing network traffic, including both header details and packet payload (a sniffer). For Gnome, KDE, or other desktops.

B

Table B-1   Command-Line Utilities, Server Daemons, and Graphical Configuration
Programs (continued)

Command name	Description
exit	Log out of a session or window.
expand	Convert tab characters in a text file into spaces.
export	Make an environmental variable available to other processes.
exportfs	Cause NFS-related networking daemons to recognize the contents of the /etc/exports configuration file.
fdformat	Format a floppy disk.
fdisk	Complex utility for managing fixed disks (hard disks).
fetchmail	A simple POP3 mail client for Linux.
fg	Move a process to the foreground of the current shell, so that the output of the process is displayed.
fi	End an *if/then/else* structure.
file	Display information about the content and file type of a file.
find	Search for a file with certain characteristics and list them or perform other actions on each one.
finger	Network service that provides basic status information via the in.fingerd daemon for any user on a system.
fips	Utility for DOS that splits a single Windows partition into two Windows partitions.
firewall-config	A graphical firewall configuration utility.
fmt	Format lines in a text file (standardize spaces, set line width, indent lines, etc.).
for	Begin a loop structure that is repeated according to the parameters provided with *for*.
free	Display the amount of free memory and swap space, with usage details on each.
fsck	Check the integrity of a file system.
ftp	Text-mode FTP client.
ftpshut	Stop the FTP daemon from accepting new connections after the specified length of time.
gated	Dynamic routing daemon that supports RIP, RIP 2, OSPF, and BGP.
gftp	Graphical FTP client in Red Hat Linux.
gpg	Manage public key encryption, including generating and managing key pairs and encrypting or decrypting files.
grep	Search for a pattern using a regular expression within a file, group of files, or other input stream.
groupadd	Add a new group.
groupmod	Modify the GID or membership of an existing group.
grpck	Check the /etc/group file to be certain that all members of groups refer to valid user accounts.

Table B-1 Command-Line Utilities, Server Daemons, and Graphical Configuration
Programs (continued)

Command name	Description
gunzip	Uncompress a file that was compressed using `gzip`.
gzip	Compress a file.
halt	Shut down all processes and halt the system so it can be turned off.
head	Display the first 15 lines of a file.
history	Display recently used commands within the shell.
host	Report basic DNS information about a hostname, such as its IP address.
hostname	Display the hostname of a system.
httpd	The Apache Web server daemon. More generally, the name used for a Web server daemon.
if	Begin an `if/then/else` structure. A test immediately follows "`if`."
ifconfig	Use with no parameters to display information on all network interfaces configured in the Linux kernel; use with parameters such as an interface, netmask, and IP address to configure a new interface. System startup scripts are normally used to configure interfaces instead of directly calling `ifconfig`.
ifdown	Script used to deactivate a networking interface in an orderly way.
ifup	Script used to activate a networking interface in an orderly way.
IglooFTP	Graphical FTP client.
in.fingerd	Server daemon for the `finger` network service.
in.ftpd	Standard FTP server daemon.
in.telnetd	Standard telnet server daemon.
in.tftpd	Server daemon for the Trivial FTP protocol.
inetd	A superserver. Listens to multiple network ports and starts the appropriate network services as needed.
info	Display documentation for a command.
init	The master control program in Linux. Started by the kernel. All programs are started by either `init` or one of its children.
innd	Standard Linux news server daemon.
insmod	Insert a module into a running Linux kernel (see also `modprobe`).
ipchains	Firewall configuration tool for Linux 2.2 kernels. Supported in newer kernels for backward compatibility.
ipfwadm	Firewall configuration tool in old Linux systems.
iptables	Firewall configuration tool in Linux 2.4 kernels.
iptraf	Text-mode menu-based IP traffic analysis and statistics utility. (Not a packet sniffer.)
ipx_configure	Enable or disable automatic IPX configuration via broadcast information from an IPX server on the same network.

B

Table B-1   Command-Line Utilities, Server Daemons, and Graphical Configuration
Programs (continued)

Command name	Description
ipx_interface	Add, delete, or check IPX configuration information (similar to the ifconfig command for IP).
ipx_internal_net	Configure an internal IPX network (similar to the loopback device for IP).
ipx_route	Manually modify the IPX routing table (similar to the route command for IP).
jobs	List processes that have been started from the current shell.
joe	Full-screen text-mode editor.
join	Merge lines from two different files based on a matching field within the files.
kfinger	Graphical finger client for KDE Desktops.
kill	Send a signal to a process; often used to end a process.
killall	Send a SIGKILL signal to all processes matching the name given as a parameter.
klogd	Daemon that processes log messages generated by the Linux kernel.
kmail	Graphical e-mail client (message reader) for KDE Desktops.
knode	Graphical newsreader client for KDE Desktops.
kppp	Graphical utility for configuring and running a PPP dial-up connection.
krn	Graphical newsreader client for KDE Desktops.
ksh	The Korn shell.
last	List the last login time for each user on the system.
lastcomm	List the last command entered by each user on the system.
ldd	List the shared libraries required by a given executable.
less	Display STDIN (or a file) one page at a time.
lidsadm	Administrative utility to manage the LIDS intrusion detection system.
ln	Create a link from one file or directory to another (both symbolic and hard links can be created).
locate	Search the internal index of the file system for any files or directories matching the given string.
logcheck	Automatically watch for suspicious activity in log files and take action when needed, such as e-mailing root.
logger	Generate a system log entry based on given parameters.
login	Log in to the system using a username and password.
logout	End a login session.
logrotate	Rotate logs automatically via a crontab entry.
lokkit	Text-mode menu-based simple firewall configuration utility.
lp	Print a file. Normally the lpr command is used; lp is the System V version of the command.

Table B-1   Command-Line Utilities, Server Daemons, and Graphical Configuration
Programs (continued)

Command name	Description
lpc	Control the lpd line printer daemon; set queuing and printing options for all defined printers.
lpd	Line printing daemon. Processes print jobs, including transferring jobs to remote hosts according to /etc/printcap configurations.
lpq	Display print jobs within a print queue.
lpr	Print a file.
lprm	Remove a print job from a print queue.
lpstat	Show the status of each print queue defined on a system.
ls	List the contents of a directory.
lsattr	List the file attributes of one or more files.
lsmod	List all modules that are part of the current kernel.
lynx	Text-based Web browser.
m4	Utility that converts the macro language of the sendmail.mc file into a standard format configuration file (sendmail.cf) for use by the sendmail e-mail server.
mail	Text-based command-line e-mail client.
make	Compile or otherwise assemble the source code of a program into a runnable binary file using a Makefile as instructions.
makemap	Convert a text file into a hashed database file for use by the sendmail e-mail server. Used with the access and virtusertable files.
makewhatis	Create a database of man pages for use by the apropos command.
man	Display an online man page for the given command.
mars-nwe	Daemon that emulates NetWare 3.x functionality.
mcopy	Copy a file or files to or from the floppy disk drive.
md5sum	Generate an MD5 hash from a file.
mdel	Delete a file or files from the floppy disk drive.
mdir	List the files on a floppy disk drive.
mesg	Enable or disable on-screen text messages from programs like talk.
mgetty	Terminal management program. (Others include getty, mingetty.) Handles login via a modem or virtual console.
minicom	Terminal emulator for Linux.
mkdir	Create a new subdirectory.
mke2fs	Format a device with the ext2 file system.
mkfs	Format a device with the given file system.
mksmbpasswd.sh	Script to convert existing Linux user accounts to Samba user accounts.
mkswap	Format a device as swap space (virtual memory on hard disk).
modprobe	Manage Linux kernel modules. Most commonly used to add a module and any dependent modules to the kernel.

Table B-1   Command-Line Utilities, Server Daemons, and Graphical Configuration
Programs (continued)

Command name	Description
more	Display STDIN (or a file) one page at a time.
mount	Allow access to a named file system via a named directory mount point.
mozilla	Web browser.
mv	Rename or move one or more files or directories.
named	DNS name server daemon in the BIND package.
named-checkconf	Validate the syntax of the /etc/named.conf configuration file.
neat	Graphical network interface configuration utility for Red Hat Linux.
netconfig	Text-mode menu-based network interface configuration utility for Red Hat Linux.
netscape	Web browser.
newaliases	Convert the /etc/aliases text file into a hashed database file that sendmail can use for processing e-mail name aliases.
nfsd	Daemon to manage file system requests from mounted NFS file systems.
nice	Start a process with a non-default priority (nice) level.
nl	Add a line number to each line of a text file.
nmap	Comprehensive port scanning utility.
nmapfe	Graphical front end to the nmap port scanning utility for Gnome Desktops.
nmbd	The NetBIOS name server daemon. Used as part of the Samba suite to interact with Windows systems.
nslookup	Query a name server. Similar to dig, but this command is not recommended. (Deprecated.)
nsupdate	Dynamically update zone information files for the named daemon.
ntpd	The NTP time server daemon. (Named xntpd in some versions of Linux.)
od	Display the contents of a file in any of several low-level formats, such as octal, hex, and ASCII.
pan	Graphical newsreader for the Gnome Desktop environment.
passwd	Set or reset the password for a user account.
paste	Merge lines from two files.
pdksh	The public domain version of the Korn shell.
perl	A complex and powerful scripting language.
pico	A full-screen character-mode text editor with on-screen help.
pine	A text-based e-mail client with a menu-style interface.
ping	Send an ICMP Echo packet to see whether a remote can be contacted via the network.

Table B-1 Command-Line Utilities, Server Daemons, and Graphical Configuration
Programs (continued)

Command name	Description
portmap	Manage network connections based on the RPC system (such as NFS connections).
pppd	The PPP daemon. Used for dial-up networking.
printconf-gui	Graphical printer configuration tool in Red Hat Linux.
printtool	Configure printers in Red Hat Linux.
procmail	An e-mail filtering tool (a Mail Delivery Agent).
ps	Display information about running processes.
pump	A DHCP client daemon. Used to lease network addresses from a DHCP server.
pwd	Display the current working directory.
rcp	Copy one or more files between any two computers on the network that support the r-utilities.
read	Read input from the keyboard (STDIN) and store it in the indicated variable.
reboot	Restart the system.
renice	Change the priority (nice) level of a running process.
rlogin	Log in to a remote host that supports the r-utilities.
rm	Delete one or more files or directories.
rmdir	Delete an empty directory.
rmmod	Remove a module from a running Linux kernel.
rndc	Manage the named name server daemon.
route	Use with no parameters to display the kernel routing table; use with parameters such as add -net to add or remove an entry from the kernel routing table. System startup scripts are normally used to populate the routing table, but some manual reconfiguration with route may be needed for complex networks.
routed	Dynamic routing daemon that supports RIP and RIP 2 routing protocols.
rp3	Graphical utility for establishing a PPP dial-up connection based on a configuration created by rp3-config.
rp3-config	Graphical utility for configuring and establishing a dial-up PPP connection.
rpc.mountd	Daemon to manage mounting of remote NFS file systems.
rpc.rquotad	Daemon to manage disk storage limits (quotas) for users who have mounted an NFS file system.
rpc.rstatd	Daemon to provide statistical data for an NFS file system.
rpm	Manage software packages, including installing new packages and verifying the integrity of package files.

Table B-1 Command-Line Utilities, Server Daemons, and Graphical Configuration Programs (continued)

Command name	Description
rsh	Execute a command on a remote computer without logging in and seeing a shell prompt.
ruptime	List the uptime for each host on the network that supports the r-utilities.
rwho	List users on the local network who are logged in. (Only those supporting r-utilities are listed.)
safedelete	Substitute for the rm command; pretends to delete a file by moving it to a hidden directory, managing all such files according to available disk space. Permits undelete operations.
sax	The X configuration utility provided by SuSE Linux.
sed	Edit files or STDIN input using patterns and commands.
sendmail	Popular MTA (e-mail server).
service	Run one of the service control scripts typically stored in /etc/rc.d/init.d.
set	List all currently defined variables.
shutdown	Shut down the system, optionally providing a message or delay for users working on the system.
smbadduser	Add a user to the /etc/samba/smbpasswd Samba user configuration file.
smbclient	Text-mode client for accessed SMB-capable servers (including Microsoft Windows servers).
smbd	The SMB server daemon. Used as part of the Samba suite to interact with Windows systems.
smbpasswd	Updates the password for a Samba user, which is typically stored in the configuration file /etc/samba/smbpasswd.
smbprint	Text-mode client for printing to SMB-capable servers (including Microsoft Windows servers).
sort	Sort lines in a file according to various options.
split	Split a single file into two or more smaller files.
ssh	The client utility for establishing a Secure Shell (SSH) encrypted connection to another host.
ssh-agent	Manage key pairs for users who use SSH on multiple systems.
ssh-keygen	Generate key pairs for use within the SSH suite.
sshd	Server daemon to which the ssh utility can make an encrypted connection.
startx	Launch the X Window System.
strings	Display the readable strings found in any file (including binary files).
stunnel	Permit secure network connections of several different protocols (e.g., POP3 and IMAP) using the OpenSSL package that Web browsers use.

Table B-1 Command-Line Utilities, Server Daemons, and Graphical Configuration
Programs (continued)

Command name	Description
su	Change to a new user account.
sudo	Execute a command with root privileges. Edit the permission configuration with `visudo`.
SWAT	Browser-based configuration program for the Samba suite.
swapon	Activate and begin using all swap partitions defined in `/etc/fstab`.
swatch	A log watching utility.
syslogd	The system logging daemon. Operates as configured by `/etc/syslog.conf`.
tac	Display the contents of a file to STDOUT in reverse order (last line first).
tail	Display the last 15 lines of a file to STDOUT.
talk	A text-based chat client using the `talk` protocol. Relies on the `talkd` server daemon.
talkd	The server daemon used for `talk`-based text-mode chat sessions.
tar	Create an archive file containing one or more files or directories, optionally compressing them all.
tcpd	The TCP Wrappers daemon. Usually called from the `inetd` superserver. Configured by `/etc/hosts.allow` and `/etc/hosts.deny`.
tcpdump	Command-line utility for analyzing network traffic.
tcsh	The TENEX C shell (a version of the C shell).
telinit	Change to a different run level.
test	Process a true/false test. Used within an *if/then/else* or *while* statement.
telnet	Make a remote connection to a system.
tethereal	Text-mode version of the `ethereal` network traffic analyzer.
then	Begin a statement block within an *if/then/else* structure, listing those commands that are executed if the "if" test succeeds.
top	Display the processes running on the system sorted with the most processor-intensive tasks listed first.
touch	Update the last-accessed-time for a file, or create an empty file if the file named does not exist.
tr	Transpose one character for another in a text file.
traceroute	Determine which routers a packet passes through to reach a destination host.
tripwire	Check file integrity.
trn	Text-mode news reader.
tty	Display the terminal device where a user is currently logged in.
ttysnoop	Capture the output of any tty. Useful for teaching situations or spying.

Table B-1 Command-Line Utilities, Server Daemons, and Graphical Configuration
Programs (continued)

Command name	Description
tune2fs	Display or alter parameters of the superblock for an ext2 or ext3 file system.
ud	Text-mode LDAP client.
umask	Set the default file permissions assigned when a new file is created.
umount	Unmount a file system that is currently mounted as part of the Linux directory structure.
uname	Display version information about a running Linux kernel.
uncompress	Uncompress a file that was compressed using the compress command.
unexpand	Convert spaces to tab characters in a text file.
uniq	Remove duplicate lines in a sorted file.
unzip	Uncompress a file that has been created using the zip command.
updatedb	Create an index of the entire file system for use by the locate command.
useradd	Add a new user to the system or modify the parameters associated with a user's account.
uucp	Use the UUCP protocol to transfer files over a dial-up connection.
vi	Powerful full-screen text editor.
vigr	Edit the /etc/group file. Used when multiple administrators might be trying to access the file at the same time. Locks the file to prevent conflicting edits.
vipw	Edit the /etc/passwd file. Used when multiple administrators might be trying to access the file at the same time. Locks the file to prevent conflicting edits.
visudo	Edit the configuration file that controls use of the sudo command.
vlock	Lock a text-mode virtual console so that the screen cannot be used without first entering the password of the person who used vlock.
vmstat	Display virtual memory (swap space) statistics.
w	List users who are logged in to the system.
wc	Display the number of characters, words, and lines in a file or STDIN input stream.
Webmin	Browser-based multifunction system administration utility.
while	Begin a loop, the statements of which are executed so long as the condition tested in the *while* command is true.
who	List users who are logged in to the system.
whois	Display information from the whois domain name database. (Requires Internet access.)

Table B-1 Command-Line Utilities, Server Daemons, and Graphical Configuration Programs (continued)

Command name	Description
wvdial	Connect to a server using PPP over a modem.
xauth	Manage permission to access an X server from a remote host using the xauth authentication scheme (based on MIT cookies).
xhost	Set permissions for access to an X server from a remote host using the xhost hostname-based authentication scheme.
xinetd	A superserver. Used to listen to multiple network ports and start the appropriate network services as needed.
xload	Display the current processor load from 0% to 100% as a small graphic.
xlock	Lock a graphical screen so that it cannot be viewed or used without first entering the password of the user who started xlock.
xlogmaster	Graphical program to manage log files.
xlsfonts	Graphical utility in which you choose from among installed fonts.
xrdb	Manage the X resources database.
xset	Display or alter settings for the X Window System such as screen blanking and keyboard repeat rate.
xterm	A graphical command-line window.
yast	A configuration tool in the SuSE Linux distribution. Can be used to configure networking.
zcat	Display to STDOUT the contents of a file (typically a text file) that was compressed using gzip.
zip	Compress one or more files into a single archive (the resulting file is compatible with ZIP files on Windows systems).

B

C

GRAPHICAL ADMINISTRATION UTILITIES

This appendix presents an overview of the graphical administration tools that accompany the Gnome and the KDE Desktop interfaces. Although this appendix is not exhaustive, it will give you an idea of what is available by summarizing the utilities described in this book. This appendix focuses on the Red Hat Linux distribution. Most of the KDE utilities are included with any product that uses KDE.

The utilities described in this appendix have been introduced to some extent within the main text of the book. Those discussions, however, have focused on using the utility for a particular task rather than providing an overview of a program's capabilities. This appendix provides that overview.

Updated versions of Linux distributions and of the Gnome and KDE desktops are likely to include additional tools that are not mentioned here. As these utilities become more stable, they will be included with standard KDE distributions, allowing administrators to rely on graphical configuration tools for more of their system management tasks. For details on new or forthcoming graphical utilities, visit *www.gnome.org* or *www.kde.org* and browse the software listings provided.

Not all of the utilities mentioned on the Gnome and KDE Web sites are fit for general consumption. Many of them are still being developed. These utilities may crash your system or may not even run. Look for information about the status of a utility (such as a version number, or a designation of Alpha- or Beta-quality software) before risking any production system on a new administration tool.

Many excellent graphical utilities are available for the X Window System that do not rely on the Gnome or KDE Desktop. A few of these are mentioned in the main text of this book. The integrated nature of the Gnome and KDE utilities, as well as the continuing rapid rate of software development that they enjoy, makes them preferable in some ways to generic X Window System utilities such as the **xfontsel** utility described in Chapter 5. Nevertheless, if you are interested in locating a graphical utility that you do not see mentioned in this appendix, consult an online index or archive of Linux utilities. For example, search *www.linuxapps.com* or *www.freshmeat.net*, or browse FTP sites such as *ftp.ibiblio.org* under the *pub/Linux* subdirectory.

GNOME UTILITIES

Red Hat Software has been instrumental in promoting the development and popularity of the Gnome Desktop for several years. It has also developed a number of useful administrative tools based on Gnome and the GTK+ graphical programming libraries (on which Gnome is based). You have seen several of these as you worked through the chapters of this book, such as **neat**, GnoRPM, and **gtop** (the Gnome System Monitor).

If you have used Red Hat Linux for several years, you may recognize that many of the utilities here are new. Previous versions of Red Hat relied on different programs, such as the Red Hat Control Panel or the large and complex LinuxConf program. Some of these tools are still included with Red Hat Linux, but are not installed by default because newer tools have replaced them.

Gnome System Monitor

The Gnome System Monitor is a process management utility. It is discussed at some length in Chapter 10. You can launch this utility from the System menu of Gnome or by entering the command **gtop** at a graphical command line. The Gnome System Monitor lets you view the same type of process data as the **ps** and **top** commands from the command line, but in a graphical interface. From this interface, you can right-click on any process to send it a control signal or learn more about its status. You can also use the column headings of the process list to sort processes based on any field.

From the menus of the Gnome System Monitor you can select which fields to display in the list of processes and how often to refresh the display. On other tabs of this program you can view memory usage information for any process or for all processes together.

Memory details you can view include how the process is using swap space, what function libraries it relies on, and how much total memory it is using.

Figure C-1 shows the main window of the Gnome System Monitor with a process list. Figure C-2 shows the Memory Usage tab displaying memory usage information on all running processes.

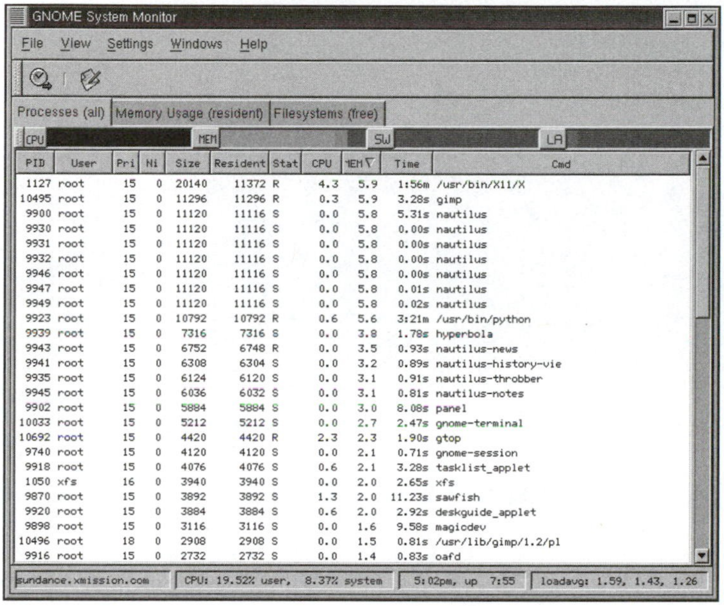

Figure C-1   The process list in the Gnome System Monitor

The Gnome RPM Management Tool GnoRPM

You can use the GnoRPM utility to manage RPM-format software packages that are installed on your Red Hat Linux system or that you want to install on your system. RPMs can be installed from a Red Hat Linux CD, from the Internet, or directly from a file on your hard disk after you have obtained the RPM file. GnoRPM is not as flexible as the multiformat `kpackage` utility described in the next section, but it provides a very nice interface for querying, installing, and deleting software packages without requiring that you know all the relevant options to use `rpm` on the command line.

GnoRPM lets you see available packages in a directory (including a directory on a CD-ROM), query a package to see what files it contains or who created it, determine if security mechanisms are in place to verify the integrity of the package, and see which package a particular file on your system came from. Figure C-3 shows the main window of GnoRPM with icons for several packages visible.

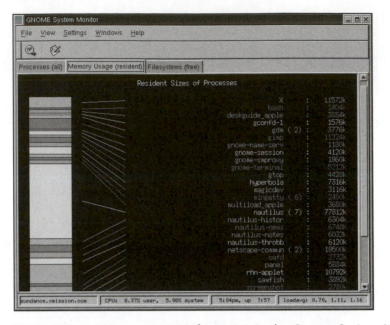

Figure C-2   Memory usage information in the Gnome System Monitor

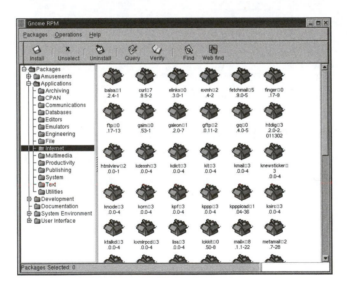

Figure C-3   Package information viewed in GnoRPM

Changing Desktop Interfaces with `switchdesk`

You can use the `switchdesk` utility to change between the different graphical desktop interfaces that are installed on your Red Hat Linux system. This utility queries your system to see which desktops are installed and presents a list of items for you to choose from. A checkbox lets you determine whether the selection you make applies to a single session or to all future sessions. This selection, however, is not always correctly applied. If you need to return to your previous desktop and cannot, you can either rerun `switchdesk` or delete the hidden file in your home directory called `.Xclients` followed by your hostname (use the `ls -a` command to see a listing of these hidden files).

The `switchdesk` utility creates a configuration file in your home directory; each user can run `switchdesk` and have a different desktop selected. The `switchdesk` window is shown in Figure C-4.

Figure C-4 The main window of the `switchdesk` utility

Setting up Printing

Setting up printer definitions in the traditional LPRng Linux printing system is best done using the `printconf-gui` utility. In this utility, described at length in Chapter 12, you define a printer by selecting a printer model and applicable filter. You can set up printer-specific configurations if the printer includes a PPD file (thousands of these are included with a standard Red Hat Linux 7.3 installation).

 A text-mode version of this utility is also available in Red Hat Linux. Enter `printconf-tui` on any command line.

The `printconf-gui` utility also lets you configure remote printers using the standard UNIX `lpd` print daemon, NetWare printing, or Windows printing based on the SMB protocol (as used in Windows XP, 2000, NT, and 98). Figure C-5 shows the main window of `printconf-gui` with a printer definition listed.

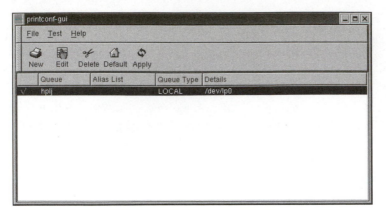

Figure C-5   A printer definition in `printconf-gui`

Gnome does not include a corresponding graphical utility to manage print jobs. You can use the KDE utility `klpq` mentioned in the next section or the command-line tools (such as `lpq` and `lpc`). Or you can use the CUPS printing system described in Chapter 12, which uses the same browser-based interface to manage both printer definitions and submitted print jobs.

Setting up Networking

In Chapters 2 and 3 during the installation of Linux you learned about basic networking information such as the IP address of your computer and the concept of a DNS server to convert between IP addresses and readable names (e.g., *www.redhat.com*). Although the installation program will be all that many users require to establish networking on their systems, system administrators will often need to use other tools to configure a server or troubleshoot networking problems. These subjects are outside the scope of this book, but the Red Hat Network Administration Tool is an important utility to be aware of.

You can launch this program from the Gnome menu by choosing Programs, then System. You can also launch it from any graphical command line using the command `neat`. In this utility you can define networking interfaces and edit the properties of any network interface, including features such as IP address, network mask, default gateway, and the DNS server addresses that the computer should use. You can set up and test multiple network interfaces and create special routing rules for complex networks. For more information on this topic, see *Guide to Linux Networking and Security* (Course Technology, 2003, ISBN 0-619-00094-5). Figure C-6 shows the main window of the `neat` utility.

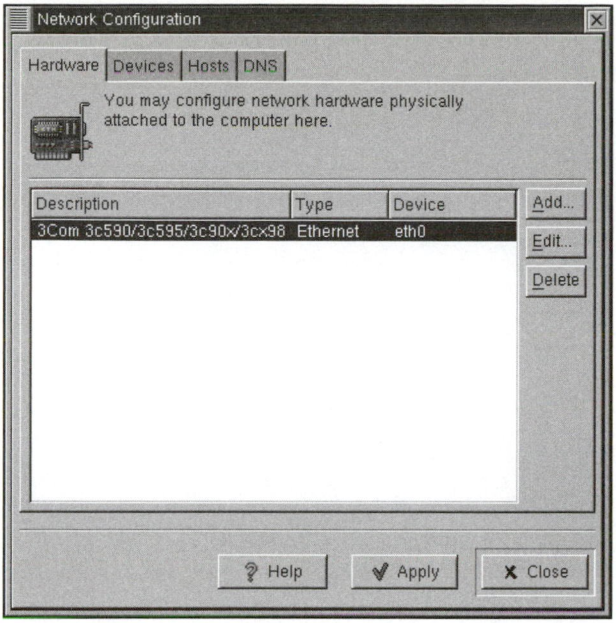

Figure C-6 The `neat` network administration utility

Configuring Gnome

The default menus of Gnome in Red Hat Linux 7.3 include many specialized configuration tools that are not discussed in this book. Examples include the firewall configuration utility, the program to set up access to the Red Hat Network update service, and
the utility to configure the graphical login screen. You can explore these utilities (carefully)
to see what other parts of your system can be graphically configured. In each case, it's
useful to read the documentation or online help for the utility to learn which text files
the graphical utility is modifying and how each is structured. This teaches you more than
simply learning which buttons to click.

The Gnome interface itself is configured using items on the Settings menu of Gnome.
You can also use the Menu Editor item to configure which applications and submenus
are displayed in the Gnome menu. This task can become quite complex, so a graphical
tool provides welcome assistance. The submenus of Gnome handle most aspects of configuring Gnome, including the following:

- Background selection
- Screen saver configuration
- Theme selections (which include background, colors, and other display
  components)
- The default editor to use for text files
- The MIME data types that Gnome recognizes and how to respond to each

- The keyboard bell
- Sound event associations
- Keyboard and mouse configuration
- Session managers
- URL handlers
- How to drag windows
- How to resize windows
- How to apply focus rules when moving between windows
- How many virtual desktops to support and how to move between them
- When to use pop-up tooltip help windows
- Special effects for window animation
- Complex background manipulation settings
- Detailed desktop theme configuration
- Keyboard shortcuts

One sample window showing a theme being selected in Gnome is shown in Figure C-7.

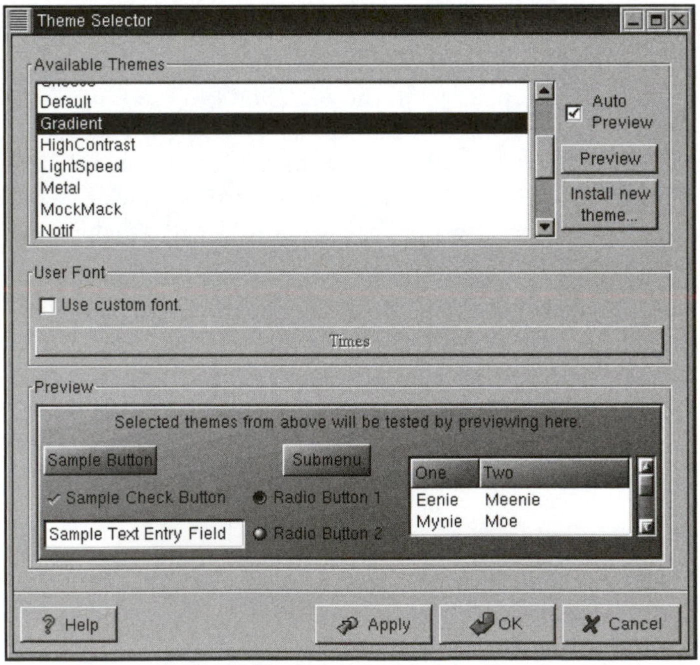

Figure C-7   Configuring a theme in Gnome

KDE UTILITIES

KDE system administration tools are found on either the System or the Utilities sub-menu of KDE. Because different Linux vendors produce their products at different times, each may include a slightly different collection of KDE graphical utilities based on which utilities that vendor feels are ready for release and what the focus of the product is. The utilities described here are those mentioned in the book, but many others are available from *apps.kde.org*; you can also explore the KDE menus to see what useful tools you can find.

Process Management in KDE

The KDE System Guard lets you manage system processes (running programs) just like the Gnome System Monitor program. The KDE program is not quite as full-featured, however, in that it doesn't let you view memory usage information or present quite as much detail on each process. Within the KDE System Guard, you can right-click on any process to select a control signal to send to that process. You can use the menu items to select which fields of information to display about each process. Figure C-8 shows the main window of the KDE System Guard.

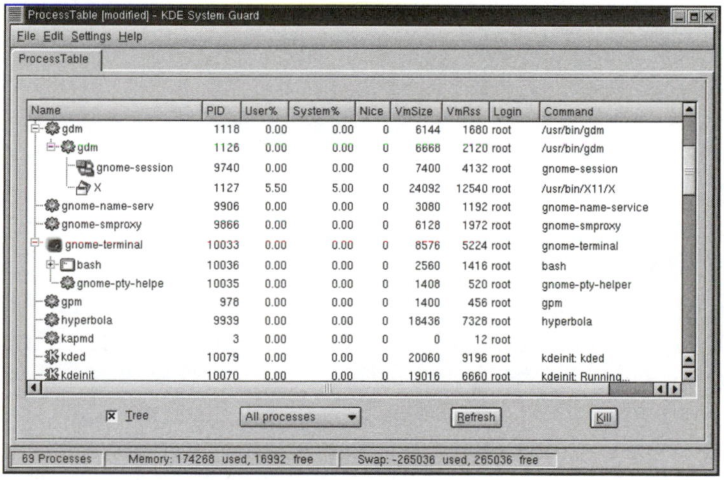

Figure C-8   The KDE System Guard

A second program for managing processes in KDE is the **kpm** program. This utility is not as powerful as the KDE System Guard, but may be included on some Linux systems that do not have the KDE System Guard.

Managing Software Packages in KDE

KDE provides a utility very similar to the GnoRPM program called kpackage. You can use this utility to view information about installed software packages or about packages you are considering installing. You can also use it to install or uninstall packages located anywhere on your system. One additional feature of kpackage compared to GnoRPM is that kpackage recognizes software package formats other than rpm, such as the deb format used by Debian Linux. Figure C-9 shows the main window of kpackage.

Figure C-9   The main window of kpackage

Using kdat to Access Tape Drives

The kdat utility mentioned in Chapter 13 provides tools to manage tape archives. This simple utility lets you control a tape drive, including viewing the table of contents for a tape and sending a new collection of archived data to a tape. The kdat program is not designed to replace more complex backup managers (free or commercial), but kdat can be a helpful tool for learning how the tape drive operates and performing basic archival tasks using programs such as tar and cpio. Figure C-10 shows the main window of kdat.

Managing Print Jobs

KDE includes a graphical tool called klpq that you can use to manage print jobs submitted using the LPRng printing architecture. Within this utility, shown in Figure C-11, you can see the print jobs for all printers or for any single printer you select. Among the print jobs, you can change the order they will print in, delete a print job, or send a job to a different printer. This utility also lets you perform tasks normally done with the lpc command: controlling whether print queues are accepting new print jobs and whether existing print jobs are being sent to the printers or held in the print queues.

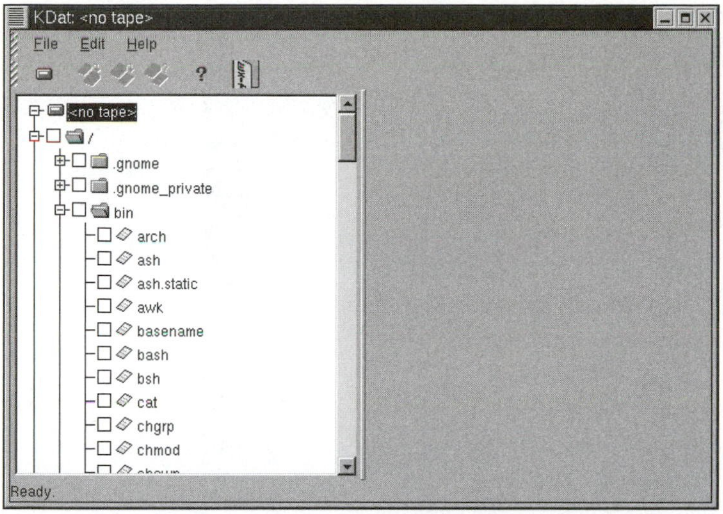

Figure C-10   The kdat tape device control program

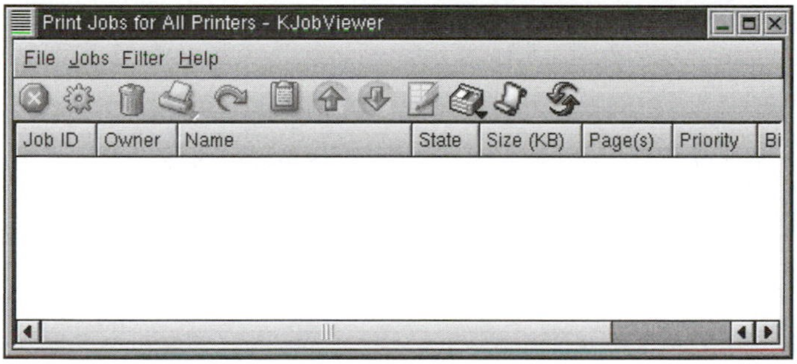

Figure C-11   Using klpg to manage print jobs

If you are using CUPS for printing instead of LPRng, you should use the KDE Control Center under Printing Manager both to set up printer definitions and manage to print jobs submitted by users. These two tasks are done using different tabs within a single window of the Control Center. Figure C-12 shows the properties of a printer within the Printing Manager tab of the Control Center.

The KDE Control Center

Many aspects of the KDE interface itself are controlled using the KDE Control Center. In this program you can also view hardware information, manage printing, and perform a few other system administration tasks. (The list keeps growing as KDE developers try to create a full-featured graphical environment.)

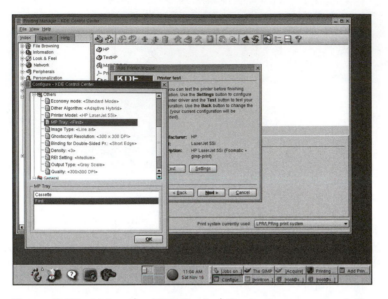

Figure C-12   Using the KDE Control Center to manage printing

Other KDE management tools you may want to explore within the Control Center or on the System or Utilities menus let you perform tasks such as the following:

- Font management

- Initialization script (run level service) configuration

- User creation and management

- Menu editing

- Compressed file archive management

- Configuration of the KDE graphical login prompt

- Setting up screen savers, themes, background graphics, and other aspects of the desktop itself

Glossary

$# — A special shell variable that holds the number of parameters entered on the command line.

$@ — A special shell variable that includes all of the parameters on the command line.

.bashrc — A configuration script that is executed each time the user starts a **bash** shell.

.profile — A configuration script that can be located in each user's home directory. This script is executed each time any user on the system starts a **bash** shell. It is not included by default on all Linux distributions, but can be created if needed.

.Xauthority — A file in a user's home directory that contains cookies defining remote access privileges for X servers and X clients.

/etc/fstab — A configuration file that contains a file system table with devices, mount points, file system types, and options. Used by the **mount** command.

/etc/group — A configuration file in which group information (group names and membership lists) is stored.

/etc/passwd — A configuration file in which user account information is stored.

/etc/profile — A script containing configuration information that applies to every user on the Linux system.

/etc/shadow — A configuration file in which encrypted user passwords and password configuration data are stored.

/etc/skel — A directory containing files that are copied to a new user's home directory at the time a new user account is created.

/proc file system — A special file system that lets users view what the operating system kernel and other programs are doing.

absolute path — A complete description of a directory, beginning with a forward slash and including all subdirectories up to the named directory. An absolute path is unambiguous, without needing to reference another directory name to give it a complete meaning.

AC power — The standard alternating current power coming into a building from a public utility; the power from a wall socket.

action — A field in the **syslog.conf** configuration file that determines what to do with messages matching the selector on that line.

active partition — The bootable partition; the partition that the MBR passes control to if the MBR does not itself contain a boot manager.

alias — A string of characters that the shell substitutes for another string of characters when a command is entered. Created in the shell using the **alias** command.

application — A program (such as a word processor or spreadsheet) that provides a service to a person using the computer, rather than simply managing the computer's resources.

apropos — A command used to show all man pages that contain a keyword.

at — A command that lets you enter one or more commands to be executed once at some future time.

atq — A command that lists each of the jobs awaiting execution by **atd**, including a job number and the date and time when the job will be executed.

atrm — A command that deletes (removes) a job from the queue used by **atd** to execute commands.

at job — A command or script that you have scheduled to be executed at a specific time in the future using the **at** command.

authentication — The process of identifying a user to a computer system via some type of login procedure.

awk — A programming language that developers use to create scripts for working on text files and completing other complex tasks.

background application — An application that does not stop the program that started it from going on to other tasks.

backup — A copy of data on a computer system.

backup level — A description of how much data will be stored in a backup operation. A backup level is only relevant in comparison with another backup level. When performing a backup operation at a given level, all of the data that has changed since the last backup of the previous level is recorded.

backup media — A device where data can be stored, such as a tape cartridge, writeable CD or DVD, or floppy disk.

backup plan — A written document that outlines when, how, and why various files and file systems will be backed up, stored, and—when necessary—restored to prevent permanent data loss.

bang — In Linux jargon, an exclamation point character.

bash — Short for Bourne Again shell, an enhanced and extended version of the Bourne shell created by the GNU project for use on many UNIX-like operating systems. `bash` is the default Linux shell.

batch — A command that executes scheduled tasks when the system load average drops below 0.8.

benchmark program — A program that provides a numeric measurement of performance for part of a system.

bg — A command used to place a job (process) in the background (either by suspending it or by preventing its output from appearing in the current shell's terminal window), thus allowing the shell prompt to become active again.

binary code — Machine-readable instructions used to execute a program.

binary file — *See* executable file.

BIOS (Basic Input/Output System) — Information stored in ROM that provides instructions to the operating system for using the devices on a computer.

bit — A binary digit; a bit can hold a value of either one or zero.

block — A unit of storage on a file system. A standard block contains 1024 characters (bytes), or two sectors.

block special file — A type of file (normally located in `/dev`) referring to a physical device that transfers data in blocks of characters, such as a hard disk drive.

bonnie — A hard disk benchmarking program.

boot disk — A disk used to launch the Linux operating system stored on your hard disk. It can be used in normal operating situations to start the Linux system.

boot manager — A program that lets you launch one or more operating systems each time you boot a computer. (Examples include GRUB and LILO.)

boot parameter — A piece of information passed directly to the Linux kernel as the system is being booted. These parameters are normally used to affect how Linux recognizes hardware devices or to enable certain features of the operating system.

boot record — A small area on each partition that contains a program to launch the operating system on that partition.

bootable CD-ROM drive — A CD-ROM drive that can launch an operating system (or other program) directly from a CD without accessing the hard disk. (This feature of the CD-ROM drive must be enabled by the BIOS.)

bottleneck — Part of a computer system that slows down completion of the task at hand.

Bourne shell — The original shell for UNIX, written by Stephen Bourne.

broadcast address — An IP address that sends a packet of data to all computers on a network.

buffer — An area of memory dedicated to holding the working data associated with a running program.

byte — Storage space sufficient to store one character; eight bits.

C shell — A shell developed by Bill Joy in the 1970s. He focused on adding easy-to-use features for interactive work at the shell prompt. (Most of these features were later added to the `bash` shell as well.) The C shell is not popular for shell programming because its syntax is more complex than that of the Bourne, `bash`, and Korn shells.

caching — The process of storing data from the hard disk in RAM so that it can be accessed more rapidly (because RAM is much faster than a hard disk).

cancel — A command supported by CUPS to delete a print job from a print queue.

cat — Command used to display the contents of a file to the screen.

cd — Command used to change the directory you are working in (the current working directory).

character special file — A filename referring to a physical device (such as a serial port) that transfers data in single characters.

chief information officer (CIO) — The executive in an organization who determines how information systems are used within the organization to further its goals or mission effectively.

child directory — A subdirectory within another directory. The directory closer to the root directory, /, is the parent; the directory deeper in the directory structure is the child.

chkconfig — Command used to configure which services are started by default when you boot Linux; modifies the contents of run level directories such as `/etc/rc.d/rc5.d`.

chmod — Command used to change the file permissions assigned to a file or directory.

chown — Command used to change the ownership of a file or directory.

CMOS RAM — A special memory chip in which computer configuration details are stored. The data is maintained by a tiny battery and is modified as needed using a BIOS utility.

command history — A feature of the shell that records in a list (the history list) each of the commands that you enter at the shell prompt.

command interpreter — A program that accepts input from the keyboard and uses that input to launch commands or otherwise control the computer system.

command-line window — A window within a graphical environment that permits you to enter commands at the keyboard.

comment — A line in a script that begins with a # character. Comments are not processed by the shell, but are only included to help someone reading the file understand the purpose of the script or how it functions.

Common Desktop Environment (CDE) — A graphical desktop interface with accompanying system administration utilities. Provides a common look and feel for many commercial UNIX systems.

Common Gateway Interface (CGI) — A method of communication between two programs using the standard input and standard output channels.

Common UNIX Printing System (CUPS) — A printing architecture for Linux and UNIX systems that lets users and system administrators browse the network to find and print to networked printers and other devices. It also lets system administrators manage printer definitions and print jobs across the network using a browser interface.

compiled language — A computer language for which the source code is converted to a binary file before the program is executed.

compiler — A program that converts the source code of a compiled language into a binary file.

computer language — A set of words and syntax rules that can be arranged in predefined ways to cause a computer to perform tasks defined by the person using the language.

cookie — A numeric token used by a program to identify information about a host or user.

cooperative multitasking — A technique in which an operating system kernel must wait for a program to yield control to other programs.

copyleft — An ironic term that refers to the GNU General Public License (the GPL), signifying a radical departure from standard copyright.

cp — Command used to copy a file or directory from one location or name to another.

cpio — A Linux archiving program. The **cpio** command also reads archive files created by the **tar** command.

cron job — A command or script that you have scheduled to be executed repeatedly at specific times in the future.

crontab — A command that lets you enter one or more commands to be executed repeatedly at intervals that you designate.

current working directory — The directory in which you are working.

cylinder — A set of tracks at the same location on all the platters of a hard disk.

daemon — A background process that handles tasks such as responding to network traffic without any visible screen output.

defrag — A utility used to defragment a Linux partition.

defragment — A procedure that arranges each file so that the parts of the file are next to each other on the hard disk; places all sectors comprising a file into contiguous disk locations.

desktop environment — A graphical application that provides a comprehensive interface, including system menus, desktop icons, and the ability to manage files and launch applications easily.

desktop interface — *See* desktop environment.

device — A hardware peripheral such as a printer, scanner, mouse, or hard disk; also some specialized parts of Linux system software, such as the devices associated with virtual consoles (tty1 through tty6).

device driver — Software used to communicate with or control a hardware component, beyond core device support provided by the kernel.

df — Short for display file systems. A command used to display file system summary information such as device, mount point, percentage used, and total capacity.

diff — A command that compares the contents of two files, displaying any differences between them.

direct memory access (DMA) channel — A communication method within a computer that allows a device to read and write directly to the computer's RAM, without going through the microprocessor first.

directory record — A special type of file that contains a list of the names and inode numbers of other files.

disaster plan — An organized written plan that describes how to respond to various threats to information systems.

disk image — A single file that contains an exact copy of a floppy disk.

disk optimization — *See* defragment.

disk quotas — Limits assigned to each user that restrict the total amount of space that the user can consume on a file system.

DISPLAY — An environment variable that defines the host whose X server will be used to display graphical applications.

dmesg — Command used to view the messages stored by the kernel during the boot process.

do — A command used with the **done** command to enclose a statement block as part of a **for** loop or a **while** loop.

domain name — A name assigned to a collection of computers on a network.

Domain Name Service (DNS) — A protocol that maps human-readable domain names and hostnames to IP addresses that correspond to individual computers.

Domain Name Server (DNS) server — A computer that uses the DNS protocol to convert from domain names and hostnames to IP addresses.

done — A command used with the **do** command to enclose a statement block as part of a **for** loop or a **while** loop.

DOS — An operating system developed for personal computers in about 1980. It gained widespread acceptance when IBM introduced the first IBM PC.

downtime — Occasions when an organization's computer systems cannot respond to requests for information.

driver — *See* device driver.

du — Short for disk usage. A command used to display disk space used by a directory and each of its subdirectories.

dual-boot system — A computer that allows a user to choose which operating system to start each time the computer is booted (turned on).

dumpe2fs — A utility used to display technical statistics and parameters about a Linux **ext2** or **ext3** file system.

duplexing — A redundancy technique in which hard disks are accessed via different hard disk controllers. Compare to "mirroring," a technique that provides identical information on two file systems but without redundant disk controllers.

Dynamic Host Configuration Protocol (DHCP) — A protocol that allows a computer to obtain networking information (such as an IP address) dynamically from a network server at the time the computer is turned on.

Dynamic Host Configuration Protocol (DHCP) server — A computer that provides networking configuration data for other computers via the DHCP protocol.

dynamic network configuration — Configuring the networking services of a computer by automatically obtaining networking parameters when the system is turned on; typically done using DHCP.

dynamically linked applications — Linux programs that do not include within themselves the library functions that they require to operate. The libraries must be installed (as shared libraries) on the Linux system on which the applications are executed.

echo — Command used to display text to the screen, converting variable names to their corresponding values.

else — A command that extends the capability of an **if/then** statement by adding a statement block that is only executed if the test after "**if**" returns a value of false (that is, if the test fails).

end user — An individual who uses the computer systems in an organization to accomplish assigned tasks, but who often relies on a system administrator to keep those systems running smoothly.

environment variables — Variables that are defined by the Linux shell so that all programs can access their values.

executable file — A file containing numeric codes that a computer can execute. Created from a source code file by a compiler, the executable file is the program that a user can run.

execute permission — A file permission that allows a user to launch a file as a program or see a file within a directory. Represented by a letter **x**.

exit — A command that stops the execution of a script immediately.

export — Command used to make a newly created environment variable available to other programs running in the same environment.

ext2 — A file system type used by Linux.

ext3 — A newer file system type used by Linux.

facility — A category assigned to a system message, identifying the type of program providing the message. Facilities are used in `syslog.conf`.

FAT — The file system type used by older versions of Windows (such as Windows 3.1).

FAT32 — The file system type used by some newer versions of Windows (such as Windows 98 and XP).

fault tolerance — The condition of being able to tolerate errors or events that might otherwise cause system failure.

fdformat — A command used to format a floppy disk.

fdisk — A utility used to create hard disk partitions and configure how they are used.

fg — A command used to bring a job (process) running in a shell to the foreground so that the job controls the shell's terminal window.

fi — A command that marks the end of an `if/then` or `if/then/else` statement.

file — Command used to display a summary of the type of data contained in a file.

file extension — The last part of a filename after a period.

file handle — An internal storage mechanism that allows a single file to be opened and used in Linux.

file manager — A graphical window that displays the contents of a directory (usually as a collection of icons) and lets you work with the files and directories using menus, mouse clicks, and dialog boxes.

file permissions — Codes that define the type of access that a user has to a file or directory on the Linux system.

file record — A record within a Linux file system that contains a filename and an inode number or else, if a symbolic link, a filename and another filename that the link refers to.

file server — A computer on which many users store their data files for access across a network.

file system — An organized arrangement of information on a device such as a hard disk.

filtering — The process of adding, removing, or altering data in a text file based on complex rules or patterns.

find — A command that searches the file system for files matching certain characteristics.

FIPS — A program that creates two separate partitions from an existing Windows partition. Used to create an empty partition that can be deleted and the resulting free space used for installing Linux.

five-nines — High availability at a statistical level of 99.999% uptime.

for — A command that repeats a statement block one time for each item in a list.

for loop — A list of commands that is repeatedly executed according to the parameters provided with the `for` command.

forking — Starting a new free software project based on an existing project.

free — Linux command used to display the amount of free and used memory (physical and virtual), with basic information about how that memory is being used.

Free Software Foundation (FSF) — An organization founded by Richard Stallman to promote his ideals of freely available software and to create and distribute that software.

fsck — A utility used to check the integrity of an `ext2` or `ext3` file system.

fully qualified domain name (FQDN) — The hostname of a computer and the domain name of the network to which the computer is attached.

function — A small task that a computer program performs.

function library — A file containing a collection of commonly used functions that any program can use as it runs.

gateway address — The IP address of the computer on a local network that can send packets of data outside that network.

gcc — A C language compiler. Probably the best-known product of the GNU project.

gigabyte (GB) — A measure of space on computers equal to 1024 megabytes, or roughly enough space to store 1 billion characters.

Gnome — A desktop interface similar to KDE; developed in cooperation with Red Hat Software and used principally on Red Hat Linux and distributions derived from that version.

Gnome System Monitor — A graphical utility for the Gnome Desktop that is used to monitor and control processes running on Linux. Also called **gtop**. Similar to the **kpm** program for KDE.

GNU General Public License (GPL) — The free software license that Richard Stallman of the Free Software Foundation developed for the programs created by the GNU project.

GNU project — An effort by the Free Software Foundation to create a free UNIX-like operating system. Many of the programs in every Linux distribution come from the GNU project.

graceful shutdown — The technique used to stop all Linux services and shut down all file access in an orderly way before turning off or rebooting the computer.

graphical libraries — Collections of programming functions that an X client can use to create and manage the elements of a graphical environment more efficiently.

Graphical User Interface (GUI) — Software that provides mouse-driven applications with menu bars, buttons, and so forth.

grep — A command that searches the contents of text files for lines containing a given regular expression.

groff — A command used to format and display documents that are created using roff markup codes.

group — A collection of user accounts that can be collectively granted access to a system resource.

group permissions — A set of three file permissions (**r**, **w**, and **x**) that apply to members of the group assigned to a file or directory.

groupadd — A command used to add a new group to a Linux system.

groupmod — A command used to modify group information.

GRUB — A Linux boot manager; used by default on Red Hat Linux 7.3.

gunzip — Command used to uncompress a file that has been compressed using **gzip**.

gzip — Command used to compress any file on a Linux system.

halt — Command used to shut down all services and then stop the computer with the message "System halted."

hard link — A file record that points to an inode that is already pointed to by at least one other file record.

hard wired — Computer functionality that is arranged in the wires and other components that make up a computer. Hard-wired functionality cannot be easily altered.

hardware-based RAID — A RAID array that is contained in a separate hardware device (a RAID subsystem) and is controlled by a CPU and other components separate from the CPU of the Linux system.

help desk — A service in many organizations that assists end users in solving problems related to information technology.

hexadecimal (hex) — A numbering system using base-16. Hex uses 0 to 9, plus the letters A through F (usually capitalized) to count the numbers 10 through 15.

high availability — Processes, products, or programs that ensure that a system experiences as little downtime as possible. The theoretical goal of a high availability system is 100% uptime.

high availability cluster — A group of servers that process the same tasks (resource groups) and take over each others' functionality in the event of an outage or failure.

history — A command used to display all of the stored commands in the history list.

history list — A list that contains the most recently executed commands. (Normally at least 100 commands are included in the history list.)

home directory — The location where all of a user's personal files are stored.

host — A computer attached to a network.

hostname — A single word used to name a computer.

hot-swapping — Removing and replacing a failed hard drive or other component without turning off the power to the device.

HOWTOs — Documents within the Linux Documentation Project that cover specific topics.

I/O ports — Special addresses (resembling memory addresses) used by a device for port-mapped I/O.

IDE — A low-cost, easy-to-manage interface used by most computers to connect hard disks and CD-ROM drives to the CPU.

IDE controller — A hardware component used to communicate between an IDE-compatible hard disk or other IDE device and the microprocessor.

if — A command used to introduce a test within a shell script. An **if** command is always followed by a **then** command.

if/then/else statement — A set of commands used to determine whether other commands in a script are executed. An **if/then/else** statement is one kind of selection statement.

incremental backup — A backup process that stores only files that have changed since a full backup was made.

index — A counting variable used within a loop statement. The index acts as a marker to count how many times the loop has executed a list of commands.

info — A command that displays online command reference information. *See* man pages.

Information Systems (IS) department — A department within many organizations. IS staff are responsible for maintaining computer and information systems for other employees. (IS is called the IT department in some organizations.)

Information Technology (IT) department — *See* Information Systems (IS) department.

init — Command used to switch the system to a different run level.

init program — A master control program that starts many other processes on the system, such as those providing a login prompt.

initialize — To set a variable to a predefined value such as zero or "" (an empty string) so a script can use the variable without uncertainty about its initial value.

inode — A file information record, identified by a unique number within a file system, which contains detailed information about a block of data commonly called a file.

insmod — Command used to copy a module file from the hard disk and add it to the Linux kernel running in memory.

install disk — A disk used to start the Linux installation program on some distributions of Linux. *See* boot disk.

installation source — The set of files from which Linux is installed. These files are normally stored on a Linux CD-ROM.

installation type — A specification indicating which Linux software to install; the appropriate installation type depends on how the Linux system is to be used.

instance — A version of a printer definition with particular options set.

interpreted language — A language for which the source code of a program is converted to numeric codes at the time a user runs the program. This conversion takes place each time the user runs the program.

interpreted program — A computer program that is converted from human-readable form to a format that can be used by a computer (numeric codes) at the moment the user executes the program.

interpreter — A program that converts the source code written in an interpreted language into numeric codes that a computer can execute.

interrupt request (IRQ) — A numbered signal that a device sends to the operating system to request service.

Internet Protocol (IP) — A networking protocol used to send packets of information across a network connection.

IP address — An identifying number assigned to a computer or device that uses IP to communicate across a network.

iteration — An occurrence of an event or process that can or must be done many times.

jobs — A command used to list jobs (processes) started in the current shell environment.

journaling — A feature of the `ext3` file system that protects against data corruption by tracking each "write" to the hard disk in a special way so that it will either be completely finished or left completely undone.

jukebox — A backup device that holds multiple backup media (such as tape cartridges or writeable CDs) and that can switch between them without assistance from a system administrator.

K Desktop Environment (KDE) — The most widely used desktop environment for Linux systems.

KDE System Guard — A graphical utility that displays a process list and lets you interact with that list to rearrange or kill processes. Can be launched from the command line with the `kpm` command.

kernel — The core of the operating system. The kernel interacts directly with the computer hardware and manages computer memory, the time allocated to each program running on a system, and other system resources.

kernel modules — Files containing computer code that can be loaded into the kernel or removed from the kernel as needed.

keyword — A word used in a computer language to define a specific task or meaning.

kill — A command used to send signals to processes, often to end them via a SIGTERM or SIGKILL signal.

killall — A command used to send signals to all processes that match a command name rather than a PID (as used with `kill`).

klogd — A daemon used to log kernel messages according to the configuration given in the `syslog.conf` configuration file.

Korn shell — A revision of the Bourne shell that includes the interactive features of the C shell but that maintains the Bourne shell programming style. The Korn shell was written by David Korn.

LaTeX — A version of the markup language TeX that includes numerous macros for easy document creation.

ldd — Command used to list the function libraries that a program uses.

legacy systems — Computer systems that an organization already owns. This term usually refers to systems that are no longer widely used.

less — Command used to display the contents of a file one screenful at a time. Permits moving around in the file and otherwise controlling the view using the keyboard.

LGPL — A special version of the GNU General Public License intended to govern both free and commercial software use of software libraries.

LILO (Linux Loader) — A Linux boot manager.

link — A special file record that refers to the same physical file data as another file record. *See* symbolic link and hard link.

Linux distribution — A Linux operating system product that includes the Linux kernel plus many software components, installation tools, documentation, and so forth.

Linux Documentation Project (LDP) — One of the first efforts to document how Linux is used. Started by Matt Welsh.

`ln` — Command used to create a symbolic link.

local printer — A printer directly attached to your computer.

`locate` — A command that searches an index of the file system for items matching a word.

log file — A file that contains detailed records of activity on a Linux system.

`logger` — A program that lets you send a message to the `syslog` function. Messages are written to the log files according to the configuration in `syslog.conf`.

logging in — The process of identifying yourself as a valid user who has been assigned a certain set of access rights.

logical partition — A hard disk partition that exists within one of the four partitions that a hard disk can traditionally manage. Logical partitions are numbered beginning with 5. *See also* primary partition.

`logrotate` — A program that manages the rotation of multiple log files at regular intervals according to the `logrotate.conf` configuration file.

loop statement — A statement used to determine whether part of a computer program should be executed more than once.

`lpc` — The Linux printer control utility. It stands for *line printer control*.

`lpd` — The print server used in the LPRng print architecture. It sends files prepared by `lpr` to the physical printer device or remote print server. It stands for *line printer daemon*.

`lpq` — A utility that lists each print job in a print queue and includes information such as the owner and size of each job.

`lpr` — A command that prepares files to be sent to a physical printer device, effectively "printing" files for Linux users.

`lprm` — A command that deletes a print job from a print queue.

`lpstat` — A command that displays a brief summary of the status of each printer.

`ls` — Command used to list the files in a directory.

`lsmod` — Command used to list the modules that are installed in the Linux kernel.

Macintosh — A computer developed by Apple Computer that integrated the operating system and the graphical interface.

macro — A set of commands that can be executed at one time by referring to the name of the macro.

magic filter — A print filter program that automatically processes a file into the correct output format based on the file's type.

`make` — A command that uses information stored in a configuration file to compile source code into a binary program or take other preset actions.

man pages — Online manual pages for Linux commands. The man pages are accessed using the `man` command.

markup languages — Computer languages that define a series of codes indicating how to format a document.

Master Boot Record (MBR) — A small area on the first hard disk partition that contains a program to decide how to start an operating system. Control passes from the BIOS to the program in the MBR when a computer is first booted.

mean time between failures (MTBF) — A reliability measurement giving the average time a device can function between breakdowns. It is typically measured in hours of operating time.

megabyte (MB) — A measure of space on computers equal to 1,048,576 bytes, or enough space to store roughly 1 million characters.

message — A description of what is happening within a program.

`messages` — The main system log file in Linux, usually stored in the directory `/var/log`.

Microsoft Windows — The leading graphical interface for DOS.

mirroring — A redundancy technique in which the contents of two file systems contain identical information. Mirroring improves data access speed and provides fault tolerance in the event that one of the file systems fails.

MIS (Management of Information Systems or Manager of Information Systems) — Another term for the IS or IT department or the staff who work in or manage that department.

MIT Magic Cookie — A type of cookie used by the `xauth` security system to control remote access to an X server.

mkdir — Command used to create a new directory.

mke2fs — A command used to format a device such as a hard disk partition with an `ext2` file system.

mkfs — A command used to format devices using various file system types. The `ext2` or `ext3` type for Linux file systems can be indicated as an option. *See also* `mke2fs`.

mkswap — A command used to format a partition as swap space for the Linux kernel.

modal editor — A text editor that uses multiple modes for editing text and entering commands to apply to that text.

modprobe — Command used to load a module with all of its required supporting modules.

module parameters — Information needed by a module to locate system resources. The parameters are added after the module name when using the `insmod` or `modprobe` command.

more — Command used to display the contents of a file one screenful at a time. The `more` command is similar to the `less` command but with fewer keyboard control options.

mount — A command used to make a logical or physical device available as a file system in the Linux directory structure.

mount point — The place or path in the Linux directory structure where a file system is accessed.

multisync monitor — A monitor that can accept data using a range of frequencies (resulting in varying resolutions and color depths).

multithreading — A technique used within multi-processing operating systems to divide a larger task between multiple processors.

multiuser system — An operating system on which numerous users can log in to the same computer (usually over a network connection).

mv — Command used to rename a file or move it to a new location.

nesting — A programming method in which one selection or loop statement contains another selection or loop statement.

network address — An address that identifies the local network that a computer is a part of. This address is used to determine how data is routed to its intended destination.

network attached printer — A printer that includes a networking interface (such as an Ethernet port), so that it is attached directly to a network instead of through a computer (such as through a parallel port).

network mask — A set of numbers that tells the networking system in Linux how to identify IP addresses that are part of the local network.

nice — A command used to set the nice level of a Linux process as it is being launched.

nice level — The priority level assigned to a Linux process.

NTFS — The default file system type for Windows NT, Windows 2000, and Windows XP.

OpenSource — A trademarked name often used to refer to software licensed under the GPL.

operating system — Software that provides a set of core functionality for other programs to use in working with the computer hardware and interfacing with the user running the computer.

option — Information added to a command that determines how the command operates.

other permissions — A set of three file permissions (r, w, and x) that apply to all users on the Linux system who are not the owner of the file or directory in question and are not members of the group assigned to the file or directory.

page — A block of 4 KB of memory. A page is the unit of memory in which the Linux kernel moves data to and from swap space.

page description language — A special set of codes that determine the graphics elements, text font, and everything else about how information appears on a printed page. PostScript and PDL are examples of page description languages.

parameter — Information added to a command that defines what the command will operate on, such as a filename or directory name.

parent directory — The directory that is one level above the current directory.

parity — A redundancy technique that allows corrupted data to be reconstructed using an extra piece of information (the parity information) that is created as the data is stored.

parity stripe — Parity information stored as part of a RAID-3 or RAID-5 system.

partition — A distinct area of a hard disk that has been prepared to store a particular type of data.

partition table — Information on a hard disk that defines the size and file system type of each partition on that hard disk.

PATH — An environment variable containing a list of directories on the Linux system that the shell searches each time a command is executed.

perl — A popular programming language developed by Larry Wall, used to create scripts for working on text files and completing other complex tasks.

pico — A simple text editor that includes on-screen information about the Control key sequences used to perform editing functions.

ping — A command used to test a network connection.

pipe — A connection between two commands (indicated by the | character) that causes the output of one command to be used as the input of a second command.

plain-text configuration file — A file containing human-readable instructions that are used by a program to define its configuration.

points of failure — Parts of an information system that are subject to failure.

port — A networking parameter that permits one application to communicate with a specific application on a networked computer.

port-mapped input/output (port-mapped I/O) — A device communication technique that uses a separate range of memory addresses called I/O ports as a place for a device to send and receive data. Essentially, each device-specific port address works like a post office box.

positional variable — A variable used within a shell script that contains data included on the command line when the script was launched.

PostScript Printer Description (PPD) file — A file containing a standardized printer description that can be used by several printing architectures on different operating systems. PPD files are used to describe many types of printers, not just PostScript printers.

power supply — The component within a computer system that converts the incoming AC power from a wall socket or UPS device to the correct DC voltage for use by components in a computer.

preemptive multitasking — A technique used by the Linux kernel to control which program is running from moment to moment.

primary partition — One of the four partitions that traditional hard disk electronics can effectively manage. *See also* logical partition.

print accounting — A method of tracking how users are using printing resources based on print job information logged by lpd.

print filter — A script that contains instructions for formatting documents using the page description language required by a specific printer. The print filter is used by the `lpr` program to prepare files to be sent to a physical printer.

print job — A file submitted for printing via the `lpr` command or a graphical dialog box.

print queue — A printer definition; also a subdirectory where files are stored to wait for a print server daemon (`lpd` or `cupsd`) to retrieve them one by one and send them to the printer. Also called a print spool directory.

print spool directory — *See* print queue.

printcap — The printer definition file used by LPRng Linux printing. This file specifies how and where files to be printed are stored and processed by `lpr` and `lpd`. It stands for *printer capture*.

printing policy — A brief document that describes how printing resources can be used and how they will be managed within an organization.

priority — (1) A value assigned to a process running on Linux that determines how much CPU time is granted to the process. (2) A label indicating the severity of a message submitted for logging. Priorities are used in `syslog.conf`.

process — A task or program running on a Linux operating system, managed by the Linux kernel.

process ID (PID) — A number from 1 to 65,000 that is associated uniquely with a process running on a Linux system.

program — An imprecise term used to refer to any process running on a Linux system.

programming language — *See* computer language.

Project Athena — The project sponsored by DEC and MIT to create a graphical environment or windowing system for UNIX.

protocol — An organized pattern of signals or words used to communicate efficiently.

ps — A command that provides information about processes running on Linux.

public domain — Creative work (such as a software program) to which no one has a copyright ownership interest.

pwd — Command that displays the current working directory.

Python — A scripting language developed by Guido van Rossum. Often used for creating graphical programs.

RAID (redundant arrays of inexpensive disks) — A storage technique using multiple inexpensive hard disks arranged in a predefined pattern (an array) to improve performance, increase fault tolerance, or both.

RAID subsystem — A hardware-controlled RAID device containing a CPU and other components to control the array of hard disks.

RAID-0 — A RAID level that uses striping to improve disk performance without adding any fault tolerance.

RAID-1 — A RAID level that uses disk mirroring to significantly improve fault tolerance. Disk read performance is also improved, but disk write performance suffers.

RAID-3 — A RAID level that uses striping with parity information to improve performance and increase fault tolerance.

RAID-5 — A RAID level in which striping with parity is spread across all disks in the RAID array (compared to RAID-3, in which the parity information is stored on a single hard disk).

RAID-Linear — A storage technique in which multiple physical devices are combined into a single logical device.

random access memory (RAM) — Volatile electronic storage within a computer.

read permission — A file permission that allows a user to read the contents of a file or browse the files in a directory. Represented by a letter `r`.

read-only memory (ROM) — Nonvolatile electronic storage within a computer. Used to store information about how the computer starts and how the devices in the computer are configured.

reboot — Command used to shut down all services and then restart the computer.

Red Hat Package Manager (rpm) — A data storage format for software packages.

redirection — The act of changing where a Linux program receives its input or sends its output.

redundancy — Duplication of a system component or piece of data. Many fault-tolerant systems rely on the use of redundant components or data; in the event of a failure, the duplicate component or copy of the data would still be available.

redundant arrays of inexpensive disks — *See* RAID.

regular expression — A system of expressing patterns using special characters that can be interpreted by many Linux programs.

relative path — The name of a directory that is only meaningful (and only sufficiently specific) in relation to another directory. A relative path does not include a forward slash.

release number — A number assigned by the company that prepares a Linux product. It allows the company to track how many times the kernel file has been altered before the final product is shipped.

remote printer — A printer attached to another computer on the network or to the network itself, rather than to the computer on which you are working.

renice — Linux command used to change the nice level of a Linux process that is already running.

rescue disk — A disk created specifically to boot a Linux system in the event of a system failure. Contains the software tools most likely to be of help in diagnosing and repairing problems with the failed system.

rescue mode — A mode of operation in Red Hat Linux. Used to repair a system failure that blocks normal booting and operation.

resource database — A file that defines how an X resource should appear on-screen.

resource group — An application or task, along with the data and system resources the task requires, defined within a high availability cluster. Each server in the cluster can take over a complete resource group if the server handling that resource group fails.

restore — To copy data from a backup location (for example, a tape cartridge) onto the file system where that data is normally used, and from which it was unintentionally lost.

rm — Command used to delete a file.

rmdir — Command used to remove (delete) an empty directory.

rmmod — Command used to remove a module from the kernel.

root — The administrative user account in Linux; the superuser. Whoever has access to this account can control the entire system.

root directory — The starting point for all access to Linux resources. It is indicated by a single forward slash: /.

rotating log files — The process of moving existing log files to another filename and location for archiving or review.

rpm — Command used to manage all of the rpm software packages on a Linux system.

run level — A mode of operation that defines which Linux system services are activated.

safedelete — A utility that makes files appear to have been deleted but actually saves a compressed copy of each one in case it is needed later.

SAGE (System Administrators Guild) — A professional organization for system administrators.

script — A list of commands stored in a text file. Instead of entering each command one by one, at the command line, a script automates the execution of a series of commands.

SCSI — A high-performance interface used by many types of devices to connect to a computer.

sector — A unit of data storage on a hard disk. Normally a sector contains 512 bytes.

sed — A command used to process each line in a text file according to a series of commands provided by the user.

selection statement — A statement that lets a computer programmer determine which parts of a program will be executed according to values that are calculated by testing as the program is executed. The `if/then` statement is a selection statement used in shell scripts.

selector — A field in the `syslog.conf` file that determines what events are being logged. A selector is composed of a facility and a priority.

service — A command that lets you launch a script in `/etc/rc.d/init.d` to control a system service.

session — A configuration that defines a set of graphical programs to run when a user logs in.

set — A command-line utility that lists all currently defined environment variables.

Shadow Password Suite — A set of password-related utilities that implement a security system used to restrict access to encrypted password text in `/etc/shadow`.

shared library — A single copy of a function library that has been loaded into memory for use by multiple dynamically linked applications.

shell — Software that accepts input from a user via a command line and processes that input to manage system resources.

shell prompt — A set of words or characters indicating that the shell is ready to accept commands at the keyboard.

shell script — An executable file containing lines of text as you would enter them at a command line, with special commands to control the order in which lines in the file are executed.

shell variable — A variable used within a shell script to store information for use by the script.

shutdown — Command used to shut down Linux gracefully.

SIGHUP — A signal sent to a logging daemon to instruct the daemon to reread its configuration files and the log file it writes to. Sometimes called HUP.

signal — A message (one of a fixed set determined by the Linux kernel) that can be sent to any process and responded to according to how that program is written.

software — Instructions that control the physical computer components, but can be changed because they reside on a changeable media such as a hard disk.

software license — A legal definition of who can use a piece of software and how it can be used.

software masters — Original copies of an application supplied by a software vendor or manufacturer, usually one or more CDs, tapes, or disks.

software package — A single file that contains all the files needed to install and use an application or group of related applications. Special data formats are used to store many files in a single software package.

sort — A command used to sort all of the lines in a text file, writing them out in alphabetical order or according to options provided to the command.

source code — A set of human-readable programming instructions used to create a piece of software. A programmer writes source code using the keywords and syntax rules of a computer language.

Stallman, Richard — Founder of the Free Software Foundation and the GNU project.

standard error (STDERR) — The communication channel used by most Linux programs to send information about errors in program execution.

standard input (STDIN) — The communication channel used by most Linux programs to collect input (normally from the keyboard).

standard output (STDOUT) — The communication channel used by most Linux programs to write output (normally to the screen).

startx — The standard command used to start an X Window System session from a text-mode command line.

statement — A command within a computer program. A statement is often a single keyword, but the term may also refer to a group of keywords that the computer language syntax requires or allows to be used together.

statement block — A list of commands (or statements) that are controlled by a selection or loop statement.

statically linked applications — Linux programs that include library functions in the program itself so that they are not dependent on the libraries loaded on the Linux system.

striping — A data storage technique in which parts of a file are written to more than one disk in order to improve performance. *See* RAID-3 and RAID-5.

su — A command used to take on the identity of a different user account. Short for substitute user.

superblock — A part of a Linux file system that contains key parameters about the file system. Numerous copies of the superblock exist on each file system; if the superblock cannot be accessed, the file system is unusable.

superuser — The root user account, which has supervisory privileges throughout the Linux system.

surge suppressor — An electronic device that prevents potentially damaging electrical irregularities from reaching a computer system's power supply.

swap partition (swap space) — A designated area on a hard disk used as virtual memory by the Linux kernel.

swapon — A command used by Linux initialization scripts to activate the swap partition defined in the `/etc/fstab` file.

symbolic link — A file record that includes a path and filename, but not an inode number. A file that refers to another filename rather than to data in a file. Also called a soft link.

symmetrical multiprocessing — A technique that allows an operating system to support multiple CPUs on the same computer.

syntax — A formalized arrangement of information to allow a Linux command to understand parameters, options, or configuration files.

syslog.conf — The configuration file used to control how and where messages are logged by `syslogd` and `klogd`.

syslogd — The background program (or daemon) that manages all of the calls to the `syslog` function, writing log messages according to the `syslog.conf` configuration.

system utilities — Programs that are used to manage a Linux system. *See also* utility programs.

tab completion — A feature of the shell that lets you enter part of a file or directory name and have the shell fill in the remainder of the name when you press the Tab Key.

tar — Command used to create a single file that contains many other files, often compressed to save space.

tar archive — A file created by the `tar` command.

target hard disk partition — The location on the system's hard disk where Linux will be installed. Also known as the *target partition*.

Tcl/Tk — A scripting language developed by John Ousterhout; often used to create graphical programs.

telinit — Command used to switch the system to a different run level.

TENEX/TOPS C shell (TC shell) — An enhancement of the C shell. This is the version of the C shell that is commonly used on Linux systems.

terminal emulator window — A command-line window (also called a terminal window) within a graphical environment.

test — A command that evaluates the arguments provided after the command name and returns either true (a value of 1) or false (a value of 0).

test — A method of examining data within a shell script and acting according to the result of the examination (or test).

TeTeX — A version of the markup language TeX that includes numerous macros for technical document creation.

TeX — A document processing system that writers use to create large and complex documents on UNIX or Linux systems.

then — A command that identifies the commands to be executed if the test introduced by the `if` command succeeds (returns a value of true).

thrashing — Excessive movement of processes between RAM and swap space, resulting in reduced system performance and excessive wear on the hard disk.

thread — A part of a process or task. Used in the context of multiprocessing operating systems.

timestamp — A record of the date and time when an event occurred.

top — A command used to view the most CPU-intensive processes running on Linux at a given moment, along with related information for those processes.

Torvalds, Linus — Originator of the Linux kernel; formerly a student in Helsinki, Finland.

touch — Command used to create a new file with no data in it or update the access timestamp of an existing file.

track — One of many concentric circles of data storage area on each platter of a hard disk.

troff — A command used to format and display documents that are created using roff markup codes.

tty — A command that displays the name of the terminal device you are currently working in.

tune2fs — A utility used to view or adjust parameters within the superblock of a Linux file system.

umask — Command used to set the file permissions assigned when you create a new file.

umount — A command used to unmount a file system that is currently accessible as part of the Linux directory structure.

uname — Command used to provide information about the operating system, including the kernel version.

uninterruptible power supply (UPS) — A device that uses batteries to provide power to a computer when the incoming AC power (wall socket power) fails. A UPS can typically also inform the Linux system of the status of the power via a serial cable.

UnitedLinux — A Linux distribution created by multiple Linux vendors as a common base product on which numerous Linux applications can be designed to run.

UNIX — An operating system created at AT&T Bell Labs (now part of Lucent Technologies) about 30 years ago by Ken Thompson and Dennis Ritchie. UNIX is still widely used, and it provided the technical basis for Linux.

uptime — The time when a computer is running and available.

user permissions — A set of three file permissions (`r`, `w`, and `x`) that apply to the owner of a file or directory.

User Private Group — A security system that creates a new group containing one user when that user is first created.

useradd — A command used to create (add) a new user account in Linux.

usermod — A command used to modify or update an existing user account.

utility — An imprecise term referring to a program used to administer a computer system rather than do work for an end user.

variable — A memory location used by a program to store a value, such as a number or a word. Each variable is assigned a name so that the program can access the value by referring to the name.

vi — The most widely used text editor on UNIX and Linux systems. Different versions of **vi**, such as **vim** and **elvis**, are usually launched with the command **vi**. Stands for *visual editor*.

vigr — A command used to edit /etc/group.

vipw — A command used to edit /etc/passwd.

virtual console — A separate login screen that you access by pressing a combination of keys on your keyboard. It allows you to start multiple text-based login sessions on the same computer.

virtual memory — A feature of the Linux kernel that allows Linux to treat a partition of the hard disk as if it were RAM, storing programs there temporarily when they are not being used.

vmstat — A command used to display detailed information about virtual memory and swap file usage.

Webmin — A browser-based graphical system administration tool to which you can add modules to configure additional programs as the need arises.

wheel — A special system administrative group, not used officially in Linux.

while — A command that creates a loop based on a test. The loop executes a statement block as long as the test returns true.

white space — Tabs or spaces included in a program or script that make the script easier for a person to read.

window manager — A special-purpose graphical application (X client) that controls the position and manipulation of the windows within a graphical user interface.

Windows NT — A business-oriented operating system product developed by Microsoft. Windows NT, 2000, and XP do not use DOS as an underlying operating system, as previous versions of Windows did (such as Windows 95 and 98).

write caching — A feature of some storage systems in which information that is to be written to a file system (particularly a RAID file system) is stored in memory temporarily in order to improve the overall read/write performance of the file system.

write permission — A file permission that allows a user to add or change information in a file or create files within a directory. Represented by a letter **w**.

WYSIWYG — A characteristic of programs that show documents on the computer screen much as they will look when printed on paper or in a Web browser (stands for what-you-see-is-what-you-get; pronounced "whiz-ee-wig").

X client — A graphical application.

X resource — The separate screen elements of a graphical application, such as scroll bars, text fonts, mouse pointers, and title bars for windows or dialog boxes.

X server — The program that communicates with the video card to create images on the screen.

X Window System — A graphical software environment used by almost all UNIX and Linux operating systems.

xauth — A security system that controls remote access to an X server by means of numeric tokens shared between users who are authorized to use a remote X server.

Xconfigurator — A utility in Red Hat Linux for configuring the X Window System.

xf86config — A standard text-based utility for configuring the X Window System.

xfontsel — Program that lets the user choose each aspect of a font definition (such as the font family and typeface) and then displays the corresponding font for review.

XFree86 Project — A free software project that creates software to provide X Window System functionality to Linux.

xfs — The font server typically used by X to process requests for font information from applications and return the requested font in the desired size.

xhost — A command-line utility that permits users on a host (or all hosts) to use the X server on the computer where the command is executed.

xrdb — A command that loads an initial X database resource file or merges additional resource configuration details.

xset — A command that adjusts the behavior of X by controlling features such as key repeat rate, EnergyStar monitor features, mouse acceleration, and the screen blanker.

xterm — A program within a graphical environment that provides a command-line window.

zcat — Command used to display the contents of a compressed file to the screen.

Index